Britain's

Britain's Empires

A History, 1600–2020

By James Heartfield

ANTHEM PRESS

Anthem Press
An imprint of Wimbledon Publishing Company
www.anthempress.com

This edition first published in UK and USA 2024
by ANTHEM PRESS
75–76 Blackfriars Road, London SE1 8HA, UK
or PO Box 9779, London SW19 7ZG, UK
and
244 Madison Ave #116, New York, NY 10016, USA

First published in the UK and USA by Anthem Press in 2023

British Library Cataloguing-in-Publication Data
A catalogue record for this book is available from the British Library.

Library of Congress Control Number: 2024939349
A catalog record for this book has been requested.

ISBN-13: 978-1-83999-310-7 (Pbk)
ISBN-10: 1-83999-310-3 (Pbk)

Cover Image: Printed for H.M. Stationery Office by Lowe & Brydone Printers Ltd

This title is also available as an e-book.

CONTENTS

INTRODUCTION

Britain's Empires grew from the moment Norman England began to unite with or colonise its neighbours. Over the centuries, Britain came to dominate the Atlantic seaboard, the Indian Ocean and the Pacific, working inland to dominate Mughal and Maratha India, planting a new Anglosphere in Australasia and in the late nineteenth century vying with European rivals to carve up the African continent. While my grandparents lived in an empire that dominated a quarter of the globe, I grew up in the flickering embers of one, always just visible in the corner of your eye – but still shaping much of British public life, as it impacted disproportionately and often destructively on the peoples of the rest of the world.

Looking at the question of Empire there are two different approaches. One looks at the *longue durée* – the more than half a millennium of conquest (1492–2019) – the other looks at imperialism as a specific epoch (1880–1914), and an 'era of transition'.

Here, we are looking at the longer span but there is a problem with the *longue durée*. In the heyday of the Empire, it was common for patriotic Britons to laud its history from Francis Drake overcoming the Spanish Armada in 1588 right through to the wonders of the British Raj in 1938 as though it was one great cavalcade of glorious victories.

Today, with a different moral judgement, many critics of European empires see them as 500 years of unrelenting oppression. Those are both judgements that situate you morally in relation to the Empire, the first positive, the second negative. There is a point to both judgements. Institutionally speaking there is indeed a continuity to the British and other European states that made empires across the world. That is what the Royal Family represents, the single line of inherited order. More, the relationship between the mother country, England (later Britain) and its colonies has as a constant feature throughout all those years, an inequality of power, whereby it dominated those other peoples that it succeeded in colonising across the world.

By taking the whole five centuries as a single continuum you can lose sight of the very different forces and motivations at work at different moments in the history of European empires. In the *longue durée* it is easy to imagine that the end result was pre-ordained in the early beginnings. Broad sweep historians are often tempted to imagine a purpose or plan where there is none, or where the plans people make have little relation to the much later outcome. (The word for such thinking is teleological, meaning 'end-inspired', and it is generally thought to be a delusion.)

Something like the *longue durée* idea is at work when critics put the label 'forever wars' on the succession of post-Cold War interventions that the United States and Britain have fought, from the 1990–91 Gulf War through to the air attacks on Syria in 2016. 'Forever wars' works as a cynical shorthand that excuses critics from looking hard at the different cases made for intervention, implying that these are mostly post-hoc justifications, not sincere. No doubt there is some point to that. Still, it is better to try to examine each conflict in its own right in the first place before deciding there is an overall pattern.

The belief that the later stages are set by the earlier is a common one, better suited to drama than history. Along with the myth of continuity there is a myth of origins – that to understand a thing you have to find its sources. History is not like biology. The later development is not coded in the original seed, like DNA. At most the earlier developments are the foundations on which the succeeding generation make their history. In the writing of history, it would be truer to say that the later development tends to shape our understanding of the earlier period than the other way around. The Empire that developed in the nineteenth century was not pre-determined by the colonial system of the sixteenth century. There is no transhistorical essence that explains the successive British Empires, whether you call that 'English genius' or 'White Supremacy'.

To make sense of the history of Britain's successive Empires I have separated them into five successive eras, the Old Empire (1600–1776), the Empire of Free Trade (1776–1870), the New Imperialism (1870–1945), the Commonwealth (1946–89) and the New World Order (1989 to date)

The first is what, following Eric Williams and others, can be called the mercantile Empire. Royal monopolies like the East India Company, Hudson's Bay Company, the Merchant Adventurers and the Royal African Company dominated world trade mostly in luxury goods from 1600 to 1776. The importance of *overseas* trade was a marker of the *underdevelopment* of British commercial life. Dominated by customary relations, the country's domestic realm did not readily yield to commercialisation. Instead, trade took off at the margins, in the port towns and with other countries. In time those monopoly companies began to be seen as a brake on further progress and were more openly criticised for their piratical excesses. In Part One we look at the role of the merchants and the monopoly companies, as well as the importance of the dynastic struggles and Renaissance characters in the transformation of British and European relations to the rest of the world. We look, too, at the importance of the early planters in the Caribbean and North America, and their spur to the slave trade.

Part Two looks at Britain's reinvention as the 'workshop of the world' – as Disraeli called it – following the repatriation of capital funds from overseas to make an industrial revolution at home. Britain's early start in commercial society, its relative openness to scientific thinking and parliamentary democracy were admired across Europe. But when it was challenged by rival modernities in the revolutions in the United States and France, and also in Ireland and Haiti, Britain's ruling class put the brakes on social change to impose a narrowly defined Empire of Free Trade. Commercial domination made the less developed world subordinate to British influence from the southern cotton fields of America to the cotton weavers of India. After the American revolution the British appetite for outright colonisation was abated. It would be wrong to say, though, that the era of free trade put an end to imperialism. That might seem a persuasive argument if you were to look at the Atlantic. In the Pacific Ocean, though, a new era of colonisation was underway, starting with the unlikely impetus of transportation, as English convicts, no longer expelled to the American colonies, were sent instead to Australia.

Free settlement followed in Australia, New Zealand, Fiji and elsewhere in the Pacific, as it did in Canada and South Africa. The settlers were different from the planters and outpost traders. Many hoped to farm for themselves like English yeomen more than to lord it over grand plantations. Many left to escape Britain and they were in the first half of the nineteenth century, much disliked in the mother country.

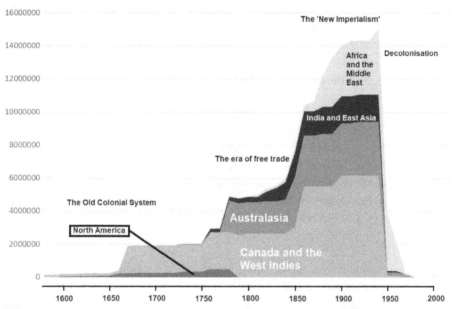

Extent of the British Empire, Square Miles

With decade intervals, including protectorates, mandates and dominions, omitting Europe and the Antarctic. Canada and Australia being large, but less populated seem yet more important than they certainly were, and I date their leaving the Empire from the point that the Commonwealth ceased to be the British Commonwealth in 1949. At the height of 1945, when Britain held Libya and Eritrea, but was on the verge of losing India, the Empire as defined above amounted to just over 26 per cent of the world's land mass.

As well as the colonies of settlement the Empire's most spectacular expansion in the 'free trade' era was into India, with the transformation of the East India Company from trading concern to political administration. Here, it pays to look not only at the drive that came from the British ideals of liberal administration, but also the collapse of the rival candidates for Indian Emperors, notably the Mughal and Maratha Kingdoms. The policy of 'free trade' was at its most naked in the actions the British took to suppress the opposition of the Chinese Emperors to the opium trade.

In Part Three we look at the era of what was called at the time, the 'new imperialism', the consolidation of the British Empire as both and economic and political system of domination, signalled in large part by the colonisation of much of Africa. The New Imperialism championed by Birmingham's Joseph Chamberlain and other late Victorian enthusiasts was part of a larger transformation of British society that, though it seemed dynamic, was an attempt to address the apparent collapse in British industrial advance. Here we look at the evidence that the New Empire was driven by the outward flow of not just capital but also moral purpose into the wider world. The New Empire subordinated much of the world to British domination, and in the process made 400 million subjects of the Empire – Indians, Africans, white settlers and aboriginal peoples across North America and the Pacific, and indentured labourers from Guyana to Malaya. The striking paradox of the New Empire was that it aspired to be a great division of labour, but that in large part it was a brake on the economic development that would make that labour productive. Britons seized control of one quarter of the land mass of the world but condemned many of its inhabitants to an impoverished life in reserved areas and protectorates or abandoned in dead-end colonies with pitifully low productivity. Cash crops like rubber, cocoa and sugar were important sources of revenue, as were tin, gold and diamond mines (and later oil wells). Labourers in these industries were harshly exploited in oppressive work regimes, but they were also a minority, since most imperial subjects were still dependent on subsistence farming in 1913.

The British drive to colonise the world brought forth rival European Empires. Imperial rivalry, the contest over who would exploit the peoples of the world, brought out the barbaric side of imperialism. World Wars between European rivals in 1914–19 and 1939–45 made the first half of the twentieth century the deadliest in human history. Seen from the colonies the European war efforts were a vast plunder of human and natural resources. The challenge of anti-Imperialism, from Ireland to Egypt and India over the era of the World Wars, and the Empire's efforts to defeat them is the subject of the last two chapters in Section 3.

Wars did not only destroy the European Empire's economies, but their moral authority, too. In Part 4 we look at the attempts Britain undertook to defend its Empire by reinventing it as a Commonwealth, the difficulties of sweating its resources, and the eventual retreat from Empire in the 1960s. Painfully aware that they had outlived their welcome, British colonialists' rearguard struggle to shape the post-colonial regimes created a new order of intervention against radical anti-imperialists, notably in Egypt and Ghana. The Commonwealth was rocked, too, by the white settler revolts in South Africa and Rhodesia. Britain's role as chief overseas investor in apartheid South Africa meant that it was generally seeking to slow down the challenge of black democracy in the region.

In Part Four we also look at the rise and fall of Third World Nationalism, the most hopeful democratic challenge to imperialism in the twentieth century. Undercut by the compromises of governing and an awkward dependence on the support of the Soviet Union, the radical nationalist regimes and movements lost impetus with a renewed campaign of western reassertion under Ronald Reagan and Margaret Thatcher in the 1980s. The collapse of the Soviet Union in 1989 fuelled a re-emphasis on western authority over Third World Nationalism.

Part Five looks at Britain's place the New World Order declared by President George H. W. Bush after the defeat of Saddam Hussein's Iraqi regime in the 1990–91 Gulf War. The end of the Cold War between the western powers and the Soviet Union greatly changed relations with the third world. It was that that led to the re-imagining of western policy as one of 'humanitarian intervention'. The wars of intervention of the New World Order looked something like the old 'gunboat diplomacy'. US-led missions were organised under the flag of the United Nations, in Iraq, Bosnia and Somalia. To the champions of these interventions, it was important that the interests of the West were not selfish but driven by a desire to protect human rights (which is why they were called humanitarian interventions). Critics objected saying that in truth the United States was fighting a 'war for oil' in Iraq. The era of humanitarian intervention begs the question whether this was an extension of the old imperialism or a new departure altogether, which we examine in Part Five.

In the main, my argument here is that there is no one overarching explanation to Britain's successive empires. In trying to understand the British Empire it is better to think of it as being driven by distinctive forces in different eras. The Old Colonial Empire saw mercantile trade reach far geographically, but in large part because Britain's domestic society was still too beholden to traditional lines of authority to yield to commercial development. The extent of that first Empire that looked so dynamic was really a reaction to the limitations of the British economy. The era of free trade was in the first instance a repatriation of investment to the United Kingdom and a downgrading of overseas interests – though the very dynamic growth of the industrial revolution soon led to a drive to secure markets for export, and a determination to dominate. Following the argument that the New Imperialism of the 1880s saw Britain compensate for its slower domestic growth by investing overseas, casts the Empire at its height as decadent, even parasitic, rather than a dynamic. There is much to this argument.

The Russian Marxist V. I. Lenin is most closely associated with the assessment of Imperialism within a stadial development, the corrupted end point of a faltering birth, dynamic youth followed by an enfeebled old age. It was a part of Lenin's argument that the era of imperialism was not only one of the decaying of the old system, but also the emergence of a new one, an era of transition. He was not wrong on the general account. The crescendo of the New Imperialism of the late nineteenth and early twentieth century saw both dramatic growth but also spectacular destruction, most clearly in the two world wars that wrecked the rival European Empires, but in the end the British Empire, too.

Lenin was right to anticipate that the shortcomings of the imperial system would lead to radical alternatives. Britain was challenged by radical nationalist movements in its Empire that would lay the basis of new independent states. Those states struggled with the continuing dominance of the mature economies in Britain and Europe, and the new hegemonic power, the United States. The argument that Ghanaian leader Kwame Nkrumah (and others) made was that even where the old colonialists conceded political independence, continuing control over private industry and world markets left those newly independent countries at the mercy of 'neo-colonialism'. Nkrumah's focus on the continuing domination of the developing world by the great powers was valuable, but it could also work as a prophylactic against looking at what was new. Those who followed Nkrumah in the 'underdevelopment' school of analysis tended to insist that third world development was impossible. And yet, in East Asia, former colonies did prosper, and even in Latin America and Africa, the story was not one of unremitting impoverishment. The emergence the so-called BRICS (Brazil, Russia, India, China and South Africa) as an alternative pole of political and economic influence says as much.

Lenin's hope that the decadence of the old imperialist system would lead to a wholly new economic order, socialist rather than capitalist, was only half fulfilled. Expanding into Germany's Eastern hinterland the Soviet Union was for 70 years a rival to the western powers, but, in the end, it proved to be no alternative. As the collapse of the Soviet Union closed off those radical ideologies that drew on its vision, the radical Third World Nationalism of the post war era was undermined. The end of the Cold War laid the basis for a re-emphasis of western authority and a new lease of life for Britain as a world leader that would have been hard to imagine in the 1970s.

If the challenge of Third World Nationalism is used up does it follow that the West is resurgent? It seemed that way in the wake of the 1990–91 Gulf War. It was, argued Francis Fukuyama, the End of History, and liberal democracy was the unchallenged victor. His later works have struck a more cautious note. The western triumphalism of the 1990s has not lasted. All around us are features that might be described as symptoms of decay. Moral redemption was aimed for in the humanitarian imperialism of the 1990s and 2000s – as much for those who wanted to reverse the 'Suez syndrome' as for those targets of western reform in the less wealthy world. From the standpoint of 2020 the history of Empire looks disreputable rather than uplifting.

In looking at the different eras of British imperialism I have foregrounded the economic questions of how Britain made use of the resources and labour of its subject peoples and enriched its domestic economy. To understand how the British Empire was a 'division of labour' (and also how it was not so) explains a lot about the motives of the imperialists. But the temptation to reduce the dynamic of expansion and domination to economic advantage alone leaves out the very important ideological and moral drives of empire. The humanitarian impulse was to the fore in the abolition of slavery, and in the colonisation of Africa, as it was in the expansion of British India. To see all of that only as an alibi for exploitation is to miss much of what was driving the people who remade much of the world according to their ideals. The ideology of colonialism, in all its complexity, was as important to the ordering of the British Empire as was the economic question.

In the recent era moral questions have loomed large in the decisions to intervene in the non-western world. The 'ethical foreign policy' adopted by Prime Minister Blair in 1997 has been dismissed by some as just a fig-leaf of humanitarianism to cover the same old imperialist plundering. That seems to me to underestimate what was new in the post-Cold War international relations. The ideological questions of how to give meaning to the world order were real ones, and the policy that emerged, 'humanitarian imperialism' deserves to be addressed as a distinctive turn.

One of the great questions of the history of the British and other European Empires is how much of what went on is down to the home country and how much was shaped by the colonised peoples. The fashion once was to dismiss the history of other peoples, outside of Europe, as not real history. The meaning was that their lives were secondary and unimportant where the 'mother country' was the North Star around which all else circled.

Today the view of non-Europeans as 'non-historic' has largely been rejected, at least explicitly – many argue it still carries on unspoken in the choice of standpoints and accounts from which the story is told. The late Samir Amin argued that in one sense Eurocentrism was unavoidable in that 'capitalism started in Europe and spread out-wards' (itself a view that has been challenged). To put it bluntly, what it meant to be colonised was that your goals were put second to the goals of the colonisers.

More recently Alex Anievas and Kerem Nişancıoğlu have argued with what they call 'self-aggrandising narratives of western exceptionalism'. They reject the idea that 'development is the product of a society's own immanent dynamics'. They say that it is 'Eurocentric' to see an 'autonomous emergence of modernity in Europe'. Critics of their work argue that fixing their view on the non-western spurs to western domination ignores those changes that did happen in Europe. Here we try to give due weight to those movements within Europe and Britain (Enlightenment, Reformation, Industrial Revolution and New Liberalism) without seeing them as being isolated from endoga-mous influences. There is a bias in the choice of topic, 'Empire', that tends to lead to a different account from those that set out to look at the history of social class, or Protestantism, or gender relations. That does not say that one is wrong and the other right, but that the topic is different.

One of the costs of writing political history is that it gives a false view of life overall. Most people's lives most of the time were not taken up with the larger political struggles of Empire-building or of national independence movements. Fixing on the dramatic conflicts where things break down can lead you to underestimate the small details of ordinary life in between the upheavals. While highlighting the injustices and depreda-tions of Empire it is always worth remembering that a great many people lived lives with much happiness and fulfilment, and of ordinary struggles and sorrows, quite apart from the larger questions. That is not a justification of the Empire, just a necessary correction to the perception that everything that took place under it was awful. Also, by choosing to tell the story of Britain's Empires, that should not suggest that the country's relations with colonised people exhausts the subject of its relations to the world – cooperation and conflict with other great powers, America, Russia and the other colonising European powers looms at least as large in the history of Britain's international relations as does its Empire.

My special thanks are due to Mark Al Dulaimi, Daniel Ben-Ami, Russell Grinker, Phil Hammond, Rania Hafez, Cheryl Hudson, Lee Jones, Spencer Leonard, Zareer Masani, Maria Morshead, Peter Ramsay, Joel Rosen and Karl Sharro.

PART ONE

The Old Colonial System, 1600–1760

Chapter One

UNITED KINGDOM

Every colonising power was once itself colonised. England between 43–410 CE was a territory of the Roman Empire. When the Romans left, German mercenaries enlarged their holdings to first challenge then conquer the Romano-British Celts. Vikings conquered and held much of Northern England – 'the Danelaw' – in the ninth century. In 1066 the Normans conquered England again and these lands paid fealty to a French King till the thirteenth century.

The key to all authority lies in the surplus, in the excess of output over base consumption. Surplus has many forms. In the pre-modern world, the name of the surplus was rent to the landlord, tithe to the Church or tax to the King. The concentration of the surplus in the hands of the lords, their courts, and in the monasteries and churches was an important step in civilising the kingdom. It might look like small beer today, and exploitative too (it was!), but the tithes and the taxes paid for the things that endure: the illustrated manuscripts, the chronicles, the music, the castles, the tapestries and jewellery. It was a world governed in the end by the appetites of the people that ruled.

In 1087 a Norman census of England's taxable resources, the Domesday Book, found that around 10 per cent of the population of one and a quarter million were slaves (the slave trade in the Kingdom – the 'negotium nefarium' – would be abolished shortly afterwards in 1171), 72 per cent were bonded peasants (Villeins or Cottars), obliged to work on the Lord's demesne and 12 per cent were free peasants.

Under the King were 12 Barons, who controlled one-quarter of the land, and in total 1,400 tenants in chief – lords or bishops who held land in lieu of the King. These raised their own armies of knights who could be called upon by the King. The Church held one-quarter of the land and there were 60 major religious houses, and 2000 churches, officiated by priests who exacted a tithe from their parishioners. The urban population was a small fraction – 18,000 in London, 8,000 in Winchester and 4000–5000 in Norwich, York and Lincoln. Townsfolk worked at crafts and trades.[1] Very little of the output of the economy in the tenth century was monetised. Villeins gave up their time to work on the Lord's demesne, or gave up vittles to the monastery. Some luxury goods were exchanged for money, and Jews lent money. Making money was so mysterious to people back then that they imagined there was a magical 'philosophers' stone' that would turn base metal into gold – not quite realising that it was just exchange that turned the one into the other.

The Union of the Crowns, Peter Paul Rubens, 1634.

From England, the Norman King Henry II seized much of Ireland in 1172 and in the thirteenth century Edward I conquered Wales and Scotland temporarily. These early dynastic kingdoms mobilised elite armies, peasant levees, and mercenaries, but had no ambition to win popular power, which was an alien idea to them. Lords exacted tribute from the land and the people on it. Emblematic of Norman power in England, the lands were lorded over from great stone castles built at the behest of a Francophone ruling class to dominate their Anglo-Saxon and Celtic subjects.

In the twelfth century Philip II of France took most of the French half of the Angevin Kingdom leaving England a Norman kingdom in its own right. In the wars between France and England (the Hundred Years War, 1337–1453) the nobility in England began to use the Saxon words of their subjects. A civil war between the Plantagenet and Yorkist Kings (1455–87) ruined both houses, and left the way for the Tudors – a Welsh Norman house to command the throne of England, through the rule of Henry VII, his son Henry VIII and his daughters Mary (whose rule was brief) and Elizabeth I.

In Wales lordly challengers contested the English crown for primacy up until the defeat of Owen Glendower in 1415. Acts of 1535 and 1542 consolidated the legal entity of England and Wales. Scotland's kings kept their independence up until the union of the two crowns under James VI of Scotland and I of England in 1603. Ireland's aristocracy challenged English primacy up until the flight of the Earls Hugh O'Neill and Rory O'Donnell to Spain in 1607.

The formation of the United Kingdom of Britain and Ireland was the creation of a 'near Empire', which had its roots in dynastic conquest. It was pre-modern. In those days all rulers were predators on the mass of the population. There was no strong sense in which the 'people' counted for very much at all, whether they were from Wessex or Dublin, Northumberland or Dumfries, Norfolk or Machllyneth. History was made by lords, whose authority grew out of the soil, or ran down the bloodlines of named families. 'The mass of the population remained serfs or villeins', says the historian Norman Davies, 'and as such played no part in political life'. Even in 1627 the Irish historian Conall Mageoghagan dismissed most of his countrymen as 'mere churls and labouring men, [not] one of whom knows his own great-grandfather'.[2]

The people known as 'Celts' – Gaelic speakers – tended to live in the hills as pastoralists in clans with cattle or sheep, while Anglo-Saxons – English speakers – were more commonly found on the plains, raising crops, with animals in pens.

This England

The Tudor kings are generally credited with the consolidation of the nation. As Angus Calder says, the 'Tudor revolution in government' meant 'that great landed noblemen lost power both to the Crown and to the gentry and merchants represented in the House of Commons'. 'This Realm of England is an Empire', wrote Thomas Cromwell in the preamble to a law of 1533, 'governed by one supreme head and King'.[3] It was a statement of independence from the authority of the Pope, who had refused to annul Henry VIII's marriage to Catherine of Aragon. Though divorce was Henry's immediate cause, the reason that the recasting of England as a Protestant state could thrive was due to more fundamental changes. Protestantism in England advanced cautiously but helped people to think individualistically.

Trade had been a marginal activity that was useful to Medieval Kings for taxing to raise war chests. Merchants sold surplus wool to northern Europe in the Middle Ages, but from 1435 exported more as broadcloth.[4] To increase output some landowners pressed for the enclosure of former arable lands for pasture, though it caused trouble.

There were other forces that threatened to break up the old obligatory social order. In 1347 the 'Black Death' (bubonic plague) killed around half of the population of England, which fell back from nearly five million to little more than two million and did not recover for a century. The shortage of labour brought about a demand for paid labour. When the European population started to boom again, it led to a price hike (which tended to undermine wages). Both of these events, or the fluctuations they represented, tended to promote the monetisation of farm goods and wages. The discovery of the Americas led to an influx of silver that boosted exchange. By the fifteenth century between a third and a fifth of the population of Norfolk, Leicestershire, and Lincolnshire was made up of farm labourers who were paid in cash.[5] Elizabeth I freed the last serfs in 1574. In Earls Colne, in Essex, most food grown was sold in nearby markets in Colchester and Braintree by 1598. (By comparison, 70 per cent of French farm goods were consumed where they were grown up to the eighteenth century.)[6]

From the early 1500s, a Reformation of the Church began taking place all over Europe, so that churchmen were appointed by civil authority and church law bent to secular purposes. After Henry's direct breach with Rome, religious properties were reformed, often meaning the destruction of monasteries. Money churches had sent to

Rome now went to the Crown. Later, under Edward VI, church lands valued at £1½ million were sold off, creating a new market in privately owned land.[7] Dissolution of the Monasteries was popular with some who could see – and sometimes exaggerated – the profligacy of the clergy.

Royal policy, though, was to rein in change. Laws were passed to limit how many sheep you could own to 2,400 (1533), against gig-mills (which raise up cloth for dressing, in 1551), banning weavers from owning more than two looms (1555). In 1563 the Statute of Artificers extended the guild regulations on access to trades from London to the whole country. The law also barred all those with less than £2 worth of land from apprenticeships. In 1624 parliament ordered the destruction of a needle-making machine.[8]

Though the Crown was resistant to change, the movement for reform pressed on. Parliament went ahead with new laws of enclosure in 1621. Enclosure – putting fences around formerly open land – carried on for many centuries. Enclosure changed not just the ways people worked, but the property relationships, too, as land with ambiguous title, or in common use was turned into private property.

From 1633 the Stuart King Charles I ruled without calling Parliament. Bishop Laud, sitting on an Enclosure Commission led a reaction against the changes, prosecuting hundreds for enclosing land. Charles I's 'personal rule' was greatly resented, as was his High Anglicanism, persecution of Puritans (prompting allegations that he would take the country back into Catholicism) and his 'ship tax' (to pay for the navy).

Though the Reformation helped to start a market in land, Elizabeth and the Stuart Kings James I and Charles I, were mulishly resistant to social change, and kept Britain tied in a life-sapping web of obligations and customs. Early economic growth tended to happen at the margins of society, in overseas trade and port towns. That was because the heartland of England was overgrown with customary duties. Under Elizabeth the integration of the English nation became more pressing. Wars with Spain forced the development of the fleet. But that nation was at its heart conservative. Innovation was forced out to the margins, until in 1642 the pressure for a new society broke through.

In 1642, the King was at war with his Parliament. Summoned to raise new taxes Parliament's merchant and improving landlord members demanded new powers for the commons. Many of those returned to the Long Parliament had been fined by Bishop Laud for enclosing their lands. On 4 January 1648, the Parliament mapped out the grounds of its authority, stating: 'That the Commons of England, in Parliament assembled, do declare that the People are, under God, the original of all just power'. The independent yeomanry of eastern England was the backbone of the Parliamentary forces under the leadership of the Cambridgeshire farmer Oliver Cromwell.

After the Civil War, the victorious Cromwell, governing as Lord Protector, pushed further in reforming state and nation than Henry or Elizabeth dared. Crown lands worth £2 million were sold off, to be followed by the sequestrated lands of Royalists worth a further £1¼ million. The Duke of Newcastle sold lands worth £56,000 in order to pay debts incurred in the Royalist cause. One Royalist wrote in 1653 that the tenants of former Church and Crown lands, 'do perfectly hate those who bought them, as possibly men can do; for these men are the greatest tyrants everywhere as men can be; for they wrest the poor tenants of all former immunities and freedoms they formerly enjoyed'.[9] It was perhaps a self-serving account, but there was truth in it too.

The Lord Protector's rule after the execution of the King lacked legitimacy in the eyes of many, and after his death, the army – rejecting Cromwell's son Richard – restored Charles I's son to the throne as Charles II. At the Restoration of the Crown in 1660, though, the power of Parliament and the economic transformation it set in train were not abandoned.

Royalists like Newcastle when they returned to buy back their estates turned improving landlord. There were 'great improvements made of lands since our inhuman civil wars; when our gentry, who before hardly knew what it was to think', wrote the agriculturalist John Houghton 'fell to such an industry and caused such an improvement as England never knew before'.[10]

Arnold Toynbee points to 'the disappearance of the small freeholders who, down to the close of the seventeenth century, formed with their families, one-sixth of the population of England, and whose stubborn determination enabled Cromwell and Fairfax to bring the Civil War to a successful close'. He writes: 'A person ignorant of our history during the intervening period might surmise that a great exterminatory war had taken place, or a violent social revolution, which had caused the transfer of the property of one class to another'. The agricultural writer Arthur Young looking back at the seventeenth century 'sincerely regrets the loss of that set of men who are called yeomen ... who really kept up the independence of the nation', and was 'loth to see their lands now in the hands of monopolising lords'.[11]

The ascent of the Catholic James II to the throne was feared by non-conformists, and the birth of a male heir raised the danger of a Catholic succession. The propertied classes welcomed the seizure of the throne by the Dutch King William of Orange in the Glorious Revolution of 1688.

Under William, Britain fought wars against James II in Ireland and then in the 'nine years war' against France. To meet the cost of war the Bank of England was founded in 1694. It lent money to the government selling bonds at interest to a growing class of rentiers. Taxes rose from two million pounds a year in the 1680s to five million a year in the 1690s. Parliamentary oversight of spending made the finances more rational. From 1689 to 1714 the new civil service grew from four to twelve thousand, most of them customs and excise men.

The Protectorate, and the Glorious Revolution after it, was a forcing house of scientific understanding of social statistics and economy, led by Nicholas Barbon, Sir James Steuart, Adam Ferguson and William Petty. They also saw a great alteration in the relation of the people to the land. Gone were the old villeinage and customary uses and obligations. Land now was property to be improved and to be bought and sold.

In the changes the people were made doubly free, in that they could go where they wanted, and in that they were no longer supported. Sir James Steuart thought that there had to be a 'separation between parent earth and her laborious children' otherwise they will 'suckle in idleness'. 'Any person who could calculate his labours in agriculture purely for subsistence, would find abundance of idle hours', he wrote. 'But the question is, whether in good economy such a person would not be better employed in providing nourishment for others...'.

The problem of 'vagabondage' – that people no longer supported on the land were roaming and hungry was first noticed in the time of Elizabeth. Agricultural improvement meant that there was a surplus of food, so that a new division of labour could emerge where more people lived in towns, specialising in trades other than farming. Those towns also drew on a steady supply of surplus labour, no longer employed in farming, but now working as labourers, craftsmen or traders in the cities. London's population grew from 80,000 in 1500 to 250,000 in 1600 then to half a million in 1670. The numbers working for a wage grew. In the past 'men were ... forced to labour because they were slaves to others', argued James Steuart: 'men are now forced to labour because they are slaves to their own wants'.[12]

Adam Ferguson sketched out a history that the rising middle classes could understand. He called it the growth of 'civil society' out of the rude state of natural subsistence. A people with a commercial bent, with manners, who sorted out their arguments in court, not in battle, and who even had liberal institutions of government. It was a story that was fanciful, but still with just enough truth for them to believe in. Social differentiation was on the horizon, but after the turmoil of the seventeenth century, the eighteenth, in England at least had solid foundations.

Acts of Union

The Acts of Union combined the English Parliament with the Scottish in 1707 and with the Irish in 1801. But they were very different in their meaning. The Union with Scotland was for the most part a success – reconfirmed in a referendum in 2014 – but that with Ireland a failure, dissolved by the Irish parliament, the Dáil, in 1921 after centuries of conflict. (The story of the Union with Ireland is told in Chapter Twelve.) Both countries had already been subject to Anglo-Norman invasions that limited their independence, but the Reformation and modernisation of England reacted more profoundly again on its relations with Scotland and Ireland. The Acts of Union of 1707 and 1801 formalised the incorporation of the 'near Empire' into the United Kingdom.

Scotland 1707

Dynastic Scotland was not so different from dynastic England. The House of Stuart was founded by a Norman lord in King David's service, and later married into the line of Robert the Bruce. James IV of Scotland married Henry VII's daughter, Mary Tudor. His grandson James VI became James I of England in the Union of the Crowns in 1603. Clan leaders like the all-powerful Campbells were Dukes, under the Crown, or they risked becoming outlaws.

The Reformation found ready soil in the Scottish Church which enthusiastically adopted it. While England's Church resisted the austere doctrine of Calvinism, it flourished in lowland Scotland. Scottish churches pushed Reformation.

The English Civil War of 1642 was pretty Scottish, too. The King who provoked Parliament was Charles Stuart – and before that he had provoked the Scottish Church trying to make them follow Bishop Laud's High Anglican liturgy. Since 1581 many Scots had entered into a 'Covenant' with God to resist 'all kind of Papistry'. Covenanting became a statement of independence of the Scottish Church, and in 1639 the Covenanters took up arms against Charles. Charles' forces were not strong enough to defeat the Scots, and the taxes he raised to make war on the Covenanters became a trigger to Parliament's opposition. In the Civil War Covenanters constituted themselves the nation and sent forces to support Parliament. Scottish Royalists led by James Graham, Marquess of Montrose, raised an army, with Irish support, to fight the Covenanters, but were defeated. In 1646 Charles I surrendered to the Covenanters, who handed him over to Cromwell's Parliamentary forces. In 1650 Charles II adopted the Covenant and lent his support to a Scottish Presbyterian war against Cromwell, which was roundly defeated in 1652, and lowland Scotland was occupied by the New Model Army. With the Restoration of Charles II to the Crown, he broke the Covenant, and persecuted the Covenanters, who kept up a militant opposition. When William of Orange took the throne, Covenanters supported him.

Scotland, though, was divided. The lowlands in the south and east of the country were enthusiastic Presbyterians, spoke *lallans* – a dialect of English – and were often arable farmers, the Highlands were less observant, spoke Gaelic and were often pastoralists. Unlike in Ireland, though, the highlanders were not so distinct from lowland Scots by religion. When Irish Franciscan friars visited the Scottish Highlands in 1620 hoping to win over Gaelic Scotland to the Catholic cause, they found that Protestantism was so entrenched that the battle was already lost (though 6,000 Catholic highlanders saw service in the British army a century later). The power of the clan chiefs was already waning. King James had forced the chiefs to pay a surety against lawlessness, and they were anyway becoming more like English lords with expensive lifestyles to keep up.[13] The lowlands largely identified with England's Reformation and modernisation. The Highlands supported their clan chiefs, many of whom rallied to the restoration of the Stuart claim to the throne as they had supported the King in the Civil War of 1642. Highlanders took part in 'Jacobite' campaigns in 1689 (and culminating in the 'Rising' of 1745, defeated at Culloden). Lowlanders, in contrast, broadly welcomed the Protestant William of Orange as their King in a Scottish Convention. On 7 June 1690 with William's agreement, Presbyterianism became the official church in Scotland.

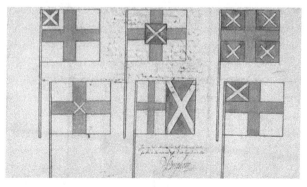

The Earl of Nottingham's earlier designs for the Union Flag, 1606.

It was lowland Presbyterian Scotland that would endorse the Union of 1707. In the background to that decision was the collapse of the Darien scheme – a Quixotic plan to create a colonial outpost for Scotland in South America – that saddled the country with onerous debts. England's offer to pay off Scotland's debt helped secure the proposal for a Union. On 2 November 1706, Lord Belhaven spoke against the proposal, wondering at,

> a free and independent kingdom delivering up that which all the world hath been fighting for, since the days of Nimrod; yea, that for which most of all the Empires, Kingdoms, States and Principalities and Dukedoms of Europe, are at this time engaged in the most bloody and cruel wars that ever were, to wit a power to manage their own affairs by themselves without the assistance and counsel of any other.

Bribery played its part, as Robert Burns wrote: 'We're bought and sold for English Gold/ Such a Parcel of Rogues in a Nation.' The Members of the Scottish Parliament who voted for the Union were not representative by modern standards, and there was rioting outside the Parliament in Edinburgh and also in Glasgow. For many the Treaty, for a Union with England, with William as its King, was a restatement of the Act of Settlement ensuring that the throne would nevertheless remain Protestant. If Scotland's support for Union was commercial, England's was dynastic – the fear that the Scots might not endorse the Hanoverian succession when Anne died led the English Parliament to push for Union.[14]

The defeat of the last serious Jacobite Rising in 1745 also meant the collapse of the clan system. A law of 1746 abolished the heritable jurisdictions that were the legal basis of the clans. Clan chiefs started to capitalise their land, pushing out the influential sub-tenants known as 'tacksmen', and selling land. In the early nineteenth century, the 'clearing' of the land of its former clans was underway. Though the Risings of '15 and '45 feature in the calendar of modern Scottish nationalism, the Stuart pretenders aimed at the English throne, seeing Scotland as a launch-pad; it was Scots who put them down, and Scottish lords who cleared the highlanders. Lowland Scotland largely identified with the campaign against the Highlands.

Support for the Union was bedded down by commercial growth, and both Edinburgh and Glasgow took off between 1760 and 1780. Scotland's elite was not at odds with England's but for the most part, sympathetic. The Moderate Party, led by William Robertson, Hugh Blair and Andrew Carlyle dominated General Assembly of the Church of Scotland, and were loyal Hanoverians. Scottish philosophers and scientists had a disproportionate influence in the eighteenth-century life of letters: Adam Ferguson, Sir James Steuart, Lord Kames, David Hume, Adam Smith, James Boswell and Lord Brougham helped frame the Hanoverian idea of a liberal and rational order; James Watt, Robert Napier and Thomas Telford helped make the industrial revolution; the *Edinburgh Review* was an important a focus for literary life. Later, Scots played a leading role in the British army – with some 48,300 Highlanders recruited between the Seven Years War and the Napoleonic Wars. Sir James Wolfe, who had helped defeat the Jacobite uprising at Culloden, led a force of Highlanders in North America. Edinburgh's Henry Dundas became William Pitt's Secretary of State for War and then First Lord of the Admiralty. The Highland-recruited Black Watch were stationed in Ireland between

1749 and 1756. In 1772, 250 of the 800 British Army officers in Bengal were Scots. With expansion of the British Empire Scots served as administrators, soldiers and industrialists, even dominating colonial trades like tobacco and opium.[15]

Ireland – the first colony

From the twelfth century Norman lords also conquered parts of Ireland. These Anglo-French lords dominated Ireland much as they did England. King Henry II granted his son John lordship over Ireland and when John became King the lordship of Ireland was a title attached to the English Crown.[16] Like the Norman lords in England they gradually adopted the English language, and in the Statutes of Kilkenny (1366) prohibited the Irish language on pain of loss of land, as they did intermarriage between English settlers and native Irish (though these laws were mostly made to stop the drift towards Gaelicisation[17]). A Parliament of Norman nobles called in Drogheda in 1494 by Sir Edward Poynings set down the statute that law made by an Irish Parliament could be overturned in England ('Poynings' law'). However, over the fourteenth and fifteenth centuries they were challenged by Gaelic lords who reduced the 'Old English' to a much more circumscribed share. Formal English rule was even more limited to that area known as 'the Pale' on the east coast around Dublin. The movement for the Reformation of the Church in England under Henry VIII found no echo in Ireland.

Edmund Spenser wrote *A View of the Present State of Ireland* in 1596 after the 'Desmond rebellion'. It painted a picture of a savage and depraved people. 'They do use all the beastly behaviour that may be', wrote Spenser:

> They steal, they are cruel and bloody, full of revenge, and delighting in deadly executions, licentious, swearers and blasphemers, common ravishers of women, and murderers of children.[18]

Much of Ireland was given over to pastoralism, mostly grazing cattle, and that suited Gaelic social structure well. The Brehon law codes held up rights of access to land more than exclusive ownership and vested these in clans not individuals. For that reason, the strict Norman laws of inheritance were less important than kinship and under Brehon law bastardy was not disinherited. Arable farming was mostly kept within the Pale and those who worked on enclosed lands were looked down upon by their neighbours as 'coloni'.[19] No strong yeomanry that might have carried the Reformation zeal grew up in Ireland, as it did in England.

In 1534, the lords gathered in Parliament in Dublin named Henry VIII King of Ireland and head of the Church (though many of those present could not follow the proceedings as they spoke no English). In the Act for Kingly Title in 1541 Ireland was made a kingdom, but a kingdom annexed to the Crown of England. Afterwards Ireland was known as a 'dependent' or 'subordinate Kingdom'.[20] As in England the King demanded the dissolution of the monasteries a policy carried on without enthusiasm, though it was also true that the conventual church had lost support. However, mendicant orders of poor friars, Franciscans, Dominicans and Augustinians were well liked, and held up the faith.

Tudor dealing with the Irish clan leaders was to impose 'surrender and re-grant' – defeat them, and then grant them back their rights on the acknowledgement of the Crown's supremacy. Chiefs of larger clans were given titles of Earl or Lord. It was in some ways a demoralising relationship, underscoring the Earls' dependency on the Crown. It was also relentlessly provocative, as the English Crown ruled by dividing the Earls against each other – which meant they were often building up rival contenders to counter the growing power of some previous favourite.

Hugh O'Neill, Earl of Tyrone; English ward, Irish chieftain.

With the Reformation in England the rule of Ireland took on an international dimension. At the Council of Trent (1545) Pope Pius V launched a *Counter-Reformation* to defend the faith, and Philip II of Spain went to war against the rebellious Dutch Calvinists. A Papal Bull of 1555 names Philip of Spain King of Ireland. By excommunicating Queen Elizabeth I (1570) Pius legitimated actions by Catholic Kings against her, at sea and at the further parts of the Kingdom, Scotland and Ireland. The Counter-Reformation gave courage and cover to Irish chiefs, who 'went out', or rebelled against the Crown.

In 1579 Hugh O'Neill, claimant to the Earldom of Tyrone built up his standing by loyally defending the Crown in the time of the 'Desmond wars', when the FitzGeralds were out. As a boy O'Neill had been protected by the Lord Deputy of Ireland Sir Henry Sidney, who raised him in his stately home in Kent, Penshurst Place, a playmate to the poet Philip Sidney. As an Irish lord Hugh O'Neill was shored up by his English patrons as an alternative to his cousin Turlough Earl of Tyrone. By helping the Earl of Essex to capture and kill his father-in-law, Brian O'Neill, who had fought against a seizure of his lands, Hugh O'Neill earned the title of Earl of Tyrone.

'Her Majesty and the State hath set up him up', said Lord Bingham of Hugh O'Neill's journey from Kentish orphan to Gaelic clan leader, 'and the State must uphold him or he will fall'.[21] It was England's divide-and-rule policy to back another, weaker claimant in reserve, and then to elevate him to compromise the incumbent. As the English did this, they created new challengers, and by 1595 O'Neill was 'out', fighting the Queen's forces.

As 'The O'Neill', Hugh won great victories over the government forces under Sir Henry Bagenal (whose sister O'Neill had eloped with, and then mistreated) at Clontibret (1595) and at the Yellow Ford (1598) where Sir Henry and 1500 of his men were killed. At the height of his powers Hugh was lauded as a hero of the Counter-Reformation. He was 'Ugo Conte di Tirone, Generale Ibernese' in Annibale Adami's *La Spada D'Orione* (1680).

In 1601 Philip III's Spanish fleet, under Don Juan del Aquila landed at Kinsale in support of O'Neill. In his demands O'Neill set out that the ancient Irish Chiefs 'may peaceably enjoy all lands and privileges that did appertain to their predecessors 200 years past', that 'all statutes made against the preferment of Irishmen, as well in their own country as abroad, be presently recalled', that the 'Catholic, Apostolic and Roman religion be openly preached and taught throughout all Ireland', and that the churches and church lands 'now in the hands of the English be presently restored to the Catholic churchmen'. 'Ewtopia' Lord Cecil scrawled over the letter, though he also said that 'if Tyrone had ever any purpose to become a subject, Her Majesty is likest to receive him with tolerable conditions, for she cares not for anything he holds in comparison with his obedience'.[22]

When the English forces recovered their nerve, under Lord Mountjoy and Sir Henry Dowcra, they broke up Tyrone's hold by surrounding him with a ring of forts and supporting rival clans against him. In time, O'Neill did bend the knee first to Elizabeth, promising to help her civilise the Irish in English ways, and then (as she had just died) to her successor James, who magnanimously restored his Earldom. Earl in name only, and at the whim of James I, O'Neill was beset on all sides by those who had been promised lands to rise against him, and English captains who were disgusted that he had been allowed to live. Sensing he would soon be betrayed, O'Neill got on a boat for the Spanish Netherlands with his old ally Hugh O'Donnell to live out his last years in Rome. Ninety more Gaelic chiefs left Ulster with him.

A 1610 scheme of plantation encouraged Scots and English to settle in Ireland, so that by 1630 there were 80,000 settlers in Ulster. Lord Strafford, who ruled the Kingdom at that time thought that 'all Wisdom advises to keep this Kingdom as much subordinate and dependent on England as possible'. He meant that Britain should hold 'them from the Manufacture of Wool', and force 'them to fetch their Clothing from thence, and to take their Salt from the King'.[23] In 1640 James Butler, Earl of Ormond, of an old Anglo-French family in Ireland, but raised a Protestant in London, was made Chief of the Armed Forces. In 1641 Sir Phelim O'Neill, till then a loyal supporter of the King, launched a campaign to save Catholic land in Ulster from settlers. Claiming

– fraudulently – that he had the support of King Charles I, Phelim O'Neill laid waste to Protestants in the north east of the country, eventually killing around 5000. If this was not bad enough the massacre became a *cause célèbre* in the growing argument between the English King and the Parliamentarians. No less a figure than the Cambridge Member of Parliament Oliver Cromwell launched an inquiry into the massacre and the King's part in it. The numbers killed were fantastically inflated in Parliamentary propaganda, to 40,000 and even to 150,000 (and 300,000 in John Temple's *History of the Irish Rebellion,* 1646). A sectarian conflict in Ireland became a launching pad for England's long Civil War, though for the first seven years the greater part of the conflict was fought in England, and then in Scotland.

Ireland's Catholic leadership, organised in a new Confederacy at Kilkenny, to support the forces of King Charles in his contest with Parliament. In September of 1643 Charles' representative in Ireland, the Earl of Ormond united with the Confederacy. Irish troops returned from the continent to Ireland, and many from there joined the Parliamentary forces fighting in England. When the King surrendered himself to the Scots Covenanters Parliament's New Model Army turned its attention to defeating the Royalists in Ireland. In January 1645, the Parliamentary 'Committee of Both Kingdoms' founded the New Model Army, saying 'God has put the sword of reformation into the soldier's hand'.

British expeditionary forces soon persuaded Ormond to give up Dublin and the Pale, but the rest of the country gave allegiance to the King or to the Catholic Confederacy. When Parliament executed Charles I Ormond was effective head of the Royalist movement, and he named Charles Stuart – the son – King Charles II, making Ireland the centre of Royalist opposition.

Oliver Cromwell, leader of the Parliamentary forces and eventual Lord Protector landed in Dublin on 15 August 1649 and on 3 September laid siege to Drogheda, just north of there. The Royalist commanders refused to surrender and when Cromwell broke through his army killed 3,000 armed defenders and around 1,000 civilians (4,000, in 'unparalleled savagery' according to some Irish sources[24]). 'It hath pleased God to bless our endeavours at Drogheda', Cromwell said: 'this is a righteous judgment of God upon those barbarous wretches'.[25] By October he had moved south to the town of Wexford where 2,000 Royalist troops were killed and many civilians. Some radicals in Cromwell's New Model Army – 'Levellers' – protested in pamphlets like *The Souldiers Demand* (1649):

> What have we to do with Ireland, to fight and murther a People and a Nation (for indeed they are set upon cruelty, and murthering poore people which is all they glory in) which have done us no harm.[26]

In the spring of 1649, though, Cromwell defeated the Levellers crushing Robert Lockyer's rebellion in London and defeating the Leveller forces at Burford, so quieting what little radical opposition there was to the invasion of Ireland. The war in Ireland was fought bitterly, but despite the moral support of the Vatican, no material help came from the great Catholic powers, Spain or France, other than the Irish soldiers returning from Spain's campaign in the Netherlands. Irish resistance to the Parliamentary forces was divided, sometimes bitterly. Ormond's Royalist army numbered many Protestant settlers, who at times turned on Irish Catholics, and he risked alienating them by making Owen Roe O'Neill general. The Catholic Confederacy had no ambition to make Ireland independent, but only to find a protector – and when Charles failed, they offered the country up to the Duke of Lorraine as his personal fiefdom if only he would defend them. Long after the Royalists had been defeated, Irish forces – who were known as 'Tories' from the Gaelic word for hunt – resisted the Cromwellian settlement.

Cromwell was for historic reasons excoriated in England as a 'Regicide' (following the Restoration of the Monarchy in 1660) but his reputation was restored by Thomas Carlyle and other writers in the nineteenth century. Not so in Ireland where the history of Drogheda and Wexford, and the very presence of the man at these two massacres, fixed his name as a curse. By the standards of the day it was not an outlandish atrocity, and the Royalists did as bad themselves. Much worse in its long-term effect was the Settlement that followed.

To raise funds for the invasion Parliament sold debentures – or bonds – to 'Adventurers' (as investors were called) that would be realised from land seized. The troops of the New Model Army were also promised land in lieu of pay. What the Parliamentarians planned was a wholesale land seizure both to finance the invasion, but also to settle the country in the belief that the Irish were too uncivilised to husband the land, and the English were, in the words of Gerard Boate's 1652 book *Ireland's Natural History*, 'introducers of all good things' – meaning the bog-draining, wood-clearing and mine-digging.[27]

William Petty, a scientific genius of the day, got the contract to map the country, which he and his surveyors did in 1655, two million and two hundred thousand acres of it. Of those fully 1,809,613 profitable acres were to be forfeited to investors or soldiers to pay off the government debts incurred invading Ireland.[28] The Catholic landowning families were threatened with an extraordinary act of ethnic cleansing whereby they were uprooted and sent to lands one tenth the size of their original holdings in a special reserved area in Connacht.

Parliament also offered former Irish soldiers to recruiting sergeants for European armies. Don Ricardo White took 7000 for the King of Spain in May 1652 – just the first shipment of many – and Lord Muskerry took 5000 to the King of Poland. In all some 34,000 were transported. Widows and orphan girls were shipped to Barbados to meet the need for companions to planters and their servants there.[29]

In the event the practicalities of clearing Ireland of all its inhabitants were too great. The entire transplantation to Connaught was unrealisable, and after some 45,000 were uprooted the plan was abandoned. Commissioner Vincent Gookin, tasked with allocating Irish land to English soldiers and investors alongside Petty, objected to the plan, in a pamphlet *The Great Case of Transplantation in Ireland Discussed* (1654). He made two arguments. The first was that it was 'barbarousness on them' which would backfire because 'crowding them all together' and 'the great injury they conceive they have in this action' would give them 'the power to rebel again'. Gookin's other argument was that 'removal' would hurt English interests because 'the revenue contribution of Ireland is generally raised out of corn and the husbandmen of that corn are generally Irish'. Those soldiers who were to take over the land 'have neither stock, nor money to buy stock, nor (for the most part) skill in husbandry'. However, 'by the labour of the Irish on their lands' the soldier-planters 'may maintain themselves, improve their lands, acquire stock'.[30] Gookin was making the case that they needed the Irish to exploit their labour. Many thought Gookin was being too soft, but the transplantation of all the Irish ground was too great an undertaking and the policy ground to a halt.

Paying for the war by seizing the land of Ireland was full of problems. The soldiers, short of money, mostly sold their debentures at a great discount to their officers. Arguments over the claims of the 'Adventurers' (investors) were part of the reason that Cromwell shut down the English Parliament altogether to rule as 'Protector'. Historian Karl Bottigheimer lists 3,043 original Adventurers who subscribed anything from A. Austin's £5, which bought him five acres to the cost of thousands of acres. London raised half the £258,000 subscribed, with merchants well represented. Members of the Long Parliament were responsible for about one tenth of the fund. Among the larger investors Sir William Brereton, the Roundhead MP for Cheshire got 2,796 acres in Tipperary and 3,750 in Armagh; George Clarke a London merchant got 7,891 acres in Tipperary and another 2,581 in East Meath; William Hawkins, a merchant tailor of London invested £4,124 in the original subscription and eventually drew 'a small empire in county Down' of 32,395 acres.[31]

Bottigheimer judged that 'in the long run the adventure was a two-fold failure':

> In a fiscal sense it failed to raise the amount necessary to repress Catholic Ireland. In a colonial sense it failed to find and tap an aggressive, enterprising stream within English society.[32]

The impact of the policy could be seen in the handing over of the land from Catholic to Protestant owners. Eight million four hundred thousand acres were taken. In 1641, 60 per cent of Ireland was still owned by Catholics. That was already less than in 1600 when 80 per cent of Ireland was Catholic-owned. But by 1688, when the full effect of the Cromwellian settlement was felt, just 22 per cent of Ireland was in the hands of Catholic landowners.[33]

The change of the country was in some ways like the changes in England and Scotland. Those that had use of the land were driven from it and brought back as paid labourers, while ownership was put in the hands of a few. Unlike England and Scotland, the land monopoly was held by lords who were a different nationality and religion from the working poor. Ireland was, said Frederick Engels, 'the first English colony'.

Share of land held by Catholics in Ireland.[34]

Year	Per cent
1641	59
1688	22
1703	14
1776	5

William Petty wrote that of the population of 1,668,000 in 1641 just 1,100,000 were left in 1652 – 568,000 were gone, 'wasted by the sword, plague, famine and hardship'. Petty recorded that the houses of Ireland were 200,000, of which 40,000 had a chimney, but 160,000 were 'nasty, wretched cabins without chimney, window or door'.[35] Ireland's path was blocked by the settlement of the land question, with the country's wealth given over to largely absentee landlords. In 1672 Petty worked out that the annual rent those landlords drew was £0.9 million – out of a national income of £4 million – climbing to £1.2 million in 1687.

When the British Parliament invited William of Orange to take the Crown in 1689, James II fought a rearguard war in Ireland, calling on Catholics to support their King against the Dutch pretender. The Irish socialist republican James Connolly took a dim view of the Jacobite cause:

> It is unfortunately beyond all question that the Irish Catholics of that time did fight for King James like lions. It is beyond all question that the Irish Catholics shed their blood like water, and wasted their wealth like dirt, in an effort to retain King James on the throne. But it is equally beyond all question that the whole struggle was no earthly concern of theirs.[36]

While Connolly had a point that the Irish people had little to gain from seeing James II restored to the throne, William's victory at the Battle of the Boyne would be celebrated by Ulster's Protestant Orangemen on the 'Glorious Twelfth' ever after.

In 1724 Jonathan Swift put Irish rents at £2 million, of which one-third went straight to English landowners. The Irish Parliament was, in Swift's day, a puppet Parliament. Only 64 of its 300 members were elected, and that on a very limited franchise, the rest were nominated, mostly by the Peers. The propertied classes of Ireland were more cautious than their European and American counterparts. The Earl of Clare, John Fitzgibbon explained that 'confiscation is their common title, and from their first settlement they have been hemmed in on every side by the old inhabitants of the island, brooding over their discontents in sullen indignation'.[37] Later, an Irish nation would assert itself. In the seventeenth and much of the eighteenth century, its possibilities were few.

Chapter Two

MERCHANTS

For 500 years the Roman Empire not only governed by military might and taxed its dominions, but it was also a trading Empire. The Empire made treaties with other states that guaranteed the rights of merchants to visit and trade. While Romans lived under the laws of the *Jus Civile* those foreign traders carried on their business under the special *Jus Gentium*, or law of peoples. In 242 BC a special judge, *Praetor Peregrinus* (*peregrinus* means strangers or foreigners), was put in charge of the merchants in Rome.

The special laws of the *Jus Gentium* covering trade are very modern. Under the rule *Locatio et Conductivo* you could hire things or employ people; under the rule of *Societas* you could make a partnership, for a special venture, or an open-ended one; the rule of *Mandatum* said that you could make someone else your agent.[1]

The right of strangers was honoured by ancient societies because merchants brought goods from other lands. If those strangers were not safe, they would not come back. The Greeks gave a name to the tavern where strangers could stay in safety, the *pandocheion* (it means 'all comers') which is mentioned in the fifth century BC. Taken up by the Romans the *pandocheion* spread through their Empire and outlasted it. In the Ummayad Caliphate it was known as the *fundunc*. To Italian merchants it was the *fondaco*.[2]

The Italian merchants knew a contract called the *commenda* under which an investor partnered with an agent, but the *commenda* was 'original with the Arabs'. Their law had two types of partnership *sharikat al-milk* (proprietary partnership) and *sharikat al-'aqd* (contractual partnership). That last was for the 'joint exploitation of capital and the joint participation in profits and losses'.[3] Muhammad himself was an agent under the *commenda*. The words tariff, check, carat are all Arab in origin. And while European thinkers like Thomas More argued that the courts ought to set a just price, Muhammad already understood that prices are in the hands of God.

By 750, the Ummayad Caliphate spread from Andalusia around the southern Mediterranean and across the Arabian Peninsula as far as modern-day India. Arab trade routes connected Europe, Africa, Arabia, India, China and the Far East. To the north the Mongol Emperors guaranteed trading rights for Genoese merchants who brought Cathay silk to the fairs of Champagne in 1257. Later scholars would call these guarantees the *Pax Mongolica* – the Mongol Peace.

The extent of the trade routes of the eleventh and twelfth centuries is impressive. Trade, though, was still the exception for most people, rather than the norm. Most people across the world farmed. They were bound to their village. They gave up all that they did not eat or use themselves to lords, as rent or taxes, and worked labour services on the lords' lands.

The *Pax Mongolica* was for merchants, but labourers were abducted from Persia and Northern China to weave, mine and make weapons in Siberia. The 'Golden Horde' in Russia imposed a 'Tartar Yoke' of harsh exploitation that plunged Russia into a culturally dark age. The European merchant could visit the *fundunc*, in Egypt, sure that his debts would be met, but at the same time the Mameluke Sultanate met their 'insatiable need for military manpower' by enslaving non-Muslims and pagans.[4] From 1770, the Yorkshire-born trader Lionel Abson lived on the West African coast for 30 years as ambassador to the Dahomey Court and raised a family with a local woman – but still he traded in enslaved Africans with his Dahomey hosts.[5] The 'right of the stranger' was only for the small minority of visiting merchants or trading partners. Strangers who were not merchants were ripe for conquest and enslavement. Trade in the middle ages was very broad, but not very deep. Most goods that were traded were luxury goods, and the buyers were among the wealthy. The greater part of a country's output never got traded, but was consumed by those who produced it, shared with others in the village, or given up as rent-in-kind. Trade was marginal to medieval society which was mostly 'tributary', that is, giving up tribute to an overlord. Markets were places that you went to, often a day or more away, or that travelled themselves, sometimes arriving just once a year. From 1312, Henry I granted a fair at the City of Ely for the feast of Saint Audrey (23 July) where lace and ribbons were sold. Its cheap but eye-catching wares were what peasants could afford and the fair gives us the modern word 'tawdry'. Only much later would trade expand to take in every aspect of life, no longer fixed to a date in the calendar or a place, but in every street, and then in our laptops and phones. For that to happen peasants who worked the land would have to leave the countryside for the towns and become employees with a wage.

Among Europeans the important mercantile powers were the Italian city states of Venice, Genoa and Florence as well as the Netherlands.

Merchant England

The medieval city was a lot smaller than its modern counterpart, not just in numbers, but also in its share of population of the country. Today most people live in cities. But London in 1300 had a population of 50,000 in a country of three million. The division of labour did not allow large-scale urbanisation. Almost everybody lived on the land, in villages that farmed. The population of London and the other – much smaller – towns like Norwich and Lincoln were for those who lived by other means. The town-dwellers needed the farmers to feed them, which meant, too, that the farmers needed the townies, or what they did, enough for those farmers to give up some of their farm goods in exchange for the goods of the town. For the most part what the people in the town did was to make those things that were too complicated to be made in the villages.

We can get some idea of what Londoners had to offer to the rest of the country by looking at the guilds – craft bodies that ran the city. They included Apothecaries, Armourers, Bakers, Barbers (also surgeons and dentists), Basket-makers, Blacksmiths, Longbow makers, Brewers, Carpenters, Candle-makers, Cutlers, Dyers, Fishmongers, Goldsmiths, Masons, Mercers (general merchants), Needlemakers, Plasterers, Plumbers,

Poulters, Saddlers, Salters, Scriveners, Skinners, Upholsterers, Vintners, Weavers and Wheelwrights.

The town was 'a self-conscious and coherent community with a distinct life of its own', wrote J. R. Green, 'a free self-governing community, a state within the state'.[6] Among the guilds, the Mercers – or merchants – and the goldsmiths would later give way to full-blown capitalists and bankers. Early merchant traders, though, were often foreigners. The eleventh century England had already set up a 'law merchant' for visiting foreigners and special *'piepoudre* courts' (*piepoudre* meaning 'dusty feet'). In England many itinerant pedlars were Scots.

Moneylending was forbidden under the medieval reading of biblical laws. Jews, being the only people in England outside the Church, were allowed to lend. The borrowers were wealthy landowners, and the loans were mostly for buying personal luxuries not investment. King Henry II owed £100,000. Interest rates were very high, 45 to 85 per cent. Loans were registered with the *Scaccarium Judaeorum* (Exchequer of Jews). The Jews were very unpopular with their noble debtors and often attacked and massacred, as happened in London, Lincoln and Stafford in 1189. The following year Richard de Malbis led an attack on Jews at York where 100–150 took their own lives rather than let themselves be killed. The King tolerated the Jews, and even gave them protection from attacks in the Tower, mostly because they were taxed at 10 per cent of all loans, making a good income for the Treasury. After the deaths at York the King collected on the outstanding loans on the grounds that the Jews were the 'slaves of his Treasury'. In 1275, the Statute de Judaismo barred Jews from lending money, forgave some debts, and made Jews wear a yellow badge in public. In 1290, Edward I expelled all Jews from England – an edict that stood until Parliament overturned it in 1655. Later, Lombard and Genoese bankers would lend money in the City of London.[7]

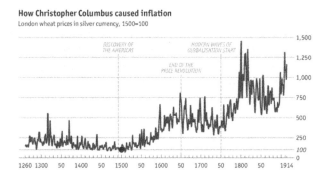

How Christopher Columbus caused inflation
London wheat prices in silver currency, 1500=100

In the sixteenth century trade was growing faster than the supply of money in England and much of Europe. The population had recovered from the Black Death and was growing. Henry VIII tried to save money for the treasury by debasing the coinage (putting less silver in each coin). Elizabeth I's counsellor Thomas Gresham convinced her to support the pound on the grounds that the 'bad money chases out the good' (now known as 'Gresham's law').

There was a need for more precious metal to act as a medium of exchange. German mines gave up too little silver. Gold could be got from Africa and helped the Portuguese to buy Indian goods. From 1493 Columbus' Caribbean gold was having a dramatic effect on prices in the Americas, and then in Spain. From 1550 to 1700 prices rose all across Europe as American silver and gold made more and more trade.

Before a larger market economy could develop, trade grew not within countries, but between them. It was in the ports that the first successful merchant businesses started. The growth of foreign trade came before that of domestic trade, against Adam Smith's expectations (see Chapter Nine). Britain sheared a lot of wool which was sold to Antwerp where it was made up into cloth. Flemish weavers were recruited so England could sell woollen cloth instead of raw wool. Enclosing open land behind fences helped turn arable land (for crops) into pasture (for livestock to graze on). Much of the land enclosed in the thirteenth and fourteenth century was turned over to sheep farming (drawing the warning from Thomas More that 'our sheep that were wont to be so meek and tame, and so small eaters, now, as I heard say, be become so great devourers and so wild, that they eat up, and swallow down the very men themselves', *Utopia*, 1516). The trade in wool had been granted to the German merchants of the Hanse, or Hanseatic League in the thirteenth century – but in 1469 British privateers fought with the Danzig merchants, leading to war between England and the League. At the Peace of Utrecht (1474), the Hanse trading privileges were restored with the Hanse outposts in the London steelyards, Boston and King's Lynn.

English merchants still clamoured for the right to the trade. William Stafford wondered 'what grossness be we of, that see it and suffer such a continual spoil to be made of our goods and treasure'. He was worried that 'everything will go where it is most esteemed; and therefore our treasure thus goeth over in ships'. Foreign merchants, warned Stafford, were buying raw materials from England and selling them back to us as finished goods, making Britons pay the customs on the outgoing goods and the re-imported goods:

> They do make us pay at the end for our stuff again; for the stranger custom, for the work-manship, and colours, and lastly, for the second custom in the return of the wares into the realm again whereas with working the same within our realm our own men should be set to work at the charges of the strangers; the custom should be borne all by strangers to the king; and clear gains to remain within our realm.[8]

Stafford's warning was a part of a wider campaign by English merchants to push out foreigners. 'The natives here', warned the Venetian ambassador in 1556, 'have laid a plot to ruin the trade of all foreign merchants'.[9] In 1557, Henry VIII tore up the Hanse monopoly and London's 'denizen' trade won out. In 1500, half of all cloth exported from London was handled by foreign merchants, but by 1561 that had fallen to less than a quarter.[10]

The company that cornered the market in cloth exports were the Merchant Adventurers (adventurer meaning investor). Their trade was taxed and raised £30,000 a year for the Exchequer – more than a quarter of all monies Parliament voted for the budget.[11] The Merchant Adventurers charged a membership fee of £66, later raised to £200 in the 1550s.

Later in the sixteenth century another company, the Levant Company was set up to trade goods from the Arab world coming through the Mediterranean. Like the Merchant Adventurers, the Levant Company had a Royal Charter which guaranteed a monopoly in trade. The number of Levant traders was limited to 53 under the charter, and from 1615 the Levant Company charter also had a clause that all goods from the Levant must come on English ships (one of the early 'Navigation Laws'). The Levant Company's main import was currants from the Greek islands (then under Turkish rule), around 49,000 hundred weight in 1610.[12]

Mercantilism

Among the Chartered Companies, as well as the Merchant Adventurers, were the French Company, the Spanish Company, the Levant Company, the Muscovy Company and the Guinea Company, later followed by the Royal African Company, the Massachusetts Bay Company, the Virginia Company, the Hudson's Bay Company, the Bermuda Company and the Providence Island Company. Under the reigns of James I and Charles I, from 1603–49, the monarchy was short of funds and one way to raise them was to charter companies of merchants, granting monopolies, for which they paid handsomely.

Mercantilism found its political twin in the theory of Absolutism. The Divine Right of Kings sat well with the gift of the Royal Charter. James and Charles both ruled – as they thought – because they were put there by God. The monopoly of the chartered company came out of the absolute rights of the King. These Kings favoured colonies, because their output was easily taxed at the port of entry by the Excise men where domestic surpluses were lost in rents and tithes to the Lords and the Church. That was why James I agreed when the Virginia Company asked for a ban on tobacco growing in England.

The East India Company

Merchants of the Levant Company helped to set up the East India Company (EIC) by Royal Charter in 1599 to take advantage of the trade opened up by the Portuguese, and by the Dutch EIC in spices from Java. The Company would live on for 258 years, in which time it did not just trade in goods but also colonised much of India in the eighteenth century.

The Thames, around 1640, as it would have looked when the first East India ships sailed.

The EIC's first voyage left London in 1601 with four ships under James Lancaster lead captain on the Red Dragon. They sailed to Bantam (Banten on the western end of Java), where Lancaster left men to found a 'factory' or warehouse. Lancaster got the local King's permission to punish 'whosoever he tooke about his house in the night' and five natives were executed. Lancaster returned to London in 1603 with a cargo of pepper and some cottons seized from a Portuguese ship.

Each of the early voyages was separately financed ventures with individual subscribers drawn from the Company's merchants. Capital was tied up in these journeys for many months, sometimes years. The rate of return on Lancaster's voyage was 87 per cent, but later voyages netted anything from 12 to 60 per cent. In 1657, the Company became a Joint Stock Company.[13]

From 1607 the EIC had ships built at Deptford and then in 1615 moved to Blackwall. In its first 40 years it built 76 ships, but from 1639 hired them – often ships built in Bombay – and from 1650 it stopped insuring the ships, meeting losses instead from its own funds.[14]

The EIC set up 'factories' in India, after the first at Bantam in Java:

- At Surat, in the North West, on the Tapi River just inland from the Hazira Creek, in 1613. Surat dealt in textiles, and also indigo and saltpetre. In 1630 Surat was in decline as the land around was in famine. In 1664 and 1670 Surat was sacked by the Marathas.
- At Masulipatam (Machilipatnam) in 1611, though it was later moved to avoid the Mughal Golconda wars.
- At Madras (now Chennai) on the Coromandel coast, facing the Bay of Bengal to the East, in 1639 where the Company built Fort St George. The settlement prospered, divided into a 'white' and a 'black' town, with a combined population of 100,000 in 1700, By the 1670s, Madras eclipsed Surat as the Company's major trading point. It had a town hall, a church, hospital and the governor's lodgings. Six aldermen and a mayor dealt with the English population, Indians went straight to the Governor.
- At the Isle of Bombay 236 kilometres south of Surat, after the island was given to Charles II as a dowry for his marriage to Catherine of Braganza in 1661 (today it is part of a much larger City connected to the mainland at Mumbai).
- At Bengal, where the Company traded from the 1650s, and in 1690 took the villages of Kalikata, Gobindapur and Sutanuti to found a settlement they called Calcutta, under Job Charnock.

EIC factory bosses were known as Chiefs up until 1619, then Presidents.

Early in the seventeenth century the EIC was boxed in by the dominant Portuguese, who had close to 50 forts in India and the Far East. The Portuguese demanded traders buy a *cartaz* or licence, charged customs at the ports they controlled, and made ship sail in Portuguese protected convoys.

The EIC also struggled against the Dutch Vereenigde Oostindische Compagnie (VOC), which raised a capital fund of £550,000 – eight times the EIC's initial fund

– for its first voyages. In the first century, the VOC sent seven ships for every three that the EIC sent.[15] The VOC put pressure on the Portuguese, too, so that their share of the spice trade fell to 20 per cent by the 1620s. The Dutch seized the Portuguese settlements at Malacca in 1641, Colombo in 1656 and Cochin in 1663. The English also clashed with the Portuguese until a peace treaty in 1653.

Though the EIC was set up to take advantage of the spice trade, it lost out to the VOC. The main trade was the importation of Indian cotton cloth, mostly chintzes, which were decorated with colourful motifs. The British craze for chintz took off in the later seventeenth century. The fine Bengal muslin was popular, too. In 1613, the company imported 5,000-piece goods, rising to 250,000 in 1664 and 1,400,000 by 1690.[16] Cotton is native to India, though it had spread to Egypt and Greece. In 1350, the Englishman John Mandeville wrote of India that 'there grew there a wonderful tree which bore tiny lambs on the endes of its branches'. The popularity of Indian textiles in London angered local silk weavers who attacked women wearing chintz in riots. England made laws to protect home-grown wool in 1660 and 1680, including a rule that all shrouds be made of wool. Cotton was chief among the goods that Royal African Company ships traded on the slave coast, and re-export of cotton was a massive business for Britain.

The Company bought cotton cloth from traders – bania – who bought it from domestic weavers. Indian weavers had invented the spinning wheel in the eleventh century and been using the treadle loom since before 750 AD. Indian crafts were the envy of Europe. Indian merchants like Pestonjee Jamsetjee and Sorabjie Javange in Bombay, or Dadabo Manockjee in Surat made large fortunes buying for the EIC as late as 1800. Later the Company would employ its own agents and take a tighter grip on trade in India.[17]

The Company in the eighteenth century was criticised for its excessive profits, and a parliamentary inquiry collated these statistics:

Accounts of the EIC.

	Exports of goods and bullion	Bills of exchange paid	Total cost of the goods received	Amount of sales of goods
1733–42	£617,283	£167,311	£784,594	£1,699,775
1743–52	£886,938	£196,160	£1,083,098	£2,058,862
1753–62	£797,318	£303,076	£1,100,394	£2,030,104
1763–72	£667,600	£323,422	£991,022	£2,298,768

Penny Cyclopaedia of the Society for the Diffusion of Useful Knowledge, Vol 9-10, p 249.

They show an average operating profit of 119 per cent, which considering the investments they had to make in factories, ships, writers and infantry is not that great.

Alongside the official trade, captains and other officials took advantage of their stay to bring back luxury goods, and saltpetre (for gunpowder) to sell at home, as well as trading in goods in the Indies. Between them the EIC, its European rivals, and the English 'Country Traders' muscled Arab, Indian and Chinese traders out of the regional market.

In time naval power would give Britain rule over the Indian Ocean and the South China sea. From 1672 EIC profits were higher than those of the Dutch EIC. Navigation Acts from 1651 gave English trade the advantage. Dutch investors put their money in London stocks. By 1750 one-fifth of all accounts were held by Dutch investors.[18]

Another land that suffered under the mercantile system was Ireland. In the House of Lords the defenders of the woollen merchants of Yorkshire beseeched King William,

> To declare to all your subjects of Ireland, that the growth and increase of the woollen-manufactures there hath long been, and will be ever, looked upon with great jealousy by all your subjects of this kingdom, and if not timely remedied, may occasion very strict laws to totally prohibit it and suppress the same.[19]

The English Government made laws banning Ireland from trading with any but Britain. There were laws, too, to stop the export of woollen cloth in favour of raw wool, so that it was worked up by woollen manufacturers in Britain.

'Mere Merchants'

One of the changes that the company charters brought to England's towns was the rule that all but 'mere merchants' were shut out. That meant that 'retailers, artificers, common mariners and handicraftsmen' were not to be investors in the Spanish Company, the Merchant Adventurers or the EIC. The Merchant Adventurers meant this rule to stop these ordinary people from 'taking the living from their brethren'. The chartered companies were kept for those who made their fortune by investing alone. In the 1620s, London's grocers, retailers to the Levant Company, refused to pay their bills for the currants they sold in protest at the 'mere merchants' provision.[20] In the debate between the Royal African Company and those independent interlopers who challenged its monopoly, the outsiders were portrayed by the Company as 'shopkeepers', themselves as 'Worthy Merchants'.[21] We look more closely at the Royal African Company's trade in slaves in Chapter Six.

Chapter Three

NAVIGATORS AND PIRATES

Britain laid claim to the world's oceans in the seventeenth century, but, notionally at least, international trade already stretched from Ireland to Japan in the thirteenth century. The trade routes of English commerce were already well established.

The Roman Empire traded in the Indian Ocean, called by them the Erythraean Sea. From the founding of the first (Rashidun) Caliphate in the seventh century European traders had no way into the Indian Ocean. The overland route from Tana (Azov on the Don) to Peking took 275 days by camel and donkey, warned the Florentine merchant Balducci Pegolotti in 1340.[1]

Trade in the Indian Ocean between Africa and India was run by Arab captains who had mastered the routes out of the Persian Gulf and through the Red Sea down the East African Coast and around India, down the (west-facing) Malabar Coast. The names of the navigators who first plotted those routes are not recorded, but the seafarers' manual written by Ibn Majid in the fifteenth century summarises an extensive knowledge of the ocean and its ports. In particular Ibn Majid's book explains the monsoon, under which winds carried dhows from the Arabian Peninsula in the late spring, and then carried them the other way in the autumn. Monsoon is from the Arabic Mawsim, meaning a part of the year.[2]

Arab influence was strong among the Gujarati merchants, who became Muslims. Arab traders favoured the settlement at Calicut (called Kozhikode today) – especially after trade in the Muslim world shifted from Persia, going through the Gulf, to Egypt by the Red Sea.

In 1405 Zheng He, admiral in the Navy of the Yongle Emperor of the Ming Dynasty sailed out of Suzhou around the Western Sea around Java, Brunei, South East Asia, India Ceylon and as far as the West Coast of Africa. It was the first of seven voyages Zheng He made carrying treasures to gift to potential tributaries of the Emperor. By contemporary accounts Zheng He's treasure ships were huge, with nine masts, four decks and a crew of 500. The whole fleet had hundreds of ships, and thousands of seamen. Zheng He's diplomatic gifting brought him to Bengal, where he was presented a giraffe to take back to China, and camels, ostriches, ivory and other treasures of the Western Sea. Maps like the Mao Kun map, a copy of Zheng He's, or the Korean Kangnido map of 1402 show that Chinese navigators had knowledge of the world extending from Japan to Europe. The Hongzhi Emperor was less favourable to these outward expeditions and the Chinese presence beyond India declined.[3]

In 1460, Henriques – King of Portugal, 'Henry the Navigator' died, having seized Ceuta on the African coast. He committed his countrymen to explore the coast of Africa, mostly in an attempt to drive south of the Muslim kingdoms and reach the source of the King of Mali's gold. Henry's legacy lived on under Jaoa, or John, II of

Portugal and his successor Manuel I. In 1482, Jaoa sent Diogo Cão down the coast. Cão got further than most, turning inwards past the land they called Guinea, and then south again, until he reached the mouth of the Congo River. In a second voyage the sailor got as far as what is modern-day Namibia.

Portuguese explorers knew of India and the spice islands, but already the Muslim traders monopolised the overground route from the Eastern Mediterranean, through the Red Sea into the Indian Ocean. Africa seemed to be an insurmountable barrier and from Ptolemy's world map they learned that the Indian Ocean was a closed sea (like the Mediterranean). The Portuguese sailors had ships called caravels, that were small and light, about 80-feet long and 20-feet wide, with triangular sails (that helped fight the winds down the coast). They would leave Lisbon out of the mouth of the Tagus (Teju) river into the Atlantic Ocean.

CHRISTOPHER COLUMBUS'S REPUTATION

> In fourteen hundred and ninety-two
> Columbus sailed the Ocean Blue

Children in North America learn the date of Columbus' voyage with this rhyme.

Columbus' reputation has changed over the years.

On the 400th anniversary of Christopher Columbus journey Antonin Dvorak wrote his Symphony 'From the New World'. A Columbian Exposition was organised in Chicago – 30 times the size of the Paris Universal Exhibition of 1855, it attracted 24 million visitors. The Exposition's publicists saw the Genoese navigator's anniversary as a showcase for American ingenuity:

> All the marvels of the world, and the products of all the master geniuses in art and inven-
> tion are gathered there to delight and instruct – a very panorama of the possibilities of
> human ingenuities and persistent effort.[4]

In an 1828 biography of Columbus, Washington Irving imagined that Columbus would have been glad to see the 'splendid empires which were to spread over the beautiful world he had discovered'. There were criticisms from the very beginning. A priest, Bartolomé de Las Casas, who was with Columbus on the third voyage recorded terrible atrocities committed against the Arawak Indians. Las Casas was named 'Universal Protector of Indians' and laws were passed against their enslavement in 1542. In 1815 the 'Liberator' Simon Bolivar could not hear Columbus' name without remembering Las Casas:

> All impartial accounts support the integrity and passion for truth of that friend of human-
> ity, who so fervently and forcefully denounced before his own government and contempo-
> raries the most depraved acts of that bloodfest.

On the 500th anniversary of Columbus voyage in 1492 attitudes were even harsher. Historian Barbara Ransby saw 'a bloody legacy of rape, pillage and plunder'.[5] Duncan Green for the Latin America Bureau in London saw Columbus' as creating 'the most unequal continent in the world', by bringing Europeans to the continent.[6] Kirkpatrick Sale saw Columbus as the product of 'A Europe that [was] in thought and deed estranged from its natural environment and had for several thousand years been engaged in depleting and destroying the lands and waters it depended on'.[7]

After Cão, Bartolomeu Dias tried to find if there was an end to the African continent, sailing out of Lisbon in the summer of 1487. The further south they went, the fiercer the winds pushing them west became. Counter-intuitively Dias turned west and south hoping that the winds would die down, which eventually they did, at 38 degrees south, allowing him to turn eastwards again around the 'Cape of Storms' – which they renamed the 'Cape of Good Hope'.[8]

Dias's successful navigation of the Cape opened up the prospect of a direct trade with the Indian Ocean, virtually unknown to Europeans, except through the wares sold them by Arab and Venetian middlemen. While the preparations were under way for the next voyage, a Genoese mariner Cristoforo Colombo landed at Portugal with the marvellous news of his successful crossing of the Atlantic Ocean, to find – as he thought – China by the western route. It was a blow to the Portuguese court, which had refused to back his voyage, and might have undermined the determination to reach the Indian Ocean around the Cape of Good Hope.

Instead, Portuguese efforts were redoubled. Vasco da Gama was appointed to lead a four-ship team. Bigger boats were built – two carracks, 80-feet long and between 100 and 120 tons, with larger, square sails, one smaller and a supply ship. They left on 8 July 1497 'to discover and go in search of spices', wrote the fleet's diarist.[9] Following Dias' westward manoeuvre around the Cape, da Gama landed at points along the East African Coast, clashing all the way with perplexed Khoikhoi and Mozambicans. He seized hostages and fired on towns when his attempts at negotiation were rebuffed.

On 20 May 1498, da Gama's fleet arrived at Calicut on the Malabar coast (today Kerala). Da Gama was presented before the Samoothiri of Kozhikode, a Hindu ruler who was contemptuous of the plain goods and trinkets the ships had brought. Distrust turned to outright conflict and da Gama's ships had to beat a hasty retreat, after some haggling over hostages and duties owed.[10]

The journeys were made harder by the monsoons, unknown to the Portuguese, and by the recurrence of scurvy, which had not yet been linked to a lack of vitamin C. The Portuguese had no idea of the extensive navigation of the Indian Ocean by Arab and Chinese merchants and were often in conflict. It took them till 4 July 1499 to return, with the return from Calicut much harder than the outward journey. Two-thirds of the crew had died.

Cristoforo Colombo – Christopher Columbus in the English history books – was born in 1451 the city state of Genoa, in modern-day Italy. Columbus worked in the Iberian Peninsula as an agent of the Genoese banking family Centurione.[11] He sailed from Lisbon, where he was staying, westwards on journeys to the Azores and Madeira, islands in the Atlantic Ocean that had been not long been settled by Portuguese. It seemed clear to him that there must be a route westward to Japan and the Indian Ocean. Columbus got the funds (from the Aragonese Luis de Santangel, and Genoese and Florentine bankers) to set off with three ships and 90 crewmen from Cadiz on 3 August 1492. After stopping at the Canaries, Columbus' ships crossed the Atlantic to land at a place he called San Salvador which is today, most likely, Watling Island in the Bahamas. From there they sailed onwards to modern-day Cuba and then what was to become Hispaniola – where he left the wreck of one boat and a small crew to build a garrison of it.[12]

On the way back Columbus was forced by bad weather to land at Lisbon (not to gloat as some thought). The event which was said by many to inaugurate the modern world was not so widely celebrated at the time. He did bring back some gold, parrots and some abducted Arawak Indians, who were thought to be Asian, confirming his claim that the lands he had discovered were the 'Indies'. In September 1493, Columbus sailed with a larger fleet of 17 ships and 1,200 men (along with 12 priests). The garrison he left behind on Hispaniola had been massacred. In 1496, he returned home from his second voyage with more Arawak prisoners – now made slaves not just specimens. Columbus made two more voyages. His third in 1498–1500 landed at Trinidad, and, for the first time, the mainland, 'Tierra Firme' of South America. In this adventure he clashed with his crew and was sent home in chains. His last voyage (1502–04) skirted around the coast of modern-day Honduras and the Isthmus of Panama.

Though Columbus' voyages across the Atlantic are credited with opening a new age, it did not happen straight away. Between 1499 and 1502 Amerigo Vespucci, born in Florence but a naturalised Castilian, explored the eastern coast of the Americas, which are named for him, and established finally that this was a 'New World'. John Cabot (born Giovanni Caboto) sailed out of Bristol in 1497, with letters patent from King Henry VII: 'to seeke out, discover and finde, whatsoever iles, countreyes, regions or provinces of the heather and infidelles, whatsoever they bee, and in what part of the world soever they bee'.[13] Cabot travelled in the North Atlantic and landed at Newfoundland, claiming it for the King. In February 1498, Cabot set out to cross the Atlantic again, with five ships laden with goods by the merchants of Bristol, but four were lost at sea. In 1521 the Portuguese explorer Ferdinand Magellan sailed across the Atlantic and around the tip of South America through the straits that now bear his name, onwards across the Pacific to the modern-day Philippines where he was killed. Some of his crew sailed back around the Cape of Good Hope to Lisbon – the first voyage around the world.

The European navigators were driven by the ambition to make great wealth. Their treatment of the peoples they encountered was often brutal. The Portuguese mariners that rounded the Cape of Good Hope bombarded the Swahili coastal cities, Malindi, Mombasa and Kilwa, as they did the Indian city of Calicut, demanding tribute, rights to trade and garrison men, and drove rival Arab traders out of their ports. Columbus captured and enslaved Arawak Indians. Europeans were often at war with each other and carried their conflicts into these new theatres.

To try to contain the conflict, the Pope had brokered a treaty on the discovery of the Americas to divide the lands beyond a meridian line (running from North to South) 370 leagues to the West of the Cape Verde Islands. The Treaty of Tordesillas (1494) was meant to keep the African coasts and the Indian Ocean, as well as some of the Atlantic islands in Portuguese hands, with the Americas going to Spain. In fact, the line cuts through South America with Brazil – which did become a Portuguese colony – on the Portuguese side. British, French and Dutch challengers rode roughshod over this agreement.

Karl Marx and Frederick Engels, in their *Communist Manifesto* of 1848 took the discoveries of the late fifteenth century as the beginning of a new era in world history:

> The discovery of America, the rounding of the Cape, opened up fresh ground for the rising bourgeoisie. The East-Indian and Chinese markets, the colonisation of America, trade with the colonies, the increase in the means of exchange and in commodities generally, gave to commerce, to navigation, to industry, an impulse never before known, and thereby, to the revolutionary element in the tottering feudal society, a rapid development.[14]

The so-called 'age of discovery' was indeed the beginning of a new age, but it was not yet the full-blown capitalist era.

Chapter Four

CONQUERORS

The Europeans who seized land beyond Europe came as conquerors. Beyond the trading outposts they set up, land they seized was almost never 'virgin land' as was claimed. Peoples who lived, farmed or hunted the land were driven off by European conquerors, or as they were called in Spain, *conquistadors.*

European dynasties of the middle ages were well versed in military conquest and plunder. They had fought and seized land from each other. In the 'Hundred Years war' (1337–1453) the House of Plantagenet in England and the House of Valois fought what was a civil and an international war, that drew in the Spanish and other European Kings. Between 1095 and 1291 Christian nobles fought successive crusades against the Muslim rulers of the Holy Lands. In the Iberian Peninsula and in North Africa Portuguese and Spanish hidalgos had fought Muslim kingdoms for land and trade. In the Indian Ocean Portuguese, Dutch and British ships raided and seized territory to get a foothold on the new lands.

The conquest of non-European lands had the character of feudal seizure in the sixteenth century, but the military conquest of a territory was not abandoned with the transition to modernity. Military conquest was not only a weapon that the new constitutional states kept, but one that in many ways became more ruthless. The military conquest of Latin America in the sixteenth century was perhaps the most decisive. Allied with mercantile organisation the conquest of India in the eighteenth century brought the greatest number of subjects under European rule. In the eighteenth and nineteenth centuries, military conquest was allied with European settlement in North America, Australia and New Zealand, and in Africa in the later nineteenth century.

The limit point to conquest was always the balance of forces between the native population and the invaders. Superior naval, military, technology and logistical organisation of resources could sustain invading forces, but where they were outnumbered and out-fought conquest was not possible. Much of what looked like outright conquest turned out to rely on alliances and native collaborators.

Spain in the New World

The first Spanish 'conquistadors' were not soldiers, but there under an *encomienda* under the crown, a kind of contract that obliged them to offer 'arms and a horse' to defend the King and granted them rights to demand tribute and labour service from the native people. It was a private enterprise under licence from the King modelled on feudal service. Where it differed from the established feudal order was that it was much more open to adventurers of all backgrounds to make their name in these new lands, so that the *encomenderos* were artisans, notaries, traders, seamen and even peasants, as well as being of the gentry.[1]

The two great federations of the continent were the Nahua (Aztecs), governed by the Mexican people, who exacted tribute from their island Kingdom of Tenochtitlan, set in Lake Texcoco (today Mexico City), and the Incas in the Andes.

Hernán Cortés was a captain who sailed from Cuba to Yucatan in 1519. Cortés made allies among the subject peoples of the Aztecs as he travelled up the Yucatan coast the Totonacs and at Tlaxcala – both in conflict with the central Aztec authority at Tenochtitlan. A joint Cortés/Tlaxcala victory over the Tenochtitlan allies, the Cholulans led to 3,000 dead and had a chilling effect on the Nahua. By the time that Cortés arrived at Tenochtitlan to confront its King Moctezuma he had the support of many subject peoples of the Nahua empire. Moctezuma had to submit to Cortés' authority. A Nahuatl lament on the fall of Mexico ran:

> Along the roads the splintered javelins lie
> Scalps are strewn around. Roofless are the houses,
> And bright red their walls.
> Vermin swarm in the streets and in the square,
> And the walls are smeared with scattered brains.
> The song ends
> Weep, my dear friends
> Know ye well that by this defeat
> We have lost our Mexican nation.[2]

In 1531 Francisco Pizzaro, illiterate and illegitimate son of a soldier ventured into Inca territory. He was reinforced by men under Hernando de Soto. The Quechua peoples extended over 5,000 kilometres and the dominant group were the Incas who ruled over several bands across the Andean valleys. But Inca power was divided between the rival sons of Huayna Capac, Atahualpa and Huascar. Pizarro and his soldiers seized the Inca emperor at Cajamarca in 1532, after staging a cannon and arquebus attack in a confined city square. The Spaniards demanded a ransom for the captive Atahualpa of enough gold and silver to fill his 22' x 17' x 9' cell. Artefacts of this fabulous civilisation were melted down to 13,420 pounds of gold and 26,000 of silver. But Pizarro did not keep his word and Atahualpa was garrotted on the dubious grounds that he had killed his brother to take the crown. Even in Spain the killing was reviled.

Pizarro's return to Seville in 1534 with the Inca treasure led many more to cross the Atlantic from Spain. Still the actual number of Europeans who were in the 'New World' were not more than 25,000 households by 1570. While they told themselves that they had conquered South America, the truth was that they held very little territory – some coastal towns and cities.

Gold – and silver – played a special part in Spain's relation to the New World. In 1521 two different groups of Conquistadores, one under Pizarro, the other under Sebastian de Benálcazar travelled north in search of a rumoured King who was dusted in gold each dusk – 'El Dorado'. The quest for 'El Dorado' – which could be a gilded man, or perhaps a golden land – became an overriding ideology of the Spanish colonists. The historian Emiliano Jos thought that more territory had been explored in the pursuit of 'El Dorado' – later 'Eldorado' – than for any other reason.[3]

In 1542 not gold, but silver was found at Potosí in the land that today is Bolivia. Until 1570 the local people themselves mined the silver and sold it to the Spanish. In 1573, the Viceroy Francisco de Toledo brought in a labour draft, the mita, under which Indians were made to work underground. Output grew by four times. In the early decades around thirteen thousand were put to work. By 1585 output was seven times what it was in 1570. 'What is being sent to Spain is not silver, but the blood and sweat of the Indians', wrote brother Domingo de Santo Tomas. Between 1596 and 1600 Spain imported treasure worth 41,314,201 ducats – around a hundred times the amount it was taking at the start of the century.[4]

At Potosí the Spanish Empire in the New World really did set the native people to work for the glory of Spain. But beyond Potosí Spanish rule was less all-encompassing. Under the banner of the Spanish King Indian communities were developing their own commercial and farming communities. The conquest dramatically overthrew the very apex of Indian society – Aztec, Inca and Maya – and it demanded its tribute as they had. But it left the next tier mostly to its own devices.

Back in Seville, the imported silver bought Andalusian grain, wheat, oil and horses; it spurred the vineyards of Jerez and the olive plantations of Jaen, the silks of Granada and Valencia. But the 'profits were not invested in the capitalist sense of the term, and the fortunate emigrants dreamed of buying land, of building castles and amassing treasure'.[5] More and more wealth was used to buy luxuries from abroad without changing production relations at home. To many Spanish critics it seemed as if the precious metals themselves were a corrupting influence that encouraged appetites but not enterprises.

EIC as Territorial Power

The EIC had fought with Portuguese and Dutch rivals for trading rights, but in its earlier years collaborated with local rulers. India was mostly ruled by the Mogul emperors, though they were increasingly pressed by the Hindu Maratha league. The EIC financed England's first ambassador to the Mogul Empire Sir Thomas Roe, who advised in 1621 'if you will profit, seek it at sea and in a quiet trade; for without controversy it is an errour to effect garrisons and land wars in India'.[6]

Historian K. C. Sharma says that because the Dutch were driving them out of the East Asia markets 'the English were reluctantly and perforce driven to develop their settlements on the mainland, little realising at the time that India itself was destined to confer on its possessors the sovereignty of the East, while the attractive Spice Islands were in reality a seductive by-path leading those who followed it astray from the road to dominion'.[7] It was by becoming a colonial power on the mainland that the EIC would come to dominate.

In 1686 the Company's administrator John Child clashed with the Mogul admiral Sidi Yakub, because non-Company 'interlopers' had been allowed by the Mogul to trade. A fleet was dispatched by the Company Director Sir Josiah Child (they were distantly related) with the wild idea of waging war on the Mogul Empire. The next year John Child seized some of Sidi Yakub's grain barges. The Mogul forces took the Company's base at Bombay and raided it. Even with the help of 3,000 Maratha troops the Company could not defend its Bombay Castle. The Company's representatives had to beg for Emperor Aurangzeb's forgiveness, pay an indemnity of 150,000 rupees, make good the missing ships and expel John Child.[8]

Two years later, on the other side of the Continent, Company administrator Job Charnock fought with the Nawab at Bengal, after a rise in duties. The Company's superior naval forces hurt the Mogul ships in the Bay of Bengal but could not hold on to their inland base at Hooghly. A timely arrival of EIC ships saved Charnock from being overrun and peace was restored with the Nawab on the promise of more trade. The peace was propitious since it founded the port of Calcutta.

After King William's 'Glorious Revolution' in Britain, EIC Directors more often looked for agreement with the powers in India, though they often clashed with their local administrators. When the men on the ground wanted to counter the influence of the French Compagnie des Indes in the Carnatic (South west coast and inland) by installing a friendly pretender to the throne of Tanjore they were reprimanded: 'You seem to look on yourselves rather as a military colony than the Factors and Agents of a Body of Merchants.'[9]

EIC grandee in the 1760s.

The French Company's energetic commander Dupleix had encircled the EIC base at Madras, but Robert Clive a company factor turned general broke out. While Dupleix's ally Chanda Sahib had led his forces to attack a British ally, Clive turned tables on him by seizing his base at Arcot, which he held.

More than a 1,000 miles away from Arcot, in Bengal, Siraj ud-Daula succeeded his grandfather, Alivardi Khan as Nawab of Bengal. Though he was on good terms with the Company, some Bengali merchants were angry at the way that English traders laid claim to the Company's trading rights, cutting them out, and prompting the Nawab to act. Siraj attacked Calcutta, where he took Fort William easily. Siraj's imprisonment of English in the 'black hole of Calcutta' was a cause célèbre in England. A company of British troops landed at Madras, but its colonel baulked at the arduous cross land route to Calcutta and let Robert Clive lead them. Clive's forces defeated the Nawab and his French allies at Plassey (Palashi) in June of 1757. Clive went further than taking Calcutta back, and restoring the company's rights. He set about undermining Siraj with the help of the Murshidabad bankers, the Seth brothers and a rival claimant Mir Ja'afar – whom Clive helped to put on the throne.

The EIC's military successes in the Carnatic and Bengal put French and also Dutch Companies at a disadvantage. The French had to withdraw from the Carnatic. In 1759 the Dutch were also overcome in clashes with the EIC. Thereafter they had to trade under EIC protection. Now the dominant power in Bengal and the Carnatic, the East India Company factors fleeced local traders and enriched themselves.

Clive was a hero in England, but a fly in the EIC's ointment. In Leadenhall Street the Directors were reluctant to take on the role of conquerors. With the backing of Bute's ministry, Laurence Sulivan was re-elected director, and Clive's own bid defeated. Clive returned to Bengal, but now as Governor. The Company, too, had to reckon with the fact that it was a lot more openly embroiled in officialdom than it had been.

Edmund Burke, who would later be classed a critic of the East India Company was bullish in the defence of conquest:

> If we make war shall we not conquer? If we conquer, shall we not keep? You are plunged into Empire in the east. You have formed a great body of power, you must abide the consequence. Europe will envy, the East will envy: I hope we shall remain an envied People.[10]

More importantly, the balance of the company shifted. The EIC began as a trading company with premises in some port towns. Later it governed towns, like Bombay. After Plassey it became a territorial power in India. The Company bought tax collecting rights to establish the security of its settlements at first.

Under the Treaty of Allahabad (1765) the much-diminished Mughal Emperor Shah Alam II granted the Company tax-gathering rights over the eastern province of Bengal–Bihar–Orissa. Shah Alam's portrait was on the Rupees the Company coined but power lay with the Company. The Company's Bengal Council wrote back to Leadenhall Street that 'your trade from hence may be considered more as a channel for conveying your revenues back to England'.[11] Instead of going forward from trade to industry, the Company ratcheted up its status as first a local and then a regional power. The company's small force became larger, with the recruitment of local troops, and from 1754 was supported by troops of the regular British army.

The Company would ally itself with the rival claimants to various Subah (provinces) and then afterwards put them in 'Subsidiary Alliance' – which meant that they were stationed with Company troops which they were also obliged to pay. After defeating the Nawab of Bengal, Mir Kasim, at the Battle of Buxar (1764) with a force made up of 860 British EIC troops, and 6,000 Indian sepoys and cavalrymen, the EIC was dominant.

The Plunder of Bengal

After the Battle of Plassey British control over the wealthy province of Bengal tightened and the Company mercilessly plundered its wealth.

In a letter to the Directors of the EIC dated 30 September 1765, Clive worked out that the EIC's revenue from taxes were 250 lakhs of Rupees (a lakh is 100,000). More, the Company's 'civil and military expenses in time of peace can never exceed 60 lakhs of Rupees' and 'the Nabob's allowances are already greatly reduced to 42 lakhs and the tribute to the King (the Great Mogul) at 26'. The Company's net revenue from Indian taxes, then, will be 122 lakhs of Rupees or £1,650,900 sterling.[12] In the event Clive was optimistic. The net balance was £1,253,501 in 1767, from a gross collection of £3,805,817.

Over and above the Diwani collection the different Nawabs that the East India Company put in charge of Bengal were honour-bound to hand out 'gifts' to Company officers. After 1757 Mir Jafir gave away £1,250,000 in one-off payments to the officers who helped elevate him. Then when he was deposed in favour of Mir Kasim, it was Kasim's turn to make more gifts. And then when Kasim was deposed and Jafir restored, there were gifts again. In 1757 Clive, hero of Plassey and later Governor of Calcutta got £31,500 and a jagir – or claim – worth £27,000 a year, and his eventual fortune amassed in England came to £400,000.[13]

Colonel Mordaunt's cock fighting a bird belonging to
Asaf-ud-Daula, the Nawab Wazir of Awadh, after Zoffany.

As well as taxation and gifts, the Company, and its writers moonlighting as independent traders, set about exploiting Bengal in other ways. After defeating Siraj-ud-Daula, the Company made a treaty with a puppet Nawab Mir Kasim. Not only were the English traders exempt from port duties but also from the duties between different Subah, or provinces of the Mughal Empire, on production of a dastak or licence to trade. Mir Kasim complained in 1762 to the English Governor of Bengal, Henry Vansittart, that in every town and village Company servants and their Indian agents 'carry on a trade in oil, fish, straw, bamboos, rice, paddy, betelnut, and other things; and every man with a company Dastak in his hand regards himself as not less than the Company'.[14]

The Weakening of the Mughal Empire

The ruling Kings of India were Mughal from a dynasty founded by Babur, a descendant of Timur, who invaded Delhi from Uzbekistan. Muslim powers had incurred on India before – Ghaznavids from what is today Afghanistan settled in the North in the eleventh century AD, and then Ghorids, who settled as far East as Bengal. The Mughal Emperor Akbar (1556–1605) was succeeded by his son Jahangir (1605–27) who first dealt with the EIC . Shah Jahan reigned from 1628–58 and was followed by his younger son Aurangzeb (1658–1707) after a dynastic struggle; Aurangzeb's son Bahadur Shah I governed 1707 to 1712, followed, after some strife, by Muhammad Shah (1719–48), but by then the Empire was in great difficulty.

The internal development of the Mughal Empire under Aurangzeb was marked by over taxation of the peasant cultivators, the ryot. Mughal officials were entitled to an income, but under Jahangir it became common to gift a hereditary grant of land revenue, a jagir to its holder the jagirdar instead, leading to many claims on the surplus output of the ryot. Under Aurangzeb it was said that the assessment grew to one-half, from the one-third of the crop under Akbar. According to Jadunath Sarkar the Mughal jagirs 'ended in a mad looting of the peasants by rival jagirdars' agents or successive agents of the same jagadir'.[15] Often the ryot left the land to avoid the collection of the jagir, so that cultivation declined.

The underlying weakness of the Mughal Empire was disguised by the wealth of its Shahs and Nawabs (viceroys). Shah Jahan commissioned the splendid Taj Mahal palace at Agra in 1623. But where Akbar's rule had been magnificent and liberal towards its Hindu and other religions, Aurangzeb's was mean and doctrinaire, with enforced loyalty to Sunni Islam. The cracks began to show with the loosening of tributary states and outright rebellion of some Nawabs. The fragmentation of the Mughal Empire was the opening of which the East India Company took advantage.

In 1647 Shivaji, a Maratha lord carved his own territory out of the Sultanate of Bijapur founding an Empire that would challenge the declining Mughals.

While Akbar granted lands to the emergent Sikh people in the sixteenth century by the second half of the seventeenth century they were, under Guru Govind Singh, in conflict with Aurangzeb. After many setbacks the Sikhs would create an independent state in the far North East around Lahore in the nineteenth century. In Aurangzeb's time the peasant Jats of the Agra–Delhi area rose up against the jagirdars and vassals of the Mughals, on the very doorstep of their capital.

After Aurangzeb's rule, his grandsons contested the throne at Delhi and the Subah (province) of the Deccan broke away from the Mughal Empire, under Nizam-ul-Mulk, who made an independent state in Hyderabad. Around that time the Subah of Oudh loosened its ties with the Mughal Empire and asserted some self-government. The Nawab of Oudh Shuja-ud-Daula would play a decisive part in the last scenes of the Mughal Empire. The Subah of Bengal asserted its independence, too, under Murshild Quli Jafar Khan, whom Aurangzeb had made Governor, and his son Shuja-ud-din Khan who succeeded him in 1727. Later Siraj-ud-Daula would become the last independent Nawab of Bengal, defeated by Clive at Plassey.

Another adventurer who rose in the decay of the Mughal Kingdom was Haider Ali, a general who established a kingdom in Mysore. His son Tipu Sultan challenged the British in their incursions into the Deccan.

Not only did the Nawab 'suffer a yearly loss of nearly 25 lakhs of Rupees' in revenue, but Indian traders were losing business to the Company, to the independent traders and their Indian agents. Warren Hastings, then a Member of the Governor's Council at Calcutta wrote that 'the oppression committed under the sanction of the English name' was a 'grievance which loudly calls for redress'. Even Clive admitted that 'the trade has been carried on by free merchants, acting as gomasthas [agents] to the Company's servants, who, under the sanction' of the Company's name, 'have committed actions which make the name of the English stink in the nostrils of a Hindu or a Musslman'.[16]

In desperation Mir Kasim abolished all inland duties so that the Indian merchants could trade on more equal terms, but the Company's General Council objected. The Company deposed Mir Kasim and put in his place as Nawab, the more compliant Mir Jafar (whom they had previously deposed).

James Mill the economist and Company historian conceded that 'the conduct of the Company's servants, upon this occasion, furnishes one of the most remarkable instances upon record, of the power of interest to extinguish all sense of justice, and even of shame.'[17]

The Dutch-born merchant William Bolts saw how the Company's control made effective slaves of the Bengali weavers, 'by fines, imprisonments, floggings, forcing bonds from them' and more. The gomasthas went to each town and made the weavers sign bonds to deliver cloth and being registered in the Company's books were forbidden from making it for anyone else or on their own account. The gomasthas would fix the price 'at least fifteen per cent and in some even 40 per cent less than the goods so manufactured would sell in the local bazaar'. If they defaulted the gomasthas would come and cut the cloth out of the loom, and in the case of some silk winders, their thumbs were cut off.[18]

The gomasthas, complained Mir Kasim 'forcibly take away the goods and the commodities of the Ryots, merchants, etc., for a fourth part of their value; and by way of violence and oppressions they oblige the Ryots, etc., to give five rupees for goods which are worth but one rupee'.[19]

Company rule not only drove the peasants and weavers to penury it greatly reduced the Indian merchant class. Dr Francis Buchanan a Company Medical Officer wrote about the district of Dinajpur in Bengal that 'a great portion of the trade of the district had passed from the hands of native traders to that of the Company. There were no longer any Saudagars or great native traders in the District'.[20] The Company and its Servants had effectively taken over the internal trade of Bengal which it carried on as an exploitative monopoly. For many years to come Bengal's indigenous traders could only work as agents of the Company and its Servants.

The plunder of Bengal was so stark that it tipped the country into famine as ryots and weavers abandoned their towns to avoid the Company's agents. From 1769 the value of the Diwani collection fell by nearly half a million pounds sterling, while the cost of company administration and the military rose. The Company's net revenue fell to £275,088 as it became clear that they were in danger of killing the goose that laid the golden egg. It was estimated at the time that as much as one-third of the population of 15 million had died.[20]

Chapter Five

THE ENGLISH FLEET

England's rivals in the fifteenth and sixteenth centuries were the dynastic families governing in Spain and France, Catholic powers, as well as Holland, a Protestant one. Henry VIII used the stones from the monasteries he demolished to build coastal forts against attack from the Catholic powers, and the cash he raised to build a navy. To establish England's independence Henry had to challenge France and Spain. Traditionalist courtiers like the Howards favoured alliance with Spain, though too close an alliance provoked England's puritans and patriots. Mary I (r. 1553–58) was reviled for her marriage to Catholic Philip of Spain. Elizabeth I (r. 1558–1603) tried to avoid war but could not.

Philip II of Spain suffered three blows from Elizabeth. English privateers in the Channel attacked Spanish ships; English forces gave help to the Protestants fighting him in the Netherlands; Elizabeth had her sister the Queen of the Scots, Mary, executed on charges of plotting to seize the crown – a Catholic martyr in Philip's eyes. Spain's armada of 130 ships threatened invasion. Lord Howard of Effingham commanded a counter force of 80 ships out of Plymouth – more than half of which belonged to the port towns or were privateers. With the armada anchored off Calais the British forces' cannon were not enough to damage the French, and they had little know-how in fighting in formation. Fire-ships were floated into the Armada to make them break their pattern and enough were isolated to attack. Luck was with England as the bulk of the Armada was carried east through the Channel into the North Sea – the 'Protestant wind' – so that many ships were lost in the arduous journey around the top of Scotland and Ireland back to Spain. It was a turning point for British sea power. It was odd, the Pope said to Philip of Spain in 1588, 'that the Emperor of half the world should be defied by a woman who was Queen of half an island'.[1]

The Treaty of London, ending the war with Spain in 1604 secured the Protestant succession (and the English negotiators refused a Spanish demand for toleration of Catholicism), which left England free to adopt a more pro-Spanish foreign policy under James I and his son Charles I.[2]

Foreign policy had a domestic dimension. The nobility tended to Spain, the lower orders preferred Holland. War with Spain was popular, according to the Lord Treasurer Burghley, because of the 'inbred malice in the vulgar against the Nobility'.[3] War was expensive. It meant that the Crown would have to raise taxes. But calling a Parliament to agree taxes would open the Crown to Parliament's counter demands.

Britain's fleet was well developed for the coastal trade as well as defence. There were 400 ships running coal from Newcastle to London in 1600.[4] In 1568, when King Philip

of Spain was sanctioning an invasion of Ireland, Queen Elizabeth retaliated by licens-
ing 'privateers' to raid Spanish ships carrying silver from the Americas.

In 1577, Francis Drake set out across the Atlantic through the Straits of Magellan. As
he sailed up the Western coasts of South America, he raided the Spanish Towns in the
Golden Hind, eventually landing in California, which he claimed for Queen Elizabeth.
On his return in September 1580 Drake had gold and jewels worth £600,000, so that
he could repay his backers £47 for each £1 invested. The Queen took all the bullion and
put it in the Tower. Ignoring the Spanish ambassadors' complaints, she knighted Drake.

From 1585 to 1604, Britain was once again at war with Spain and Elizabeth sanctioned corsairs' raids on enemy ships crossing the Atlantic. In 1592, English privateers
seized a large Portuguese carrack off the Azores carrying jewels, silks and spices worth
£500,000. The voyage promoters, including Elizabeth I, took their share of the profits:
£140,000 of which the Queen took half. Walter Raleigh the previous year had made a
200 per cent profit on one privateering voyage around the Caribbean.[5]

England was not the only power to use privateers to wage war. The Dutch Republic
sanctioned the seizure of ships when its war with Spain resumed, taking 547 Spanish
and Portuguese ships crossing the Atlantic between 1623 and 1636, with a total value
of 37 million guilders. The Spanish retaliated from their northern port of Dunkirk seizing 3,000 vessels over 25 years, costing the Dutch as much as all their customs receipts.
Military–company competition between states really was a zero-sum game in the seventeenth century.[6]

The long line of English Sea Lords.

'Whosoever commands the sea, commands the trade', wrote Walter Raleigh, and
'whosoever commands the trade of the world commands the riches of the world, and
consequently the world itself'. He was looking at the growing conflict over resources
among the maritime powers. Elizabeth I's minister Walsingham recommending the
granting of a monopoly to the Levant Company on the grounds that 'you shall set a
great number of your greatest ships in work, whereby your navy shall be maintained,
one of the principallest strengths and defence of this realm'. In 1622 James I created
a Commission for Trade, 'because the Maintenance of our Navy and the shipping of

our kingdom, is a principal means to advance the Honour, Strength, safety and Profit thereof'.[7]

England's naval supremacy was eventually formalised in the Navigation Acts. These date back to the twelfth century and according to Francis Bacon, Henry VII ordained 'that wines and woads from the parts of Gascoin and Languedoc, should not be brought but in English bottoms', meaning English ships' holds. After the civil war in England between supporters of the Crown on the one side, and Parliament on the other the Navigation Acts were made into a war policy. Early American settlements in Bermuda, Antigua and Virginia declared for the King. Cromwell's Parliament answered by a trade embargo. Not only English ships but 'All Ships of Any Foreign Nation whatsoever' were forbidden from trading with the rebel colonies (mostly, this was addressed to those Dutch ships selling guns to Virginia). In time the Parliamentarians subdued their reluctant settlements. But the militarisation of Atlantic trade was a successful policy, and Parliament made it permanent. Navigation Laws passed from 1650 onwards forbade any foreign ships from carrying goods to or from English colonies. Only English ships were to carry that trade. The Navigation Laws were upheld by naval power. It was a policy aimed first at Holland, but one that locked rival powers out of trade with English colonies. With government support the merchant navy tripled its tonnage between 1629 and 1686 to 340,000 growing at 2.5 per cent a year from 1660 to 1690.[8]

The Navigation Acts have been seen as the height of the mercantilist policy, which they were. But they were also a sign that the unfettered rule of the Chartered Companies was coming to a close. 'The Navigation Act of 1651 represented the victory of a national trading interest over the separate interests and privileges of the old companies', wrote Christopher Hill.[9]

Cromwell set out to drive Spain from the New World in 1655, claiming as his justification that he would free its indigenous people from the 'Miserable Thraldome and bondage both Spirituall and Civill' – the so-called 'Western Design'.[10]

England's naval accomplishments were patchy. Under the amateurish and venal command of William Penn (father to the founder of Pennsylvania) the navy was humiliated in Hispaniola by the Spanish. Even in the eventually successful taking of Jamaica, the costs seemed higher than the prize.

The English piratical tradition was kept up by 'buccaneers' – seamen expelled from St Kitt's by Spain in 1629. They earned their name by drying bacon ('boucan') on the northern shore of Hispaniola, where they settled. They raided ships from Providence Island (near Nicaragua) or Tortuga. In 1656, Edward D'Oyley, Britain's governor of the colony newly seized from Spain, Jamaica, invited the buccaneers to defend Port Royal, raiding Spanish ships under letters of marque.

Cromwell's Commonwealth did not long survive his death, but he did leave a strong navy to the restored Crown: a fleet of 157 ships. Cromwell's Parliament built up the state anew. They brought in land taxes, an excise and customs that paid for the New Model Army and made a professional Navy. No longer were armed forces made up by lordly retinues. On the restoration of the monarchy in 1660 Charles II came close to frittering away Cromwell's military machine. He allied Britain with France against Holland, and in 1667 a triumphant Dutch fleet sailed up the Thames to attack the Royal Docks at Chatham.

The amateurishness that dogged the British Navy was addressed on the Restoration by 'Secretary of the Marine' Samuel Pepys, who put the Navy Board on a more professional footing. The return of the Monarchy did not lessen the naval monopoly over the colonies. Charles raised taxes on sugar and other colonial goods that came from non-English colonies, while guaranteeing the British West Indies open access, though they in turn had to buy English goods. Charles thought that the way to the 'greatest Dominion in the world' was to 'win and keep the sovereignty of the seas'.[11]

Under the Restoration a special committee of the Privy Council was set up called the 'Lords of Trade and Plantations' to enforce the Navigation Acts. They could 'command the respect, attendance, or opinion' of the Admiralty and Treasury and it acted as an executive over the colonies.[12] In 1664 the governor of New Amsterdam, Peter Stuyvesant, surrendered to a small fleet under James, Duke of York. In 1675, Charles founded the Greenwich Observatory setting down the meridian line. In 1686, Edmond Halley published a table of wind movements, trade winds and monsoons that greatly helped Britain's ships navigate around the world. John Harrison's chronometers helped eighteenth century sailors work out their longitude at sea, by comparing the time set at Greenwich with the time they observed.

Britain's naval power rose in the years following William of Orange's succession to the English throne, and under the Hanoverian Kings. The war over the succession to the Spanish throne ended the threat of a united Spanish-French Kingdom, and the Peace of Utrecht (1713) guaranteed British access to Spanish and Portuguese colonies in the New World. At the end of the war the Royal Navy had 131 ships of the line – 20 of them three-decked ships with 96–100 guns. Her sea power was greater than either of her nearest rivals France and Holland, while Spain was in decline. Britain clashed with France in wars over colonial possessions. French and English colonists fought in the Ohio valley in 1754. The following year, the English fleet attacked a convoy of French ships going to Canada, seizing 300 ships. The English Navy and the East India Company seized Calcutta and Chandernagore in 1757; British forces grabbed Louisburg and Fort-Duquesne (1758); Québec (1759); Montréal (1760) and Pondicherry and Mahe (1761). In the treaties following this Seven Years war, Britain gained Florida from Spain, the territories that would become Canada, the Antillean Islands (Dominica, St Vincent, Tobago, Grenada, and the Grenadines), Louisiana east of the Mississippi, Saint Louis and the French outposts in Senegal.[13] The year 1763 proved to be the high-point of British influence in North America.

Chapter Six

THE SLAVE TRADE

The first black men taken as slaves in European-owned ships were seized by Portuguese traders in the 1440s. Lançarote de Freitas founded a trading company in Lagos in Portugal with the licence of Henry the Navigator. João de Fernandes and Antão Gonçalves bought enslaved Africans from a merchant Ahude Meyman. By 1448 around 1,000 enslaved Africans had been traded by Portuguese captains, who brought them to Lisbon, or to the Portuguese islands of the Azores, Sao Tome and Madeira.[1]

In 1562, Elizabeth I's naval hero John Hawkins intercepted a Portuguese shipment of enslaved men, seized them and sold them in the West Indies. Other voyages on the Jesus of Lubeck carried slaves again from West Africa to the West Indies. England's slave trading would take off in the 1620s.

In 1626, the Dutch West India Company overturned its old ban on slave trafficking to supply enslaved Africans to Virginia, and to the sugar colonies that the Dutch had established on territories in Brazil taken from the Portuguese.

In 1631, Charles I granted a patent to the Guinea Company headed by the courtier merchant Sir Nicholas Crispe to trade with the African coast. His partners were Humphrey Slaney, John Wood and William Cloberry. For the first 10 years the Company imported redwood, Ivory, hides and gold. But in the 1640s the Guinea Company brought enslaved Africans to the West Indies. The Company had rivals – colonial merchant Samuel Vassall, who brought slaves to Barbados between 1642 and 1645, Michael Cawton, a sea captain and merchant who had traded to Virginia and the West Indies brought enslaved men from Guinea. The Company tried to defend its monopoly in the courts, without success and many more joined the loathsome trade.[2]

In the Anglo-Dutch War of 1652–54 the Dutch fleet was stationed off the coast of West Africa threatening England's trade in the enslaved. Britain's slave trade got a new boost with the restored Crown. The returning Stuart court was short of money and looking around for any means to boost their incomes. Samuel Pepys overheard Charles II's brother the Duke of York 'speak of a great design' that involved 'sending a venture to some part of Africa to dig for gold and ore there'. The Duke, who would later be King as James II, proposed an initial investment of not less than £250.[3]

King Charles II set down the Charter giving the Royal African Company the exclusive right to trade slaves in 1672. Under the monopoly, the Royal African Company had extraordinary powers. The Company had the rights to set up Admiralty Courts on the African coast, and in the colonies, to prosecute interlopers who broke its charter.[4]

The Royal African Company was quickly overcome by the great many independent traders. They were often ships captains, or retailers who had a hand in trading to the colonies before they turned to slave trading. Without any intended irony, the champions of the independent traders complained that the African Company monopoly was 'destructive of the Native Liberty and Freedom of the Subjects of England', and so 'contrary to the true Interest of the Nation'.[5] The Royal African Company lost its monopoly in 1698 when rivals had to pay a duty to the Company, and in 1712 that, too, was abolished.

In 1708 the Board of Trade wrote to the governors of all Britain's Atlantic Colonies:

> It being absolutely necessary that such a trade so beneficial to the Kingdom should be carried on to the greatest advantage, there is no doubt but that the greatest consideration thereof will come early before the Parliament at their next meeting.

As the Board saw it 'the well supplying of plantations and colonies with sufficient numbers of negroes at reasonable prices, is, in our opinion, the chief point to be considered in regard to that trade'.[6] In 1713, at the peace talks at Utrecht the British were awarded the 'Asiento' – the right to trade slaves to Spanish America.

The political journalist and pamphleteer Daniel Defoe (best known today for his novel *Robinson Crusoe*) wrote:

> Whatever can be said for a Trade, that is the Essence of our Colonies – the Support of our Sugar and Tobacco Works, that brings much Home and carries little out; that Exports nothing but what we can spare, and brings Home nothing but what we cannot be without – That sets our Poor to Work, for Manufactures, Employs our Shipping, and extends our Dominions; That carries out our woollens to Africa, carries Slaves to America; That barters Gold for Glass-Beads, and the Riches of Africa, for the Baubles of Europe, may be said for this Trade.[7]

The Royal African Company did not make the profits that were expected. In 1750, a new Company of Merchants Trading to Africa was founded. From the 1640s to the abolition of the slave trade by Parliament in 1806, 3.2 million enslaved Africans were carried on British ships, around 2.7 million of them sold in the Caribbean islands (and around 25,000 in North America) – one-third of the total 9.2 million Africans carried out of the continent in slavery. In that time, British-based companies traded many more enslaved Africans than any of their rivals, having quickly eclipsed the Portuguese and Dutch. The importance of slavery to the sugar colonies shaped British priorities. There were around 60 voyages made each year, but sometimes as many as 100. Until 1724 most ships left from London, when Bristol's slave traders overtook the capital, and then in 1744 Liverpool took the lead.[8]

The 'middle passage' as the journey from Africa to the Americas was known was inhuman. Enslaved Africans were chained below deck without room to turn or stand. 'From the year 1789 to the year 1805, two years before the abolition of the slave-trade by this country, the average number of negroes exported from Africa to the English, French, Spanish and other colonies and countries was 85,000', explained the Anti-Slavery Society's secretary John Scoble: 'and the average mortality connected with this export of slaves was 14 per cent; 14 in every hundred'![9] – in earlier years as many as a quarter died. They died from thirst, dysentery, and other diseases, made worse by the squalor they were kept in below decks, or at the hands of their captors, through violence, or being thrown overboard.

Slavery on English soil was officially outlawed in 1171. Six hundred years later, in 1771 the case of James Somersett versus his master Steuart, before Lord Mansfield reaffirmed that, when Mansfield freed Somersett. It was, though, common before 1771 to read notices like this, in the *Liverpool Chronicle:*

> A fine negro boy, to be sold by auction. He is 11 years of age; the auction will take place at the Merchants' Coffee House, Old Church Yard. Sale to commence at 7 o'clock by candle-light. By order of Thomas Yates who hath imported him from Bonny. Auctioneer, James Parker.

Or, this, in the *Liverpool Advertiser*, 8 September 1766: 'To be sold at the Exchange Coffee House, Water Street, this day, the 12th Sept. inst., at 1 o'clock precisely, eleven negroes imported per the Angola.'[10]

The Royal African Company had a fort at Cabo Corso (Cape Coast, in modern-day Ghana) that was built by the Swede Henrik Carloff but was seized by Britain in 1664. It had many buildings, including slaveholds for 1,000–1,500 enslaved Africans. Nicholas Buckeridge was chief agent there in 1700, and after him, Sir Dalby Thomas.[11] A second fort was just East of Cape Coast, Fort William at Anamabu, where Richard Brew was governor in 1761, followed by Lionel Abson.

From the Ouidah coast, most of those enslaved had been captured by the Dahomey Kings, Agaja (regnant, 1704–40), his son Tegbesu (1740–74) and his son Kpengla (1774–89), and sold to Portuguese, French, Dutch or English traders. The Dahomey wars with their neighbours were fuelled by the guns and other goods that the European slavers traded with them for men. To the Dahomey the slaves were defeated peoples of rival polities, that they thought of as prisoners-of-war.

One of the larger London-based companies was under William Camden, Anthony Calvert and Thomas King, based at Red Lion Street in Wapping. They traded slaves from 1760, and after abolition shifted to transporting convicts.

The new Company of Merchants 'inherited all of the Royal African Company's forts, settlements, territory and property' – but could not impose a monopoly.[12] The new Company was a trade body and did not trade in its own right. It got a grant from the government of £13,000 a year to the upkeep of the forts.

Many different Britons took part in the slave trade. Some, like the investors of the Royal African Company were well-connected gentry, or army men who moved in Royal circles. Others, like the independent traders were self-made men, sometimes non-conformists, like the Lancaster Merchant and Quaker Dodshon Foster (1730–93) or dissenters Benjamin Way of Bridgeport or John Burridge of Lyme Regis. Ship's captains like Peregrine Brown of the Olive Tree galley and Robert Cruickshank traded in slaves on their own account.

Chapter Seven

PLANTATIONS

European settlements outside of Europe were originally mercantile outposts, usually at bays and estuaries on the coasts. Those were set up to trade with native peoples.

At some settlements Europeans seized or claimed land for planting. Later we will look at those homesteaders who farmed the land themselves. But some of the earlier plantations were large-scale estates that settlers claimed, set out and farmed with indentured and then enslaved labour. The most important areas of plantation in the seventeenth and eighteenth centuries were in Virginia, the Carolinas and Georgia on the American mainland, and on the Caribbean islands. In the later nineteenth century Europeans seized and developed land in the East to plant rubber, gutta percha, tea, coffee and bananas.

Sugar

Sugar cane is a giant grass with a high sugar concentration in its sap. It is native to Indonesia and from 500 BC was grown in India. By the sixth century AD it was grown in Persia, and then later in Cyprus, Crete and Sicily – though it thrives better in the hot and humid tropics. The explosion of sugar planting in the new world in the seventeenth century was down to the conquest of Brazil and the Caribbean by Europeans, and the enslavement of Africans who were made to work the cane rows. It was due, too, to a demand-side change in Europeans' diets.

More and more Europeans were moving from the country to the town. For most Europeans, who dwelt in the country, grains made up 80 per cent of calorie intake.[1] Natural sugars they found in fruit, honey and malts. As people moved to the town, they had more money to spend, but less access to natural sugars. In London they bought currants from the Levant Company, and later they bought cane sugar from the West India merchants to make up what was missing from their diet. A great source of energy and wealth, sugar was doubly important at the beginning of the age of manufacture, which was driven by muscle-power. Later with mechanisation first coal, then oil, would be the machines' energy sources.

The Portuguese had two settlements in the Atlantic, Madeira (1425) and the Azores (1433), and a third off the Gulf of Guinea, Sao Tome (1493). By the 1550s there were

3,000 slaves on Madeira and more on the other islands tending sugar cane. From 1630 the Dutch conquered much of Brazil and made it a sugar colony. It was Dutch expertise that James Drax, the first English sugar planter in the West Indies, drew upon.

English Planters in the Caribbean

The merchants of the EIC were, in the mid-seventeenth century, opposed to planting and any kind of colonisation. Though they used Madagascar as a stopping point on the route to the Indian Ocean, they wanted no part in Prince Rupert's (Quixotic, as it turned out) plan to colonise that island. To those merchants, planting was not their business.[2]

In 1623, Thomas Warner and a small group landed at St Kitts (St Christopher), funded by the London merchant Charles Jeaffreson. They had an uneasy peace with the Arawak leader Tegreeman, but not trusting him, they killed him and his people, treacherously, after laying on a feast. A good crop of tobacco was swept away in a hurricane, but a second crop took. In April 1626, Maurice Thomson and Thomas Combes sent three ships carrying 60 slaves to their thousand-acre plantation in St Kitts.[3]

On the 17 February 1627 a ship, the William and John, landed at Barbados. The journey had been funded by the Anglo-Dutch Courten family. On board was James Drax, a clergyman's son from East Anglia. The goal of the mission was to settle and plant the island. The would-be planters struggled, hungry in 1630–31, sometimes fighting with Arawak natives and other Europeans (Spanish and French). Tobacco grew at Barbados, though it was a poor smoke.

In 1656 as part of Lord Protector Oliver Cromwell's 'Western Design' a naval force took Jamaica at great cost. Grenada, Dominica, St Vincent and Tobago were ceded to Britain by France in 1763.

In Barbados the important sugar families were the Draxes, James and his son Henry (there were Draxes in Jamaica, too, who were distant cousins and heirs to the estates) and the Codringtons. In Jamaica, the main sugar family was the Beckfords.

Between 1640 and 1660 Barbadian planters spent one million sterling importing enslaved Africans to the colony, and half as much again on servants, equipment and livestock. In 1663–64 the Royal Adventurers shipped 3,075 slaves to Barbados, though often they were bought on credit. Henry Drax had a labour force of 327 Africans and seven white servants – 'the fewer the better' – in 1680.[4] The Barbadian planters' profits were around 20 per cent return on their investments.

With larger estates the social character of Barbados changed. The white population shrunk from 30,000 in 1650 to 18,000 in 1690 – though there were 358 sugar works whose exports were worth more than all of North America's combined. Josiah Child said that the West India colonies were useful to the mother country, whereas abstemious 'New England is the most prejudicial plantation to the Kingdom'.[5] Sugar cane robs the soil, which can be fought with manuring, but diminishes the crop over time. Barbadian yields fell from 1.35 tons an acre in 1649 to less than one ton in 1690. It was worked out that the virgin soil of Jamaica needed one slave for each acre, while those of Barbados needed two.[6]

Jamaica took over from Barbados as the lead sugar colony. By 1673 the population of Jamaica was 4,000 white men, 2,000 white women and their children, together with 9,500 Africans – almost every one of them enslaved. Over the next seven years the African population grew to 15,000 (rivalling the 20,000 in Barbados). Demand was so high that an enslaved man in Barbados was sold for £17, but in Jamaica, £24. By 1780 in the West Indies just 50,000 white settlers and planters governed over an enslaved population of half a million.[7]

The life of a slave on a West India sugar plantation was brutal. The enslaved were not seen as human and treated with great cruelty. Whipping was common. Enslaved Africans who in any way resisted the authority of their masters could be tortured, mutilated and murdered. Instruments of torture like iron collars, tethers and chains, the 'scold's bridal', stocks and the gibbet were used. The enslaved in the West Indies were worked until they died. Unlike those who were transported to North America, they did not as a rule have children, so they were replaced by newly bought slaves. Jamaica planters imported three-quarters of a million Africans but less than half of that number were there when slavery was abolished, 311,692.

Across the British West Indies as a whole there were 673,953 enslaved people at the abolition of slavery overall. Thirty years earlier the number was 775,000 just before the abolition of the transatlantic slave *trade* in 1807. By the 1820s the value of a slave was around £45 in Jamaica, as much as £60 in St Vincent and Grenada and even went up to £120 in Honduras – though by that time there were no more shipments.

Barbadian planters exported 8,000 tons of sugar to England in 1655, rising to 15,000 tons by the 1660s – around 85 per cent of all British sugar imports. By 1690 it was up to 23,000 tons of sugar a year, to go in tea, jams, biscuits and other processed foods. Sugar was not only for English mouths, but also the first important colonial re-export, sold on to Europe.[8] The Crown made £300,000 a year in sugar duties by the mid-1670s on imports valued at £6,667,000.

In 1783, exports from the West Indies to Britain were 90,710 tons – and after the rebellion in France's Saint-Domingue colony (modern day Haiti) they rose by 11,6501 tons in 1794, though that artificial boost disguised an underlying problem.[9]

The planters were known as 'absentee landlords' who made their money in the West Indies but lived and spent their wealth in Britain.

From 1654 a committee of West India Planters and Merchants met at the Jamaica Coffee House in St Michael's Walk, James Drax among them. The planters had different clubs over the decades. In the 1740s William Beckford kept up with the club of planters and merchants 'at Lebeck's'. In 1780, the Society of West India Planters and Merchants was formed. There were West India Clubs in Bristol and Glasgow, too.[10]

In Parliament Sir W. Codrington and Sir W. Stapleton represented the West Indians in the Commons from 1737. Later, between 1785 and 1830, the West Indian interest in the Commons ballooned. These were the major pro-slavery legislators:

Edward and Henry Lascelles (later Earls of Harewood)   Sir Michael Stewart
William Beckford (MP and Mayor of London)   Joseph Birch
Bryan Edwards (Southampton)   W. R. Keith Douglas
Charles Ellis (later Baron Seaford)   Sir William Young
George Hibbert (head of the West India dock company)   Henry Bright
Joseph Marryat   Ralph Bernal
John Gladstone (father to Prime Minister William Gladstone)   W Dickinson
William Manning   Sir Rose Price
James Blair   Henry Dawkins
John Mitchell   Richard Pennant,
Sir Alexander Grant   John Irving
Sir Edward East   Robert Gordon
Sir Bethel Codrington   John Plummer
                                                           J. J. Ward

Many other Members of Parliament (MPs) had plantations, like James Modyford Heywood, MP for Fowey, who owned the Heywood Hall Estate in St. Mary, Jamaica with 232 slaves, and two other estates. The MP Henry Lascelles, the 2nd Earl of Harewood owned six plantations in Barbados and Jamaica. His son William Lascelles was also an MP.

In the Lords the Marquis of Chandos, the Earl of Balcarres, the Earl of Airlie, Lord Hatherton, Lord Rivers, Lord Shelborne, Viscount St Vincent and Earl Talbot were all sponsors.[11]

Many wealthy houses were built by the 'West Indians' – the Beeston Long's mansion in Bishopsgate Street, Robert Hibbert's Birtles Hall in Cheshire, William Beckford's gothic castle at Fonthill. Edwin Lascelles had John Carr and Robert Adam build Harewood house in West Yorkshire with the money from his West Indian plantations. Thomas Onslow, the Second Baron Onslow, had Clandon Park House in Surrey rebuilt in the 1730s by Giacomo Leoni in the Palladian style, and gardens by Capability Brown, with a fortune based on Jamaican plantations. Baron Seaford, Charles Ellis, who bought Claremont House in Surrey, inherited plantations of 404 acres with 349 slaves, and was the long-standing chairman of the Standing Committee of The London Society of West India Planters and Merchants and a leading promoter of anti-abolitionist, West Indian interests in Parliament. Felix Bedingfield of Oxburgh Hall bought the Amershams Estate in Montserrat when he was the island's legal representative.[12] The All Saints Church in Southampton and Bath Abbey have many memorial plaques to West Indian Planters. Roger Hope Elletson, who had been a Governor of Jamaica, and died in 1775, owned Merrymans Hill with 600 acres and 93 enslaved people is memorialised in Bath Abbey, as is Matthew Munro, who owned a 500-acre plantation on Berbice, and died in 1797.

By the late eighteenth century, the 'West India interest' was seen as a problem in Britain. Their great wealth had long been disliked, and they were mocked for being vulgar. Worse still, those fortunes were sliding, and many of the estates in the Caribbean were over-mortgaged and losing money. The anti-slavery campaign shifted public opinion against the planters. Economists complained that the colonies were soaking up funds that could be put to better use in British industry. Statesmen saw the 'West Indians' parliamentary lobby as a brake on reform.[13]

America

Though the early English colony in Virginia had been set out as a Company venture the investors in London tended to lose control to the settlers in America. The 'mere merchant' provision in the Company statutes was left behind as planters worked at their own fortunes.[14]

An allegory of Africa and America.

Virginia planters grew tobacco, much of which they sold back to England. In 1619 a Dutch captain sold 20 enslaved Africans in Virginia, but the real take off in the American slave trade did not happen until the 1680s. Before then the planters relied mostly on indentured English labour.

Tobacco sales grew from 20,000 lbs in 1619 to 38 million lbs in 1700, thereafter rising to anywhere between 25 and 60 million all through the eighteenth century. Tobacco, and slavery, blossomed in Virginia, Maryland and the North East of North Carolina. South Carolina planters, from 1690 raised rice, and were followed by those in Georgia. Rice exports grew from 12,000 lbs in 1690, to 18 million in 1730 and 83 million in 1770. South Carolina's capital Charleston, with a population of 12,000 was the fourth largest city in North American. Many of those who settled in South Carolina and Georgia had come from the West Indies, bringing their slaves with them.[15]

The slave culture in the South was, like that in the West Indies, reliant on barbaric punishments – whipping, mutilation, torture and chains. In other respects, though, slavery in North America's southern provinces differed from the West Indies. Pointedly, the enslaved population on the North American continent, managed to create a family life, so that the enslaved Africans raised children, who were, by law, themselves the property of the owners of their parents. As a share of the enslaved population, fewer came across the Atlantic, and more were born in America. From the middle of the eighteenth century, slaves were encouraged by their masters to go to church and learn the ways of Christianity. More substantially than their West Indian counterparts, southern slave owners identified with their locale, and even imagined themselves patrician and kindly masters to 'their people'.

Slavery was common in the northern provinces, too, though there was not the same plantation-driven demand. In the northern settlements enslaved men and women were often put to work as domestic servants, farmhands, craftsmen and labourers. Peter Stuyvesant's Dutch colony of New Amsterdam first imported enslaved Africans in 1646 – and New York, as the city became known had more slaves than any other northern state. In 1741 a panic about a negro plot to overthrow their white masters gripped New Yorkers, when one in every five households there owned at least one slave.[16]

By 1750, the tobacco planters and other masters of Maryland and Virginia held 144,872 in slavery, 61 per cent of the North American total. In South Carolina and Georgia, another 40,000 slaves worked the rice plantations, or farmed indigo. The enslaved population had grown to one-fifth of all the people living in the colonies.

Chapter Eight

BRITAIN'S MERCANTILE RIVALS

In the sixteenth century the great dynastic empires were breaking up. Holy Roman Emperor Charles V (1500–58) divided his territories between his sons – Ferdinand taking the Habsburg lands in Austria, while Philip II inherited lands that extended from Holland in the North to its colonies in North Africa, and as far West as the New Spain in the Americas. From 1554 to 1558 he was, by marriage to Mary I, King of England, too.[1]

Philip ruled from Castile, making that Spanish region the centre of the Empire, which is why it is often called Spanish Empire, or Spanish Habsburg Empire. Castile, dominant in Spain, had the one great advantage that the silver (and gold) of the new world passed through there. Despite that great wealth, Philip's Spain had serious shortcomings that made it an awkward seat of power. Castile itself was backward in technology and government. Philip relied on Milanese and Genoese bankers to raise cash and had to raise large armies by a levee on the Castilian nobility. The loans helped pay for large mercenary armies to augment the Castilian troops. The different territories in the Empire were for the most part self-governing, though Philip tried to place as many loyal Castilians in positions of power as he could.[2]

As the effective leader of the Christian world, it fell to Philip to face the attacks of the Ottoman Empire. Victory over the Turks at Lepanto in 1571 cost five million ducats, but only 60,000 silver ducats were paid by the treasury at Castile, and the balance was met by Genoese bankers' bills of exchange. The credit for the victory was, in any event, claimed by the Venetians and by Rome.[3]

Philip faced a more existential challenge in the West. In 1558 Mary Tudor had died, so that the throne reverted to the very Protestant Elizabeth I, whose Kingdom would go on to challenge Philip's Catholic authority. In the Netherlands, Philip refused an appeal to relax the Holy Inquisition provoking sharp protests from Dutch Calvinists. Mobs attacked Catholic churches in the summer of 1566. A group of Calvinist nobles withdrew and made alliance with German Lutherans. Philip sent the Duke of Alba with a force of 10,000 to suppress the revolt. In 1572 a naval force of Dutch exiles, called 'Sea Beggars' captured the port of Brielle. The Duke of Alba pressed the advantage that October and attacked the City of Mechelen, and then Zutphen, Naarden and Haarlem leaving thousands of dead.[4]

Three years later the overburdened Spanish treasury was bankrupt. The Spanish (and mercenary) troops stationed in the Netherlands had dwindled from 60,000 to 8,000, and the remaining core, unpaid, mutinied, sacking the City of Antwerp destroying property and killing 6,000 people.[5] It was in response to this 'Spanish Fury' that the

17 provinces of the Netherlands assembled at Ghent in the States-General to demand an end to the Spanish occupation. At that time Don Juan's forces were in no position to fight and the United Provinces were effectively self-governing. In 1584 a pro-Spanish fanatic killed William of Orange, the Dutch Stadtholder, and then the Duke of Parma led a Spanish force that took Antwerp, dividing the country between the Spanish-governed South Netherlands and the independent North Netherlands.

In 1580 the King of Portugal, Henry I, died leaving no heir, at which point Spain occupied and Philip II made himself King of that land as well. The Papal Bull that had divided the New World between Portugal and Spain now effectively gave the entire Western Hemisphere to King Philip so that by 1600 Spain was drawing around 40 million Ducats of silver a year from America, of which the crown got 13 million. To both the new Dutch Republic and the English Kingdom Spain's mastery of the world was intolerable.

Dutch Courage

Four years after the assembly of the Estates-General at Ghent the United Provinces signed a Treaty at Utrecht making themselves a self-governing nation. Holland was well-placed for the European trade, having already served Philip's Empire as master shipbuilders, exporters of farm goods from a healthy hinterland, and traders of wood to the Baltics. Town-based merchants had invested in land reclamation and trade before independence, and many man-made waterways connected the inland farms to the ports. William of Orange was leaning towards alliance with one of the German protestant principalities, but his death and the accession of Maurits as Stadtholder paved the way to an independent state. Elizabeth I of England's ambitions to challenge Philip's Empire had tempted her to give quiet support to the Dutch and after 1588, with the defeat of the Spanish Armada, the way was open to both Britain and Holland to challenge Spain in the New World.[6]

Merchants who had fled the sack of Antwerp brought capital and knowledge north to Holland. Some of them were involved in a new venture the Far Lands Company, which raised a capital of 300,000 guilders, got a patent from Stadtholder Maurits and sent four ships to the Indies to buy pepper. They were following the routes that had been laid out by the Portuguese – as they learned from Dutch seamen like Dirk 'China' Gerritsz and Jan Huygen van Linschoten, both of whom wrote up their eastward journeys on Dutch ships. The 'Far Lands Company' voyage only just broke even and scurvy killed most of the crews (only 87 out of 240 survived). Still, the temptation of breaking the Portuguese pepper monopoly was high and in the six years from 1595 to 1601 65 ships made the journey, in 15 different fleets – some were highly profitable, others were disasters. The States-General, the Dutch Government, stepped in and persuaded them to combine as the *Vereenigde Oostindische Compagnie* (VOC) or 'United East India Company', with a combined capital fund of 6.5 million guilders.[7] Maurits led a coup in 1618 for a more orthodox Protestantism, and coincidentally, a more belligerent challenge to the Dual Iberian Crown overseas, so that the war was resumed in 1621, just as Philip IV succeeded his father to the Spanish throne.[8]

Dutch factory in Hoogly, India, 1665, by Schuylenburgh.

Early Dutch VOC settlements were at Banda Islands (1602) at Ambon (1625) and Batavia (1619). The Dutch demanded Bandanese families sell their Mace and Nutmeg but when they later traded with the British, Jan Pieterszoon Coen slaughtered many of them and deported the rest. They replaced the population with slave plantations and built Fort Hollandia. At Ambon they obliged each family to plant and maintain 10 clove trees. They also dragooned the Ambonese into *hongitochten* – war parties – to burn down rival English and Portuguese plantations.[9]

On Java (modern-day Indonesia) the Dutch built a small fort with the agreement of the local Prince Jayawikarta, before turning on him and razing his town of Jacatra (Jakarta) and raising up instead their own new town of Batavia.[10] Batavia grew up to be a city of 70,000 by 1700, and it more than doubled by 1800 – but only 6,000 of its inhabitants were Dutch. There was a military force of 1,200. Overall, the Company employed 3,000 soldiers and 3,500 seamen in 1600, rising to 17,000 troops and 12,000 seamen by 1750.[11]

The Dutch VOC obliged natives to let them build warehouses, a small shipyard and a hospital at Table Bay in the Cape of Good Hope in 1647–48, where ships would break their voyage for around four weeks. The Company's Jan van Riebeeck became the first Dutch colonial administrator on 6 April 1652 (300 years later he was celebrated in an apartheid-era festival as the founder of South Africa).

The Company had outposts in Sumatra, and on the Malay Peninsula, won through blockades and gunboat diplomacy, and they controlled the Malacca Strait between those two from 1641, after taking Malacca from the Portuguese that year. In 1667, they won control of Macassar on Celebes. With these possessions they had a monopoly on the Cinnamon trade, and control over the pepper and clove trade to Europe. They had outposts at Surat in the north west of India, on the Coromandel Coast in the south east and in Bengal in the north east. In 1608 the Company built its first trading post at Ayutthaya in Siam, with the agreement of King Ekathotsarot. Though the trade meant the post closed down more than once, the Dutch did exploit tin mines and Sappanwood from the 1640s. Though they were there by agreement, it was not equal, and over the winter of 1663–64 the Dutch blockaded the mouth of the Chao Phraya River to force King Narai to limit Chinese trade out of Siam.[12]

The Company's other significant colony was in Ceylon – modern-day Sri Lanka – where at the invitation of Rajasingha II of the inland kingdom of Kandy, they drove the Portuguese out in 1647. Presenting the King with a bill of 7,265,460 guilders the Dutch demanded control of all of Ceylon's coast isolating the Kandy uplands. Cinnamon prices rose 1.5 guilders to the pound in 1660 and rose to 8 or 9 guilders to the pound by 1780. The monopoly profits were untaxed in the colony but sent straight back to Holland. The Salāgama caste were tasked with delivering and peeling the Cinammon under strict *plakaats*. Oppressive as the work was the Dutch later rewarded the Salāgama with generous farming rights, so that other castes would seek to have themselves registered as Salāgama. In the mid eighteenth century, Dutch governors banned subsistence farming where it encroached on land that would yield cinnamon, so that the island was dependent on rice imports from India. The Dutch eventually gave up Ceylon to the British in 1796.[13]

As well as challenging Portugal in the Far East, the Dutch pushed into the Atlantic and the Americas with their own West India Company founded on 3 June 1621. Though the Dutch West India Company was organised like the VOC, it never did become a wholly profitable enterprise and more than its Eastern counterpart leaned on Dutch Government money and soldiery to support its plans, which were, all the same, warlike. At the same time, and conscious that they would need slaves to work plantations in Brazil, the Dutch took the Portuguese slave port Luanda on the West African coast (in modern-day Angola). Dutch privateers played havoc with the Spanish and Portuguese trans-Atlantic trade. One lucky attack on Matanzas Bay in Cuba in 1628 netted silver and other goods to the value of 11.5 million guilders. In 1629, the Dutch sent 67 ships to seal its control over Brazil with an attack on Pernambuco. Though the West India Company managed the conquest of Brazil for the Dutch Republic they were unable to keep up the costs or man-power to keep it, and called for the help of the States-General.[14]

Further north the Dutch colony of New Netherland, spread along the Hudson River (named after Henry Hudson, the Englishman who navigated it while working for the Dutch VOC). The Dutch West India Company was responsible for these settlements, which grew into the lands of the Munsee, who they fought through the 1640s.

From 1645, the Portuguese-Brazilian settlers rose up in a revolt that would throw Dutch rule in the Americas into permanent decline. Though the revolt was launched by slave-holding planters (many of whom were at that time deeply in debt to the Dutch West India Company), its leader the Jesuit father Antonio Vieira promised freedom for any enslaved blacks who enlisted. Before the end of 1645 the rebels had captured much of the sugar producing area of Brazil, which also meant that the slave trade with Africa was stopped. A Portuguese fleet was sent to recapture Luanda and Sao Tome from Dutch rule.[15] A peace treaty in 1660 shrank Holland's possessions in the Americas to Dutch Guyana – Surinam (which only became independent in 1975).

After the wars with Spain and Portugal, the Dutch were challenged by their former ally, Britain. Anglo-Dutch wars in 1652–54, 1664–67 (when Peter Stuyvesant surrendered New Amsterdam to the Duke of York), and again in 1672–74 were fought primarily over trade, after Britain made the first Navigation Act (1651) excluding foreign ships from English ports. The Dutch Empire in the later seventeenth century was reduced to

Batavia and Malacca in the Far East, their forts on the Gold Coast, Cape Town, the towns on the Malabar and Coromandel coasts of southern India as well as Ceylon.

Portuguese Decline

English and Dutch expansion into the Far East, and into the Americas followed, but largely destroyed, the Portuguese Empire. In the East, the Estado da Índia was at its height around 1550 when Portuguese sea power overcame their Arab rivals, undercutting the overland trade through Venice and the Ottoman Empire.

The Estado da Índia, unlike the British and Dutch colonial companies, belonged to the King. It had around 50 armoured forts around the Indian ocean, the four most important being Goa on the west coast of India, Ormuz, controlling the access to the Gulf, Mozambique, which served as a way station for fleets travelling East, and the island port of Malacca. It had between 6,000 and 7,000 Portuguese troops. They had allies in the Sultan of Melinde, the Ethiopian Kings, the Shah of Ormuz, the Sultan of Diu, the rulers of Cochin and Kotte (in Sri Lanka) and the Sultan of Ternate in the Moluccas. The Estado da Índia subcontracted shipping (the Indies contracts) on the condition that the goods were delivered up to the King in Portugal – a monopsony. Then other merchants (the European contracts) marketed the peppers, spices and other imports in Europe.

Abandoned today, Yashwantgad Fort, in Redi, Maharashtra is called the Portuguese fort locally, though it was built by the Marathas in 1713, before being captured by the Portuguese in 1746.

The moral character of the Portuguese settlements is much abused in historical sources. Rival imperialists tended to talk about their anxieties as European overlords by describing their own flaws, as exhibited in an exaggerated way, by the Portuguese. There was no doubt a big element of truth in these accounts, but you can also see the guilty projection.

It was said of the Portuguese that they were of low character, with common backgrounds, until they rounded the Cape of Good Hope, when they became noblemen in other people's countries.[16] British, French and Dutch accounts also emphasise the great cruelties that the Portuguese did, most of all in their trade in slaves. These complaints were no doubt true, but as true of the English, French and Dutch as they were of the Portuguese.

Another theme that is strong in rival European reports of the Portuguese is that they intermarried with native peoples and, in some versions, were degenerating as a race because of it. Early mercantile empires, of which the Portuguese is the earliest, did not send women out, only men (later there was a programme for sending girl orphans to the colonies, but they were not prized as partners, and themselves often married natives). Portuguese settlers all across the Empire had sexual relations and later children with women of Goa, Macao, Africa and the Americas.[17]

On the one hand, the Estado da Índia's Portuguese-born servants numbered no more than 7,000. On the other hand, the Portuguese gave local administrators a lot of independence of action, under the system of 'donatory captain'-ship. These donatory captains organised their own districts.[18] When the coherence of the Estado da Índia broke down under the pressure of rivalry from the colonial companies of rival powers, the captains were often making their own little fiefdoms.

Around Goa a large community of Portuguese ex-soldiers, and their families grew up to be a thriving community. So too did the Chinese concession in Macao become an important mixed Portuguese Asian city and district. Other parts of Portugal's overseas Empire were more piratical in character. Venetian merchant Cesare Fedrici recorded that the 90 Portuguese in Martaban (today in Myanmar) killed the King of Pegu's men, had their warehouses attacked, and then tried to bombard the city with cannon. It was 'a strange thing to see the Portugales use such insolencie in another man's citie', thought Federici.[19]

However, 'in 1595–6 there appeared in Asian waters an ominous threat to the Portuguese in the shape of Dutch ships' K. M. de Silva tells us. The Dutch 'had ousted the Portuguese from the Spice Islands, besieged Mozambique and Malacca and blockaded Malacca and Goa all within four years of the foundation of the VOC' – the Dutch EIC.[20] Through most of the seventeenth century Portugal was losing territory and outposts: Ormuz (1641); Formosa to the Dutch (1642); Muscat (1650); Sri Lanka (1656); Bombay to the English in (1662); towns on the Malabar Coast (1663) to the Dutch; Mombasa and the towns on the Delgado Coast north of Cape Delgado (1698) to Oman. In the eighteenth-century Portugal lost Bassein (1740) and Chaul (1742) to the Marathas.

Portugal's rivals in the Indian Ocean were a check on her power, but the home country itself was governed by Spain when Philip II imposed the Union of Crowns in 1580. Philip told the Cortes at Tomar that Portugal would be independent within the Empire. Portuguese traders brought slaves to the Spanish Empire in the Americas and prospered under Philip II. Portuguese merchants and bankers prospered in Madrid where they were financiers to the Crown, with contracts of more than 40 million ducats. The Portuguese Empire, however, withered under the Union of Crowns, and the Estado da Índia's captains had reason to complain that the Spanish Kings had failed to defend or secure their territories in the East.

The Union of the Crowns ended in 1640 after the strains of supporting Spain's wars with France and Catalonia proved too much for Portugal. The demand for troops to fight in Catalonia sparked another rebellion in Portugal, where the House of Braganza declared a new King, Joao IV.[21] The Portuguese had military help from the French. Their determination to secure their own Portuguese Empire can be seen in the revolt against the Dutch in Brazil, and the retaking of Luanda.

Portugal's Empire in the eighteenth century was centred on Brazil and Angola on either side of the Atlantic, tied together by the slave trade out of Luanda and Brazilian sugar. Charles II married Joao's daughter Catherine of Braganza in 1661, and Portugal would become a subordinate ally of Stuart and Georgian England, and an important market for English manufactures.

War and Peace

At the Peace of Westphalia, in 1648, after the Thirty Years War, fought between Catholic and Protestant princes in Europe, it was agreed that they would recognise each other's sovereignty. The issue was what religion people would follow, so the rule of thumb to stop the war was *cuius regio, eius religio*, literally, 'who's realm, his religion'. What it meant was that rival faiths could not interfere in the sovereign realm of another principality. Sovereignty took off because European powers needed to stop fighting, so they recognised the geographic limit of their authority. The shift matched a real inward focus in the building up of nation states.

There were voices in Holland that doubted the virtues of peace: A pamphlet from 1650 asked:

> What certainty has peace brought you? War has made you great, peace makes you small. War has brought you splendour, authority, deference from all potentates. Peace makes you suspicious to all, including the least, even Portugal. War has expanded your boundaries to the East and West, peace leads to their loss. War, impoverishing all other nations and Empires, has made you rich, has flooded your country with silver and gold, peace makes you poor. War has made all industries and traffics grow and prosper, peace makes them disappear and decay. War has been a bond of union and accord, peace of strife and discord.[22]

The wars of the seventeenth century had many aspects, as dynastic, or as religious conflicts, as wars of independence, commercial and colonial rivalry. Many of the seventeenth century wars were wars of succession, that is between Dynastic Houses, over their alliances, where the immediate cause is who inherits the crown. But they were often also religious wars. The conflicts between the Dutch Republic and Britain, on the one hand, and Spain on the other are wars of the Reformation and Counter-Reformation. The Spanish fleet's actions against England and the Dutch are reactions to their breach with Rome. On the other hand, co-religionists waged war against each other, as the Catholic Portuguese and Spanish did, and as the Protestant British and Dutch did.

The wars of the seventeenth century might also be seen as wars of national independence. Certainly, for the Dutch Republic and Portugal, waging war against the Spanish Habsburg Empire came as they laid (or reclaimed in the case of Portugal) independence. England was largely a self-governing state, but it, too, was asserting its independence from the Catholic world, and its wars with Spain were fought in the fear of subordination. The course of the seventeenth century sees the declining influence of the multi-state Kingdom of Habsburg Spain, and the emergence on the Atlantic seaboard of jealously competitive nation states: England, the Dutch Republic, Portugal, France and Spain.

As well as being dynastic wars of succession, religious conflicts and wars of independence, these conflicts were also mercantile wars. The 'mercantilist craze for seizing new markets and shutting out all possible rivals brought about most of the wars that desolated Europe', thought J. Holland Rose.[23] Merchants played a significant role in making the case for war. Privateers fought in many of the conflicts. English privateers raided Spanish ships between 1588 and 1604. The wars can be seen as the clash between the great colonial companies. The Royal African Company of England clashed with the Portuguese over control of the Slave Coast; the British and Dutch East India Companies fought over the control of trade between India, Java, China and Europe; the Dutch West India Company fought with the Portuguese over the plantations in Brazil.

The wars of the seventeenth century can also be seen as colonial wars. England fought with Holland over New Amsterdam leading to its transfer to Britain in 1667. From 1688–97 England and France fought a war in North America, alongside their respective native allies. Between 1654 and 1660 Oliver Cromwell sanctioned war over Spain's Caribbean possessions in his 'Western Design' (only in 1670 was a treaty signed, in which England took Jamaica and the Cayman Islands).

These different causes of warfare were not all that different. The religious conflicts had their own inner meaning, but they were also ways that people understood their competing interests. The Duke of Alba fought to reimpose Catholicism on the rebellious northern states, but he also advanced the interests of Spain, and therefore of the Spanish merchants against their Dutch rivals. Mercantile interests were not always the same as those of Kings, but merchants prospered in the territorial spaces and trading routes that nations protected. Territorial conquests enhanced the status of Kings and filled the holds of merchants' ships. Commercial fleets could be turned to military ones.

While the wars stand out in history seeing European and world developments only through the lens of 'power politics' can deceive. Throughout the seventeenth century Europeans cooperated as well as fighting. Trade took off. Prince Philip II's Empire would have been immobile without the assistance of the many states that made it. Even as they made war, the different states made alliances to cooperate in mutual defence. The Spanish and Portuguese worked together, as did the British and Dutch. In 1651, Oliver Cromwell proposed a 'closer union' between the Dutch Republic and England, not yet a merger, but something more than just a diplomatic treaty. The Great Assembly in the Hague replied:

Commerce and traffic are often most plausibly mixed with great jealousy, especially between neighbouring republics. As two twins, the constantly fight and wrestle with each other over their primogeniture, that is profit.

The Assembly went on to outline a hydraulic theory of mercantilism proper to a country that reclaimed so much of its land from the sea: 'Therefore it can also be compared to connected waters, where the growth at one place is the erosion at another.' Proud Republicans themselves, the Dutch wondered whether that was what they wanted for England, saying 'many wise and far-sighted persons have judged, that commerce would be driven with more profit and security by this state, if England would remain a kingdom, than if it is turned into a republic'.[24] Shortly after this too-honest reply Cromwell brought in the Navigation Laws that kept Dutch shipping out of British ports.

The last Spanish Habsburg Emperor Charles II died in November 1700, with no heir, naming the Bourbon Duke Philip of Anjou as his successor, confirming Spain as a French ally, if not a French satellite. In the conflict over the succession, in which Holland, France, Britain and Savoy invaded her territory, Spain was reduced from the seat of an Empire to a single country. Under the impetus of war, and with French advisors, Philip V modernised the tax-raising and military organisation, centralising power as other modern nation states had. Much of Habsburg Italy passed to Savoy, while Britain took Gibraltar. What survived of the Habsburg Empire was the New Spain in the Americas, and the Philippines.

It was an irony that the breaking up of Europe's largest Empire, the Spanish Habsburg Empire, and the independence of the Dutch and English from Spanish domination, was the lead up to new English and Dutch Empires in the Americas and Asia. In the eighteenth century there was a new rival. Just as Spain's power waned Bourbon France grew to challenge Britain not just across the channel, but across the world.

Chapter Nine

THE LIMITS OF THE
MERCANTILE SYSTEM

The old colonial system boosted Britain's exports. The colonies as they produced and exported raw materials to Britain were becoming the market for British goods. In 1730 British exports to Europe were valued at £6,224,000. Exports to Ireland, the British West Indies, North America and the East Indies were £1,654,000. By 1770 Britain was still exporting £5,965,000 to Europe, but exports to Ireland, the West Indies, North America and the East Indies had grown to £6,495,000.[1] Good as these numbers were for British industry the merchant companies were open to criticism and it was getting louder.

Mercantilism and Its Critics

The growing power of the merchants in the cities of London, Bristol, Liverpool and Southampton made them some enemies. One of the complaints against them was that they were getting rich at everyone else's expense. Many were dismayed by the money flowing out of the country to pay for the luxuries that the companies brought back. Pamphleteer Robert Kayll said that, like the Portuguese, the East India Company 'were the enemies of Christendome, for they carried away the treasure of Europe to enrich the heathen'. It was true. In the first 23 years of its existence the East India Company exported £753,336 in coin and bullion, but only £351,236 in other commodities.[2]

Thomas Mun, who was the chairman of the East India Company, took issue with the idea that 'the gold, silver, and Coyne of Christendome, and particularly of this Kingdome, is exhausted, to buy unnecessarie wares...'[3] Of the £500,000 of goods that the country imported, Mun claimed, only £120,000 were consumed here, and the rest destined for re-export, at profit. Thomas Mun and the merchant capitalists were already changing the nature of their trade, by turning from imports to re-exporting, and to the carrying, or triangular trade. The consumer gained because the prices were lower by sea than by the overland route. Aware of the charges that the Chartered Companies were just importing luxuries and damaging the balance of trade, their defenders insisted otherwise, that foreign trade increased wealth. Defensively, they argued that it was austerity at home that would help the country profit. Hoping to distract attention from the luxury goods market they had created, the merchants counselled abstinence. This early economic theory was known as 'mercantilism' and its chief proponents were members and supporters of the East India and the other Chartered Companies.

Mun wrote that 'the ordinary means therefore to increase our wealth and treasure is by Forraign Trade, wherein we must ever observe this rule; to sell more to strangers yearly than we consume of theirs in value'.[4] According to D'Avenant, the balance of trade thesis meant that it was better that consumption within the kingdom be held down, since all expenditure at home would be a loss of profit. He wrote that it is

> the Exportation of our own Product that must make England rich; to be Gainers in the Ballance of Trade we must carry out of our own Product what will purchase the Things of Foreign Growth that are needful for our own Consumption, with some Overplus either in Bullion or Goods to be sold in other Countries; which Overplus is the Profit a Nation makes by Trade, and it is more or less according to the natural Frugality of the People that Export, or as from the low Price of Labour and Manufacture they can afford the Commodity cheap, and at a rate not to be under-sold in Foreign Markets.[5]

D'Avenant also wrote that 'by what is Consum'd at Home, one loseth only what another gets, and the Nation in General is not at all the Richer; but all Foreign Consumption is a clear and certain profit'. William Petty wondered at the mercantilist doctrine, pointing out that 'Ireland exporting more than it imports doth yet grow poorer', while Thomas Mun pushed the point to its abstemious conclusion: 'as plenty and power do make nation vicious and improvident, so penury and want to make a people wise and industrious' – begging the question, as to which people it was who would live in penury and want.[6]

The mercantilists tended to see trade as a zero-sum game, because they saw gain largely as 'profit upon alienation', which, as Sir James Steuart thought was 'relative profit', 'it marks a vibration of the balance of wealth between parties but implies no addition to the general stock'.[7]

Mercantilist economic ideas were closely tied up with the colonial outposts that had been established in the seventeenth and eighteenth centuries: the East India Company outposts in India and the Far East, the colonies in the Americas and the Caribbean Islands and the slave forts on the West African Coast. Together these were later called the 'Old Colonial System' – a model of trading posts across the world, serving British Chartered Companies. According to Josiah Child, a chairman of the East India Company, the point of colonial policy was to keep the 'external provinces and colonies in a state of subjection unto and dependency upon their mother-kingdom'.[8]

Criticisms of mercantilism were made forcefully by Adam Smith and after him, Lord Brougham. By then the mercantile interest was on the wane. To Smith, writing in 1776, the capital 'employed in the home trade of any country will generally give encouragement and support to a greater quantity of productive labour in that country, and increase the value of its annual produce more than an equal capital employed in the foreign trade of consumption'. Domestic investment, he goes on to write has a 'still greater advantage over an equal capital employed in the carrying trade'. Against the mercantilists Smith says, 'the power of every country must be in proportion to its annual produce, the fund from which all taxes must ultimately be paid'. So, he argues, 'the great object of the political economy of every country is to increase the riches and power of that country'. More, 'it ought to give no preference nor superior encouragement, to the foreign trade above the home trade, nor to the carrying trade'.[9]

Adam Smith complained that 'the monopoly of the colony trade has drawn from those other branches a part of the British capital which would otherwise have been employed in them' and that 'it must evidently have subjected Great Britain to a relative disadvantage in all those other branches of trade'.[10] Smith thought that countries ought to follow 'the natural progress of opulence', where 'the greater part of capital of every growing society is, first, directed to agriculture, afterwards to manufacture and last of all to foreign commerce'. He was frustrated to find, though, that Europe's course of development was 'entirely inverted': 'The foreign commerce of some of their cities has introduced all their finer manufactures, or such as were fit for distant sale; and manufactures and foreign commerce together have given birth to the principal improvements of agriculture', This was an 'unnatural and retrograde order', he thought.[11]

Lord Henry Brougham, in 1802, when he was a radical Whig, wrote that 'the means by which, with a very few exceptions, all the colonial territories of Modern Europe have been acquired are such as reflect no great honour, either upon the honesty, or the humanism of the different nations'.

Before they were colonies, thought Brougham, 'those distant countries were peopled by independent tribes, either united in society under regular governments and advanced in government, or living in a rude but free state'.

However, 'as soon as their existence became known to the more powerful communities of the old world, an intercourse was established which terminated in the subjection or extirpation of the ancient possessors, after a succession of cruelty and fraud'.

'The title, then, by which the different powers now hold their colonial territories', wrote Brougham, is 'the right of the strongest'.[12]

Brougham was nonetheless impressed with the colonial enterprise: 'It is wonderful how large a proportion of the capital employed in raising, as well as that employed in the transporting and circulating the commodities of any colony, belongs to the monied interest of the mother country.' But he also points to a problem which is that the merchants 'engaged in the colonial trade' are tempted by 'a higher rate of interest than is ever given in the home money-market'.[13] As long as returns on capital invested overseas were higher than those at home, the overseas market would attract all the capital.

Smith's criticisms of overseas trade were a sign that the balance of the British economy was changing, from investment abroad to a new-found determination to build up industry at home, at the end of the eighteenth century. More than a sign of that change, it was Smith and those who shared his views that were leading the change. Already the Royal Africa Company monopoly had been abolished as had the South Sea Company's.

The mercantilist policy of monopoly was seen more and more as a dam to trade. Andrew Ure railed against the 'extremely foolish' rule of the Lord Mayor of London in 1662 'for the regulating the cloth markets of the city and for preventing foreigners buying and selling' – to which he adds a great exclamation mark. 'Door-keepers were to attend strictly at the halls, and turn out all foreigners and aliens coming to purchase cloth', Ure reports, in disbelief.[14]

Clamour against the East India Company

In the seventeenth century the East India Company paid out loans and gifts first to the King's treasury, and then later to the Government's. But in the later eighteenth century it began to draw on loans and subsidies from the Bank of England and the Government. Robert Clive's victory over the Nawab of Bengal, and the Treaty of Allahabad grant-ing the East India Company the Diwani was a cause for celebration, but it also brought problems. Expectations of great riches drawn from Indian taxation sent demand for stock very high, but the returns were disappointing. There were criticisms that the Company was going too far towards dictatorship. In 1766 William Pitt ('The Elder', and Earl Chatham) announced an inquiry into the Company.

Between 1769 and 1772 the Company borrowed £5.5 million from the Bank of England. Then they had to rely on a Government loan of £1.2 million. Those loans were paid off, but then more drawn both from the Bank of England and the Treasury.[15] Government oversight of Company business was harder to fend off when the Company relied so heavily on cash injections, and criticisms mounted. Investors demanded high returns but the onerous taxing of Bengal had helped drive the province into famine under Robert Clive, as we have seen.

A 'Secret Committee' to inquire into the East India Company was defended in Parliament. 'In the east the laws of society, the laws of nature have been enormously violated', John Burgoyne told the House of Commons: 'Oppression in every shape has ground the faces of the poor defenceless natives; and tyranny in her bloodless form has stalked abroad.'[16]

In Parliament the criticisms mounted against the East India Company and its Bengal President Warren Hastings, pursued by the MP Edmund Burke. Adam Smith made another criticism of the Company when he wrote that it would be better if Britain were to pay over the odds for East India goods from the Dutch than suffer 'the distraction of a large portion of its capital from other employments more necessary, or more useful, or more suitable to its circumstances and situation, than a direct trade to the East Indies'.[17] It was a clue that the colonies were more and more being seen as a limitation on invest-ment in Britain, as well as a drain on India. In March of 1784 bailiffs were sent to East India House to try to recover Government debts of £100,000.[18]

Charles Fox's government did set out to abolish the East India Company court and replace it with government appointed commissioners and passed a law in the Commons saying so in 1783. But the Company's supporters in the House of Lords, led by King George III vetoed it. The King dismissed Fox – criticism of the East India Company could only go so far – and William Pitt's government brought in a weaker version of Fox's reforms.

The South Sea Bubble

The South Sea Company was founded by the Earl of Oxford Robert Harley in 1711. The Company bid for the exclusive right to 'trade and traffick from 1 August 1711, into and unto and from the Kingdoms, Lands, etc. of America, on the east side from the river Aranoca, to the southern-most part of the Terra del Fuego' – and also trade on the western side of the Americas and 'into unto and from all countries in the same limits reputed to belong to the crown of Spain, or which shall hereafter be discovered', – that is, the right to trade in slaves, the 'asiento de negros'. In exchange for this right the South Sea Company undertook to pay off all the Government debts.

The apparent advantage of the trade monopoly was clear, and when the monopoly was granted in 1720 the company issued shares to the value of £12,750,000 in April, followed by further issues of £50,000,000 in June and £12,500,000 in August. As they traded the shares rose in price from £128 to over £1000 in the space of six months. Tradesmen and improving landlords were looking for place to invest their cash. A great many other speculative ventures were launched around that time, promising new kinds of soap, perpetual motion machines or even 'for carrying on an undertaking of great advantage, but nobody knows what it is'.[19]

Among the investors in the South Sea Company were Isaac Newton (who was said to have lost £20,000), John Gay and Alexander Pope. Sadly, there was no venture. The monopoly trade was not the Government's to gift since it was still Spain's. The value of the shares climbed on expected earnings that never appeared.

The investors did not just lose their savings, but their dignity as well. Hogarth made a moral fable in a print that showed the foolish investors on a swirling merry-go-round. Jonathan Swift wrote a poem about the terrible South Seas and Change Alley, where the favoured share trading coffee house of Garroways was:

There is a gulf, where thousands fell,
  Here all the bold adventurers came,
A narrow sound, though deep as Hell--
  Change Alley is the dreadful name.

The following year the Government passed a 'Bubble Act' that forbade Joint Stock Companies not created by Royal Charter (though it was widely evaded).[20]

Anti-Slavery

The moral argument against the slave trade in England arose out of a religious feeling that the enslaved Africans were God's creatures as much as those who enslaved them. The American Quaker Anthony Benezet's pamphlet *Caution and Warning to Great Britain* (1767) set out the argument and was followed by John Wesley's cautious, but condemnatory *Thoughts on Slavery* in 1767. A Cambridge student Thomas Clarkson took up the cause in 1785 in an essay *Is it lawful to make slaves of others against their wills?* Clarkson was a driven man and went around the country gathering stories from slavers to show how bad the trade was. He found the plan for putting slaves in a ship's hold that when copied shocked many. Poets like Southey, Wordsworth, Charles Lamb and Coleridge supported Clarkson.[21]

The founding of the Society for Effecting the Emancipation of the Slaves in 1787, with Clarkson and the York MP William Wilberforce, was a turning point in the public relations campaign. Sir Thomas Fowell Buxton remembered being 'impressed, when young, with the resolution of his sister-in-law, one of the Gurney family, in refusing slave sugar'. He remembered the campaign to boycott slave-grown sugar 'passing through the land like an electric shock'.[22]

Clarkson explained why it was that the Anti-Slavery Campaign supported abolition with the compensation of the slaveholder (which strikes people today as so wrong). It was, he argued, the whole country's sin, not just the slave-holders: 'Can we ask of the slaveholder the sacrifice of his property without being prepared ourselves some cost and inconvenience in dissevering ourselves from the system we condemn?'[23]

Three hundred thousand were boycotting slave-grown sugar and displayed their (pricier) Indian sugar in bowls made by Josiah Wedgwood's pottery, decorated with the image of a pleading slave, in chains, over the slogan 'Am I not a Man and a Brother?'

The moral campaign against the slave trade came when many were growing more critical of the 'West India Interest' in Britain. Henry Brougham painted a harsh picture of the West India colonies in his *Enquiry into the Colonial Policy of the European Powers*. Showing that the 'great proportion of those whose capital has planted the West Indies, have in fact, continued in their native country', Henry Brougham argued that they 'had no connection with the property, except that of receiving their interest, or selling the produce on commission'. For Brougham, 'the great strength of every country, the landed interest, is almost wholly wanting in the West Indies':

> Its place is supplied partly by proprietors loaded with debt, who are little more than commissioners for the European creditors; partly by factors, so-called, acting for the non-resident population.[24]

Planter society, he said, was corrupt:

> The witnesses of the planters' actions, are the companions of his debaucheries, who reek with the same lust, and wallow in the same gluttonous mire; or the wretched beings, who tremble at his nod, while they minister to the indulgence of his brutal appetites.[25]

Brougham – who spent much of his later life campaigning against slavery and highlighting its cruelty – was in 1803 deeply worried about what it was doing to Britons: 'the most disgusting contamination with which the residence of the new world stains the character of the European – a love of uncontrolled power over individuals'.[26]

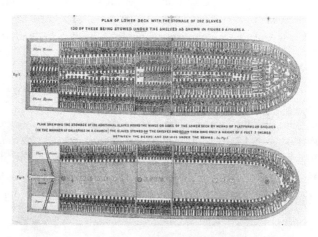

'Men of a respectable character', he despaired, 'remove to these settlements' and 'by degrees they partake of the general contamination'.[27] Worse, 'upon return to their native country, their habits are too deeply rooted to be shaken off', and 'their influence is not inconsiderable upon the societies in which they mingle'. Brougham underlines the point, writing 'they return still more depraved in principles and taste, armed with an influence they did not before possess'.[28] Here, Brougham was attacking the 'West India interest' which by the later eighteenth century was generally Tory and hostile to liberal reform, most particularly the struggle to end the slave trade. Though the war with Revolutionary France worked against reform, the moral argument against slavery had already been won with much of the country's middle classes and the elite. 'Instead of being very advantageous to Great Britain', said William Pitt in the House of Commons in 1792, the slave trade 'is the most destructive that can well be imagined for her interests'.[29] James Stephen, a former Solicitor General of St Kitts, found a way to bring it to the heart of British policy. Stephen had written a pamphlet denouncing American trade with France in 1805, and two years later he helped to draft a bill that would marry economic warfare with anti-Slavery. The Foreign Slave Trade Act forbade Britons from working for the slave trade to French and American colonies. The Act would give the Admiralty the legal basis to stop and search American ships trading between the Caribbean and France. Anti-Slavery yoked to British diplomatic and naval dominance was very effective.

On the 10th of June 1806 Charles Fox moved the resolution in Parliament, 'that this House, considering the African slave-trade to be contrary to the principles of justice, humanity, and policy, will, with all practicable expedition, take effectual measures for the abolition of said trade, in such a manner, and at such a period, as may be deemed advisable'. The Tory Navy Treasurer George Canning said, he would vote for it, though he should have been better pleased with a bill which would strike at once at the root of this detestable commerce. Fox died in October 1806. On his death-bed he said, 'I wish earnestly to see accomplished ... the abolition of the slave-trade'.[30]

Abandoning the Myths of the Mercantile Age

European rationalists like Voltaire and Humboldt made light of the Spanish myth of Eldorado, thinking that it was a clue to the primitive attitudes of the Conquistadors – and of Seville. It was the geographer Charles de la Condamine who persuaded them that 'El Dorado' was a 'belle chimère' in an address to the French academy of Sciences in 1745. Still, however primitive, Spanish gold and more importantly silver, helped to oil the wheels of international commerce in the sixteenth century, as we have seen.[31]

By the early nineteenth century Simon Bolivar spearheaded a movement of national liberation against Spain. Britain backed these independence moves hoping for an 'opening to our manufactures [of] the markets of that great Continent', wrote Lord Castlereagh.[32] To the naturalist Humboldt the myth of Eldorado belonged to the past: 'The real wealth of this country is founded on the care of the herds and the cultivation of colonial produce.'[33]

With the parliamentary scrutiny of the East India and West India interests, the Old Colonial System was being reformed and put on a more rational footing. The company-led colonies that owed their existence to Royal Monopoly were giving way to new administrations under governors and local assemblies, that gave their allegiance to the government in Westminster. Under William the Board of Trade and Plantations was re-established, made up of civil servants and privy councillors so that its day-to-day operations were removed both from King and Parliament.[34]

Mercantilism would in time give way to a new doctrine of Free Trade, and the Old Colonial System would be overturned by the American Revolution of 1776. A very different relation between Britain and the world was on the horizon.

Chapter Ten

THE MEANING OF 'PRIMITIVE ACCUMULATION'

The era of the Old Colonial System could be said to run from Columbus' voyage across the Atlantic in 1492 when the seeds of the European domination of the world were planted, through to the American Revolution of 1776, when the system was overthrown. Or, for a less expansive idea, you could say from the founding of the EIC and the Virginia Colony 1600–07 through to the industrial revolution, 1760.

The merchants were capitalists. They had a stock of money, or goods, that they turned into more money by advantageous trades. That was their capital. But they were not yet industrial capitalists. Their capital was not invested in the production process. Trade changed a lot. Things that had not been there, then were. But it did not change the way that people worked.

The social critic Karl Marx coined the term 'primitive accumulation' to describe this era. He said that in its early development capital had plundered the non-capitalist world, seizing slaves and precious metals by force as its fund for 'primitive accumulation'; hence 'capital comes dripping from head to foot, from every pore, with blood and dirt'.[1] Marx was not piling up atrocity stories to damn the capitalists – at least not just that. He was intervening in a discussion about 'original accumulation' in political economy, challenging the orthodox view that initial capital funding came from prudent saving.

Marx coined the term 'primitive accumulation' as a rejoinder to the mystifying concept of 'original accumulation' found in economic textbooks of his day, arguing that capital funds came about through frugality. Marx shows that the original funds for investment, primitive accumulation, were instead plundered from the new world (as gold), from Africa (as slaves), or from Asia (as spices), but always through extortion and violence. Marx's reworking of the conventional economic category 'original accumulation' as 'primitive accumulation' was meant to show that the origins of capitalism were steeped in barbaric expropriation.

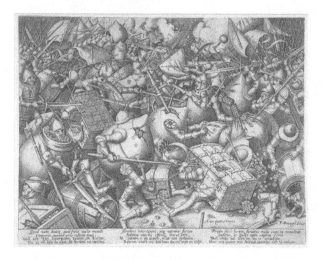

Peter Bruegel, The Battle of the Moneybags and the Strongboxes, 1570.

The idea of 'primitive accumulation' appealed to Third World critics of colonialism because it linked their history to a wider cause. Among them were the Trinidadians C. L. R. James and Eric Williams and the Indians Ramkrishna Mukherjee and Rajani Palme Dutt. Eric Williams' book *Capitalism and Slavery* (1944) connected the era of the slave trade the Royal African Company and the West Indian plantations to the Old Colonial System and what he, after Marx, called 'Mercantile Capitalism'. The meaning of his book was that the system of direct slavery raised the initial funds for the industrial revolution. In doing so, it also undermined its own basis. Once the capital generated from the slave trade and the plantation system was redirected towards investment in British domestic industry, the direct domination of slavery was superseded by wage slavery. As well as explaining the necessary connection between slave trade and origins of capitalism, Williams was also explaining the abolition of slavery as itself a necessary further step in the development of capitalism. This was a very different argument from the one that British historians had been used to hearing. For them, the moral awakening of the anti-slavery movement was the real reason that slavery was abolished. Williams was showing that the moral awakening went hand in hand with the ordinary business of making money.

Ramakrishna Mukherjee used Marx's account of 'primitive accumulation' as a way to understand the founding, years of success, and then the failure of the EIC. He was arguing that the Company was part of the era of 'primitive accumulation', and further, that its end had come about because it was not right for the new era of free trade that followed.

Williams and Mukherjee's ideas were not well liked in British and American universities in the 1960s and 1970s. Pointed rebuttals were written by people including Paul Bairoch and Seymour Drescher. Paul Bairoch argued that the colonies were not important as a source of capital funds for the industrial revolution.[2] Seymour Drescher dismissed the argument saying that 'the slave trade was not inordinately profitable to imperial investors, and that its profits simply could not have been large enough to be considered the or even a "major contributing factor" in British capital formation'. Drescher went on to say that 'a few individuals in Lancashire might have funnelled slave trade profits into the new manufacturing sectors, but they were no more than incidental in financing British economic growth'.[3]

More recently a greater interest in colonial history has found the judgement on 'primitive accumulation' leaning the other way. Against Drescher, Robin Blackburn argues that the 'profits from the triangular trade could have furnished anything from 20.9 per cent to 55 per cent of Britain's gross fixed capital formation in 1770'. Utsa Patnaik estimates that the transfer of wealth from both the West Indies and India is as great as 57 per cent of domestic savings in the UK in 1770 rising to 86 per cent in 1801.[4]

Like the West India interest in Britain, the East India traders, known as 'Nabobs' (a corruption of the Indian title 'Nawab') were known and often criticised for their great wealth. The historian and EIC administrator Thomas Macaulay said that they had 'sprung from obscurity' to acquire great wealth, 'spent it extravagantly' and 'exhibited it insolently'. One such was Ann, the daughter of the EIC's Sir Streynsham Master, who married Gilbert, the 4th Earl of Coventry; her wealth helped pay for Capability Brown and Robert Adam to build Croome Court in the 1740s (the seventh earl's second son William Coventry also married wisely, to Mary Laing, heir to the vast Goshen estate in Jamaica).

The Whig MP Horace Walpole said of the Nabobs: 'They starved millions in India by monopolies and plunder, and almost raised a famine at home by the luxury occasioned by their opulence'. Like Macaulay, Walpole blamed the excessive spending of the British Nabobs for pushing up prices in England, 'till the poor could not purchase bread'![5]

There is no way of knowing how much of profit made on trade, taxation and investment in the colonies was invested in British industry, and how much just wasted on conspicuous consumption. Even the luxury spending of the wealthy West Indian planters – or of the EIC Nabob – could add to the Mother Country's wealth, as it seemed to Lord Brougham:

> The demand for the production of the more elegant arts which such men create, however ridiculous in them, and however indiscriminate, tends to improve the manners of a community, by encouraging a species of industry, not much favoured in a country merely commercial or agricultural.[6]

Local historians, and institutional histories in recent times have tended to support the argument that colonial profits had a marked impact on investment on the building of docks in London, Liverpool, Bristol, Southampton and Glasgow, in the development of banking, as well as financing schools, colleges and churches around the country.

The Egyptian social analyst and activist Samir Amin used the phrase 'primitive accumulation' in another way. He wrote:

> Whenever the capitalist mode of production enters into relations with pre-capitalist modes of production, and subjects these to itself, transfers of value take place from the pre-capitalist to the capitalist formations as a result of the mechanism of primitive accumulation.

Amin went on to say 'these mechanisms do not belong only to the prehistory of capitalism; they are contemporary as well'.[7] Amin's point subtly shifts the meaning of Marx's
idea. It was no longer an explanation of the original source of capital investment but a
general term for exploitation of the less developed ('pre-capitalist') world by the wealthy
west. What is set aside in Amin's idea is primitive accumulation as a historically specific
era that comes before the industrial revolution.

For Karl Marx, though, the point was to give an historical account of the development of capitalism, from its more bloodthirsty origins to the cooler domination of its
later incarnation. For Marx:

> the discovery of gold and silver in America … expiration, enslavement and entombment in
> mines of the indigenous population of that continent, the beginnings of the conquest and
> plunder of India, and the conversion of Africa into a preserve for the commercial hunting
> of blackskins, are all things which characterise the dawn of the era capitalist production.[8]

Marx thought that mercantilism was a barrier to full-blown capitalism:

> Wherever merchant's capital still predominates we find backward conditions. This is true
> even within the same country … The independent and predominant development of mer-
> chant's capital is tantamount to the non-subjection of production to capital, and hence
> capital developing on the basis of an alien mode of production which is also independent of
> it. The independent development of merchant's capital, therefore, stands in inverse propor-
> tion to the general economic development of society.[9]

Eric Williams also saw the era of mercantile capitalism as historically distinct from
the later development of industrial capitalism. Slavery was important to capitalism,
but it was not the only source of an economic surplus. 'It must not be inferred that the
triangular trade was solely and entirely responsible for the economic development', he
wrote. Rather, 'the growth of the internal market in England, the ploughing-in of the
profits from industry to generate still further capital and achieve still greater expansion,
played a large part'. What was more, he wrote 'this industrial development, stimu-
lated by mercantilism, later outgrew mercantilism and destroyed it'.[10] Williams shared
Marx's view of an historical development out of the Old Colonial System into the industrial revolution.

Marx saw the relation between merchant capitalism and industrial capitalism as a
kind of shift, where: 'capital arises out of circulation and posits labour as wage labour'.[11]
He means that the cash funds that were concentrated in the hands a few merchants were
the wealth that was used to put men and women to work in factories.

For Marx 'primitive accumulation' is not just about the colonies. In sixteenth-century
England harsh laws, known as the 'Bloody Legislation' against vagrancy and enforcing
longer hours at work were passed. Marx writes that in developed capitalism 'direct force'
is exceptional. But it 'is otherwise during the historic genesis of capitalist production':

> The bourgeoisie at its rise, wants and uses the power of the state to 'regulate' wages, i.e. to
> force them within the limits suitable for surplus value making, to lengthen the working day

and to keep the labourer himself in the normal degree of dependence. This is an essential element of the so-called primitive accumulation.[12]

He also wrote:

> As long as capital is weak, it still relies on the crutches of the past modes of production, or of those that will pass with its rise. As soon as it feels strong, it throws away those crutches, and moves in accordance with its own laws.[13]

For Marx, then, 'primitive accumulation' is what comes before full-blooded capitalism. The funds gathered by enclosing the commons, by seizing new lands, and by trading on the margins are all the original seed capital for the industrial revolution. His substantial argument is that once industrial capitalism was set in train it was less important where the *original* accumulation fund had come from, since it was the exploitation of labour in the factory that made the wage fund for the next day. Later writers have found Marx's evolutionary model less useful and fixed on the *longue durée* instead. But for our purposes the periodisation of the history of colonialism illuminates the differences between the Old Colonial System and the Free-Market imperialism that follows.

Colonialism and the Idea of Race

Any twenty-first century reader of sixteenth-century ideas about the colonies will understandably be taken aback by the racial prejudices that recur throughout them. We come to these discussions after racial thinking has for us long since been exposed as a fraud. The Old Colonial System is right at the beginning of the chasm between Europeans and the non-European world.

The end point of the primitive accumulation was a world where black slaves worked under white overseers on American plantations, and where Indian peasants' rents were handed over from the Mughal Emperor to EIC directors. Some of the foundations of the racial division of the world that would reach its climax at the beginning of the twentieth century were already being laid.

At the same time the mercantile connections that were at the heart of the new colonialism meant that Europeans often met non-Europeans as contracting parties. That meant that they had to recognise each other as free agents. Even in the trade in enslaved Africans, the European masters of forts on the Bight of Benin kept up friendly relations with the Kings of Ouidah, Dahomey and other slave-trading peoples. The forts were not held by force, but with the agreement of these Kings. Even as the dungeons of the slave forts were filled with enslaved Africans, white slave traders met with, entertained and often married into African families.[14]

European slave traders were honoured guests at Dahomey festivals where captured enemies were sacrificed to 'water the graves' of ancestors. At the Danish fort at Christiansborg, white officers of the West India and Guinea Company were united with Ga women in 'cassare' – a marriage, in a Ga ceremony that was, all the same honoured by the Lutheran chaplain. Other leading slave traders like Lionel Abson, Pieter Woortman and Richard Brew had African wives and children they loved.

The Ga and Ouidah women who married European slave traders, had slaves themselves. All the Africans who dealt with the Europeans, in trade and more intimately,
held fast to the difference between themselves and the enslaved. The wives never set
foot on a visiting ship because they knew that the ship captains would not honour that
difference in the way that the fort captains did. They might be seized and sold. Nor did
Europeans take their African wives back to England or Denmark, though some children did go to Europe.

English relations with the natives of North America also swung between conquest
and compact. In 1670, Charles II's Instructions to the Council of Foreign Plantations
were that 'Forasmuch as most of our colonies do border upon the Indians, and peace is
not to be expected without the due observance and preservation of justice to them, you
are, in our name, to command all the governors that they, at no time, give any just prov-
ocation to any of the said Indians that are at peace with us.' From the Dutch concession
of the Hudson's Bay lands in 1664 to American Independence in 1776, Britain was in
a 'Covenant Chain' or friendship with the Iroquois. Newly installed British Governors
would meet with Iroquois leaders to reaffirm the alliance that they kept up against
France and later against the colonists. Native Americans leaders were received at the
Court of St James: Tiyanoga (Hendrick Theyanoguin) and other Mohawks by Queen
Anne in 1710; Ookounaka (or Oukandekah) and six other Cherokee by King George in
1730, who also met Tomochichi of the Yamacraw four years later. Treaties of friendship
were signed.

In Asia, the EIC writers and soldiers of the seventeenth century were dependent
upon the good will of Indians to survive. The outposts of the British and Dutch East
India Companies were first set up by agreement with local leaders. Many Europeans
lived among natives, took up native customs, even converting to Islam, as Josua
Blackwelle did in 1649, or marrying Indian partners as James Kirkpatrick, the EIC's
Resident at the court of Hyderabad did with the young noblewoman, and descendant of
Muhammed, Khair un-Nissa.[15]

Professor Holden Furber of the American Association for Asian Studies thought
that the period from the sixteenth century was an 'Age of Partnership' where relations
between the non-western world and the west were based on mutual respect which was
very different from the later Age of Imperialism.[16] That was an idealised view of a relationship that was always self-serving and would often break out into conflict. It also tells
something true about the mercantile connections, that they were relations of trade, and
not yet outright domination.

The idea of racial difference did not yet have the fixity that it would have later.
Britons had prejudices against each other, against other Europeans, as strong as they did
against people outside of Europe. Faced with excommunication from Catholic Europe,
Queen Elizabeth proposed common cause with Ottoman Sultan Murad III. Right up to
the last quarter of the eighteenth century, the English – and later the British – national
identity was decidedly Protestant, meaning that in so far as there was an enemy against
whom the Britons differentiated themselves, they were Catholic Europeans: Spanish,
French and Irish. Early modern Europeans were less democratic in outlook, and more
admiring of status, so that the Mohawk chiefs struck Londoners as aristocratic in their

mien. Europeans even enslaved other Europeans from time to time, as Cromwell did some of the defeated Irish, setting them to work in the West Indies (where they were known as 'redshanks'), or the Spanish did to Dutch boys taken prisoner in Tortuga in 1635. On the whole, though, the system of slavery worked on the basis of the colour divide, with transported Africans making up the statistically significant workforce. Pointedly, the condition of slavery was hereditary for the African enslaved, but not for the white indentured servants. The plantations were the original site of racial differentiation, in a way that often shocked visitors from non-slave-holding regions.

Where white settlers lived among native populations the racial identity became more mutually exclusive when white women joined them. Native concubines were abandoned for supposedly more upright English wives. Their arrival marked the shift to a more rigidly demarcated social sphere of white and brown. As we shall see later, the full ideological imposition of systems of racial difference was closely related to the democratisation of western societies – but that did not happen until late in the nineteenth century.

PART TWO

Empire of Free Trade, 1760–1870

Chapter Eleven

THE 'GREAT DIVERGENCE'

In the eighteenth century, European powers pulled ahead of their rivals in the East and South, and in the nineteenth century came to dominate the world. Europeans pulled ahead in economic terms, with the industrial revolution, or what some called the 'birth of modern capitalism', and they also pulled ahead in military power. 'Asia fell back in the race of life because of the industrial revolution', Jawaharlal Nehru told the Asian-African Conference at Bandung on 23 April 1955.[1]

Europe – and in particular Britain's 'take-off' is not doubted as a fact, but what people make of it has been argued over. Many accounts draw implied or explicit moral lessons along the lines that economic success shows that Europeans were better people than non-Europeans. What made them 'better' in these ways of explaining what happened could be different things. Some people thought that European success showed that Europeans were chosen by God, others thought that they were naturally cleverer with higher Intelligence Quotients (IQs), others still think that the European institutions were superior (the institutions people have in mind are often scientific inquiry, free markets, Christian conscience, parliamentary government and obedience to laws).[2]

To others, though, the idea that Europeans were better people than those in the rest of the world was shameless hype and prejudice. The idea of European superiority was just an ideological cover for the imperialist exploitation of the non-European world, they objected. The wars and atrocities of the twentieth century, undertaken by the European powers, and by America, have made the argument for a European moral superiority ring hollow. The challenge that non-Europeans raised, first in the anti-colonial movements, and then, afterwards in successful nation-states, like China and India, make the idea of a natural European superiority implausible.[3]

For historians, though, the problem remains how to explain what Samuel Huntingdon (and after him Kenneth Pomeranz) called 'the Great Divergence'[4] – the growing gap between European economic and politico-military power on the one hand, and the relatively diminished power of non-European powers? One important point is that European success was in large part due to outright plunder of the non-European world, and that this was often done at gunpoint. The conquest of Latin America and the brutal exploitation of its silver mines, the taking of twelve and a half million enslaved Africans, the piratical trade in the East Indies all put non-European wealth in the hands of Europeans. The origin of the investment funds that helped British and other European powers' businesses take off were often robbed from overseas, say the radical critics.

Allowing that the European powers leapt ahead with the help of plunder from the rest of the world, it is still worth looking at West Europe's internal dynamics. To understand the way that Britain and the other European powers came to dominate much of the rest of the world, we ought to understand what were the internal resources they drew upon, as well as the external ones.

Britain

Britain went through a bruising time in the second half of the seventeenth century. The Cromwellian commonwealth fostered a great democratic movement and strong ideas of individual conscience – mostly connected to religious puritanism. The Commonwealth, though, was unstable, and riven by factions. London merchants who had supported it wanted the return of Charles II to the throne in 1660. Restoration brought its own problems. The Church of England drove out non-Conformists while the King, harbouring Catholic sympathies, promised England's loyalty to France's Louis in his war against the Protestant Dutch. Parliament invited William, Stadtholder of Holland, to invade in 1689 and establish a Protestant succession. Eighteenth-century Britain was ruled over by a succession of Hanoverian Kings all called George: George I (r. 1714–27), George II (r. 1727–60) and George III (r. 1760–1820).

After the conflicts of the seventeenth century the Georgian era was looked on as a peaceful and stable time when the country enjoyed its wealth – at least for the growing and stable middle classes. Robert Walpole was Prime Minister and the state was run by an oligarchy, sometimes called the 'Robinocracy' in honour of his assiduous promotion of allies.[5] Those allies were for the most part large landowners, and also called 'Court Whigs' because they governed with the support of King George II, steering between the twin evils of a Stuart Restoration and radical democracy.

George II (Metropolitan Museum of Art, NY).

The Court Whigs had critics – High Tories like Bolingbroke and his ally Jonathan Swift, who railed against the corruption of Old England by the monied interests. They appealed to the country squire. There were more radical Whigs who spoke up for democracy, like William Pitt and his backer William Beckford. Their social base was in the towns. The unlikely alliance of radical Whigs and High Tories gave birth to a Patriot opposition that called for rearmament against Bourbon France.

On the face of things, Britain's overseas trade was still oriented to Europe, which took around four-fifths of her exports. That was not the full picture, though. The trade with Europe was at a standstill, while as much as 95 per cent of the increase in exports in the years from 1707 to 1767 was in the colonial markets outside Europe. Yet more telling, by 1750 as much as 40 per cent of exports to Europe were re-exports, colonial goods that had been imported into Britain, and then sold on to Europeans, like sugar, tea and tobacco.[6]

In 1759, Joseph Massie worked out that there were in England 866,000 families living on less than the £40 a year it was thought would make for a comfortable middle-class life. There was also a large middle class of 567,500 families with an income between £40 and £200, and there were 41,070 wealthy families with incomes above £200.

Of the wealthy there were 2070 esquires and entitled; 16,000 gentlemen, 20,500 merchants and traders and 2,500 master manufacturers.

Of the middle classes there were 65,000 in the professions (lawyers, clergy, army officers and the like), working the land were 265,000 freeholders, farmers and cottagers, and there were 77,500 master manufacturers, and 160,000 tradesmen.

Of the less well off, there were 520,000 working the land, as farmers and farm labourers, in town were 248,000 manufacturers and labourers, 20,000 tradesmen and 78,000 seamen and soldiers.[7]

At that time the total population of Britain was eight million (making Massie's total an underestimate even if it described the social classes). Another four million lived in Ireland. The East India Company ruled haphazardly over some 30 million people in Bengal. There were more than one and a half million people living in the British American colonies, of whom 325,000 were enslaved Africans, and a further 300,000 in the British West Indies, of whom 250,000 were enslaved.

Enlightenment

The poet Alexander Pope in a dedication to George II, George Augustus, called the times an 'Augustan Age' linking George to his namesake the Roman Emperor Augustus. Augustus was known as a benign but absolute ruler, who guaranteed the *Pax Romana* so that culture and the arts could flourish. What came to be called 'the Augustan Age' in England was a time of relatively open liberal inquiry where the arts and sciences flourished. The focus of cultural life shifted from the Court to the Coffee House. A number of debating societies, clubs and scientific circles were set up. Addison and Steele founded the *Spectator* which showcased the litterateurs of the Augustan Age. Differences could be sharp, but they were more often worked out in debate, which could be very cutting, than in violence.

Chief among the propagandists of the new age was Anthony Ashley Cooper, the Third Earl of Shaftesbury. He wrote to a friend in 1706: 'There is a mighty light that spreads its self over the world especially in those two free nations of England and Holland on whom the affairs of Europe now turn.'[8] Shaftesbury was Chancellor in 1672 and put his physician and friend John Locke on the Board of Trade. For a while Locke was out of favour and had to take shelter in Holland.

Locke's writings were central to the Augustan Age. In 1689, he published the *Two Treatises on Government* which argue the case for a liberal order, with minimal government. In 1690, he published the *Essay on Human Understanding* which set out a stridently empirical account of consciousness as a sensual reflection of reality (in disagreement with both religious obscurantism and also the speculative metaphysics of René Descartes). Locke's defence of human reason and individual rights resonated with the age. His work was popularised in the *Spectator* and widely read.

In France, the English writers were greatly admired. Voltaire and Diderot (who translated Shaftesbury) sung their praises, as, further afield, did Rousseau (whose *On the Social Contract*, 1762, draws on Locke's Two Treatises). Ephraim Chambers' *Cyclopaedia* (1728) was the model for what would become the *Encyclopedie* (1751–64) that Diderot edited, a founding document of what came to be called the French Enlightenment. Though the word was not used in England, scholars since have thought that it is easier to understand the Augustan Age as the English Enlightenment.

The 'Augustan Age' was a literary thing. Unlike the more ideological struggle of the French intellectuals against the *Ancien Régime* the English had already had their revolution in 1649 and shrunk from its excesses to flourish under the Georges. Its later work included Jonathan Swift's mockeries of excessive rationalism, *The Tale of a Tub*, and 'The Voyage to Laputa' (in *Gulliver's Travels*, a parody of Francis Bacon's *New Atlantis*), Hume's *History of England* (1762) which cautiously warned against fanaticism, Dr Johnson's *Dictionary of the English Language* (1754) which smuggled in many of his value judgements on non-Conformists and the barbaric Scots, and Gibbon's *Fall of the Roman Empire* (1776).

Britons thought that their version of liberty was better than France's.

The English Enlightenment was much more than a literary movement. Natural philosophy, as science was called then, had been put on a sound foundation with Francis Bacon who died in 1627. Robert Boyle (1627–91) was a part of the Anglo-Irish plantocracy, the son of the Earl of Cork. He developed early chemistry and in particular showed the relation between the volume of gas and pressure and was known for demonstrating the vacuum. Isaac Newton (1642–1727) published his *Philosophiæ Naturalis Principia Mathematica* (1687). It was there that he set out his laws of mechanics for the universe, which deal with forces, inertia and momentum. In it he shows how gravitation can account for the laws of motion of the planets as set out by Kepler and Galileo. Edmond Halley (1656–1742) observed the stars and gives his name to Halley's Comet. The biologist Erasmus Darwin (1731–1802) wrote several works of botany, with an impressive theoretical compendium *Zoonomia* (1794), as well as being an accomplished engineer and inventor. The polymath Joseph Priestly (1733–1804) identified several gases among his many pedagogical efforts. Joseph Banks (1743–1820) was an important botanist who travelled with Cook on his Pacific voyages. Scientific bodies, like the Royal Society and the Lunar Society in Birmingham, supported these scientific speculations, as did a wide scientifically curious public among the better-off.

Economics as a distinct discipline was founded around this time, through the work of Sir James Steuart, Adam Smith, Thomas Malthus and Josiah Tucker. Smith's celebrated book *Wealth of Nations* (1776) was to economic theory what Locke's *Two Treatises of Government* were to political theory. Smith set out to show how the categories of labour, land and capital were related, dethroning the prejudice that only the land was truly fruitful, and showing instead that labour in general was productive of wealth. Smith's view that the economy worked through the operation of the 'invisible hand'[9] of the market put the policy of 'free trade' on a philosophical footing.

The Limits of Enlightenment

Nowadays John Locke is often criticised for his racial views. He was one of the early investors in the Royal African Company, and, in 1669 helped draught the Fundamental Constitutions of Carolina. The constitution guaranteed liberty to all regardless of religion – who were free. But clause 110 said that 'every freeman of Carolina shall have absolute power and authority over his negro slaves, of what opinion or religion soever'. Locke's defenders make the point that he was only a clerk working on the draughting with many others – as they also say that he sold his shares in the Royal African Company.

It is perhaps the wrong way to look at the question to look for race discrimination in Locke's philosophy. With his 'blank slate' idea of the mind, Locke did not think that native peoples were naturally incapable of reason.

'Had the Virginia king Apochancana, been educated in England', Locke wrote, he would be 'as good a Mathematician, as any in it':

> The difference between him, and a more improved Englishman, lying barely in this, That the exercise of his Faculties was bounded within the Ways, Modes, and Notions of his own Country.[10]

To the modern reader this passage is contemptuous of native American culture. But it also shows how Locke's blank slate sees no racial inequality in nature.

The limitation to Locke's humanism was not race but the ownership of property: 'the great and chief end, therefore, of Men's uniting into Commonwealths, and putting themselves under Government, is the Preservation of their Property'.[11] Locke understands this property as based on claim and improvement. 'As much land as a Man Tills, Plants, Improves, Cultivates, and can use the Product of, so much is his Property'. The enclosure of the commons, and the transfer of wealth from the community to the individual as private property was a change Locke had lived to see, and to him, the property owner 'by his Labour, does, as it were, inclose it from the Commons'.[12]

As a member of the Board of Trade dealing with the Colonies Locke wrote to Governors telling them not to encroach on native lands, which was the British policy (except when it was not). On the other hand, Locke's view of private property was not in principle hostile to expansion into Indian territory, because of the distinction he made between worked-up, farmed land and more scarcely occupied land, as in hunting lands. He wrote, 'Where there being more Land, than the Inhabitants possess, and make use of, anyone has liberty to make use of the waste'.[13]

One important political scientist who used something like a Lockean argument was Emer de Vattel (1714–67). In his *Law of Nations* Vattel asks 'if a nation may lawfully occupy any portion of a vast country in which are to be found only errant tribes incapable because of the smallness of their numbers of inhabiting the whole'? Vattel thought that 'we are not departing from the intentions of nature when we restrict the savages within narrower bounds'.[14]

For Locke the 'law of nature' teaches only those 'who will but consult it'. Those who do not declare themselves 'to live by another Rule than that of reason and common equity' and so become 'dangerous to Mankind'. Anyone who lives outside of the law of nature 'becomes degenerate, and declares himself to quit the Principles of Human Nature, and to be a noxious Creature'.[15] Here Locke was talking about those who break the law, but it was not hard to see how the theory could be extended to those 'naturals' who live 'outside of civil society' in the Americas.

Industrial Revolution

Manufacturing in the early eighteenth-century Britain was not more technologically advanced than manufacturing in India or China. Chinese pottery (chinoiserie) and Indian calicos were imported because they were better and cheaper than the goods made in England. (Controls on the import of Indian calicos were brought in in 1700 and 1720.) The fine bronze statues of Benin were as good as any European bust. By the end of the eighteenth century, Britain was in the throes of what would later be called the industrial revolution.

The industrial revolution did not really get going until the late eighteenth century though many of the technologies at its centre were invented much earlier. In 1668 'Brewer with about fifty Walloons came over to England, and received encouragement in the working and dyeing of fine cloths from Spanish wool', wrote Andrew Ure, marking the beginning of domestic cloth working.[16] While it is true in the later eighteenth century that Cotton Lords put thousands to work in their mills, domestic spinning and weaving not only carried on but increased with the increases in demand right up to the end of the eighteenth century.

Georgian England saw a strong rise in population from around 5.29 million in 1700 to more than 7.57 million in 1780, with corn output rising from 13 to 16 million quarters over the same period. Threshing machines, the seed drill, steel ploughs and eventually traction engines all greatly increased agricultural output, as enclosure crop rotation and selective breeding had in the sixteenth century. Before the age of the machines, the eighteenth century was an age of manufacture where the productive force was the skill of her craftsmen and women.[17]

The key improvements in technique were a number of innovations in spinning thread (Hargreaves' 'Spinning Jenny', Crompton's 'mule' and Arkwright's Water Frame); John Kay's 'flying shuttle' which brought loom weaving down from a two- to a one-man operation, and Cartwright's power-driven loom and the Jacquard machine (that programmed patterned weaves). There were mechanical innovations in the preparation of fibres and cloth finishing, with fulling, carding and napping machines.

Woollen production grew by one and a half times over the eighteenth century. Wool was eclipsed by the cotton industry, which only added £600,000 in value in 1770, but by 1802 accounted for a fifth of industrial value added, at £9,200,000.[18]

Abraham Darby worked out how to make iron with coke instead of charcoal greatly increasing the output of cast iron at his Coalbrookdale works in 1709. The output of pig iron in England and Wales grew from 18,000 tons in 1717 to 61,000 in 1788, but then leapt again to 109,000 tons in 1796, and then more than doubled to 235,000 tons in the following 10 years. By 1790, there were only 25 charcoal furnaces left as against 81 coke furnaces.[19] Henry Cort found out how to lower the carbon in iron by 'puddling' it, so that it became malleable enough to work – 'wrought iron' instead of too-brittle 'pig iron'.

Thomas Savery and Henry Newcomen made atmospheric pumps that used the contraction of steam into water in a cylinder to pump water out of mines. James Watt, repairing a Newcomen engine in Glasgow, made it more efficient (with a separate chamber for cooling the steam) so that it worked as a steam-pressure engine. With the addition of a Sun and planet gear, the piston action became rotary and the steam engine was a moveable power source.

Later Richard Trevithick worked out that iron working improvements meant that the pressure in the steam engine could be much higher, so dispensing with the need for the separate condensation chamber. Steam engines replaced water wheels as a source for powered machinery, and, with Robert Stephenson's 'Rocket' became a viable locomotive.

Pumping made deeper mines but beyond that there were no great increases in productivity. Coal output grew to meet the demands of the new iron and steam demands, from 3 metric tons in 1700, 5 metric tons in 1750, 10 metric tons in 1800 to 50 metric tons in 1850.[20]

The Enlightenment clearly had a big impact on the industrial revolution that followed. Many of the technologies that had an impact sprang out of practical demands, like the flying shuttle. But the Augustan Age had created a general climate of openness to 'improvement' and the application of science to labour processes. Watt's steam engine was built at Glasgow University, where he was working repairing scientific instruments. Josiah Wedgwood was close friends with the scientist Joseph Priestly and with Matthew Boulton supported the Lunar Society where scientific papers were read.

Though it is common to set out the industrial revolution like this in a set of mutually reinforcing steps historians like Maxine Berg and David Edgerton have emphasised that the existence of 'cutting edge' technology is not the same thing as its application, which can lag behind by many decades.[21] A simple steam engine, the aeolipile was built in Roman Egypt, as described by Hero in the first century, but without the social conditions that would favour replacing slave power with steam 'Hero's Engine' was just a remarkable toy.

In 1719, John and Thomas Lombe built a silk mill at Cromford on the river Derwent. It was not the first factory – the Gobelins Manufactory had been set up in France a half century earlier and Chinese Emperor Zhenzhong built a porcelain kiln complex at Jingdezhen in 1004. The Lombe brothers silk throwing factory was all the same the model for the English factory system at the heart of the industrial revolution. Gathering work processes under one roof not only saved in economies of scale: on heating, centralised power sources, use of idle time; it also took ownership of the tools and machines so that jobs once done by craftsmen in their own workshops were now carried on by hired 'hands', under the discipline of the factory manager.

Other important factories included Arkwright's cotton-spinning factory also at Cromford that employed 200 (a second, larger mill had 600) and Josiah Wedgwood's Etruria pottery works in Stafford. To grind the colours, Wedgwood first got Erasmus Darwin to build a windmill then replaced it with a Boulton and Watt steam engine in 1784. He also brought in 'clocking on', setting out to 'make such machines of Men as cannot err'.[22] The Boulton and Watt Soho foundry near Birmingham opened in 1796 to make engines.

A pool of cheap labour (a 'labour market') was needed to turn the English countryfolk into wage labourers, but that meant a revolution in social conditions. Early factory founders scoured the poorhouses buying up job lots of orphan girls to work in their factories.[23] Over time the numbers the factory owners could call upon grew. Those drawn from farms to the town would find it harder to return if their factory or workshop closed and become instead part of the floating 'reserve army' of the factory owners. The sociology of the country was changing. By 1801, the number of people employed in industry was for the first time higher than the number in agriculture.

Turning Inward

One of the key features of the industrial revolution was the way that the geography of the country changed. Britain became less rural and more urban. The balance between the South and North shifted. London, which had been the industrial centre lost out as other towns took advantage of their distance from the capital to evade the prohibitive terms of the Statute of Apprentices. Spinning and weaving wool moved from East Anglia and Norfolk north to West Yorkshire (which accounted for just a fifth of output in 1700 but three-fifths a century later). The most dramatic change was the way that industry and population shifted from the port towns by river mouths (like Bristol and Southampton) inland to new urban centres, like Manchester, Leeds, Sheffield and Birmingham.

In the nineteenth century the growing population of the towns made the new geography of Britain.

Town	1801	1831	1851
Liverpool	82,000	202,000	376,000
Glasgow	77,000	193,000	329,000
Manchester	70,000	238,000	303,000
Leeds	53,000	123,000	172,000

A transport revolution made it possible for these new industrial centres to grow. In 1663 the first of many Turnpike Acts was passed allowing Justices of the Peace in Hertfordshire, Huntingdonshire and Cambridgeshire to charge travellers for the use of the road. Later on, it would be seen as an awkward solution, but the use of turnpikes got roads built in the eighteenth century. John Metcalfe (1717–1810), known as 'blind Jack of Knaresborough' built 180 miles of turnpike road in Lancashire and Yorkshire; Thomas Telford (1757–1834) built the London-Holyhead road and many other things besides; John Macadam (1756–1836) developed the small stone compound that compacts down into a solid mass (which, sealed with tar to make tarmacadam, or tarmac is how modern roads are built). By 1830 there were 22,000 miles of new roads and 30,000 men working 3,000 coaches on them. These new roads carried the first Royal Mail, by horseback from 1720 and coach from 1784.[24]

In the House of Commons in February 1762 a Bill was debated allowing the Liverpool to Manchester Canal. Francis Egerton, the third Duke of Bridgewater paid for the works, with James Brindley his chief engineer. Bridgwater used it to carry coals to the port, halving the price, which helped him repay his £2500 loan in 4 years of completion. Brindley had between 400 and 600 men in gangs of 50 digging the canal, which relied on a remarkable aqueduct over the River Irwell. Later Brindley built the Grand Trunk canal that connected Runcorn on the West coast to the River Trent, and to Derby, Stafford and Birmingham. He had the help of Josiah Wedgwood who saw it as a way to move his pottery business to 'Etruria' in Stafford, secure in the knowledge that his plates could be floated down the canal. The canal mania would only end with the railway boom of the 1840s, which resolved the need another way.[25]

The new infrastructure brought down transport times and freight prices, and, more importantly created a national commerce where all parts of the kingdom were in touch with each other. The map of the new roads, canals and railways showed how commerce was extending from those concentrated points around the coast to penetrate deep into the centre of the country. The transport revolution represented a great refocussing of the new trading economy back into the country, withdrawing from the colonial focus of the preceding era. In 1747, Lord Pelham brought in open bidding on government debt. It was a sign that the old system of discretely raising money from the colonial chartered companies like the East India and the South Sea was at an end. Bonds were open to all investors.[26]

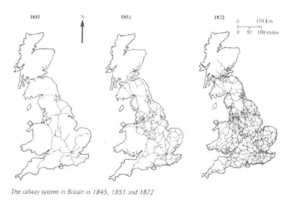

The railway system in Britain in 1845, 1851 and 1872

Britain's railways helped consolidate the national economy.

The rate at which British capitalists invested in their domestic industries climbed from 6 per cent of output in 1760 to 12 per cent – or £65 million a year – in 1840. The domestic investment boom began in 1760, so that industrial output rose from £23.6 million to £39.9 million between 1760 and 1780. By contrast exports hardly increased in those first twenty years, from £8.3 million to £8.9 million, which is to say that the share of exports in output fell from more than one-third to just over a fifth.[27]

Among those who redirected their business was the firm of Boulton and Watt that had supplied steam engines to West Indian plantations, but saw the orders dry up as the plantations went into decline. Hearing that an order from Messrs Beguye and Co. for a steam engine was unlikely to go ahead, Watt wrote on 31 October 1791 to say it would not be shipped, adding 'we heartily pray that the system of slavery so disgraceful to humanity were abolished'. Watt's father, James Watt Senior was a ship owner who traded between Greenock and the slave economy in the West Indies, and even imported slave boys to work as servants in Scotland (and in at least one case James Watt the future engineer took payment for a servant boy on his father's behalf).[28]

As the economy turned inwards the labour force changed, too. In 1806, on the eve of the abolition of the slave trade there were 775,000 slaves working to make Britain rich – more a tenth of the working classes of England. By 1851 there were no slaves, but the working class in England had grown by one-third to nine million over 20 years.

Inward investment drove the integration of the nation. Politically, nationalism seemed quite a weak idea but over the eighteenth century the middle classes became more patriotic. Tory alienation from the Whig-favouring George II did not carry over into support for the Stuart pretender, Charles Edmund. His surprise victories in 1745, after landing in Scotland and marching as far as Derby were undone as his forces were driven back to Culloden, where the Jacobite army was defeated. Englishness was at the heart of Garrick's Shakespeare revival and the landscape gardening of William Kent and Capability Brown. Patriotic feeling would become more important as Britain was challenged in the world and in 1785 William Pitt made the case for Britain and Ireland to become one free trade area.

An age of improvement shored up the idea of progress. 'No man can set bounds to the Progress that may yet be made in Agriculture and Manufacture', wrote the Welsh churchman Josiah Tucker, 'is it not much more natural and reasonable to suppose, that we are rather at the Beginning only, and just got within the Threshold, than that we are arrived at the *ne plus ultra* of useful discoveries'?[29] Adam Smith was confident that the 'very meanest person in a civilised country' was, thanks to cooperation and the division of labour, better accommodated than 'many an African King, the absolute master of the lives and liberties of ten thousand naked savages'.[30] Where Vasari caught the spirit of Florence by replacing the *Lives of the Saints* with the *Lives of the Artists,* the popular writer Samuel Smiles wrote *The Lives of the Engineers* (1862), with biographies of Watt, Brindley and Stephenson for the edification of nineteenth century Britain.

The phrase 'industrial revolution' was probably first coined as late as 1837, by the French economist Jérôme-Adolphe Blanqui, and not popularised in Britain until Arnold Toynbee's lectures published under that title in 1884. People did have a sense that a great change was taking place even if they did not have the modern phrase for it.

Dr Olinthus Gregory, mathematics teacher at the Royal Military Academy at Woolwich, gave a speech to the Deptford Mechanics' Institution in 1826, outlining how much things had changed:

Agriculture, manufactures, commerce, navigation, the arts, and sciences, useful and ornamental, in a copious and inexhaustible variety, enhance the conveniences and embellishments of this otherwise happy spot.

Dr Gregory described 'cities thronged with inhabitants, warehouses filled with stores, markets and fairs with busy rustics; fields, villages, roads, seaports, all contributing to the riches and glory of our land'.

To Gregory it seemed clear that 'every natural and every artificial advantage is susceptible of gradual progression':

New machines to advance our arts and facilitate labour; waste lands enclosed, roads improved, bridges erected, canals cut, tunnels excavated, marshes drained and cultivated, docks formed, ports enlarged.

As he put it, 'these and a thousand kindred operations which present themselves spontaneously to the mind's eye'.

'Man', Gregory argued, 'is in his nature an improveable being'. He thought that natural resources were important. Britain's coal is 'more valuable to us than the gold mines ever were to Spain'. But it was the community of inventors and scientists who were improvement's primary cause. He listed the Boultons and Watts and Trevethicks and Maudslays, who within living memory had brought about extraordinary changes. He exhorted his working audience to emulate them. Many of the great inventors of the 1820s, after all, had originally been of humble means. Every extra person inspired to educate themselves, Gregory argued, led to the 'augmentation of the national stock of happiness, prosperity, and peace, as well as to its stock of mechanical knowledge, of beneficial invention, and of practical skill'.[31]

At the heart of the industrial revolution a new dynamic was being created that would make Britain the leading power in the world. What drove it though was an intense relationship between the propertied classes and the labourers. The sociology of Britain had, by 1851 changed overwhelmingly. In England and Wales 1,790,000 worked in agriculture, there were 1,380,000 working in textile factories or workshops, another 1,200,000 working as builders, labourers and miners, and more than a million in domestic service.

The journey from the farm to the factory was often a bewildering fall for the people who had lost out in the enclosure of the commons and found themselves no longer tenants but wage labourers. Each mechanisation entailed a reordering of the work process in which many people found that they were no longer needed. Social ties that they thought were built on the solid rock of custom were torn up and remade. The old system of guilds was undermined but in time the factory operatives made themselves new trade unions, though these were outlawed under the Combination Acts of 1799 and 1800. The followers of the fictitious 'Ned Ludd' attacked napping and other machines in Derby between 1811 and 1816. In 1830, farm labourers destroyed threshing machines in the name of 'Captain Swing' risking a sentence of transportation. Workers' organisations would later take part in political movements for the Democratic Charter (1839–48) and for the Union Cause in the American Civil War (1861–65). The social war between capital and labour over hours and wages carried on throughout the nineteenth and into twentieth century. That was the secret of Britain's leap forward, that it was carried on the backs of the labouring population.

The Free Trade Debate

We are often told that the best way to grow the economy is for the authorities to play as little a role in the day-to-day decisions of individuals. According to the doctrine of 'laissez faire', choices are best left to self-interested actors. 'It is not from the benevolence of the butcher, the brewer, or the baker that we expect our dinner', wrote Adam Smith, 'but from their regard to their own interest'. The idea of free trade had been set out in Adam Smith's book *The Wealth of Nations* of 1776. He argued that all the different self-interested choices would add up to a public benefit. It was an argument that won most forward-looking men over. Smith gave voice to the new industrial class when he railed against the chartered companies saying that 'exclusive companies' were 'nuisances in every respect'. Adam Smith's name is often attached to the policy, but he himself thought that perfectly free trade was an unrealisable ideal.[32]

The great clashes with America and France in the late eighteenth and early nineteenth centuries derailed free trade as a policy. They were marked by blockades and government purchases – not what Smith had argued for but as it seemed, a spur to the industrial revolution all the same.

It is often claimed that the industrial revolution happened because of the policy of 'free trade'. The historical record is that the policy was not fully embraced until sometime after the industrial revolution had happened, in the 1850s.

The industrial revolution changed the balance between Britain and the rest of the World. Now sure of winning the English manufacturer turned his mind from protection to free trade. Even then, as the economic historian John Vincent Nye explains, Britain's tariffs against overseas goods were higher than France's.[33]

While the industrial revolution drew investment capital back from the colonies to Britain, increased output greatly accelerated the trade in goods. One of the big differences between the mercantile and 'free trade' eras is the volume of goods crossing the seas. As important as foreign trade was in the seventeenth century it was limited by the capacity of ships. Smaller and more expensive shipping meant that it was economical to ship goods that were high in value relative to their weight (and volume). Sugar, raisins, spices, tea, coffee, silver and gold, metal goods out of England, and enslaved Africans were all cargoes with a high price/weight ratio. Trade in these goods made the West India traders, the Royal African Company and the EIC rich. But the tonnage was by later standards, modest. Between 1689 and 1791 Britain shipped home some 4.75 million tons of sugar, less than 50,000 tons a year (France, with the colony of Saint-Domingue shipped home 5.25 million tons over the same years). The EIC's China tableware imports were 24,000 tons in total between 1684 and 1791. The Company's tea imports, in a single year, 1750 were 3,000 tons. These look like large amounts, and they were for the time. They made Britain's share of world trade substantial. Overall that world trade is estimated to come to a million tons by the year 1800. By 1840, though, world trade had increased to 20 million tons, and by 1870, 80 million.[34]

One of the big changes in shipping was the end of the Napoleonic wars in 1815. The centuries of war in the Atlantic and the North Sea before then made shipping very expensive. In the War of American Independence Britain lost 3,836 merchant ships, 2,861 more in the French Revolutionary War (1793–1800), and another 2,000 in the Anglo-American war of 1812. These attacks made freight costs high, with the loss of ships and cargoes and increased insurance costs. The Vienna peace of 1815 meant that world shipping would for the most part be free of conflict among the Christian powers up until 1914 (though economic blockades and gunboat diplomacy would still be a weapon in the domination of African coastal towns, India and the East Indies).

As the peace made shipping a lot cheaper, the war that came before led to big developments in the shipping industry. Napoleon's continental blockade cut off vital timber supplies for Britain from the Baltic Sea. To make up the shortfall British ships carried timber from the North American colony of New Brunswick (part of modern-day Canada). New Brunswick's timber exports grew from 5000 tons in 1805 to 100,000 tons in 1812. By 1825 – after the war was over – Britain was importing 417,000 tons, three-quarters of it from North America (where in 1803 only 6 per cent crossed the Atlantic). The timber imports showed that basic goods could by this time be profitably transported, not just high-value goods like sugar, silver and tea.

The revolutionary American clipper Prince de Neufchatel was seized by the British off Newfoundland in 1814 and taken to dry docks at Deptford where her measurements and structure were analysed. Later these were the model for the East India Company clippers beginning with the Red Rover, that were strong enough to beat up against the north-east monsoon. The Red Rover managed the round trip between Calcutta and the Gulf of Canton in 86 days.[35]

Shipbuilding had been spurred on by the demands of war. By the 1850s cargo carriers were three times the size of those built in the 1820s and often reinforced with iron – all iron hulls were made from 1860. Sailing clippers, first developed in America in the 1840s, cut down transport time so that the voyage to Australia with 300 tons had taken around 200 days; but in 1852 a 1,652 ton-clipper made the trip to Melbourne in 68 days. The British ocean-going merchant fleet grew from a tonnage of 2.3 million tons in 1818 to 5.7 million tons in 1860.[36]

With the end of the Napoleonic wars it might have seemed that the case for opening up trade would follow, but it did not. Farmers and landlords pressed for limits on imports after the war. They were afraid that once Europe was free of Napoleon's continental system and Pitt's Orders in Council that cheap imported corn would undercut them. The 'Corn Laws' were granted and ran from 1815 to 1846. They were not well liked by the working classes, who saw that they pushed the price of bread upwards. They were not liked by manufacturers either, who had to pay higher wages, or they could not get people to work for them. The Anti-Corn Law league gathered free marketeers like John Bright but also won the support of working-class leaders. In Parliament the Tories were mostly for protection and the Whigs for free trade. Free trade was a question that would shape domestic and international policy.

In 1842 Robert Peel won his Conservative Party over to 'free trade'. Tariffs on wool, linen, flax and cotton were taken down – so that Peel could say 'there hardly remains any raw material imported from other countries, on which the duty has not been reduced'.[37]

The practical end of the Corn Laws came with the Irish famine. Conservative Prime Minister Robert Peel was himself for free trade but knew his party would split over it. When he planned to buy maize for famine relief he knew it would be wrong to buy it at inflated prices. That was why the Corn Laws were repealed in 1846 when the Irish famine was under way. As we shall see the 'free trade' doctrine would in other ways be disastrous for Ireland. The free trade policy did split his party and briefly put his Liberal opponent John Russell in office. In 1850 the Navigation Laws were repealed so that any foreign merchant could trade to the colonies or Britain in their own ships.

At first free trade policies hurt British shipping, and the economy was slow to respond to the new stimulus. But in time the economy boomed. In 1851 a great exhibition of British and world industry opened its halls in London. By then Britain mined two-thirds of the world's coal, wrought and cast half of the world's iron and 70 per cent of the world's steel, and wove half of its textiles.[38]

Frédéric Bastiat wrote that:

> England opens all of its ports; it has broken down all the barriers which separated it from other nations; England had 50 colonies, and now has only one, the universe.[39]

The 'free trade' era is not just sales patter but does describe the way that Britain was orienting to the world in the nineteenth century. It was different from the old mercantile policy which dominated by upholding monopoly. It meant, too that British industry was part of a much larger – and deeper – international division of labour that had been pointedly recast.

Total costs of British Wars, 1688–1868, £ millions, adjusted to 2013 prices.

		Total cost	Cost per year
1688–97	War in Ireland and France	4,885	539
1702–13	War of Spanish Succession	6,792	564
1718–21	War with Spain	602	151
1739–48	War with Spain (right of search) and of Austrian Succession	6,230	623
1756–63	Seven Years War	10,742	1,343
1776–85	American War	11,218	1,122
1793–15	War with France	83,496	3,630
1838–43	Insurrection in Canada	191	-
1840–53	First Opium War	206	-
1848–53	Eastern Cape Frontier Wars	209	-
1854–56	Russian War	6,698	3,349
1856–57, 1860–61	Second Opium War	641	-
1856–57	Persian Expedition	87	-
1864–65	New Zealand War	67	-
1866–68	Abyssinian Expedition	769	-

Commons Library Briefing, 20 March 2018.

For Britain the years after the Napoleonic wars were less warlike than those before. War spending in the mercantilist era was high – it was the reason that the Bank of England had been founded, to pay for William I's wars. The era of democratic revolutions was very costly, too. But after the defeat of Napoleon Britain dominated through trade more than it did through naval power.

The Industrial Revolution and the World

The industrial revolution changed Britain's relations to the world. First, the industrial revolution was a change in the British economy, making it more inwardly focussed.

Second, the industrial revolution made Britain a more formidable power in Europe, which emulated and adopted British industrial technique where it could.

Third, the industrial revolution greatly changed the British economy's use of raw materials reducing its dependence on imported goods like porcelain and calicos, but greatly increasing its dependence on imported raw materials like raw cotton, whale oil, sugar and palm oil.

Fourth, over time the increased output of British industry would make it more important to secure and guarantee a hinterland of territories where goods could be readily be sold – a 'free market'. The impact of British exports on domestic markets could be very destructive.

Fifth, Britain's new domestic policy, 'free trade', was made the rationale for its new diplomatic policy, which claimed to put free trade across the world at its centre – though as we shall see, Empire of Free Trade relied heavily on gunboat diplomacy and force. While the exceptions seem greater than the observances, there was scepticism over colonial annexations between 1832 and 1880.

Lastly, the industrial revolution by its cycles of growth and contraction constantly dislocated settled peoples, undermining their subsistence farming, recruiting them as factory workers, then often abandoning them when work was scarce. This *sturm und drang* of British industry over time threw more and more people beyond the country's shores, to settle in other parts of the world, even as other people were being drawn in. We look at the great export of white settlers and its relationship to the Empire later on.

Chapter Twelve

REVOLUTION AND COUNTER-REVOLUTION, 1776–1815

The mercantile colonialism helped turn Dynasties into States. The Merchant Companies had been first made by Royal decree. But the competing rights of rival companies was decided by Parliament. Adjudicating the claims of merchant companies demanded impersonal authority. No longer family dynasties, the seat of power was in national parliaments. But nation states to develop had to overturn the old mercantile colonialism. Nation-building was a turn inwards, away from the colonies. Attention turned to building the nation, and so too did investment. The colonial system was in crisis, but the nation state was resplendent.

The underlying theory of the nation state was 'sovereignty'. Seventeenth- and eighteenth-centuries lawyers rooted out an ancient precedent for their modern idea in the Justinian Code of 533 as, *extra territorium jus dicenti impune non paretur*, meaning 'the judgment (or the authority) of one who is exceeding his territorial jurisdiction is disobeyed with impunity'. In the mid-nineteenth century it was summed up by the Government lawyer Sir Henry Jenkyns. 'The essence of political sovereignty' according to Sir Henry, 'is that it is legally omnipotent within its own territory, but that it is legally powerless within the territory of another state'.[1] It is often argued that 'sovereignty' is something of a delusion because the British nation was not something that grew out of the soil but rather is all mixed up with other parts of the world. To look at it the other way around, the modern idea of sovereignty came about because dynastic states were mixed up in each other's business and extended across the world. That early, expansionary dynamic is why the idea of sovereignty was needed, as a way of demarcating the limits of authority.

Britain's inward focus of the Hanoverian era was largely a retreat from military engagement in European politics. Prime Minister Robert Walpole hoped to stay out of the wars on the European mainland. 'If I can keep this nation out of war a year longer', he wrote in 1734. Still, he dreamed, 'I know it is impossible but England must give law to all Europe.' His rival Sir John Carteret negotiated the agreement between Maria Theresa and Frederick II of Prussia after the war of the Austrian succession. 'It is my job to make Kings and Emperors and maintain the balance of Europe', he said, outlining the emerging British foreign policy.

The balance of power doctrine was to avoid permanent alliances and to prevent rival powers allying among themselves against Britain. 'To suppose that any nation could be unalterably the enemy of another, was weak and childish', the younger William Pitt told Parliament in 1787. Sea power, the 'blue water policy' would guarantee British dominance. That was not a pacific but a militant policy. American John Rutledge visited parliament after Spain had challenged British possession of Nootka Sound, in modern-day British Columbia. He was surprised: 'in my life I do not remember to have been among such insolent bullies'. They 'talked much of Old England and the British Lion' and looked forward to exacting millions from Spain for having 'insulted the first power on Earth'.[2]

In the sixteenth and seventeenth centuries, Britain's diplomatic stance was often seen in religious terms – championing Protestant princes in Europe and taking on Spain's colonial might. At the Peace of Utrecht (1713) Britain was seen by some to have let down its Protestant Dutch allies, backing Catholic France for pragmatic reasons. Though international rivals tried to champion the Stuart pretenders to the Throne, with France backing a Scottish rising in 1715 in support of the Pretender James Stuart, and Spain backing another in 1745 in support of the Young Pretender Charles Edward Stuart – both ended in failure. Conservatives opposed to the Hanoverian Crown did not dare go as far as risking a Catholic restoration.

The shock of the Jacobite rebellion had a marked impact on England. Among townspeople popular 'Patriot' societies took off, at first as a would-be militia to take on the Scots. In London a group of tradesmen set up the Laudable Society of Anti-Gallicans in 1745, mindful of the threat of a French invasion. At the beginning of the Seven Years' War in 1756 Jonas Hanway set up the 'Marine Society' to get paupers and orphans dressed up and into the Navy – some 10,000 were recruited. The backers of the Patriot societies challenged the Court Whig oligarchy with a popular campaign to take the war to Bourbon France. 'The public spirit of persons in the middling rank of this kingdom', said Yorkshire MP and militia leader William Thornton, 'and the depravity and selfishness of those in a higher class was never more remarkable than at present'.[3] First Minister William Pitt (the elder) came to power on the back of the Patriot movement.

By the time George III took the throne in 1760 Britain was confident, glorying in victories over Spain and France. George brought the Tories back into power, clipping the wings of the radical Whigs.

Under the Old Colonial System Europeans went far from home looking for windfall profits from overseas 'trade'. In their eyes trade was a zero-sum game where you were a winner or a loser. They forced the people they met to trade on poor terms if they could. They clashed violently with each other fighting over exclusive trading rights in different parts of the world. Throughout the mercantilist era the leading powers fought each other in near-continuous warfare.

The wars of the eighteenth century were fought in Europe, but also in the Caribbean, on the American Continent and in India. The French EIC and the British EIC fought three wars over which European power would be dominant in India, known as the Carnatic Wars between 1746 and 1763. From 1754 to 1763 the French and the native Americans fought to limit British settlement to North America's Eastern Seaboard, behind the 1763 Proclamation Line agreed at the end of the war. Other powers were in the conflict, which had many sides to it. In Europe it was called the 'Seven Years War'. British forces were triumphant in both the Carnatic and the 'French and Indian' wars.

It was a short-lived victory. The colonial war of the mid-eighteenth century tested the Old Colonial System to destruction.

Just 13 years after the Peace Treaty in Paris confirmed her global pre-eminence, Britain's colonial subjects in America rose in revolt against the Empire. In the war Britain fought to try to head off the rebellion between 1778 and 1783. Britain's European rivals France and Spain supported the rebels, as did Holland, and in Mysore Tipu Sultan and Hyder Ali rebelled against the East India Company.

The American War of Independence was waged against British rule and also against mercantilism, with the excessive duties and taxes England laid to pay off its Seven Years War deficit a particular target – even to the point that the East India Company's tea was thrown into the Boston harbour as a symbolic act of defiance. Worse for Britain and the old powers, the American Republic became a model for revolutionaries across the world.

The colonists' grievances were part of a mood that the mother country had become indifferent to them. Edmund Burke likened British Policy from 1721–42 to 'salutary neglect', in a speech in the Commons in 1775. British exports to the Americas were strong – almost all iron and nails went to the colonies and four-fifths of linen in the mid-century – but at the same time Americans were stopped from buying from the West Indies under the 1733 Molasses Act, and from selling exports (notably hats and iron). The conflict came about around the same time that Britain was turning its attention inwards, away from colonial investments towards domestic growth. To the colonists the British seemed high-handed and distant. The French and Indian Wars were to the British a big cost that had to be recouped.

Revolutions inspired by America's Declaration of Independence followed against the Dutch Stadtholder William V of Orange in Holland's Patriot-led Batavian revolution (1785); against Louis XVI of France (1789–99); for Ireland's independence from Britain (1798–1804); and for Haiti's independence from France (1791–1804).[4]

The revolutions at the end of the eighteenth century shook the world. Where the wars that came before them were harsh, they did not draw in as many people as these democratic revolutions. The ideologues of the revolutionary movement fought for democracy, freedom and reason. The social conflict over who was to rule was followed by a new round of wars between nations, known in England as the Napoleonic Wars.

The revolutions of the eighteenth century provoked counter-revolutionary movements. These drew on the old order that lost its place and on the support of more conservative nations – Britain chief among them. Even where the revolutions were successful, the leaderships installed by those revolutions retreated from many of the liberal and democratic aspirations. The eventual settlement of the social and national conflicts at the end of the eighteenth century brought in a new order that was largely committed to private property, free trade and 'mixed constitutions' with constituent assemblies under authoritarian rulers.

It was the death-knell of the Old Colonial System, but that did not mean decolonisation, so much as the construction of a new colonial system, which has been called the 'imperialism of free trade'.[5] The most marked difference was that the European powers lost much of their territory on the North American Continent, making India, and the

Southern hemisphere, much more central to the British Empire. Looking from the per-spective of today many people draw the conclusion that the War of Independence was also the birth of a new Imperial Power that would come to dominate in the twentieth century.

In the century following the American Revolution Britain's policy was to have 'no permanent alliances'. Throughout that time, though, its main rivals were France and America, and Britain often promoted France's rivals, in particular the German states, as a counterweight to French influence.

America's War of Independence

In 1776 there were 2,400,000 people living in the 13 English colonies – 10 times the number a century before – of whom nearly half a million were slaves (mostly living in Virginia, Maryland and the Carolinas). The white colonists were from England, Germany and other parts of Europe. They were a settlement of farmers, craftsmen, traders, with Governors appointed from England among the large landowning class. Their culture was shaped both by a European heritage but also in large part by a Protestant background.

In the 'French and Indian Wars', the colonists had rallied behind the British flag against France thinking that England was the home of liberty, and, optimistically, that the British Crown would let them advance westwards. After that war the British King set out to raise revenue to pay off the deficit. A Stamp Act taxing contracts and other legal documents was felt keenly by the settlers. The mercantile system of shutting out other suppliers meant that the Americans had to buy English goods at monopoly prices. A Boston Committee was organised to boycott English in favour of American-made goods, or failing that, imports from Holland and France. In mid-December of 1773 Bostonians disguised themselves as native Americans and threw EIC tea into the harbour. The protests brought down harsh repression in the Coercive Act, the Boston Harbour Act and the Massachusetts Government Act (which banned public meetings).

In their different town assemblies and colonial assemblies, the settlers tried out their own ideas of self-government. The Patriots drew on different intellectual traditions. Some like John Adams, Hamilton and James Madison were impressed with the idea of a 'mixed government' which combined elected and aristocratic elements, modelled on Britain's own Government. 'Mixed Government' came recommended by continental thinkers like Montesquieu, for whom the English Constitution was a model. Others, like planter Thomas Jefferson and colonial agent Benjamin Franklin were more impressed by the idea of radical democracy. They, like many Americans, were inspired by the Norfolk-born pamphleteer Thomas Paine's compelling book *Common Sense*. In it, Paine, who had only landed in Pennsylvania in 1774, set out the case for democratic self-gov-ernment, freedom of conscience and liberty.[6]

By 1775 the Patriots were gathering militia and British troops under Thomas Gage set out to disarm them, opening the war. A Continental Congress of delegates of 12 of the 13 colonies made a Declaration of Independence, opening a war across the Eastern seaboard that lasted until 1783 at the cost of more than 100,000 lives.

British military organisation and power was initially superior, and forces under William Howe and George Clinton took Patriot positions in New York and Long Island, while Washington withdrew inland. The Battle of Bunker Hill in 1775 saw Britain hold Boston but at some cost. In 1777 John Burgoyne's force coming down from Quebec was overstretched and made a humiliating surrender at Saratoga. In the long run popular support for Congress and the Patriots' mobility counted more.[7] The loss of America was a terrible blow to British prestige, but for the economy the loss was not so great. Lost sales to America were made up by European markets and war spending was a spur to domestic industry.[8]

Two Views of the War of Independence

This whole civilization was swept in the last four decades of the eighteenth century by a single revolutionary movement, which manifested itself in different ways and with varying success in different countries, yet in all of them showed similar objectives and principles. … this forty-year movement was essentially 'democratic', and that these years are in fact the Age of the Democratic Revolution.

R. R. Palmer[9]

To the extent that 1776 led to the resultant U.S. which came to captain the African Slave Trade – as London moved in an opposing direction toward a revolutionary abolition of this form of property – the much celebrated revolt of the North American settlers can fairly be said to have eventuated as a counter-revolution of slavery.

Gerald Horne[10]

Whether the War of Independence is seen as a war of liberation or the reaction of a slave-settler state might tell us more about present-day attitudes than those of 1776 and afterwards. However, both accounts do tell one side of the story. Palmer's version of the War of Independence as part of a revolutionary wave across the world fits the views of people at the time. Horne's account of the victory of the slave owners' reaction also tells an important story about the limitations of 1776.

At the outset Thomas Jefferson wanted to put a line into the Declaration of Independence attacking the British Crown for bringing black slavery into America as 'a cruel war against human nature itself' – but Congress struck it out. Pennsylvania did put a gradual abolition into its legislature in 1780 and Benjamin Franklin's last act before his death was to send a petition to Congress for abolition.[11]

The Patriots' silence on slavery stands in stark contrast to the lines in the Declaration 'that all men are created equal, that they are endowed by their Creator with certain unalienable Rights, that among these are Life, Liberty and the pursuit of Happiness'. Many Patriots were themselves slave owners. Even those who spoke out against slavery were slaveowners. Thomas Jefferson owned a plantation at Monticello where 150 slaves worked at his command. He even had children by one of his slaves, Sally Hemings. George Washington also had a slave plantation. Even Benjamin Franklin had two enslaved men with him when he came to England (one of whom ran away, while the other lived with him in London).

Patriot leaders knew that many slaveowners in Virginia, Maryland and the Carolinas would not support Independence if it meant the loss of their human property. More, the British did, as Gerald Horne explains, offer liberty to the slaves of rebel patriots (though this was more opportunistic than principled). Thousands left rebel plantations for a new life in Nova Scotia or Sierra Leone, even some from Jefferson and Washington's own estates. At the request of the planters the American negotiators at the 1783 peace talks in Paris called for compensation for the loss of their property at the hands of the British forces – including their human property.

Nikole Hannah-Jones, as part of the *New York Times*' '1619 Project' summed up:

> Conveniently left out of our founding mythology is the fact that one of the primary reasons the colonists decided to declare their independence from Britain was because they wanted to protect the institution of slavery.[12]

Answering Hannah-Jones, historian Gordon Wood said

> The idea that the Revolution occurred as a means of protecting slavery—I just don't think there is much evidence for it, and in fact the contrary is more true to what happened. The Revolution unleashed antislavery sentiments that led to the first abolition movements in the history of the world.[13]

If the Patriots' idea of liberty overlooked slavery, it was harsh, too, on the rights of the indigenous peoples of the North American Continent. As they took the anti-slavery line out of the Declaration, Congress put another one in cursing the King of Great Britain because he 'has endeavoured to bring on the inhabitants of our frontiers, the merciless Indian Savages whose known rule of warfare, is an undistinguished destruction of all ages, sexes and conditions'.

That the founding declaration of the United States carries a slander against the Native Americans tells us that the state was fundamentally at odds with their culture. The meaning of the clause is that the King did indeed support Native American land claims because they set a limit to colonial expansion. Native American bands often sided with whichever European power offered the least threat of land expansion, such as the French in 1754 and then the English in 1778. Westward expansion was a popular demand for homesteaders that put them on a collision course with native Americans.

The founders' prejudices against native Americans were all the more tragic since – according to Benjamin Franklin – one inspiration for the declaration came from the Treaty of Confederation of the Five Iroquois nations of 1712. It read: 'A large bunch of shell strings, in the making of which the Five Nations League chiefs have equally contributed, shall symbolize the completeness of the union.' In 1744, Canasatego told the English:

> Union and amity between the five nations have made us formidable. We are a powerful confederacy, and by your observing the same methods our wise forefathers have taken you will acquire fresh strength and power. Therefore, whatever befalls you, never fall out with one another.[14]

It was good advice for the colonists, but in the end, bad for the Iroquois.

At the core of the American revolution's limits were not fundamentally questions of race, but of property. As the Republic stabilised it was a Government of men of property. Property in men, and property in land – though it was true that only men of colour were ever property. For all their blind spots the Patriots were themselves rising up against British oppression in the colonies and were for that reason a model to other freedom fighters.

France in Revolt

France's development from dynasty to nation state in some ways mirrored Britain's. The internal market was poorly developed, and trade grew up at the margins. Baron Montchretien's *Treatise on Political Economy* (1616) set out a similar mercantilist policy to England's: 'We must have money, and if we have none from our own productions, then we must have some from foreigners'. Montchretien saw colonisation not only as a duty, calling on France to 'make known the name of God, our creator, to so many barbarous peoples'; but it was also an opportunity, 'as God himself promises to those who seek out his Kingdom he will add to it', so 'he would open up in his way, as much here as there, great and inexhaustible sources of wealth'.[15]

Cardinal Richelieu told the Royal Council that 'there was no kingdom so well situated as France, and so rich in all the resources necessary for making her master of the seas'. 'In order to arrive at this goal', he said, 'it as necessary to see how our neighbours managed to do it – by creating large companies and obliging merchants to make use of them through the bestowal of valuable privileges'.[16]

Companies were set up on the English model, like the 100 Associates Company (with the Government monopoly on trade to Canada), the Cape Verde Company trading to Senegal, the Islands of America Company trading to the Antilles, and the EIC in Madagascar.

Jean-Baptiste Colbert, Minister of Finances under Louis XIV saw 'the trading companies are the armies of the King and the manufactures of France are his reserves'. Like the English mercantilists Colbert thought that 'one cannot increase the money of a kingdom without at the same time taking away the same quantity of money from neighbouring states'.[17] French colonial policy had been successful in the West Indies, in Louisiana and Canada in North America and in India. French colonial trade grew faster in the first half of the eighteenth century than British and was a real challenge. In the Seven Years War (1757–63), however, Britain won out over French settlers in America, and the Royal Navy kept French ships in their harbours costing them the Atlantic trade.

The French court was changed by the mercantilist policy. The older feudal nobility, the *noblesse d'epée* (of the sword) were losing out to the appointed functionaries of the court, known as the *noblesse de robe* who were gathered under the King's watchful eye at Versailles.[18] The wealth of the court was in sharp contrast to the impoverishment of peasantry and artisans. It did, however, make sources for the patronage of a large intelligentsia. Scientists and philosophes lived on the whim of a leisured class of nobles. Finance Minister Ann Robert Turgot tried to open up the land and labour markets in

1774–76, but 'Turgot's Carnival' led to bread riots as prices rose, and the measures were rescinded.

The French philosophes were admirers of the English Augustan age writers and scientists. They believed in the power of reason and free thinking, which came collectively to be known as the Enlightenment. With the War of Independence many French intellectuals shifted their allegiance to the colonists. The American minister in France Benjamin Franklin was introduced by Thomas Paine to the leading lights of intellectual and political life Condorcet, Chastellux and Le Rochefoucauld. Franklin had been a colonial agent in London where he was friends with Priestley and Richard Price, radicals and men of science. In 1778, an elderly Voltaire came to meet Franklin at the Academy of Sciences.[19] Free-thinker, scientist and humbly dressed man of the people, Franklin was a great ambassador to pre-revolutionary Enlightenment France. In 1785, he was replaced by Thomas Jefferson, main author of the Declaration of Independence.

The social question in France overturned the authority of the court at Versailles. The Parisian crowds rallied to the cause of a new constitution, where the formerly separate Estates General would be united under one Convention, and the feudal powers of the aristocracy abolished. The old order struggled to regain control unleashing repression on the mob, but failed and the nobility was driven into exile, to plot their return in the capitals of England and Austria. In the French Convention the philosophes wrote a constitution for the people that was even more comprehensive than the American Declaration of Independence, the Declaration of the Rights of Man and Citizen. Its first clause echoed the Jefferson's document: 'Men are born and remain free and equal in rights.' (1791) America's ambassador Jefferson thought that the French Revolution's success was 'necessary to stay up our own' and would help to stop America 'falling back to that halfway house, the English constitution'.[20] In time the French Revolution would shake Europe and the world as profoundly as it did France.

The United Irishmen

Ireland in the eighteenth century was under the political domination of a Protestant Assembly. Three-quarters of the country was in the hands of English landlords. Penal laws put Catholics out of the professions, forbade them to trade in any charter town, barred them from any lease longer than 31 years, compelled them to give up their land to any Protestant heir, barred them from owning a horse above £5 in value, barred them from practising their religion and barred them from voting or holding public office. The penal laws impoverished and demoralised Catholics. Even the non-conforming settlers who could vote and stand were barred from holding public office so that the Irish Parliament was dominated by the narrow strata of landlords who were in the Church of Ireland – an Episcopalian adjunct of the Church of England. There was a Whig party in Parliament, led by Henry Grattan that was largely in opposition to the Government but all laws passed there had been sent to the Privy Council in England to be approved under Poynings' Law, and from 1720 the Declaratory Act made gave Westminster legislation priority over Dublin. From 1728 to 1793 Catholics were denied the vote under the Disenfranchising Act – passed by the Irish Parliament. The country was ruled from

Dublin Castle by a Lord Lieutenant appointed by the British Government, so that his realm was called 'the King's business'. 'If I were called upon to describe a colony', said the Chief Secretary for Ireland Lord Castlereagh in 1800, 'I would describe it as something very like the present state of this country, enjoying indeed a local Legislature, but without any power entrusted that Legislature ... an Executive administered by the order of the Minister of another country, not in any way responsible to the colony for his acts or his advice.'[21]

Some English reformers like Arthur Young, who toured the country in 1776, and Adam Smith thought that the best outcome would be a union of Britain and Ireland. After some lobbying the Irish Whigs did manage to open the Empire trade to Irish exporters (mostly linen and wool) in 1780 to stiff opposition from English manufacturers.

As troops left Ireland to fight in the war against America, Protestant gentry organised volunteer militias to defend the country around 1782–83. Northern Presbyterians were the backbone of the militias which became an extra-Parliamentary opposition that was – surprisingly – influenced by the democratic sentiments of the American revolution. The Whig Clubs in Dublin and Belfast studied the books of John Locke and even Thomas Paine.

Theobald Wolfe Tone, a lawyer from a Presbyterian family, wrote a pamphlet in 1791 'An Argument in Favour of Catholics' in which he argued that the Volunteers' agitation would not succeed because 'no reform can ever be obtained which shall not comprehensively embrace Irishmen of all denominations'. That year Tone set up the Society of United Irishmen with Robert Emmet, Henry Joy McCracken, William Drennan, Thomas Russell and others. Tone helped to organise a Catholic Convention to promote emancipation in December of 1792 that threatened the 'Protestant Ascendancy' by appealing over their heads to the British Parliament. The United Irishmen organised a convention of thousands of Volunteers in Dungannon on 15 February 1793, where resolutions calling for complete Catholic emancipation and reform of Parliament were passed. The British Government supported moves by Dublin Castle to draw the volunteers away into a professional army. Wolfe Tone recalled that 'to break the connection with England, the never-failing source of all our political evils, and to assert the independence of my country – these were my objects'. More, 'to unite the whole people of Ireland, to abolish the memory of all past dissensions, and to substitute the common name of Irishman, in place of the denominations of Protestant, Catholic and Dissenter – these were my means'.[22]

London appointed a reformer, Earl Fitzwilliam, as Lord Lieutenant in January 1795, but then fearing he was moving too fast, withdrew him in favour of Earl Camden who brought in an Insurrection Act in March 1796 to put down the United Irishmen. By then there were 28,577 United Irishmen in County Down and 22,716 in neighbouring County Antrim and 1,600 in Belfast. In September 1796 Dublin Castle seized its leaders in Belfast. Preparations for an Ulster Directory of the United Irishmen had been laid in Randalstown in February and membership climbed to 117,197 in Ulster alone.[23] In 1795, Arthur O'Connor sought help from the French Government for an invasion in support of a general uprising, and in the Christmas of 1797 Tone and General Hoche of the Revolutionary Army boarded ships with 14,450 troops to land in Ireland. In the event storms stopped the fleet from landing and the plan was broken.

Revolution did break out on 30 March 1798, but the leading United Irishmen were in jail or exile. A short-lived Republic was declared in Wexford and in June Antrim and Down were in revolt. Henry Joy McCracken declared a Republic of Ulster, but the United Irishmen were defeated at the end of the month. General Jean Humbert of the French army landed at Killala in County Sligo and marched on to set up a Republic of Connacht with 4,000 Irish volunteers in August 1789. Four hundred United Irishmen were hanged. In October the French fleet were intercepted by the Royal Navy and captured after a ten-hour battle. On board was Wolfe Tone. He was tried for treason and told the court on the subject of Ireland that 'looking upon the connexion with England to have been her bane I have endeavoured by every means to break that connexion'. Tone continued 'I have laboured in consequence to create a people in Ireland by raising three millions of my countrymen to the rank of citizens'.[24] He was sentenced to be hanged but cheated the executioner by cutting his own throat.

The Black Jacobins of Haiti

The West Indies had been remade by European planters in the sixteenth and seventeenth century. The indigenous Caribs were all but exterminated. The population of the Caribbean islands and the Guianas on the South American continent were a mix of enslaved Africans, white settlers and some free blacks and mixed-race or mulatto offspring of both. The most populous islands were Cuba, Hispaniola and Puerto Rico – Spanish colonies – Jamaica, Trinidad and Barbados which were British colonies and Saint-Domingue (the western half of Hispaniola), Martinique and Guadeloupe which were French colonies. By 1739 there were 117,000 enslaved Africans working in Saint-Domingue serving 450 sugar mills, making it the richest of all the Caribbean colonies. The Saint-Domingue planters had a special law, the Code Noir, which denied equal rights to blacks.

Slavery in its nature is coercive and the enslaved resisted in many ways, often breaking out into rebellion. As oppressive as plantation life was the enslaved sidestepped the blows where they could and most of the larger islands had communities of runaway slaves living inland in the hills, known as maroons. Slaves generally had provision grounds and sometimes traded produce with free blacks and poorer whites. The intercourse between the enslaved and the masterless blacks was a source of information about events beyond the plantation, in the towns and in the wider world. The masters were often surprised that enslaved Africans were keenly aware of events in England, the American colonies and France that bore upon their condition.[25]

The wars between the European colonisers, the American War of Independence and the French Revolution of 1789 were all events that shook the awkwardly balanced plantations. In some conflicts blacks were encouraged to abscond or rebel against their masters, and sometimes were recruited into European armies. In the War of Independence Britain recruited black troops from among the slaves of the southern planters to fight, while other black Caribbeans were recruited to fight in French forces on the American side. Planters feared that their slaves were encouraged by the War of Independence (and just stopped an uprising in Hanover, Jamaica in July of 1776).

The French Revolution of 1789 upturned the French Caribbean first but then all of the slave-holders in the Americas. In France there were two forces pulling in different directions – the port-based merchants who were for the Revolution but depended on the sugar trade to Bordeaux and Nantes, and the radical philosophes. The merchants wanted the Revolution but did not expect slavery to end. Their leaders in the Constituent Assembly were Vincent-Marie Viénot, Count of Vaublanc and the deputies Pierre Victurnien Verginaud and Marguerite-Élie Guadet of the maritime towns. The radicals saw slavery as a defining issue in the Rights of Man. Brissot, Mirabeau, Pétion, Condorcet and Abbé Gregoire set up the *Société des amis des Noir* – the Society of the Friends of the Blacks to lobby the new Constituent Assembly. They were inspired in part by the British anti-slavery movement. They supported the Saint-Domingue mulattoes who demanded their rights in Paris, Vincent Ogé and Julien Raimond.[26]

When the slave owners of Saint-Domingue claimed 18 seats in the Constituent Assembly Mirabeau turned on them:

> You claim representation proportionate to the number of inhabitants. The free blacks are proprietors and tax-payers and yet they have not been allowed to vote. And as for the slaves, either they are men or they are not; if the colonists consider them to be men, let them free them and make them electors and eligible for seats.[27]

The mulattoes in Paris and the Friends of the Negro did not get their way. The merchants pushed for a committee to consider the matter, which they dominated and eventually decided for slavery. The Constituent Assembly wavered. Vincent Ogé made his way on a ship, the Léopard, with a few hundred men back to Saint-Domingue to make a revolution there – but he was surrounded by loyal forces, and he and his men were tortured and executed.

Equality of Rank, Equality of Colour – the Revolution at its most optimistic.

In Saint-Domingue the news of the Revolution disturbed the social order, but not as might be expected. Poorer whites rallied to the makeshift Convention forces in the colony. To defend his position the Royalist governor rallied the free mulattoes to his cause, promising them political rights that the white Saint-Dominguans refused. The rights of the slaves were not yet at issue.

Dutty Boukman, who had been taken from the Gambia and had been a slave in Jamaica before being sold on to Saint-Domingue, led a revolt in Cap Français in 1791. He gathered many hundreds of slaves in revolt against the owners. Boukman was killed early in the fighting and his head displayed as a warning. But his revolt was well-organised and he had put lieutenants in place, Jean-François Papillon, Georges Biassou and Jeannot so that the revolt was not stopped.[28] Toussaint Louverture (1743–1803) joined the revolt a few months in and became its general. Louverture had been a slave on the Breda plantation but was freed in 1776 to work as a coachman, and as an overseer of slaves. Toussaint was well-read and knew Abbé Raynal's *Philosophical and Political History of the Establishments and Commerce of the Two Indies*. In it he would have read this passage:

> Already are there established two communities of fugitive negroes, whom treaties and power protect from assault. Those lightnings announce the thunder. A courageous chief only is wanted. Where is he, that great man whom Nature owes to her vexed, oppressed and tormented children?

Raynal felt sure that 'he will come forth and raise the sacred standard of liberty', and the words rang true for Toussaint.[29]

The Chiefs of the Revolt wrote to the General Assembly of Saint-Domingue in July 1791:

> Under the blows of your barbarous whip we have accumulated for you the treasures you enjoy in this colony; the human race has suffered to see with what barbarity you have treated men – yes, men – over whom you have no other right that you are stronger and more barbaric than we; you've engaged in the slave traffic.

They went on,

> We are black, it is true, but tell us, Gentlemen, you who are so judicious, what is the law that says that the black man must belong to and be the property of the white man?

They praised the 'fortunate revolution that has taken place in the Motherland which has opened up for us the road which our courage and our labour will enable us to ascend, to arrive at the temple of liberty, like those brave Frenchmen who are our models and whom all the universe is contemplating'. And they asked the colonists 'have you forgotten that you have formally vowed the declaration of the rights of man which says that men are born free, equal in their rights?'[30]

The Government in Paris though was equivocal. Millet told the Legislature on 30 November 1792 that the life of the slaves was 'pleasant and easy' and more to the point that if the slave trade were abolished 'the profits which can result from it for French commerce will be delivered to foreigners'. Even Brissot was half-hearted in making the case against slavery.[31] Instead the Legislature decided to send Commissioners,

Léger-Félicité Sonthonax and Etienne Polverel to reassert control over Saint-Domingue's colonial assembly and institute equality for the mulattoes.

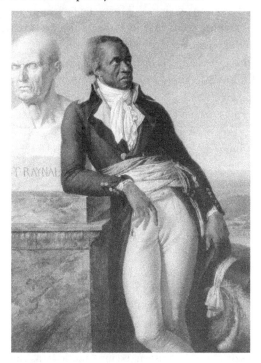

Jean-Baptiste Belley, by Girodet.

Reluctantly, the colonists accepted Sonthonax's reforms for the mulattoes and the rebellious slaves were isolated. To sustain their forces Toussaint, Biassou and Jean-François made an alliance with the Spanish governor of neighbouring Hispaniola (Spain was at war with France). Sonthonax's honeymoon was over when the old Royalist Governor Galbaud led an uprising of colonists against the new Revolution-aligned Saint-Domingue administration, at Cap-Français on the north coast of the colony in June 1793. Sonthonax only managed to defeat the slave-holders' revolt by the extraordinary measure of freeing the slaves, who joined the attacks on the colonists. Thousands were killed on both sides in the fighting and the surviving colonists escaped by sea. The stories they took with them of the slaughter of whites by rebellious black slaves later became part of the legend of the barbarity of the revolution in Saint-Domingue.

In France the revolution had overtaken Vaublanc's resistance and Brissot's caution. In August 1792, the Parisian crowd invaded the King's Tuilieries Palace and a Republic was proclaimed. In January 1793, Louis XVI was executed. That September Jean-Baptiste Belley a black Saint-Dominguan took his seat as a Deputy in the National Convention (Girodet painted Belley's portrait). The Convention understood the symbolism. Citoyen Camboulas announced that 'since 1789 the aristocracy of birth and the aristocracy of religion have been destroyed; but the aristocracy of the skin still remains'. With the seating of the deputies from Saint-Domingue, said Camboulas, 'equality is consecrated', and the Convention rose in applause. Belley addressed the Convention in February 1794 for the resolution 'the National Convention decrees that the slavery of Negroes is abolished in all the colonies'. More, the Convention 'decrees that all men without distinction of colour, domiciled in the colonies are French citizens and will enjoy all the rights guaranteed by the constitution'.[32]

France's abolition had a great impact on the Saint-Domingue revolutionaries. Toussaint Louverture changed sides to fight for France. From being outcasts, the black generals became the effective power in the land, working with Sonthonax to stabilise the colony.

From Jamaica, Lord Maitland's British army invaded as part of William Pitt's war with France. The Secretary of State for War Henry Dundas' policy was to defeat France in her colonies. Lord Dundas' poured men and money into the campaign so that by 1797 it had cost 80,000 casualties (including 40,000 dead) and £4,400,000 but was not enough to defeat the forces under the mulatto captain Rigaud.[33]

A Worldwide Reaction

The democratic wave that swept across the world from 1776 to 1791 crashed against the rocks. Britain waged war against the Americans and later took up arms against revolutionary France. That was a grave disappointment to many who admired Britain as the leading power in the Age of Reason. In 1775, there were defenders of the colonists in Parliament but the clamour against the rebels was rising. They were 'a Mob and a Rabble led by mad Enthusiasts and desperate republicans' or just 'Sons of Anarchy'.[34] Once the French King took the side of the colonists to be for America was close to treason.

Among London's more radical journeymen there was a strong sympathy for the American revolution. The Radical and Unitarian Richard Price ran a 'Club of Honest Whigs' that kept support for the colonists, and he published a popular pamphlet *Observations on Civil Liberty* in 1776 which made the case for rights in Britain and America.[35]

With the French Revolution the dividing line was yet more decisive. From the outset the British Government ran agents in France like Francis Wickham who handed out funds to emigré French aristocrats and Royalists.[36] In February 1793, after Louis XVI was executed the French ambassador was expelled from the court of St James and France declared war on Britain.

Prime Minister Pitt suspended the *habeus corpus* law against imprisonment without trial and suppressed the radical London Corresponding Committee that had agitated for peace with revolutionary France. Pitt's network of spies included Bethnal Green landlord Joseph Merceron who sent back reports on the Corresponding Committee meetings in his public houses. Other radical groups that were suppressed were the United Englishmen – built on the model of the United Irishmen – and sailors at two anchorage's Spithead in Portsmouth and the Nore in the Thames Estuary who rebelled under their leader Richard Parker in 1797, inspired by the French Revolution. Parker called his committee of mutineers the 'floating republic', put the ships under democratic control and even blocked the mouth of the Thames, but in the suppression of it 59 were hanged.[37]

In Britain itself many positive, liberalising trends were sent in reverse. The impeachment of the EIC's Warren Hastings for the depredation of Bengal was dragged out and allowed to fall in 1795. Pitt had summoned a Parliamentary inquiry into slavery which educated liberal opinion supported, but the West India interest in London fought back and the fear that abolition would undermine Britain's position in the Caribbean put anti-slavery on hold. Charles Fox's Whigs had been bullish in their support for democracy in France and even worked with the radicals of the London Corresponding Society – but as the war with France wore on, they became isolated.[38] In Europe Britain allied itself with the more reactionary powers to stop the French revolutionary forces exporting democracy across the Continent. In Economic policy Prime Minister Pitt had said to Adam Smith, the champion of free trade that 'we are all your disciples'. But the war policy meant economic blockade of Napoleonic Europe and so protection for British farmers which, after the end of the Second Napoleonic War were firmed up into 'Corn Laws'.

In America the more radical trend of the revolution, led by Thomas Jefferson, Benjamin Franklin and Thomas Paine was losing ground to the supporters of bicameralism and a natural aristocracy, like Adams, Hamilton and Washington. Hamilton's tax on imports stirred a revolt in Pennsylvania that was called the 'Whiskey rebellion' to mock the Paineite radicals who backed it. At the same time a Baptist movement known as the Second Great Awakening undermined those like Paine and Jefferson who saw the new Republic as a secular state. People flocked to the Baptist chapels and favoured a Republic 'under God'.[39]

Across the Caribbean planters struggled to keep the news of the changes in Europe secret from their slaves – who showed a marked ability to find out what was going on. In Martinique slaves refused to work arguing that if the English slaves were about to be freed by Wilberforce, then they should be too. Jamaican slaves hearing of the French revolution declared they would not work and took to wearing the Republican cockade. All over the Caribbean planters had Thomas Paine burned in effigy at large public gatherings, sometimes with an effigy of William Wilberforce beside him. A Jamaica planter worried that after the French Revolution 'the Ideas of Liberty have sunk so deep in the Minds of all the Negroes that, wherever the greatest Precautions are not taken, they will rise'.[40] Revolutionary Saint-Domingue's victory over Maitland's army led the British to reverse their policy and back Toussaint Louverture's leadership, while inviting him to rebel against France.

The Revolution in France though had run out of steam. The intensity of the Jacobin leadership of the Convention left little room for doubt – doubt seemed like too much of a luxury while the Revolution was beset by enemies on all sides. The trials and executions of enemies of the state became central to Robespierre's rule. Paranoia gripped the revolutionaries until Robespierre himself was denounced as a traitor, tried and executed. The possibility of a restoration of the monarchy was real, but the heir Louis XVII died at the age of 10, of tuberculosis, while imprisoned. With the revolutionaries in disarray, the General Napoleon Bonaparte imposed a ruling Triumvirate with plenipotentiary powers – which put him in effective control of France.[41]

Listening to the colonial planters of Paris's Massaic Club, Napoleon was persuaded to attack British and Spanish forces in the Atlantic. For them he favoured the end of the Revolutionary decree against slavery. Napoleon's brother-in-law General Paul Leclerc went to Saint-Domingue to persuade the revolutionaries to accept French rule. The unhappy rebels were tasked with keeping order for Napoleon, until, as they feared, Leclerc arrested Toussaint Louverture and shipped him back to France (where he died in a prison cell in 1803). In May 1802 the French legislature voted to restore slavery in the colonies. 'I am for the whites, because I am white', Napoleon told Laurent Truguet. The repression of the black and Mulatto Saint-Dominguans turned into an orgy of violence, even more so under Leclerc's successor the Vicomte de Rochambeau. Hearing from Martinique and other islands that slavery was being restored, the surviving revolution- ary leadership in Saint-Domingue rebelled, with a new goal of independence, under Dessalines. In 1803 Dessalines accepted Rochambeau's surrender, and in 1804 declared himself Emperor of the new country of Haiti.[42]

The loss of Saint-Domingue was a painful blow to France's ambitions in the Americas. It opened the door to the transfer of France's territory on the mainland, Louisiana, to the United States. Seeing that Napoleon was in difficulty Congress raised $15 million (or 50 million Francs) to buy the 828,000 square miles (which today are Louisiana, Arkansas, Missouri, Kansas, Oklahoma, Nebraska and the Dakotas). The Louisiana purchase got France out of North America and was a stabilising, even conservative influence on America's political development. Jefferson's Government withheld political representation to Louisiana fear- ing the influence of a local Catholic polity, ruling instead through an appointed Governor. At the same time the US government bent to the demands of Louisiana planters, many of whom were refugees from Saint-Domingue, to import slaves into the territory. As a British captive on St Helena, Napoleon admitted that 'the Saint-Domingue business was a great piece of folly on my part'. 'I ought to have treated with the black leaders', he wrote.[43]

In Ireland the defeat of the United Irishman laid the basis for a fateful step: the Union of Great Britain and Ireland. Grattan's Parliament was built on a narrow franchise but the members there still had to be persuaded to give up their Dublin seats. In the debates First Minister Lord Castlereagh accused the elderly Grattan of Jacobinism and giving succour to the United Irishmen. Castlereagh managed the transition with wholesale bribery even- tually winning a majority for the change in 1801. He thought that Union would put an end to the problem of governing the Catholic population which while a majority in Ireland would become a minority in the Union. The Catholic clergy were told by Castlereagh's advisor Edward Cooke that if they avoided 'any unconstitutional conflict' then 'their object can finally and advantageously obtained' – which was understood to mean that with Union the Catholics would get emancipation.[44] George III stamped on the suggestion and Castlereagh insisted that he had given no undertaking, whatever the Catholic clergy believed. The drift away from democracy rebounded on Britain as the new Irish MPs were, as Charles Grey feared 'supported by the Treasury' and therefore the 'constant and unal- terable supporters' of the government. To William Wilberforce the new Irish MPs were 'a very considerable addition to the influence of the Crown'. The Government of Ireland from Britain was as repressive as before. For the government, Lord Hawkesbury boasted that in Ireland 'there will be no more parties but the parties of the British Empire'.[45] In 1803 *habeas corpus* was suspended once again as the United Irishmen resurfaced under the leadership of Robert Emmet and Thomas Russell. On 23 July, they launched an insur- rection. Emmet told his trial that he had sought to deliver 'my country from the yoke of a foreign and unrelenting tyranny' for which he was hung in September 1803.[46]

The war between Napoleonic Europe and the British led alliances carried on – with some interruptions – till 1815. Napoleon's army smashed autocratic rule, abolished church tithes and emancipated the Jews of France and Italy. France's Loi le Chapelier (1791) abolishing guilds was rolled out across Europe opening up trade. As the Napoleonic Code unified the laws of Continental Europe from Brest to Galicia he was welcomed by the middle classes. Later the imposition of order from above, most markedly in Spain where Napoleon's brother-in-law Joseph was imposed as an Enlightened despot, and eventually in Germany, provoked national movements to rise up against army rule.

The British fleet managed to defeat France at sea in the battle of Trafalgar – though it cost Admiral Horatio Nelson his life – and was matched by land victories. The sixth coalition drew on those that the French had provoked, including Count Bernadotte in Sweden, Austria, the Spanish King and the patriots that fought alongside him as well as Alexander of Russia. Britain paid tens of millions to keep its allies in the fight. Under Wellington the British Army forced its way up through Spain. With defeat in sight Napoleon was overthrown in favour of a government led by Talleyrand, committed to the restoration of the Bourbon throne.

The 'Holy Alliance' of Russia, Prussia and Austria agreed to 'a paternal alliance of monarchs over their peoples' in September of 1815 and the Paris Treaty of that year saw the British-sponsored reaction triumphant in Europe. Poland was divided between Russia and Prussia. Much of Italy was given to Austria. In Spain the restored King Fernando turned on the Patriots of Cadiz – democrats who fought to free their country from France – and jailed them. He sent troops too across the Atlantic to suppress the democratic revolutions in Caracas and Chile. Over time, though, it became clear that there would be no return to the old order in Western Europe. Even in France very little church property was returned and many of the revolutionary era politicians and leaders returned to play a role. Private property rights and trade were too well rooted in the growing middle class to be limited by the restoration of the old nobility.

Castlereagh's policy was to steer between the twin dangers of democracy and arbitrary power.

One lesson of the Napoleonic Wars was that France failed to unite Europe. Though the abolition of feudal obligations and opening of markets was welcomed by the middle classes in north-west Europe, French political domination was resisted in Spain, Germany, Sweden and Russia. The anti-Napoleonic coalitions also failed to unite Europe. Where England's Augustan Age thinkers were the model for many of the reformers in France, Holland, Switzerland and Germany, Britain reacted to reform with horror. To suppress the democratic national movements Britain bolstered deeply reactionary dynasties in Russia, Prussia, Austria and Spain. The outcome was that Europe from 1815 remained divided politically in a 'System of States'. The underlying social order of western Europe was surprisingly similar: increasingly urbanised on the basis of private property, where the dynamic was with industry and commerce rather than land; Christian in faith but with a greatly curtailed church; largely open to scientific inquiry, with a commercial press; with individual rights and qualified representation, but harsh repression of plebeian opposition. For all that the continent was divided against itself as rival powers and would continue to be so into the twentieth century.

Britain pressed its advantage in the colonies by taking Cape Colony and Ceylon from the Dutch and Mauritius from France, but other colonies were returned to their former European overlords – so Java was returned to Holland, Guiana and Guadeloupe to France. Outposts were consolidated in Gibraltar (which Britain had initially won in the Peace of Utrecht), the Island of Malta, which thrived as a naval port and the Ionian Islands of Greece. With these bases Britain held the balance of power in the Mediterranean. When the Egyptian Viceroy Mehemet Ali rebelled against the Ottoman Empire, the British Navy tipped the balance against him – notably in the bombardments of Beirut, Sidon and then Acre in autumn 1840.

The war itself pushed Britain to develop its industry changing the make-up of the country, to be more urban and driven. Expectations of reform that had been sat on under the exigency of fighting the war re-emerged at its end. The reaction that Britain led, alongside Prussia, Russia and Austria, did not take the world back to that point before the revolutionary upheaval. However chastened, the townsfolk expected things to open up. On the face of things, the revolutionary hopes of 1776 and of 1789 had been narrowed down to a more cautious property-based liberalism. That said, the spirit of democratic revolution and a wider liberty got shape in the upheavals at the end of the eighteenth century. Later rebels would have a rich stock of ideas and lessons to draw on. American abolitionists and Lincoln-era Republicans, British Chartists, Irish and Indian rebels, and in time much of the colonised world would have the watchwords of liberty, democracy and independence, and the experiences and memoirs of the Jacobins, the United Irishmen, the London Corresponding Committee, Toussaint Louverture and the Haitian Republic to hand. Revolution was derailed into safer channels, but its early drive was still felt. The end of the Napoleonic Wars was the beginning of a new period, a *Pax Britannica* that was conservative but not reactionary – not in western Europe, anyway.

The role of the armed forces changed over the eighteenth century. Before then the unhappy years of army rule under Cromwell's Protectorate had left a strong feeling against a 'standing army'. But a century of wars – mostly against France – bedded down a common-man's patriotism. The regular army grew from a high point of 70,000 in 1760 to as much as 226,000 in 1810, and the Navy grew to 140,000 men. Over and above the regular army the 1757 Militia Act sanctioned the recruitment of local reserves. Under the spur of the Napoleonic Wars, the irregular forces, militia, yeomanry and fencibles, ballooned to half a million in 1814 before falling back. A commonly used policy was to dragoon awkward populations into the armed forces, as Scots were into Highland regiments, Irish were across the British Army (so that they made up 42 per cent of it in 1830) and English radicals were pressed into the Navy. Not yet on the scale that they became in the later nineteenth and the twentieth century, the Armed Services were already a conservative influence in British society and were still used to put down bread riots and early labour protests. Though the rank-and-file soldier hoped to earn respect by his service, he got little. Ordinary ranks could be flogged or even executed for indiscipline, cowardice or desertion. They were drawn from people who had no vote and recruiters learned that the urban unemployed were an easy target. Many were pressed into naval service or tempted by a bounty. Recruiters shared most of the government award for each recruit with officers. The officers, who were drawn from the gentry or aristocracy, mostly bought their commissions and could recoup some of their investment by selling uniforms to the men. An Ensign's Commission in an infantry regiment cost £450 and a lieutenant-colonel's commission cost £4,500. Prices were higher in the cavalry, ranging from £850 for a cornet's commission to £6,175 for a lieutenant-colonel's. The Officer's Mess was an exclusive club as the barracks was largely a refuge for hopeless men.[47]

The armed forces were also the mainstay of Britain's influence overseas, both the Royal Navy and of growing importance the army. 'By 1815', writes historian Lawrence James, 'British troops were stationed at Halifax, Bermuda, Gibraltar, Malta, Cape Town, Mauritius and St Helena'. As well as those naval bases, the army were stationed in garrisons to protect colonies. Around that time 'British armies fought against native Americans on the frontiers of north America, rebellious slaves in the West Indies, Xhosas in Cape Colony and Maoris in New Zealand'.[48]

In 1812, Earl Bathurst became Secretary of State for War and the Colonies and Henry Goulburn his undersecretary. Bathurst and Goulburn rationalised the colonial office on modern administrative lines. The Charter Act of 1813 took away the monopoly over trade that the East India Company had since 1600. The West Indian sugar colonies were exposed to free competition, too. In 1836, James Stephen (whose father, also James, played a key role in abolishing the slave trade) took over from Goulburn as undersecretary, launching another round of rational reorganisation, and earning himself the nicknames 'Mr Over secretary' and 'Mr Mother Country' among his critics. A new Colonial Office, now separate from the War Office, was putting relations with the Colonies on a more systematic and professional footing. Central to those changes were new rights for colonists. In 1839 an influential report on the situation in Canada by Lord Durham set in motion the course of 'responsible self-government' in the colonies. It was still a relatively small operation. In 1857 the Colonial Office was in two ramshackle houses in Nos. 13 and 14 Downing Street, with just 62 employees, including nine copyists, five messengers and four porters.

Chapter Thirteen

COMBINED AND UNEVEN DEVELOPMENT

The industrial revolution in Britain changed the balance between the European and world powers. Once the impact of the greater rate of investment in British industry began to tell exports grew in value from £9 million in 1780 to £25 million in 1800 and then £125 million in 1850.

Though British ministers said they were in favour of free trade since Pitt's day, fighting the war against France led them to suspend that policy in favour of economic warfare and protection. The 'Orders in Council' between 1783 and 1807 attacked French trade and blockaded French-controlled ports. Defending these Lord Castlereagh pointed to the Continental blockade against British trade. Because the war interrupted trade with America the US President Jefferson ordered an embargo on all trade with Britain and France. In 1812, the Orders were withdrawn after stinging attacks in the British Parliament led by the Whig Lord Brougham.[1] Even then trade restrictions were tough. Until 1825 the emigration of skilled British artisans was forbidden and major technologies like textile machines were forbidden from export until 1841.[2]

Continental Emulation

The north-western corner of Europe mirrored the British patterns of industrialisation. This 'inner Europe' was close enough in its economic, cultural and political make-up to answer the flood of British imports by emulating British industrialisation. Farther from the inner European core, German historians talk about a *Gefälle,* or gradient of difference. Beyond the core, the European periphery in the East was faced with a very different challenge: how to survive in the face of West European export domination.

Between 1793 and 1815, warfare and the commercial warfare that ran alongside it encouraged innovation as well as limiting it. Many manufacturers' sales were boosted by army and other government purchasing. Marc Brunel's innovative factory in Portsmouth made blocks for ships – the pulleys that held the rigging in place. Warships used thousands of these blocks taking up tens of thousands of man-hours to make. Brunel's factory used a steam engine to drive a shaft from which leather belts drove lathes and drills in jigs to cut the blocks. For Napoleon's army Nicholas Appert built the first bottled food business where cooked meat and vegetables were sealed in air-tight containers after heating. The Leblanc soda process and getting sugar from beet were both answers to the British blockade of French ports. Behind the embargos and blockades some European industries blossomed, sheltered from the harsh wind of British competition. According to the economic historian David Landes the industrialising regions of northern Europe were 'the greatest beneficiaries of the "new order" – those small industrial states long locked in a tight tariff cage and now released into the huge spaces of Napoleon's Europe'. French cotton spinning took off around Lyon and north of Paris (and cotton exports grew after the war). 'We are both fighting the English', Napoleon flattered France's cotton manufacturer Oberkampf, 'but yours is the better war'.[3]

Despite the bar on emigration around two thousand skilled British artisans and engineers went to work on the Continent building and working on machinery that was exported or copied from British manufacturers.[4] Northwest Europe's legal and cultural conditions, as well as its human and natural resources, were close enough to those in England that the industrial revolution could readily be cloned, before, during and after the Napoleonic wars. For west European countries industrialisation could happen more quickly because many of the technologies had already been developed in Britain. In the first place a lot of the work of industrialisation was speeded up by copying over British inventions.

In the Sambre-Meuse region of Belgium and the Sheldt valley coal owners built a Newcomen engine in the Borinage in 1720 to help deep mining; 10 more by 1812, and 13 in the Charleroi. A Boulton and Watt engine was installed at Jemappes in 1785. By 1838, pits were around 210-metres deep and yielded five million tons of coal by 1846. At Charleroi Paul Huart-Chapel built a reverberatory furnace and in 1820 ironmakers helped by Englishman Thomas Bonehill built a puddling furnace in 1821. In nearby Verviers mechanic William Cockerill helped build textile machinery for the woollen manufacturer J. F. Simonis before setting up his own workshop in Liege making machines all across the woollen industry. His son John Cockerill took up iron and machine making. In Verviers, from 1801, woollen makers installed spinning machines and frames, and flying shuttles, exporting to Germany, Italy, Russia, Scandinavia and Holland. Lieven Bauwens smuggled a set of cotton mules with a steam engine out of England to set up at Ghent and set about making his own versions. The blockade saw a massive increase in woven cloth with 3600 looms and 103,000 mule spindles set up in 25 mills in France in 1812.

In the Nord in France the Anzin coalmining company exploited one of the largest fields from 1717 and built a Newcomen pump to get deeper in in 1732. By 1830 the district was mining 390,000 tons rising to 945,000 in 1845 – or about a quarter of all French coal (protected from cheaper Belgian coal by tariffs). The woollen industry took longer to get going, helped by a William Cockerill-built carding machine at Reims, so that worsteds grew fivefold between 1808 and 1848. France's cotton industry was spread over Nord, Flanders, Picardy, Normandy and Paris.

To the North the Duchy of Berg (around modern-day Dusseldorf) had relatively free commerce that helped ironmakers set up to serve the towns on the Rhine. The Wupper towns of Elberfeld and Barmen worked linen from as far afield as America and Africa. J. G. Brugelmann went to England to see Arkwright's mill and built his own water-powered mill at Ratingen in 1783, which he called Cromford, after the English model. Manufacturers built a steam powered cotton mill at Elberfeld in 1821. Iron smelters worked north of the Ruhr, though their great expansion began late – the first blast furnace was built in 1826 and the Friedrich Wilhelm ironworks blasted iron in Mulheim from 1849. Later in the century Krupp built the first Bessemer converter in Essen in 1862.

Up the Rhine in Alsace factories were set up to print calicos, six million metres of them in 1806. Weavers took up the loom to serve that industry, and Sainte-Marie – which had been a mining district – was home to 6000 looms in 1832. Alsatian manufacturers brought in power looms in 1820 and by 1846 there were 15,000 of them.

By 1807, there were four mechanised spinning mills in Saxony rising to 84 by 1831. Saxony was one of the most densely populated and industrialised areas in Europe at that time despite the harsh Prussian tariffs raised against it. Silesia, which Frederick the Great had seized from Austria for Prussia in 1742 saw its linen and woollen industries decline in the face of Irish and Dutch competition. Coal miners and iron masters took up the slack. Scotsman John Baildon set up a coke smelting furnace at Gleiwitz in 1796, and more followed.

The industrial development of North West Europe between 1780 and 1840 was remarkable. At that time, though, it was still in Britain's shade. Even by 1860 British pig iron output per head was almost twice its nearest rival (Belgium), as was its consumption of coal and raw cotton. Steam power per head was four times its nearest rival. All the same the extension of the industrial revolution across Europe was a compelling example of emulation and transfer of technology. These industrial centres in Europe were following the same pattern of economic development as Britain's, making capital-intensive manufactured goods and machines for European and world markets. Other parts of the world would be forced to adapt to European industry in ways that would put them at a disadvantage.

Uneven Development

In 1815 David Ricardo set out the 'theory of comparative advantage' in his book *Principles of Political Economy and Taxation*. He was broadening the theory of the 'division of labour' that Adam Smith had popularised. Where Smith looked at the different tasks undertaken within an economy (the 'division of labour'), Ricardo proposed that there could be a division of labour between economies: 'Under a system of perfectly free commerce, each country naturally devotes its capital and labour to such employments as are most beneficial to each'.[5]

In his book Ricardo uses the example of wine from Portugal and woven cotton cloth from England. The Portuguese have the right climate for growing grapes and so the better place for winemaking. The English have put money into cotton spinning and weaving. It is better for both to specialise and trade in an international division of labour. Ricardo's example was based on the Methuen Treaty of 1703 under which Portuguese wines and English textiles both had access to the markets of the other country without taxation. It was a harmonious picture of the growth of the world market where exchange would benefit both nations.

Thomas Babington Macaulay drew out the way that the terms of trade might be more weighted in Britain's favour, writing that 'while other nations were raising abundant provisions for us on the banks of the Mississippi or the Vistula', Britain would 'supply the whole world with manufactures, and have almost a monopoly of the trade of the world'.[6]

In Europe, though, there were doubts whether the 'free trade' panacea that Britain favoured really helped them. The German-American economist Friedrich List (1789–1846) took a more sceptical view of international trade. He argued that it was better to make goods at home even if they could be got for less abroad:

> Politics demands, in the interests of each separate nation, guarantees for its independence and continued existence, special regulations to help its progress in culture, prosperity, and power, to build its society into a perfectly complete and harmoniously developed body politic, self-contained and independent.[7]

His argument was that national interest called for policies to protect native industries against overseas competition. He put into words what a lot of people feared – that the level playing field of the free market would not lead to mutual benefits but favour that country that was already in a stronger position. He charged the British in particular with carrying on a policy of punishing rivals from behind a mask of benevolence. 'It is indeed strange to see at the same time the present Ministry of England', List wrote, 'jealously watch to prevent every progress of other rival nations, particularly of the United States'.[8] The free trade policy as List warned was very good for Britain, though it was not always as good for Britain's rivals to open their markets to British competition. What was more, the British free trade policy was often broken by Britain itself when it used force to sort those problems that trade could not.

Not all Europe emulated Britain's industrial revolution. In the East many rural elites adapted to it by securing the farm surpluses to feed the growing urban centres in Europe. It had been argued by Adam Ferguson and others that the growth of 'civil society' would be largely a progression towards greater liberty. But for the peasants of much of eastern Europe the industrial revolution in the west, and the urban and liberal trends that were associated with it led in a different direction altogether. Faced with the rapid industrialisation of western Europe, East European society had to accommodate to a world that had changed. In Prussia the landowning military caste called Junkers owned the land east of the Elbe River. The developing countries in the east had to fit themselves into a European division of labour where west European countries already occupied the advanced industry niche. To trade with them east European countries had to create another niche – and that tended to be sending primary goods to the west to trade for their worked-up goods.

Where the trend in the west was to end servitude in the East the Junkers brought in what has been called a 'Second Serfdom'. On the face of things Prussia would see serfdom abolished, but the terms of the changes were even more onerous than what had gone before. While the feudal obligations were lifted, the lords who granted the land to the peasants demanded as compensation more of the land, in edicts of 1811 and 1816, leaving the peasants worse off. As a description the 'Second Serfdom' captures something of the subordinate status of the peasant on Junker lands. The onerous conditions though, were not just a hangover from the past. From 1830 the Junkers large estates, the *Gutswirtschaft*, were exporting the surplus rye to feed the growing urban populations of western Europe, in particular Britain. In Moldavia the Boyars (landlords) used their power as magistrates to increase the peasants' burden of labour service. Even in Austria peasants had to give up labour service to their landlords, the 'robot patent', and though these were limited by successive decrees, there were still 38.6 million days of Hand-robot and 29.4 million days of Team-robot due in 1853.[9]

As in Prussia, the peasants were locked in a feudal-like relation with their landlords, complete with compulsory service. But it would be a mistake to see this as the survival of feudalism. On the contrary, it was a re-birth of feudal-like oppression bent to meeting the west European demand for farm goods to feed urban populations.

Even industry was twisted by the patriarchal social order. A Russian government commission into peasant conditions found that they were paying between 200 and 270 per cent of their farming income in rent to the landlord – which would have been impossible but that the peasants were also working for wages, a share of which was then given up to the Boyars. In Silesia linen weaving was a thriving cottage industry but the weavers themselves were subject to feudal duties to their landlords, including a weaving tax, as well as control over their trade. When the abolition of serfdom was announced at Martinmas in 1810, the King of Silesia issued an order in council explaining that 'forced labour and socage, payments in money and in kind, ground rent and dog fees, hen, goose, egg, broom, watchmens' and silver dues were by no means abolished along with serfdom.[10] The weavers were supplying goods for commercial sale, often handled by their landlords, but they worked under patriarchal domination.

Those things that were signs of modernisation in western Europe, like railways and banks, in much of eastern Europe worked only to highlight the uneven development of the region. In Russia railways were built to carry wood, rye and iron westwards, there were very few passenger trains and the people who travelled on them most often were soldiers. Ironmaking in the Urals had prospered in the eighteenth century, outstripping even England in pig iron, but by the time the railways were built the steel was imported as the Urals' ironworks were unresponsive to demand, being worked by peasants under feudal obligation. Banks in Russia and Hungary did little for local industries and were for the most part subordinate to western banks, with local currencies tied to west European currencies like the British gold standard or the Franc to make exports easier. Major cities in the East, like Moscow and even Vienna had a marked sex imbalance because they were for the most part garrison towns, not commercial centres. Uneven development was a curse on Eastern Europe, locking the region into backward-looking social and cultural practices. But it was not an historical hangover: it was the modern condition of capitalism. Development in West Europe, and in Britain in particular, meant East Europe could not compete in manufactured goods, but tended instead to be pushed back into exporting primary goods, raw materials and farm goods, to feed the industrial revolution in the west. The East was locked into a subordinate relationship that was not ameliorated but rather became more fixed over time.

Cotton Is King

Between 1785 and 1861, a sea borne trade bound two work sites to each other. Raw cotton grown in the southern states of the North American republic was carried by ship to Britain's western port towns and to the industrial regions of Lancashire and Clydeside. There it was worked up into thread and woven into cloth in Britain's growing number of textile mills. The two efforts rested on each other. The southern planters needed the English mill owners to buy their cotton, and the mills would be useless without it. Though this was a job of work carried on in two places with 800 miles or more between, their cooperation was managed through trade. The United States of America was by this time an independent country and the plantation owners and the mill owners had no hold on each other apart from their contracts.

It had been hoped that the spread of trade across the world would bring greater freedom with it. But in the case of the cotton trade the very opposite happened. The mill workers at the outset of the industrial revolution were not truly free, though over time they did get the rights to strike a bargain with their employers over their work. The plantation workers were not in any way free. They were enslaved Africans carried to America on ships or bought up from other (often tobacco) planters. The French radical Élisée Reclus suggested that 'the industrial prosperity of England appears to be intimately tied to the progress of slavery'.[11]

When the textile industry started in England the mill owners did not get their cotton from America. They bought it instead from the Ottoman Empire and then from planters in the Caribbean. The Ottoman cotton growers and pickers were not slaves but peasants and the paternal relations in Izmir and Salonika meant that they were not able to turn over enough land and labour to growing cotton to meet the growing demand. Some Caribbean planters turned to cotton, and before the revolution Saint-Domingue was a big exporter, but sugar was still a more lucrative crop and land was limited. English merchants scoured the world for cotton and found some grown in South Carolina and Georgia meant for local markets. The merchants Peel, Yates and Co brought cotton to Liverpool in 1786 and shortly afterwards Stockport manufacturer John Milne set out to talk American planters into growing more.[12]

Cotton growing in America got a boost from the slaver-refugees from the Saint-Domingue revolution, and from the Louisiana and Florida purchases. Thomas Baring, London banker and cotton merchant helped raise the capital for the Louisiana Purchase. He checked with the British Prime Minister Henry Addington if he was doing the right thing. Addington told him that he was, and Louisiana in American hands would be a valuable trading partner.[13]

Encouraged by British merchants many American planters switched from tobacco to cotton. South Carolina exported 10,000 pounds of raw cotton in 1790 which grew to 6.4 million pounds in 1800. Cotton cultivation spread westward to upland South Carolina and Georgia, then to Alabama and Louisiana, and eventually to Mississippi, Arkansas and Texas. Eli Whitney made an engine for pulling the cotton fibres apart from the seeds, the 'Cotton gin', in 1794, which saved a lot of time and labour. From the outset cotton cultivation was mostly slave driven. American planters took it as an act of faith that only slaves could be made to do the onerous work.

British cotton mills imported just over one million lbs of cotton in 1700, rising to 40 million in 1800, but by 1859 that had risen to more than a billion pounds. By 1802, most of the cotton came from the slave plantations of the United States. In 1824, according to the trade industry minister Huskisson raw cotton cost the industry £6 million, but the finished product was worth £32 million – making an added value of £26 million for wages and operating profit. At the point that the tariffs on raw cotton from America were lowered in 1859, the *Anti-Slavery Reporter* in London condemned the annual payment of £30,000,000 to the slave owners to buy seven-fifths of all American cotton.[14] By 1850 there were 1,800,000 enslaved men and women growing and harvesting raw cotton in America's 15 slave states, most of which was destined for England's cotton mills.[15]

Raw cotton imported from the United States and cotton goods exported from the UK.

	Raw cotton imports to the UK from the United States lbs 000s	*Cotton goods and yarn exported from the UK £000s*
1840	487,857	24,669
1841	358,241	23,499
1842	414,031	21,679
1843	574,739	23,448
1844	517,219	25,805
1845	626,650	26,119
1846	401,949	25,600
1847	364,599	23,333
1848	600,247	22,681
1849	634,504	26,775
1850	493,153	28,257
1851	596,639	30,089
1852	765,631	29,978
1853	658,452	32,713
1854	722,151	31,746
1855	681,629	34,779
1856	780,040	38,233
1857	654,758	39,073
1858	833,238	43,001
1859	961,707	48,202
1860	1,115,891	52,012
1861	819,501	46,872
1862	13,524	36,751

Some of the shortfall during the civil war was made up by imports of raw cotton from India, which grew from 132,723,000 lbs in 1858 to 506,527,000 lbs in 1864.

Historians like Jairus Banaji and Sven Beckert have argued that the cotton plantations were modern capitalist businesses just like the English cotton mills that they served. They take issue with the (late) historian of the slave south Eugene Genovese who argued that slavery was different from wage labour and worked according to different rules. Banaji and Beckert are right to say that the growth of the cotton plantations in the years from 1790–1860 was so closely connected to modern capitalist system that it should be thought of as a part of it. Slaves were property against which you could raise a loan. 'When the price rises in the English market', said the fugitive slave John Brown, 'the poor slaves immediately feel the effects, for they are driven harder and the whip is constantly going'.[16] But the enslaved were not wage labourers and the relations of domination on the plantations were also quite different from those in the cotton mill (however onerous). Genovese was right to point to the peculiarity of the southern custom. Cotton slavery was run like a capitalist business, but it was peculiarly limited.

The planters' hunger for profit drove them west, conquering more land, to make more cotton and between 1836 and 1845 they doubled the amount they harvested. At the same time the value of the raw cotton crop dropped from $71,284,925 to $51,739,643.[17] Critics of the south like Frederick Law Olmstead pointed out that the slave plantations were crowding out industry so that southerners' invested very little in manufactures; Olmstead talked to southerners who worried that the south was dependent on Europe and the north for 'almost every yard of cloth, and every coat and boot, and hat we wear; for our axes, scythes, tubs, and buckets – in short for everything except our meat and bread'. John Greenleaf Whittier warned that 'millions of northern capital must be sunk in southern bankruptcy' and that 'the cost of raising cotton now so nearly approximates its value', that 'the planters cannot live much longer without a change'.[18]

While the slave economy grabbed land but choked off economic growth, it made sure to dominate government. The northern Yankees were busy building up their industry and banking, and they were happy to leave the Senate, the Presidency, much of the military and the magistracy in southern hands.[19] The conservatism of Presidents like Franklin Pierce (1853–57) and James Buchanan (1857–61) helped the south dominate. The persistence of slavery up to 1863 in the heart of the young American republic showed that the industrial revolution was not all progress. Modern capitalism did not always pull in the direction of liberalisation, in some cases it threw up its own systems of patrician domination. Chattel slavery in America's southern states was not a hangover from the past, it was a distinct feature of the now-global market economy.

Famine in Ireland

The Union with Britain in 1801 did not help Irish industry. The Penal laws had done their work hobbling the mostly Catholic population. Absentee landlords took £6.5 million annually off to their English homes from their Irish tenants by the 1840s. Improving landlords were few in Ireland. The agreements they struck with their tenants were demeaning. Much land was let in 'conacre' – a one harvest contract – often with a 'hanging gale', meaning on credit so that a single crop failure would lead to ruin. The balance of power between the landlord – or more often his agent – and the tenant was very much in the landlord's favour – they were 'tenants at will', meaning they could be readily evicted. There were eight million two hundred thousand people living on the island of Ireland in 1841 and the competition for land was great. Without any push for improvement the trend was for the subdivision of the land into smaller and smaller plots to accommodate the demand from a growing population. The leases were so short that tenant farmers had no reason to invest in land that they could lose in a season. What improvements they did make were the property of the landlord that they had no right to a share in. The poor state of their land left a great many on the edge of ruin.

Irish tenants farmed oxen, sheep, wheat, barley and oats which they sold to pay the rent. But they lived mostly on potatoes that grew in 'lazy beds' and would keep a family through most of the year (summer being a hungry season). The Irish people did not consider wheat, oats and barley as food, the government official Sir Randolph Routh wrote in 1846, they were grown to pay the rent and the rent was the first necessity of life in Ireland. Without making rent the tenants could be evicted and would be left with no means to live. So great was the dependence on the potato that in the south and west there were barely any bakers or domestic bread ovens, nor mills to grind the wheat. The Irish farmer in the United Kingdom gave up his farm goods to feed England while he depended on potatoes to make-up his own meal.

In 1807, half the potato crop was lost through frost bringing hunger. In 1817, and again in 1822, people starved in Ireland – the potato crop failed in 1820 bringing misery to Munster and Connaught. There were many blights to the potato through the 1830s that brought people close to starvation. While the people went hungry for want of potatoes their own farm goods went abroad to be sold on the English market. In 1817, while people ate weeds 695,600 quarters of grain and much cattle was exported. William Cobbett wrote in 1822 that 'since this famine has been declared in Parliament, thousands of quarters of corn have been imported every week from Ireland' – 1,063,000 quarters in fact.[20]

In Ireland the settlement of 1801 was long resented and in time a movement of Irish Catholics aggrieved by their subject state rose up under a compelling campaigner Daniel O'Connell. O'Connell's movement alarmed Tories, but Whigs were also pushing for reform in England and were willing to work with 'the great liberator'. In 1829 the English Government conceded Catholic Emancipation – meaning that Catholics would be free to stand in an election to the Westminster Parliament, and to practice in the professions and hold land. It was an important a step forward that the law would not discriminate against the Catholic professional, property-owner or aspirant Member of Parliament. But in place of discrimination on confessional grounds, the new law brought in a far stricter property qualification. Under the old rule anyone holding a freehold to land of forty shillings (£2) or more could vote. Under the new rule the property qualification was brought up to £10. The net effect was that the old electorate of 216,000 was brought down to just 37,000. O'Connell re-launched his campaign as an Association to repeal the Act of Union. *The Times* in 1836 thought O'Connell's new campaign was just the 'scum condensed of the Irish bog'.[21]

From London there was a strong feeling that Ireland's agriculture should be reformed, though their idea of who the reform should help and who should pay for it was not in the Irish tenant's favour. Looking at the model of the improving landlord in England economists were sure that the land could be more productive with investment, on which score they were right. But they also thought that the only way to get to that goal was to rid themselves of a great many of their tenants. In 1836, *The Times* gave voice to English prejudice against the Irish, who, hate our free and fertile isle. They hate our order, our civilisation, our enterprising industry, our sustained courage, our decorous liberty, our pure religion. This wild, reckless, indolent, uncertain and superstitious race has no sympathy with the English character.[22]

Many would answer that it was the way that English landlords and militiamen had denied the Irish their liberty and ruined their industry. Most of all these complaints showed how those who ruled Ireland from Westminster were driven to blame the Irish character for what were more obviously the failings of the administration.

In 1843, a government report was commissioned to look at the question of land occupation under Sir William Courtney the tenth Lord Devon and other English landlords ('a jury of butchers trying a sheep for his life', said Daniel O'Connell). The commissioners reported that: 'We find that there are at present 326,084 occupiers of land, whose holdings vary from seven acres to less than one acre; and are, therefore, inadequate to support the families residing upon them.' They worked out that 'the consolidation of these small holding to up to eight acres, would require the removal of about 192,368 families'. John Mitchel, editor of the *United Irishman,* quoted these numbers to say 'that is, the killing of a million of persons'.[23]

Those landlords with ambitions to turn their land to raise more profit saw the answer in reducing the tenants. In their eyes the tenants ate but they did not raise much beyond that to pay a rent. 'The sooner Ireland becomes a grazing country, with the comparatively thin population which a grazing country requires, the better for all classes' one landlord told Nassau Senior.[24] The landlords pressed Parliament to change the law to make it easier to evict. The law was changed in 1815 and then again in 1822 to make evictions easier.

On 11 August 1845, the potato blight (*phytophthora infestans* – a kind of fungus) was first reported in Kent, and then in Ireland in September – and already by October it was clear that the crop as a whole was at risk. At first it was not clear how bad the impact would be. A brown leaf showed that underneath the tuber was turned to a slimy dark grey mass. Though many tried you just could not eat the rotten tubers. As more reports came in it became clear that the blight was not just in some places but had spread right across the country. Even stores of potatoes opened up showed most were rotten. The following year the whole crop failed in the spring and then again in the autumn. People were falling ill with hunger. Soon they fell prey to diseases like dysentery and typhus. Children grew downy hair on their hands and faces. People started to die, families in their cottages, or fallen in ditches by the roadside.

Eight years before the Government had made provision for poverty with a Poor Law of 1834. The law though was modelled on England's poverty problem – and a particular idea of what that demanded. In England many of the poor were already dislocated from the land and collecting in towns and cities. The Workhouses that were made for British towns were punitive, made as brutal as they could be out of a fear that people would choose welfare over work. Workhouses were brought in instead of 'outdoor relief' – payments to people off site. Workhouses were vicious in England. In Ireland they were wholly destructive. Claimants had to give up their farms to stay in the workhouse.

In 1998, the British Prime Minister Tony Blair apologised for the way that the British Government dealt with the famine. His main point was that the welfare that the

Westminster Government put in place was not enough to meet the scale of the famine. But the strain on the workhouses and soup kitchens was just the end-point of the problem. It was the rent payments and the failure to reinvest the surplus in improvements that made the conditions of the famine. As the scale of the famine became known it was clear that there were not enough places in the workhouses to meet the need. To meet the loss of a potato crop valued at £3,500,000 the Government spent £100,000 on Indian corn (maize) to make up the difference. It was true that the workhouses struggled to meet the needs of the 300,000 that called on them at their height. It was also true that the workhouse system itself made the position of the Irish tenant worse. Under the quarter acre or Gregory clause in the Poor Law a man and his family could not get help until they had given up all their land back to the landlord, to pay off all outstanding debts and tithes. John Mitchel called it 'passing paupers through the workhouse': 'a man went in a pauper came out.' Nassau Senior's landlord friend said, 'well we have got our Poor Law and it is a great instrument for giving victory to the landlords.'[25]

While the tenant farmers' own meals were lost they still had to pay the rent or risk losing their farm and starving. Evictions mounted as tenants failed to meet their rents, but in many cases landlords decided to rid themselves of the tenants anyway. Lord Lucan evicted 400 families – 2,200 people – from his estates in County Mayo, and then used the land for sheep grazing. On 30 March 1846 Mrs Gerrard called on troops and police to help her clear the tenants from 61 stone cottages in Ballinlass in the West of Ireland. The tenants had of their own cleared four hundred acres of bogland that all fell to Mrs Gerrard on eviction. At Ballinlass the tenants were not in arrears but the land was claimed anyway. Soldiers were sickened by what they were called upon to do. But still the houses were broken, their roofs pulled down and windows broken. Later many tenants were to be seen hiding in the wreckage of their old homes, or in 'scalps' (makeshift shelters of peat covers propped against a wall or tree) or sheltering in ditches.[26]

Just before Christmas 1847 a landlord called Walshe cleared three villages on the Mullet peninsula in Mayo. At one of the villages, Mullaroghue 102 families were evicted in a terrible gale, so that 'after the eviction only the walls of three houses remained', according to an eye-witness, the Quaker James Hack Tuke. It was the first time that Walshe had visited his estate in Mayo. On 27 April 1846 the Radical MP George Scrope told the House of Commons that 'ejectment is tantamount to a sentence of death upon them, death by slow torture'. During the famine 84,123 families were evicted.[27]

On the 3 November 1846 the Lord Lieutenant of Ireland, Lord Heytesbury, met a delegation of concerned citizens including the Duke of Leinster, the Lord Mayor of Dublin, Daniel O'Connell, Henry Gratton son of the late First Minister and many others. O'Connell demanded action to help the people beginning with a bar on the export of food. The Lord Lieutenant was unmoved. The exports went on. In each of the famine years 1846, 1847 and 1848, Ireland exported 15 million pounds worth of wheat, barley, oats, oxen, sheep and poultry, out of a usual output of £41 million. In 1846 1,875,393 quarters of grain, and eggs to the value of £1,000,000 were exported to England. The *Daily News* of 3 October 1847 reported that in the London market the 'receipts of oats chiefly consist of the new Irish crop', and in one day 11,050 quarters of Irish oats landed in London. In one week that October there were shipped from Drogheda 1,200 cows,

3,500 sheep and wine, 2,000 quarters of grain, 211 tons of meal and flour, 130 boxes of eggs and more. Similar cargoes were sent from Waterford, Newry, Derry, Coleraine, Belfast, Dundalk, Dublin, Wexford, Cork and Limerick.[28]

When the grain was bagged and warehoused in towns, angry crowds gathered and troops were placed to guard the export-destined crop. From Waterford an official wrote on 24 April 1846 that 'the barges leave Clonmel once a week for this place, with the export supplies under convoy which, last Tuesday consisted of two guns, 50 cavalry and 80 infantry escorting them on the banks of the Suir as far as Carrick'. One farmer Simon Dunane of Gurtnahaller, County Limerick wrote to his landlord on 20 September 1846 that he could only meet his rent by thrashing and selling his oats, and that since he has no potato crop left he and his family would leave and seek help.[29] 'Do not encourage the idea of prohibiting exports', wrote the Assistant Chief Secretary – the effective overlord of Ireland – Charles Trevelyan on 3 September 1846, 'perfect free trade is the right course'.

The *Times* in 1846 welcomed the potato blight as a means for changing the nature of the Irish Celts:

> We regard the potato blight as a blessing. When the Celts once cease to be potatophagi, they must become carnivorous. With the taste of meat will grow an appetite for them; with the appetite the readiness to earn them.[30]

Economic change was sped up with the Encumbered Estates Act which made it easier to sell off over-mortgaged estates, which led to much land changing hands from bankrupt landlords to improving landlords for sheep and cattle farming. The starvation of the Irish tenant farmers was not something that Britain failed to prevent, but something that the British landlords and their agents, the merchants and authorities made happen. The potato blight ruined the crop but it was the domination of Ireland by Britain that caused the famine. The threat of eviction was the lever that forced the surplus product, the 15 £millions of agricultural goods that were exported to England each year, out of the Irish tenant farmer even as he was starving to death.

Nassau Senior's landlord companion told him 'No friend to Ireland can wish the war to be prolonged – still less that it should end by the victory of the tenants for that would plunge Ireland into barbarism worse than that of the last century.'[31] He meant something very different by 'Ireland' than its people. Victory for the landlords in their war against the Irish tenant farmer was the latter's starvation or emigration. The records show that 985,366 people died. The population fell from 8,200,000 to 6,500,000 in the ten years from 1841 to 1851. As a million died nearly as many more left for Britain's burgeoning industrial towns – Liverpool, Manchester, Birmingham, Glasgow and London – or they left for America.

In Ireland the shock transformation of the country was very much as the economists had hoped: the population was less and more of the land was given over to grazing where it had been arable land. The number of farmers on holdings less than five acres fell from 45 per cent to just 15 per cent. Holdings of over 30 acres were now one quarter of the total, where they had been seven per cent.

The administrators, politicians and many of the landlords in Ireland believed in the new god of Political Economy as much as they had the Church of England. But then, as the MP and writer Edmund Burke had told them, 'the laws of commerce are the laws of nature, and therefore the laws of God'.[32] From 1828, in Ireland it was money not religion that sorted who had the vote and who did not. Guiding the administration were Charles Trevelyan (1807–86) the Assistant Secretary to the Treasury – but effectively the British Government in Ireland – and Nassau Senior, Drummond Professor of Political Economy at Oxford University, and a part of the Poor Law Commission of 1832. They drew on the ideas of Adam Smith, or more often the Economist Thomas Malthus. Charles Trevelyan gave copies of Smith's *Wealth of Nations* to his officials as he told them not to indulge the Irish hunger with famine relief because it would be undermining.

The economists preached a harsh sermon. According to Malthus a man who 'cannot get subsistence from his parents, on whom he has a just demand, has no claim of right to the smallest portion of food, and in fact no business to be where he is'. Malthus' own contribution to economics was the theory that poverty was caused by overpopulation, and that it would be checked by starvation. He thought that Ireland was the proof:

> The land in Ireland is infinitely more peopled than in England; and to give full effect to the natural resources of the country, a great part of the population should be swept from the soil.

Looking back, John Russell remembered that it was the common sense of the day:

> Many years ago the Political Economy Club of London came, as I was told, to a resolution that the emigration of two million of the population of Ireland would be the best cure for her social evils. Famine and emigration have accomplished the task beyond the reach of legislation or government.[33]

Critics thought that Malthus' theory of overpopulation was a convenient excuse for bad policy that shifted the blame for government failure onto the victims of that failure. The economists J. E. Cairnes and John Stuart Mill broke with the mainstream view when Cairnes argued in articles in the *Economist* that a free market in land (the Unencumbered Estates Act) might be right for England, but not for Ireland, because the circumstances were different. Cairnes, who lived in Dublin, advised Mill on the hardship of the cottiers. Mill was persuaded that the cottiers were too much at the mercy of the landlords. He concluded that 'the social economy resulting is intolerable, unless either by law or custom the tenant is protected against arbitrary eviction, or arbitrary increase of rent'.[34]

Karl Marx poring over the statistical reports in the British Library saw that the rents and profits of the landlords and larger farmers had grown. Even though the population had been decimated and the total output of the country was less after the famine than before, still 'the surplus produce increased though the total produce of which it formed a fraction decreased'. The forties showed that 'Ireland at present is only an agricultural district of England', wrote Marx, 'marked off by a wide channel from the country to which it yields, corn, wool, cattle, industrial and military recruits'.[35]

India's Weavers

India's cotton and silk weavers led world output in the sixteenth century. As we have seen, from the time that the East India Company began trading between the sub-continent and Europe cotton goods were their most important staple – and because of that British weavers successfully pressed to have Indian goods excluded from the domestic market.[36]

With the industrial revolution in Britain the balance of power between the Indian and British weavers shifted. The flying shuttle, the Jenny and later Cartwright's power loom gave British weavers the advantage. By 1825, it took British workers 135 hours to produce 100 pounds of cloth compared with 50,000 hours to produce the same by hand in India. English export of cottons grew in value from £766,000 in 1780, to £3,380,000 in 1790 and then to £15,871,000 in 1800. British import of textiles from Asia altogether fell from £1,687,000 in 1790 to £827,000 in 1800. India's cloth exports fell from £2,521,000 to £976,000 in 1810. British cotton exports to India grew by a factor of 700 between 1794 and 1813.[37]

In 1813, the EIC's charter was renewed but its monopoly in trade with India was abolished. In the Commons debate on the charter in 1812 the industrial interests of Lancashire were upheld. The 'free trade' measure was backed up with a swingeing tariff on Indian imports of calicos and muslins. The Sanskrit scholar and former East India Company surgeon Horace Hayman Wilson wrote that without the tariff 'the mills of Paisley and Manchester would have been stopped in their outset' and that they owed their growth to 'the sacrifice of the Indian manufacture'. Moreover:

> Had India been independent, she would have retaliated; would have imposed preventive duties upon British goods, and would thus have preserved her own productive industry from annihilation. This act of self-defence was not permitted her; she was at the mercy of the stranger. British goods were forced upon her without paying any duty.[38]

Under these terms British textile exports to India grew even faster. Between 1824 and 1837 export of British muslins to India grew from one million to 64 million yards. In 1824, British exporters sent 121,000 lbs of cotton twists to India, but by 1828 they sent 4,000,000 lbs. The blow to Bengal's cotton weavers was disastrous. Unable to sell they were ruined and hungry. William Bentinck, Governor-General of India, wrote in a report of 1835 that the 'misery scarcely finds a parallel in the history of commerce': 'the bones of the cotton weavers are bleaching the plains of India'. As Jawaharlal Nehru wrote 'the machine did not come to India as it might have done in the ordinary course; but machine-made goods came from the outside'.[39]

The East Indies kept on buying British cotton, taking in a third of all British cotton exports after 1850. By the 1870s India alone was importing between 40 and 45 per cent of all British cotton exports.[40]

Britain's Informal Empire in Latin America

While Spain was under Joseph Bonaparte the Spanish Empire in South America was weakened. National liberation struggles in Chile and Argentina under O'Higgins and Simon Bolivar set up independent American states. British leaders saw the opportunity. In 1806 and 1807, British forces under William Beresford blockaded the estuary of the Plata and even tried to invade Montevideo as a part of the war against Napoleonic Spain. Afterwards British Foreign Secretary Castlereagh promised that Britain would act as 'auxiliaries and protectors' not 'conquistadors' to the Latin American republics breaking free from Spanish rule.[41] From Argentina's Estanceros Britain imported cattle hides – rising from 150,000 in 1776, to 874,000 in 1796 and to 2.3 million in the 1840s.[42] Sir Woodbine Parish, British Consul, wrote in 1839 that,

> the manufactures of Great Britain are becoming articles of prime necessity. The gaucho is everywhere clothed in them.[43]

Britain's Barings Bank extended loans that stabilised Argentina's debts in 1857. British investors took shares in many of the railway schemes and development ventures, including the Central Argentine Land Company and the Central Argentine Railway Company Limited.

From 1822 Brazil, too, declared its independence from Portugal. In 1849, the MP John Bright claimed that 'between £4,000,000 and £5,000,000 of British capital was invested in various commercial undertakings' in Brazil.[44] British investments in Brazil were controversial because there was still slavery there. The *Anti-Slavery Reporter* published an editorial that highlighted slaves owned by mining companies which were part-owned by Britons:

> the number of slaves belonging to the Imperial Brazilian Gongo or Soco Mine to be 418; to the Brazilian Company Cata Branca Mine, 406; to the Brazilian Company Concéicáo, 50; to the Macaubas and Cocaes Company, 619; to the St. Joaò del Rey Company, 360; and to the Condonga Mine, 240; in all 2,093 slaves owned by the proprietors of these several mines. ...

'O, generous directors'! wrote the *Reporter,* 'Pray, tell us by what right you hold these Africans as your slaves'?[45]

World Money

The Napoleonic war cost the British government a great deal of money that it raised by borrowing. At the end of the war £54 million of the £56 million the Government raised in revenue (customs and taxes on goods, but not on incomes) went on the interest on the national debt, and a 'sinking fund' for future interest.[46] These were years of great hardship across the country. For the financiers in the City of London, however, there was money to be made lending to the Government.

War in Europe was good for London's bankers. The French occupation of Amsterdam in 1795 tipped the competition in London's favour. London firms like Barings took their business. London's financial district was the safe place for Europe's merchants and bankers. Nathan Rothschild, son of the Austrian banking family, moved to Manchester in 1798 to trade cotton, but in 1804 set up trading in government bills in London. Johann Heinrich Schroeder moved between Hamburg and London in 1817. The revolutionary wave of 1848 brought more money – £20 million was moved to London. C. J. Hambro of Copenhagen and Alexander Kleinwort of Holstein set up in London in 1839 and 1855 respectively. In the war of 1871 Prussia beat back a French invasion and occupied the north of the country. Defeated France was nearly bankrupted and suspended convertibility of the Franc for eight years – leaving Britain to dominate the world bullion market. Money flowed to London and continental banks Erlanger and Co, Crédit Lyonnais and Deutsche Bank set up in London.

These merchant banks raised money for loans for trade and bought and sold government debt to make their profits. Baring Brothers raised loans to help stabilise the Talleyrand-led Bourbon Government in France in 1817 (that is they sold interest-paying bonds to the value of £12 million in the City of London). Rothschild raised £5 million for the Prussian government. Financing the post-war reconstruction opened the merchant banks to criticism. The *Commercial Chronicle* decried 'the base and wretched avidity of the Monied Interest, which, at the prospect of gain, is ready to forget all claims of patriotism'.[47]

The foreign loan business took off in 1824 when Barings and Rothschilds offered investment opportunities in Brazil, Mexico, and less reputably Columbia and Peru. These loans were a way for London-based investors to participate in ventures across the world. Brokers made up a fictitious issue, 'Chinese Turnpikes', to make fun of overenthusiastic investors. But in 1825 the failure of some of the South American loans led to a sudden shortage of loan capital, so that the Bank of England's reserves were only saved by the shipment of 150,000 gold sovereigns from France, arranged by Rothschilds. When confidence was restored, Barings, with the help of their Boston-born partner Joshua Bates, floated stock in US states and railroads, which made a lot of money in the city. Another marketer of US stocks was George Peabody, who had originally set up to import dry goods for the American market from Britain in 1838. Over 1841 and 1842, eight American states defaulted on their loans in succession. Around that time British industry was making a surplus of £60 million a year, capital that was looking for a good return.[48] By 1852 George Peabody had overcome doubts again to raise loans for US investments, this time in Railway Bonds, beginning with the Ohio and Mississippi. Loans were raised, too, by Barings, for Russian railways in 1850, though Cobden denounced it as a disguised war loan.

By 1853 foreign offers made up £101 million of the £1215 million quoted securities on the London Stock Exchange. Schröders secretly helped the French firm Erlangers float a £3 million bond on behalf of the American Confederate States in 1863 – with the City acting more on prejudice than common sense. The American Minister in London Henry Adams took comfort from the collapse of the bonds. In the wake of the Franco-Prussian War George Peabody's partner, and successor, Junius S. Morgan raised loans for the French reconstruction, which looked like a bad bet, but French commitment to honour the bonds rewarded Morgan well.

The City returned Whig and then Liberal MPs up till the 1870s, but it was quite conservative in its relations with the Government. The City spoke out against Huskisson's free trade measures and were hostile to the 1832 Reform Act until it became clear that the property qualification would keep poorer Britons' hands off the levers of power. When the Chartist movement's last great protest in 1848 petered out, the City rallied, putting an end to a long era of caution. The Government allowed joint stock banking outside of London after the 1827 crash, and in London later on. Slowly, chartered monopolies were lifted allowing trade in insurance and to the East Indies. After the repeal of the corn laws grain was imported from the Black Sea and the Mediterranean. Greek shipping merchants of whom the Ralli Brothers were the most successful, set up as importers in London – taking advantage of the end of the Navigation Acts. Pandia Ralli perfected the art of realising investments by raising credit on 'bills of lading', the note of the cargo, while it was in transit.

Generally, the City resisted Government efforts to limit liability. Huskisson's return to the gold standard after the Napoleonic wars was resisted as an unnecessary disturbance likely to lead to money shortages and interruption of trade, though it was in the end very successful. The Bank Charter Act of 1844 was brought in after the failure of US loans and the strain on the banks. It set a fixed ratio between notes and bullion held by the Bank of England and set a limit of £14 million on the amount that notes could be issued against securities. It was likened to a machine that took all the politics out of the Bank of England's role, by fixing the amount that it could extend in credit. Banks like Overend and Gurney put a lot of pressure on the Bank and the Government to suspend the Bank Charter Act, more so when the credit markets seized up. In 1866, Overend and Gurney's cavalier investments ended in a crash 'felt in the remotest corners of the kingdom'.[49] The Bank had hoped to disguise its debts, with assets of just one million to cover debts of four million, by floating as a public company, raising good money to send after bad. The collapse of Samuel Gurney Jr's business promoting a trans-Atlantic cable were instrumental in the collapse, when it was discovered that the company existed mostly on paper.

Trade in securities, loans and shares took place on different sites. The Royal Exchange (which burned down and was rebuilt by William Tite, re-opening in 1844), was never much favoured by traders. Stock trading, which had for many years gone on in coffee shops was moved to a dedicated exchange in Capel Court from 1802. The new exchange excluded non-members, to some protests. Undersea telegraphs carried news of bond and share prices from Europe from 1850 and across the Atlantic from 1866.

In January 1872, the *Quarterly Review* boasted that London was becoming the financial centre of the old world and the new. They contrasted 'political distrust and Revolution in France, the absence of unity between North and South Germany, and the want of a great Teutonic financial metropolis' with London's superior position:

> the unquestioned stability and credit of English institutions, the benefit of firm and equal laws, and the facilities and inducements of the freest ports, the lowest tariff, and the cheapest manufactures in the world

All of which,

> render London the place of ultimate settlement of the largest part of the business of both
> hemispheres. Hence the accumulation here of foreign capital and the growth of a powerful
> class of banks and financial houses...[50]

Even as this great system of international finance was coming together, there was some intimation that it would not last forever. The *Economist* editor Walter Bagehot wrote that 'most men of business' had forgotten the collapse of Overends and think: 'Anyhow this system will probably last my time. It has gone on a long time and it is likely to go on still.' 'But', Bagehot cautioned, 'the exact point is that it has not gone on a long time. The collection of these vast funds in one place is perfectly new'.[51]

Chapter Fourteen

WHITE FLIGHT

In Britain's industrial revolution the towns drew people from the countryside, just as the country drew capital funds back into its growing industrial cities (see 'Turning Inward', in Chapter Eleven). People came from further and further afield. At first the cities drew on the near countryside for more people. Later English cities drew on people living in Scotland, Wales and Ireland – which gave up many to the growing industrial centres.

A report on the Irish Poor in Great Britain, of 1835 found that there were 24,156 Irish living in Liverpool, 30,000 in Manchester and 6,000 in Birmingham, 10,000 in Edinburgh, 35,554 in Glasgow and perhaps 30,000 in London.[1]

Even as the new industrial towns were drawing people in, others were leaving. In the eighteenth century around half a million people left Britain for the colonies. After the American War of Independence official policy was against emigration to the Americas, and governors of the Canadian colonies were told to dissuade incomers. Then, in the years from 1815 to 1924 the United Kingdom alienated fully nineteen million people to settle permanently overseas.[2]

How could it be that industrial Britain was both drawing people in and at the same time forcing them out? The answer is that the growth of the new industrial society was antagonistic. It did draw people in to waged labour in its growing towns and cities. But it also drove people off their small plots of land. The industrial revolution put many people to work but it also led to clashes, sometimes violent clashes, between the common people, the employers and the authorities. There were centripetal forces drawing people to Britain's cities but centrifugal forces throwing them outwards.

In the minds of the propertied, the reason that people found it hard to live was that there were too many of them. That was what Thomas Malthus had taught them: over-population was the reason people were poor or starving. It did not entirely make sense. The factories were recruiting more and more people, and in the countryside around the towns, like in Kent and Dorset, demand for food led to a boom. But other parts of the country, like Cornwall and the Scottish Highlands, were badly disrupted. As well as being different according to what part of the country you were in, work was easier or harder to get in different times.

The Bank of England's historic estimate of gross domestic product (GDP) growth shows just how marked the business cycle was in Britain in the eighteenth and nineteenth centuries. What poverty looked like was more people than there were opportunities for them.

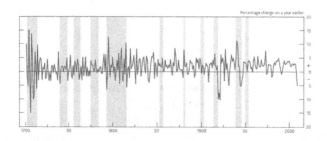

Annual UK GDP change and major war periods. Source Bank of England.

Regional disparities and the economic cycle mean that even in an economy that was growing overall, there could be severe downturns that would leave many people out of work and therefore surplus to the economy. The big downturns were in the Spanish War of Succession, at the end of the Napoleonic Wars up until 1821, in the hungry forties, 1845–48, 1857–58, 1867–69 and the long depression 1879–93 which we will look at in part three. Joshua Bates, a partner at Barings Bank, judged that the emigration was the answer to surplus population: 'Emigration seems the natural cure for excessive population in old countries'.[3]

Much emigration was forced. Bristol Aldermen were told in 1654 of 'the inveigling purloining carrying and stealing away boyes, maides and other persons and transporting them beyond seas' without their parents knowing. Cozeners like the Bristol mariner Michael Diggens took people off to the new lands – but then so did the Government.[4] In 1666, the parliament passed 'An Act to continue a former Act for preventing of theft and rapine upon the Northern Borders of England', that gave magistrates the right 'to transport or cause to be transported the said Offenders and every of them into any of His Majestyes Dominions in America there to remaine and not to returne'. The Transportation Act of 1717, 'for the further preventing Robbery, Burglary, and other Felonies, and for the more effectual Transportation of Felons' let magistrates commit criminals to indentured servitude in the colonies. Fully 50,000 were sent to North America between 1717 and 1775.[5]

Convicts Exiled, 1614–1864

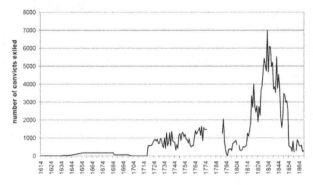

Source: 1614–1717: figures are based on Abbot Emerson Smith, *Colonists in bondage: white servitude and convict labor in America 1607–1776* (New York 1947)

The founding fathers of the North American republic saw transportation as another wickedness of King George's treatment of them and stopped it after 1776. From then on those who were transported were sent to Britain's colonies in Australia. There the transported were made to work as servants of the government – often sent to work on farms until they had worked their 'ticket'. Once free they settled so that the convict population of between 2,500 and 3,000 was a minority of the 8,300 convicts and ex-convicts, but still more than those who migrated freely, 931 in 1810. Transportation was awful. Transportees travelled chained in boats for weeks, in overcrowded and filthy conditions.[6]

It seems surprising that English magistrates sent so many people abroad. But then those same magistrates hung thousands of people, too. Capital offences in England before 1820 were many. You could be hung for treason, arson, frame-breaking, sending threatening letters, rioting, 'pulling down' houses, shooting at a revenue officer or a game-keeper, destroying turnpikes or silk in the loom, malicious maiming, killing cattle, certain types of smuggling and cutting down trees in an avenue.[7] The laws, called the 'Black Acts' have been described as a kind of warfare against the poor. As well as judicial executions disorderly towns were often occupied by the militia and scores of people were killed in protests. One hundred and twenty thousand troops occupied the Luddite protest districts between Leicester and York over 1811 and 1812 and eight rioters were killed. Eleven were killed at St Peter's Field in the 'Peterloo massacre' of 1819 and another 400 wounded; a dozen rioters were killed at Bristol and 16 striking ironworkers were killed in the same year; 11 Kentish labourers were shot dead in the battle of Bossenden Woods in 1838 and 24 people were killed in the Newport Rising of 1839. Between 1735 and 1799 6,679 people were hanged in Great Britain.[8] From the 1820s reforms under Peel meant far fewer people were hanged (3,872 between 1800 and 1899) and many were transported instead. As well as transporting people, from 1832 the authorities shut the poor in workhouses, wilfully made onerous and hateful to persuade people not to make themselves a burden on the public funds. In 1850, 123,000 people were confined in workhouses, while another 885,696 were living on public relief. And as we have seen, in Ireland hundreds of thousands starved in famine.

In 1838, the Molesworth Committee into transportation found that the conditions were cruel and degrading and it was wound down (but not ended until the 1860s). Around the same time a Board of Colonial Land and Emigration Commissioners was set up that promoted emigration to Australia and New Zealand. There were private companies, too, set up by people in the colonies to promote further colonisation, like the New Zealand Company, the West Australian Company and the South Australian Association.[9]

Champions of settlement thought that it could be the 'cure and prevention of pauperism, by means of systematic colonisation' (the title of an 1830 pamphlet written by the New Zealand Company's E. G. Wakefield). In the five years after the Napoleonic Wars, from 1815 to 1820, when wages were falling, as many as 170,000 left Britain and Ireland. A government scheme of 1819 set out to plant 4,000 in South Africa – but 80,000 applied.[10]

In the Scottish Highlands crofters and cottars living on large estates were seen by the owners as a burden, reduced to charity after the potato-crop failure of 1846–47. Landlords looked forward to clearing them in favour of sheep runs. As with Ireland, Assistant Secretary to the Treasury Charles Trevelyan argued that 'the only immediate remedy to the present state of things is emigration', and the *Scotsman* agreed, calling emigration 'the removal of a diseased and damaged part of our population'. The estates of the Dukes of Argyll and Sutherland, John Gordon of Cluny, and James Matheson, the opium baron who owned much of Lewis, set about selecting tenants for emigration, threatening them with eviction if they did not agree. Over 10,000 were 'assisted' to move to Canada.[11] Thomas Douglas, Fifth Earl of Selkirk, guiltily helped crofters he had dispossessed to settle in Rupert's Land with the help of the Hudson's Bay Company.

Scots and Welsh made up a good share of emigrants, but most of all it was Ireland that was marked by emigration. Ireland's Catholic Royalists were among the first transported to Barbados at the end of the Civil War, and transportee ships were burdened with those convicted of the land wars of the early eighteenth century – supporters of the factions called 'Whiteboys' and 'Ribbonmen' caught under the Insurrection Acts of 1822 that made it a transportable offence to be out of your house at night; later they were joined by many of the Young Irishmen of the 1848 rising, including John Mitchel (who later made his escape to America); 62 Fenian rebels of 1867 arrived in Fremantle, Australia in January of 1868, carried in the Hougoumont. Those Irish that emigrated 'freely' chose America over Australia or Canada. Their numbers were swelled by the threat of famine.

Emigration from the United Kingdom, 1815-1877

Emigration from the United Kingdom peaked above 100,000 in 1832, 1841–42, and then between 1847 to 1854 climbed above 250,000 a year. Most emigration was to the United States, followed by Canada, Australia and New Zealand.

In Dublin and London officials called for emigration to deal with the hunger in Ireland. 'I do not know how farms are to be consolidated if small farmers do not emigrate', said Sir Charles Trevelyan.[12] Landlords like Baron Monteagle paid their tenants to emigrate and he set up a Committee of the House of Lords on Colonisation. Already by 1846 more than a thousand Irish tenants had been shipped to Quebec. One landlord Francis Spaight of Limerick had a share in a shipping line and paid his tenants £2 a family to emigrate. Around 109,000 migrated to British North America (modern day Canada) in 1847, almost all Irish.[13] Of 477 passengers on the Lord Ashburton travelling from Ireland to Quebec in 1847, 107 were buried at sea after fever spread through the ship. The vessels were later called 'Coffin Ships'. Other Irish tenants were sent to the United States. Lord Lansdowne, seeing his Kerry tenants starve, was persuaded by Matthew Trench that it would be cheaper to get them to emigrate. New York newspapers railed against the Marquis who had shipped his surplus tenants there on the Sir Robert Peel: 'grey haired and aged men and women, who had spent the heyday of their life as tillers of their native soil, and are now sent to this country to find a grave'.[14]

Though poverty played its part, there were other reasons people emigrated. The British Isles were a limiting place in many ways. Among the educated middle classes religious non-conformism or political radicalism were reasons to seek a better life. For those second sons who did not take to the clergy emigration often seemed a better way to find your fortune. Bankrupts and others who had tarnished their reputation found a new life in the colonies. William Lyon Mackenzie fled Glasgow after the radical uprising of 1820 was put down – and went on to publish the *Colonial Advocate*, serve as Toronto's first mayor, and then to lead the revolt in Upper Canada in 1837. Edward Gibbon Wakefield, from a professional background was jailed in Newgate Prison for abducting and marrying a young heiress but went on to be active in the colonisation of New Zealand and Canada. New settlers were tempted to emigrate with the promise of grants of land. Hundreds upon hundreds of brochures were printed up by the colonial companies to tempt new settlers.

Throughout the eighteenth and the first half of the nineteenth centuries, the British establishment loathed the emigrants. 'Emigration is the natural recourse of the culprit and those who have made themselves the objects of contempt and neglect', said Lord Sheffield in 1763. Emigrants were paupers, fools or 'malignant outcasts', editorialised the *Times* in 1816, 'execrably base in their natures'.[15] To the Quaker gentlemen of the Aborigines' Protection Society, the emigrants were Europe's 'surplus population', the 'unhappy outcasts' or 'the dregs of our countrymen'. Over the years the British Government often clashed with the settler societies that these unhappy outcasts made, most shockingly in the War of Independence 1776–82, also in the revolts in Canada in 1839 and the wars with the Boers 1880–81 and 1899–1902.[16]

'The Last of England', Ford Madox Brown, 1855.

It caused some irritation to those who so patronised and reviled the emigrants that often they prospered in exile. In the second half of the nineteenth century voluntary migration took over from transportation. Settler Australia grew from 12,000 people in 1810 to 1.25 million in 1860, while Ontario grew from 60,000 to 1.4 million over the same years. By 1860 there were already five million emigrants living in the British Empire and many more in the United States of America. Outside of the British Empire, California's European population grew from 15,000 in 1848 to 380,000 in 1860, while the old North West grew from 250,000 in 1810 to seven million in 1860.[17] As James Belich has explained, these settler frontiers grew 'explosively' – that is in sudden and speculative booms. These were driven as much by hope and expectation as they were by strict economic sense. In their letters the new colonists wrote of their hopes as well as letting us know what it was they were getting away from. The words that are echoed again and again are 'Jack is as good as his master here'.[18] Letters home invited family and friends to join the emigrant in the new life. Often people sent back money so their families could join them. Back in England the figure of the emigrant or convict made good was an unnerving figure, like Abel Magwitch in Dickens' 1861 novel, *Great Expectations*, who terrifies Pip in the graveyard, but much later turns out to be his secret benefactor, having made his fortune in Australia. The emigrants' success seemed like a reprimand to the stay-at-homes. 'How dare these exiles prosper?' was the question that staid England asked.

The settler societies that the emigrants made thrived. The native peoples that lived where they settled were subject to severe pressure, through competition for resources – land and game – and by direct attacks and massacres. The settlers were colonists but more than those who went before they meant to husband the land.

The old colonial system made trading outposts where rivers met the coast, but the settlers moved inland. Those earlier colonies traded with native peoples and guarded their stockades. Even trade changed native communities dramatically. The Dutch traded guns to the Mohawk of the Iroquois Confederacy from 1626 which gave them significant advantage over rival bands.[19] The Naskapi of Labrador lost their Caribou-tracking skills when they bought rifles from the Hudson's Bay Company, and later found that they had no time to hunt Caribou because they were trapping the bony Marten to trade its fur, so that many starved in 1843.[20]

Before 1776 native American peoples fought successive wars with colonists. In 1636, the Pequot fought the colonists of Massachusetts losing around 700 killed or captured. Throughout much the seventeenth century the Iroquois fought a series of wars with France and their Algonquin and Huron allies around what today is New York and Albany.[21] In 1655, the Susquehannock Indians fought against the New Netherlands settlements along the Hudson River. Further south the colonists of Jamestown fought a series of wars with the Powhatan Confederacy between 1610 and 1646. In 1676, Nathaniel Bacon led a revolt of Virginia Settlers that united white indentured servants and even black slaves against the English Governor William Berkeley – though the common programme of the rebellion was a more aggressive policy to the Doeg and Susquehannock peoples.[22] In 1722, the Wabanaki Confederacy of Abenaki, Mi'kmaq and others joined with French colonists fighting against the New England colonies and their Mohawk allies. What was the Seven Years War in Europe was the 'French and Indian War' to the English colonists. Between 1754 and 1763 the Wabanaki Confederacy, the Algonquin, Lenape, Ojibwa, Ottawa and Shawnee Indians supported France in their struggle against the British colonists and their native American allies, the Iroquois Confederacy, the Wyandot and Cherokee. Many native Americans preferred the French to the English colonists because the French tended to trade furs whereas the English were more committed to planting, and so threatened more incursions.

The Iroquois backed the English in part because of their having already clashed with the French. The Revolutionary War was similar in that many native Americans preferred the British to the colonists because the colonists threatened more development and more pressure on native American territory. The low-born settlers wanted a more forward Indian policy because land was their route out subservience to their masters; the well-born governors and masters tended to promote peace treaties with the Indians to hem the settlers in. The conflict got worse after independence, when Andrew Jackson was elected President with a promise to remove Indians from the land east of the Mississippi River. The forced relocation of around 60,000 Cherokee, Seminole, Chocktaw, Winnebago and other peoples led to thousands of deaths between 1830 and 1850, and a sustained war with the Seminole between 1835 and 1842.[23]

White settlers were not born hating natives and early contact could be cooperative. Maori chiefs 'adopted' early settlers so that they would act as ambassadors to Europeans. In Western Australia aborigines worked as whalers and farm labourers for settlers for a wage. At Port Phillip (modern day Melbourne) the original white settlers aimed to buy territory from native chiefs to secure the legitimacy of their claims. Early relations between Mfengu and the British Cape Colony were good and the Africans prospered as peasant farmers from 1835.[24]

As settlements grew the settlers did not embrace natives but pushed them back. In Tasmania settlers turned violently on aborigines in successive slaughters culminating in governor Sir George Arthur's 'Bounty Five' (for the £5 reward for capture of a native) campaign to clear the island in 1830. On the Australian mainland as settlements expanded they clashed sharply with each native group whose lands they came into. Aborigines were killed in hundreds of different clashes, like those on the Camaspie in 1839, at Loddon in 1840 right up to the massacre of 150 by a troop under Corporal Montague in the Northern Territories in 1884. In New Zealand settlers clashed with Maori in 1844 and then again in 1860, as the settlement pressed on native land.[25]

In 1870 British Colonel Garnet Wolseley, Deputy Quartermaster General in North America led a force of 2,213 officers and men, and another 700 local constabulary to take the Red River colony, newly transferred from the Hudson's Bay Company to the Government of Canada, from Métis – or mixed race – hunters and fur traders (see left). A gang of outraged settlers attacked some Métis, including Norbert Parisien, who they took prisoner, and then shot, when he tried to run. When the Métis riflemen arrested the ringleaders, 28-year-old Thomas Scott was found to have killed Parisien. Scott was executed for the murder, which was taken by the settlers and the Government in Ottawa as an outrage. Though Wolseley's men met no resistance the troops looted, raped and murdered the Métis they found – including Elzéar Goulet and his seventeen-year-old daughter.[26]

Dutch settlers in Southern Africa who were moving inland as the Cape changed hands to Britain clashed with the Tswana from 1840 onwards, the Sotho in 1867, and successive Southern African peoples.

Just as settlers were often seen as an unfortunate overspill of the scum of society the Government viewed their settlements with some distrust. Colonists were demanding, often calling on the Crown for military support as well as loans. Many settlements were outside of Britain's colonies and pressed for the incorporation of whole territories even if they only occupied a part. The pressure for incorporation was a slippery slope. Under nineteenth century diplomacy it was common for expatriates to fall under the sovereignty of their home countries, as did, for example, Britons in the Turkish Porte from 1844, in Siam (1856), Morocco (1857), China and Japan (1865), Zanzibar (1866), Madagascar and Muscat (1867). Demands for 'concessions' – that is self-governing British trading enclaves in other territories would also become the jumping off point for newly incorporated colonies. There was some scepticism in the Foreign Office to new colonies up until the 1880s, when a new era of expansion began.[27]

Where settlements were already in territories claimed by the Crown the clamour for 'Responsible Government' was generally conceded in those lands where settlers were the majority of the population. Lord Durham's 1839 report on British Affairs in North America set out the principle of self-government was accepted by the UK Government in 1847; New Zealand and the Province of Canada got Legislative Councils in 1841; Australia's states got Legislative Councils individually between 1824 and 1860.[28] The Legislative Councils were a modest concession to manage distant communities. Later the white settler territories would become much more important to the British Empire as Dominions.

Other Europeans settled outside their homelands. Thirty-seven thousand French had settled in Algeria by 1841, and that number grew to 279,000 by 1871. French social-ists, followers of Etienne Cabet, disappointed by the failure of the National Workshops scheme of Louis-Napoleon Bonaparte made a utopian community they called Icaria in Texas, Illinois, Iowa, Missouri and California in the 1840s. Around the same time many German radicals disappointed by the failure of the revolution of 1848 moved to the United States, settling in St Louis, Chicago and New York.[29]

Chapter Fifteen

CIVILISING MISSION

After the loss of the American colonies, there were more objections raised to taking territory overseas. But Britons' interest in other people grew as their own belief in their own moral mission to help them towards civilisation grew. In the first instance this was a religious calling, and from there it extended outwards to other schemes for improving the lives of the benighted natives, from civilising India to the protecting aboriginal people.

Mission Societies like the Baptist Mission Society (1792) London Missionary Society (1794), Church Mission Society (1799) were founded with a goal of bringing the gospel to native people outside of Britain. The Baptist Mission Society led the way. William Carey had asked 'whether the command given to the apostles to "teach all nations" was not obligatory on all succeeding ministers to the end of the world', at the Northamptonshire Baptist Association's ministers' meeting in 1785, but it was dismissed then as unworthy.[1]

One hurdle that had to be overcome was the strong Calvinist belief in the 'elect' among Baptists. The idea was that the people in the church were those who God had chosen, which worked against the feeling that the faithful had a need to bring others to God. That view was changing. A great Baptist revival had swept Britain and the thirteen colonies in the 1730s and 1740s swelling congregations. Then in 1790s a second great awakening started in America. In 1754, Jonathan Edwards' pamphlet *An Inquiry into the Modern Prevailing Notions Respecting that Freedom of the Will Which is Supposed to be Essential to Moral Agency* put the case that faith was an act of the will. In 1784. Andrew Fuller's tract *The Gospel Worthy of All Acceptation* made the case against the Calvinist exclusion of unconverted sinners. Then, in 1791, Carey published a sermon he had given under the title *An Enquiry into the Obligations of Christians to use Means for the Conversion of the Heathens* at the prompting of Fuller and Samuel Pearce. That was the beginning of the Baptist Mission.[2]

Carey began the first overseas mission in Serampore, in West Bengal in 1793 with a handful of co-religionists, John Thomas, John Marshman, William Grant and William Ward. They found the work hard going in the face of Hindu belief (which they loathed) and challenging circumstances – illness took two families and William Grant. Converts were few. Between 1800 and 1821, 1,407 were baptised. But Marshman did build a successful school network that was, by 1811 teaching 10,000 children in 92 schools.[3] The mission had to work with the EIC, which was indulgent until 1806, when a mutiny broke out in Vellore at least in part because the Indian troops believed they were going to be made to take up Christian symbols. For a while the Company barred mission preaching until lobbying at home persuaded them to relax the ban. Among those in Britain who spoke up for the missions in India was the renowned anti-slavery campaigner William Wilberforce, who told Parliament in 1813 that it was 'the greatest of all causes, for I really place it before Abolition'. 'Our religion is sublime, pure and beneficent', he said, 'while theirs is mean, licentious and cruel'.[4]

Apart from the schools, the English missionaries put their efforts into translating the bible into Bengali, Oriya, Hindi, Marathi, Sanskrit and Assamese. They lobbied the Governor William Bentinck to ban Sati – the ritual burning of widows on the funeral pyre – which he did in 1829 and complained about the Company's grants to the Hindu temple at Puri in Orissa.[5]

More successful than the Bengal mission was the Methodist Church in the West Indies. The Baptists had some influence in Jamaica because of the migration of the black Americans John Liele, a preacher, and his convert Moses Baker in 1791, who gathered congregations among slaves. In 1806, the Jamaican House of Assembly forbade preaching on plantations. Appealing to John Ryland of the Baptist Academy in Bristol, Liele was sent student John Rowe. Rowe's instinct was to appeal to the planters and Baker's benighted congregation grew from around 800 to 1000. No matter how hard the English Baptists tried to reconcile the faithful with the island's governing planter class, the native congregations were distrusted by their owners. When the campaign against slavery revived in England the news encouraged and discouraged the enslaved and the planters respectively. The House of Assembly again took measures to suppress worship.[6]

Elsewhere, in Demerara (in modern-day Guyana) a slave uprising of 1823 was blamed upon another mission, sent by the London Missionary Society. In Jamaica the Baptist Mission's John Phillipo was refused accreditation to preach by the House of Assembly. The English missionaries were alarmed by the enthusiasm of the black congregants – called 'native Baptists' – and called on them to abstain from the political question. But native Baptists like Sam Swiney and Sam Sharpe were persecuted by the authorities and the latter was charged with inciting the slaves to rebellion and hung along with 311 others at the end of March 1832. 'I would rather die on yonder gallows than live in slavery', Sharpe said. In England that summer the missionary William Knibb who had seethed under the injunction to stay out of politics told a meeting at Spa Fields that 'slaves would never be allowed to worship God till slavery had been abolished' and made it clear that he would rather leave the church than defend slavery. Knibb's intervention helped push the newly elected Parliament to abolish slavery in the West Indies – which happened piecemeal in two acts, one in 1833 and then a further in 1838 (of which more below).[7]

As well as Baptists, Congregationalists were active in mission work. The London Mission Society was mostly made up of Congregationalists. The best-known mission was perhaps David Livingstone's. 'I only did my duty in attempting to open up part of Southern intertropical Africa to the sympathy of Christendom', Livingstone explained to the Royal Geographical Society on 15 December 1856, 'a pledge that the true negro family, whose country I traversed will yet become a part of the general community of nations'. In 1865, Queen Victoria appointed Livingstone 'to be Her Majesty's Consul in the territories of all African kings and chiefs in the interior of Africa, not subject to the authority of the King of Portugal, or of the King of Abyssinia, or of the Vice-Roy of Egypt'.[8]

The London Missionary Society played a key role in managing the conflict between the Boers, the Tswana and the British Empire. Robert and Mary Moffatt talked the mixed-race people known as the 'Basters' into adopting the name 'Griqua' and to settle by the Tswana. In the conflicts between Tswana, Sotho and Griqua first the Moffatts, then the missionary couples that followed them the Ashtons and the Helmores played a key role persuading those African people that they would be safer if they accepted the protection of the British Empire. The British colonial officer Charles Warren over-saw the building of the Moffatt institute as a British redoubt in Tswanaland. Far to the South, Bishop John Colenso's appointment as the Church of England's Bishop of Natal in 1853 led to schism, when he argued for the accommodation of Zulu polyg-amy. Colenso embroiled his parishioners in controversies over the literal truth of the Bible and his advocacy for the Zulu families under Cetshwayo. Colenso clashed not only with the Church in Cape Town over religious doctrine, but with the Natal Native Administration under Theophilus Shepstone, too.[9]

The Anglican Church Missionary Society set up in Badagry by Lagos in West Africa in 1842, and other missions in Abeokuta and Calabar soon afterwards, and then in Igboland in 1857. The West African mission struggled to make recruits but played an important part in formalising written Yoruba and Igbo in translations of the bible, the Book of Common Prayer, and written dictionaries. As with other lan-guages, from Fijian to Xhosa, missionaries played a major role in the translation of spoken language into written in such a way as to significantly impact upon the culture. While baptisms came slow in West Africa, where the Church of England was overshadowed in Northern Nigeria by Moslem proselytisers the educational and linguistic legacy lasted, so that the Anglican Church today is larger in Nigeria than in Britain. By 1884 it was estimated that the Protestant missions in the Empire put some 900 missionaries in the field.[10]

The East India College

In 1800 Richard, the Marquess of Wellesley set out the case for a college for the East India Company. 'To dispense justice to millions of people of various languages, man-ners, usages and religions', he wrote, 'no qualifications more various or comprehensive can be imagined, than those which are required of every British subject who enters the seat of judgement within the limits of the Company's empire in India'. Wellesley's pro-posal for an East India College in Calcutta was thought too difficult, and the existing universities in Britain did not address the need, so the Company set up its own college at Haileybury in Hertford, with two cohorts of 40 students studying over two years from the ages of 16 to 18 years. The company subsidised the college by around £10,000 a year though students paid to be qualified as writers.[11]

The young men of the Hertfordshire East India College were high-spirited and after they rioted in town there were calls to close it down. In their college magazine, the *Hertfordian,* the boys complained about learning Persian grammar, in verse:

These curs'd terms of grammar fall on us like rain,
I confess they confoundedly puzzle my brain;
Whilst all men declare 'tis a horrible tool,
Of the Mazi Kharib, and the ya-i-majhoul.

(in the last line the Mazi Kharib are 'ancient ruins' and the 'ya-i-majhoul' is the silent 'y')[12]

Other verses mocked the East India College curriculum

... the stern Koran cramm'd with pious rules,
(Read by few else than prizemen – or by fools)
Ope's its dry page: where Rustam and his horse,
(A better never trod Newmarket course)
Ferdousi's lines in orient grandeur show,
And Sadi says, king morals are so so.

This rhymester dreamed of the day the 'term expir'd they're banished from the brain'.

In 1805, Thomas Malthus was appointed to teach history at East India College. He was known by the students as 'old Pop' (a play on his interest in population). The population question was one that had a bearing on colonialism, and clearly played on Malthus' mind. 'To exterminate the inhabitants of Asia and Africa is a thought that could not be admitted for a moment', Malthus said. However, 'to civilise and directed the industry of the various tribes of Tartars and Negroes would certainly be a work of considerable time and variable and uncertain success'.[13] A student called J. D. Inverarity kept notes of one of his lessons, which was on Adam Smith, though with the qualification, in keeping both with his own 'phsyiocratic' bias and the balance of the Indian economy, 'as to the superior importance of agriculture there is no doubt but that agriculture is the original source of all wealth'.[14]

In 1835, the economist Richard Jones took up Malthus's position as lecturer at the East India College. Jones' lectures in great part argued with the claims of his predecessor. Jones saw a greater flexibility both in agricultural outputs and in population than Malthus allowed, which made him more optimistic about avoiding famine. He also saw economic questions as more historically variable than the system-minded David Ricardo. His essay on the different kinds of rent collection promoted by the EIC was alive to the errors of imposing systems – as had happened when the Company sought to elevate the Zamindar class of tax-farmers into landowners, only to discover they enjoyed no such status in the eyes of the land-tending Ryot peasant.[15]

Other teachers at the college included Monier Monier-Williams, who went on to become chair of Sanskrit at Oxford University, Mirza Muhammed Ibrahim who spent 20 years in Britain teaching Persian at East India College before returning to tutor the future Shah, and Alexander Hamilton, who was the first head of Sanskrit after serving in the EIC Navy. From 1857, the EIC was wound up and East India College was reopened as an independent school, the Haileybury and Imperial Service College, that served to staff the Empire.

The East India College was at the forefront of the emerging 'orientalist' scholarship in Britain. The teachers and scholars who translated Asian languages and
studied the literature of the Indian sub-continent added greatly to the sum of knowledge. They are also, though, open to the objection that their interest was a part of a
programme that was self-serving. Ranajit Guha argues that 'the aim of mercantilist historiography was merely to educate the East India Company', and the interest
in land tenure in the precolonial period was intended to 'equip the Company with
a knowledge that would help it to extract the highest possible amount of revenue
from the conquered territories and use it to finance its seaborn trade'. Manan Ahmed
Asif, comparing native histories, like Firishta's, shows that Company histories liked to
paint the Hindus as indolent victims of Muslim invaders, rather than coevals in the
culture of Hindustan.[16]

Macaulay and the Civilisation of India

The outlook of the East India College was 'orientalist', meaning that they looked on
Indian civilisation like collectors of rare books and art works. The Company had been
committed to teaching its servants some vernacular Indian languages – or at least
enough to issue orders.

The relationship between the Company, India and the British Government, however, was changing. In 1813, an Act of Parliament renewed the Company charter, and at
the same time asserted British sovereignty over British India and ended the Company's
monopoly over trade in India, apart from tea and opium. The Charter Act of 1833
'effectively nationalised the East India Company and created a centralised government
of British India accountable to the British Crown', says the historian Zareer Masani.[17]
The EIC still had a Board of Directors, but its governmental powers in India had been
overtaken by the Board of Control set up in 1784 - though the rents it extracted still went
to private investors even after 1833.

In 1833, speaking on the renewal of the Charter, Thomas Babington Macaulay laid
out a very different idea of the British mission in India than the orientalist approach
of the East India College. To Macaulay the early Company years were 'chequered
with guilt and shame' because of the 'rapacious, imperious and corrupt' English merchants.[18] The new approach Macaulay outlined was very different. The liberal and
middle-class Macaulay was the son of the anti-slavery campaigner Zachary Macaulay
and was raised in the Anglican evangelical 'Clapham Sect'. He told parliament that: 'It
is scarcely possible to calculate the benefits which we might derive from the diffusion of
European civilisation among the vast population of the East.' As Macaulay saw it the
new Government in India would be 'an enlightened and paternal despotism'. It was
duty bound to rid India of 'bloody and degrading superstitions' and save 'a race debased
by three thousand years of despotism and priest craft'.

At some future date it might be that:

> The public mind of India may expand under our system till it has outgrown that system; that
> by good government we may educate our subjects into a capacity for better government;

that, having been instructed in European knowledge, they may, in some future age, demand European institutions.

Until that time, thought Macaulay, it was the job of the British administration to rule without selfish purpose, but for the good of the Indians themselves.[19]

After this speech Macaulay set out a Minute on Education in India, in which he argued forcefully to abandon vernacular languages in administration and teaching. Instead, he said that government should be conducted in English. In a letter to his father Macaulay said that 'if our plans for education are followed up, there will not be a single idolator among the respectable classes in Bengal thirty years hence'.[20]

Macaulay's idea of government in India was that it was a calling that Europeans should take on to raise up what he saw as a people degraded by superstition.

Anti-Slavery Diplomacy and the Africa Squadron

Returning from the Vienna Congress which ended the war, Wellington was surprised to face criticism at home for not having made agreements to end the slave trade part of the treaty. The veteran anti-slavery campaigner Thomas Clarkson went to the Congress of Aix-la-Chapelle in 1818 'and he brought before the Plenipotentiaries at that Congress a memorial urging the adoption of a measure for bringing about a reciprocal right of search on the part of the Powers', and also 'that the Slave-trade should be recognised as piracy by International Law'. At Verona in 1822, the Duke of Wellington got 'an emphatic declaration against the slave-trade'. Lord Castlereagh, thought of as a tyrant at home, enforced the anti-slavery system abroad as Foreign Secretary and Britain insisted on anti-slave trade clauses in treaties with other nations. Castlereagh started the publication of treaties and news about the suppression of the slave trade in the Blue Books. By 1842, slave trade diplomacy had become 'a new and vast branch of international relations', said Foreign Secretary Lord Aberdeen.[21]

Britain had effectively created an international system for the suppression of the slave trade, in which the British Navy was the leading actor. To enforce the system the Government founded the African Squadron of the Royal Navy, from the point that the Act abolishing the slave trade was passed in 1808, but then reorganised with more ships in 1811. The squadron had, by 1867, 25 ships with 2459 men. When slave ships were seized their fate was decided first in Admiralty Courts, but then later in 'Mixed Commission' courts. In these British judges sat alongside judges from Spain, Portugal and the Netherlands. Allies were made to take part in Mixed Commission courts in West Africa, Havana, Brazil and the Cape to enforce the ban on the slave trade.

One of the earliest encounters was in 1809, Commodore Columbine sent 120 seamen under Captain Parker to seize the French base at St Louis on the Senegal River on 13 July. After that there were regular clashes with slavers, as when Lieutenant Robert Hagan on the Thistle attacked slaver Thomas Curtis's forts and barracoon on the Rio Pongas in May 1820. The following March Hagan seized Captain Mateo Sanchez' slave ship Anna Maria, in the Bonny River, releasing 500. In 1826, Captain William Purchas in the Esk seized the Brazilian ship the Netuno in March off Benin. That

September, Lieutenant William Tucker challenged the slave ship Principe de Guinea out of Whydah, eventually boarding her and freeing 587. His ship was the Hope, which had been a Dutch slaver, the Hoop, until she was auctioned off in Freetown and was bought by Commodore Charles Bullen. In 1831, Sir William Ramsey on the Black Joke set off after the Spanish brig Marinerito coming out of the Calabar River. After fierce fighting Ramsey prevailed. The Black Joke went on to seize 21 ships and free 7,000 slaves. But by 1832, the ship was so rotten that she was condemned by the Admiralty and broken up.[22] Between 1819 and 1846, 498 ships were seized of which 473 were condemned, and 63,436 slaves freed.[23]

A curious outcome of Britain's 'anti-slavery' policy was the founding of the settlement of Sierra Leone in West Africa in 1792, as a refuge for those formerly enslaved Africans who had fought for Britain in the war against America. Africans seized from slavers by the West Africa Squadron were disembarked in Sierra Leone, which was made a colony in 1808, or later in the British West Indies, or sometimes Canada. Often the African Squadron went inland to challenge slavers and their native allies. In November of 1840 Joseph Denman led an attack on King Siaca's stockades on the Gallinas, forcing him to sign a treaty abolishing slavery. Then in 1851 Commodore Bruce led two successive attacks on Lagos's usurping King Kosoko, and restored Akintoye to the throne, with a new anti-slavery treaty. There were wars with the Ashante, too, from 1823 to 1831, and again in 1863–64. And though there were some ambitions to build Christian colonies for the most part Britain's elite wanted no great responsibility for inland Africa. An 1865 Commons Select Committee said that 'all further extension of territory, or assumption of government, or new treaties offering any protection to native tribes would be inexpedient', and looked forward to 'ultimate withdrawal from all, except, probably, Sierra Leone'.[24]

Britain's overseas rivals understood that by putting itself at the head of the struggle against the slave trade, Britain had also made itself policeman of the world's oceans as well as keeper of the world's conscience. Sometimes the suppression of slavery was less urgent than official statements claimed, and exceptions made for pragmatic reasons. Britain put anti-slavery clauses into its treaty with Brazil in 1826 and even pressed Brazilians to participate in the Mixed Commission Courts. But Brazil remained an ally even though slavery was not abolished there until 1888. Britain's alliance with the Sultan of Zanzibar was made in 1856, but for the next fifteen years it was accepted that slavery would not be disturbed there.[25]

Though the British slave trade to the West Indies was abolished in 1807 slavery itself was not abolished in the British colonies. Without new imports the slave population of the West Indies fell from three quarters to two thirds of a million enslaved. The 'West India interest' fought off attempts to abolish slavery through its influence in parliament. After the Reform Act of 1832 the parliamentary arithmetic shifted, and the anti-slavery campaigners forced through abolition in 1833. The anti-slavery case was helped by the economic decline of the sugar plantations which was already clear at the beginning of the century. Cheaper sugar from Brazil and Cuba brought prices down, while underinvested plantations yielded smaller crops, becoming heavily indebted. Planters were beset, too, by slave risings, of which the most challenging was the 'Baptist war' of 1830.

Where West India sugar profits had poured into Britain at the end of the eighteenth century, by the beginning of the nineteenth planters were often appealing to Parliament for relief.[26]

The Government took the decision to abolish slavery with compensation to the slave owners, to the sum of £20 million, about a fifth of the entire country's output. (Slave-owner and statistician James McQueen claimed the actual value of the enslaved as £45,281,738.[27]) Even at the time people spoke out against compensation, but the leader of the Parliamentary anti-slavery movement Thomas Fowell Buxton argued that all of the country was responsible for slavery not just the slave owners and that the money was the price of freedom for the slaves. The practical meaning was that abolition without compensation was seen as 'expropriation of property' which was as great an anathema to the Reform Parliament of 1832 as it had been to previous governments. Once the compensation was paid, the money passed from the hands of the West India planters straight back into the hands of their creditors, who were mostly in Britain. Looked at cynically, the compensation was a bailout to secure loans extended to the planters.[28]

The slaves were still not free, though. Under the 1833 Slavery Abolition Act they were kept under a system of 'apprenticeship', a kind of officially sanctioned and regulated forced labour. No longer 'property' they were still made to work for their former owners. 'Apprenticeship' was supposed to be a temporary, intermediate measure, ending after six years. But as it turned out opposition in the West Indies and from a revived anti-slavery movement in Britain brought it to an abrupt close in 1838. In their lobbying the West India interest had always claimed that abolition would impoverish the islands. It turned out that abolishing slavery was a great advantage for Britain. Lord Palmerston reflected 'from the time when this country first began to abolish the slave-trade, followed up by abolishing slavery within the dominions of the Crown... from that period this country has prospered in a degree to which it had never experienced before'. The same was not true of the West Indies. No one could regret the end of slavery, but the conditions under which it happened left the former slaves impoverished squatters on the old plantations. What had been the greatest source of wealth in the Old Colonial system was in the era of free trade one of the very poorest parts of the Empire. Many of the anti-slavery campaigners tried to ameliorate the former slaves' lives but the investors abandoned the islands.[29]

Protecting the Aborigines

The humanitarian lobby that campaigned against slavery had other things to do after abolition. An alliance of Quakers, Baptists and other non-conformists were very active drawing attention to the humanitarian disaster in the white settlements. In the House of Commons, in 1834, Thomas Fowell Buxton called for a select committee to be set up to ask 'what measures ought to be adopted with regard to the native inhabitants of countries where British settlements are made, and to the neighbouring tribes' to protect them 'and to lead them to the peaceful and voluntary reception of the Christian religion'? In those days the word 'Aborigine' was used for all native people not just those of Australia, and so the select committee was commonly known as the 'Committee on Aborigines'.

Among the members of the select committee were the Undersecretary for War and the Colonies, Sir George Grey, the soap-heir Benjamin Hawes, anti-slavery campaigner Lord Charles Lushington and the young W. E. Gladstone. Like the anti-slavery campaign before it, much of the dynamic inside the House of Commons was driven by a campaign outside of it. One man in particular, Thomas Hodgkin (1798–1866) did much of the work to prepare the committee, finding witnesses and gathering evidence to put before the committee – work that he was to continue as the driving force behind the Aborigines' Protection Society, which lobbied over the issue over the next 73 years.[30]

Three events around the world were at the forefront of the Select Committee's deliberations. The first was the dramatic collapse in the population of Tasmanian aborigines. The Committee noted Bishop Broughton's view that 'within a very limited period, a few years, those who are most in contact with Europeans will be utterly extinct – I will not say exterminated – but they will be extinct'. The Aborigines' Protection Society warned of the 'generally fatal results of the present system of intercourse with' native people: 'this contact has almost invariably resulted in injury to, and often extermination of, the Aborigines'.

The second event was the collapse in the livelihoods of the Native Americans in the Hudson's Bay Company territory (Canada today). The Committee heard evidence from the surgeon Richard King who had taken part in an expedition to the Arctic that 'even peaceable trade with the Indians, by encouraging in them improvident habits which frequently bring large parties of them to utter destruction and to death by starvation'.[31]

Finally, two witnesses from Britain's colony in South Africa, John Phillip of the London Missionary Society, and Andries Stockenstrom painted a damning picture of Sir Benjamin D'Urban's administration there. Phillip pointed to the persecution of the Africans. The Report of the Select Committee on Aborigines condemned the course 'of petty encroachments and acts of injustice committed by the new settlers' that is 'not sufficiently checked in the outset by the leaders of the colonists'. The purchase of land from natives was 'illegal and void' and, they ordered 'new Territories not to be acquired without the Sanction of the Home Government'. The Report emphasised:

> The protection of the Aborigines should be considered as a duty peculiarly belonging and appropriate to the Executive Government, as administered either in this country or by the Governors of the respective colonies. This is not a trust which could conveniently be confined to the local legislatures.[32]

Around the time of the Committee the Secretary of State for the Colonies Lord Glenelg sent a searing memo to Sir Benjamin D'Urban rejecting his report of native attacks on settlers pointing out that they had only been retaliating. Dramatically Glenelg ordered the lands known as Queen Adelaide's Province (modern-day Transkei) be returned to its native inhabitants – the kind of decolonisation that would not be seen again until more than a century later.

Glenelg also put clauses in the charters of the Australian colonies ordering that they should appoint officers as 'Protectors of Aborigines'. The first Aborigines' Protector was

George Robinson who had some success bringing Tasmanian Aborigines in from the countryside. Robinson gathered the remaining Tasmanians in a compound in nearby Flinders Island but torn from their own lands the Aborigines were demoralised and many died while no children were raised. Robinson moved the handful of survivors to the mainland where he had been put in charge of a new 'Protectorate' at Port Phillip (modern-day Melbourne).[33] The Port Phillip Protectorate and the others that followed in it Western Australia, New South Wales and the Northern Territories were hampered by confused ambitions and resentment from settlers. At their best the protectorates provided a temporary shield from the incursions of the settlers, at their worst they were oppressive reservations where native people were subject to patrician and violent oppression.

In New Brunswick native Mi'kmaq Indians were pushed onto the Lennox Island, just by the larger Prince Edward Island in the Gulf of St Lawrence. The land was reserved for them by its titleholder James Montgomery and then later bought for them by the Aborigines' Protection Society. Over time the authorities saw the reserved land as the only place Indians should be allowed to settle, and while it was enough land for them to live on, it was not enough to keep them by hunting or farming and the population fell.[34]

The policy of 'Protection' never gave lasting security to nativepeople. Practically speaking it was mostly a strategy for setting limits on white colonists – sympathy for natives in Britain being in large part an upside-down way of disliking settlers. The British government tended to recognise native land claims where the settlers were getting too big for their boots. Reserved territories set limits to settler expansion. In some cases, the British went so far as to arm natives to protect their land claims against settlers who were at odds with London. Britain backed the Sotho against the Boers from 1843 and in 1879, the British backed Zulu territorial claims to stop the Boer republics from establishing a seaport to the north east of the Cape Colony So, too, was it the Tswana's 'loyalty to Great Britain which has rendered them hateful to their restless neighbours'.[35]

The Civilising Mission in Retrospect

The civilising mission seen from today looks patrician and oppressive, but it did spring from a humanistic intent. The missionaries' conviction was that natives were also the children of God. Their determination to see the common humanity of the natives gave rise to real advances, like the abolition of slavery and the protection of aboriginal people. Alongside that theological view was the incorporation of more and more of the world's people into a global market, under the government of the British Empire. The missionaries were among the first Europeans to see native people as moral agents in their own right. As such they were potential subjects to laws, contracts of labour and even rights.

The civilising mission became something more like an ideology of control in the era of the New Imperialism in the later nineteenth century. The later imperialists trumpeted the claim to be civilising the colonies at the point that their claim looked less persuasive. The anti-slavery campaign had European traders in its sights in the first part of the century. Towards the end of the century the anti-slavery campaign fixed on the African slave traders, with dramatic results. So, too, would the policy of protecting the Aborigines become more like the management of native people and native labour regimes, as we shall see.

Chapter Sixteen

INDIA – FROM COMPANY TO RAJ

The idea that the era of 'free trade' was at odds with territorial expansion has little meaning outside the Western hemisphere. The change in the British Empire from the end of the eighteenth century was a 'pivot to the East' as much as it was about a change in trade policy. While Britain lost territory in the Americas, East of the Ottoman Empire it expanded greatly. As well as the acquisition of extensive Australian territories between 1825 and 1859, and New Zealand under the Treaty of Waitangi in 1844, British territories grew at an astonishing rate in Asia, outwards from the EIC's outposts in India.

In 1758, after the Battle of Plassey the Governor of Bengal commanded a territory of 26,000,000 people.[1] In 1783, Edmund Burke reckoned that the Company commanded 30 million people overall. By 1836, after major conflicts with the Maratha Federation in the West and the Mysore Kingdom in the South, there were reportedly 83 million living directly under British rule of whom 57.5 million were living under the Bengal Presidency of the EIC, in a territory of 328,000 square miles. The Bengal Presidency was the territory that Clive had taken from the Nawab Siraj ud-Daula, with some additions. As well as the Bengal Presidency, there were the territories of the Madras and Bombay Presidencies, which swelled the EIC holdings in 1836 to 533,000 square miles.

Beyond those territories directly controlled by the EIC, in 1836 there were 15,000,000 people living under British allies and tributaries, on 550,000 square miles. The main 'allies and tributaries' were The Nizam, governing 10,000,000 in a territory of 96,000 square miles; the Najpoor Raja, the King of Awadh, the Mysore Raja and the Satara Raja. That made British India and its tributaries a total of 123,000,000 people on territories covering 1,103,000 square miles.

Beyond British influence were around a million people living on 10,000 square miles under the Nepal Raja, the Lahore Raja (Runjeet Singh) the Amirs of Scinde, the dominions of Sindia and the Kabul sovereign, east of the Indus.[2]

After 1836, the EIC took many other large and populous territories, including most dramatically, the Punjab, after the second war with the Sikh Kingdom in 1849, and Awadh (Oude to the British) in 1856.

The chronological list of British territorial gains in India.

	Year	Districts	Taken from
1	1640	Site of Fort St George, Madras	Rajas of Beejanuggur
2	1650	Site of factories at Hooghly	Shah Jahan
3	1661	Bombay	Portuguese
4	1700	Site of Fort William in Bengal	Viceroy Azim, grandson of Aurangzeb
5	1756	Bankote, &c	The Peshwa

Under the Government of Lord Clive

6	1757	Twenty-four Pergunnahs	Nawab of Bengal
7	1759	Masulipatam, &c	The Nizam
8	1760	Burdwan, Midnapore and Chittagong	Nawab of Bengal
9	1765	Bengal, Bahar &c	Shah Alam
10	1765	Chingleput, Company's Jaghire, near Madras	Nawab of Arcot
11	1766	Northern Circars	The Nizam

Under Warren Hastings

12	1775	Zemindary of Benares	Vizier of Oude
13	1775	Island of Salsette	The Mahrattas
14	1778	Nagore	Rajah of Tanjore
15	1778	Guntoor Circar	The Nizam
16	1786	Pulo Pinang (Prince of Wales' Island)	King of Queda

Under Lord Cornwallis

17	1792	Malabr, Dindigul, Salem, Baramahl &c	Tippoo Sultan of Mysore

Under Marquess Wellesley

18	1799	Coimbatore, Canara, Wynaad, &c	Sultan of Mysore
19	1800	Districts acquired by the Nizam in 1792 and 1799 from Sultan of Mysore	The Nizam
21	1802	The Carnatic	Nawab of the Carnatic
22	1802	Gorruckpore, Lower Doab, Bareilly	Vizier of Oude
23	1802	Districts in Bundeleund	The Peshwa
24	1805	Districts in Gujerat	The Guicowar (Gaikwad)

Under the Marquess of Hastings

25	1815	Kumaon and part of the Terraje	Rajah of Nepal
26	1817	Saugur and Huttah Darwar &c.	The Peshwa
27	1817	Ahmedabad Farm	The Guicowar (Gaikwad)
28	1818	Candeish (Khandesh)	Holkar
29	1818	Ajmeer	Dowlut Rao Scindia
30	1818	Poonah, Concan, Southern Maharatta Country &c	The Peshwa
31	1820	Lands in Southern Concan	Rajah of Sawant Warree

Under Lord Amherst

32	1826	Assam, Arracan and Tenasserim Provinces	Burmese

Under Lord William Bentinck

33	1830	South Cachar	Lapsed on the death of Raja
34	1834	Koorg	Conquered from the Raja
35	1835	Jynteea, in Assam	Conquered from the Raja

	Year	Districts	Taken from
36	1836	Loodiana and Ferozepore	Lapsed in default of heirs
37	1840	Jaloun, in Budelcund	Lapsed in default of heir
38	1841	Kurnoul, on the southern bank of the Kistna	Taken from the Nawab

Under Lord Ellenborough

	Year	Districts	Taken from
39	1843	Sindh	Conquered from the Ameers

Under Lord Hardinge

	Year	Districts	Taken from
40	1845	Danish settlements of Serampore and Tranquebar	Purchased from Danes
41	1846	Julinder Dooab	Conquered in the first Sikh War

Under the Marquis Dalhousie

	Year	Districts	Taken from
42	1848	Sattara	Lapsed in default of heirs
43	1849	The Punjab	Annexed at the close of the second Sikh War
44	1849	Jeitpore, in Bundelcund	Lapsed in default of heirs
45	1850	Sumbhulpore (south-west frontier of Bengal)	Lapsed in default of heirs
46	1852	Pegu and Martaban	Annexed at the close of the second Burmese War
47	1852	Khyber in Sindh	Resumed from Ali Morad
48	1853	North Cachar	Resumed from the rebel Toola Ram Senna-puttee
49	1853	Odeipore (south-west frontier of Bengal)	Lapsed in default of heirs
50	1853	Berar or Nagpore	Lapsed on death of Raja in default of heirs
51	1854	Jhansi, in Bundelcund	Lapsed in default of heirs
52	1855	Boodawul, in Kandeish	Lapsed in default of heirs

Sources: George Trevor, *India: An Historical Sketch*, 1858, Appendix and *Penny Cyclopaedia of the Society for the Diffusion of Useful Knowledge*, Volumes 9–10, 1837, p 250.

British India in Indian History

The EIC became a powerful player in the history of India. There is no way of knowing whether India would have followed a path of development like Europe's if it had not been for the influence of the Company. What can be said is that it could not do so because of the way that the Company impacted upon India.

From early on India's rulers lost out in the sea borne trade that was so decisive in the development of European economies. First Arab, then Portuguese, and ultimately the English ships of the EIC dominated the overseas trade. Portuguese and English trading ports took the lion's share of India's trade with the world. In Europe those trading ports had been the nursery of capitalism. But in the case of India, they fell under the command of a foreign power: the EIC. (Though the Gujarati traders' Bill of Exchange, or Humdi, was still honoured by communities around the Arabian sea and down the east coast of Africa.)

With the command of the Bengal territory in Company hands from 1765 and then the territorial expansion of over much of India in the later eighteenth and the nineteenth century the history of India and the history of British India were no longer separable. The British governed in India though the country remained overwhelmingly Indian.

In what were to become the Dominions of Australia, New Zealand and Canada the settled, white population became the majority. In India white settlers were relatively few, a few hundred among millions, according to the historian and British India administrator Thomas Babington Macaulay. In 1836, estimated James McQueen, there were around 40,000 whites settled in India. Most of those were officials of the EIC, or they were European soldiers in the EIC army, some were independent traders and Christian clergymen and missionaries, and their families.

The ascendance of the British EIC to become the pre-eminent power in the sub-continent is not easy to explain. The precise history of the conflicts, alliances, treaties and concessions suggests that the Company's dynamic was at least in part driven by the decline in the authority of the Mughal Emperor and the emergence of regional rivals, principally the Maratha Federation in the West, but also the Sikh Kingdom in the north-west, and scores of other Nawabs and Rajas who went from being viceroys of the Mughal Empire to becoming independent princes.

In this collapse and conflict, the strategic intervention of the EIC was to ally itself to emergent rivals, or to sponsor weaker claimants to enhance their advantage. In most of these contests the EIC forces were less numerous. And in each the different rivals for power had their own ambitions only seeing the Company's role as secondary. Anievas and Nişancıoğlu make the argument that, 'in this rather perverse sense, "Eastern agency" was then a significant part in how the British succeeded in their colonisation efforts'.[3] Another way of looking at the question would be to say that the EIC, and the British Raj after it, summed up Indian society as it was at that time. The unity of the nation was not yet a reality and imposed from outside by the British conquerors. The piecemeal and fragmented state of the Company and its presidencies mirrored the state of India itself.

For many millions of people living in the Indian sub-continent British-India was – at first – as distant as Mughal India was before it. It is not that Company rule had no impact at all upon their lives, but that the web of social relations that they were in were almost wholly Indian. There was a profound sense in which Indians living under Company rule were woven into the British Empire. A share of the Diwani tribute that they gave up to the Company, after administrative expenses were met in India, went back to Britain where it was re-described as Company 'profits' from which a dividend was paid to investors.

'India', thought of as a whole, was a vast region of 123 million people who individually were of modest means but collectively yielded up large surpluses to those who governed them, whether Mughal or Briton. India under Company rule might be thought of as part of a much larger division of labour, with the British Empire, but for the most part Indians collaborated with other Indians, whereby they were fed and clothed, giving up relatively meagre amounts to the tax collectors of the EIC, and participating only marginally in the global economy that British merchants controlled.

The Company employees and the other Europeans living in India undoubtedly enjoyed great luxury relative to Indians, and in relation to most Britons. Even quite a lowly soldier or writer could afford a house and servants. Thomas Malthus saw that the 'young men who go out as writers to India have the power of borrowing to almost any extent' and find themselves 'members of a privileged caste'. Malthus worried about the 'almost arbitrary control which they exercise over the persons they chiefly see about them', the 'temptations' and the 'tendency to foster their caprices'.[4]

The most important institution of the EIC's government in India in the nineteenth century was its army. Clive first recruited Indian soldiers known as sepoys (from the Persian sipahi) into battalions in 1757. By comparison with any army in Europe the EIC army was vast – bigger than the British army by 1823. As a share of the population, on the other hand, it was tiny – perhaps two in every thousand Indians.

EIC army

	Bengal	Madras	Bombay	Total
1763	6,680	9,000	2,550	18,230
1782	52,400	48,000	15,000	115,400
1805	64,000	64,000	26,500	154,500
1823	129,473	71,423	36,475	237,371

Source: Ian Barrow, East India Company, 2017

Overwhelmingly it was – until after 1857 – Indian. The Company recruited Indians in part because the cost of recruiting and keeping Europeans in India would have been too much, whereas many former Mughal warriors were at a loose end. The army also made a strong bond between the Company and Indians. Soldiers in Mughal India were of high status or caste if they were Hindu. The EIC army carried on that tradition, recruiting from higher Brahmin and Kshatriya castes. Sepoys fought in the Company's wars against Mysore, the Marathas, in Burma, in China and against the Sikhs.[5] From the perspective of today's Indian nationhood it does not make sense that Indians should fight Indians. But Indian nationhood did not exist in the early nineteenth century. Fighting Sikhs or Marathas for a local Nawab or for the Mughal emperor was not much different from fighting them for Britain in the eyes of the sepoys.

The territorial expansion of the Company Presidencies in the first half of the nineteenth century did for given districts and territories at specific turning points, have a marked and dramatic impact. The battles that took place were many though the armies engaged in them were for the most part numbered in the thousands so that much of day-to-day life went on regardless of the question of who was the Governor, Rajah or Nawab. At times Company historians exaggerated what they saw as the timeless endurance of the Indian village, but it was true that most Indians lived by farming small plots and were tied into social orders that were often very distant from the ruling authority. The history of Company rule and its expansion read very much like the conflicts in dynastic Europe. In the first instance the transfer from a Mughal or a Maratha overlord to a Company might have little impact. Over the transition from Company rule to the British Raj that would begin to change.

The era of Company rule, and the transition to the British Government in 1858 would in time lead to a great transformation in social relations in the sub-continent. The laws of land ownership and the social power of elites would change pointedly. The disintegration of the Mughal Empire opened the way for an economic integration of British India, with a significant communications revolution. The political integration of India under British rule would be profound, though always with significant limits.

The Development of the East India Company

The EIC was still in name the same organisation that had set up its trading factories in Fort St George, Bombay, and Fort William in the seventeenth century. By the nineteenth century it was a very different beast.

The arguments in England about Company Monopolies had a big impact on the direction of the EIC. The EIC persisted as a governing power until 1858, long after the other important Companies had gone, but it was substantially changed by Parliament's decisions.

A succession of Acts in 1773, 1784, 1786, 1793, 1813 and 1833 changed the Company. In the Regulating Act of 1773 Parliament asserted that the 'acquisition of sovereignty by the subjects of the Crown is on behalf of the Crown and not in its own right'. The following year Pitt's India Act put the Company under a Board of Control made up of the Chancellor, the Secretary of State and four nominees of the King. The Act of 1786 enlarged the powers of the governor-general over the council in Calcutta. The 1813 Charter Act asserted authority over Indian territories held by the Company and removed the Company's monopoly over trade with the exception of the trade in tea and opium.

The key change in the Company's function came with Clive's victory at Plassey in 1757 and over Mir Kasim in 1764. From that point Clive could say to the Company Court in London that 'the Company's government in Bengal' was 'a military government as well as a civil one'. As Spencer Leonard explains 'neither bullion nor any other commodity was, after 1757, sent in large quantities from England. Instead, the Company's investment was supplied from the tax revenues paid by the peasants of districts ceded to the Company'.[6]

With the change of Company rule in Bengal from a trading to a taxing regime London and Manchester merchants raised protests against its monopoly on trade. Reports like William Bolts' *Consideration on India Affairs* (1772) galvanised demands for India under the Company to be opened up to imports from British merchants and manufacturers. Adam Smith's criticisms of the confused role of the EIC – as both government and merchant – were part of the demand to open up Company-governed India to British exports, that made the case for the end of the Company monopoly in the 1813 Act. The impact was marked, as the Company's exports to India (but not its exports from India) dwindled to a small share of the total. The Company by this time was not a trading company primarily but an arm's length corporation for the British Government of India.

Value of Exports from the UK to all places east of the Cape of Good Hope, excluding China, selected years, Sterling.

	By the EIC	By private traders	Total
1815	996,248	1,569,132	2,565,761
1820	971,096	2,066,815	3,037,911
1825	598,553	2,574,660	3,173,213
1830	195,394	3,891,917	4,087,311

Penny Cyclopaedia of the Society for the Diffusion of Useful Knowledge, Vol 9–10, p 250.

The Company's Wars against Its Indian Rivals

Clive's victory in Bengal and the consolidation of the Bengal Presidency were decisive gains for British Rule, but Britain still faced significant rivals for dominance in India. The most important were the Maratha Federation in the West and the Mysore Kingdom in the South.

The Mysore Kingdom was governed by a Muslim general who had risen to power, Haider Ali. With his son Tipu Sultan Haider Ali built up a remarkable state that challenged the Maratha Federation and also the British in the Carnatic and even in their base at Madras. The Madras Presidency's alliance with the Nizam of Hyderabad to the north of Mysore threatened Mysore, and to meet that Haider Ali challenged the Company in the Carnatic. In 1769, Tipu Sultan attacked as far as the suburbs of Madras, and the Company had to sue for peace. Mysore's authority grew pressing on the Maratha Kingdom to the West. In 1780, Haider Ali again challenged Britain in the Carnatic and that September Tipu Sultan wiped out an EIC army of 4000, taking Lieutenant Colonel William Baille and other officers' prisoner. Haider Ali took Arcot, the seat of the Nawab of the Carnatic, marking his ascendancy. The Madras Presidency, which had taken on Haider Ali was relieved by troops from the EIC in Bengal, and the war continued inconclusively for three years. It took two more wars to dislodge Mysore, governed by Tipu Sultan after Haider Ali's death in 1782. The third Mysore war fought by Cornwallis ended with Tipu defeated but still in power. Then, in 1799, Governor-general Richard Wellesley launched a renewed attack – on the pretext that Tipu was allied with Napoleonic France and therefore a strategic threat – under the command of his brother, Arthur. Wellesley's forces were hit with Tipu's iron-cased rockets (samples of were sent back to the Royal Armouries where they were reworked as Congreve rockets, and later used to great effect against the United States in the 1812 war). But the Company army prevailed, with thousands killed, including Tipu, and the sack of the Mysore capital Seringapatam. After the victory, the Nawab at Arcot surrendered the Carnatic, and the Nawab of Hyderabad gave up other territories to Wellesley who also took territories from Mysore. France's Governor Dupleix had already shown how a well-drilled infantry combined with a mobile artillery gave European troops the advantage in the 1740s, and in 1760 Sir Eyre Coote brought the two-deep formation known as the 'thin red line' to India.[7]

The conflict with Mysore forced the Company into alliances with the Marathas who were also enemies of Haider Ali. The Marathas Federation was made up of many different ruling families, the Holkars of Indore, the Scindias of Gwalior, the Gaikwads of Baroda and the Bhonsles of Nagpur. All recognised the peshwa in Pune as a titular leader, while exercising considerable power on their own accounts. The Marathas united with the Mughal emperor in a defence of Delhi against the Afghan invasion led by Abdali (Ahmed Shah Durrani, 1722–72) but were defeated at Panipat in 1761. Britain played no part in the conflict though the changing balance of power opened up new possibilities. Afterwards the Emperor was little more than a dependent of the Nawab of Awadh. The Peshwa at Pune was significantly weakened as power unifying the Marathas.[8]

In 1775, the Bombay Presidency made an alliance with Raghunath Rao, a rival for the Peshwa at Pune hoping to get the concession of the island of Salsette across from Company Fort. The Council at Calcutta stopped a joint army of Company troops and supporters of Rao invading Gujarat. In 1778 the Company forces in Bombay defended Rao against a rival Maratha attack on Pune but were defeated. Heavily outnumbered they had to surrender.[9] In Pune, Nana Phadnavis rallied a new Maratha alliance that alarmed the Company, though they did manage to pull the Gaikwad in Gujerat into an alliance. When Phadnavis died in 1800 the British again backed a challenger for the status of Peshwa, Baji Rao II. In the ensuing war over the succession at Pune, Arthur Wellesley – the Governor's younger brother – led forces that defeated the Scindia's army at Assaye, a conflict that the future Duke of Wellington thought tougher than facing Napoleon at Waterloo. Successive battles against the main Maratha families ended with a decisive victory in 1843, including the capture of the Mughal Emperor, who was at that time under the protection of the Marathas at Delhi.[10] Richard Wellesley, who was architect of these victories, was seen in London to have overreached and was called back. The Company extended its rule over Delhi, Agra and the Ganga Jamuna Doab in the North West. Bands of former Maratha soldiers, known as Pindaris, raided much of central India in the aftermath of these conflicts. In 1817, the British forced the remaining Maratha leaders to support them in an extensive policing operation against the Pindaris.

In 1837, Lord Auckland entertained an alliance with the Afghan leader Dost Muhammed to defeat the Sikh territory that was being built by Ranjit Singh. The fear that the Afghan Amir was in alliance with Russia persuaded them to reverse that idea and invade Kabul in alliance with the Sikh leader. It was a disaster that cost the – mostly Indian – invasion force heavily and damaged the Company army's prestige. A second invasion overthrew Dost Muhammed and replaced him with Shah Shuja in 1843. Britain exacted Sind from the Amir as the spoils of war.[11]

In the 1830s, the British avoided outright conflict with Ranjit Singh's Sikh Empire. His death, in 1843, saw conflict for leadership and an opening for the British. A war in 1846 cost the Sikh army many thousands, and at its end they were made to surrender part of the Punjab. In 1849, under the pretext of attacks on British agents in the territories surrendered in 1846, a greater force was sent against the Sikhs by Governor-General James Ramsay, the Marquess of Dalhousie. The British victory at Gujrat led to a surrender treaty signed by Maharaja Dhalip Singh giving the Company control of the whole of the former Sikh Empire – and the Koh-I-Noor diamond was sent to London where it was worn, guiltily, by Queen Victoria.[12]

British India's reach stretched into the Far East. After Burma's expansion incurred on Assam and then the Raja of Chachar in 1823 the EIC sent a force of 10,000 to Rangoon from Bengal and Madras. Alarmed, the Burmese court withdrew. Even Count Bandula's elephant cavalry was no match for the EIC's Congreve rockets and Rangoon was occupied.[13]

Governor-General Dalhousie revived Bentinck's 'doctrine of lapse' in India in 1848, taking over those states that had no hereditary heir. These seizures were controversial, since it had been common practice for Indian nobles to pass on their offices by adoption where there was no heir. In Satara and in Jhansi the Company's claim to govern by the lapse of the hereditary rulers was bitterly resented. Dalhousie's last seizure, the great territory of Awadh, on the premise that the Wajid Ali Shah's rule was anarchic and profligate was seen as high-handed and unjustified not just by his many subjects, but also by Company sepoys in the Bengal infantry (of whom many were recruited from Awadh) and also in London. Dalhousie had annexed over a quarter of a million square miles of Indian territory.[14]

British strategy was generally opportunistic and aggressive. The motivations were territorial and ideological rather than economic, though the outcomes were to enlarge the Company's tax base. The British in India would impose themselves on 'friends' as much as foes. Subsidiary Alliance, the policy where allies would be saddled with a local force of Company sepoys and British officers and be expected to pay for them was often the first step towards incorporation or at least subjugation by the Company Government.

One by one India's Shahs and Nawabs had been brought to heel – first yielding up trading rights and trading posts, then conceding tax-collecting rights, and relying on the Company's army to defend them from their rivals, until at last they were made into pensioned decorations on Company rule.

India's Farmers and the Rent

There were serious flaws in the EIC's revenue-raising. In Bengal the Company assumed that the rights of the Zamindar, or pensioned tax collectors, were analogous to English landlords and supported land rights they had never before enjoyed. The Company's invented land titles stirred opposition in Rajput and other places, 'threatening to break out into overt rebellion'.[15] This was the failure of the 'Zamindary System', or as it came to be called the Permanent Settlement of Zamindary Land'.

In the Madras Presidency, where the Zamindars were not a force, the Company adopted a Ryotwary system, brought in by Thomas Munro. The Ryots were the peasant farmers of India. As the Company took on the tax-raising duties it made each Ryot individually responsible for paying directly to the Company. The Ryotwary system was as dysfunctional as the Zemindary system in the Bengal Presidency.

The Company took on a quixotic task of mapping land and allotments – only to discover that the people had over the years misrepresented landholdings to avoid payment to Princes and could not meet the more comprehensively accounted rents. They also struggled with the Company's assumption that rents were fixed over time, where their customary system had been to underpay when crops were poor.[16]

Seeing that was a problem, the Company then tried to recreate the village community, but in doing so only broke it. British administrators were impressed – perhaps too much - by the timeless endurance of independent village life in India. Charles Metcalfe who was British Resident at the Court of Nizam told a House of Commons Select Committee that,

> the Village Communities are little Republics, having nearly everything they can want within themselves, and almost independent of any foreign relation. They seem to last where nothing else lasts. Dynasty after dynasty tumbles down; revolution succeeds to revolution; Hindu, Patan, Mogul, Mahratta, Sikh, English are all masters in turn.[17]

Arguably this was as much a justification for the EIC's indifference to social welfare as it was an objective survey.

The new village communities were to be built under a system called the Mouzawar, or sometimes, the Mahalwari system. The East India College political economy teacher Richard Jones wrote about the village headmen: 'The old village system which we had rashly destroyed, had provided checks to their power'. But 'when we were building up a new system in imitation of that old one, we ignorantly, or carelessly left out those checks'. As it turned out 'the new set of headmen turned out exceedingly avaricious and oppressive; and it was deemed necessary to relinquish the Mouzawar system'.[18]

The Company's experiments in tax gathering often laid claim to being based upon local traditions, which is why they were called Ryotwary, Zamindary and so on. For the most part they tore up well-founded relationships of authority and order, and put newly-minted, artificial ones in their stead. Lord William Bentinck, wrote in 1806, before he assumed the office of Governor-General, 'I am satisfied that the creation of zamindars is a measure incompatible with the true interest of the government and the community at large.' These new systems were more rigid and more coercive. As a rule, the taxes increased, often greatly. The intermediaries the Company appointed were not restrained by local ties and often acted without measure. Assessments that were rigidly enforced could push the peasant farmer off the land. The Zamindar of old was a hereditary title, that had claim to a rent or tax, but did not have the same right to sell off the land as the Company's invented Zamindars did. These new titles were auctioned, to raise money, and to create a class of landlords to act as a buffer between the Company and the Ryot. The same Lord Bentinck as Governor-General, wrote on 8 November 1829:

> If security was wanting against extensive popular tumult or revolution, I should say that the Permanent Settlement, though a failure in many other respects, and in most important essentials, has this great advantage at least of having created a vast body of rich landed proprietors deeply interested in the continuance of the British Dominion and having complete command over the mass of people.[19]

What they often did was to evict defaulting peasants in a way they would not have been able to before, making a growing class of landless labourers.

Famine years would lead to famers vacating their land because they could not pay the assessment and live. But even good years could be a curse. In 1847-8 in Ahmednagar 'to pay his rent' a Ryot 'had frequently to part with a bullock or other property'. That year there was a good harvest, but the demand was increased so that more grain was sold 'until the market was glutted and prices so ruinously low' that farmers had to rely on money lenders or sell-up. The strict pursuit of the assessment, with the Company looking over its shoulders at the shareholders in Britain, would over time break the bond between the Ryot and the land, as he struggled to make payment.[20]

From the north eastern corner of modern-day Uttar Pradesh to the south-west corner of Bihar the EIC installed an Opium Department to trade with China. Around a hundred separate offices were scattered over the area, with 2,500 clerks gathering the crop from farmers who were largely at their mercy. In Bihar every other household was working on opium.[21] Later in the nineteenth century the opium farmers would see their prices driven so low that they were losing money by farming, but still unable to get out. For other Indian farmers, the break-up of customary social relations, meant many more were made property-less labourers.

Railways and Other Developments

The Marquess of Dalhousie made it his mission to revolutionise communications in India. He kicked off a railway revolution across the continent that would change the country for ever. There would be 'commercial and social advantages', Dalhousie promised, 'beyond all calculation'. The *Railway Times* lauded 'the iron road that is probably destined to change the habits, manners, customs and religion of Hindoo, Parsee, and Mussulman'. The first train left from Bombay to Thane on 16 April 1853. By 1855, there were 325 kilometres of track. By 1870 that had grown to 8,000 kilometres. The following year Bombay, Allahabad, Calcutta, Delhi and Madras were all connected by rail. As well as railways, Dalhousie commanded the laying of 4,000 miles of gutta percha encased telegraph wires, so government and commerce were in communication across the whole territory.[22]

It was a good imperial myth that 'Britons built India's railways'. The truth was very different. The railways were built by Indians – around 490,000 Indians were digging and laying track in the peak year of 1861, and the numbers hovered around 250,000 to 350,000 for most of the next twenty years. In 1857 20,000 were exhausting themselves digging tunnels and viaducts to cross the Bhor Ghat ridge near Bombay. Two years later, when the contractors were late with the wages, the Bhor Ghat labourers armed themselves with sticks and attacked their European overseers. Lieutenant Corporal Crawford, investigating the incident wrote privately that it was a wonder that trouble had not broken out before: 'it is evident that the labourers have been most grossly abused in the matter of their wages'. That same year 4,000 rail workers were killed in a cholera epidemic, made worse by their onerous working conditions. In Sind 12,000 labourers digging earth works went on strike asking for higher pay, and another strike in the Trichinopoly district of Madras broke out over a contractor absconding without paying the men.[23]

The railway revolution was made possible by the breach between the labourer and the land. As these landless labourers swelled the numbers of the railway labourers, others joined the army. The Company, and then the British-India Army grew until it was larger than the British Army, at more than a quarter of a million troops. As well as fighting against successive Indian princes, the Company Army was sent to fight in the Opium Wars in China, to fight in Burma in 1852, and the British-India Army was sent to Ethiopia in 1868.

While landless Indian labourers were dragooned into the building of the railways, Indian capitalists were not invited to invest. British investors were guaranteed returns against the British Indian Government's budget, raised from the taxation of the masses. Nor were the Indians made welcome as passengers, most of them allowed only as 'Third-Class' fares. For all that the Third-Class fares raised the sums that paid off the British investors, quickly becoming the mainstay of rail company earnings – and also accelerating the migration from the villages. At the time many made the point that the rails had not really been built with the interests of India in mind, but with the twin goals of taking raw materials from the countryside and then distributing Manchester's manufactured goods. Karl Marx said at the time that this assessment of motives was true, but once built the railways would be an engine for the transformation of the country that British rule could not contain.[24]

The end of the Company monopoly did open up India for investment, though capital was scarce to finance it. From 1857, the stabilisation of the legal system helped encourage European industrialists like James Finlay in Calcutta (Jute and Cotton), Thomas Parry (sugar) and the Assam Company (tea); Indian entrepreneurs like Dinshaw Petit and Jamsetji Tata also set up cotton mills, and Ranchhodlal Chhotalal set up a textile factory with imported British looms in Ahmedabad in 1863.[25]

The Drain on India

Already in 1783 Edmund Burke called the economic relationship with the EIC a 'drain' on India, pointing to the loss of wealth the sub-continent suffered with the transfer of the Diwan. Dadabhai Naoroji, who opened a cotton trading company in Liverpool, but then in 1892 was elected Member of Parliament for Finsbury Central, wrote a book three years later analysing the economic drain. Naoroji found that the EIC's own estimates of the 'drain' were between three and six million pounds stirling a year. Naoroji, who carried his estimate on to 1872 found that it was as great as £27.4 million.[26]

There are different ways of working out the value of the 'drain'. One way is to sum up all the different income streams, like the value of the Diwan itself (pre-1857), remittances and so on. The other is to look at the difference in the balance of payment between Britain and British India. Ordinarily a positive balance of payments is an advantageous position. But quite early on EIC directors worked out that in the case of Presidency India this was a measure of the transfer of wealth from one place to another.

The nineteenth century statistician James McQueen worked out India's entire output, in 1837 as £566,000,000 (which is certainly an underestimate). Around that time, estimates Indian parliamentarian, Shashi Tharoor, the tribute India gave up to Britain was around £18,000,000. That would mean that the 'drain' was around three per cent of India's entire output. Economic historian Angus Maddison looked at the different measures of the economic drain from India to Britain. He argued that by comparison to the Mughal Empire, which taxed around 15 per cent of all output, the EIC taxation was less, allowing a greater share of the surplus to go to an emerging landlord class in India. By Maddison's more cautious calculations the export surplus in the period 1868 to 1872 was a loss of one per cent of India's net domestic product, and a gain for Britain equivalent to 1.3 per cent of its domestic product, or about £10 million in 1872.[27] In the era of classical imperialism the drain would be even deeper.

Dominance without Hegemony

The British administration of India, both as Company and later as the British India Government faced two ways. Like the orientalists of the East India College, many administrators fancied themselves to be nurturers of the authentic Indian culture. Others, like Thomas Macaulay, saw themselves as agents of the modernisation of the country, uprooting its ancient superstitions to bring a new enlightenment on Christian foundations. In truth, neither was exclusively a sound foundation for the administration of 123 million people, but both captured something of the challenge of governing a people to whom the British were alien.

In the years after Clive's tempestuous government of Bengal Warren Hastings struck a very different note. He stated that the Company Government in India would rule through Indian custom, not against it. The 1781 Act of Settlement stated that where British authorities were called upon to decide cases of inheritance, succession or contract they would decide 'in the case of the Mahommedans by the laws and usages of the Mahommedans and in the case of the Gentoos' – the collective name 'Hindu' only came into fashion later – 'by the laws and usages of the Gentoos'.

Hastings employed some 'learned professors of the Mahomedan law for translating from the Arabic into the Persian tongue, a compendium of their law, called Hedaya'. He also arranged a printing of the 'Code of the Gentoos' in 1776.[28] In the preface, translator Nathaniel Brassey Halhed praised Hastings' policy of 'a well-timed toleration in matters of religion, and an adoption of such original institutes of the country as do not immediately clash with the laws or interests of the conquerors'. This was, he thought, the best way to 'conciliate the affections of the natives', and to 'ensure stability to the acquisition'.

Under Hastings, Indian languages were taught on the understanding that the Company would rule in what they called the 'vernacular' languages, and the Government paid £20,000 a year towards native education at a Sanskrit College and a Madrassa in Calcutta. As well as paying for translations into Urdu and Sanskrit, the Company Government contributed to the upkeep of Hindu temples, as fitted their status as holders of the Mughal's Diwan. Hastings' 'orientalism' was in keeping with the earlier days of the EIC writers in India. The chief writers and administrators were collectors of art and literature in the regions where they dwelt. Many took on Indian dress and Indian consorts – wives in all but name.[29]

The goal of governing in the grain of Indian society was one that the British often claimed. In practice the act of governing dramatically changed the customs to which Hastings' administration appealed. The reinvention of Zamindars and village head-men as agents of the Company meant that they took on the name of the traditional authority, but with a very different meaning and effect. Even India's religious castes took on a different meaning when they became a part of the 'caste system' that the English incorporated into institutions like the EIC army. Indeed, some scholars have argued that Britain made the different castes into a system. U.S. academic Sanjoy Chakravorty writes:

> The 'ethnographic state' created by the British erected a knowledge structure for ruling and control in which Hinduism was the foundation and caste the reinforced steel that held it together.[30]

Certainly, the Hastings and other administrations incorporated Indian customs includ-ing caste into their system of government.

Later administrations took issue with Hastings' approach. One issue that became a scandal was the custom of Sati, in which widows were encouraged to commit suicide by burning themselves on the funeral pyres of their husbands. In the Gentoo Code that Hastings had promoted it says:

> It is proper for a Woman, after her Husband's Death, to burn herself in the Fire with his Corpse; every Woman who burns herself, shall remain in Paradise with her Husband Three Crore and Fifty Lakhs of Years, by Destiny; if she cannot burn, she must, in that Case, preserve an inviolable Chastity; if she remains always chaste, she goes to Paradise; if she does not preserve her Chastity, she goes to Hell.[31]

Sati was not universal, but it did happen. The EIC recorded 7,941 cases recorded in Bengal between 1813 and 1828.[32]

In 1829, a new Governor-General Lord William Bentinck set a very different tone from those that preceded him. Bentinck followed the 'Clapham Sect' of Evangelists in the Church of England (like William Wilberforce). Bentinck thought that the role of the British in India was to improve along Christian lines. Bentinck passed a law against the 'Thugees' – highway bandits whose threat was sensationalised in lurid stories.[33] He also brought in a law in 1829 banning Sati in Bengal. (Horace Hayman Wilson, the Sanskrit scholar, representative of the orientalists, opposed the ban, thinking it would lead to disaffection.)

While Bentinck was Governor General he was sent Thomas Babington Macaulay, who had been a Member of Parliament and advocate for widespread reform, to serve as 'Law Member' on the Governor's Council. As we have seen Macaulay favoured the teaching of, and Governing in, the English language. Though his proposal to shut down the Sanskrit College and the Madrassa in Calcutta were prevented by petitioning stu-dents, funds were redirected to the more pro-English Hindu College.

Some of Macaulay's reforms were meant to make the administration more liberal. These reforms included a Press Act affirming freedom of speech and an act taking away the exclusive right of English settlers to bring civil appeals to the Supreme Court at Calcutta. For both of these Macaulay was criticised in London. Macaulay also gave up a lot of time to re-writing the penal code, which was eventually adopted in 1860, after he had left. It was a liberal document, though not quite as liberal as the younger Macaulay would have hoped, carrying a clause against sedition that overthrew the commitment to free speech in his own Press Act of 1835.

As we have seen, the Marquess of Dalhousie's Governor General-ship between 1848 and 1856 was marked by a policy of technical modernisation and the extinction of several Royal houses under the revived 'doctrine of lapse'. The Indian Sepoy Revolution of 1857 (see Chapter Eighteen) can be seen as a reaction to the 'civilising mission' that administrators like Dalhousie, Bentinck and Macaulay represented. The revolt was severely repressed, and afterwards the Government of India became openly what it already truly was, a British Government of India, under Queen Victoria. In a Proclamation in 1858 Victoria sought to assure Indians that the 'civilising' policies would be put in abeyance, promising that her Government had no 'desire to impose Our convictions on any of Our subjects', and ordered officials to stop interfering with Indian customs and beliefs 'on the pain of Our highest displeasure'.

Secretary of State for India Sir Charles Wood outlined the problem as it looked to the British authorities after the Mutiny:

> We reduce the natural gentry and persons of hereditary influence, to raise mere money-lenders and traders. The latter cannot help us. The former are all indifferent if not against us. We must endeavour to enlist on our side the classes naturally possessing influence in the country.[34]

The clearest sign of the reversal of the 'civilising mission' policy was the incorporation of the Rajahs and Nawabs into the administration of India. Under the Crown treaties the recognition of five hundred different princes would be 'scrupulously maintained'. It was a promise not to return to the rapacious 'doctrine of lapse'. Indian ruling families were to be honoured as loyal allies, and a special knighthood, the Star of India, was created in 1861, to share the honours.[35]

Though the successive policies of the Governors-General of India do seem to show a dramatic swing from one policy of native collaboration to another of top-down 'civilising mission' and then back to native collaboration, that is not quite what happened. It would be more accurate to say that both policies were in play at the same time, with different emphases. The Bentinck and Dalhousie Governorships worked with the supposedly traditional Zamindars. Under the new dispensation of Queen Victoria modernisation measures carried on. Modernisation and traditionalism were not wholly opposed, but different sides of the problem of British administrators trying to govern a country of 123 million Indians.

Bernard Cohn, commenting on a great imperial procession of India's 'sixty-three ruling princes' and 'three hundred titular chiefs' in 1877 shows how British rule was to be preserved as a kind of Imperial pageantry: 'The British conception of India history, thereby was realised as a kind of "living museum", with the descendants of both the allies and the enemies of the English displaying the period of the conquest of India.'[36]

The historian Ranajit Guha argued that the enduring question about British rule in India was 'why two paradigms and not just one?' He meant that it was a clue to the underlying weakness of the project of colonisation that British rule was neither wholly traditional nor wholly liberal. He poses the question another way, 'why did the establishment of British paramountcy in South Asia fail to overcome the resistance of its indigenous culture to the point of being forced into a symbiosis?' Guha sees the arresting of the Bentinck/Dalhousie programme, and the reversion to cooperation with traditional Indian figures of authority as a sign that colonialism is a 'failure of the universalising project', which he argues is implicit in market expansion. Looking at the way that those civil rights promised in Macaulay's speeches were in practice withheld, Guha says that for Indians 'colonialism amounted to dominance without hegemony'. What Guha meant was that Britain neither incorporated India into its own realm of liberal society, nor did it excuse India from British authority. Britain dominated India by force but did not in the end recognise the civil rights of those subjects to which it had laid claim.[37]

Chapter Seventeen

OPIUM WARS

In the seventeenth century Britain lost out to its mercantile rival Holland in the contest for the Far East market. Having overcome Portuguese and French rivals on the Indian sub-continent the EIC's influence grew, putting them in the right place to dominate European trade with the Far East. The Company was inserting itself into a complex web of local and regional trade. After the withdrawal of the Sung dynasty fleet, Portuguese and Dutch traders had dominated the regional trade. Along the China coast trade was carried on by local merchants and junks.[1]

After France's victory over the Dutch in Europe in 1795, Britain invaded Malacca and Amboyna, and then in 1810, with the Dutch EIC out of action, Governor-General Minto invaded Java, leaving Thomas Stamford Raffles in charge of the island. When the Dutch Company returned Raffles persuaded his superiors to press to keep the small island of Singapore. Raffles' vision was that it would prosper as a free port in the middle of the Dutch monopoly, and in time it did. Britain also took Mauritius from the French in 1810, landing a party of EIC troops under Governor Sir Robert Farquhar. A less official intervention was James Brooke's commission as governor of Sarawak from the Sultan of Brunei. Brooke had been an officer in the EIC army in Bengal and was inspired by Raffles' book *The History of Java* (1817) to make his own kingdom in the East. Brooke had the occasional support of the British navy to suppress pirates and contenders to the Sultan's throne, so securing his own position as the 'white Rajah of Sarawak'. Brooke's dynasty passed down the male line until 1946.[2]

The most important trade that the EIC initiated east of India was the export of tea to Britain. Britain's appetite for tea was growing from the end of the eighteenth century. Tea consumption per capita grew from half a pound a year in 1730 to a pound a year in 1740, to one and a half pounds in the 1780 and more than two pounds in the 1790s.[3] From the 1820s a number of different temperance movements were at work persuading people to switch from beer to tea which was by then cheaper than a mug of beer. The EIC auctioned five million pounds of tea in 1760 and 30 million a year in the 1830s. The East India trade was valuable to the British Exchequer. In 1784, the duty on tea was reduced from 100 per cent to 12 and a half per cent. The reduced duty greatly increased the market, so that even at that lower rate tea tariffs raised three million a year, about a half of the cost of the British Navy.[4]

At that time, tea came exclusively from China. The problem was that there were no obvious goods that the Chinese wanted in exchange. Cotton and ironworks were plentiful in China. The EIC's tea-buying was only moving British coin to China. The answer the Company hit upon was to sell Indian-grown opium to the Chinese – in defiance of a Qing Government ban that dated back to 1720. The Company could not afford to risk its standing in China by breaking the Daoguang Emperor's rules. While many of the monopolies resisted 'interlopers' the EIC actively encouraged some off-book trading by its writers and many old Company hands took part in the so-called 'Country Trade' within the East Indies. These independents were the ones who sold the opium that they had bought in EIC auctions to Chinese addicts. The most successful of the opium companies were Magniac, Dent & Co and Jardine Matheson.[5]

The opium poppy was grown in Bihar and Uttar Pradesh, in India. At the height of the colonial opium industry almost 1.5 million small peasant households cultivated the labour-intensive poppy plant on their fields and then they delivered the harvested raw opium to the nearest government opium office.[6] The EIC factories in Patna and Benares formed the sap into balls of opium. Around a thousand people worked in an opium factory, working in shifts in the hot months of April and May, making around 20,000 balls a day. Each chest of opium contained 40 three and a half pound balls of opium. The price of Patna opium grew from 466 rupees a chest in 1788 to 4,259 rupees in 1821.[7]

The economics of the opium business can be seen in one year, 1828. British imports into China were to the value of $20.3 million, of which $4.5 million were those of the EIC (which sold half European goods, like woollens, and half eastern, like Indian cottons). The imports that did not come from the EIC, the 'Country Trade', were made up of $11.2 million worth of opium, and $2.5 million worth of raw cotton.

China's exports totalled $18.1 million in value, which is to say $2 million and more in deficit. The EIC bought $8.5 million of goods from China, almost entirely tea, which it then exported to Britain. Of the other $9.6 million exported, $6.1 million was in specie, silver, which the private traders used to buy opium from the EIC, so that they could sell it to the Chinese. Of the other goods the Chinese sold to English and other white traders, the important exports were around $1.1 million of raw silk, as well as decorative Chinese pottery and cloth (though this 'Chinoiserie' so important in the eighteenth century, fell out of favour from the 1830s and played a much smaller part in Company trade to Britain). What is clear is that the sale of opium was largely EIC opium, brought from the EIC by smaller firms. The silver they got in return was used by the Company to buy tea from China for export to Britain.[8]

English traders were watched closely by the Emperor's officials, and only allowed to set up shop in a compound on the Pearl River, a quarter of a mile square outside the city walls of Canton. Thirteen long narrow factories were shared between the English, French, Dutch and American traders. They were not allowed to interact with the Chinese population and teaching the Europeans Chinese was expressly forbidden. Traders and sailors could drink a local brew of alcohol, tobacco and arsenic in taverns in

Dog Lane, that ran behind the European compound. From Canton the traders bought tea, and some silk. They dealt with a small Chinese traders' guild, the Cohong and the Superintendent of Marine Customs, or Hwai Kwan-pu (that the English pronounced 'Hoppo').[9]

Indian opium exports to China, chests[10].

1822–23	7,773
1833–34	20,486
1838–39	40,000
1855	80,000

The official ban on opium by the Celestial Emperor was widely broken by the trading companies who docked at Lintin island (today Nei Lingding), in the Pearl River estuary that the European traders controlled, and sold their cargoes to Tanka rivermen in ships called 'scrambling dragons' or 'fast crabs' (the English translation of their Chinese names). Chinese traders were outside the law. In the 1820s, the EIC monopoly on opium was challenged by the rulers of the still-independent Princely States of India. The Company opium was branded Patna or Benares, while that grown in Western India outside of direct company control was marked 'Malwa'. The more open competition greatly increased supply and brought down prices. Exports of opium to China doubled between 1830 and 1840 from 20,000 to 40,000 chests.[11] From 1832, Jardine Matheson sent ships, first the Sylph, followed by the Jamesina, up the Chinese coast to trade directly at Quanzhou and Fuzhou (in modern day Fujian province).

As duties on imported tea were helping to keep the British Government, the opium trade was helping to pay for the EIC administration. A report from the House of Commons in 1831 stated that 'the monopoly of opium in Bengal supplies the Government with a revenue amounting to ...Rupees 84,59,425, or sterling money £981,283, per annum'.

A British official weighing opium in India.

The Select Committee's conclusion was to bless the Company's opium trade to China, remarkable as that seems today:

> In the present state of the Revenue of India it does not seem advisable to abandon so important a source of revenue as the E.I. Co.'s monopoly of opium in Bengal.[12]

Later the Company lost its monopoly over opium trading from India, but Britain continued to support the opium traders, leading to a show down with the Celestial Emperor. In China a growing anger at the opium trade led a group of officials to petition the Emperor for a strict enforcement of the ban. As well as increasing addiction, even among the civil service, the negative balance of payments was leading to a drain of silver from the country. The Governor-General of Hunan and Hubei, Lin Zexu led these and was made Imperial Commissioner on 31 December 1838 with a brief to stamp out the opium trade. Even before he took office a clamp down on sales was under way and thousands of addicts were arrested and many executed.

Lin was a lot more decisive than the English traders were used to. He blockaded their colony at Canton and refused to let them go until they handed over the opium that his informants told him they were hiding there. A panic-stricken Captain Charles Elliott surrendered 20,291 chests of opium to the value of £1,250,000, for which he was lambasted by the British Prime Minster Palmerston. The English merchants had made the condition that they should be indemnified by the British Government – conveniently getting paid for the excess stock they were finding impossible to sell under the suppression. It took almost four months to pour the seized opium into the sea.[13]

After the destruction of the opium, Imperial Commissioner Lin Zexu wrote to Queen Victoria:

> We have reflected that this noxious article is the clandestine manufacture of artful schemers under the dominion of your honourable nation. Doubtless, you, the honourable chieftainess, have not commanded the growing and sale thereof.

Lin continued:

> We have heard that in your honourable barbarian country the people are not permitted to inhale the drug. If it is admittedly so deleterious, how can to seek profit by exposing others to its malific powers be reconciled with the decrees of Heaven.

More, he advised the young Queen:

> You should immediately have the plant plucked up by the very root, cause the land there to be hoed up afresh, sow the five grams and if any man dare again to plant a single poppy, visit his crime with condign punishment.[14]

There was another flashpoint in the stand-off with the Chinese Imperial Commissioner Lin. On 7 July 1839 British and American sailors went ashore at Hong Kong and killed a local man in a brawl.

Lin Zexu.

Commissioner Lin demanded that the man, who had made his way back on board, be given up to the Chinese. Elliott refused. Lin answered by sending a force of Chinese troops into Macao. The British residents had to flee the outpost to take refuge on the anchored ships. In September, Lin himself, was greeted by the Portuguese Viceroy. Macao's Chinese inhabitants lined the streets with flowers and silk banners. They were there 'in order to manifest', said one of their number, 'their profound gratitude for the visit of his Excellency, the High Commissioner, who had saved them from a deadly vice and removed from them a dire calamity by the destruction of the Foreign Mud'.[15]

'Free Trade'

As tensions rose between English opium traders and the Chinese Government the issue was seen in London as one of 'free trade'. Britain's conversion to free trade policy was well underway, with tariffs being reduced, but was by no means complete. In particular the EIC's monopoly had been abolished in 1833 (it was their bad luck that the licence agreed for a twenty-year term came due just as the new Reform Parliament of 1832 was sitting). One of the chief lobbies against the renewal of the EIC's monopoly was the Manchester Chamber of Commerce, focal point of the Free Trade movement.

James Matheson, partner in the most important of the opium trading companies in the Far East, Jardine Matheson, was a loud champion of free trade. He had been educated in Edinburgh before his uncle bought him a free merchant's indenture from the EIC. He was an enthusiastic supporter of Adam Smith's doctrines and of free trade generally, which he argued in the journal he edited, the *Canton Register*, and in a book, *The Present Position and Future Prospects of Trade in China* (1836). In it he wrote that

> the vast and lucrative trade between Great Britain and China, with all its extensive dependencies both at home and abroad, is liable to be, and frequently has been, suspended on the most frivolous and ridiculous pretences that could be devised by the capricious and unprincipled local authorities of Canton.[16]

Jardine knew the trade intimately. In 1823, Matheson had personally sold $80,000 worth of opium in Chinzhou from the San Sebastian, and always had a hands-on approach to the trade.

Among Jardine's allies were the Chairman of the Manchester Chamber of Commerce James MacVicar. He wrote a briefing paper for the Foreign Secretary arguing that the Government should help the East India trade that was supporting a £3 million market for British goods and employment for 100,000 tons of shipping.[17]

While Jardine Matheson were arguing for a 'forward' policy of challenging the Qing Government, they were hampered by the stand-offish views of the Tory Wellington, and indeed of the Viceroy Charles Elliott, another Tory, who looked with disdain on the opium trade. With Lord Melbourne as Prime Minister and Palmerston as his Foreign Secretary the Whig merchants had a Whig Government they could depend upon. James Matheson visited England in 1835, and returned full time in 1839, where he set about lobbying Lord Palmerston, alongside James MacVicar, for decisive action against the Emperor.[18]

'Wherever the real demand for commodities imported into Asiatic countries, does not answer the supposed demand', wrote Karl Marx, looking back:

> commercial men, in their eagerness at securing a larger area of exchange, are too prone to account for their disappointment by the circumstances that artificial arrangements, invented by barbarian governments, stand in their way, and may, consequently, be cleared away by force.[19]

Palmerston wrote to the Daoguang Emperor, saying on the one hand that the Chinese had the right to punish opium smuggling, and on the other that he still expected them to compensate for the cost of the opium Lin had destroyed. Further, he demanded the cession of an island off the coast to Britain as compensation for the insult to Viceroy Elliott in forcing him out of Canton. He sent a note to Elliott ordering him to seize the island of Chusan to hold until the British Government's demands had been met.[20] The Emperor later wrote in an edict reviewing his policy:

> If I should be content with peace for the time being, and not seek for the great and the far, and let the evil of the opium go its way without any prohibition, that would mean that I am betraying my ancestors who entrusted to me the care of the empire, and that I am unable to afford due protection to the lives of my subjects. Thinking about these points, how can I rest without strictly prohibiting it?[21]

In Parliament the Conservative opposition tabled a motion of censure. In the debate Lord Aberdeen was cautious, only complaining about the lack of clarity in the Government's instructions to the Viceroy. The Government spokesmen avoided defending the trade in opium but argued that the encirclement of the traders at Canton was intolerable, and that free trade was generally good for Chinese who wanted to sell goods to British traders, and that without it many would go hungry.

Thomas Babington Macaulay, the historian, and at that time the Secretary of War, argued that the Chinese in hoping to suppress the evils of opium had committed an even greater evil, an interference in private property and free trade. Macaulay also pointed to the insult to British prestige as well as to free trade. He bade Parliament to look upon the flag as a reminder 'that they belonged to a country unaccustomed to defeat'. Macaulay's meaning was that if Britain did not defend her flag against insult, they would lose authority in the eyes of the world. A young Tory backbencher, William Ewart Gladstone (who would later become a Liberal Prime Minister) challenged the Government on the morality of this 'unjust and iniquitous war'. Gladstone accused Palmerston of hoisting the British flag 'to protect an infamous contraband traffic, and it if were never to be hoisted except as it is now hoisted on the coast of China, we should recoil from its sight in horror'. (It was often claimed of Gladstone that he was motivated by a horror of the drug to which his sister was addicted, though that seems to be a way of diminishing his arguments.) The vote of censure was defeated.[22]

At first it seemed as if the Qing Government would back down under threat, and the trade was resumed. But in September 1839, Lin ordered armed junks to refuse British ships access to Kowloon for food and water, and Elliott fired upon them. Then in June 1840, a British naval force of 16 ships of war, 4 armed steamers and 28 transports carrying 4,000 soldiers assembled of Macao. After attacking Canton the British forces brought China's envoy Ch'i-shan to the negotiating table (while Lin was dismissed to a provincial outpost). Ch'i-shan and Elliott agreed an indemnity of $6 million against Qing Government and the cession of Hong Kong.[23] As it turned out neither the British nor the Qing Government approved of the settlement. Elliott was dismissed by Palmerston for surrendering Chusan – but before the letter arrived he did, on 21 May, open fire on the Chinese navy destroying 71 junks after an attack on his ships. The new Viceroy Sir Henry Pottinger pressed the attack on China, landing a force of 4,000 British and a further 6,000 Indian troops. Over the following summer Pottinger's forces inflicted overwhelming defeats on the Emperor seizing Chapu, Shanghai and Chinkiang, and then blockading Beijing. The Imperial Court surrendered on 29 August 1842.

Under the Treaty of Nanking China agreed to pay an indemnity of $21 million to cover the cost of the war, as well as compensation for the seized opium. Canton, Amoy, Fuzhou, Ningpo and Shanghai were to be opened up to foreign trade and there would be a British consul at each Treaty Port. Further, Hong Kong was to be ceded under British sovereignty. Though Pottinger condemned smuggling, the opium trade immediately started up again.[24]

Hong Kong grew quite quickly from being an under-populated island into a thriving port and trading point. Though it was later styled a colony, it was always a concession on the model of the original European settlements at Macao and Canton. These trading ports on the seaports of the continent mirrored the way that the market economies had developed in west Europe, on the margins, connected to trade. It was because the mainland of China was relatively underdeveloped and rigidly organised that the merchants could only thrive at the ports on the coast. 'In the Qing dynasty', reflected Deng Xiaoping, 'there was no open policy to speak of'. He added, 'As a consequence the country declined into poverty and ignorance'.[25]

John Francis Davis, the British Plenipotentiary in China and Governor of Hong Kong wrote in 1843 – before his appointment – that Hong Kong was 'a real British colony ... planted on the very threshold of China',

> There they may see commerce flourishing in the absence of restrictions, property and person secure under the protection of equal laws, and, in a word, all the best fruits of science and civilisation transplanted direct from European headquarters.[26]

Britain's position in China was challenged again in 1856 when the British Consul Harry Parkes leapt to the defence of the seamen of the British-registered Arrow, who had been detained for piracy. Though the captain, an Ulsterman, was released his Chinese crew were not, and as it turned out the British registration had expired: it was indeed a pirate ship. Governor Sir John Bowring ordered the British Navy to bombard Canton.[27] The Cantonese Commissioner Ye Ming-chin ordered all-out war on the English. Many warehouses were burned down, and Europeans attacked by outraged Chinese. The Navy kept up the pressure on Canton, but Beijing did not move and the revolt failed. Lord Palmerston, who had faced down votes of censure in the Commons fought an election the following year decrying the opposition for their lack of patriotism.[28] In 1860, a Franco-British military force under Lord Elgin invaded inland as far as Beijing. China was forced to cede the Kowloon territory just north of Hong Kong.

Chinese concessions went further. In Shanghai in 1854, during the Taiping rebellion, both the rebel 'Small Swords Society' and the Imperial Army threatened the International Settlement of European traders. British Consul Rutherford Alcock mustered a militia of 400 English and Russian volunteers and got them to back down. The International Settlement's own Shanghai Corps, a force of 127 under Alcock was born, as well as a Municipal Council for the Europeans. In the Chinese struggle for power the collection of port taxes was abandoned, and when the Imperial Maritime Customs was reorganised in 1863, it was under the British Inspector-General Robert Hart.[29]

In Hong Kong the Cohong had been abolished. Over time, though, the servants of the European merchants, the 'comprador', took over more and more of the responsibilities of the trading house until they left and even displaced their old masters. The 'comprador capitalists' were later seen as beholden to Europeans, but they thrived as rivals to English merchants in Hong Kong, Shanghai and Macao. Free trade it turned out did not secure Europeans exclusive control over retail. English merchants still sold opium to the Chinese – the Shanghai Opium Combine traded until 1917. Dent and Co. went broke. Jardine Matheson lost a lot of its trading business to Chinese merchants, and its shipping empire of sail-driven clippers could not compete with the steamboats of the Peninsular and Oriental Shipping Company, once the Suez Canal reduced the journey time from London from eighty to forty days. Over time Jardine Matheson moved into banking and insurance. China's small traders, struggling to thrive on the mainland, spread across what would become the British Empire in the East Indies, serving communities of Malays, Javanese, Burmans and Fijians.

China's Qing Emperors suffered greater humiliations. The Taiping Rebellion conquered a large territory around Nanjing and to the south for Hong Xiuquan and his 'Heavenly Kingdom' from 1854. Hong's 'God Worshipping Society' mixed up bits of Confucianism and the Christianity he had learned second hand from Chinese converts. Hong challenged Manchu authority and it took a considerable struggle to eventually overthrow the Heavenly Kingdom. The Qing Emperors recruited foreign military men to help, including Frederick Townshend Ward and Charles Gordon, who was in Beijing as part of the British forces. Nanjing was taken by the Qing 'Ever Victorious Army' in 1862 by which time the rebellion was broken, though Taiping rebels carried on for some years after. The conflicts left the Qing Empire severely weakened before the European powers.[30]

Chapter Eighteen

FIGHTING BACK

It was not easy to fight back against the Empire of free trade.

Unfree people all over the world took part in the democratic revolutions at the end of the eighteenth century – Irish Republicans as well as English democrats; French revolutionaries and Haitian slaves; American patriots and southern freedmen.

The societies that emerged from the struggle though were dominated by the European and North American colonisers. Britain, France and the United States laid claim to the banner of freedom while burying the rebellious Irish in an oppressive Union and isolating the Haitian Republic. Freedom was contagious, all the same. The language of liberation that Toussaint Louverture, Wolfe Tone, Tom Paine and Saint Just worked up was a powerful weapon for any people determined to be free.

The new elites that clambered to the top over the democratic wave were cautious, and then later enthusiastic, champions of free trade. Lowered tariffs and the end of feudal duties, as well as the deregulation of labour markets were the conditions of the new wealth concentrated in the cities. Royal dynasties that survived, like Britain's, did so by making themselves defenders of urban commerce and industrialisation.

The dynamism of the new commercial elites made them a difficult target for their critics. Laying claim to liberty – now reimagined first and foremost as the freedom of the property owners – these new elites had a powerful ideological appeal. If they were cautious of universal suffrage, they still offered themselves as champions of parliament. Rationality and science, too, were embraced as evidence and results of the English genius.

Those who fought for their freedom against the new commercial elites tried different strategies. They could appeal to older traditions that seemed to offer a more compelling loyalty. They could collaborate with the 'new money' elites and hope to win a better deal for themselves as society was remade. They could also lay claim to the democratic and liberal ideals of freedom and self-government and argue for a truer commitment to them – one that extended those rights to all. All of these different ways of coping with the new society were tried, and for the most part oppositional strategies drew on all of them in different measure.

In England, the democrats were lively but often wrong-footed by the confidence of the new order. Early working-class organisations threw themselves into the campaign for the suffrage at the end of the Napoleonic War, rallying to the monster meetings addressed by Henry 'Orator' Hunt. At St. Peter's Fields in Manchester in 1819, the militia charged a suffrage meeting that left 19 dead and hundreds injured. Rural and working-class protestors drew on folklore. They conjured up imaginary generals to lead their protests, like Ned Ludd, Captain Swing and in Wales, Rebecca. Against the new threshing machines, they appealed to early statute law fixing prices. George Loveless was one of six transported for their attempt to organise a farm workers union in 1834. When his sentence was up he came back and wrote a pamphlet *The Victims of Whiggery* to try to put a name on his oppressor:

> Arise, men of Britain and take your stand! rally round the standard of Liberty, or for ever lay prostrate under the iron hand of your land and money-mongering taskmasters![1]

In common cause with the middle classes, working people fought for the vote in the great Reform Movement. But when the Reform came in 1832, they were shut out, denied the vote by a property qualification that enfranchised the town merchants but not the labourers and artisans. In the decade and a half that followed, the growing working class in Britain's towns committed themselves to the People's Charter, a radical democratic programme of Universal Manhood Suffrage. Their paper, the *Northern Star*, went further, putting a name to the enemy that stood in their way. It was not enough to fight the 'aristocracy', working men must fight 'the plutocracy', too. In 1839, the Chartists' uprising spread from Newport to Newcastle, as thousands rose up in arms against the militia, but were beaten back. The movement rallied over and over again in the 1840s, organising monster marches and monster petitions. By the great demonstration in South London in 1848 the movement was exhausted by the unwillingness of the authorities to give one inch.[2]

Strident opposition to the 'plutocracy' was at one extreme of working-class reaction. Many more struggled to get on in the new conditions. Working people dedicated themselves to 'self-help' organising the original 'cooperative society' (to buy wholesale and hold down prices), and educational classes at the many Working Men's Institutes, Owenite Halls and Schools. Weavers evaded the ban on workers combinations by organising delegations to a Parliamentary inquiry. They lent support to the Tory Radical champions of factory legislation to limit the working day and for safer conditions. From 1867 they had legal trade unions whose membership blossomed.[3]

Young Ireland and the Fenians

Daniel O'Connell's monster meeting at Clontarf in 1843 was the high point of his campaign to repeal the Union. The depth of the famine in the 1840s stirred animosity towards Britain, but it demoralised people, too. O'Connell in his seventies was too close to Lord Russell's Whig government in the British Parliament to mount a fight against the British Government's famine policies. When O'Connell died in 1847 the movement lost a great figurehead with no clear successor.[4]

Those who followed were journalists and lawyers who gathered under the banner of Young Ireland. Chief among them was Thomas Davis, who wrote in the *Nation*. John Mitchell published polemical articles and did much to expose the famine atrocities in the *United Irishman*. James Fintan Lalor coined the most strident case for 'The Reconquest of Ireland': 'My object is to repeal the conquest – not any part or portion of it but the whole and entire conquest of seven hundred years'. As Lalor saw it 'the absolute ownership of the land is vested of right in the people of Ireland' and they 'are the first landowners and lords paramount as well as the lawmakers of this island'.[5] His goal was 'Ireland her own, and all therein, from the sod to the sky'.

William Smith O'Brien, Thomas Meagher and other Young Irelanders took the rebellions across Europe in 1848, and the terrible impact of the famine as good reason to rise up in revolt, calling for independence. They were defeated at Ballingarry. The leaders were transported to Tasmania, though Mitchel had already been arrested and was sent to Bermuda where he was put to work building the Royal Naval Dockyard. Lalor was arrested, released in ill-health, fought on ambushing police barracks and outposts, and died of bronchitis a year after the rising.[6]

Many of the Young Irelanders having served their term of transportation, or escaped them, ended up in America, making a life among the Irish emigrants. It was there that they made a new organisation, the Fenian Brotherhood to fight against the old Enemy, England. The Fenians drew on great organising skills and ambition, planning an invasion of Canada from America that was only stopped by the American authorities. In February 1867, Fenians returned from America to launch uprisings in Dublin, Cork and Limerick. The uprising was undermined by the infiltration of police spies so that the British were well prepared.[7]

In September 1867, Fenians Thomas Kelly and Timothy Deasy – both veterans of the Union Army – were arrested in Manchester. But later that month they were sprung from a police wagon taking them to court. In the fighting a policeman, Sergeant Brett was shot dead. Twenty-six Fenian sympathisers were arrested in the dragnet that followed. Three of them, Michael O'Brien, William Philip Allen and Michael Larkin, who were almost certainly innocent of the shooting of Sergeant Brett, were hung in Salford, while many of their supporters protested.[8]

In November 1867, Richard Burke, a Fenian leader was arrested in London. His comrades planted explosives and blew open the Clerkenwell Prison, killing many innocent bystanders but failing to free their man. The bomber's leader Michael Barrett was hanged, and Burke sentenced to thirty years. The Fenian Brotherhood's failure showcased the weaknesses and the strengths of Ireland's expatriate nationalists. On the one hand, the activists could be cut off from the people in the country. On the other hand, they swam in a vast diaspora created by England's uprooting that nurtured an enduring movement.[9]

Fighting the Settlers

Among non-white populations all over the world the arrival of English and other European settlers was disruptive and often destructive. In the early days white traders and drifters could cooperate well with local peoples. Maori chiefs valued the white settlers that were adopted into their bands as valuable ambassadors and traders to the European world.[10] Where settlers secured their own farms and compounds, however, they generally clashed with natives over resources and rights.

The conflict with the settlers and the natives had a third component, the British Colonial Government. Seen in the long span of history it is clear that the British Crown helped the settlers to dominate indigenous peoples. In the first instance, though, the British Government, through the Colonial Office, and other representatives (Consuls, Residents and Governors) often acted to restrain the settlers from encroaching upon native rights, adopting the policy of 'aborigine protection' (see Chapter Fifteen).

Polynesian and Micronesian peoples faced strident and quickly successful settlements, particularly in Australia and New Zealand. Tasmanian resistance to Governor Arthur's brutal 'Bounty Five' campaign was sporadic but a Bruny woman Truganini (1812–76) negotiated a peace with the Protector of Aborigines George Robinson. Truganini was saved from the impending collapse of the Aborigine protectorate on Flinders Island, by Robinson, who brought her and a few surviving members of her band to the mainland, to act as negotiators. In Port Phillip, Truganini, another Tasmanian Tunnerminnerwait and her compatriots fought with settlers, some of whom were shot. Truganini was wounded and escaped execution, leaving her one of a handful of surviving Tasmanians.[11]

Across mainland Australia Aborigines challenged settlers but were often undermined by the pressure for resources and the settlers' determination to defend their extensive sheep farms. Collaboration was another strategy. The Yarra elder Billibellary helped the Protectors to build a 60-strong Aborigine police force which acted as a buffer between the two communities, though generally on the settlers' terms. Billibellary turned against the force saying that it tended to turn men against their own families. Where the settlements recruited fewer Europeans, notably in Western Australia, Aborigines worked as farm hands, pearl divers and whalers for European employers.[12]

The settlers of New Zealand were drawn from a different stock from the Australians. There were no convicts and the number of independent farming families was high. Maori society was very different from the Aborigines of Australia too, with substantial bands and more common language. Maori leaders commanded large settlements with considerable resources for husbandry and if needed, warfare. Forty chiefs signed the Treaty of Waitangi with Captain William Hobson representing Queen Victoria on 6 February 1840. The meaning of the Treaty is still contested today, in particular whether the word 'kawanatanga' meant sovereignty or lordship. The Crown did promise to extend the rights of citizenship to the Maori and to protect their lands. Over time, though, the settler community grew to 100,000-strong, while the Maoris' numbers fell back from 56,000 to 40,000 in the 1860s.[13]

Maori King Tawhiao.

The first breach in the Treaty came three years after Waitangi at Wairau when Chief Te Rauparaha's men opened fire on a group led by Arthur Wakefield, killing 21. On that occasion Governor Fitzroy found that the New Zealand Company that Wakefield was representing had provoked the fighting with a false land claim, much to the disgust of the settlers. In 1844, the Ngapui Chief Hone Heke, believing (not without cause) that the British had repudiated the treaty rallied opposition, adopting the United States' Stars and Stripes as his flag. The new Governor George Grey defeated Hone Heke by rallying a Maori rival to help.[14]

Grey oversaw the expansion of the white community in the South Island (which had been the less settled) with extensive land buying, especially after the discovery of Gold in Otago. The new settlements put pressure on the Maori from Waikato in the north, to Taranaki in the West. In 1860, fighting broke out between the followers of Wiremu Kingi and the settlers' own militia, after Kingi repudiated the sale of a plot by a subject of his, Teira. There were many stand-offs and feints in the battles that followed, and relatively few were killed on either side.

To the consternation of the settlers and the Governor, the Maori's pre-eminent chief Te Wherowhero was named King by many, after he offered Wiremu Kingi protection.[15] The settlers and the Governor were widely criticised in Britain for their mean-spirited evasion of the Waitangi Treaty, but in time the King movement was undermined and pushed back. Later opposition to the settlers took on a more millenarian character like the Huahua led by the Taranaki prophet Te Ua Haumene, or the followers of Te Kooti's 'Pai Maarire' faith, which were violently suppressed.[16] Maori in the later nineteenth and twentieth centuries became adept political actors in New Zealand and won more lasting concessions.

Princes and Mutineers in India

In India there was every kind of opposition, protest, negotiation and collaboration. As we have seen the Mughal, Maratha, Bengali and Mysore Kingdoms and Sultanates sometimes fought against and sometimes worked alongside the East India Company Presidencies.

One of the most dramatic challenges to British power came from Haider Ali and his son Tipu Sultan. The Kingdom of Mysore Under Haider Ali covered some 80,000 square miles (about the same size as Britain), through acquisitions in what is today Tamil Nadu and southern Karnataka. Haider Ali made successful alliances with the Maratha Federation, on occasions with Britain and also with the French court. Mysore had an ambitious policy of international diplomacy, with missions in France, the Ottoman Empire and Burma – made possible by the access that the Marathas gave to the sea. To boost the technical base of his Kingdom Tipu Sultan recruited craftsmen from France, including gunsmiths, porcelain-workers, glass-makers, watchmakers, tapestry-makers, engineers, linen-weavers and two printers to his capital in Seringapatam. Tipu had factories for making silk, sugar, paper, knives and scissors, as well as ammunition factories. In the capital Tipu commissioned large panoramas to celebrate his victories over Britain. It was little wonder that the EIC found Mysore so challenging an opponent, nor that it was determined over time to defeat Tipu.[17]

While Haider Ali and Tipu Sultan fought against Britain, they did hold out the hope of alliance – the British failure to honour a mutual defence treaty against the Maratha confirmed Mysore's opposition to the British. Other ruling powers followed the policy of cooperation where they could. The Nizam of Hyderabad, Mughal Viceroy in the Deccan, governed a state north of Mysore of a similar size. Nizam Ali Khan made Hyderabad a British ally in the wars with the Maratha and with Mysore.[18]

In 1857, the EIC faced another challenge – this time from within its own Army. Significant sections of the EIC army launched a general mutiny. The trigger for the mutiny was the widespread belief that the new Enfield rifle paper cartridges, holding the charge and bullet, that the sepoys were to bite had been greased with a mixture of cow and pig fat. Were it so 'biting the bullet' would breach dietary law for both Hindu and Muslim, for whom the cow was sacred on the one hand and the pig unclean, on the other hand. Whether it had happened is still not clear, but the British officers quickly set about trying to show their troops that it was no longer, and that they need not fear polluting their bodies.[19]

British officers' assurances had little effect because the cartridge was emblematic of an underlying belief that the army was being reorganised on 'Christian' lines. Even when sepoys were taken to see the cartridges made, they explained that even if they knew the greasing was beeswax everybody else believed it was tallow and pig fat, so they would 'lose caste' anyway.[20]

When they began to recruit for their army, the EIC was still in name anyway acting as Diwan of the Mughal, and honoured established practice relating to caste – that for Hindus it would be limited to the higher castes, Brahmins, Bhumihars and Rajputs (about 20 per cent of the army was Muslim). This was a commitment that army service would be honourable. Religious observance gave the men a measure of control over their working conditions. Sepoys were paid bonuses ('batta') if they were sent outside their region, or if they had to sail on the sea (crossing the black waters, 'kali pani' was not strictly taboo to Hindus, but it was customarily thought to risk loss of caste). The sepoys were paid much less than their English officers, but in India seven rupees was an honourable wage that could keep a family, and status, in the home village.[21]

The British commanders relied on traditional authority to order the army, but they also challenged it. In 1824, at Barrackpore British commanders clashed with sepoys who were being sent out to fight in Rangoon. Already frustrated that the sepoys would not board ships to cross the Bay of Bengal, the officers abused the men, who refused orders. The British officers ordered artillery fire on the men and hundreds were killed. The massacre taught sepoys that they should guard against being disarmed by their British officers.[22]

In 1834, the army changed its recruitment policy allowing lower castes to join. By 1857, around one eighth of the army was made up of lower castes. That meant that serving as a sepoy in the Company Army was no longer a sign that you were of high caste undermining their status. The 'batta' payments were also being withheld. The annexation of Awadh had a big impact on the status of the sepoys. Many of the Bengal Presidency sepoys were recruited from Awadh, so that their families lived in villages there. The high status they enjoyed as sepoys before was hurt by the occupation. These changes all laid the basis for the widespread belief that the Enfield cartridge was greased with pork fat and tallow – a belief that was emblematic of the loss of caste the sepoys feared in the reformed company army.[23]

All through the early months of 1857 sepoys took part in clandestine meetings where defection to other armies and outright mutiny were discussed. The 34th Bengal Native Infantry were interrupted in an attempt to take Fort William. An old prophecy that the Company Rule would last one hundred years after Clive's Victory at Plassey in 1757 was retold. Sepoys rallied at night with their faces covered in Barrackpore. The 19th Foot Regiment at Berhampur refused the cartridges. An unsigned petition of March 1857 read:

> We will not give up our religion. We serve for honour and religion; if we lose our religion, the Hindoo and the Mahomedan religions will be destroyed.[24]

The manifesto granted that the English were 'masters of the country' but warned that 'a king or any other one who acts unjustly does not remain'.[25]

On 18 March, at Barrackpore Captain Hearsey tried to persuade the assembled brigade that the cartridges were not polluted, and also that there was no truth in the rumours that European troops were coming with cavalry and artillery to attack them. This was warning enough for Mangel Pandey, a Brahmin sepoy of the 34th Bengal Native Infantry to produce his rifle and call on the assembled men to refuse orders. To the dismay of the British officers, the men hovered, unwilling to take Pandey down as they were urged, though not yet joining his rebellion. Pandey was about to be taken when he shot himself. The 19th Bengal Native Infantry and several companies of the 34th were disbanded. In the Bengal Army's summer headquarters at Ambala, the next month there were arson attacks on native huts.[26]

At Meerut eighty-five sepoys were court-martialled for refusing the cartridges and humiliated in front of the entire garrison. Then on 10 May the British officers lost control of the 11th and 20th Bengal Native Infantry. Colonel Finnis challenged the men of the 20th and was shot dead. The Havildar Major of the 11th ran into the officers mess saying 'fly sahib, fly at once, the Regiments are in open mutiny and firing on their officers'.[27] Historian Kim Wagner says that the likeliest candidate for ringleader of the Meerut mutiny was Ghulab Shah, and officer of the Third Bengal Light Cavalry.[28] That evening many British soldiers and their families were killed by the mutineers – around forty dead in total.

From Meerut, mutineers marched to Delhi, seat of the now pensioned Bahadur Shah II, heir to the Mughal Empire, calling 'Dohai Badshah!' – 'Help O King!'. Bahadur Shah was alarmed and asked the British what to do, but effectively abandoned, he threw in his lot with the mutineers.[29]

Other centres of opposition were at Lucknow, where the 7th Oudh Irregulars refused to drill and offered to support the Bengal National Infantry; 'We are ready to obey the directions of our brothers of the 48th'.[30] At Jhansi, the R____, frustrated by Dalhousie in the succession of her son to the throne was met by mutineers. They had killed 48 Europeans. At first, she, like Bahadur Shah, was reluctant, and sent message to the Company asking for help. So, too, did Nana Sahib, Peshwa of the Maratha at

Cawnpore baulk at the mutineers at first, but their invitation was difficult to refuse: 'a kingdom was prepared for him if he joined them with all his wealth; or death if he sided with the Europeans'.[31] Though the Sepoys fought for military control from the British they did not get to change the country all that much. Abdul Rahman Khan the rebel Nawab of Jhajjar set out to raise taxes to pay to the Emperor Bahadur Shah, sending a force of cavalry to the villages.[32]

The suppression of the mutiny was decisive and barbaric. Thousands of Indians were executed for mutiny, or merely on suspicion of disloyalty. The British troops, stirred by an intense press campaign at home, sought retribution for the affront. Rebellious sepoys were executed in the most violent and degrading way. They were held alive across the mouths of cannon and then blown apart. In Britain the anger and outrage concealed a profound self-doubt that was answered with the abolition of the Company, made a scapegoat for the rebellion. Bahadur Shah, pleading innocence of rebellion, was exiled to Rangoon – but his sons, Mirza Mughal and Mirza Khizr Sultan, grandson, Mirza Abu Bakr, and thirty more Mughal princes were executed to destroy the line. Both the Rani of Jhansi and Nana Sahib disappeared in the reimposition of British rule, either killed or escaped, but potent symbols of a national sentiment that that sees the events of 1857 as the beginning of a national revolution not a mutiny.

Felice Beato's photograph of the remains of slaughtered rebels.

As remarkable a blow against British rule in India the mutiny of 1857 was, it was limited mostly to the North West, with the sepoys Bengal Native Infantry at its core. The Sikh regiments fought to defeat of the mutineers and would play a big part in the reorganised British-India Army. The Bengal Native Infantry had helped in the defeat of the Sikh Kingdom in 1846 and some 36,000, mostly Hindu troops were stationed in the Punjab – many of whom were sympathetic to the mutiny, and even had plans to seize the Sikh capital, Lahore for the mutineers. Sikh princes on the other hand rallied to the British cause against the mutineers, contributing four Sikh regiments to the taking of Delhi from the supporters of Bahadur Shah. When Company Sepoys rebelled in Jullundur, the Raja of Kapurthala sent his troops to support the British. General Campbell's 20,000 strong army marching into Awadh in February was made up of British and Sikh troops. The British Indian Government thanked them in a General Order of 8 October 1857:

> These true-hearted Chiefs, faithful to their engagements, have shown trust in the power, honour, and friendship of the British Government, and they will not repent it.[33]

In March 1858, the Prime Minister of Nepal Rana Jang Bahadur, led a force of nearly ten thousand Nepalese troops to support the final British assault on Lucknow. Some Sikhs, on the other hand, did join the mutiny, as in Benares.

So, too, did the Nizam of Hyderabad oppose the mutineers. For the Bengal National Infantry and their supporters, rebellion looked like the best option, but for other parts of India, collaboration, whether from fear, opportunism or outright identification, seemed the better route.

The Morant Bay Rebellion

In the years following the abolition of slavery European authority had suffered a real blow in the Caribbean as black West Indians largely withdrew from the plantation economy to live inland, or squat land in peasant villages.

Without slavery the white planters struggled to control the islands. Under abolition former slaves were not excluded from the franchise and would stand for election to the Legislative Councils contesting for power. In Jamaica Edward Vickars – 'Vote for Vickars, the black man' was his slogan – led thirteen black and mixed-race members elected to the House of Assembly, including Edward Jordon (who had been editor of a local newspaper, the *Watchman*) and George W. Gordon.[34]

Island legislatures adopted property qualifications, like those in Antigua (where the threshold was an annual income of £75) and Jamaica (where you had to pay ten shillings to vote). Around the same time, these Legislative Councils passed authoritarian rules for policing which were called 'class legislation', including the Jamaica Vagrancy Act, or Antigua's 'whipping bill'. In Jamaica the 'custodes', or Governor-appointed magistrates enforced the law.[35]

After the close of the American civil war the West Indies were in the throes of a sharp recession, which fell heavily on the black population. A Methodist missionary Edward Bean Underhill wrote a report on poverty in the island meant for the Governor but publicised across the island in what were called 'Underhill Meetings'. Assemblyman George W. Gordon chaired some of these. Others were organised by Paul Bogle, Deacon of the Native Baptist Tabernacle in St Ann's. At some of these meetings, according to the

Governor's informants, it was said that the people of Jamaica were told 'you must do what Hayti does' – meaning rise up like the Haitians did under Toussaint Louverture against their white masters.[36]

One placard for an 'Underhill meeting' in August 1865 read:

> People of St Ann's,
> Poor people of St Ann's
> Starving people of St Ann's
> Naked people of St Ann's.
> You who have no sugar estates to work on, nor can find other employment, we call on you to come forth, even if you be naked, come forth and protest against the unjust representations made against you by Mr Governor Eyre and his band of Custodes.[37]

Paul Bogle organised military drills in St. Anns. On 7 October 1865, at the Court of Petty Session a boy was fined and in the court room James Geoghegan protested, upon which he was ordered arrested. But outside Bogle had gathered a crowd of 150, who freed Geoghegan and set about the police with sticks. The following week Lewis Miller, a cousin of Bogle's, was to appear for letting his horse stray onto land that the old planter James Williams owned (though his title was not accepted by the 'squatting' farmers). Miller was released on Bogle's surety, but later a warrant was issued for Bogle's arrest. The police were overpowered by a large crowd (300 it was claimed) armed again with sticks.

After these clashes Bogle's makeshift army marched from Stony Gut to Morant Bay. They killed the Custo Baron von Ketelholdt and then moved on to the Plaintain River District where they attacked Duckinfield House and Hordley House before moving on to the town of Manchioneal. Bogle appointed officers, including his brother Moses, James McLaren and Scipio Cowell and had command of much of St Anns.[38]

A panicked Governor Eyre gathered his forces off the shore and attacked the rebels. The repression was rightly called a 'reign of terror' as hundreds were summarily executed Eyre having declared martial law. Captain Hole was sent to put down the revolt in Manchioneal, while Captain Hobbs was dispatched to St Thomas in the East and Stony Gut. Assemblyman George W. Gordon tried to speak to Eyre but was instead pushed onto a boat so that he could be sailed into the area under martial law. Gordon was tried in a mockery of a tribunal and executed. In all, around 200 were hanged by Eyre's courts martial, including Paul Bogle, his brother and Scipio Cowell. Hundreds more were slaughtered in the fields and left there.

The Morant Bay rebellion was crushed by military might. The measures Governor Eyre took were a scandal to many even in Britain, where the old Anti-Slavery Society and other radicals tried to force his prosecution. On his return Eyre was cheered by conservatives and jeered by radicals all over England. Captain Hobbs was also called back, but on the ship he began hallucinating, and shouted at his wife:

> Go away! I don't want you near me. You are Paul Bogle's widow! Go away! Go away![39]

After that, he jumped in the sea and drowned. Bogle and Gordon were remembered rather better. Today they are heroes of Jamaica's national story.

After the Morant Bay Rebellion the Foreign Office cut through the gordian knot of black representation in the colony, by making it a Crown Colony under Sir John Grant, who had been an administrator in India. The rebellion became the occasion for a more open imperial rule over the West Indies, where the other islands followed suit, becoming Crown colonies – that is colonies directly governed over the heads of the people who lived there.

These were some of the episodes of outright challenge to Britain's 'Empire of free trade'. Highlighting opposition alone can give a distorted picture of what the times were like. For most of the time conflict did not break out into outright opposition, but rather was contained, and even productive of a developing Empire, that only crudely contained a multiplicity of lives and communities. Later, when the Empire settled into its fully made form it was more definitively integrated, dominant, and by virtue of that, challengeable.

PART THREE

Modern Imperialism, 1870–1947

Chapter Nineteen

'THE NEW IMPERIALISM'

On the eve of World War I, the British Empire had expanded to govern over some 431 million people on 12.7 million square miles of territory. In 1861, the estimated land mass of the Empire had been eight and a half million square miles. By 1891 it had grown to 11.9 million square miles. By 1920 it covered 13.7 million square miles and contained 449 million people – one quarter of the world's land mass and of its population. In Africa alone Britain added 4,065,398 square miles of territory by 1900. Britain's colonial land grab was mirrored to a lesser extent by rivals, France, Germany, Belgium, the United States, later Italy and Japan. The great colonial expansion between 1880 and 1914 was not just a quantitative continuation of the past, but a new era of imperialism, the 'new imperialism' as it was called at the time.

The imperialist ethos did not appear fully formed straight away but instead emerged out of a number of dramatic clashes on the periphery of the Empire, in Africa mainly, but also in Asia and the Pacific. For this reason, historian John Seeley said in his book *The Expansion of England* (1883) that 'we seem, as it were, to have conquered half the world in a fit of absence of mind'.[1] Many since have protested at Seeley's claim as a bad faith excuse for what in truth were deliberate policies of domination.

The Marxist critic of Imperialism, V. I. Lenin came to a similar conclusion to Seeley, but from a different starting point. Lenin took issue with those who thought that imperialism was a bad policy that ought to be abandoned. It is not just a policy option, he argued but a fundamental characteristic of capitalism in its maturity and decay.[2] He was saying that the drive to Empire was bigger than anyone's biases or even choices, that it was in the zeitgeist.

There were deliberate policy decisions behind the growth of imperialism. Each treaty made and broken, each mobilisation, bombardment and incursion, every Governor appointed, every land tribunal set up, Legislative Council or Council of Chiefs called was a deliberate choice.

Those choices were made, however, in a new context. How Britons thought about the world, and their place in it had changed, in ways that predisposed them to choose the option of annexation over *laissez faire*. This new mood emerged out of different elements, but all tended towards the conclusion that the answers to the challenges that Britain faced would be found beyond its borders.

The New Liberalism and the Social Question

The mainstream ideology of free market capitalism, of liberalism, the small state, and laissez faire had come to dominate from 1776 to 1866. In the later nineteenth century those ideas were much more widely questioned.

It was poverty in the first place that caused people to question the idea that the free market would tend to help everyone. Studies like Charles Booth's *Life and Labour of the People in London* (1892) and the Reverend Andrew Mearns' pamphlet *The Bitter Cry of Outcast London* (1883) drew attention to the persistence of poverty – which they painted in lurid and sometimes apocalyptic colours. The idea that rising prosperity would help everyone was harder to defend. The social reformer Arnold Tonybee said,

> we now approach a darker period – a period as disastrous and as terrible as any through which a nation ever passed; disastrous and terrible, because side by side with a great increase of wealth was seen an enormous increase of pauperism; and production on a vast scale, the result of free competition, led to a rapid alienation of classes and to the degradation of a large body of producers.[3]

In 1881, Thomas Hill Green, Whyte Professor of Moral Philosophy gave a lecture on 'Liberal Legislation and Freedom of Contract'. Green was active in the Liberal Party and taught and influenced many political and social reformers, including Toynbee and the future Prime Minister A. J. Balfour.

In his talk Green argued that real freedom might be better won by interfering with the 'freedom of contract'. He takes as his examples the laws that stopped parents from putting their children to work, that stopped landlords evicting 'tenants-at-will' in Ireland, and labour laws:

> Act after act was passed preventing master and workman, parent and child, housebuilder and householder, from doing as they pleased, with the result of a great addition to the real freedom of society.[4]

Toynbee followed Green in challenging the 'reckless abstractness' and 'unwarrantable assumptions' of the laissez faire economic theory, that 'the economic interest of the individual is in fact identical with that of the community', and that 'he knows his own interest and follows it'.[5]

The editor of the *Economist* despaired of the status of political economy, that 'younger men either do not study it, or do not feel that it comes home to them, and that it matches up with their most living ideas'.[6] In 1874, for the first time, the Conservative Party won control of Manchester, where the cotton interest had for many years been the most vocal champion of free trade.

The philosophical scepticism towards the free market ideal was one thing. The underlying dread that there was a growing underclass was a yet more pressing reason for a more muscular state intervention. The Reverend Mearns, in *The Bitter Cry of Outcast London*, dreaded that 'in the very centre of our great cities, concealed by the thinnest crust of civilisation and decency, is a vast mass of moral corruption, of heartbreaking misery and absolute godlessness'.[7]

The right-wing journalist Arnold White feared that 'there is a married pauper class, growing in numbers, who drag along during the summer with hopping, hob-jobbing, and casual labour, depending for subsistence in the winter time on the rates and on the charity that maintained and propagates the evils it blindly hopes to extinguish'. What was worse, he said, the 'criminal and pauperised classes with low cerebral development renew their race more rapidly than those of higher nervous natures'.[8]

With doubts about the 'invisible hand of the market' and its ability to fix problems came a social activism which Toynbee, Green and other championed. Philanthropists like housing activist Octavia Hill and the Salvation Army's Edward Chad Varah worked to help the poor. It was work that gave them a greater sense of moral purpose when the general direction of society seemed less clear.

The outlook of the governing and educated classes in the mid-century was broadly optimistic, putting its faith in the free market to raise society. Free trade went hand in hand with (moderate) reform, widening the franchise gradually and letting people govern their own lives. Man was essentially good and would improve with better prospects. Towards the end of the century the liberal ideal was shaken by doubts. Persistent poverty seemed to show up the failures of the free market to improve people's lives. Small government might have to give way to greater intervention. 'We are all socialists, now', the Liberal Party Chancellor William Harcourt joked in 1887 (as Parliament discussed a Tory bill to stop labourers' allotments being turned into commercial farms). He did not mean that Parliament had become socialist. He meant that the taboo against government interfering between contracting parties and acting for the social good had been broken. The new social activism would go on to have a big impact on the Labour Party, which was by the end of the century becoming a movement in its own right.

The New Liberalism was an attempt to forestall the rising demands of democracy. Conservative and Liberal parties both had conceded to working class demands for a wider franchise. Now they had to develop a political appeal to the less well-off to forestall the challenge of socialism. For the Liberals that meant social reform. For the Conservatives it meant the spectacle of Empire. The two came together in the 'New Imperialism'.

The New Imperialism

As the British establishment's own belief in free trade as a policy for Britain had changed, so, too did they change their attitude towards the wider world along similar lines. The case for a more interventionist state applied to those non-European territories. 'After 1870', wrote L. C. Knowles in her book *Economic Development of the Overseas Empire*, 'this policy of laissez faire was gradually superseded by an era of active intervention on the part of the Government'.[9]

The imperialist ethos came from different places. The humanitarian and missionary campaigns played a big part in shaping the new idea. Church Missions were militant in making the case for annexations. 'We accepted the Word of God in our youth', the Tswana Chiefs told the Missionary John Mackenzie, 'but we did not know all that was coming behind it'.[10] The Aborigines' Protection Society, though it campaigned for the well-being of native peoples across the world, generally thought that they would be safer under British protection. They lobbied the government for the annexation of Zululand, Basutoland, Botswana, Fiji and Tonga. For quite different reasons investors in the City of London were very active champions of annexation where their investments were at stake (discussed in the next chapter). So, too, were the industrialists of Lancashire, Birmingham and Glasgow keen promoters of colonisation, which they hoped would help exports.

A number of key players promoted the idea of Empire. Some of these were called the 'liberal imperialists' (or 'limps'). Among them were the Birmingham Mayor Joseph Chamberlain, who had risen to influence as a 'new liberal', known for what was called the 'gas and water socialism' of the Birmingham authority's public works. Chamberlain tried but failed to get the Liberal Party to support a far more radical programme of state intervention, trade union protection and land nationalisation. (Chamberlain's inspiration for the 'Radical Programme' was a pamphlet by his friend Frederick Maxse, proposing broad social reform to forestall the kind of revolution that had taken place in Paris in 1871, *The Causes of Social Revolt,* 1872).

Chamberlain broke with the Liberal Party over Gladstone's proposal for Home Rule in Ireland. His Liberal Unionist group became a vehicle for the campaign for a more forward imperial policy. Between 1895 and 1903 Chamberlain was Secretary of State for the Colonies in Arthur Balfour's Conservative government, and at the forefront of the anti-Boer campaign that culminated in the second Boer war. On 1 August 1895, Chamberlain gave a speech in which he argued that 'No longer have we to read the annals of a kingdom – it is the history of an Empire with which we will have to deal'.

A promising Liberal MP, Charles Dilke, a supporter of Chamberlain's 'Radical Programme', played an interesting role in the policy move towards the new imperialism. Dilke's book *Greater Britain* (1868) written after a tour of first America and then Canada and Australia was pointedly liberal and democratic in its attitude to the settlers, making the case for self-government, and for an English-speaking union of freely associating states. Dilke was an active campaigner for the protection of native peoples, a leading representative of the Aborigines' Protection Society, speaking out against Sir Henry Bartle Frere's treatment of the Sotho people, and other colonialist oppressions. His view of these native peoples was that they were owed protection more than that they were independence, and his view that the Anglo-Saxon race was destined to rule became more explicit in old age.

Alfred Milner studied at Oxford where he fell under the spell of Arnold Toynbee, and then later worked as a journalist for W. T. Stead and for the Liberal Party, before being made finance secretary in Egypt and then in South Africa. Milner wrote up the campaign against the Egyptian nationalist 'Urabi and the reorganisation of the country's finances that he helped to engineer in a book, *England in Egypt* (1892). In South Africa, Milner organised a group of up-and-coming colonial officials who were known as 'Milner's Kindergarten'. They included future Governor General of South Africa Patrick Duncan, future ambassador to the United States Philip Kerr, the novelist and later Governor General of Canada John Buchan, Lionel Curtis, Royal Institute of International Affairs founder, George Geoffrey Dawson, editor of *The Times* (1912–17), and Fabian Ware who would go on to run the Imperial War Graves Commission from 1918. Many of the key members of Milner's Kindergarten had, like him, developed their ideas in South Africa. Like the Fabians after them, they wanted to influence existing officials in directions worked out in their discussion group. Funding came from the mining magnate Cecil Rhodes.

A Kindergarten paper of 1907, published under the name of Lord Selborne, was in fact the outcome of a group discussion on the future of South Africa. It talked about practical matters, like railways, but also about race relations. On the conflict between the English and 'Teuton' races in the Boer war, it argued 'the fusion between them is merely a matter of time, as it was with the Saxons and Normans, who were related to one another in a similar degree of kinship'. The Kindergarten campaigned for the Union of the whole of South Africa. One spin-off of Milner's Kindergarten was the *Round Table Journal, A Quarterly Review of the Politics of the British Empire*, which published from 1910, and its meeting, the 'Round Table moot'.

Other important champions of the New Imperialism included the historian John Seeley. His book *The Expansion of England* underplayed the novelty of colonialism, claiming instead it was a continuous expansion, though one that had been overlooked by historians before him. And there was Earl Cromer, a cousin of the banking family Baring, who became the British Controller General in Egypt, nominally under the Khedive, though secretly the power relation was the reverse. He wrote up his experiences in *Modern Egypt* (1908) and a biography of the Khedive Abbas Hilmi, *Abbas II* (1915).

As well as the political and literary promoters, there was a growing pantheon of heroes of the Empire, living and dead. These included Gordon of Khartoum, the missionary David Livingstone, the American explorer Henry Morton Stanley. They were assiduous publicists as well as explorers and spoke in meeting halls and churches, and published articles and interviews in the newspapers. There were a great many more who were well-known at the time, though less so today, including the men of the anti-slavery squadron, like Commodore Leopold Heath and Captain Edward Meara, 'Emin Pasha' (born Eduard Schnitzer) who was surprised to be the subject of Stanley's Emin Pasha Relief Fund, not believing he was lost in Equatorial Africa. Military men, who were figures in their own right, were also known (like Gordon) for Imperial wars that caught the popular imagination. Lord Kitchener's attempted relief of Gordon at Khartoum in 1884 was too late, but in 1898 he took revenge on the Mahdists in the Battle of Omdurman. Field Marshall Garnet Wolseley served for 48 years and was associated with all the major colonial wars of the second half of the nineteenth century, from the Indian rebellion of 1857 to the campaigns in Egypt. Colonial governors like Sir Henry Bartle Frere (who governed in India and the Cape) and Hercules Robinson were also keen publicists at home as they were administrators abroad.

Through their actions and self-publicity, the leading lights of the new imperialism changed the balance of colonial policy from one of caution towards expansion, to a predisposition to expansion. As 'the new imperialism' became less of a project and more of a reality, the case for Empire became more coherent, until it got the character of common sense.

Transformation of the Armed Forces

The era of modern imperialism also saw the transformation of the armed forces. New fears of foreign invasion in 1859 (from France) and 1871 (from Germany) saw a revival of the volunteer regiments, drawing on the urban middle classes and skilled craftsmen

– many of whom had won the vote in the Reform Act of 1867 and the Representation of the People Act of 1884. Between 1859 and 1877 818,000 served with the volunteers, around 16 per cent of the adult population. The regular army still drew on the poorer classes, who had no vote, and it grew to around 165,000 by 1880. The domestic garrison was around 40,000 on the mainland and 20,000 in Ireland in 1847; in Britain, but less so in Ireland, the army gave over its public order role to the new civilian police force that had been created in 1829.[11]

The officers were still drawn from the elites, but they were changing, too. By 1912 just nine per cent of officers were from titled families, and a further 32 per cent the sons of country landowners. Almost all, though, were educated in public schools, including the military academies at Sandhurst, Woolwich and Dartmouth (for the navy), with the new middle classes sending their sons to serve. Douglas Haig, who graduated from Oxford and then Sandhurst in 1885 and would rise to command the British Expeditionary Force in World War I was heir to the Haig's Whisky distillery. In 1870, Gladstone's Liberal government abolished the sale of officer's commissions.[12] Gilbert and Sullivan's comic opera The Pirates of Penzance portrayed 'the modern major general' who knows 'the kings of England, and I quote the fights historical/From marathon to Waterloo in order categorical'.

In the later nineteenth century, the army fought outside of Europe, against Zulus (1879), Boers (1880–81 and 1899–1902), Ndebele (1893, 1896–97), in Egypt (1882), Sudan (1884–85, 1896–98), Burma (1885–89), the North-West Frontier of India (1897–98), Northern China (1900) and in many other conflicts. In these wars, the army fought alongside native auxiliaries and had the advantage of breach-loading rifles and machine guns. An 'Imperial Yeomanry' was raised to fight in South Africa in 1899, though the top brass were disappointed by both their, and the regular army's showing against the Boers. Around a third of recruits to the regular army were rejected on health grounds which leant force to public health campaigns at home.

Flogging was restricted in the army in 1859, and eventually abolished in 1881 – a sign that the rank-and-file soldier had more rights than his eighteenth-century predecessor. Soldiers were seen more as heroes in distant wars than a locally garrisoned menace. A further change in the status of the armed forces would come in the twentieth century, when the army was once again transformed, this time into a mass, citizen's army that would win itself the right to vote *in toto* in 1919.

Popular Imperialism

The wider franchise in Britain led government to bring in compulsory schooling to age 11 years from 1870. Literacy rates climbed and many more newspapers and magazines for adults and children were published. One paper that was doing very well in the new market was *Tit Bits,* published by George Newnes, and selling 900,000 copies a week. Alfred Harmsworth said of it that there are:

> thousands of boys and girls … who are aching to read. They do not care for the ordinary newspaper. They have no interest in society, but will read anything which is simple and is sufficiently interesting.[13]

Titbits was Harmsworth's model for the *Daily Mail* which he launched in 1896, and which popularised the heroes of Empire.

From 1879 to 1967, the Religious Tract Society published the *Boys Own Paper,* which was soon selling one million copies a week, and was imitated by the *Union Jack* (from 1880), *The Boy's Friend* (1895), *The Gem* (1907) and *The Magnet* (1908). The children's papers were filled with stories of great British explorers 'discovering' new lands, like Livingstone, Mungo Park, Burton, Speke and Grant; there were heroic tragedies, like the Siege of Khartoum, and victories, like the Battle of Omdurman and the relief of Mafeking, or the voyages of the anti-slavery squadrons.

Robert Brown, an Edinburgh trained botanist wrote serialised collections like *The Races of Mankind,* that cost 6d an issue (1873–76). Brown's attitude to the Native Americans, Aborigines and Africans he described was patronising rather than vicious, though he thought it was wiser to let nature take its course and extinguish less civilised peoples than for missionaries to save them. Later he wrote *Countries of the World* (1884–89) and *The Story of Africa and Its Explorers* (1892–95).

Augustus H. Keane a lecturer in Indian languages and ethnology at University College London was also a popular writer and published school textbooks, like *School Physical and Descriptive Geography* (1892). Keane found an audience for books like *Ethnology* (1896) *Popular Races of Mankind* (1905) *The World's Peoples* (1908) and *The Boer States* (1900) which he filled with highly racialised descriptions of Africans as 'treacherous and cruel hordes, accustomed from old to raid, plunder and murder'.[14]

According to the Amalgamated Press the boys' papers were 'aimed from the first at the encouragement of physical strength, patriotism, of interest in travel and exploration, and of pride in our empire'. They thought that 'the boys' papers of the Amalgamated Press have done more to provide recruits for our Navy and Army' than anything else.[15] As well as the popular papers and journals there were thousands of postcards, cigarette cards (that you could collect) with subjects like peoples of the empire, armies of the empire, battle ships and more.

Popular entertainment thrived on Empire themes that brought exotic adventure to English towns. Astley's theatre put on 'The War in Zululand' and the 'Kaffir War' (both in 1879). Many plays took Indian themes, like 'The Great Mogul', 'The Saucy Nabob', 'Lalla Rookh and the Indian Mutiny', all staged in the 1880s and 1890s. 'The Zulu Chief' and 'Cetewayo at Last' were both staged in 1882 to take advantage (and parody) the great interest in his visit to London. South Africa was highlighted in adventures like 'The Kimberley Mail', 'The Diamond Rush' and 'The Raid on the Transvaal', and 1894 saw plays about the Sudan, 'The Dancing Dervish' and 'The Mahdi'.[16]

Whereas Britain put on industrial exhibitions in 1851 and 1862, the later century saw the Colonial and Indian Exhibition of 1884 (with five and a half million visitors) the Greater Britain exhibition of 1899 and the Coronation Exhibition of 1911, all with a strong colonial theme. Fixed displays at the Crystal Palace exhibition ground featured a Chinese Court and a Grand Panorama of the Battle of Tel-el-Kabir (the Crystal Palace housed the Great Exhibition of 1851 in Hyde Park, was rebuilt in South London in 1854 but burned down in 1936). Imre Kiralfy founded London Exhibitions Ltd which put on 'Greater Britain' at Earls Court in 1899, which featured a 'Kaffir Kraal', and exhibited 174 Africans, purportedly representatives of Zulus, Basuto (Sotho) and Matabele, with exotic animals and a re-enactment of the Matabele war. Kiralfy developed the White City site which put on the Imperial International exhibition of 1909 and the Coronation Exhibition of 1911. The biggest was the British Empire Exhibition after the Great War, 'to stimulate trade, strengthen bonds that bind mother Country to her Sister States and Daughters, to bring into closer contact the one with each other, to enable all who owe allegiance to the British flag to meet on common ground and learn to know each other', at Wembley in 1924. Twenty-seven million visitors came over the year and a half that it was open, but at one shilling and sixpence, only a fraction of the £12 million costs were recouped in ticket sales.[17]

The spectacle of Empire let people express emotions that were mostly kept under the lid in polite society, like a yearning for violence in the re-staged battles or sexual longing, more easily expressed towards the native women of imagination. In 1924 Billy Merson sang 'In My Little Wigwam Wembley Way', about 'dusky Eves' in 'nothing but leaves', and 'the girls from Africa': 'All they wear is beads and a grin; That is where the exhibition comes in.'

The exhibitions featured spectacle and a wider world, where British Patriotism was reaffirmed. Mixed up with the patriotic feelings were often brutal expressions of racial superiority. Empire propaganda played an important part in the campaign for more arms. In 1909, plays called 'Wake Up England', 'Nation in Arms' and 'A Plea for the Navy' were all staged.[18]

In 1911, John Nash's processional route, the Mall was remodelled with the unveiling of Sir Thomas Brock's baroque memorial to Queen Victoria, in marble with the figures of Victory, Courage and Constancy, and the ornamental gates given by the Dominions: Australia Gate, South Africa Gate and Canada Gate. At the other end of the Mall Aston Webb's imposing neoclassical Admiralty Arch was completed the following year. At the same time a towering statue of Robert Clive was put up on Horse Guards Road, more than 150 years after his victory at the Battle of Plassey (though only 46 years before India's independence). The Victoria Memorial was on display in the Coronation of George V in June 1911, when 45,000 troops lined the route from Buckingham Palace to Westminster Abbey. The Monarchy knew how to put on a grand display of imperial might as well as any promoter.

Chapter Twenty

LITTLE ENGLAND, EXHAUSTED

Britain's industrial revolution between 1790 and 1840 had wrought great change. By the later nineteenth century, it was exhausted.

There was a marked fall-off in the value of British exports, from £311 million in 1873 to £245 million in 1878. From then on, they rarely exceeded £300 million until they started to climb again in 1900. Growth rates per head in British industry were low right through from 1874 to 1913. Between 1875 and 1895 Germany's exports grew by 30 per cent, as a greater share of them came to be in finished goods than raw materials. Rivals on the Continent and in America were cutting into British overseas markets.[1]

The slower growth of the later 1870s and 1880s was marked by a fall in prices by about 20 per cent between 1870 and 1890. Prices had generally been falling through most of the nineteenth century because of increased productivity – but the fall was greater in the mid-1870s because of weaker demand for British goods. Anxious Lancashire manufacturers lobbied for a policy of 'bimetallism' – meaning the issuing of additional currency backed by silver – vainly hoping that the increased money supply would shift their stocks. The cotton merchants campaigned, too, against tariffs the British Indian Government put on goods, in the hope that Indian sales would clear their inventories. Factories were closed and in 1879 unemployment reached a peak of 12 per cent, and then in 1886 again topped 10 per cent. However, for those in work, lower prices mitigated any reduction in wages.[2]

The slowdown in growth also led to a rise in emigration. From 1881 to 1893 more than 200,000 people were leaving the country every year. Then from 1900 emigration numbers started to rise again, until around 450,000 were leaving every year. From 1895 to 1913 around 25,000 were leaving each year just for the Cape or Natal. The United States was still the most common destination, though from 1906 emigration to Canada kept pace, and then outstripped it. In Empire propaganda it was a moment of pride that while more people went to America than the British colonies between 1884 and 1893 (980,337 to 421,149), from 1904 and 1913 the position was reversed, with 622,773 going to the US and 1,291,406 to the colonies.[3]

Child emigration was promoted by the Child's Friends Society and Barnardos, both of which shipped off orphans and destitute children to work on farms and 'industrial schools' in Canada, Australia and the Cape. According to a later government report Britain 'exported as many as 100,000 Home Children to Canada between 1869 and the Great Depression to serve as cheap farm labour'.[4]

Understanding the slowdown of the British economy between 1873 and 1890 has troubled many historians. There were real technological advances but on the whole its seems that the outlay on fixed capital in many of the larger industries was so great that it did not readily yield to re-investment, and it took a much larger investment to increase productivity. It became common to talk about the British economy as 'mature', as if it were no longer in its youthful growth phase, or even 'over-mature', or 'senile'. Edwin Cannan, in the *Economic Journal,* revived an old fear of David Ricardo's which he called 'the law of diminishing returns' – the fear that over time greater investment would yield falling profits. There were exaggerations in that, but it was clear that there was a change in the rate of industrial growth in Britain.[5]

The slower growth in Britain was understood at the time to be connected with the country's relation to the world economy. One of the features of the British economy that stood out was the far greater role that overseas investment played compared to other economies. In the decade before the slowdown of 1873 overseas investment was fully forty per cent of British investment. That fell back after 1873, but then in the decade from 1885 to 1894 overseas investment was equal to half of all domestic investment. By comparison, German overseas investment was equal to 12.9 per cent and then 20 per cent of domestic investment in the same decades.[6]

P. J. Cain and A. G. Hopkins make the point that 'before 1870, home and foreign investment fluctuated more or less in unison', on a seven-year cycle. But after that 'the paths of home and foreign investment diverged, each setting into a pattern of swings … which were inverse to each other'.[7] Arguably, though, this was a return to the older pattern of the mercantilist era, when, as Smith complained, overseas investment ate up domestic. In this new imperialist era, investment overseas was a refuge for Britain's surplus capital when the domestic economy was in trouble.

The City of London played a great part in the promotion of overseas investment, with the flotation of loans to overseas governments and industries. The big merchant banks in London, Barings, Rothschilds, Kleinwort and Hambro sold shares in these overseas flotations to British investors looking for a good return on their capital. It was to the great advantage of the British investors that the City of London had come to dominate the world market for capital investment. Throughout the mid-century loans raised in the City helped to finance the governments and nascent industries of many parts of the world. The surpluses that the industrial revolution had generated were now being loaned out to grow industries overseas. Chief among the places the British capitalists invested in was the United States. British loans helped build America's railroads, and open up the West.

Per cent share of World Manufacturing Output.[8]

	1880	1900	1913
Britain	22.9	18.5	13.6
United States	14.7	23.6	32
Germany	8.5	13.2	14.8
France	7.8	6.8	6.1

Both the United States and Germany were important places for the export of British industrial goods. British loans to Russia and Turkey helped the German economy expand eastwards. By 1870, though, both countries' railway and industrial expansion had reached a natural plateau. Both had expanded to the point that they were significant rivals for overseas markets with the United Kingdom. Both pursued more protectionist policies in the 1870s to defend their markets. These rivals had grown up in part with the help of British investment but having become mature economies they were competing with Britain for a share of world trade. America's share of world manufacturing output exceeded Britain's in 1900. Germany's manufacturing output exceeded Britain's in 1913. These rivals cut into Britain's share of the world export market undermining the advantage the country had enjoyed in the heyday of 'free trade'.

The other way that the City's appetite for American and Russian railway stocks impacted on her domestic industry was that these were rivals for investment funds. The City in the 1880s was largely unmoved by domestic flotations. In 1887, Barings and Rothschilds promoted a £4 million share offer in the proposed Manchester Ship Canal, but only one fifth was sold, and interest mainly came from Lancashire not London. The historian of the City, David Kynaston argues that this was the point that Rothschilds Bank 'decided that British industrial promotions were not for it'. Early plans to light London by the Brush Company were sabotaged when the issue was first oversubscribed, and then later undermined by mischievous rumours spread by City traders. 'The confidence of the public in electricity was almost destroyed' by the traders' huckstering, Alexander Siemens told the Institution of Electrical Engineers.[9]

The City's taste for overseas investments was often highly speculative. Investors had lost on defaulting American railways in 1841–42 but their enthusiasm for distant ventures was undimmed. Loans were raised for the Egyptian Khedive for £9 million in 1885 (by Rothschilds), £2 million for Peking Field Force (by Barings, Jardine Matheson and the Hong Kong and Shanghai Bank) for the Ottoman Court. That year Argentina's finance minister Carlos Pellegrini restructured debts of £45 million with Barings and Morgans on the condition that their Finance Ministry accept oversight from London.

In 1887, after gold was discovered on the Witwatersrand in South Africa, a number of mining companies were floated, and the one that secured the best price was Cecil Rhodes' Consolidated Gold Fields. Rhodes followed that up with De Beers Consolidated that had the concession on the Kimberley Gold Mines. The most dramatic of all foreign purchases was not floated at all. Prime Minister Benjamin Disraeli finding out that the Khedive of Egypt was aiming to raise cash by the sale of his share in the Suez Canal, by-passed the Stock Market and the Bank of England to raise the purchase price of £4 million from Rothschilds. A cartoon in the satirical *Punch* pictured Disraeli less than heroically extending the Empire by handing over a sack of cash to the Khedive, but the sharp rise in the share price confirmed the success of the venture. British control over the gateway to India and influence in Egypt was stepped up.[10]

In 1888 the 'independent journal of finance and trade', *The Statist,* did a breakdown of Barings' offers showing that all but two were overseas, the brochures were misleading, and Barings' own fees undeclared. Other signs that some of the flotations were untrustworthy was the failure of the Chilean Nitrate Rails offer organised by Colonel North – the proposed rail to carry the nitrate across difficult terrain came unstuck because of political instability in the country. In 1890 Barings came close to bringing the whole City down when its Argentine loans defaulted. Barings' losses were greater than the Bank of England reserve, and it was only by persuading the Russian Government, the Joint-Stock Banks and other traders who were holding Barings' bills not to try to cash them in that the Governor in Threadneedle Street stopped the run.[11]

The key to all of these seemingly adventurous speculations was that while the country was suffering from low growth and factory closures, the City of London was enjoying a bull market, thanks to a great glut of capital; the reserves that British companies and investors were reluctant to plough back into their own businesses were burning holes in their pockets. If mills and canals in Britain looked like yesterday's news, the prospect of generous returns on the Ottoman court or a Chinese railway was much more novel.

The City in the mid-century was whiggish but by the 1870s it was returning three Tories and one Liberal MP. The City traders were very much against Gladstone's Home Rule for Ireland proposal and resisted, too, the reform of local Government that would demote the Lord Mayor of London. To resist Gladstone, Robert Fowler stood for Lord Mayor. Fowler set up the Imperial Federation League with the help of another former mayor William McArthur. The Imperial Federation League campaigned to keep the French out of the Suez Canal, and championed the annexation of Upper Burma to stymie the Gallic enemy there. Already the City had risen up in protest at the nationalist revolt in Egypt, motivated, thought the *Economist*, by 'the prices of Egyptian securities' rather than any higher interest. Gladstone promised that 'the bondholders' interests would be protected' and when a rumour went round that Admiral Seymour's fleet was bombarding Alexandria, the bonds rose in value. David McLean of the Hongkong and Shanghai Bank wrote 'I want to see England take Egypt and hold it'.[12]

'The Bondholders are now in possession of Egypt', protested the Radical publisher Frederic Harrison, speaking for the 'Anti-Aggression League':

> Does it follow that, because certain Englishmen hold large sums in Unified bonds, and because they have invested much capital in Egyptian works, that Europeans are to be guaranteed as a dominant caste?[13]

Fowler's Imperial Federation League invited Lord Salisbury to a dinner at the London Chamber of Commerce in 1889, where he promised them that, 'our greatest duty is to provide the material for defending the splendid commerce which your enterprise has created'. Fowler and McArthur were not typical Gung Ho imperialists: both were active in the Aborigines' Protection Society. Fowler, in his role as Lord Mayor, invited Tawhiao and the other leaders of the Maori King movement to the Mansion House, to help them press their claims against the English settlers in New Zealand.

In 1882 the British fleet bombarded Alexandria, to put down the 'Urabi revolt'.

By the new century the forward policy that the City clamoured for had a name, the New Imperialism. Radicals like Henry Fox Bourne (who took over as Secretary of the Aborigines' Protection Society after Robert Fowler died) were making the connections, as he did in his pamphlet: *The Struggle For Markets: The First Report Of A Commission To Inquire Into The Causes Of Modern War* (1903). The radical John Hobson argued that the driving force behind imperialism was 'excessive capital in search of investment', and 'the endeavour of the great controllers of industry to broaden the channel for the flow of their surplus wealth by seeking foreign markets and foreign investments to take off the goods and capital that they cannot sell or use at home'.

Hobson copied Mulhall's estimate of Britain's overseas investments:

1862	£144,000,000
1872	£600,000,000
1882	£875,000,000
1893	£1,698,000,000

Which, as he said, meant that fully 15 per cent of all UK wealth was overseas.[14]

There were flaws in Hobson's thesis (including a tendency to see the controlling hand of the Jews behind high finance). What he did understand was that the New Imperialism was a new stage in Britain's relationship to the world, where the problems at home could no longer be contained, but would instead drive outwards looking for solutions in the wider world, under the sign of Empire.

The rush to claim colonies in Africa had been so fast that the government entrusted the exploitation of some of these new territories to chartered companies, in an echo of the chartered companies of the mercantilist era. These were not all successful. The British East Africa Company was more of a political vehicle than a money-making enterprise. On its board were some of the Anti-Slavery Society activists that lobbied for its franchise, like the younger Thomas Fowell Buxton. They were captivated by the dream of a railway from Lake Victoria to the coast. In September 1891, the Company wrote to the Colonial Secretary to say that it had little chance but to retrench, having spent three quarters of its capital, and was losing £30–40,000 a year.[15]

George Goldie Taubman's Royal Niger Company, formed as the United African Company raised one million in investments when it became a government chartered monopoly in 1886. Taubman traded in palm oil but depended on anti-competitive treaties with local chiefs to sustain his business. When King Jaja of Opobo organised his own trading network, he was lured onto a Royal Navy ship, seized and then exiled to St Vincent, charged with breach of treaty. The company was eventually wound up and its assets transferred to the British government when the protectorate was declared in 1900.

The African companies that did succeed were those in South Africa, notably, De Beers, the British South Africa Company, created by charter in 1889, and like De Beers, largely controlled by Cecil Rhodes till his death in 1902. In the Rand Gold Fields many mining companies succeeded including those of Alfred Beit, Sir Lionel Philips and Samuel Marks – so that they were known as 'Randlords'.

Chapter Twenty-one

SCRAMBLE FOR AFRICA

Before 1871 British colonial territories in Africa were negligible. Britain had occupied Cape Coast Castle and Bance Island in West Africa since the late 1600s. In 1806, they took the settlement at the Cape of Good Hope from the Dutch.

Between 1871 and 1900 British colonies and protectorates (including Egypt and Sudan) grew to territory of 4,065,398 square miles covering 61,503,360 people. The 'protectorates' were self-governing but having agreed to let the Crown organise their international relations and other aspects of government.

Other European powers also laid claim to African colonies in these years, notably the Belgian 'Congo Free State', some 900,000 square miles with a population of three million in 1903; German East Africa; and French Algeria.

Each of these territories, peoples and designations had their own history and definite events led up to the moment that they were annexed by Britain or the other European powers. It makes sense to put them all together because over and above the unique national questions there was a 'scramble for Africa' among the European powers. Apart from developments in Africa the colonising trend pushed on through into Asia and the Pacific, too.

The colonising trend on Britain's part rose to a great crescendo around the turn of the century. Its causes were a seemingly contradictory mix of high and low motives. Exploiting Africa's economic, human and natural resources was high on the agenda. And there was a competition for territorial gains between the Great Powers – the 'scramble'. But so, too, were there goals of freeing Africans from slavery and also from superstition (that is, converting them to Christianity).

These motives jar in the minds of modern students of those events, and it is common, and understandable, to think that the 'high' motives were just a disguise for baser greed. For Victorians, though, the difference between making money and acting morally was not so great as it is for us. To them, free labour was morally enriching. Free markets encouraged self-sufficiency and independence.

British colonisation of Africa.[1]

Name		Finally acquired	Area, Sq. miles	Population
Ashanti		1901	70,000	2,000,000
Gambia		1888	3,550	215,000
Lagos		1899	42,217	688,049
Niger Coast	A protectorate	1898	500,000	40,000,000
Egypt	A 'veiled protectorate'	1882	400,000	9,734,405
Sudan		1882	950,000	10,000,000
Zanzibar		1888	1,000,000	200,000
East Africa	A protectorate	1895		250,000
Uganda	A protectorate	1896	140,000	3,800,000
Somali Coast	A protectorate	1885	68,000	
British Central Africa	A protectorate	1889	42,217	688,049
Griqualand West		1880	15,197	83,373
Zululand		1897	10,521	240,000
Bechuanaland	A protectorate	1891	326,424	161,952
Transkei		1885	2,535	153,582
Tembuland		1885	4,155	180,130
Pondoland		1894	4,040	188,000
Griqualand East		1885	7,511	152,609
British South Africa Charter		1889	750,000	321,000
Transvaal		1900	117,732	1,354,200
Orange River County		1900	50,000	385,045

The discovery of diamonds at Kimberley (1868) and then the excavation of the gold fields led Lord Carnarvon, Secretary of State for the Colonies to push for a confederation of the southern African colonies and protectorates. The drive towards a Union of South Africa reversed the policy of disengagement that Lord Glenelg had pushed at the time of the Aborigines' Select Committee of 1835. Diamond miner and later Prime Minister at the Cape, Cecil Rhodes championed British control, eventually provoking war with the Dutch settlers.

Britain's manufacturers often dreamed about beckoning overseas markets, but economic ambitions for Africa beyond the mines at Kimberley and Witwatersrand were often fanciful. In 1878, the Lancashire MP Thomas Bayley Potter looked forward to selling cotton to 400 million Africans, though the population would not reach that figure for another century.[2] After withdrawing from the Atlantic slave trade, Britain bought palm oil (for soap) and ivory on the former slave coast, and the City of London invested in Egyptian debts, and from 1888 fostered a boom in South Africa's recently discovered gold fields. The Suez Canal was from its opening in 1869, and the British purchase of the Khedive's share in 1875, a big help to Britain's East India trade.

Africa was morally important to Britain. Having been the greatest slave trading nation in the eighteenth century, anti-slavery became core to Britain's idea of itself, and its diplomatic and military push to police the seas. The middle classes in Britain campaigned hard against slavery in the United States between 1840 and 1860, marrying moral outrage and patriotic anti-Americanism. Missions to Africa were of growing importance.

One thing that the missionaries and the investors agreed was that it was a great thing to be governed by Britain, which was an enlightened power and the enemy of oppression everywhere. There were critics who argued against this view, but they were very much in the minority in Britain in the nineteenth century.

The Civilising Mission in Africa

Right at the forefront of the imperial mission was the goal of civilising Africa, and of freeing Africa from Arab slavery.

In 1866, with the American civil war over, the British West Africa Squadron was reporting that the trans-Atlantic slave trade was at an end. The Anti-Slavery Society was talking about winding up. They were challenged, though, by the missionary David Livingstone, who having returned to Britain in 1864, was telling anyone who would listen that the Arab slavers were trading as many as 30,000 Africans a year out of Zanzibar, and that they had depopulated an area 100 miles wide around Lake Nyasa.

Livingstone argued that Britain was complicit because they had through different treaties helped Sayyid Sa'id bin Sultan (1791–1856) to power in Muscat and Oman, and also supported his son the Sayyid Majid (1834–70) to the Sultanate in Zanzibar. The treaties that Britain and the Sultans of Oman and Zanzibar signed put limits on the slave trade but did not ban it. Under these treaties, slaves were not to be sold to Britons, nor between January and May.[3]

A number of Royal Navy officers who had served in West Africa Squadron wanted to take the campaign to the other side of the continent to challenge the slave trade out of Zanzibar. Commodore Leopold Heath and midshipman (later captain) Edward Spencer Meara had served together on the West Africa coast. They were joined by George Sulivan (who had fought in an attack on an Arab slave fort in the Mozambique channel) and Lieutenant Philip Columb in the squadron Heath gathered to enforce the ban on slave trading in the Indian ocean.[4]

This new anti-slavery squadron had success breaking up the slave trade out of Zanzibar, but it upset relations with the Foreign Office (FO), Arab traders up the African coast, and at Oman and Aden. The British India Office was also keen to keep up a trade that many Indian expatriates in Zanzibar invested in, as well as keeping the trade round the Arabian sea going. At a FO meeting in November 1869 Commodore Heath was attacked by Henry Rothery, a lawyer for the treasury, and William Wylde who was head of the 'anti-slavery' desk at the FO, for jeopardising trade relations with the Arabs. The Foreign Secretary Lord Clarendon had new instructions issued to the Navy that greatly limited its 'stop and search' powers East of Cape Town.[5]

The limitations were misjudged. Heath and his anti-slavery squadron were heroes to a revived anti-slavery campaign, in church halls, and in the popular press, which retold their stories of daring deeds to liberate enslaved Africans. In England, waiting for new commissions, George Sulivan and Philip Columb wrote popular books about their adventures. Gladstone and Queen Victoria both denounced the Arab slave trade. At a great meeting of the Anti-Slavery Society, on the 29 May 1872, Sir Henry Bartle Frere trumpeted 'only where the Christian religion has extended and shed its influence that you find an end put to slavery and the desire to make slaves'.[6] Empire, anti-Slavery and Christianity were all brought together in a wave of self-righteousness.

Formally Egypt was a part of the Ottoman Empire and the Khedive Ismail Pasha sent £7 million in tribute every year. The Khedive's ambitions to modernise the country were expensive, as was the life of his court, and he was greatly in debt to bankers in London and Paris, who exacted their own tribute in interest repayments (though the Khedive would borrow more to meet these).

It was the Khedive's uncle Mohammed Said who on coming to power as Wali of Egypt in 1854 agreed to Ferdinand de Lessep's plant to dig a canal from Port Said in the Mediterranean to Suez on the Red Sea – opening the route from Europe to the Indian Ocean. It took fifteen years and much forced labour to dig the 101-mile-long canal which opened on 17 November 1869.The company admitted that 1,390 fellaheen died digging the canal, though Egyptians said the number was in the tens of thousands (120,000 according to Prime Minister Gamal Abdel Nasser in 1956[7]). De Lesseps accompanied the French Empress Eugenie on the imperial yacht down the canal and Giuseppe Verdi was commissioned to write the opera Aida to celebrate it. The canal cut the journey from Liverpool to Calcutta from 11,600 miles, when ships went around the horn of Africa, to 7,900.

Under the original terms, the Compagnie Universelle du Canal Maritime de Suez awarded Egypt 44 per cent of the company stock, a 15 per cent royalty, and an option to buy it out after 99 years. But only six years after the opening the Khedive Ismail was so heavily in debt that he had to sell his share of the stock to Britain for £4 million. (In 1880, the Khedive Tewfik had to sell his 15 per cent royalty to a French group for 22 million francs.)[8]

The Khedive had another problem in the lawlessness of his southern province of Sudan, that he met by recruiting European officers to lead his Egyptian army south. Understanding European sentiment, the Khedive covered this landgrab with the fig leaf of anti-slavery. Among those European officers was Charles Gordon, called 'Chinese Gordon' for his leadership in the campaign of the Ever-Victorious Army over the Taiping Rebellion. The Khedive made Gordon Governor General of Sudan, with a mandate to rid the country of slavery – though many were sceptical of Egypt's observation of its own anti-slavery laws. On a second tour, Gordon confronted Muhammad Ahmad, proclaimed the Mahdi, redeemer of the Islamic faith, and founder of an Islamic state in Sudan, the Mahdiyya. The Mahdi's supporters included slave-traders among the Baggara and Dongolawi peoples. Gordon's trek to Khartoum left him isolated from his supply routes to the north. Gordon's messages out got to England, where a great movement gathered demanding his relief, and Sir Garnet Wolseley was sent to the Sudan. In January 1885, the Mahdi's forces broke into Khartoum and on the 26th Gordon was killed, with Wolseley's relief expedition just a fortnight away. (The characterisation of the Mahdiyya as a slave-owner's regime was justified by the alliances the Mahdi and his successors made with slave traders, though as it turned out, the isolation of the Sudan from Egypt also disrupted and greatly dampened the slave trade.)[9]

In Europe the clamour for united action against the Arab slave trade grew stronger. With the end of slavery in Brazil the Vatican was at last free to denounce the trade, so that Christians from the non-conformists, through the Church of England to the Papal See were united in condemnation of Arab slavers. England's Cardinal Manning joined the anti-slavery platform to claim that:

> the great Mahometan Slave-trade was far worse, far more atrocious, far more outrageous, far more cruel, far more degrading, far more brutal to man, woman and child that was the Slave-trade of the West, horrible as were the cruelties of the Middle Passage.[10]

It is hard not to see the defensiveness about Europe's own record in the determination to decry the 'Arab slave trade'. There were some hypocrisies in the way that the British addressed slavery. The slaves freed by Leopold Heath and other Africa Squadron boats most often were disembarked in Mauritius or the Seychelles, where they were made indentured labourers on sugar plantations; Gordon in office in Sudan did not abolish slavery; even Livingstone was accused of flogging his bearers. Those who set themselves up as moral icons are open to charges of hypocrisy. The harder question was whether European authority over Africans would make their lives better or worse.

These public demands for action helped the European powers to frame their overseas policy towards Africa. A number of conferences were held ostensibly to address the problem of slavery, though they all concluded by agreeing the division of the continent between European powers.

1. **Brussels Geographic Conference of 1876.** King Leopold of the Belgians, Victoria's uncle, laid claim to govern a Congo Free State. Hosted by the Association Internationale Africaine. Leopold claimed the new Congo Free State would rid the country of slavery and help the natives. Leopold had the support of the Aborigines' Protection Society in London and the explorer Henry Morton Stanley.[11]

2. **Berlin Conference of 1884–85.** The Conference was hosted by Otto von Bismarck with the support of the British Government. Once again, the explicit cause of the conference was to promote an end to slavery, but it ended up parcelling up authority to European powers to act as custodians for African peoples. The great powers bound themselves 'to watch over the preservation of the native tribes'.[12] Leopold's Congo Free State was agreed. Around this time Britain was preoccupied with stalling French influence, so saw the attraction of supporting Belgium and Germany as counterweights to French influence.

   'We are forced by German, French and Portuguese ambitions to extend our direct political influence over a large part of Africa', explorer Harry Johnston told the *Times* in 1888. Africa's great wealth meant that it was 'destined to be exploited by the white races'. Johnston's article had been agreed by the British Secretary of State for Foreign Affairs, Lord Salisbury.[13]

3. **Brussels Conference of 1889–90.** In August 1889 Queen Victoria announced:

   > At my suggestion, the King of the Belgians has consented to summon in the autumn a Conference of the European Powers at Brussels, which will consider the present

condition of the Slave-trade both by land and sea, and will deliberate upon measures for arresting or mitigating the evils which it still inflicts on mankind.[14]

'In 1889 sixteen of the principal nations of the world agreed at Brussels to suppress the
internal slave trade', wrote economist Lilian Knowles: 'Meanwhile, the extension of
European rule in Africa gave effective means for carrying this out.'[15]

Today the Brussels conference is remembered as the carve up of Africa – which it
was – and for the 15-feet-high map of Africa that loomed over it. Less well remembered
is that the map was put there by the British Anti-Slavery Society which prepared the
conference papers with the Foreign Office. The map was meant to show the main slave
routes, though as people suspected, it helped the delegates decide how to divide the continent between them. At the time, the British Prime Minister insisted that 'the matters
with which on the present surface of the world we are most concerned, strange to say,
are the interests not of Europe, but of Africa'.[16]

In a bilateral meeting with Germany in 1886 Britain agreed to divide up the Sultan
of Zanzibar's mainland territories between the two European powers, becoming the
bases of British East Africa (Kenya today) and German East Africa (Tanzania) – an
agreement that was rubber-stamped in Brussels in 1890.

In the middle of the conference, Henry Morton Stanley, explorer and promoter of
Leopold's Congo Free State – the man who had found Dr Livingstone in 1871, returned
from another relief expedition. He had been sent to find Emin Pasha, in Equatorial Africa,
and now returned, to great acclaim. In a speech in Brussels on 23 April, Stanley said that
he 'returns from the Black Continent and finds assembled at Brussels a Conference of the
Powers, pledged to war against the scourge of Africa, and a Society existing in Belgium
devoted entirely to the extirpation of that evil'.[17]

The fall-out of the Berlin and Brussels conferences was profound. British and
German East Africa Companies set up in Mombasa and Pangani town respectively,
and they provoked a Swahili-Arab revolt led by Abushiri ibn Salim al-Harthi up the
East African coast. Egypt, which had caused anxiety on the London stock exchange by
the revolt against onerous interest payments in 1882, was put down. Egypt's national
debt was stabilised at £100,000,000 on which the Egyptians paid £4,500,000 interest
each year, and a special Slave Trade Department under Colonel Schaeffer was imposed
to reform the country. Earl Cromer described the arrangement under which he, as
British Consul General effectively governed while the Khedive stayed in place as 'a
hybrid form of government to which no name can be given because there is no precedent'. It was often called the 'veiled protectorate'.[18]

Britain also claimed the lands that are today Nigeria at the Berlin Conference of
1885. They had already control of Lagos after installing Oba Akitoye and accepting
Deed of Cession from him in 1852. The Royal Niger Company of George Taubman
Goldie managed the territories for Britain until 1900 when they were made into two
Protectorates, North and South, and then united as a colony in 1914.

Southern Africa

'You will take one slice of Africa after another, till you get to Delagoa Bay', Andries Stockenstrom, a Commissioner of the Frontier told the Aborigines Select Committee of the House of Commons, in 1835[19] – 70 years later his prediction had come true.

The drive to colonise southern Africa followed different lines from the campaigns in the Sudan and East Africa. Slavery was not the main issue in the British mission there. Most of the pressure for change came from the clash of the Boers, the British and black South African peoples, the Zulu, the Xhosa, the Tswana, and the Sotho – and from the discovery of valuable minerals from 1867, diamonds and then gold.

In the first half of the nineteenth century, the English and Dutch settlers fought successive wars first with the Khoisan and then with the Xhosa over the land to the East of Cape Town, from Port Elizabeth to the Kei River. Khoi and Xhosa challenged settlers from 1799–1803 around Bethelsdorp, and after settlers clashed again in 1812, 1819, 1834–35 and 1846–47.[20]

Each of the extensions of British authority had their own story, but the underlying dynamic was this – the Dutch settlers, called Boers, had trekked northwards out of the Cape Colony from 1836 to evade British rule.[21] They clashed with native peoples over land and resources as they moved further inland. The British colonial authorities sought to keep control over the Boers and through the 1870s and 1880s backed native land claims to limit their 'voortrek'. Britain played a dangerous game of 'divide and rule' with the Boers and the natives which made their relations more antagonistic than they already were. Inviting Sotho, Tswana and Zulu to accept British protection against Boer incursions turned out to be a trap. Each people were successively subordinated to British rule, indirectly at first, through compliant native chiefs, and then directly put under white command.[22]

Zululand

After a conference in London in 1876 Lord Carnarvon set out the plan (worked out by James Froude) for a South African Union that would take in the Boers' Orange Free State, but their leader Jan Hendrik Brand walked out. Natal administrator Theophilus Shepstone, who was also there, had instructions to take over the Transvaal, if he could get the Boers' approval. Shepstone overstated Boer support for the annexation and went ahead but was straight away faced with opposition. To placate the Boers, Shepstone promised a war against the Zulu, whose chief, Cetshwayo, he had helped enthrone. Sir Henry Bartle Frere was pushing for them to be brought under a Confederation of South Africa. On 11 January 1879, Bartle Frere sent a force of 18,000 British troops into Zululand. Just 11 days later the British were surrounded on the hills at Isandlhwana, and 900 English troops and another 470 of their native allies were killed by the Zulu.[23] To Queen Victoria's dismay, Prince Louis Napoleon, who had volunteered for service in the British Army was among the dead. The defeat at the hands of a Zulu army was a tremendous shock to the British Army and to the public back home.

Cetshwayo.

After pulling back into Natal, the British re-invaded and took their revenge at Ulundi, in July, where the main Zulu force was defeated. The invasion was brutal and led to many atrocities. King Cetshwayo was eventually defeated, but the mood in Britain turned as Gladstone criticised the overreaching policy in the 1880 'Midlothian' election campaign. A repentant Cetshwayo promised to accept Shepstone's tutelage. But to the discomfort of Shepstone and his secretary, H. Rider Haggard (who went on to write popular adventure stories of Empire), Cetshwayo went to England on Lord Kimberley's invitation, where his gracious manner and good looks made him a big hit with fashionable society, and with the Queen.[24]

Back home Cetshwayo's status was greatly limited as Shepstone promoted other, rival chiefs, Zibhebhu principally, and handed land over to the Boers. Cetshwayo died in 1884, poisoned by the British said some, but certainly he was already a hunted man, his Usuthu clan having been attacked and harried by Zibhebhu.[25]

Cetshwayo's son, Dinuzulu assumed leadership of the Usuthu, but clashed with the Resident Commissioner Melmoth Osborne, refusing to accept British rule. He was tried and exiled to St Helena from 1890–97.[26]

Tswana

The Tswana territory was coveted by English miners after diamonds had been found on the Vaal riverbeds. In 1872, the British adjusted the borders of Griqualand, already a British protectorate, when a new mine (which became known as 'The Big Hole') was found. Under a proclamation of that year natives were forbidden from holding diamond claims. Judge Sidney Shippard dismissed the Tswana Chief's claims abruptly: 'the idea of Jantjie's royal rights to minerals and precious [stones] is ludicrous in the extreme'.[27] The miners called their claims 'Barkly West' after the Cape Governor Henry Barkly, and then 'Kimberley' after the Secretary of State for the Colonies.

In 1884, the British created a Protectorate in Southern Bechuanaland with the agreement of some of the Tswana chiefs. The land was under pressure from Boers and the British claimed to want to defend them. In the event Shippard's Land Commission reserved just eight per cent of Bechuanaland for 50,000 Tswana, while handing over the best farms to white settlers. Luka Jantjie (pronounced Yanki) rose up against Shippard's land commission in 1896, and despite leading a heroic resistance, was killed.[28]

Sotho

King Moshoeshoe (1786–1870) founded the mountain kingdom of the Sotho (which the English called Basutoland) signing a mutual defence pact with the Crown in 1843. The British Resident Major Warden over-interpreted his authority and tried to overthrow Moshoeshoe in a row over farmland. Warden was quickly overwhelmed and withdrew in disgrace. Later, Britain armed the Sotho to stymie the Boers. When Moshoeshoe's son Malapo made a separate peace with the Boers, Theophilus Shepstone invaded and annexed his territory – which the English called Alfred County – to Natal. Then, in 1868, the Cape Governor Wodehouse annexed Basutoland claiming that conflict between them and the Boers was too threatening. Later the British used the pretext of a revolt by a rival chief Morosi as a reason to disarm all the Sotho.[29] The ensuing 'Gun War' cost many lives, including 39 British Army lancers killed in an attack in October 1880.

Cape Colony Governor Henry Bartle Frere was widely criticised in Parliament and made to stand down by Lord Kimberley. Basutoland, mostly made up of inhospitable mountainous territory left over after white farmers had grabbed the best land, was made a crown colony in 1884. As colonial subjects the Sotho were used as a labour resource for the Kimberley mines and gold mines on the Reef after 1886.[30]

Settler Colonialism

White settlers had made colonies in other parts of the Empire. Settlers in North America, Australia and New Zealand had tended to drive the native peoples off the land they farmed. Settlers in the Caribbean had imported slave labour to work their plantations. Settlers in India played the role of governing administrators and reserved some industries for their own. Settlers in Malaysia became the class of planters and mine-owners.

Settlers in southern Africa made a distinctive colonialism that rested on the continuing exploitation of the native peoples as farm labourers and miners. Proportionately, the white settlers of southern Africa were a large minority that monopolised political power. Unlike those settler colonies of Australia and Canada, the settlers of southern Africa marshalled much of the native population into an engine of production.

Boer Wars

The conflict between the Boers and the British was real, and explosive, leading to wars in 1880–81 and then again, and at terrible cost, in 1899–1902. The second Boer war was marked by brutal oppression. Lord Kitchener's Army destroyed 30,000 farms and drove 160,000 women and children into concentration camps, where 28,000 as well as a lot more African labourers starved to death.[31]

Driving the British determination to control South Africa was the discovery of first diamonds, and then later Gold in the Rand. A febrile group of investors in the City of London were led by Barney Barnato and inspired by Cecil Rhodes to push hard for military action. Gold mining stocks were known on the exchange as 'Kaffirs', and the traders were called the 'Kaffir Circus'. Their raucous agitation led at one point to a great protest by stock traders in Threadneedle Street, after some of their number had been arrested.[32]

The Boers' brutalisation of black South Africans featured heavily in British war propaganda. Joseph Chamberlain, facing criticism from war sceptics, protested that 'the laws of the Transvaal are harsh, arbitrary and cruel', and asked, 'are we to reject the whole history of South Africa and say the Boers are the friends of the natives?'[33] Once the Boers were defeated Chamberlain's attitude changed. The settlement of the war meant that the Boers would be brought into a new South African Union, that governed all the native protectorates. On Chamberlain's instructions, Kitchener wrote to the Boer leader General Louis Botha (1862–1919) promising that the settlement would 'secure a just predominance of the white race'.[34] The Boer second-in-command Jan Smuts replied: 'two such peoples as the Dutch and the English must either unite or try to exterminate each other'. They needed to 'start a Union here and to rule the country from here to the Congo, and even beyond that'.[35] White unity was bought at the price of discrimination against black Africans.

In 1913, the South Africa Land Act imposed a harsh settlement on black South Africans who were restricted to 7.3 per cent of the land in native reservations, mostly on the poorest agricultural land, so that they were dependent on work from the white South Africans for subsistence. Taxes were also imposed so they had to work for white farmers and mine owners to earn wages to pay them.[36]

Rivals

At the end of the 'Scramble for Africa' most of the continent, apart from the Ethiopian highlands, was nominally occupied by Europeans, and the important economic centres of Egypt, Mombasa, Lagos, the Gold Coast and Cape Colony were clearly under British control. France had already colonised Algiers in 1840, invading the coastal city after a dispute over debts owed to Algerian grain merchants escalated into a diplomatic row. By 1871, France defeated the last resistance to her rule in Algiers, led by Sheikh Mohamed el-Mokhrani. In 1881 the French took the opportunity of raids by Khroumir tribesmen into Algeria to invade Tunis (though in the medium term they were more worried by Italian and British purchases of rail and land). By May they had obliged the Bey – whose Ottoman overlords were losing influence – to grant the Treaty of Bardo, making Tunis a French Protectorate.[37]

French West Africa in 1915.[38]

Colony	Area Sq. M.	French population	Total population
Senegal	74,000	4,226	1,247,979
Guinea	93,000	1,082	1,812,579
Ivory Coast	125,000	910	1,417,029
Dahomey	39,000	617	911,759
Upper Senegal and Niger	301,000	1,134	5,598,973
Military territory of the Niger	502,000	79	850,094
Mauritania	344,000	163	600,164
Total	1,478,000	8,905	12,486,567

In West Africa France expanded inwards from the slave trading capital of Senegal into sugar-growing Casamance in the 1880s. French Guinea was expanded northwards into the Islamic state of Fouta-Jalon, made a Protectorate in 1881, and exclusive trading party from 1891. From the 1860s France had concessions on the old Slave Coast from the Dahomey chief Gléglé and Grand Popo and Porto Novo. In 1890, they attacked his son Béhanzin – 'how many French villages have been attacked by me?' he asked, rhetorically. Béhanzin was eventually defeated in 1893 and exiled to Martinique, and Dahomey made a French colony. Marcel Treich-Laplène, who worked for a trading company, and Louis-Gustave Binger, an officer in the colonial army, raised a campaign against Samory Touré for the territories that became the Côte D'Ivoire in 1893. Samory was finally defeated in 1898 and interned in Gabon where he died two years later. French power extended into Mali, Niger, Cameroon, Togo Chad, Djibouti, and the territory called French Equatorial Africa.[39]

The British had favoured German colonisation in South-West Africa and in Tanganyika, as a barrier to French expansion. Towards the end of the nineteenth century, Britain came to be more alarmed by German expansion and started to favour France as a counterweight the other way. In an agreement of 1890 Britain and France acknowledged their respective rights to Zanzibar and Madagascar, after many years of mutual suspicion. In 1897 the War Office was already preparing a *Scheme for Operations Against German East Africa*.

German Africa in 1913.[40]

	Acquired	Area (Sq miles)	White population	Native population
Togo	1884	33,700	368	1,032,978
Kamerun	1884	191,300	1,871	2,648,720
South West Africa	1884–90	322,450	14,830	79,556
East Africa	1885–90	384,180	5,836	7,645,770
Total German Africa	1884–90	931,460	22,405	11,406,024

The United States at that time, backed Britain in Africa. American investors and mining engineers were active in East and South Africa. The archaeologist Charles Waldstein spoke for America's Anglophile ascendancy when he wrote:

> The expansion of England and its opening out of the world's ports to commerce is *ipso facto* the expansion of American commerce without the cost of blood and substance to the United States.[41]

Britain would clash with France and Germany in Africa, but not America.

The Consolidation of British Africa and the Re-creation of Chiefly Power

In 1854, Parliament received reports on the African colonies of Sierra Leone, Gambia, the Gold Coast, the Cape of Good Hope and Natal. By 1937, British tropical Africa included the Union of South Africa (which included Natal from 1910) and its territories of Swaziland and Tswanaland (then Bechuanaland, today Botswana), Southern Rhodesia (today Zimbabwe), northern Rhodesia (today Zambia), Kenya (which had been British East Africa), Nyasaland (today Malawi) and Uganda (which had been British Central Africa); in the West there was Nigeria (including Lagos), Sierra Leone and the Gold Coast. After World War I the German colony of South West Africa (Namibia) was governed by South Africa, and Tanganyika, otherwise known as German East Africa or Tanzania was a British colony, as were the Cameroons. Britain also governed in Somaliland from 1920, in Sudan (jointly with Egypt from 1899) and had effective control of Egypt (the 'veiled protectorate').

European settlement in British Africa was not extensive with the exceptions of Cape colony, where, in 1892 one third of a million Europeans settled alongside more than a million Xhosa, Mfengu and other African peoples on 200 square miles of territory; Natal and Zululand, where in 1898 55,000 settlers lived alongside 800,000 Africans (including more than 200,000 Zulus) on not quite 30,000 square miles; the main Witwatersrand gold reef was discovered in June 1884 and Johannesburg founded in 1886. The discovery of gold rapidly attracted people to the area, and within 10 years, the city of Johannesburg included 100,000 people. Southern Rhodesia where, by 1921, 34,000 Europeans lived alongside 830,000 Matabele and other peoples in lands totalling 150,000 square miles; Northern Rhodesia, where 10,500 Europeans lived alongside 1,366,425 Africans, in a land larger than England; and Kenya, where, in 1921 just over ten thousand whites lived among two and a half million Africans on territories of 250,000 square miles.[42] The settler populations in the other African colonies were negligible.

Picking pyretheum at Loldiani in the 'White Highlands' of British East Africa.

European settlers in Africa ran farms in the first place, and later managed mines and other businesses. Though Europeans were a small share of the population in a small share of the British colonies they demanded a remarkably large share of the land – often more than they could possibly farm.

Britain claimed East Africa on the basis first of the grant of the Sultan of Zanzibar in 1887 and the protectorate it declared in 1895. The Maasai people of the Rift valley were weakened by cattle epidemics in 1883 and 1889, followed by internal feuding. The British forced them out claiming the fabled 'White Highlands', Kenya's choice farming land for themselves. That the White Highlands were 5,000 feet above sea level, and so cool, was given as a reason that they should be reserved for Europeans. Fully 16,000 square miles were earmarked for 10,000 white settlers. In the end just over ten thousand square miles were taken possession of, and of those only a little more than half were farmed or grazed by Europeans. That was a loss to Africans of one third of the arable land. The 2.5 million Africans were moved onto 'reserved areas' of a little under 50,000 square miles of poorer quality land. The larger reserves were Kavirondo, Kikuyu, Wakamba and Masai. Land hunger, leading to hunger, were a great pressure, particularly on the Kikuyu reserves, and many Kikuyu went to work on European owned farms in exchange for the use of some of the land for themselves.[43]

In Southern Rhodesia, in 1920, 21,595,000 acres were reserved for Africans, against 47,176,700 acres held by settlers – meaning half the land was owned by the white six per cent of the population, while Africans were granted just 21 per cent of their own country. Just over half a million lived in the reserved areas while 122,460 lived and worked on white farms, and others lived in towns or by mines. White farmers in Northern Rhodesia, in Uganda and Tanzania were less successful.

South Africa's settlement between Boer and Briton was a disaster for the Africans. The Land Settlement Act of 1913 left only around 11 per cent of the land to the native peoples. As territories were added to the Union of South Africa the reserved areas were increased in size but remained as a share under 13 per cent. Under the 1936 Land Act 39,417,000 acres were given over to 'native reserves', 12,791,000 in the Cape, 5,880,000 in Natal, 2,256,000 in the Transvaal and 157,000 in the Orange Free State. The 'High Commission' territories Lesotho (Basutoland, then), Tswanaland (Bechuanaland) and Swaziland were truncated territories, like overcrowded annexes serving as more 'reserved territories'.[44]

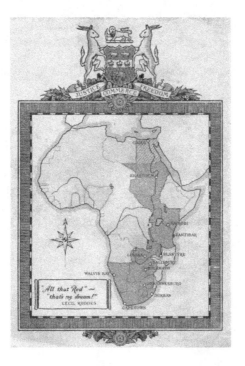

British South Africa Company catalogue,
Empire Exhibition of 1936, Johannesburg.

The reserved territories were often thought of as a surplus labour pool – which they were. Migrant labourers from the reserved areas, and from Swaziland and Bechuanaland worked on European farms and mines. Without them the white-owned concerns would have failed. But the share of territory in the reserved areas, and of the people living on it – not just in the settled territories but across British Africa tells us that the reserves were much more than just a labour pool.

A far greater share of the British Empire's African subjects, in the years from 1880 to 1960, lived and worked under the system of Native Administration than for white farmers and mine-owners. The basic pattern of British rule in Africa was that British-backed chiefs ruled over tribes in districts within the reserved areas under a Native Administration with its own native code of by-laws.[45]

Though the different kinds of leaders that the British met in Africa had different titles in their own languages, from the Emirs of Northern Nigeria to the Induna of the Zulu, to the British they were all 'chiefs', like the Scottish clan leaders that had been defeated in 1745. The British pushed hard against any chiefs who held out against them, but when they did win, they worked hard to recreate chiefly authority to make it work for them. Chiefs were re-purposed as agents of the British Empire. It was through the chiefs' concessions and grants of land, brought cheaply from leaders with a narrow span of resources, that Europeans governed and settled.

The British made the chief into the native counterpart of the District Commissioner. Where the original rulers often had to share power with village elders, or relatives, the Empire needed local chiefs who ruled absolutely. Chiefly authority was supposed to be undiluted. It was on the other hand wholly dependent on the patronage of the Governor though he was careful not to be seen to undermine the chief, because his authority was an important prop for the authority of the Empire. District commissioners and magistrates and local colonial police forces ruled in conjunction with chiefs.

The Native codes gave leeway for punishments including corporal punishments and fines. They generally included the obligation of labour services as a tax due to the chief, for the upkeep of the village and of the roads, and often a contribution in labour or produce to a store for hospitality and for the upkeep of the chief. In theory the native codes embodied native custom, which it was claimed, was handed down from the past. But the native codes were changeable, often in line with circulars that chiefs were sent from the Native Administration about the need to raise levies for special projects, or for the dipping of animals or other practical exigencies.

The system of native administration was codified by Frederick Lugard who had been an agent of the British East Africa Company and then an administrator in Northern Nigeria. Lugard's book *The Dual Mandate* set out the claim that 'European domination' over another race could only be understood as a 'trusteeship', where 'the control of the land … should be exercised in accordance with native law and custom'.[46]

The 'Dual Mandate' made for a dualism between the towns, where the law governing Europeans and even some natives was closer to English law, with a strong presumption of individual agency, and the villages and reserves where the chief governed despotically and personally on the basis of 'custom'. The people in the town were citizens of the colony and indeed of the Empire, whereas those in the villages were subjects. The rights of villagers to private property in land, or to contract freely, even to leave the reserve or tribal area were overruled by the arbitrary power of the chief. Land was – in theory – held as the property of the tribe, administered by the chief and the native authority. Customary rule might seem to clash with the 1865 Act 'to remove Doubts as to the Validity of Colonial Laws', which said that any that were repugnant to an Act of Parliament were 'void and inoperative'. But there was no clash. The Acts creating the colonies allowed for such rights as Britons might enjoy, to be put to one side.

In claiming that the African colonies rested on a mandate to protect, the authorities went so far as to say that in the colony the interests of the African peoples, were 'paramount'. In practice that meant that the colonial authorities were paramount, in so far as they presented their own policies as being meant to look after the natives.

Making native interests 'paramount' was a good way of sidestepping the rights of Indian petitioners, and even of setting limits to European land purchases. Most of all the claim that native interests were 'paramount' was used by the Governors and administrators to tell Africans what their interests were. 'The main object of keeping natives under their own law', explained Natal administrator Theophilus Shepstone, 'is to ensure control of them'.[47]

In 1929 General Jan Smuts, the South African leader who served in Lloyd George's war cabinet, gave a lecture at Oxford University. Equal rights would 'de-Africanise the African and turn him either into a beast in the field or into a pseudo-European':

> The principle of equal rights was applied in its crudest form, and while it gave the native a semblance of equality with whites, which was little good to him, it destroyed the base of his African system which was his highest good.[48]

Though he claimed to be concerned for natives, his own record as a colonial officer was stained with blood. Smuts was responsible for the Bulhoek massacre on 24 May 1921, in Ntabelanga in the Cape Province (today part of Eastern Cape), when 500 supporters of the 'Israelite' sect were attacked by 800 police on his orders. One hundred and sixty-three were killed. The following year Smuts government attacked a group of rebellious Khoi Khoi who were called the Bondlewarts, bombing them from the air and killing more than a hundred. His theories of native administration never meant that Africans could rule themselves free of white control.

A 1930 memorandum on Native Administration in Tanganyika set out that 'every African belonged to a tribe, just as every European belonged to a nation'. 'Each tribe must be considered a distinct unit', and 'each tribe must be under a chief'. The small problem of those familial groups that had no chiefs was met by appointing chiefs for them.[49]

The chiefly system under British colonialism was neither wholly African, nor was it wholly alien. It was a re-creation of African authority under British rule. The claim was that the Empire so stood on African custom. But the customs were not really African – they were a mixture of African and British needs. The unit of the tribe and district might be in the grain of how people lived, but sometimes it was not. In the Sahel and the Horn of Africa transhumant cattle herders roamed widely to chase what grazing there was – but that took them out of the bounds of the 'reserved areas' and the Native Administration wrecked those customs.

The Swazi Royal House changed the labour service to a cash payment – khonta fees – to meet the way that their subjects' lives had shifted from subsistence farmers to migrant labourers in the South African mines. An anthropologist asked about the payment and was told 'this is the custom today, though not in the past'.[50]

In many ways the 'dual mandate' was pragmatic. At the start of World War II there were 1,315 European officials 'governing' twenty million Nigerians. Clearly the only way that could happen was that much practical authority, having been first conceded to the British Crown, was then derogated back down again to local leaders – 'chiefs'.

Once it was formalised, the allocation of Africans into native reserves meant that their rights as citizens in the towns were jeopardised. The 'Stallard Commission', in South Africa reported infamously in 1922 that 'the native should only be allowed to enter the urban areas, which are essentially the white man's creation, when he is willing to enter and minister to the needs of the white man, and should depart therefrom when he ceases so to minister'. There had been a significant reform movement campaigning for the rights of Africans in Cape Colony, the Native Electoral Society, led by John Tengo Jabavu. But the prospect of black civil rights was crushed under the policy of separation.[51]

Each of the settlements that gave rise to the reserved areas and the recognition of chiefs were distinct to the people, their society and the terms of colonisation. Still, a general pattern emerges. The British colonial administration rested on many chiefs and peoples.

Sotho chiefs with Joseph Chamberlain in London in 1907.

There were the Sotho and Swazi chiefs, who came to London in 1907, concerned to assure their place in the new South Africa; Lewanika who brought Barotseland (in today's Zambia) under British control in 1890 and went to Edward VII's coronation in 1902; Siyanbola Ladigbolu the Alaafin of Oyo in Yorubaland managed to secure the sponsorship of Captain William Ross in the colonial administration of Nigeria between 1914 and 1931 to the great disadvantage of other Yoruba chiefs by the forced reading of the Alaafin's primacy among them; to the North Lugard made already made allies of the Fulani Emirs after the defeat of the Sokoto Caliphate at Kano in 1903; after the defeat of the Ashante Kingdom in 1898 the British invited the exiled Prempeh to restore the authority of the Kumasi chiefs in 1926. These were just some of the many chiefs who were first undermined and then re-installed to consolidate British pre-eminence in Africa.

Chiefly rule was an important prop for Britain, and it did give leeway to Africans to local self-government, though with the influence of the Colonial Office on the side of the conservative forces in African society. After the Second World War, with the rising tide of national independence, mostly drawing on modernist and radical leaders in the towns, the chiefs' councils became bulwarks of reaction, and not very strong ones.

Chapter Twenty-two

ASIA

Cyprus

Britain tried to hold the balance of power in the Mediterranean to frustrate French, Egyptian and Russian influence, generally propping up the weakening Ottoman Empire. Britain had naval bases in Gibraltar and Malta but its governorship of the Ionian Islands of Greece had been abandoned in 1864 in the face of a clamour for union with Greece. For strategic reasons, and as an experiment in rallying popular support through Imperial expansion, Prime Minister Disraeli sought to expand Britain's reach over the Eastern Mediterranean by the accession of the island of Cyprus, agreed with a weakened and indebted Ottoman Sultan Abdul Hamid. Announced at the Berlin Congress the handover to Britain was agreed on 1 January 1878, with a ceremonial lowering of the Ottoman standard and raising of the Union Jack.

After the British invasion of Egypt, the strategic advantage of holding Cyprus was less obvious, though the 'Eastern Question' – what would happen to the Balkans if the Ottoman Empire collapsed – was still a major concern. The islanders were 137,631 Greek Orthodox and 45,458 Muslims according to the 1881 census, and the former were at first glad to be out from under Ottoman rule, and hopeful that the British would let them join the Greek mainland. By the letter of the treaty the British only exercised authority in the name of the Ottoman Empire and an annual tribute of £92,000 was exacted each year, though since the British Treasury used the money to pay the English and French holders of its debts, the money never arrived in Turkey. Under High Commissioner Sir Garnet Wolseley the administration spent little and its annual tribute was deeply resented. Under the 1882 constitution there were elected representatives but the Governor-nominated council members usually combined with the Turkish representatives to block any assertion of independence by the majority. The island's police force was mostly Turkish as its population was mostly Greek Orthodox. High Commissioner Wolseley loathed what he called 'these dirty and very ignorant but grasping churchmen of the Greek faith'.[1]

The Gulf

Britain's presence in the Gulf of Aden dates back to the Treaty with the Sultan of Muscat in 1798 and many more treaties with local sultans followed as Britain set out to secure the route into the Arabian Sea and on to India. With the opening of the Suez Canal those treaties got more important.

Captain Haines surveyed the South Arabian coast to find a coaling station for ships going to and from the East India Company territories. In 1839, Britain conquered Aden and later imposed a protectorate on the hinterland. The hostility of local tribesmen was tempered by the port's success, as it grew to a population of around 200,000. Later, the colony would be run from India, not London, because it had been built up to help the trade to that part of the Empire.

A truce with the sheikhdoms of Abu Dhabi, Dubai and others in 1842, made permanent in 1853 created the 'Trucial States'. In 1880, Bahrain signed an agreement of exclusive diplomatic relations with Britain, as did the Trucial Sheikhs in 1887 and again in 1892, and a similar treaty was signed with Muscat and Oman in 1891 (by which the British blocked a planned French coal depot there).

Aden was the biggest port in the Gulf and in 1850 the British made it a free port, lifting all duties. The through trade rose eight-fold to around one million sterling a year. For the most part Britain's policy towards the Gulf Sheikhdoms was for control at arm's length. The British Navy (with the help of the Royal Indian Navy) policed the gulf. In the 1840s the Egyptian viceroy Muhammad Ali impinged upon Yemen, as did the Ottoman Empire in the 1880s – but not significantly.[2]

India

After the Mutiny, British Administration in India was generally conservative in outlook. In the Parliament, Disraeli had blamed the mutiny on excessive reforming on the part of liberal dogmatists, unwilling to let things lie. Caution rather than reform became the norm. 'Labour steadily', Gladstone told Lord Ripon on his appointment as viceroy in 1880. His successor Lord Dufferin said he hoped for an 'uneventful' time in the post where he would keep up a 'low and steady pressure' on the machinery of government.[3]

The Indian Civil Service was run by an elite of around 1,000, who, since 1855 had been chosen by competitive examination. Two thirds were drawn from landowning, military or professional backgrounds, about a fifth from trade backgrounds. Originally the candidates were to be aged 19 years, but the rules were changed to allow university graduates, of whom around half were from Scottish universities. After 1878, apprentice administrators took a two-year course at Balliol College, Oxford. Pay for the Indian Civil Service was high, ranging from £300 a year for an assistant commissioner, £2,700 a year for judges and collectors, £8,000 for a lieutenant governor. The pension for all grades was £1,000 a year after 25 years' service.[4] Beneath them were more than 120,000 Indian and Eurasian clerks. In the summer months the elite of the Raj withdrew from the cities and plains of India up to the Hill Fort at Simla, with its alpine climate, 7,467 feet above sea level in the Himalayan foothills, building Scottish-styled baronial castles and half-timbered Tudor cottages.

British rule in India was often justified on the grounds that it would bring progress and social advance. A comparison of the British and Indian economies shows that evidence of progress was not great. In 1820, Britain's total output was £0.478 billion, while India's was £2.4 billion. By 1913, Britain's output was £2.2 billion, while India's was 2.7 billion. Britain's population had grown from ten to 33 million over that time, and its productivity had increased by 2.5 times. India's population had grown from 200 to 300 million, but its productivity had only increased by a quarter, and only around five million were literate.[5]

One sign that India's economy had not changed was that the overwhelming share of its people lived from the land. In India, the peasants' share of all incomes earned was two thirds, in 1895 (while artisans earned only one tenth).[6]

In the census of 1901 of an Indian population of 294 million, 195.6 million lived from pasture and agriculture; 152 million were the families of landholders and tenants, the families of tenants being 106 million. Around a quarter were landless labourers, working for hire. Only some 2.6 million were the families of cash crop growers. The much-vaunted railways supported just half a million employees and their families. In 1918, the Montagu-Chelmsford Report found the situation hardly changed: 'In the whole of India the soil supports 226, out of 315 millions, and 208 millions of them get their living directly by, or depend directly upon, the cultivation of their own or others' fields.'[7] To the colonialists it seemed that India was the conservative force resisting reform. To the Raj's critics it was the other way around. Rajani Palme Dutt argued that India's large and impoverished agrarian society was 'not an inherited characteristic of the old, primitive Indian society surviving into the modern period, but is, on the contrary, in its present scale a *modern* phenomenon and the direct consequence of imperialist rule'.[8]

The British rules tended to change the customary land and tax administration so that they were more like English ideas of alienable land ownership. Land titles changed hands more often. A lighter tax burden than was typical under the Mughals meant that the class of landowners prospered. In Bengal the number of Zamindari estates grew to 154,200 by 1872 where there had been only 100 a century earlier.[9] Over time those who got land titles were mostly higher castes, and those who ended up as tenants of landless labourers were lower castes. Later the British would pass legislation to protect tenants' rights so as to forestall social struggles.

In 1873, in Pabna, Ryots fought with the Zamindar 'lathiyals' (literally, men with sticks) when their taxes were raised. Later, the British administration brought in the 1885 Bengal Tenants Rights Act. In 1875, Deccan agriculturalists burned rent books and attacked money lenders. After a commission into the disturbances the Deccan Agriculturalists Relief Act made it harder to evict cultivators over debts.[10]

The life of the Indian cultivator was hard and precarious. In 1876 and 1877, poor rainfall across a large swathe of land from Punjab in the North West down to Mysore, with crop failure in the Deccan led to a terrible famine. Fifty-eight million people were without food and the number who died were, according to some estimates, as high as ten million over India as a whole. The famine relief that the British Administration organised was poor. Sir Richard Temple organised camps where people were set to work on roads and drains, but these were out of the way and the ration was just one pound of rice a day. Many died before they got to the camp.

The photographer Willoughby Wallace Hooper took harrowing pictures of famine victims, posed in family groups. He also took a photo of grain at the harbour at Madras, waiting to be exported while the famine was on (above). 'Grain merchants, in fact, preferred to export a record 6.4 million cwt. of wheat to Europe in 1877–78 rather than relieve starvation in India', explains Mike Davis.[11] After the 1876–77 famine the government directed more public works on canals and irrigation, especially in the Punjab.

Just how precarious was the life of the undercapitalised subsistence farmer's is shown in Malcolm Darling's study on indebtedness in the Punjab. He found that only 17 per cent of cultivators had no debt, and on average the debts were 12 times the value of the land. Too much of the debt was incurred to fend off hardship and too little for future investment.[12] The dangers were underscored by the return of famine to northern India in 1896–97 – a famine in which five million died.[13]

Though India's hand loom weavers had suffered sharply under competition from Manchester in the eighteenth century, in the later nineteenth century some textile mills prospered. In 1854, Parsi Cowasji Davar founded the Bombay Spinning & Weaving Company at Tardeo, Bombay. Five years later the Borneo Jute Company of Calcutta opened. By 1875 there were 27 textile mills working in Bombay. Many Scots owned jute mills in India. Between 1879 and 1913 there were ten times as many jute spindles working. By 1900 there were 80,000 working in jute mills.[14]

The Indian cotton mills provoked Manchester's cotton interest who lobbied against tariffs that the British Indian Government put against British cotton goods. The Lieutenant Governor of Bengal, Sir Richard Temple, on returning to Britain told a group of Manchester businessmen that Bombay was turning out excellent cotton goods, and getting markets in the Persian Gulf, Africa and Asia, 'which as a patriotic Englishman, I should say rather belong to Manchester'.[15] The Manchester cotton interest were denied a lifting of the tariffs, and in revenge sponsored a campaign to impose British-style Factory Acts on their Indian competitors, to limit the exploitation of women and children so levelling the playing field.

The Bombay Mill Owners Association was formed to answer a visit of the Under Secretary for India Louis Mallet to Calcutta: 'the representations of interested persons or mistaken philanthropists, in England, of the condition and system of work in Indian factories has been grossly exaggerated', they said.[16] Despite Manchester's fears there were only around 200,000 working in cotton mills in 1900, while there were still ten times that number of hand weavers. By 1913 Indian mills were making a fifth of all cloth bought, and after the war that grew to 62 per cent in 1936 and 76 per cent in 1945. The first steel mill was built by the Tata Company at Jamshedpur in Bihar in 1911 and coal mines, mostly in Bengal, dug up 15.7 million tons in 1914 – most of which was for the railways. Even though the workforce was still mostly farmers, commerce was taking off, so that railway cargo grew from less than 20 million tons in 1883 to 120 million by 1927.[17]

India exported jute, cotton, indigo and tea to Europe, and rice and opium to the far east. Exports of these cash crops increased five times between 1870 to 1914. In the 1890s British manufactures made up 85 per cent of all of India's imports, leading to a balance of trade greatly in Britain's favour. The way that India could afford to pay for the British exports was that India in turn had a positive balance of trade with other colonies in the Empire, notably Ceylon, the Straits Settlements and Mauritius, and also with China.[18]

Outside of the Europeans working for the government, either in the civil service or in the army, were some 29,000 Britons who were in private industry, as managers and overseers on tea, coffee and indigo plantations; engineers and administrators on the railways and in other employment. They were an aggressive minority who agitated hard against Sir Courtney Ibert's proposed change to the law that would have allowed Indian judges to try Europeans – and defeated it. Even in the Bombay Textile Mills, where most of the capital was Indian, expatriates managed to take 42 per cent of the managerial and supervisory positions in 1895. In the Tata Steel Works in 1921-2 the average salary of an English supervisor was 13,257 rupees a year, compared to just 240 rupees for the Indian workers. An insight into the privileged lifestyles of the British in India is given in William Beveridge's memoir of growing up in Rangpur, the son of Henry Beveridge of the Indian Civil Service. Even when he was a single man, Beveridge had 18 servants who cost him just six per cent of his salary. By the time that he had a wife and three children, he had no less than 39 servants.[19]

British managing agencies recruited European personnel for administrative roles, and these had much better access to government, suppliers and other markets so that Indian businesses had to use them, even though they tended to serve European interests more than Indian shareholders, according to Angus Maddison. These connections gave Britons a stranglehold over indigenous Indian industry, and also banking.[20] The National Bank of India was founded in Calcutta in 1863. In 1866 it moved its head office to London. It had offices all over India and also in Burma and East Africa. Though it raised cash in India its Board of Directors was stuffed with former India Civil Service officials. Even the Government of India's official mail contract was held by Sir William Mackinnon's shipping company.

India was not only a captive market for Britain's surplus goods, it also financed the Mother Country in other ways. British investors put money into Indian concerns, looking for a return and £286 million of the capital raised on the London Stock market between 1865 and 1914 was invested in India. In Cain and Hopkins' estimation around half of the value of India's exports were siphoned off by the British, around 30 per cent in interest and other charges on private investments, and another 20 per cent in the 'Home Charges' – which were the costs Britain charged India for running its government, being wages, pensions, and other payments, including interest on the British-India Government debt.[21] Angus Maddison worked out the total annual 'drain' from India to Britain was around 1.5 per cent of national income, or about £40,500,000 in 1913.

East Asia

As well as consolidating control over India, Britain pressed out eastwards into Burma. Britain had invaded the coast in 1824–26 and again in 1853. Then in November 1885 a 15,000 strong force of the British-Indian Army under General Harry Prendergast pushed up the Irrawaddy to the ancient capital of Ava, near Mandalay and King Thibaw was sent into exile. British rule beyond the coast was far from popular. Pleas for collaboration from the Burmese nobility were ignored by the new Governor Lord Dufferin. As the British destroyed much of Ava the nobility withdrew into the forests to join up with bandit leaders like Hla-U, Yuan Nyun and Bo Cho – now endowed with the status of national heroes. With an army of 40,000 Indian and Gurkha troops, the British tried to put down uprisings of villagers in 1892 and 1895–96. The British developed teak and then oil industries in Burma – in 1901 the Burmah Oil Company pumped 170,000 tons which was just a small drop of the world's oil and aimed at the Indian kerosene market. The traditional relations of Burmese noble families and their bondsmen were broken up as the economic centre of the colony shifted from Mandalay to Rangoon. Under British rule the rice fields of the Irrawaddy became the main exporters, supplying markets as far afield as Bengal and the Straits settlements. A great influx of migrants, labourers and middle classes, made Rangoon a majority-Indian city. Though the former nobles of Thibaw's court met up at village weddings and funerals into the 1920s, the territory was ruled by the British Indian Government until 1937, when it was made a colony in its own right.[22]

From 1874, Britain tightened its control of the Malay States obliging the sultans to accept a permanent resident in their courts, a British official whose 'advice must be asked for and acted upon in all questions other than those touching Malay religion and custom'.[23] In 1895, the sultans made the Federated Malay States with British tutelage.

British mining companies encroached on the Chinese tin mines in Malaya. In the 1870s, Brazil was the only source of rubber worldwide, but Henry Wickham managed to smuggle seeds out, and cultured them in Kew Gardens. Rubber saplings were sent to Ceylon and some to Singapore. In 1888, botanist H. N. Ridley saw that the Singapore rubber plants were flourishing and set out to replant them in Malaya. Early planters were Tan Chay Yang and the Kinderley Brothers. Many that followed them had been coffee planters, who were looking to diversify because that market was glutted.

The fields were generally cleared by contracted Chinese labour, while the cultivation was carried out by Indian indentured servants (mostly Tamil). By 1929 there were 258,000 Indian labourers working on the Malay rubber plantations. English planters once they made some money, left the estates in the hands of supervisors, and managing agency houses, like Guthrie and Company, Harrison and Crossfield and Sime Darby (Sime Darby, now incorporating Guthrie, was valued at 31.6 billion Malayan ringgit in 2007). By 1913 rubber output was as much as Brazil's and by 1928 with more than 1,400,000 acres planted Malaya tapped 95 per cent of the world's rubber. Rubber was in high demand as a component in the 'Second Industrial Revolution' – as an insulator, for tubing and, since John Dunlop's invention, in pneumatic tyres. Rubber companies often paid out dividends of 200 per cent.

The government barred Ethnic Malays from selling their own land to rubber planters out of fear that 'our Malay subjects, deluded by visions of all but transitory wealth, have been divesting themselves of their homestead and family lands to anyone willing to pay in cash for them'. Land outside the rubber plantations was reserved for Malays:

> The rulers of the Federated Malay States and their Advisers conclusively feel that unless a better judgement is exercised on their behalf, the result will be the extinction of the Malay yeoman peasantry.[24]

The Malay Reservations Act of 1913 put them outside of the rubber economy, which carried on as a cash crop, with migrant labour and British capital. In Anthony Burgess' mystified telling the (fictional) Sultan of Lanchap

> had few illusions about his own people: amiable, well-favoured, courteous, they loved rest better than industry; through them the peninsula would never advance – rather their function was to remind the toiling Chinese, Indians and British of the ultimate vanity of labour.[25]

In truth the Malays were shut out of the cash economy and relegated to less rewarding farming.

Penang, as the English saw it.

In 1875, Augustus Margary was exploring overland trade routes from Shanghai to Burma, and on his way back was challenged by Chinese officials at Manwine for his lack of official papers. Margary was killed along with his four Chinese staff. Thomas Wade the British Minister forced an apology and concession from the Chinese court, including an enhancement of International Settlement in Shanghai. By 1919 the Shanghai Municipal Corporation controlled an area of just under nine square miles. The settlement had grown larger than the Chinese city to the south. It had a population of 18,519 non-Chinese, of whom just 4,822 were Britons, and 620,401 Chinese (1920 census). For all that the British, or Shanghailanders as they called themselves, dominated the Corporation, while the Chinese were not allowed a vote on the council. In 1919 in a sop to Chinese demands the Corporation set up a Chinese Advisory Committee with five representatives of Chinese residents.[26]

The impact of the European and Japanese concessions on the Chinese coastal towns was destabilising. While the growing commercial China was largely under foreign control, the greater realm of rural China was cut off from that wealth. In a bid to modernise the country the Guangxu Emperor (1871–1908) issued a flurry of reforming edicts in 1898 – but these were simply ignored by the Manchu officials. The Empress Dowager Cixi had the Guangxu Emperor put under house arrest and locked down a reactionary regime. By the time the Dowager Empress died in 1908 China was in danger of fragmenting.

The Western Pacific

In 1869, the Queensland Parliament passed a law against 'blackbirding' – the rounding up of Pacific islanders to work on Australian and Fijian plantations. The following year Captain George Palmer of the Royal Navy intercepted the 48-ton schooner the Daphne at Levuka in Fiji with a cargo of 100 islanders. The ship was owned by Pritchard, Strickland and Sterne, and the Fiji planters Smith and Bates had bought the men.

To Palmer's dismay the Australian judge Sir Alfred Stephen – refusing to hear native evidence – found that the men were not slaves but contracted labourers.

Palmer's published account of 'blackbirding' in the Pacific began a clamour for a Western Pacific Commission to stamp out this new slave trade. The Aborigines' Protection Society, and in particular the Lambeth MP and Sheriff of London, William M'Arthur, made common cause with the many Wesleyan missions on the Pacific Islands lobbying for a Western Pacific Protectorate. In Fiji, the authority of King Cakobau over natives and settlers alike was shaky at best. Missionaries and planters took advantage of the King's weakness to lobby for the cession of sovereignty to the English Crown. Gladstone declined the offer but in 1874 Disraeli accepted the deed of cession from Cakobau and 13 other chiefs. Sir Arthur Hamilton Gordon, was sent out as Governor of Fiji and head of the Western Pacific Commission, arriving in 1875.

Gordon was the son of the former Prime Minister, the Earl of Aberdeen, and had been governor in New Brunswick and Mauritius, where his autocratic rule led to clashes with the settlers. 'Nothing but a despotism is thought of' in Fiji, Sir Robert Herbert told Gordon, 'and you are the man to do it'.[27]

In Fiji, Gordon based his government on a special relationship with the Bose Vakaturaga – the Great Council of Chiefs. He led them in a 'little war' against the Tevoro (devils) of the inland. Gordon's overwrought native policy placed villagers under the authority of the chiefs, so that the white sugar planters had to recruit Indian farm labourers.

In the nearby Tongan islands King Tupou ruled though unrecognised by any European power. Tongans enthusiastically took up the Wesleyan Church which raised £5,460 in collections in 1869. The Reverend Shirley Baker and King Tupou between them decided to break free and name their own independent church to keep the funds on the island. 'Tonga for the Tongans' was their slogan. The Wesleyan Church in London agitated against Baker's breakaway and charged him and Tupou with despotism. But Tupou's government, with Baker as an advisor won recognition from Germany's Chancellor Bismarck, and soon after from a nervous Foreign Office. In 1890, Fiji governor and West Pacific High Commissioner John Thurston got Baker removed and forced Tupou into retirement. Ten years after that the Tongans were made to accept the status of a British protectorate.[28]

In 1893 Resident Commissioner Charles Morris Woodford imposed a British Protectorate in the Solomon Islands by smashing the chiefs or 'big men' in a campaign against head-hunting. In 1885 Britain annexed southern New Guinea (today Papua New Guinea), Australia annexed more of it in 1888 and there was a German colony, too. In 1902, the British Government handed over control to Australia.

The expanding powers of the Western Pacific Commission were justified through a series of measures against 'blackbirding' and to protect natives from exploitation at the hands of unscrupulous settlers. As a rule, the end result of any engagement between natives and the British Empire would lead to an extension of British authority.

Chapter Twenty-three

THE COLONIAL LABOUR QUESTION

Most colonial subjects lived from agriculture. While Britain's urban workforce had outgrown its rural workforce by 1801 that was not true for most British colonies until after they had become independent, if at all.

Relations between landlords and tenants were often oppressive, and the peasant's life was vulnerable to famine. In India the landlords were generally Indian and were taxed to pay for the administration. Cash crops like tea and coffee plantations were generally English-owned. In Southern and East Africa labourers who had been pushed off fertile land were often reduced to the status of tenant farmers or hired labourers on European-claimed farmland.

Farming, mostly on small plots, was the lot of most non-white subjects of the British Empire. Hunger was the discipline that made them work. The number of landless labourers was growing but the people of the colonies had not been proletarianized or urbanised to anything like the extent that Britons had. Plantations and mines, where native peoples were made into wage labourers were an important source of tradeable commodities for the empire. But most people were working at keeping themselves and their landlords fed. The persistently large share of subsistence farming in the Empire was both a measure of how colonisation put the brakes on development, and also an upper limit on the surpluses that the metropolis could extract from its subject peoples.

When the British took over other countries that meant they were responsible for what happened in them. One of the most important things that the colonial administrators had to manage were the labour relations in the countries they colonised. The societies that they took over and began to shape had work to do even if it was just to gather their own subsistence, and a great deal more if they were to meet the expectations of the Chartered Companies, private companies, their investors, and, increasingly, of the many European settlers who were living among them.

It was a big claim that the British made that they would make the colonies more civilised. Most of all the British colonists had said that they would set the people free from slavery and oppression. When they were in charge things did not always turn out that way.

The economist Lilian Knowles argued that 'in the first half of the nineteenth century England considered that if she had freed the slave and stopped the slave trade on the high seas she had done her duty towards the coloured population'.

This was not good enough, Knowles thought, because, 'merely to free slaves was to produce idleness and economic chaos, as in the West Indies'. The problem, in Knowles' mind, was that 'the freed negro did not want steady work', and 'the Indian peasant, delivered from the heel of the conqueror, merely multiplied and became a helot to the money-lender':

> Great Britain began to recognize that she had a civilizing mission and not merely a freeing mission to all indigenous peoples under her control.[1]

Another view of the shift from slavery to Empire came in the pamphlet *Buganda Nyafe* ('Buganda Our Mother', 1944). 'The slave trade was abolished in one way and then it was introduced in another', wrote the authors:

> the old slave trade was better because only a few were taken and those who remained home lived in peace, but the modern slave trade includes children and women and English laws put yokes around our necks even though we think we are in our native home.[2]

One general rule that the Colonial Office held to was that 'wherever possible colonies should be expected to pay for themselves' That meant that the upkeep of the local government should come from locally raised taxes. In that way Governors had to make sure that native peoples raised a surplus over and above what they needed to live to pay for the colonial administration. Beyond raising the cost of running the government through their taxes, native peoples worked the mines and plantations for mostly British owners to make money for them. Often the British had pushed aside, or made subordinate, local rulers who lived by the efforts of the peoples they ruled. To keep the European planters, mine-owners, industrialists and landlords, as well as the local rulers and intermediaries, native peoples often worked even harder than they had before colonisation. The economist Herman Merivale, who went on to be Under Secretary for the Colonies argued that 'in civilised countries the labourer, though free, is by a law of nature dependent on capitalists'. But, 'in colonies this dependence must be created by artificial means'. To make them work harder colonial administrations relied on some harsh labour regimes, including indentures and forced labour.[3]

Indentured Labour

As we have seen indentured labour played a big part after the abolition of slavery in the British Empire (between 1833 and 1845). Planters lobbied colonial administrations to import indentured labour from India and China to make up the shortfall. Indentured labour was mostly used for cash crops like sugar and later rubber, where the produce was high in value and exported, so that planters could not easily afford a break in production.

Indenture – which is a long-term labour contract – was not the same as slavery, but it was not free, either. By contracting to work for three, five or seven years indentured labourers lost control over their ability to strike a bargain. It was the opposite of a free labour market. They were at the mercy of their employers. The indentured workers of China and also of India were often called by the racially derogatory word, 'Coolie', or 'Coolies'.

A big part of the subordination of the indentured labourer was being moved from one place, where you knew people who could help you get out of a bad fix, to another place where you knew no-one and had to do what your employer told you. The sea voyage from India, or China, to the West Indies or elsewhere in Asia, or to Africa, changed people in a similar way to the move from the countryside to the town in England, that is from a rural life governed by custom, to work in a factory where the overseer ruled. The differences were first that the journey across the sea was much greater and more isolating, and second, there was no free labour market at the other end. Your contract, struck with a labour agent, was often sold on to a planter. Indians called the sea, Kala Pani, the black waters, and it was said that you 'lost caste' when you crossed the Kala Pani – the status you had was gone and you were the lowest of the low. The Calcutta labour agents Gillanders, Arbuthnot at Co. told the former slave owner (and father of the future Prime Minister) John Gladstone that there would be no difficulty recruiting labourers for his Guiana plantation because the Indians were 'perfectly ignorant of the place they agree to go to and the length of the voyage they are undertaking': 'a newly arrived simpleton, in his blissful ignorance, will have to grin and take what is given him'.[4]

Between 1834 and 1920 one million Indians were sent across the seas.[5] Looking at the migration of indentured labourers from Calcutta in 1872 we can get an idea of where they were going. More than 17,000 left Calcutta that year. The number going to Demerara was 6,087, to Trinidad 3,850, to Jamaica 1,562 and to Surinam 410; another 5,626 went to Mauritius. Labourers also went on seasonal contracts from Mysore and Malabar to the coffee estates on the hills of Coorg and Wynaad in Burma – fully 97,679 in 1871–72.[6] The growth of indentured labour from India came around the same time as the famine of 1875–76, which ought to be counted as a 'push factor' for the migration.

After 1879 Governor Arthur Gordon recruited indentured Indians to Fiji. The native administration did not raise enough to pay for the colony, so Gordon saw sugar planting as a way to make money. From 1882 the Colonial Sugar Refining Company of Australia organised the plantations. Up until 1920 60,965 made the journey. An indenture contract was called 'girmit' – for 'agreement' – so that the indentured were called 'girmitiyas', and would usually be for a nine-hour day, with a day and a half off on Sunday and Saturday. They were also entitled to a free fare back to India after their contracts for five or ten years of service, though only 24,000 did go back. Nearly half came from the North Western Provinces, and another 13,207 came from Awadh. Three quarters came through Calcutta and the rest through Madras. Labour relations were starkly oppressive on the plantations, with 'overtasking' and poor rations, often leading to poor health, so that they were described as 'narak' – hell. The Colonial Sugar Refining Company set prices and wages, and a great deal of the colony's policy. Governor John Thurston looked on the Indians as 'a working population and nothing more'.[7]

Between 1834 and 1920, 453,063 Indians were recruited to work in Mauritius mostly on sugar plantations. In the 1860s there were around 72,960 plantation workers under contract. By the 1880s that number had reduced to 42,632. Magistrates heard thousands of complaints against planters who had held back wages. The colony and the planters waged a vicious war of attrition with those Indians who had fulfilled their indenture contracts, the so-called 'old immigrants'. The 'old immigrants' felt they ought to be free to get work where they could, in Port Louis or other towns. The planters thought they ought to renew their indentures. Planters laid around 8,000 complaints a year against labourers for absconding from the plantation or breaking contract. Even in 1871 the non-indentured were made to carry identity cards with photographs.

The colony used vagrancy laws to punish the 'old immigrants' who would not re-contract themselves to a plantation. Between 1860 and 1871 206,000 Indian immigrants were charged with vagrancy. Adolphe de Plevitz was an overseer for his father-in-law at the Nouvelle Decouverte estate, in Pamplemousses. He was moved by the plight of the harried Indians and set himself up as an alternative to the official 'protector of immigrants'. In his pamphlet, *The Petition of the Old Immigrants of Mauritius,* based on interviews, de Plevitz alleged that the more the labour recruiters 'lie, the greater the profits'. The Protector of Immigrants' office 'was instituted to facilitate oppression'; the planter pays 'very nearly what he chooses'; and nearly all the magistrates were 'more or less directly interested in the sugar plantations'. The legislative council deprived the Indian 'of the rights of citizenship' and 'almost put him without the pale of humanity' while Governor Barkly was charged with discriminating against Indians and breaking the terms of his commission from the Queen. The planters and the legislative council bullied and threatened de Plevitz, but a Royal Commission afterwards found most of his charges were true.[8]

Labourers under indenture in 1906.[9]

Destination	Number	Main origin	Main work
Transvaal	49,877	China	Rand mines
Natal	32,586	India	Agricultural
East Africa	1,350	India	Railway works
Gold Coast	4,000	Elsewhere in West Africa	
British Guiana	11,921	India	Sugar
Trinidad	10,600	India	Sugar
Jamaica	1,392	India	Bananas, sugar
Straits Settlements	1,731	China	
Straits Settlements	1,854	India	
Fiji	8,684	India	Sugar
Australia	2,152	East Asia	Pearling
Mauritius	Unknown	India	Sugar

Between 1855 and 1930 the rice paddies of the Irrawaddy delta in Upper Burma grew ten times to cover four million hectares. Labourers were recruited from the Madras Presidency – mostly Tamils – and Bengal, so that Indian migration into Rangoon and the delta climbed from 136,504 in 1872 to more than a million in 1930. As well as working as cultivators on contracts of between one and three years, the Indians were recruited under the 'Maistry' labour contracting system to work in processing mills, like those owned by William Strang Steel, from Glasgow. In Ceylon, as Sri Lanka was then called, the number of Indian labourers working on coffee plantations and building roads and railways grew from 123,000 in 1871 to 195,000 in 1881, to 235,000 in 1891. [10]

In 1904, some 30,000 Chinese indentured labourers were recruited to work in the Rand mines in the Transvaal. Their conditions were mean and oppressive. They were 'imported for unskilled labour in the mines only, and are not allowed to trade, or to acquire lease or hold any land or building, directly or indirectly'. The Chinese labourer was not allowed to work for anyone other than those who had brought them, and 'must always carry a passport, and must obtain a permit if he wishes to leave the mine premises'.[11] In June and July of 1904 there were some 29 violent clashes between the Chinese, the employers and the authorities, often beginning with protests over safety or being locked in.

As relations between the Chinese and the mine owners broke down, white South Africans protested against the use of 'coolie' labour. Meetings and delegations against the Chinese were held all over South Africa. The issue was even taken up in the British General Election of 1905. In the popular press the Chinese were called a 'Yellow Peril'. The main complaint was that they were taking well-paying jobs from white settlers at much less pay. The riots, as well as fanciful stories against them, were used to paint the Chinese as a threat. In 1907, Winston Churchill announced the 'winding up of the Chinese labour experiment'.

Indian and Chinese immigration had a big impact on many colonies. In Mauritius 100,000 descendants of Indian immigrants, making up around one third of the colony were living there in 1906. In Guiana there were three times as many formerly indentured Indians as indentured, and in Trinidad nine times as many.[12]

There were more and louder voices raised against indenture so that an official inquiry was commissioned by the Government of India under James MacNeill and Chimman Lal, who visited the West Indies and Fiji. Their report on indentured labour was that 'on the whole favourable to the system, the advantages of which in the opinion of the commissioners have far outweighed its disadvantages'.[13] Many thought that the MacNeill-Lal Report was a whitewash, and soon after Charles Freer Andrews and W.W. Pearson's investigation into indentured labour in Fiji was more damning. In India there were protests and anti-Indenture leagues founded. In 1920 the British Government abolished the indenture system.

Labour under the Colour Bar

Throughout the Empire there were 'colour bars'. European settlers kept themselves isolated from native peoples with clubs and special areas, by segregating socially, and, in the colonies of settlement by forcing indigenous people into native reserves. Some of the most egregious colour bars were set up in those African colonies of settlement from 1870 onwards – South Africa, Rhodesia and Kenya. Formalised discrimination on grounds of colour were so marked there because of the way that black labour was exploited.

Digging for diamonds.

In the Boer Republics and Natal, the conditions for African labour were not far from slavery, though it was generally called 'apprenticeship' to get around Britain's abolition laws. When mining took off in South Africa black labour was recruited to do a lot of the heavy lifting and digging. The men were paid but the terms were pointedly oppressive.

The discovery of diamonds in Kimberly in Griqualand drew thousands to the newly declared British Protectorate. By June 1871 some 37,000 had come of whom 21,000 were African. The Boer and English claim holders organised themselves as the Diamond Diggers Protection Society, and barred Africans and those of mixed race from holding claims on 23 July 1872 – a rule that Governor Barkly effectively agreed with the proviso that the colour stipulation was not written down in the law, but that instead a local magistrate would agree a mining licence. The white claim owners pressed too for a Pass Law obliging all Africans to carry papers.

De Beers Compound at Kimberley in the 1890s.

The mining claims at Kimberley were consolidated down from 3,600 to 98 in 1885 and then into one giant De Beers Consolidated Mine. De Beers created labour compounds in 1888 for fear that African miners would steal diamonds. Men lived twenty to a room in an enclosure surrounded by a high corrugated iron wall and covered by wire netting for the four or six months of their contracts. They bought food from the company store and ate in the compound, leaving only by a tunnel to the mine itself. When their contract was up the men were kept for a week for any diamonds they might have swallowed to pass through them. White miners refused the forced searches.

De Beers extracted £300 million-worth of diamonds over seventy years. Its four life governors – Rhodes, Beit, Barnato and Phillipson Stow – took 40 per cent of the profits.[14]

After diamonds South Africa's mining lords had gold dug for them at Witwatersrand. Fifty-three companies employed 3,400 whites and 10 times that number of Africans. The mining code set down a colour bar excluding Africans from jobs as banksmen, onsetters and engine drivers, while a blasting certificate was effectively a colour bar, too. Among the mine owners many would have preferred certification rather than an explicit colour bar, but the miners' union insisted on it.

Death rates for African miners at 69 per 1,000 were a scandal, even in South Africa and Alfred Milner's administration imposed standards for diet, housing, sanitation and hospital care on mine owners.

The key to the recruitment of black miners were the reserved areas and Protectorates. Sotho chiefs told commissioner for Native Affairs Sir Geoffrey Lagden 'we do not like our men to go to Johannesburg, because they go there to die'.[15] The Swazi Royal House, having conceded so much of their land to Europeans encouraged labour migration to the mines, taking a quarter of labourers' wages in tax for themselves. The gold mines recruited from Portuguese Mozambique anywhere between 74,000 and 118,000 labourers a year from 1908 to 1975. From 1932 the mines had government approved access to the vast labour pools of northern Bechuanaland, Northern Rhodesia and Nyasaland.

In the ten years to 1897 the mines gave up more than three million ounces of gold, valued at £10.5 million and paid out £2,817,000 to investors. John Hobson, who went to the Transvaal to investigate thought that the mine owners were the main lobby calling for Britain to wage war against the Boers, and that their 'one all-important object' was 'to secure a full, cheap, regular, submissive supply of Kaffir and white labour'. Between 1913 and 1921 black miners' wages grew by 13 per cent, but the wages of white miners grew by 50 per cent. African nationalist leader Abdul Abdurrahman estimated that twenty thousand white men earned £10,500,000 between them, while two hundred thousand Africans drew wages totalling £6,500,000 in 1922.[16]

The colour bar in industry was a powerful lever for its spread over the rest of society. Governor Sprigg's Parliamentary Registration Act of 1887 disenfranchised thousands of Africans in the East Cape. In 1903, the Transvaal Municipalities Election Ordinance set out the first all-white franchise, and the first election under it was held on 20 February 1907. In 1904, the Native Locations Act segregated urban Africans.

Segregation filled the lives of black South Africans with impossible choices. Work drew them to the cities, but they were excluded from most of the city. Between 1939 and 1952, the urban African population doubled, but municipalities made no new land or homes available. One James Mpanza led a group of overcrowded families out of Newclare and Cliptown onto open land in Orlando, to set up homes for themselves in the Veldt (he organised his campaign under the slogan 'Sofasonke', meaning 'we shall all die together'). The 'squatting' movement exploded. By 1947, more than a million urban Africans were living in accommodation without services – fully 57.5 of the urban African population. Mpanza's settlement became 'Soweto' (South Western Township) and is today home to 1.27 million. The perverse geography of South Africa meant that black Africans, the majority of the population and the original inhabitants, were restricted first to 'reserved areas', then to work compounds by the mines, and finally to unofficial 'townships' outside the city boundaries. The colour bar in South Africa – which would later be called 'apartheid' – made it easier for the farmers, mine-owners and later on a growing industrial sector – to exploit black labour intensively.

In Southern Rhodesia, to the north east of South Africa, mining was only peripheral but the settler economy boomed on agricultural output, with tobacco to the fore. By 1922, 64 per cent of the African population was penned into 'tribal areas'. White farmers were helped by laws like the Masters and Servants Act that kept wages low and barred African farm hands from leaving work. In 1922, a white-only referendum voted to make the colony self-governing. With more working, the 1934 Industrial Conciliation Act barred Africans from wage bargaining with a clause saying that the term employee 'shall not include a native'.

The Rhodesian government did want to make sure that Africans were working to enrich the colony. Prime Minister Huggins supported married accommodation for African labour in urban areas so that 'the native is more efficient at his job'. The number of African wage-earners grew from 254,000 in 1936 to 377,000 in 1946 and half a million (out of an African population of three million) in 1954.[17]

ALFRED MILNER'S PLAN FOR A WHITE SOUTH AFRICA, 1903

'Our welfare depends upon increasing the quantity of our white population, but not at the expense of its quality. We do not want a white proletariat in this country.

The position of the white among the vastly more numerous black population requires that even their lowest ranks should be able to maintain a standard of living far above that of the poorest section of the population of a purely white country.

But, without making them the hewers of wood and drawers of water, there are scores and scores of employments in which white men could be honourably and profitably employed, if we could at once succeed in multiplying our industries and in reducing the cost of living.

However you look at the matter, you always come back to the same root principle – the urgency of the development which alone can make this a white man's country in the only sense in which South Africa can become one, and that is, not a country full of poor whites, but one in which a largely increased white population can live in decency and comfort. That development requires capital, but it also requires a large amount of rough labour. And that labour cannot to any extent, be white, if only because, pending development and the subsequent reduction in the cost of living, white labour is much too dear.'

Quoted in Bernard Magabune, *The Making of a Racist State*, Africa World Press, 1996, p 354

In Kenya's 'White Highlands' – the territory around the Rift valley that settlers had seized from the Maasai, growing numbers of Kikuyu were attracted by the offer of land in exchange for labour on white farms. The challenge for the European settlers was that they had bitten off much more land than they could chew. Most of the land was not farmed at all. The white settlers' farms were undercapitalised and they depended on African labour to make the concerns work. Kikuyu settled land in the White Highlands sometimes by invitation but increasingly they squatted empty land out of necessity. Chief Koinage recalled that 'I received a letter from Mr Northcote saying that I may ask people to help cultivate on European farms to increase friendship': 'the Europeans requested that Kikuyu men should be collected and get free tickets to go to the Highlands to work on the farms'.

The Kenya police force.

The European farmers and the Kenyan authorities pulled in different directions at different times. In 1929 they tried to evict Kikuyu squatters and drive them back to the reserved areas, but these could not sustain the returnees. While they complained of Kikuyu incursions, white farmers still needed their labour. The wages, though, were very poor, and the conditions brutal, so that the Governor had to rein in white excesses, too.[18]

Jamaica's Return to the Plantation

In the years after the Morant Bay rebellion former slaves kept themselves living on independent plots, so that there were 72,000 of ten acres or less in 1897. The islands' governors, and a Royal Commission under Sir Henry Norman conceded that this was not such a bad result and praised the islanders' self-sufficiency.[19] Jamaica's peasants kept fowl, pigs and goats, grew cassava, potatoes, yams, plantain and bananas. Peasants could make sixpence on a bunch of bananas carried down and sold to small ships working the coast. From 1880, the Atlas Steamship Company reserved cargo space for four hundred tons of fruit on its twice-a-month mail ship to New York.

Jamaican banana exports were disdained by the island's planters who saw the fruit as a 'backwoods n****r business'. It took an American Lorenzo Baker, founder of the Boston Fruit Company (that would become the United Fruit Company in 1899) to exploit the peasant growers' industry. The United Fruit Company bought up 42 per cent of all of Jamaica's bananas for export to America's growing consumer market by 1886. By the turn of the century fruit made up 56 per cent of Jamaica's exports while sugar and rum was down to just one seventh of the island's production. At the same time the American market overtook the British as the main destination for Jamaican exports.[20] Baker's company bought mostly from small planters, but it also bought up old sugar estates for conversion.

The United Fruit Company was challenged by Elders & Fyffes, which was set up with the help of the colonial office, but over time was reduced to an English marketer of United's fruit until they bought it up completely in 1913. In 1929 the Jamaica Banana Producers' Association, a cooperative of 7,694 small farmers was set up with the help of the Imperial Economic Committee. The JBPA challenged United exporting 32 per cent of Jamaica's bananas in 1932, having grown to employ 11,628 contractors. Despite its successes the Association was undercapitalised and less resilient to disasters like the hurricanes of 1934 and 1935 and the collapse in US demand in 1936. United's lobbyists persuaded the colonial authorities that the Jamaica producer was not ready for economic independence and the JBPA was restructured as a limited company, now buying fruit for United to export. Throughout its growth United Fruit fought off competitors by raising prices, but when it had the monopoly its attitude to producers changed. 'Tell the people if they wish to sell their fruit they must bring it down', Baker told his son Loren.[21]

From World War I with sugar beet treatment in Europe disrupted Jamaica's sugar cane plantations and factories revived. Output had fallen from 24,000 tons in the 1850s to 17,000 in the first decade of the twentieth century. In 1928, it had grown to 59,000 tons and then to 118,000 in 1938, reaching 180,318 tons in 1948.[22] The falling number of plantations in the second half of the nineteenth century was symptomatic of the decay of the business. But by 1926 the 38 factories still operating were each producing 12 times those of 1896, 1,620 tons. Productivity increased to an output of 11,650 tons per factory in 1951. Governors had for decades tried to persuade planters to invest, but the estates in the nineteenth century were still run by attorneys and agents trying to cover old debts. By 1929, around a third of the sugar was grown at the behest of the West Indian Sugar Company (WISCO), that was effectively a subsidiary of the Tate and Lyle Company. Its two largest planters were Moneymusks in Vere and Frome in Westmoreland.

The United Fruit and WISCO plantations were paying wages that drew the surplus workers of the peasant villages to come down from the hills. New employees found that their hope for a provision ground, as on the old estates was refused. WISCO's managing director R. L. M. Kirkwood set out a prospectus of model employers building housing, health and leisure facilities for their workers. A Colonial Office investigation of 1938 found that of 381 estates in Jamaica 117 were given over to sugar and 94 to bananas. Fully 22,620 people were living in 2,513 barracks on the estates, fewer than half of which were thought to be acceptable, being overcrowded, lacking latrines and water. The sugar planters of Westmoreland were among the worst.[23]

As the West Indian peasant was led into wage labour in the twentieth century, there were clashes. There were riots all across the West Indies in 1935. In 1938 canecutters struck out the Serge Island estate in St. Thomas. In 1937 WISCO started building a new sugar mill at Frome in Westmoreland. Reports of high wages drew so many to the site that those not taken on camped on land nearby. On 29 April 1938 workers were kept waiting for their pay at the office for hours and when they threw stones were fired upon. They struck on the Saturday. One hundred armed police were sent from Kingston to reinforce the local officers. When the workers marched on the overseer's residence on Monday the police opened fire, killing four and injuring 13 more. The strikers burned 156 acres of sugar cane.[24]

The following month, on 21 May 1938, a dock-workers strike in Kingston was widened into a general strike. Kingston rioted burning shops and overturning cars. A hunger march in Islington, in St. Mary, was fired upon by police killing eight people and injuring 39.

Two of the leaders of the unrest of 1938 went on to be political leaders who won the campaign for independence. They were cousins: Alexander Bustamente, the trade union leader, and Norman Manley, the socialist. Bustamente's Jamaica Labour Party would win the first free election, and Manley's People's National Party came second.

Forced Labour

Over and above the use of indentured labour and segregated labour, colonial authorities in different conditions also used directed or forced labour. Forced labour was not the norm, but it was common. Governors and District Officers often commanded work details for special projects, like roads. Colonial authorities gave their blessing to native leaders who commanded forced labour and drew on their authority to summon crews.

A Parliamentary paper of 1908, titled 'Forced Labour in British Possessions', admitted that people were made to work in Northern and Southern Nigeria, Uganda, Gambia, Fiji, Ceylon and Natal. Questioned in the House of Commons Winston Churchill said that forced labour was a 'universal and immemorial custom' in Nigeria, where Chiefs ordered work crews to repair roads and defend towns, and admitted that where these were ordered by the authorities, payments were made to the Chiefs, not to the labourers.[25] In Nigeria, Gambia, the Gold Coast, Uganda and Fiji, chiefs and labourers could be fined or imprisoned for failure to meet the tasks set by the Colonial Officers.

In Egypt under the 'veiled protectorate', tens of thousands of fellaheen were made to work the corvée, usually of one hundred days, on the repairing of the Suez Canal at the end of the nineteenth century and the beginning of the twentieth, as they were on other public works. Officially the corvée had been banned in 1892, but it carried on right through till 1911.[26]

Fiji

Native Fijians, unlike the indentured Indians who worked the sugar cane plantations, were organised in 'customary' village structures known as mataqali, and their Chiefs were integrated into the Native Administration. The Chiefs exacted 'lala' – or obligatory labour – farming in the Chief's provision grounds, or other services, for around 60 days a year. The villages' farm output was taxed by the Colony and helped pay for the administration. The Chiefs disciplined the villagers, who were not allowed to leave the village. The Fijian sociologist Rusiate Nayacakalou was sceptical about the customary authority of the Chiefs, which he explained most came from their relationship to the colonial authorities.[27] There were protests against lala and the authority of the Chiefs, led by Matanitobua, chief of the Namosi in the early century, and then by Apolosi Nawai and his Fiji Produce Agency in 1915, but the authorities suppressed these as challenges to their authority.

Kenya

On 23 October 1919 Kenya (British East Africa) Governor Northey issued a circular, 'Native Land Required for Non-Native Farms and Other Undertakings'. The point of the circular was that 'officers who are in charge of what is termed labour supplying districts', should 'induce an augmentation of the supply of labour to various farms and plantations in the protectorate'. It also said that 'where farms are situated in the vicinity of a native area, women and children should be encouraged to go out for such labour as they can perform'. The circular said that native chiefs and elders should assist, and that district commissioners should collect the names of those who did not help. The district commissioners were to hold local meetings to tell the native authorities what their duties were. As critics pointed out at the time this was a policy of forced labour.

'Their mothers were crying as they went', Leah Kurungu remembered of the time the headman came to take away young men from her village: 'Ropes were put through their ears and tied together'. Sydney Olivier, the Governor of Jamaica spoke out: 'to many in this country it was a new and startling discovery that forced labour, including unpaid forced labour, was an institution prevalent in the British Empire'. Kenya Governor Northey was backed by Colonial Secretary Lord Milner, who said 'it is desirable that young, able bodied men should become wage earners and should not remain idle in the reserves for a large part of the year'. Archdeacon Owen campaigned for many years over the issue, highlighting cases of children being called on to make a road; of around fifty men whipped with Kibokos (hippo-hide whips) to dig ground for cotton-growing; or men whipped to cut wood for European contractors, on the pretext that this was to clear tsetse flies.[28]

Nigeria

In March 1904, District Commissioner for Owerri in South East Nigeria Harold Morday Douglas ordered a sustained campaign of burning homes in the town of Eziama after locals protested against his onerous demands for labourers to build roads.

Douglas' forced labour details were commonplace in Southern Nigeria, and Governor Walter Egerton told his officers to avoid 'undue leniency' when commanding labour details, because it was 'apt to by misconstrued by the natives and regarded as weakness'. Nigerians were made to work building roads, railways and telegraphs for the colony, and even homes for British personnel, and most often to work as carriers. That was brutal work and often carriers died of thirst or from infected wounds. Often they were made to work against their own best interests, set to clearing their own farmland or as carriers for the British army in campaigns against their neighbours. In Parliament in 1906, Winston Churchill defended the practice, saying 'in West African Colonies and Protectorates there is a legal power to demand labour on roads and waterways, the Governor or High Commissioner alone can make and order that such work shall be done'.[29]

Merchant Seamen

From the repeal of the navigation acts in 1849 Britain's merchant shipping was free to recruit colonial seamen. Most were got from India, Malaya and some from Aden and East Africa. Indian seamen were known as 'Lascars'. They were recruited on very unequal rates and terms to British seamen, often called 'Asiatic' or Lascar articles of agreement. The MP and shipowner Thomas Brassey said in 1877 that 'foreign seamen keep wages down'. From pay scales published in Parliament in 1928 English sailors were paid four times as much as sailors recruited in Bombay, who themselves earned one-and-a-quarter times as much as sailors boarding in Calcutta. Rations for non-European seamen were less, and even the cabin space was set at 72 cubic feet compared to 120 cubic feet for an English seaman. In the early twentieth century, more and more seamen were contracted in China. In 1933 Ship owner Charles Ainsworth reckoned that 'the food and wages required to maintain one British seaman equals the needs of six or more Chinese; moreover, native crews work longer hours and can eat and sleep anywhere'.[30]

In 1891 there were 186,176 British sailors, and 24,037 lascars in the British merchant fleet. The number of Britons fell back to around 175,000 from 1897 to 1904, and then climbed again to 212,640 in 1914. The number of lascars kept climbing by around ten thousand a decade until it reached 51,616 on the eve of the First World War. After the war, the number of British seamen fell sharply to a low of 126,000 while lascars were still around 50,000. Lascars were often abandoned in London and other seaports. They were cared for in the Strangers' Home in East London. Adenese and Somali sailors made communities in Tyneside and Cardiff's Tiger Bay.

From 1939 to 1945, Alfred Holt and Company (the so-called Blue Funnel Line) and Anglo-Saxon Petroleum (Shell) ran their reserve pools of Chinese seamen out of Liverpool. After the Second World War, many Liverpool wives of Chinese seamen were shocked to find they and their children had been abandoned – only later learning that their partners had been rounded up and sent back to China on Winston Churchill's orders, to make way for the British merchant seamen released from the Royal Navy. Two thousand Chinese who served in the merchant navy during the war were expelled by a government order in 1946, as 'an undesirable element in Liverpool'.

Other People's Colonies

As well exploiting native labour in the British Empire, British investors exploited labour in other people's colonies. At number 100 Victoria Embankment, on the north side of the Thames is striking art deco building. The headquarters of Unilever House are decorated with several motifs of the African origins of its financing, especially in the two grey metal pillars either side of the main entrance. On these you can see panels with profiles of African heads, Africans in loin cloths and Africans climbing palm trees to cut their fruit.

The palm *Elaeis guineensis* yields a fruit that is rich in oil and William Lever of Lever Brothers marketed 'Sunlight Soap' made from palm oil at their 'model village' Port Sunlight, from 1888. The palm fruit were cut by Congolese labourers at their three main sites Barumbu, Basongo and Lusanga. The exploitation of Congolese labour had been a humanitarian disaster under the King of the Belgians' own colonial rubber company, exposed by Roger Casement and Henry Fox Bourne in 1908. William Lever's choice of the Congo as the base for his subsidiary company *Huileries du Congo Belge* (HCB, huilerie, meaning oil refinery) came at the right time for a Belgian government that needed to develop its colony. William Lever's reputation as a model employer, it was said, would carry over into the HCB's treatment of the natives. It was not to be.

The HCB exploited the natives cruelly. To force them to climb the palms and cut the fruit the company had many incentives of which payment was the least. Under the accord with the Belgian authorities the HCB had control of three circles with a radius of 60 miles around (later expanded to five), and within them imposed a monopoly so that natives could not sell their own palm fruits to any merchant but the HCB. The HCB laid claim to native planted and tended palm groves arguing that they were natural resources that they had ownership of under the contract. The HCB persuaded the Belgian authorities to impose and to raise the 'hut tax' so that natives would have to get cash to pay, where the company was the only source of cash. The HCB put pressure on the Belgian authorities themselves to recruit labour for the company, which meant drafting labourers from villages. Finally, the HCB made 'tripartite' contracts with the Belgian authorities, the company and the native chiefs to supply labour. This way the chiefs were tasked with rounding up the unfortunate villagers who were to be sent up the palms to cut the fruit. By these methods the HCB put some 26,000 Congolese to work by 1930. An internal company memo recounted:

> The chiefs supplied slaves. The slaves, once designated, were resigned to their fate. They were given a work-book, a blanket and a machete. They were told what work was expected of them, and in general they do it fairly willingly.

Just how willing these 'slaves' were was questionable. Their three year contracts were renewed automatically, marked only by 'a new blanket and a new machete': 'In practice, a cutter is never set free but cuts fruit until he dies, or until his manager lays him off because of old age'.[31] The 'decorated' chiefs, explained the former Belgian colonial official Jules Marchal, who documented the story of the HCB, were themselves mostly usurpers who got a bonus from the company for the labour they supplied. In the HCB's 'circles' all labour was monopolised by the company, so that natives went hungry.

Backing up the labour discipline of company officials and the chefferie were the native Force Publique, as in the old days of King Leopold's rubber company. When the Pende rose up against the HCB (they made up a religious movement that demanded a withdrawal from all work for the Europeans) they were put down in a brutal massacre, where more than 500 were killed, and a military occupation of their lands.

Lever Brothers exploitation of the Congolese labourers was disguised as the profits of the HCB were very poor throughout the history of the company (£72,000 in 1919–20, but lossmaking thereafter). That was because the parent company Lever Brothers paid under the odds for palm oil from the HCB which was, after all, the basis of its Sunlight Soap. In 1930, the English company made profits of £1.8 million rising to £7.6 million in 1939.[32]

British companies had other investments in overseas territories and European colonies. The Great Gold Zone Mining Exploration & Estate Co Ltd exploited the gold in the Lombige river and nearby mines in Angola from 1884. British owned companies had telegraph connections built for Portugal's African colonies, and railway companies in Portuguese Goa, too.[33] And while they were not actual colonies, British investors also employed labour in a lot of Latin America, as we have seen.

Chapter Twenty-four

HIGH NOON OF THE EMPIRE

'Merrie England, an age away from us, lies lapped in its long Edwardian summer's evening',
John Raymond, *England's on the Anvil*, 1958, p 132

Queen Victoria lived into the twentieth century before handing her crown on to
Edward VII in 1901. He only lived till 1910 but the Edwardian era is remembered
as that late perfection of Britain's Empire, before the cycle of World Wars consumed
it. The 'long Edwardian summer' summons up a time of innocent, languid reverie
before the Great War.

On the face of things, the Edwardian era was that long summer with handsome
men and women looking wistfully out of the canvases of William Holman Hunt or John
Singer Sargent, paid for by energetic Scotsmen making pneumatic tyres with Malaysian
rubber.

England since 1895 had been enjoying a recovery as its industry was reorganised
around steel, lighter industries and, though behind Germany, the beginnings of a chemical industry, diesel power and electricity. Newer industries, often for consumer goods
drew on colonial products, like Lever Brothers (founded 1884) which used African palm
oil for soap, Dunlop Rubber's pneumatic tyre (1889), the City of London Electricity
Company was founded in 1891, Fry's had already made the first chocolate bar in 1866,
and Cadbury's made Dairy Milk in 1905. In 1898, the British Admiralty began the first
trials of oil fuel in ships, and in 1905 started to build dual use oil and coal burning vessels, signing a contract with Burmah Oil for 10,000 tons of oil a year.

Britain was not entirely at ease with itself. In 1905 and then again in 1910–11
labourers rose up against employers and government in a number of sharp clashes. The
'great unrest' in Britain saw strikes by miners, seamen, dockers, carters, tramwaymen
railway workers and even school children, and between 1911 and 1914 seventy million working days were lost through strike action. The upsurge was so shocking that
the Government went to war against its own people. In 1910 troops were used against
rioters at the Rhondda Valley coal pits, with Hussars and Fusiliers invading the pit
town of Tonypandy. Home Secretary Winston Churchill also sent a cavalry column
into the East End to threaten striking dockers. Troops were called out against a rail
strike in Chesterfield. In 1911 a general strike in Liverpool so alarmed Home Secretary
Churchill that he anchored a battleship off the port to intimidate the strikers.

The long Edwardian Summer.

The social turmoil was not only in the factories. Women, too, were on the march, fighting for the right to vote. The Women's Social and Political Union led by Emmeline and Christabel Pankhurst fought for women's suffrage. The Suffragette campaign had snowballed, turning from constitutional lobbying to militant campaigns that included the burning churches and letterboxes, and smashing shop windows in the West End. The government answered with repression arresting women – many of whom went on hunger strike, and many of whom were force fed. On 18 November 1910 – 'black Friday' – Home Secretary Winston Churchill told the police to make no arrests at a Suffragette demonstration outside parliament, meaning instead that they were to beat the protestors into submission, which they tried to do in fighting that went on for five hours.

Not just domestic unrest threatened Edwardian security. There was a real fear that Britain would lose its world trade advantage. Books like Williams' *Made in Germany* (1896), Mackenzie's *American Invaders* (1902) and A. Shadwell's *Industrial Efficiency* (1906) warned the public of the problem. A *Times* editorial of 1902 warned of 'The Crisis in British Industry'. The Liberal-turned-Unionist Joseph Chamberlain stumped the country whipping up support for 'Tariff Reform' – an appeal to strengthen the ties of Empire and protect British industry against German competition. Agriculture was 'practically destroyed', 'sugar has gone, silk has gone, iron is threatened; the turn of cotton will come', Chamberlain warned. His campaign had the backing of all the big newspapers, the *Daily Mail,* the *Times,* the *Telegraph* and the *Express.* Protecting British industry against foreign competition was a big concern.[1]

Elite Britain at the fin de siècle was prey to some morbid fantasies. There was a decadent undercurrent. In Oscar Wilde's *Picture of Dorian Gray* (1891) the immoral and dissolute anti-hero heads off to Chinatown in Limehouse to find solace: 'There were opium dens where one could buy oblivion, dens of horror where the memory of old sins could be destroyed by the madness of sins that were new.'[2] Influenced by the French 'Decadents' like Felicien de Rops and Joris Huysmans, Wilde and Aubrey Beardsley explored ideas of a retreat from duty and morality into a more aesthetic and pleasure-seeking life.

The earnestness of the Pre-Raphaelite Brotherhood gave way to the more sensual Art Nouveau explorations of Charles Rennie Mackintosh.

At Cambridge University a long-standing discussion group, called the 'Cambridge Apostles', met, for whom the mild-mannered philosopher G. E. Moore was an unlikely champion of freethinking. Moore's big idea, summarised in his 1903 book, *Principia Ethica* was that there was no essential foundation to morality, which was really a utilitarian consideration of what was more or less pleasurable. The appeal to a transcendant 'good' was, he argued, a 'naturalistic fallacy'. Moore was a contemporary of Bertrand Russell, who was himself falling out of love with the German-influenced idealism that had been popular in Cambridge, in particular the English followers of G. W. F. Hegel. Russell reacted against the holistic and purposeful philosophy of English Hegelianism and emphasized instead the fragmentary world he saw:

> Hegel had maintained that all separateness is illusory and the universe is more like a pot of treacle than a heap of shot. I therefore said, 'the universe is exactly like a heap of shot'.[3]

'My position, in all its chief features, is derived from Mr G. E. Moore', wrote Russell in his preface to *Principia Mathematica*. From Moore he had taken 'that pluralism which regards the world, both that of existents and that of entities, as composed of an infinite number of mutually independent entities'. The holistic morality that bound the old world together was gone and there were to be no more 'naturalistic fallacies' to ground us. The roster of those who listened to Moore's papers at the Cambridge Apostles circle included John Maynard Keynes, who would later jettison the belief in an equilibrium in economics, and in balanced budgets. In his essay, *My Early Beliefs*, Keynes would write that Moore's 'influence was not only overwhelming ... it was exciting, exhilarating, the beginning of a renaissance, the opening of a new heaven on earth, we were the forerunners of a new dispensation, we were not afraid of anything'. 'We had no respect for traditional wisdom or the restraints of custom', Keynes explained: 'We lacked reverence ... for everything and everyone'.[4]

Another Apostle was Lytton Strachey, whose book *Eminent Victorians* – published in 1918 but conceived in 1912 – mocked the Victorian heroes Cardinal Manning, Thomas Arnold and General Gordon. So, too, was Leonard Woolf, who would serve in the Ceylon Civil Service. Like Keynes and Strachey he was one of the 'Bloomsbury set' of writers and intellectuals.

Moore, Russell and the Cambridge Apostles, like Wilde, Beardsley and Mackintosh, were not mainstream figures (though Keynes, especially, but also Russell and Woolf would play a big role after the Great War). They were emblematic of one strand of the intellectual elite that had lost its belief in the ideal of Britain and its world mission. Others, like Joseph Chamberlain, reacted with a more bombastic assertion of the importance of the British ideal, and in particular the ideal of Empire.

Robert Cecil, Conservative Prime Minister and former Secretary of State for India was apprehensive of change as he was conscious that Britain's position was overstretched: 'Whatever happens will be for the worse, and therefore it is in our interest that as little should happen as possible', he said. The New Imperialism had been driven by Liberal Imperialists, but the business of holding and governing the Empire was more suited to Conservatives.

Anxiety about losing the top position was clear in the growing fear of Germany, and other rivals. 'In view of the pan-Germanic aspirations, the British Empire is today confronted by a danger unparalleled in history', warned military historian C. Stuart Linton. When J. K. O' Connor talked to German officers in East Africa in 1913 he felt 'it was evident that the possession of the African continent was the greatest desire of the Teutons', as he wrote in his book *The Hun in our Hinterland*. Pro-war journals like Horatio Bottomley's *John Bull* and Noel Pemberton Billing's *The Imperialist* demanded more Dreadnoughts, and more scholarly journals like the *Commonwealth and Empire Review* were hardly less jingoistic.

The Navy's capital ships programme was lauded in a great propaganda campaign built around the first of the new battleships, the Dreadnought. There was a cult of the Dreadnought, which featured in newspapers and magazines, and there was even a boys' comic called the *Dreadnought*. The Admiralty had a full publicity campaign with booklets and press releases. When the Dreadnought visited the Thames in 1909:

> there were chaotic scenes at Southend where the flagship was moored. The main pier to the Dreadnought had to be closed again and again because of overcrowding. On the morning of 18 July, an estimated 20,000 people tried to get on to the pier.[5]

When war was declared against Germany in 1914 the British Chancellor was relieved that the social conflicts in Britain would have to take a back seat to the more pressing conflict. Lloyd George recorded 'in the course of a single day angry political passions were silenced and followed by the just wrath' of patriotism. The Labour Party, which had only just emerged from under the wing of the Liberals was profoundly shaped by the wartime experience. Though it had a strong pacifist wing, and Labour leaders like McDonald and Lansbury were pacifists, the trade union leadership that was the bedrock of the party was drawn into the industrial war. Under the 'treasury agreement' of 18 March 1915 union leaders undertook to support the war with a 'no-strike' agreement. They were rewarded with official status by the Ministry of Munitions. The incorporation of the trade unions and the Labour Party leaders into the war effort consolidated the patriotic and pro-imperial outlook of the Party in the decades that followed.

The British Empire

The British Empire in 1909 was at its height. Though it would cover more territory after the 1914-18 war, imperialism as an ideal was in the eyes of many compromised after then, and even more so after the Second World War. With authority over a quarter of the world's population, and over a quarter of its land mass, the Imperial Crown was resplendent – the hubris before the nemesis.

Britain's economy in 1913 was more globalised than any had been until then and would be the high-water mark of globalisation until the 1970s. The falling cost of shipping and on-board refrigeration made it possible to meet more of the country's food needs by importing butter and lamb from New Zealand and Australia. Sugar came from Fiji and Australia, and cane cultivation would soon revive in the West Indies. Tea, coffee and chocolate came from Assam, Ghana and the West Indies. Rubber and Gutta Percha for components in the 'second industrial revolution' came from Malaya and Ceylon, Jute for sacks came from India to Aberdeen. Those colonies in turn were captive markets for Britain's industrial exports.

Britain's exports between 1873 and 1899 had stagnated, but from 1899 to 1913 they grew again by five per cent per year. Between 1850 and 1875 only a little more than a quarter of Britain's exports went to the Empire, but from 1881 the share was more than a third – with about half of that going to the 'settlement colonies' and the other half going to Indian and the other non-white colonies.[6] In 1897, Canada brought in a preferential tariff rate for British goods, New Zealand and South Africa followed suit in 1903 and Australia in 1908. From 1906 to 1913 British exports to the colonies climbed from £93 million worth to £157 million, whereas the growth in trade to the rest of the world was much more modest, and depended in part on the re-export of colonial goods, directly, or as components of British manufactures.[7] In 1911, scientific advisor to the colonial office Sir Daniel Morris lectured that 'the productions of the tropics' were in increasing demand and that that it was 'not beyond the mark to state that our commercial supremacy may largely depend on our maintaining control of them'.[8]

Britain was still in 1914 the biggest exporter of capital to the world. Of all foreign investment, Britain's made up 44 per cent of the total (compared to France's 20 per cent, Germany's 12.8 per cent and America's 7.8 per cent). The British Empire was an important site of British investment, but more than half of overseas investments were elsewhere. British overseas investment was, between 1905 and 1914, greater than British investment in domestic industries.[9]

William Woodruff worked out that of the $20 billion Britain invested overseas, $4.25 billion was invested in the United States, $2.8 billion in Canada, $1.5 billion in Argentina, $1.7 billion in Australia, $1.85 billion in India and Ceylon and $1.5 billion in West Africa ($2.45 billion in Africa as a whole).[10] George Paish put the estimate somewhat lower at around $18.8 billion, or £4 billion, generating an income of £200 million a year: around eight per cent of Britain's total GDP.[11]

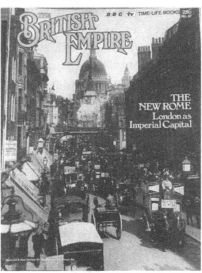

1913 – As it looked in 1975.

The whole of the British Empire in 1913 had an output £6.467 billion, of which Britain contributed £2.497 billion, the colonies £3.97 billion. Colonial output was 1.59 times British output.[12] Not all of that colonial output was at Britain's disposal. Most of what the colonies produced they consumed. That was necessarily so since so many of the people in the colonies were subsistence farmers, and only a very small minority farmed cash crops or manufactured goods for sale.[13] Abercrombie found that two thirds of the farmers in the former British colonies of Malawi and Kenya were still subsistence farmers in 1954.[14] The subsistence farmers paid a modest tax individually, but in aggregate that was a large sum, which financed the colonial administration and Britain. But it was limited by the small surpluses that the farmers gave up over and above their subsistence. The low capital investment in agriculture meant that output was low. The colonies of settlement were distinctive, with more capital investment in agriculture and also some larger manufacturing sectors.

The cash crops were important money makers, including Indian tea, coffee, jute and opium; Malaysian rubber, tea and coffee; Fijian, Mauritian, Australian and West Indian sugar; West African palm oil; East African sisal. Mining, too, was important, in particular diamonds and gold in South Africa, and Gold in Australia; tin in Malaya. H. G. Wells' parodied the outlook of the British statesman in Westminster in his 1910 book *The New Machiavelli*:

> I see quadrangles and corridors of spacious grey-toned offices in which undistinguished little men and little files of papers link us to islands in the tropics, to frozen wildernesses gashed for gold, to vast temple-studded plains, to forest worlds and mountain worlds, to ports and fortresses and lighthouses and watch-towers and grazing lands and corn lands all about the globe.[15]

Those colonial countries and regions where cash crops and commodities were widespread were faced with a problem. The crops – sugar, tobacco, tea, coffee, opium and rubber – and the mineral resources like tin, copper, zinc and oil, were all developed for the British and the international market, and subject to wide price swings. Those colonies' economies had grown in a lop-sided way where a large part of the workforce was given over to one output, like sugar or rubber. Their economies had developed more in accord with the needs of the 'mother country' than of their own. Changes in the world market could have a dramatic impact in a way that a more rounded economy, where domestic demand for a broad mix of goods would cushion exporters, would be more secure. The 'terms of trade' between those colonies that exported mostly raw materials in exchange for British-made manufactured goods were against them.

These colonial goods were on display in the publicity that the colonies and manufacturers put out. The picture of the British Empire as a vast division of labour was only half true. With so many colonial subjects living as subsistence farmers, most of their output was not made part of the wider division of labour – only the surplus over and above their subsistence would be taken from them as rent or in tax. The tax would mostly go to pay for the administration of the colony and the rent kept a growing class of landlords, native and European.

The whole of the cash-croppers' output, like those of craftsmen and wage labourers were traded as Empire produce. The total inter-imperial trade of the British Empire in 1913 was £551,527,000, or just 8.5 per cent of its output. The persistence of subsistence farming and the poor capitalisation of agriculture shows the extent to which the Empire acted as a brake on economic progress. As an example, between 1891 and 1921 the share of the Indian population who lived by farming actually went up from 61 to 73 per cent.[16]

In many cases the distinction between cash-cropping and subsistence was institutionalised in the colonial native administrations. Malays and native Fijians were formally excluded from the cash economy and directed to subsistence-based village economies, while migrant Indian labour (indentured labour) was put to work on the revenue-raising plantations. In the 1911 census there were 87,096 Fijians, subsistence farmers under the native administration, and 40,286 Indians, mostly planting cane for the Colonial Sugar Refining Company, who sold 62,776 tons of sugar in 1910, worth about $5.6 million (up from 11,859 tons in 1890[17]). The large parts of the community excluded from the cash economy, were a protected native 'yeomanry' according to the colonial administrators, but they were being held back by negligible capital investment in their farming. In 1907, the Chief of Bau called the native policy the 'digging stick' policy – 'forty years ago our people used the digging stick', Ratu Epeli said, adding: 'Today they are using the digging stick still.' Malaya had a parallel ethnic divide, where Chinese and Indian migrants in the tin and rubber industries were just short of one million in 1911, while the Malayan subsistence farmers were 1.3 million. In Ceylon, dependent like Fiji on its cash crops, governor Sir Hugh Clifford promoted peasant subsistence farming to mitigate hunger when prices fell between the two world wars.[18]

British investment could be a spur to development but white planters and mine-owners were often half-hearted investors. Indigenous capitalists filled the gap. In Ceylon the sale of government land was meant to encourage Europeans but locals, particularly of the Karāvas caste, pooled cash to buy estates for coffee and later arrack farms. Governor Gordon imported Indian labour thinking it would be put to work by European cane farmers, but as it turned out the Indians themselves bought leases and farmed cane. The 'comprador' intermediaries in Hong Kong gradually displaced western traders like Jardine Matheson to set up companies of their own. Indian Jute and cotton mills took off when British owners withdrew. Though they often faced discrimination from the colonial authorities, at the urging of those English investors who were struggling on, indigenous farmers, traders and industrialists would later go on to help build independent countries.

The Empire, then, was an important cushion for Britain. They sold their goods to the Empire, they sold on some of the goods they bought from the Empire, and the dividends on investments they made in the Empire paid handsome returns. If the 'new imperialism' was in some ways a defensive reaction to the loss of confidence in Britain, it seemed to have paid off. For the colonial subjects that was less true. There is no way of knowing what would have happened without British rule, but it is apparent that under British rule, economic development was comparably far weaker than development in Europe, or the Americas.

Colonial Service

In 1857, the Colonial Office was in two ramshackle houses in Nos. 13 and 14 Downing Street, with just 62 employees, including nine copyists, five messengers and four porters. The 50 colonies were run by post: everything was written down in instructions to the colonies, and the reports back to the Colonial Office were also written down and published in what were known as the Blue Books.

At the top of the Colonial Service were the Governors, who were political appointments.

Some of the Governors were controversial. Edward John Eyre's role in the Morant Bay massacre ended his colonial career. Bartle Frere was pilloried for his role in the Basotho gun war at the end of his career. George Grey, who was a governor in South Wales, New Zealand and Cape Colony confounded the colonial office by his involvement in New Zealand's local politics, and he was briefly elected premier there. Many Governors, like John Pope Hennessy and Arthur Hamilton Gordon were criticised by the English settlers for being too solicitous of native interests. The Governors-General of India were not often governors elsewhere. The position was on a higher plane.

Officially there was not one Colonial Service, as the Secretary of State for the Colonies, Leo Amery, explained in 1927: 'I deal in this office with twenty-six different governments, each entirely separate from the rest, each administratively, financially, legislatively self-contained.'[19] Internally, Lord Selborne reported for the Secretary of State for the Colonies on the Colonial Service in 1899 that it was made up of 434 higher administrative officers, 310 legal officers, 447 medical officers, and just over 300 under the heading, 'other' – making around 1500 colonial officers running the British Empire. The legend that the British Empire was just 'a Thin White Line' is not really true. Anthony Kirk-Greene estimates that 'at least ninety per cent of the staff of colonial governments were locally employed officials'. Characteristically the Colonial Office defended the European monopoly over civil senior Civil Service posts, as they did in Ceylon, in the face of calls to open up to native candidates.[20]

Given that there were more than two million people working for the Indian Government according to the census of 1901, the ratio of native employees to European officers was most likely even greater. As well as the Colonial Service and its locally recruited officials there were locally recruited armies, permanent, like the British-Indian Army, and later local constabularies, white and native, and also *ad hoc* forces recruited from local levees of natives or settlers, according to the needs of the time.

Some of the governors and High Commissioners.

Henry Barkly	Guiana, Jamaica, Victoria, Mauritius and Cape Colony	1848–77
John Grant	Bengal (Lieutenant Governor) and Jamaica	1859–74
Bartle Frere	Bombay and South Africa (High Commissioner)	1851–80
Arthur Hamilton Gordon	New Brunswick, Trinidad, Mauritius, Fiji, New Zealand and Ceylon	1866–90
Hercules Robinson	Hong Kong, New South Wales, Fiji, New Zealand and Cape Colony	1859–97
John Pope Hennessy	Labuan, Sierra Leone, Bahamas, Barbados, Hong Kong and Mauritius	1867–89
William Des Vœux	Fiji, Newfoundland and Hong Kong	1880–91
Alfred Moloney	The Gambia, Lagos, British Honduras, Windward Islands and Trinidad and Tobago	1884–1904
Matthew Nathan	Gold Coast, Hong Kong, Natal and Queensland	1900–25
Frederick Lugard	Nigeria and Hong Kong	1900–19
Earl Cromer	Consul-General of Egypt	1883–1907
Garnet Wolseley	Gold Coast, Transvaal and Natal	1873–75
Harry Luke	Palestine, Western Pacific and Fiji	1928–42
Sydney Olivier	Jamaica and India	1907–24
Ronald Storrs	Jerusalem, Cyprus and Northern Rhodesia	1920–34
Herbert Plumer	Malta and Palestine	1919–26
Herbert Samuel	Palestine	1920–25
Shenton Thomas	Nyasaland, Gold Coast and Straits Settlement	1929–46
Miles Lampson	High Commissioner to Egypt and Sudan	1934–46
John Macpherson	Nigeria	1948–55
Robert Armitage	Cyprus and Nyasaland	1954–61
Alan Burns	Bahamas, Nigeria and Honduras Gold Coast	1924–47

The Colonial Service, which made up the District Officers, Protectors of Aborigines, Medical Officers, Judges and tax collectors was only the next level down of the colonial elite, who commanded a vast governmental machine, or rather several parallel machines, the different colonial administrations. By 1949, it was calculated that there were 300,000 colonial staff, under 20,500 senior officers.[21]

Many who served in the colonial service went on to describe their experiences in memoirs and novels. They include Leonard Woolf, who was a cadet and then a government agent in the Ceylon civil service, before becoming an advisor on Labour's colonial policy. Woolf wrote a novel about Ceylon called *The Village in the Jungle* (1913). George Orwell was an Assistant District Attendant in the Indian Constabulary in Burma, which authority he ridiculed painfully in the essay 'Shooting an elephant'. Anthony Burgess was an education officer in Malaya in 1965 which he made into three novels, all published together as *The Long Day Wanes*.

In Malaya the Sultanate employed 1,700 British civil servants who 'held the key posts in all departments and determined the political and economic directions Malaya would take'.[22] Expatriate Britons had control of the Shanghai Municipal Corporation in the International Settlement. It was, admitted the British Minister to China in 1919 an 'anachronism', but a 'most useful one'. In 1919 the Corporation recruited 74 demobilised British troops to boost its local police force.[23]

In Tropical Africa the Colonial Service had between 1900 and 1909 recruited 261 administrative officers for Nigeria and 82 for Kenya, 47 for the Gold Coast. In West Africa by 1910 there were 30 officers serving, in Gambia, 150 in Sierra Leone, 400 in the Gold Coast, 850 in Southern Nigeria and Lagos, 680 in Northern Nigeria. Other services that were drawing on the pool of Britain's trainee colonial administrators included the Indian Civil Service, the Indian Political Service and the All-India Services; the Egyptian Civil Service, the Sudan Political Service, and the Hong Kong Civil Service.[24]

In 1909, the Colonial Office set up a training course for new recruits to its African Administrative Services, covering colonial accounts, tropical economic products, hygiene and sanitation, criminal law and procedure, international law and Mahommedan law, elementary surveying, African languages and ethnology – all in three months.

On 23 February 1917, King George V opened the 'Oriental School' of the London University with funds raised in an appeal by Lord Cromer. Funders included Anglo-Persian Oil, Burmah Oil, Lloyds Bank, the Hong Kong and Shanghai Bank, the Chartered Bank of India, Australia and China, as well as the Bombay Burmah Trading Company. A small share of the students studied for a degree while most were colonial administrators, military officers, businessmen and missionaries on short courses. Student numbers fluctuated from 539 in 1919–20 to 611 in 1927–28. The Secretary of State for India also sent trainees to Oxford, Cambridge, and Trinity College Dublin to study for the one- and two-years Indian Civil Service probationers' course. The Colonial Office sent its Straits Settlement and Federated Malay Cadets to the Oriental School to learn Malay in 1927–28, but later sent them to Oxford. Probationers for the Malay Police, agriculture and education service went to the Oriental School, while candidates for the Hong Kong and Tropical Africa Service went to Oxford and Cambridge. In 1937, the Oriental School moved to Bloomsbury and the following year was renamed the School of Oriental and African Studies. Funds were boosted with contributions from colonial governments.[25]

In the Public Records Office in Kew there are collected millions of pages of reports drawn up by the Colonial Service Officers, in quarterly reports, annual reports and special incident reports. From these Governors condensed very detailed reports of the state of the colonial societies and their economic resources. To read these is to see the world through the eyes of the colonial service. The reports are for the most part empirically robust and filled with detail. They also often betray a sardonic even misanthropic view of the native peoples the British governed, a barely disguised hostility towards missionaries and other Europeans who might intercede on behalf of the native peoples, and often a distaste for the grasping settlers. The virtues of the British mission overseas are rarely stated in anything but the most guarded terms unless it is in contrast to the undeserving character of the natives.

Many more files would exist but that the Colonial Office launched a programme of destroying records that would be embarrassing to Britain called 'Operation Legacy'. In 1961, Colonial Secretary Iain Macleod sent instructions to those administrators on how they should burn or dump files in the sea. Tens of thousands of files that were repatriated to Britain were withheld from the public collection at Kew and kept in a secret site in Hanslope Park, Buckinghamshire, and many of these later destroyed.

Native Administration

Before they were Dominions, the colonies of settlement had become self-governing colonies through Legislative Councils. Britain was not only the Mother Country, it was the 'Mother of Parliaments'. For white settlers, the path to self-government and Dominion status under the Crown echoed the Whig view of history as institutional progress.

For the non-white colonies the path was different. The assumption was that European ideals of political representation were not applicable to native peoples. In 1914, Lord Milner argued 'that nation will in the long run be most successful which exhibits the greatest wisdom in its efforts to promote the welfare and progress and contentment of its subject peoples'. The British role was to look after the non-white races in their own best interests.[26]

For the Royal Institute of International Affairs, H. A. Wyndham explained that British experiments in 'introducing representative institutions into West Africa' were 'to encourage "habits of self-reliance" among Africans rather than to train them to fit into a planned and imperial structure'. Wyndham saw the British policy as very different from the French, because it was 'looking forward to the evolution of a distinctive African polity' where France was 'aiming at the eventual assimilation of West Africa to her language and culture'.[27]

Wyndham describes the Native Jurisdiction Ordinance of 1878 in West Africa. Under it those who were 'not subordinate to any other chiefs' were recognized as 'Head Chiefs' and the British Governor then put them under 'Divisional Chiefs' and gave them 'authority to pass by-laws with the concurrence of divisional chiefs and headmen'.[28] It was less an indigenous than a colonial hierarchy.

A Parliamentary inquiry was held over the settlement of land in British East Africa, with Sir Frederick Lugard's direction in 1925. A Native Lands Trust Board reserved 47,000 (out of 245,000) square miles 'for the use and benefit of the native tribes forever' and 'the control of the land ... should be exercised in accordance with native law and custom'. In practice that meant that the land was controlled by a 'native administration' of white colonial officers working through collaborating chiefs.[29]

Governing through native administrations had already been tried in Fiji where Governor Arthur Gordon made a native administration with the Great Council of Chiefs (Bose Vakaturaga) at the head with men of chiefly families recruited as local administrators, thirteen Rokos (District Commissioners) and Bulis (Village Headmen). 'The organisation is almost wholly that of native organisation, and all that I have done with it is to take hold of it and formulate it', Gordon thought – though sociologist Peter French later explained that Gordon's system markedly altered Fijian society as it formalised grades and organisations that were very different from anything that had previously existed in Fiji.[30]

Sir Frederick Lugard who played an important role in the colonisation of Nigeria argued that without giving natives an 'active share in the control of their own affairs under their own native leaders', 'the servile races would not long be content to occupy their present subordinate position'.[31]

The principle of separate development in a native administration had already been modelled in India, where the halt on new territories after the Mutiny left some 675 Maharajas governing semi-dependent states within India. Collectively these 822,000 square miles of territory had 72.5 million inhabitants. The Maharajas were honoured in British ceremonies like the Durbar and enjoyed local independence as long as they remained loyal.

Native administrations, Dual Mandates, and reserved areas were all a recipe for arrested development. In the 1950s and 1960s the national independence movements would take on the Great Councils of Chiefs and Princely states for what they were, local collaborators with the Empire. But from 1880 till 1939 they were still an important mainstay of British authority in the Empire. Practically speaking they cemented the racial division between traditional native village and largely urban-based white settler society.

The Ideology of Race

The British Empire brought many English people to meet people of other races, often in contested settings. When that happened people were a lot more conscious of racial differences. The idea that white people were naturally superior to black people was often voiced then. West Indian planters and Indian Civil Servants often called the people that they ruled over by the 'n' word, and treated them as such (Thomas Carlyle called his article on emancipation 'The N****r Question' in 1849, Queen Victoria ordered Lytton to stop his officers using the word[32]).

By the 1880s the idea that the world was divided into white and black, and that the former were destined to rule over the latter was widely taken up in Britain. The colonial experience of governing non-white peoples was the main driver of racial thinking. The racial ideology was consolidated with the defence of the British Empire and the appeal to the white settlers of Australia, New Zealand, Canada and South Africa to come to Britain's aid.

In his book *The Expansion of England* (1883) historian John Seeley argued that the settlers 'are of our own blood, and therefore united with us by the strongest ties'. In 1899 John Robinson, who had served as Prime Minister of Natal, gave a lecture to the Royal Colonial Institute saying that 'a Canadian or an Australian, or a South African need not be the less ardent British subject because he is devoted to his own land'. In the discussion it was agreed that 'Briton' was the collective word for all of these white peoples.[33] Among the settler communities in the British Empire there was a strong belief that not only were they Britons, but they were *better* Britons, a younger, more vital addition to the stock. As historian John Mitcham explains views of the settlers had changed: 'Abandoning an earlier liberal view of the white colonies as strategic liabilities and unwanted nuisances, many Britons began to see them as valuable reservoirs of strength against European adversaries.'[34] As we have seen attitudes to settlers were often vicious in England in the mid-century, but by the turn of the next century the colonials were admirable and manly adventurers. These colonies by settlement were called *Dominions* from the late nineteenth century (officially from the 1907 Colonial Conference).

Prime Minister Balfour set up the Committee for Imperial Defence in 1902. He aimed to integrate the command of all the armed services of Britain and the Colonies – 'the Dominions' must 'realize more fully that their security from attack', said Viscount Esher, 'is inextricably bound up with the security of Britain'.[35] Politicians and newspaper editors in the Dominions were flattered and promised support in men and cash. Initially, the support was token, but with the Great War, the Dominions offered up more than a million troops.

Just as the Imperial appeal emphasized the solidarity of British settlers and the mother country, it made a sharp distinction between the white and the black Empire. Lord Alfred Milner saw the Empire as two, separated by a colour line, of which the more important part were the white settler communities, bound together with 'the bond of common blood, of common language, common history and traditions'[36] Milner had already trialled this policy of white unity at the end of the Boer War, where he had won the support of the rebellious Boers by promising them that the natives would be denied political rights.

In the propaganda lead-up to the 1914–18 war the volunteers from the Dominions were lauded in the British press as young lions come to aid the Mother Country. The British reaction to the Dominion soldiers was very different from an earlier use of colonial troops. In 1878, in the middle of a panic about a potential Russian invasion, Disraeli sent 7,500 Indian troops to Malta (Indian troops had often been used overseas, in Rangoon and in Omdurman).

The use of Indian troops in Europe caused difficulties. The *Spectator* thought 'in asking Sepoys to fight for them in a quarrel outside Asia, Englishmen are putting upon subject races a duty which, if it is obligatory, they ought to perform themselves, and rendering themselves in no small degree dependent on their own subjects'.[37] This was an early statement of what would later become a semi-official principle among Europeans, that native troops should not be used in conflicts between Europeans. As it turned out Indian troops played a considerable role in the war of 1914–18 – greater than any of the Dominions. They fought on the Western front, too, though overwhelmingly they were used in non-European theatres of war.

The ideology of race was not just the bombastic appeal of Empire solidarity. At least as important was the underlying idea that the European race was in danger of being overwhelmed. In 1905, the Japanese defeated the Russian Navy. On hearing the news Oxford history teacher Alfred Zimmern changed the title of his lecture, as he explained to his class, because 'I feel I must speak to you about the most important historical event which has happened, or is likely to happen, in our lifetime: the victory of a non-white people over a white people.' Fear of the eclipse of the white race was a strong theme in Jeremiads like Oswald Spengler's *Decline of the West*.[38] More ambitiously, the solidarity of the white race could be imagined as a common endeavour of subduing the non-white. Cecil Rhodes set out a plan to recruit leaders from the 'Nordic race' to govern 'the entire continent of Africa, the Holy Land, the valley of the Euphrates, the islands of Cyprus and Candia, the whole of South America, the islands of the Pacific', and even 'the whole of the Malay Archipelago, the seaboards of China and Japan' and 'the ultimate recovery of the United States'. This madcap plan gave birth to the Rhodes-endowed scholarship at the University of Oxford.[39]

Racial ideology was popular not just in the Dominions, but in Britain, too. Alarms were raised when many volunteers for service in the Boer War from Britain's cities were rejected by the army as being unfit. A Liberal MP challenged on his argument for free meals and free baths for schoolchildren said 'all this sounds terribly like socialism. I'm afraid it is ... because I know Empire cannot be built upon rickety and flat-chested citizens'.[40] Social reform was often justified on the grounds that it was needed to reverse the 'decline of the race'.

Cecil Rhodes said in 1885, after attending a meeting of the unemployed in the East End of London, after listening to 'wild speeches that were just a call for "bread, bread, bread"', that he had become convinced of the importance of imperialism as a solution for the 'social problem':

> The Empire is a bread and butter question. If you want to avoid civil war, you must become imperialists.[41]

A sceptical Jack London wrote about the splendours of the Coronation Day parade in 1902 as a compensation for the impoverished state of urban Britain:

> So it was along the whole line of march – force, overpowering force; myriads of men, splen-
> did men, the pick of the people, whose sole function in life is blindly to obey, and blindly
> kill and destroy and stamp out life. And that they should be well fed, well clothed, and well-
> armed, and have ships to hurl them to the ends of the earth, the East end of London, and
> the 'East End' of all England, toils and rots and dies.[42]

Working class identification with Britain's mastery of the world, as Jack London saw it, did not do all that much for the poorer denizens of the East End.

Joseph Chamberlain's protectionist campaigns against foreign competition also led to racist campaigns against foreign labour. In 1905, the Aliens Act was passed to stop Jewish immigration, at the urging of the British Brothers League and the National Union of Boot and Shoe Operatives. That was the year there was a great campaign in England, against Chinese labour in South Africa. The Dominions adopted legislation against non-white immigration at the end of the nineteenth century. The *Sydney Morning Herald* explained 'that by a White Australia we mean a British Australia'.[43]

The 'Keep Australia White' campaign

Scientific Racism and Cultural Anthropology

It has often been argued since that the racial ideology in Britain owed its strength to the ideas of Francis Galton's Eugenic Society. Galton, a cousin of Charles Darwin's, was a keen science populariser. He was a leading light in the British Society for the

Advancement of Science, the Royal Geographical Society, the Royal Society, and many others. For all his many accomplishments in statistics and cartography, Galton dedicated much of his energy to the promotion of the science to which he gave the name 'eugenics' (from the Greek eugenes, meaning 'well-born'). Sometimes this is called 'social Darwinism', meaning the use of Darwin's ideas about natural selection in animal species to explain sociological problems, like the persistence of poverty.

Galton used his official positions to spread the idea that the human species was differentiated according to its mental, moral and physical capacities, which were innate, inherited characteristics. Eugenics also held up the (illusory) prospect that social problems could be overcome by sterilising 'idiots'. Birth-control campaigner Marie Stopes argued for the reduction of the 'hordes of defectives' through contraception. 'The time is surely coming', argued the socialist academic Harold Laski, 'when society will look upon the production of a weakling as a crime against itself'.[44]

Charles Temple who served as a colonial administrator in northern Nigeria in early century saw his mission as through the lens of race, as he explained in his 1918 book *Native Races and Their Rulers*:

> The destiny of nations has placed under our control during the immediately preceding generations so great a teeming mass of dusky humanity that history furnishes no parallel to the weight of national responsibility which we carry, and on our proper discharge of those responsibilities doubtless depends not only the maintenance of the position which we now occupy but our very existence as a distinct race.[45]

It was a view of the racial difference between Briton and Nigerian that served to justify acts of domination and at times great cruelty.

Not just eugenics but also anthropology also lent itself to policy of race discrimination. Economic historian Lilian Knowles explains in her 1924 history of the Empire that England in the era of free market capitalism believed that 'the coloured races were fundamentally the same as the white, only a little darker, and that once slavery was removed there would be a marvellous progress attained under a regime of freedom and order'. This earlier, naïve view gave way to 'the scientific stage':

> Anthropology and ethnology developed, and after 1870 men began to realize that human beings were fundamentally different, not merely in the shape of their heads, their colour and hair, but in their institutions, religious beliefs, likes, dislikes, economic and social structure.[46]

In Knowles' view the native administration and indirect rule policies adopted by Frederick Lugard in Nigeria were a proper example of government in keeping with the scientific findings of anthropological diversity.

British service in native administrations in the Empire was a great spur to anthropology. Edward Evans-Pritchard's studies of the Azande in Central Africa and the Sanusi in Libya in the 1930s were ground-breaking. Evans-Pritchard's determination not to reduce the beliefs of native peoples to imperfect understanding, but to try to see them in their own terms mirrored the colonial policy of native administration and its stress

on native autonomy. After the war Evans-Pritchard was made Professor of anthropology at Oxford and his emphasis on cultural (as opposed to racial) difference was widely
taken up.

Eugenics was an important influence on social policy, but it was not the cause of the
ideology of racism. Racial ideology came about without too much rational reflection,
as a spontaneous explanation of the inequality of subject and governing groups. Slave
owners tended to explain their right to dominate their slaves as a natural outcome of
racial superiority, because skin colour was the marker of difference between European
slave-holders and enslaved Africans. Later, English District Officers, when pushed to
account for their social status, would say that they were from a naturally dominant race.
Social reformers struggling with the poverty of London's East End would be tempted
to see the persistence of poverty in terms of the degeneration of the race. These were
for the most part unthinking generalisations. Later on, natural scientists like Francis
Galton and the government advisor Frederick Lindemann, Lord Cherwell, would dress
up these prejudices in scientific theories, drawing too freely on Charles Darwin's ideas of
natural selection. Though they were tempting, they were also repellent to many Britons,
in particular the more traditionally-minded, for whom Social Darwinism and Eugenics
were un-Christian. Those intellectual, pseudo-scientific explanations did do a lot of
harm later on, but they did not give rise to the ideology of racial difference and superiority – that was already there in the organisation of Britain's Empire. Darwin's name was
loosely invoked to explain the clash of nations as a Darwinian struggle for survival.[47]

Chapter Twenty-five

THE EMPIRE AT WAR

The 1880s opened a new era of colonial expansion that saw the British Empire seize territories across Africa and Asia. Though it seemed dynamic, this new expansion was a displacement for the lost drive in British society. It would meet its limits in the colonial rivals that challenged Britain's global pre-eminence. Those rivals had grabbed land across the world in imitation of, and in defence against British domination. In 1914, and then again in 1939, the competition of Empires broke out into world war.

By 1914 the French Empire was 4,300,000 square miles with a population of 48 million.[1] Germany's overseas Empire was home to 11 million on 931,460 square miles in Africa, mostly claimed in 1880–90, and covered a further 94,927 square miles in New Guinea and Samoa.

Holland governed 35 million in Java and the outer Indonesia islands, covering some 730,000 square miles; and Surinam, with 63,000 square miles. In 1898 after the Spanish-American war Spain ceded the Philippines to the United States, which consolidated the territory under what was called the Insular Government in 1901.

The Austro-Hungarian Empire combined 28.5 million Austrians and 20.8 million Hungarians on a territory of 241,474.5 square miles, governing over 1.9 million in Bosnia-Herzegovina (19,702 square miles) and 135,000 Serbs in the 3244 square mile territory of Sanzak. Austro-Hungary had aspirations to govern Serbia, whose population was at 4.5 million.

The Russian Empire in the 1870s and 1880s had taken territory in Turkmenistan, Tajikistan, Kirgizstan and Sakhalin (lost to Japan in 1905) after the slow incursion into Kazakhstan was completed in the 1860s.

The Ottoman Empire was on the eve of the 1914–18 war the most compromised. Its high point had been in 1566 when it covered 877,888 square miles. Then the Sublime Porte was the centre of a tributary regime that governed by raising taxes and levees on its dependent Sanjaks. In the nineteenth century its Eyalets in Egypt and Tunis had become more independent as they became fiscally dependent on French and British loans. By 1913 the territory covered was 710,224 square miles and a population of 21 million including 5.6 million Arabs in Syria, Iraq and Arabia and another 2.4 million in Armenia and Kurdistan.

Ottoman empire, 1913.

	Area square miles	Population
Europe	10,882	1,891,000
Asia Minor	199,272	10,186,900
Armenia and Kurdistan	71,990	2,470,900
Mesopotamia	143,250	2,000,000
Syria	114,530	3,675,100
Arabia	170,300	1,050,000
Total	710,224	21,273,900

Statesman Year-Book, 1917, p 1347.

The growth of European empires worldwide had to stop at the point that they abutted one another. Those new borders in Africa and Asia were flash-points for inter-European conflicts. More so were the economic barriers towards European rivals that colonisation came to represent.

Like Britain, France raised tariffs against foreign imports. In 1892 Algeria, Indochina, Tunisia, Madagascar, Gabon and the vielles colonies of the Antilles and the Indian Ocean were brought into the French tariff zone so that they could trade freely in France, while others had favoured nation status and generally lower tariffs.[2]

Britain had shifted from a German-sympathetic foreign policy to a French-sympathetic one in the 1880s, alarmed at Bismarck's domination of Europe. The 'Entente Cordiale' struck in 1902 between Britain and France was at first an agreement that each would allow the other a free hand in Egypt and Morocco respectively. The agreement, which would later commit Britain to war in 1914, was a direct challenge to Germany, both economically and diplomatically. As a counterweight to the Anglo-French accord, Germany sought to shore up its alliance with the Austro-Hungarian Empire, supporting Austria's claims in the Balkans.

In 1911 Kaiser Wilhelm challenged the terms of the Entente Cordiale by sending the warship Panther to Agadir on the Moroccan coast. Wilhelm claimed the right to trade freely or for compensation in money and territory. It was another territorial claim on the other end of Europe, though, that began the war that everyone anticipated.

The Austro-Hungarian Empire sought to conquer Serbia, a state that had claimed its freedom in the decline of the Ottoman Empire. The assassination of the Arch-Duke Ferdinand in Sarajevo, by a team of South Slav liberation fighters was the pretext for Austria's demand to control Serbia. The diplomatic agreements that the European countries made to try to control Great Power rivalries divided them into two camps, the Entente Cordiale (which had been expanded to include Russia alongside France and Britain) and the Central Powers of Germany, Austria-Hungary and the Ottoman Empire.

The growing international rivalry gave rise to an arms race in the production of 'Dreadnought' class battleships, and the anticipatory building of railways to carry troops. The mobilisation of troops under the terms of mutual defence pacts over the summer of 1914 put Europe on the precipice of outright war.

Territorial competition for colonies, and following that, trade war, turned into outright warfare between the major European powers. The war waged between 1914 and 1918.

The theatres of war were: Europe, where a four-year stalemate on the 'western front' cost millions of lives; on the eastern front, a protracted war between Russia and Austria, then strengthened by German support raged back and forward through East Europe deep into Russian territory; West and Central Africa, where Paul von Lettow-Vorbeck led a force of European and native troops out of Kamerun in a prolonged guerrilla war against British and Portuguese colonial forces; the Ottoman Empire, where Arab tribesmen with British support rebelled from 1916, and the troops of the British-Indian Army occupied Mesopotamia (Iraq) from late 1914. Even Japan used the war as a pretext to invade the German colony of Qingdao in Shandong, China. Only the Americas survived unscathed. Ten million combat troops were killed and seven million civilians, followed by five million who died in the flu epidemic that followed. Another twenty million were wounded. The bare numbers only begin to tell the story of a fall into barbarism never seen before.

Volunteers

'An Empire that has been defending India and of which India aspires to be the equal partner is in great peril and it ill befits India to stand aloof at the hour of its destiny' – the speaker was Mohandas Karamchand Gandhi, later known as the Mahatma, and the Empire was Britain. Gandhi had been asked by the Viceroy to support a campaign to rally Indian support for the war effort, and in 1918 he did. 'India would be nowhere without the Englishmen', Gandhi said: 'if the British do not win who shall we go to for claiming equal partnership?'[3]

Indian fighters on the Western Front, World War I.

Years before Gandhi's appeal Indians had rallied to the British-Indian army: one and a half million served in 1914–18. They went for many reasons. War was a chance to prove one's courage, or to find a more fulfilling life. For many, like Gandhi, the war was a chance for India to prove itself worthy of the goal of 'home rule'. This was the aim of the Indian nationalists in the 1914–18 war, to persuade the British by their commitment to the Empire that they were worthy of self-government when the fighting was over.

Indian troops fought courageously at Ypres, Neuve Chapelle, the Somme and Gallipoli. On 15 March 1915 Sir John French wired the Viceroy that he was 'glad to be able to inform Your Excellency that the Indian troops under James Willcocks fought with great gallantry and marked success in the capture of Neuve Chapelle'. 'Their tenacity, courage and endurance were admirable and worthy of the best traditions of the soldiers of India', he added. In the Middle East and East Africa, Indian troops shouldered the lion's share of the Empire's war efforts.

Indian nationalists were not the only people who hoped that fighting for Britain would earn them respect. 'Is it too much to hope that out of this situation there may spring a result which will be good not merely for the Empire but good for the future welfare and integrity of the Irish Nation?' asked the Irish Nationalist member of Parliament John Redmond. He said

> no people can be said to have rightly proved their nationhood and their power to maintain it until they have demonstrated their military prowess; and though Irish blood has reddened the earth of every continent, never until now have we as a people set a national army in the field.

This was in a propaganda pamphlet *The Irish at the Front,* published in 1916 and circulated by the Department of Recruiting in Ireland, which sent copies out to every household in Waterford. In all 210,000 Irishmen served in the British Army. Recruitment from the 'loyal' protestant community, and the 'nationalist' Catholic community were in competition. Protestant leader Edward Carson was aiming to show the British that Ulster's loyalists were their proper allies against the nationalist claim for 'home rule', while Redmond was aiming to show the opposite.

Nine men who stowed away on the SS Danube from Barbados aiming to sign up in London were instead arrested and sent home by the Magistrate at the West Ham Police Court, who made fun of them. Afterwards the Colonial Office, seeing things differently, decided that they would recruit a British West Indies Regiment, which numbered 16,000 in 1915.

The King's African Rifles recruited in Kenya and Nyasaland first saw service in the Somaliland campaign against the Dervish movement in Sudan. In the 1914–18 war the K.A.R. fought against Lettow-Vorbeck's Askari force, alongside Baluchi troops of the British-Indian Army.

The colonial troops of the 1914–18 war were often abused by their officers. Joining up they found they were under the same overlords as before. The 1914 Manual of Military Law said 'alien soldiers' were prohibited from 'exercising any actual command or power' while the 1912 Short Guide for Obtaining a Commission in the Special Reserve of Officers (1912) said that 'all officers must be of pure European descent'. Fiji's Ratu Lala Sukuna, was at first turned down by British Army and volunteered in the French Foreign Legion in 1915. Returning with the Croix de Guerre he was allowed to train for a Commission, but Defence Force Regulation 28 was amended to read 'officers in uniform shall salute the governor and every *European* officer in uniform', so that no English racist would be embarrassed.

Soldiers of the West Indian Regiment were sent on the Verdala to arctic waters off Nova Scotia with only tropical uniforms so that 600 suffered exposure and frostbite and five died of hypothermia. In France, the West Indians found they were often used as a labour battalion rather than fighting.

The Kings African Rifles sent out to hunt down Lettow-Vorbeck's Kamerun Askaris were put under the Boer commander Jan Smuts who was fighting to secure white South African domination over the continent.

Catholic Irish recruits found that the army they joined was officered almost wholly by the sons of the Protestant Ascendancy that lorded over them in civilian life. Britain's military commanders – Sirs Henry Wilson, John French and Hubert Gough – were all from long-standing planter families (the French, or DeFreyne family had owned estates in Roscommon since the fourteenth century). While the protestant-recruited battalions had their own 'Red Hand of Ulster' badges, Redmond's plea for an Irish Harp on a banner was turned down. In the barracks the Irish soldiers were often insulted and punished by English officers who hated them. Many in Ireland believed that Catholics were cannon-fodder in Churchill's lost cause of taking Gallipoli in Turkey.

Redivision of the World, 1919

The end of the Great War saw a massive redivision of the world between the imperial powers. Under the agreements that followed – the treaties at Versailles, Sevres and Lausanne – the British Empire absorbed 1,800,000 square miles and an additional 13 million subjects. The territories of the Ottoman Empire in the Middle East and the German Empire in Africa were shared out between France and Britain. Britain's territory increased to 13,700,000 square miles – almost a quarter of all land in the world – and those living in its dominions, overseas territories, crown colonies, protectorates and mandates numbered 460,000,000. The modern French empire covered 5,020,000 square miles of territory, home to 110,631,000 – 41.5 million of whom were in France itself. By 1930 the population of Dutch Indonesia had grown to 60,727,233, mostly through migration.

A negotiation between Sir Mark Sykes and M. F. Georges-Picot started at the Foreign Office in London in the war. The 'Sykes-Picot' agreement divided Ottoman Arabia between a French and a British sphere of influence. France would dominate in those lands that today are roughly Syria and the Lebanon; Britain in those lands that are Iraq and Jordan. They further stipulated that there would be direct French rule in western Syria and Lebanon, and direct British rule in Basra, Baghdad and the land thereabout. They did concede that there could be a degree of self-government in some parts of these French and British spheres of influence (Zones A and B on their map). Under the Versailles terms these were 'Class A Mandates' that is territories that were governed by Great Powers, on behalf of their peoples who:

> have reached a stage of development where their existence as independent nations can be provisionally recognized subject to the rendering of administrative advice and assistance by a Mandatory until such time as they are able to stand alone.

That meant that they were to be ruled on their behalf for the meantime, by Britain, or France. In Palestine, Britain patronised the small Jewish community. According to Ronald Storrs, who described himself as 'the first military governor of Palestine since Pontius Pilate', he would build 'little loyal Jewish Ulster in a sea of potentially hostile Arabism'.

British Military Recruitment in 1919.

Former German colonies Tanganyika and Cameroon were handed over to Britain and France respectively. South West Africa (today's Namibia) was put into the hands of Britain's Dominion in South Africa. In the Pacific the government of the German colony of Samoa was handed over to that other British Dominion, New Zealand. The Mandate system was created to solve a problem:

Namely, how could the Allied powers which had seized (or in the modern jargon 'liberated') German and Turkish dependencies be allowed to keep their gains without affronting people, especially in the United States, who wanted to break free from old-fashioned imperialism?[4]

The imperial share-out had to be dressed up as if it was a matter of 'taking up the white man's burden'.

On the other side of the world another stitch-up was being made against the Chinese. Secretly, the Japanese and Americans had already agreed in the secret Lansing-Ishii protocol of 1917 to recognise each other's 'interests' in China. That meant that the Japanese occupation of Qingdao had the approval of the post-war Versailles conference.

Though the armistice was declared on 11 November 1918 the world was not at peace. After World War I, in January 1919 British Chief of Staff Henry Wilson reported to the Cabinet that the only policy was to 'get our troops out of Europe and Russia and concentrate all our strength in our coming storm centres, England, Ireland, Egypt, India'.[5] As well as those stationed in Europe, and in Russia, where Britain was fighting a war of intervention against the new Bolshevik Government, British troops were deployed as follows in September 1919: 'Egypt and Palestine 96,000, Mesopotamia 21,000, India, 62,000, Ireland 60,000.'[6] For the next twenty years Britain waged low intensity warfare against the colonial peoples that it held.

Between 1919 and 1922 Britain fought a war against insurgent Ireland. From among its demobbed soldiers Britain recruited an 'Auxiliary' force of 14,000 to back up the Royal Irish Constabulary, known, because of their mix of black police and khaki military uniforms, as the 'Black and Tans'.

The auxiliaries and the RIC imposed 'a state of government terrorism' according to the *New Statesman*. In September 1920 they carried out the Sack of Balbriggan, terrorising the citizens of that town, murdering two Irish nationalists, beating many others and burning many shops and houses in the town. On 21 November – Bloody Sunday – the Auxiliaries and the Royal Irish Constabulary opened fire on the crowd at a Gaelic Football match at Croke Park. Fourteen were killed and around 60 wounded.

In India, faced with demands for self-government, the British puppet legislative council passed the 'Anarchical and Revolutionary Crimes Act of 1919', known as the 'Rowlatt Act' after the judge Sir Sidney Rowlatt, whose committee drew up its provisions. Under the Rowlatt Act, suspects could be detained indefinitely, tried in camera and allegations made anonymously – all adding up to a fearsome set of measures to silence and intimidate Indian nationalists.

In March and April of 1919, a number of stoppages – hartals – were made to protest the Rowlatt Act. On 9 April, the government responded by jailing two nationalist leaders in the Punjab: Dr Saifuddin Kithclew and Dr Satyapal. There were riots in the town of Amritsar. The police opened fire on the crowd killing 10, and in the rioting that followed five Englishmen were killed. The town was shut down by Brigadier General Reginald Dyer. On the 13 April a religious festival, Baisakhi, drew crowds of ten thousand or more, who were gathered in the walled gardens called Jallianwala Bagh. Dyer ordered his men to surround the garden and open fire on the crowd, until their ammunition was spent. Three hundred and twenty-nine people were killed outright and 1,179 were wounded after 1,650 rounds were fired.

Shocking as it was, the Jallianwala Bagh massacre was only the culmination of Dyer's reign of terror. He arrested students and teachers and made them crawl on their bellies in the street. He had hundreds of people flogged and built an open cage in the town centre to detain people. He had Sadhus painted with quick lime and left to dry in the sun. And he had aircraft bomb villagers as they worked in the fields. [7]

An uprising of Arabs and Kurds against the imposition of the Sykes-Picot division of Arabia came quickly after the end of the war. In May 1920, they rose against the 100,000 British and Indian troops that were holding the territory.

The Royal Air Force:

> flew missions totalling 4,008 hours, dropped 97 tons of bombs and fired 183,861 rounds for the loss of nine men killed, seven wounded and 11 aircraft destroyed behind rebel lines. The rebellion was thwarted, with nearly 9,000 Iraqis killed.

The Air Minister, Lord Thomson, wrote about one district of 'recalcitrant chiefs' in the Liwa region on the Euphrates in November 1923: 'As they refused to come in, bombing was then authorised and took place over a period of two days. The surrender of many of the headmen of the offending tribes followed.'[8]

'Here ! What's all this ? Move along there !'
(Sketch by the Chief Scout)

Aerial bombardment was trialled in Iraq, as a 'policing operation', as this cartoon shows.

In the course of the Great War, the British military chiefs stationed in Salonica were contemptuous of what they saw as the dilatory efforts of their Greek allies based in Athens. They intimidated Constantine's Greece and supported the Venizelist revolt that overthrew him.

World War II

Between 1939 and 1945 the British Empire was again at war. Britain, with the United States, the Soviet Union in Russia (from 1941), and the 'Free French' fought against Nazi Germany, Italy, Bulgaria and Japan. The Second World War is properly understood as very different from the first, for being fought between democracies on one side and the dictatorships on the other.

In the British colonies the difference between the dictatorships and the democracies was not so well delineated. Many colonial peoples viewed the appeal of the war against Fascism with some scepticism and some, like the mass Quit India! movement (see Chapter 27) actively opposed it. Others volunteered to fight for Britain. Arguably, Britain's war aims gave a platform for anti-colonial movements after the war, but at the time there was no question that Britain was fighting to defend the Empire.

Germany it was often said broke the accepted rules of imperialism by taking colonies in Europe itself (though many Irish subjects of British rule would see things differently). By the end of 1940 Germany's New Order had engulfed Austria, the Czech Republic, Poland, Norway, Denmark, Holland and northern France 'almost 1,000,000 square miles of territory and 225,000,000 white people' in January 1941, reported *Flight*.[9] That year the Third Reich added the Ukraine, Estonia, Lithuania, Latvia, Greece and Serbia. The Nazi chancellor Hitler had already written in 1926 that 'our aim in foreign policy' is 'to secure for the German people the land and soil to which they are entitled on this earth'. Italy had colonies in Eritrea, Somaliland and Libya – and invaded Abyssinia in 1935.

Imperial Japan occupied 460,265 square miles of territory in Manchuria in 1931, subjugating a population of 43 million. In 1941 Japanese troops conquered the Philippines, French IndoChina, Thailand, Burma, Malaya, the Netherlands East Indies, British Borneo and Portuguese Timor. The additional territory was 1.7 million square miles and a population of 150 million. The commanded territory was called by the Japanese the Greater East Asia Co-Prosperity Sphere.

On 10 June 1940 Italy declared war on Britain. At that time General Wavell, Middle East commanded 36,000 troops in Egypt, 28,000 in Palestine and 22,000 in Kenya, Aden, British Somaliland and Cyprus. Both the Egyptian and Iraqi native governments resisted British demands to join the war on the allies' side. On 4 February 1942 British troops invaded King Farouk's palace, threatening he would be deposed if a new government was not installed.

Tommy Atkins in Palestine.

In January 1941 Rashid 'Ali, Prime Minister in the quasi-independent government of Iraq protested at the British decision to site the British-Indian army in the oil fields at Basra. The British pressured Crown Prince Abd al-Ilāh to depose him, but that backfired when the Iraqi military rallied to 'Ali's cause. A general revolt swept the Arab lands in support of 'Ali. Royal Air Force squadrons and Wellington bombers sent from Sha'iba attacked Iraqi troops at Habbaniya, and went on to attack bases at Baghdad, Baquba and al-Mussayib. The revolt was only narrowly defeated by the British-Indian army and the Royal Air Force.

In the North Africa campaign Britain fought Italy, and then the German desert army under Rommel. The Arabs, whose lands and cities were the prize, were for the most part victims of the war rather than protagonists. The Libyan cities of Tobruk, Benghazi and Tripoli, over which Italy, Germany and Britain fought throughout the desert war were thoroughly destroyed and the country was left with a deadly legacy of mines that took thousands of lives in the decades after the war had ended.

From 1943 the Axis powers were on the defensive and Germany's collapse in the face of the renewed Soviet-partisan offensive from the East left Japan's brief Empire the target of British pressure from the West and American from the East. The 'Co-Prosperity Sphere' was a signal failure as all resources in the occupied countries were directed to fighting the war under the domination of the Japanese military police, the Kempetai. British forces landed in Penang, Malaya on 1 May 1945 and installed a police force 'many of them old Malaya hands' – policemen, planters and game wardens.[10] In the re-occupation of Malaya the British army suppressed Communist guerrillas who had been fighting against the Japanese occupation and put down hunger marches in Singapore and at Sungei Siput, Ipoh and Batu Gajah in Perak state in October. The British deputised surrendered Japanese troops to help them. As the British moved into Burma tensions were high. Officers of the King's Own Yorkshire Light Infantry summarily executed 27 Burmese civilians claiming that they had collaborated with the Japanese in the 1942 retreat. Indochina and Indonesia were returned to their pre-war French and Dutch overlords at gunpoint.

At the conclusion of World War II seventy-five million people, soldiers and civilians had been killed. The war was fought in the name of democracy, but it was waged between Empires and it had a lasting consequence for the reputation of imperialism that was played out in the post war years.

Material Impact of Two Wars on the Colonies

War can be seen as an exceptional state where ordinary rules do not apply. But the cycle of conflict between 1914 and 1946, particularly in the colonies, was so relentless that warfare cannot be thought of as an exception. Conflict and military occupation were always at hand for colonised peoples. What the world wars did was to make the impositions of being colonised sharper.

The world wars of the twentieth century were fought by heavily industrialised European powers that were increasingly dependent upon colonial goods. They also drew on colonial armies to fight for them. The wars put tremendous strain on all peoples as every resource was turned to fighting.

India

The British-Indian army mobilisation in 1914–18 took many people away from agriculture. India was not only expected to feed itself but also to feed the army occupying Mesopotamia. After a failure of supply to the Mesopotamia mission the Indian Munitions Board was founded and spent £48.2 million buying up stores for the army. Government demand boosted industry. The Tata Steel Works in Jamshedpur was set up with 4000 workers in 1907. By 1922 it had 30,000 employees and had increased its output 100-fold. To demonstrate their loyalty the British-Indian Government granted £100 million to the British Government to finance the war. By the end of the war Indian producers were selling much more to Japan and America than they were to Britain.

By 1918 the war sucked up so many goods and men that there was not enough to go around. Prices sky-rocketed – so that food and clothing were one-and-a-half-times as costly and people were starving. In Baluchistan and Sind food prices doubled, and the United and Central Provinces were declared a famine zone.[11] Viscount Chelmsford wrote to the Secretary of State for India that 'stocks of all food grain will barely suffice to meet internal demand'.

Between the wars the British-India government fixed the exchange rate of the Rupee too high (to protect the pensions of colonial officials returned to Britain). With the world-wide fall in demand it was a policy that damaged Indian exports. Industrialisation was sent into reverse. The percentage of those dependent on industry fell from 5.5 in 1911 to 4.3 in 1931.[12]

In World War II, India was the greatest single contributor to the British war effort after Britain herself, giving up £2 billion in goods and services. Indian manufacturers made munitions and supplies for the troops, while her farmers gave up grain to feed the rest of the Empire.

At the same time as denuding India of goods, the British exchequer was accumulating debts to India that reversed the historic relation and laid bare the true dependence of the metropolitan power on its colonial hinterland.

Throughout the war India was made to lend the British what Churchill called 'a million pounds a day' so that by the end they had extended credit of £1,300,000,000 – money they could not afford. With bad grace, the Prime Minister moaned throughout about 'Indian money lenders'.[13]

Early in 1942 with the Japanese already in Burma the British set out to deny them means to invade India by a policy of 'rice denial' in a 25-mile deep band at the border. Instructions came to say that rice should be destroyed. If rice could not be burned 'dumping in the sea will suffice'. Secretary of State for India Leo Amery cabled on 27 March 1942 Governor-General Wavell that not just rice but boats and bicycles should be destroyed: 'it is essential that destruction should be ruthless and should achieve without fail total denial of such resources as would assist enemy operation'. Across Bengal rice output was falling, but still the war cabinet insisted that what there was should be exported to Ceylon to feed the rubber planters there. Warned that Bengal would starve Churchill, with the backing of his scientific advisor Frederick Lindemann, argued that hunger was the outcome of Indians having too many children, not their own policies of seizing, and even destroying rice.[14] When the famine came in 1943 three and a half million people died.

Far East

In 1922 Sir John Stevenson brought in a plan to restrict the British Empire's rubber output. Falling demand was hurting prices, but as Stevenson explained 'quite frankly, I did not embark on this proposition with any regard for the Rubber Growers' Association' but rather because 'I am deeply interested in the development of the British Empire'. Later the Stevenson plan was expanded into an international agreement – first and foremost with the Dutch whose East Indies plantations were almost the only other source at that time – which ran from 1934 to 1943, when the Japanese overran Malaya and Indonesia.

During the war, the restrictions on output were thrown into reverse as the industry was subsumed into the war effort. In Ceylon in March 1942, 'the British Ministry of Supply became the sole purchaser of rubber' and local prices were determined by a Rubber Commissioner: 'he fixed a price that was likely to secure as large an output as possible'. After years of underinvestment, growers were told to take up 'slaughter tapping'.

The Middle East

In the 1914–18 war the pressure on agriculture in the Middle East led to a famine that spread across Syria, the Lebanon and Palestine. *The Times* reported:

> People were found in the streets, unconscious, and were carried to hospitals. We passed women and children lying by the roadside with closed eyes and ghastly, pale faces. It was a common thing to find people searching the garbage heaps for orange peel, old bones, or other refuse and eating them greedily when found. Everywhere women could be seen seeking eatable weeds among the grass along the roads.[15]

It was estimated that from 60,000 to 80,000 had died of starvation in Northern Syria.

Oil was a major consideration at the start of the 1914–18 war as Britain's Navy already depended upon it. Lord Curzon saw Britain 'floating to victory on a sea of oil'. On 6 November the Anglo-Indian Mesopotamia Expeditionary Force seized the Basra oil fields. The Expeditionary Force's chief political officer, Sir Percy Cox blithely concluded 'I don't see how we can well avoid taking over Baghdad'. In November 1922 at the Lausanne conference America had come out against Britain and France for trying to carve up Middle East oil between them. Britain's claim on Iraq in the post-war settlement gave them access to the most developed oil fields then known. Between them France and Britain made what was known as the 'Red Line' agreement sharing out the oil. Sir E. Mackay Edgar, chairman of British Controlled Oilfields Ltd, boasted to the *Times* that the agreement would give Britain the dollars it so badly needed:

> To the tune of many millions of pounds a year, America, before very long will have to purchase from British companies and to pay for in dollar currency, in increasing proportions, the oil she cannot do without and is no longer able to furnish from her own store.[16]

In World War II the determination to defeat Rashid 'Ali's revolt came from Britain's need to control the oil. On 4 May 1941, Churchill wrote to General Wavell:

> A commitment in Iraq was inevitable. We had to establish a base at Basra, and control that port to safeguard Persian oil ... it is essential to do all in our power to save Habbaniya and control the pipe-line to the Mediterranean.[17]

As well as Iraq, Britain was determined to deal with Persia (Iran), too. The Foreign Office's Eastern Department said that Britain should 'come out into the open and say frankly that we must look after the oilfields for the duration of the war'.[18] In an agreement with the Soviet Union, Britain invaded and they divided the country between them.

The British landed at the Abadan refinery at dawn on August 25, having assembled the 8th Indian Infantry division under General Harvey, the 9th Armoured Brigade under General Slim, one Indian regiment of tanks, four British battalions and one regiment of British artillery. 'At Abadan there was considerable opposition', wrote Sir John Hammerton: 'For seven hours hand-to-hand fighting continued between the Persian soldiers and Indian troops'. According to the Shah Mohammad Reza Pahlavi 'the Royal Air Force bombed military targets such as Ahvaz, Bandar-Shapur and Korramshahr, taking pains however to avoid petroleum plants'. H.M.S. Shoreham sank an Iranian frigate off Abadan, while the Soviet Air Force bombarded Tabriz, Ghazvin, Bandar-Pahlavi, Rasht and Fezajeh.[19]

The Anglo-Soviet occupation of Persia was a disaster for the people. As a natural supply route between the Soviet Union and the British Empire all of Teheran's railways were taken up with military supplies so that grain could not be imported. At the same time the troops billeted there bought up all the food that was available. Prices climbed 400 per cent bringing starvation and bread riots in the winter of 1942–43. Student protestors were gunned down in the streets.

Forced Labour in War Time

In the two world wars authorities used forced labour sure that they were doing what needed to be done to save the Empire. In Britain workers were directed to work in given industries, under the Treasury Agreement in the First World War, and under the Executive Work Order regime of Ernest Bevin in the Second. So, too, in the colonies.

In 1915, Britain recruited labourers under an agreement with China's Finance Minister Liang Shiyi to supply 300,000. The men were contracted under indentures that lasted for five years. Once they had signed on, they were under military discipline as the Chinese Labour Corps, and imprisoned in barracks, working ten hours a day, seven days a week. The work was dangerous – 752 were killed when their ship, the Athos, was hit by a German torpedo. Researcher Chen Ta for the US Bureau of Labor Statistics listed 25 riots and strikes by Chinese in the Labour Corps between November 1916 and July 1917. Of the 140,000 labourers sent to France, 10,000 died. Twenty-one of them were executed for mutiny. After the war the Chinese Labour Corps were still under their indentures so that while British troops returned it was left to the Chinese to bury the great many dead.

In August 1915 the British administration in Kenya brought in the Native Followers Recruitment Ordinance, a law that allowed for compulsory recruitment of men to work as carriers. Thirty thousand Kenyans were pressed into service in 1916, growing to 65,000 by June 1917 – with other British African colonies, notably Uganda, Nigera, Nyasaland swelling the numbers. The death rate in the Carrier Corps was astonishing.

The Carriers died from exhaustion, infected wounds and other diseases, as they were weakened by malnutrition. Historian David Olusoga estimates the total Corps to have been around one million, and the deaths as high as one quarter of a million. At the end of the war the Imperial War Graves Commission chose not to mark the mass graves of the Carrier Corps in Dar es Salaam out of fear of acknowledging the number who died.

In World War II, the colonial authorities again relied on forced labour to meet shortages in supply. On 1 August 1942 the British colony of Rhodesia passed a Compulsory Native Labour Act to force people to work on settlers' farms and as labourers at the large air force bases. Indigenous chiefs selected the unhappy victims, or if not, the Native Commissioner would have to 'hunt the natives in the reserves until the required numbers were obtained'.[20]

In Tanzania the British authorities brought 6,000 hectares of Ceara Rubber plantations, abandoned when the colony passed from German hands after the First World War, back into production. 'Conscription for periods of twelve months was introduced in Central Province, mainly targeting the Gogo' writes William Clarence Smith:

> Many died, especially in the early months, when conditions were particularly poor. Although workers' compounds were guarded, others managed to desert.[21]

Though Belgium was occupied by Germany the Belgian government-in-exile based in London agreed to supply Britain with palm oil on 21 January 1941. War time labour discipline was imposed on cutters and the compulsory labour service demanded from Congolese villagers for tending the palms was raised from 60 to 120 days a year under the ordinance of 10 March 1942.[22]

With the loss of Malaya and Burma to the Japanese in 1942, the British used forced labour to 'expand the production of tin in Nigeria and food crops in other African dependencies and declared that forced labour was necessary' to do so. The British Anti-Slavery Society pointed out that 'in Kenya, Nigeria, Sierra Leone, and the Seychelles Islands' as well as Northern Rhodesia, forced labour was not only used for government war work, but also for private farms. Even after the war conscript labourers were working on sisal plantations in Kenya. In Burma, officials impressed labour to build military supply roads under the 'Defence of Burma' rules, starving the countryside of farmers.[23]

Chapter Twenty-six

DECLINE OF 'WHITE PRESTIGE'

In the General Act of the Berlin Conference on West Africa, 26 February 1885 articles 10 and 11 set out that the territories covered by the conference would not go to war, and that if the colonial powers did, then those territories would remain neutral throughout the war. In the East Africa War of 1914–17 the German governor of Tanganyika, Heinrich Schnee and the governor of British East Africa, Sir Harry Belfield, both hoped to stay out of the war under those articles. Paul von Lettow-Vorbeck's determination to bring the war to Britain stymied them.

Articles 10 and 11 were more than just woolly humanitarian clauses snuck into the conference resolution. The thinking behind the goal of avoiding conflict was that European powers ought to avoid going to war in front of native peoples. The fear was that the white race would lose that prestige that gave them authority over native peoples.

'White prestige' was a curious quality. It was supposed at one moment to be unassailable, and at the next so fragile that it would collapse under the slightest pressure. The claim was that Europeans ruled over natives because they were looked on with awe. There was something in it. Prestige meant that you did not have to use force but as long as it was understood that you could use force others would avoid that happening. In the European imagination the prestige was more than just force, though, it was the superiority of European civilisation. Perhaps they were deluding themselves about that. On the other hand, Britain was dominant over the Empire and it was wealthier which all added to the image of a 'higher civilisation'. That was the idea that the colonial authorities carefully nurtured with their great displays of grandeur and Royal Tours.

The thing that was thought to threaten 'white prestige' was a loss of face in front of native peoples. That might happen because Europeans behaved badly, with cowardice, or even with excessive cruelty, or in ways that revealed their baser characters. Sexual relations between Europeans and natives that were already unequal and even oppressive, became taboo when English women joined men in the settlements overseas. Most of all Europeans feared that they would lose face in front of the natives because they failed to maintain an attitude of superiority. As far as military conflict went the two distinct taboos were that natives must not be armed to fight against white Europeans; and that Europeans ought not to fight one another in front of natives. That latter taboo arose because it was feared that Europeans killing one another would encourage natives to believe that Europeans could be attacked, and also that European civilisation might not be as superior as it claimed. World War I fractured those taboos and World War II ripped them to shreds.

Bernhard Dernberg, Germany's Secretary of State for Colonial Affairs, published a book *England: Traitor to the White Race* in America in the First World War. In it Dernberg claimed that 'in the colonial domain, every member of the white race is answerable to every other for the maintenance of his purity, culture and prestige of this greater community'. Dernberg's complaints were self-serving. They were meant to persuade Americans that Britain had 'let the side down'. To succeed his argument had to mesh with real fears. Those fears are not hard to divine in his argument. Dernberg continues 'it is a question of dealing with great masses of undeveloped beings' – the natives, he means – 'far superior to the whites in number'. He goes on to say that 'this task of the colonizer can be accomplished only if he succeeds in maintain the prestige of the white race morally and culturally'.[1]

Dernberg's fears were not uniquely German. After the 1914–18 war French troops occupying German territory included some small number of Moroccan and other African soldiers in the French colonial army. This was a great scandal. Leo Chiozza Money, who was a government minister and protégé of David Lloyd George, wrote a tract *The Peril of the White* in 1924, that warned 'whites in Europe and elsewhere are set upon race suicide and internecine war'. In particular Money was dismayed by 'the spectacle of France looking to Africa for troops with which to support her military power in Europe'. The 160,000 native soldiers he claimed were in Europe were 'an ill service to European civilisation for which not only France but all the White Man's World will have to pay'. In Money's imagination 'Europeans cannot expect to teach Africans to use modern arms and to employ them against other Europeans, without creating a weapon against themselves and their posterity'.[2]

The scientist Julian Huxley was also depressed about the damage to the reputation of European civilisation. He started with an arrogant claim that 'in 1914 we Europeans could have pointed with some pride to the fact that we had for all practical purposes suppressed the constant violence of intertribal war in Africa'. That was a self-serving view of European colonisation though it was just the preamble to a moment of guilty self-reflection. 'By 1919 that boast seemed a little empty', thought Huxley: 'The native has lost his belief in the white as an inherently superior being.'

In 1938 the future British Prime Minister Harold Macmillan, wrote about the war of 1914–18 that 'the Great War, which by the horror and waste fully displayed to Africans, cost Europeans some of their old prestige in native Africa'. Worse, he thought, the war had 'caused widespread disillusion in Europe about the bases of our own civilisation and gravely weakened faith in the universal efficacy of our democratic institutions'.[3]

Harold Macmillan's feeling about the way that European wars looked to non-Europeans did not improve after World War II. He thought that 'what the two wars did was to destroy the prestige of the white people.' As Macmillan saw it, 'not only did the yellows and blacks watch them' – the Europeans he means – 'tear each other apart, committing the most frightful crimes and acts of barbarism against each other, but they actually saw them enlisting their own yellows and blacks to fight other Europeans, other whites'.[4]

Over and above the fear that Europeans had forfeited their claim to supremacy by waging war against each other, World War II presented a marked challenge to British authority in the colonies. The most dramatic reversal came with the Japanese invasion of Singapore in February of 1942. Singapore was by then a strategic and symbolic outpost of the British Empire, sometimes called the 'Gibraltar of the East'. General Yamashita's attack on Singapore was audacious and unexpected (he invaded from Malaya to the north, rather than by sea). Prime Minister Winston Churchill understood the symbolic weight of the attack. He ordered that 'there must at this stage be no thought of saving the troops or sparing the population', but instead, 'the battle must be fought to the bitter end at all costs'.

Britain's officer in command in Singapore General Wavell did not honour Churchill's appeal to sacrifice and surrendered. In the Empire the fall of Singapore was understood to be a fatal blow to white prestige, the worst defeat of the war according to Churchill.

Margery Perham at the Colonial Office was forced to admit that 'Japan's attack in the Pacific has produced a very practical revolution in race relationships', because 'an Asiatic people has for the moment successfully challenged the ascendancy of three great white imperial powers' – Britain, France and Holland.[5] The feeling was that that Britain's defeat at the hands of a non-European people, the Japanese, would embolden colonial peoples to turn on their European 'masters'. Japan's successes in the war up to 1943 underscored the problem of colonial legitimacy.

Even before the fall of Singapore, however, the British Cabinet held a gloomy assessment of the authority that the Empire rested upon. Leo Amery prepared a paper for discussion in January 1942. In it he set out a damning assessment of Britain's standing arguing that:

> India and Burma have no natural association with the Empire, from which they are alien by race, history and religion, and for which as such neither of them have any natural affection, and both are in the Empire because they are conquered countries which had been brought there by force, kept there by our control, and which hitherto it has suited to remain under our protection.

This was a remarkable admission of the failure of Britain's civilising mission in the East Indies. It was all the more remarkable considering that as many Indians were fighting to save the British Empire as Britons were, with two million volunteering by the end of the war. In the context of the war, Amery's fears were that India would fall before the Japanese advance. 'I suspect that the moment they think that we may lose the war or take a bad knock, their leaders would be much more concerned to make terms with victor at our expense than to fight for ideals to which so much lip-service is given', the Secretary of State wrote. Amery's judgements were made to the background of a rising protest movement calling for Britain to 'Quit India!' It was in that mood of resignation set out in Amery's paper that the British acted so destructively over the Bengal famine. They had already decided that the Indians were unreliable allies and did nothing for them.

The feeling at the Colonial Office that Britain's reputation was substantially damaged by reverses in the Second World War had a big impact on policy afterwards. The reactions swung from a strong desire for revenge against those they deemed to have

betrayed the Empire by collaborating with the Japanese enemy, to a drive to accommodate native demands.

Reflections on the Holocaust

As we have seen, 'eugenics', the racial science became popular among the middle classes
in Britain in the first half of the twentieth century. Eugenics gave some intellectual support to race discrimination in Britain and in the British Empire (as the older 'science'
of Malthusianism did in nineteenth century). The most grotesque application of racial
science in policy did not take place in the British Empire, but in Germany's empire in
the East.

Securing control over Poland, Ukraine, Byelorussia, Russia and Greece, and over
Holland and France, the Nazi Empire conquered countries with large Jewish populations. The race laws that Germany applied from 1934 under Ernst Rüdin led to the persecution and imprisonment of Jews in the Third Reich. From January 1942 the policy
of concentration was turned into one of extermination. At a conference of senior Nazi
officials at Wannsee in Poland Governor Hans Frank said, 'We must annihilate the Jews
wherever we encounter them and wherever possible, in order to maintain the overall
mastery of the Reich here'. The eventual death toll of Jews slaughtered by the Nazis was
six million. In word and deed the Nazi regime had damned itself.

Stopping the extermination of Jews was not an allied war aim at the time. When
Russian, American and British troops liberated the remaining survivors of the Nazi
death camps the full horror of what had happened there was unavoidable. News reel
footage from the camps showed the world the culmination of Nazi policy.

The allied victors of World War II saw the justness of their cause strikingly confirmed in the prosecution of Nazi war criminals at the Nuremberg trials. For all that,
the horror of the death camps meant that the racial science that had been endemic in
the western world from Texas to London became properly a hateful taboo. The founding conference of the United Nations Educational, Scientific and Cultural Organization
(UNESCO), published the statement:

> That the great and terrible war which has now ended was a war made possible by the
> denial of the democratic principles of the dignity, equality and mutual respect of men, and
> by the propagation, in their place, through ignorance and prejudice, of the doctrine of the
> inequality of men and races.[6]

Five years later UNESCO published a short book on *The Race Concept*, in which they
argued that 'for all practical social purposes "race" is not so much a biological phenomenon as a social myth', and 'the myth of "race" has created an enormous amount of
human and social damage'.[7]

As radical as the UNESCO document seems, the champions of the world commu-
nity were not quite done with the idea of human differentiation. A 1947 proposal for a
Declaration of Human Rights that anthropologist Melville Herskovits sent to the United
Nations began: 'The individual realizes his personality through his culture, hence

respect for individual differences entails a respect for cultural differences', and carried on to say that 'the applicability of any Declaration of Human Rights to Mankind as a whole' was questionable. It was an echo of Evans-Pritchard's re-imagination of racial differences as cultural differences.[8]

The reflections on the holocaust had no immediate consequences for the British Empire. Britons could reasonably argue that it was the Empire that had defeated Nazism. The concept of race on the other hand was, at least in the more thoughtful arenas of diplomacy, characterised as a 'social myth' without scientific foundation, and one that was destructive to man and society.

For all the talk in the UNESCO and academia, 'white prestige' would go on to be a defining goal for the post-war Empire, even if it was more openly stated by colonial settlers than the Foreign Office in London. The racial underpinnings of the British Empire, already compromised by the Japanese victories in the Far East were less easy to defend after the Holocaust.

Chapter Twenty-seven

FROM HOME RULE TO INDEPENDENCE

From the first Norman invasion of Ireland the British Empire has faced opposition. In the first half of the twentieth century the British Empire reached its fullest extent and its most complete shape. Perfection came before the collapse.

As a complete system, covering one quarter of the world's land mass, the British Empire was ripe for attack. Attack came in the shape of rivals, but more lastingly, in the shape of national liberation movements.

The national liberation movements challenged the fundamental meaning of the British Empire – rule over other territories. By making themselves free of British rule the national liberation movements overthrew the British Empire, country by country.

National liberation did not happen all at once. Before there were national liberation movements there were Home Rule campaigns. The Dominions, Canada, New Zealand and Australia got to be self-governing nations under the Crown earlier. They got legislative councils in the nineteenth century. In the twentieth they were named Dominions as a marker of their self-governing status. In 1931 the Statute of Westminster created the British Commonwealth of Nations made up of the six self-governing Dominions – Canada, Newfoundland, Australia, New Zealand and – as we shall see – the Irish Free State.

The Dominions were the model for the 'Home Rule' demands of the earlier national movements. The demand for self-government proved more challenging for Britain in the non-white colonies than those of settlement.

Home Rule – 1880–1920

Charles Stewart Parnell, himself a landlord and a Protestant, had joined agitation in a new Irish Land League in the late 1870s. Joined in Parliament by Catholic Irishmen elected under the 1884 country franchise, Parnell was wooed by William Ewart Gladstone's offer of Home Rule for Ireland, and he organised his peers as the Home Rule Party.

In 1885 the Congress Party of India was formed in Calcutta, under the initiative of retired civil servant Allan Hume and the Presidency of the barrister Umesh Chandra Bonnerji. The Congress was a moderate project to inculcate a sense of leadership among educated Indians. The following year Dadabhai Nairoji who wrote about the 'drain' on India, was president.

Around the same time John Tengo Jabavu, a Mfengu Methodist and editor of *Imvo Zabuntsundu* (Native Opinion), took up the campaign for votes for non-whites in the Cape, along with A. Abdurrahman, A. Effendi and Alan Kirkland Soga. In 1889, John Casely Hayford, and J. P. Brown founded an Aborigines Rights Protection Society in Freetown, in the Gold Coast of West Africa.

These early, moderate bodies were aiming for civil rights for natives and for native representation within the Empire. In time the moderate, Home Rule-oriented lobbies became a focus for broader national aspirations.

The Boer War was a focal point for critics of the Empire. Some Irish patriots backed the Boers, like John MacBride who was a major in the Irish Transvaal Brigade. The Irish Nationalist Party's 2000 strong national convention of 1907 rejected the British Government's modest reforms.

Expatriates nurtured a strong national sentiment. Nationalists like Thomas Clarke of the Irish Republican Brotherhood, James Connolly of the Irish Socialist Republican Party, the founder of the Hindustani Ghadr Party Har Dayal were all living in America – Connolly and Clarke returned, while Har Dayal was arrested. In North London Shyamji Krishna Varma, set up India House, where a group of Indian students prepared for a revolution against the Empire (one of them Madan Lal Dhingra assassinated a British-India government official in 1909). Mohandas K. Gandhi had been active as a lawyer fighting for Indian civil rights in the Cape in the early century.

In 1905 Lord Curzon's plan to partition the old Province of Bengal stirred a protest that began with a boycott of British goods, and quickly spiralled into an underground campaign of bombs and assassinations. Activists Lajpat Rai and Bhal Gangadhar Tilak of Mahratta were deported; Bipin Chandra Pal, Chidambaram Pillai, Abdul Hasan Hasrat Mohani and many other activists were imprisoned in 1908.

Donald McGill's optimistic view of Home Rule.

In Egypt, in 1905, there was the Denashwai incident: triggered when English officers shot villagers' pigeons and wounded a local woman, provoking a riot that was later punished with summary executions. Shortly afterwards Mustafa Kamil founded the National Party, with the discrete support of Khedive Abbas Hilmi II.

In 1912, alarmed by the growing support for the Nationalist Party in Ireland the judge Sir Edward Carson drilled 100,000 loyal Protestants to defeat the 'nefarious conspiracy' to impose 'Home Rule'. Ominously, Carson's militia had the backing of the Conservative Party leader Andrew Bonar Law and many senior military men.

Carson warned the British Government that they could not afford to give way:

> If you tell your empire in India, in Egypt, and all over the world that you have not got the men, the money, the pluck, the inclination and the backing to restore order in a country within 20 miles of your own shore, you may as well begin to abandon the attempt to make British rule prevail throughout the Empire at all.[1]

Britain's exchequer David Lloyd George shared Carson's fear of Irish self-government: 'It will give the impression that we have lost grip, that the empire has no further force and will have an effect on India and throughout the empire.'[2]

It was in response to the 'loyalist' parades of Carson that the Irish Nationalist Party leader John Redmond sanctioned the mobilisation of a force of 168,000 national volunteers. Alongside the Home Rulers a more militant republicanism was nurtured by the teacher and Irish language campaigner Padraig Pearse, the Irish Republican Brotherhood and James Connolly's Irish Socialist Republican Party.

The outbreak of World War I had the immediate effect of stilling the nationalist challenges to British rule around the world. Home Rule champions like John Redmond in Ireland and Mohandas K. Gandhi in India were keen to show that their peoples would prove worthy of national rights. In India Bal Gangadhai Tilak, owner of the Maratha weekly *Kesari* said, 'if you want home rule you had better be willing to defend your home'. Not everyone agreed. 'Stop at home', said trade union leader Jim Larkin: 'Arm for Ireland. Fight for Ireland and no other land.'[3]

As the war went on the tensions it put on Indian society broke out in Bihar in 1917. Farmers there were made to plant indigo by their English landlords. Gandhi, who had returned to India to campaign for support for the British war effort, helped to organise protests for the farmers.

It was in Ireland where the Home Rule demand ran out of road. The rising number of casualties and lack of respect for Irish volunteers in the British Army were focal points for anti-British feeling. The militant Republicans got more of a hearing as the war dragged on. In time they succeeded in infiltrating the leadership of Redmond's National Volunteers. At Easter of 1916 some 1500 Irish volunteers rose up against the Empire and fought for control of Dublin for four days. Another 700 volunteers under Liam Mellows secured the town of Athenry in County Galway.

James Connolly taken to his execution by stretcher.

Most of the leaders of the Irish rising were executed, but sympathy for their cause grew. The surviving leaders Eamon De Valera, Constance Markiewicz and Michael Collins were a beacon for a risen people. Plans for conscription that were uncontroversial in Britain were shelved for Ireland because of the mass protests of the Anti-Conscription League. An All-Ireland Labour Committee organised a general strike on 23 April 1918 and the Irish Trade Union Congress called on workers in other countries to follow Ireland's example and 'rise up against their oppressors and bring the war to an end'.[4] At the end of the war the Easter Rising, which had been widely denounced for its adventurism, was retrospectively vindicated. The *'Sinn Fein'* party ('Ourselves Alone') of the Republicans won 73 of 105 Parliamentary seats in Ireland, reducing Redmond's party to six and isolating the Protestants in the 22 seats in the north east. Home Rule was finished in Ireland and a new and tempestuous era had begun.

After World War I Ireland's newly-elected Sinn Fein MPs did not take their places in the Palace of Westminster, but sat instead in a new assembly, *Dáil Éireann* in the Mansion House in Dublin. Declaring themselves to be a Republic the Sinn Feiners had to fight a harsh war of Independence from 1919 to 1921 before coming to terms with Britain in an Anglo-Irish Treaty. The 'Free State' that emerged was compromised in its independence, but the example of a subject people overthrowing the British Empire encouraged anti-colonial movements, none more so than India's.

Women of the Congress Party at the Marian Esplandade, 1913.

India's emerging national movement was electrified by the Republicans' success in freeing themselves from the British yoke. 'Bravo!' the Indian paper *Ghadr* saluted the Easter Rising: 'O Irish, you kept your sword on high and did not show the white feather'.[5] Indian nationalists like Subhas Chandra Bose went to Ireland to meet De Valera, Sean Lemass and Maud Gonne MacBride. In India no less than four translations of Dan Breen's memoir *My Fight for Irish Freedom* were published, in Tamil, Hindi, Punjabi and Burmese. The War of Independence even spilled over onto Indian soil as the Irish Connaught Rangers, stationed at Jullundur, rose in mutiny for Ireland. Afterwards Indian nationalists kept a shrine for James Daly who was executed for leading the revolt.

The Congress Party was underwhelmed by the Montague-Morley reforms proposed in 1918. These were for more regional assemblies chosen by a restricted Indian electorate to handle local services like health and education. Home Rule was dead in Ireland and looking increasingly untenable in India.

The Arab Revolution 1915–17

Ireland's republicans saw that 'England's adversity was Ireland's opportunity'. Arabs living under the Ottoman Empire saw that the Sublime Porte's difficulty was their opportunity. In this case the British Empire was for a time the ally of a national revolution.

On 14 July 1915 Sharif Hussein wrote to Sir Henry McMahon, British High Commissioner in Egypt, asking whether Great Britain would 'recognize the independence of the Arab countries' and set out the territory that today is divided between Syria, Iraq, Lebanon, Jordan, Israel, Saudi Arabia, The United Arab Emirates, Bahrain, Qatar, Oman and Yemen.[6]

On 24 October 1915 McMahon wrote to Sharif Hussein, that 'the districts of Mersin and Alexandretta, and portions of Syria lying to the west of the districts of Damascus, Homs, Hama and Aleppo, cannot be said to purely Arab and must on that account be excepted from the proposed delimitation'. He went on to say that 'I am authorised to give you the following pledges on behalf of the Government of Great Britain: ... subject to the modifications stated above, Great Britain is prepared to recognise and uphold the independence of the Arabs in all the regions lying within the frontiers proposed by the Sharif of Mecca'.[7]

On 10 June 1916 the Sharif's forces attacked Turkish troops garrisoned in Mecca. The fighting lasted till the Turks surrendered on 9 July. A force of 3,500 tribesmen under the Harb federation led by Sharif Muhsin attacked the Turkish troops at Jedda, who surrendered on 16 June. The Arab revolt had begun. By 30 September 1917 the Turks withdrew from Damascus in the face of the Arab and British advance, ending 400 years of Ottoman domination. Arab hopes for the post-war settlement were high.

While Arabs grabbed their chance of overthrowing the Turks, the British Empire's Muslim subjects heard the declaration of the Sultan Mehmed V in November 1914 that the war against Britain was jihad, a Holy War. In Singapore, in 1915 the Muslim Rajput soldiers of the 5th Light Infantry, angered by constant discrimination, mutinied, killing their officers and taking control of the territory. Their victory was brief and 47 were killed by firing squad.[8]

Egypt's nominal independence had been suspended in the Great War but the nationalist movement revived at its closing under the leadership of Saad Zaghloul and his Wafd Party – Zaghloul had organised a delegation, ('wafd') of Egyptian leaders to represent the country at the Versailles conference, but their credentials were refused. The British exiled Zaghloul to Malta. On 28 February 1922, High Commissioner Viscount Allenby conceded independence to sultan Fu'ad, who became king, albeit with important powers reserved to Britain. Though Britain ruled *de facto* in Sudan to the South, the fiction was that it was upholding Egypt's claims there – an arrangement known as the 'Condominium'. Egyptian nationalists were dismayed to find that among the powers Britain reserved were continued rule in Sudan. To Allenby's frustration Sudan's young nationalist movement led by 'Ali 'Abd al-Latif joined up with the Egyptian Wafd Party. Events came to a head when Governor General Sir Lee Stack was shot dead by protestors in Cairo on 19 November 1924. In the stand-off between Britain and Egypt that followed Allenby ordered the evacuation of Egyptian officials and troops from Sudan, leading to several clashes. Having claimed to rule Sudan jointly with Egypt, Britain reversed its policy to adopt a strategy of 'Sudanisation' – promoting Sudanese officials and politicians to block the threat of Egyptian-Sudanese unity. With feelings running high, Allenby threatened to redirect the Nile waters by redirecting them to irrigate Gezira, on the Sudanese side and create drought in Egypt.[9]

Sun Yat Sen and China's National Revolution

The student and Christian convert Sun Yat Sen led a movement of national renewal in the dying days of the Qing Empire to rid China of its Tatar (Manchu) overlords. Creating a Provisional Chinese Republic in Nanjing in 1912 he was briefly elected President until his Republic was overthrown by the northern general Yuan Shikai in 1915. Sun Yat Sen's party was called the Kuomintang, and though it was defeated Sun returned after the close of the First World War to lead a renewed national movement.[10]

After the war students protested at the Versailles decision to hand Japan control over Shandong on 4 May 1919 and also attacked pro-Japanese government ministers. The Kuomintang led the revived Chinese national movement.

The impact of the foreign concessions – the coastal port towns that Britain and other powers (Japan, Russia, America, France and Portugal) controlled was destabilising China. 'The capitalist is a rare specimen in China and is only beginning to make his appearance in the treaty ports', Sun Yat Sen wrote in his ambitious programme of economic development. 'Shall we follow the old path of western civilization?' he asked. He hoped that 'all will enjoy, in the same degree, the fruits of modern civilization', China's working masses, its business leaders, and lenders of foreign capital – though that proved optimistic.[11]

In 1925 there were large labour protests and strikes aimed at foreign owned businesses in Canton and Hong Kong. On 30 May of that year the British Shanghai Military Police fired on a student and labour protest killing twelve. A general strike paralysed Shanghai and the British authorities had to smuggle the policeman involved out of the country. The Kuomintang carried on the agitation and in January 1927 reclaimed the British concessions in Hankow and Kiukang without any opposition from London.

With the 'Northern expedition' of 1926 the Kuomintang succeeded in taking half the country from the warlords. This was the last successful collaboration between the left and right wing of the Kuomintang as the Communist Mao Tse-tung created a stronghold in Wuhan. On 12 April 1927 Chiang Kai-shek who had replaced Sun Yat-sen (he died of cancer in 1925) as leader of the Kuomintang repudiated the Communists in Wuhan. Late in 1928 the last of the warlords Chang Hsueh-liang acknowledged the authority of the Kuomintang government in Nanjing, so that the nationalists could claim to have united the country.

Marxism and National Liberation

While the anti-colonial movements were making their impact Europe was more fixed on the conflict of capital and labour. An underground revolt in the nineteenth century had built up into a mass labour movement by its end. In the twentieth century the workers' movement's challenge dominated the politics of Europe and America. In Europe especially, the labour movement gave rise to large socialist parties. The socialist parties' doctrines were shaped by Christians, liberals and the followers of Karl Marx. At times socialists sympathised and identified with the struggles of the colonial peoples which they thought were analogous to their own, but by no means consistently.

Among the Marxists William Morris of the Hammersmith Socialist League, the Irish labour leader James Connolly, the suffragette Sylvia Pankhurst and the Russian V. I. Lenin all saw the struggle of colonial peoples against imperialism as part and parcel of the social struggle against capitalism. Other socialists who identified more deeply with the social reforms that the labour movement had won through legislation were less sympathetic to the 'enemies of Britain'. Connolly struggled to explain to sceptical English socialists why it was he had thrown his lot in with the Irish Republic. They thought that he had gone soft on nationalism. He thought that they had gone soft on the British Empire, asking ironically if socialists were supposed to support the Crown.[12] In Connolly's mind the struggles were connected – in the colonies the national question and the social question were at root the same.

The differences between the reform-minded socialists and the Marxists were dramatically spelled out in October 1917. In February 1917 the Russians had overthrow their Tsar in large part because of dismay at the cost of fighting the war against Germany. When the Kerensky government that replaced the Tsar failed to pull Russia out of the war, the Marxist 'Bolshevik' party supported a second revolution. The regime that they created was unstable and loathed by the ruling classes across the world, committed as it was to worldwide revolution. The leader of the Bolshevik Party Lenin also committed his movement to supporting the struggles of colonial peoples against imperialism.[13]

The impact of the Russian revolution was electric. All over the world people rushed to join new communist parties allied to the Union of Socialist Soviet Republics, as the old Russian Empire was renamed. The nationalist revolts in the British – as in the

French and other Europeans' – Empire took succour and more practical support from the new Soviet state.

The Soviets' early ambitions that their revolution would carry over into war-torn Europe looked possible. By 1920, though, the European powers had stabilised, and the Soviets were isolated. The policy of promoting world revolution made the Soviets turn towards the East. From 1924 the Soviet Union moderated its policy and dedicated itself instead to Stalin's idea of building 'socialism in one country'.

The anti-colonial movements found that the new policy meant the Soviet Union adopted a much more pragmatic attitude to them. The Leninist rhetoric of anti-imperialism was still there, but Moscow saw the nationalists more as leverage in their diplomatic efforts to avoid isolation than part of a common struggle. The USSR could still be a useful source of funds and other assistance for national liberation movements, and the ideology of Marxism, particularly as Lenin reworked it, had a big impact on them. But at key turning points the nationalists found that the Soviet leadership would not just abandon them, but sometimes directly sabotage them when it suited their foreign policy alliances.

The most dramatic zigzags in Soviet policy over the colonies came in the Second World War. From 1939 to 1941 the Soviet Union allied itself with the German Nazi regime waging war against Polish and Finnish nationalists alongside the Nazis. Soviet propaganda at that time was stridently hostile towards British imperialism in India and elsewhere. Then after Germany betrayed their alliance and invaded the Soviet Union in June 1941 the Soviet policy towards Britain changed. Instead of being imperialist the British Government was reimagined as the leader of the 'Freedom loving peoples'. Accordingly, anti-colonial movements were told that they must support Britain, and local communist allies did all they could to undermine any who dared to take the opportunity to press their claims for independence.

The socialists who did not become communists were also often unreliable allies. As the communists tended to put the USSR's interests first, most Labour Party MPs and trade unionists, like railwaymen's leader J. H. Thomas and *Labour Leader* editor John Bruce Glasier, put Britain's interests before those of colonised peoples. On the other hand, many British socialists, like the Labour Party's George Lansbury and Ellen Wilkinson, and James Maxton and Fenner Brockway of the Independent Labour Party, did carry on raising the rights of people in the Empire. The greater organisational drive and ideological certainty of the communists, and their extensive international links still meant that even despite the sharp U-turns in policy, they tended to attract the more militant anti-imperialists to their side of the divide. Most of the pamphlets and meetings denouncing imperialism were put together by the communists who, in alliance with nationalists, for the most part 'owned' the issue.

The League Against Imperialism

The German communist Willi Münzenberg organised the 'League Against Imperialism' in 1927 – a successful rallying point for different national movements across the British and other Empires. The name was a mock of the League of Nations which was sanctioning the re-allocation of colonies as mandated territories at the time. Jawaharlal Nehru the rising star of the Congress Party was there along with the Indian communist Virendranath Chattopadhyaya, and so was Mohammed Hatta, who would go on to be deputy prime minister in Indonesia in 1951, J. T. Gumede of the South African National Congress, Messali Hadj of the Algerian *Etoile du Nord* organisation, and Lamine Senghor, of Senegal and the French Communist Party. English socialists Lansbury, Maxwell Wilkinson and Brockway all supported the League and Brockway chaired the first meeting.[14]

The League Against Imperialism was a great success in its first few years and was a big headache for the British intelligence officers who were tasked with watching and, if they could, undermining it. The tensions between the Soviet sponsors of the League and the different national movements it rallied eventually became too much and it fell into paralysis before being shut down by the Nazi takeover in 1933.

The Soviet organisers got Münzenberg to pressure Nehru to criticise the mainstream leaders of the Congress Party (Gandhi, effectively) in ways that only hurt his attempts to build an alliance. At first the Soviet leadership were keen that the League should give the spotlight to the Kuomintang representatives, who they supported eagerly. But in 1928 the Kuomintang in Shanghai turned on the Chinese communists and killed thousands of them, in a struggle for the leadership of the national movement. Embittered, the communists in the League Against Imperialism argued that only communists could be trusted to lead the fight. In a sharp sectarian turn they denounced and expelled their blameless socialist supporters and carried on all kinds of witch-hunts against those nationalist leaders who they characterised as inconsistent. It was a disaster for the communists who only lost support. It hurt the nationalist movements that looked to communist leadership only to be tasked with denouncing their closest allies as 'bourgeois nationalists'.

There was a point to the communist criticisms. It was often the case that nationalist leaders who were drawn from the business class would look at mass mobilisation as a greater danger than the Empire and turn on their former allies. But that was not something that could be assumed before the event as a reason not to find common cause in the struggle – not without paralysing the movement with sectarianism. In any event, the record of the communists, if not their rhetoric, proved at least as unpredictable as that of the 'bourgeois nationalists'.

In the aftermath of the League Against Imperialism Soviet policy on the British Empire was yet more erratic. In the Second World War the turn to embrace Britain as an ally saw anti-colonial movements all through the Empire told to shelve plans for liberation. In some cases that instruction cost them dear. In India, in particular, the communists lost all standing by opposing the Congress Party's campaign to make Britain 'Quit India!' In Japanese occupied Malaya, on the other hand, the Malayan People's Anti-Fascist Army under the communist leadership of Chin Peng enjoyed the awkward support of British intelligence – at least up to the end of the war.

There were other important left-wing anti-imperialist organisations that avoided the sectarianism of the official Communist and Socialist groups. The Trinidadian leftists George Padmore and C. L. R. James allied with African students in England like

Kwame Nkrumah and Jomo Kenyatta who would become presidents of Ghana and Kenya respectively. They edited a journal *International African Opinion* which rallied critics of British rule in Africa.

Quit India!

Quit India movement by Beohar Rammanohar Sinha, c. 1952, Jabalpur, India.

India's nationalist movement was galvanised by Dyer's attack on the Jallianwala Bagh in Amritsar in 1919. A Swaraj, or self-rule campaign adopted the tactic of boycotting English goods in favour of home grown, led by Mohandas K. Gandhi.

The two main leaders of the Indian Congress Party were Gandhi and Jawaharlal Nehru. The former had from his early life as a lawyer moved to become more self-consciously ascetic and spiritual in his approach; the latter had disappointed his father by withdrawing from the law to become a left-wing political activist, influenced by the English socialists he met while living in London.

Nehru often urged Gandhi to go further, and was critical of the homespun Swaraj appeal, for its lionisation of small craft production. When the Second World War came it was Nehru who counselled India join the fight against Nazi Germany, but Gandhi said no. Gandhi was reminded of a story from the Mahabharata about a mighty war in which the Pandavas are laid low. 'The warring nations are destroying themselves with such fury and ferocity that the end will be mutual exhaustion', Gandhi wrote in the *Harijan* of 15 February 1942: 'And out of this holocaust must arise a new order for which the exploited millions have so long thirsted.' Congress's most dangerous step, the 'Quit India!' campaign was taken.

The British Cabinet sent the socialist Sir Stafford Cripps, who knew Nehru from his days in England. Cripps promised more representation but nothing approaching the independence that Congress was by this time committed to. 'I would advise you to take the next plane home', Gandhi told Cripps. The offer was 'a post-dated cheque' he told journalists (one of whom made the quote stronger by adding 'on a failing bank').

The British response was barbaric. Protestors were gunned down in the street. A contemporary report put the numbers killed at 940 – but later estimates put the numbers killed over all at as many as ten times that. In Bihar hundreds were killed when planes strafed protestors. In the first wave 60,222 protestors were arrested and 18,000 jailed under the Defence of India Rules. The total eventually jailed rose as high as 90,000. In an orgy of sadistic brutality the British forces got an Emergency Whipping Act passed into law. Gandhi's wife Kasturba died in prison in Pune in his arms. Nehru's brother-in-law Pandit Ranjit died in jail, as did Gandhi's Secretary Mahadev Desai and scores of others. 'Quit India!' brought the country to the brink of revolution.

Indian National Army

In Singapore, on 17 February 1942 thousands of Indian troops who laid down their arms on General Wavell's surrender were marched to the Farrer Park Racecourse wondering whether they were to be executed. Instead they were addressed by Japanese Major Fujiwara:

> We hope you will join the Indian National Army. The Japanese Army will not treat you as prisoners, but as friends. We will recognise your struggle for freedom and give you all-out assistance.[15]

The Indian National Army (INA) had been founded with Japanese support by Mohan Singh to fight against the British Empire. Their leader from 1943 was Subhas Chandra Bose, who had been chair of the Congress Party (though opposed by Gandhi for his radicalism). Though his politics were socialist he had become an admirer of Fascist action against Britain while in exile in Germany. He led the Indian National Army to fight against the British Army in the war for Burma.[16]

The Indian National Army was not a decisive force in the war being just 50,000 strong compared to the more than a million who joined the British-Indian Army. The INA's only major battle was for the hill at Imphal. As a propaganda weapon the INA was a stark demonstration that India was not loyal, as the British feared. The Rani of Jansi Brigade of women fighters under General Lakshmi Swaminathan added to the INA's prestige.

The INA was not the only party in Asia to get help from the Japanese in their fight with the British Empire. Aung San led a group of the national party, the Thakins into a Japanese trained Burma Independence Army in December of 1941. Joining with the Japanese to rid the country of the British was fraught with danger but growing to 200,000 the Independence Army was the effective government of Burma outside of the cities. Later Aung San's army clashed with the Kempetai, and early in 1945, after a secret agreement with Louis Mountbatten the Burmese nationalists attacked the Japanese. In Malaya British officials were disappointed to discover that the ethnic Malay leaders they nurtured were happy to work with Japan, while the Chinese labourers were led into a Malayan Peoples Anti-Japanese Army led by the Communist Chin Peng. Peng's forces fought for their independence alongside the British, but at the end of the war they quickly found that they were to be side-lined in favour of a renewed British alliance with the Malay leader Tunku Abdur Rahman.[17]

At the end of the War the British tried to prosecute the INA leaders at the Red Fort in Delhi. The Congress leader Nehru defended the INA men in court, while tens of thousands protested on their behalf outside. Soon all India was in protest, with the Royal Indian Navy mutinying. Attlee conceded that the reaction to the Indian National Army prosecutions and the Navy mutiny meant that Congress had won. India would get its independence.

The success of the anti-imperialist movements was not a secondary question in the world wars. The question of who would be the victors and who the vanquished was decided by their ability to hold territory beyond their borders. The Central Powers weakest flank in the First World War was the Ottoman Empire in Arabia, of which Britain and France took advantage. Britain was lucky that the withdrawal of Irish support for the war came as Germany's ally Austria was sickening, or the cost could well have been higher.

Britain's defeats in Asia in the Second World War came because the Empire they built there had no broad base of support, as Leo Amery's paper to the British Cabinet admitted. Japan was no true friend to the peoples briefly dragged into its Co-Prosperity Sphere. Still, the Japanese invasion and the later British re-invasion of East Asia fatally weakened not just the British, but also the French and Dutch holdings in Vietnam and Indonesia. Britain was fortunate that the rule of Germany's empire in East Europe was so barbaric that it collapsed before Britain lost control of India and Africa. As it was the Britain that emerged from the Second World War would have to make some kind of peace with the nationalist revolt that had shaken its Empire to the core.

Chapter Twenty-eight

DEFEATING NATIONALISM

British strategies towards challenges to its rule were many. Colonial administrators' natural instincts were to resist any sign of weakness – because they were weak and feared that showing that would encourage more challenges.

Where facing down opposition failed the British would try to ameliorate opposition by making concessions. In the middle of the twentieth century it had become clear that the Native Administration and a seat on the Legislative Council was not enough to buy off the opposition. Decolonisation surrendered ground to the formerly colonised.

Even where it conceded decolonisation Britain was not necessarily withdrawing gracefully. The perceived cost to British prestige of giving way to anti-British nationalist movements seemed too high. Where the challenge to her rule was militant Britain tried to punish nationalists for their effrontery. As they left the British forces would often inflict lasting damage to the conceded polity.

Ireland Divided

In August 1920 the Restoration of Order in Ireland Act was passed giving Sir John French special powers for a crackdown. The First Lord of the Admiralty Sir Walter Long had written to French the year before saying he should use the demobilised servicemen to shore up the Royal Irish Constabulary (RIC). In June 1920 the Ministry of Labour reported that there were 167,000 ex-servicemen on unemployment benefits. Ex-servicemen were recruited into the RIC – more than 10,000 of them between 1920 and 1921.[1] Though the war that followed was bitter, Britain was unable to defeat the nationalist movement directly.

In peace talks the British proposal, a Treaty, was well calculated to divide the moderate and militant Republicans, offering self-government in the South, but with the loss of the North East, and with an oath of allegiance to the British Crown. The Irish nationalists were divided along pro and anti-Treaty lines, with the former winning the civil war that followed at great cost. The pro-Treaty Irish army lost nearly a thousand men, and the anti-treaty rebels around half that number, though by the end 12,000 of them were jailed in a bitter conflict that divided families and comrades between June of 1922 and May 1923. Anti-treaty leaders Liam Mellows and Erskine Childers were executed, and the pro-Treaty leader Michael Collins was killed in an ambush by his former comrades, leaving W. T. Cosgrave to impose an armed and paranoid peace. The liberators of the war of independence were robbed of their victory. Not at that time an Irish Republic, but *An Saorstat*, the 'Free State' in the South, Ireland was denuded of its

industrial base in the northern Six Counties, in the province of Ulster. In final settlement talks with Cosgrave in 1925, the British even got the Free State to pay £1,500,000
a year in 'land annuities' for the grants made under the land reform of the 1880s. From
1923 to 1945 Britain kept up economic sanctions against Ireland.

The Northern Ireland state was an artificial creation, made up of six of the nine
counties of the historic province of Ulster, cut off from the rest of Ireland. The six
counties were set apart on the basis that this was the territory that the predominantly
Protestant and loyal community of the area could hold against the Irish rebels. In
the six counties in 1920, 840,000 Protestants dominated 430,000 Catholics. Catholics
were driven out of the shipyards, and most of industry in a long campaign of terror. Jobs in Northern Ireland were allocated according to religion, on the assumption that the Catholic minority were disloyal. The Northern Ireland government at
Stormont was what its leader Viscount Craigavon would call 'a Protestant State for a
Protestant people'. That meant that Catholics were excluded from most positions of
public authority.

Under the government of Taoiseach de Valera from 1937 the Irish Free State's economic policy was for self-sufficiency in an accommodation to the South's now shrunken
industrial base and its rural bias. Social policy was backward and relied on the Catholic
Church to do the job of giving welfare to the destitute and running the schools. The
lively and creative nationalist movement of the early century became ossified and parochial. 'De Valera himself officiated in his priestly function with austerity and dignity',
wrote the historian Owen Dudley Edwards, to create a 'martyrology', dedicated to
the executed leaders of the Easter Rising, that underpinned his own authority as their
heir.[2]

Britain's official position was that the six counties would remain in the United
Kingdom as long as it was the 'will' of the people there. In the Northern Ireland Act
of 1949 it is stated that 'in no event will Northern Ireland or any part thereof cease to
be part of His Majesty's dominions and of the United Kingdom without the consent
of the parliament of Northern Ireland'. Republicans complained that the border was
drawn up to guarantee the 'loyalist' majority (with the arbitrary surrender of three of
the nine counties of Ulster to the South that was true). While they claimed the artificial
state of Northern Ireland on the basis of consent, in private the British government took
another view. The Cabinet Secretary Sir Norman Brook wrote in a memo to Prime
Minister Attlee in 1949 that:

> It will never be to Great Britain's advantage that Northern Ireland should form part of a
> territory outside His Majesty's jurisdiction. Indeed, it seems unlikely that Great Britain
> would ever be able to agree with this even if the people of Northern Ireland desired it.[3]

Britain's reaction to the Rising of 1798 had been to make Ireland a part of the United
Kingdom. Their reaction to the War of Independence was to divide Ireland but also to
incorporate Northern Ireland more definitively into the United Kingdom. The silent
doctrine that Northern Ireland should not be surrendered at any cost governed British
policy and was set in stone for the next 70 years.

India Partitioned

Overshadowing the whole question of a political settlement in India was the division that Britain had sowed between Mohammad Ali Jinnah's Muslim League and the Congress. In the 1931 census the population of British India included 67 million Muslims or 24.7 per cent, of the population, as compared to 178 million Hindus, or 65.5 per cent. In March 1940, Jinnah had given a speech to a crowd of 40,000 Muslim League supporters at Minto Park where he said 'the Musulmans are a nation by any definition'.[4]

That year the British Cabinet talked about a proposal from Lord Linlithgow about Home Rule for India. Prime Minister Churchill did not agree with those who wanted 'to promote unity among Hindu and Moslem communities', whose 'immediate result would be that the united communities would join in showing us the door'. He saw 'the Hindu-Moslem feud as the bulwark of British rule in India'.[5]

In the war and the 'Quit India!' campaign that ran alongside it, the British-India Government leant on the loyalty of Muslims. Muslims were over-represented in the Army (about 37 per cent in 1940), and where Congress-supporting Hindus boycotted local government, Muslims took on positions of local authority. On the other hand, the fear that they would be sold out in a settlement between Britain and Congress worried supporters of the Muslim League.

Muslim refugees from India in 1947.

A British Cabinet Mission made two proposals, both of which made communal division the constitutional foundation. The first, in May proposed two autonomous regions, one predominantly Muslim in the North, and the other predominantly Hindu under a central government. This was vetoed by the Muslim League. The Second proposal in June was for partition, which was rejected by Congress. With few options, Nehru ruled through the Congress majority in the Indian Parliament.

'Today we have said good-bye to constitutions and constitutional methods', Jinnah announced, naming 16 August 1946 as 'Direct Action' day. When the day came Huseyn Shaheed Suhrawardy, Bengal's Chief Minister and Muslim League member declared a 'public holiday' and all police and other officials were withdrawn from duties.[6] Gangs of Muslims attacked Hindus, and Hindus attacked Muslims. Thousands fled the city, and over the next ten days 10,000 people were murdered in Bengal alone. In October anti-Muslim rioting began in Bihar again leading to an even greater number of deaths. Wavell argued that British forces should withdraw from Hindu India and defend Pakistan. By December Nehru was presiding over an Assembly whose Muslim League members had withdrawn.

Britain's last Viceroy in India was Louis Mountbatten (known to his friends as 'Dickie') who replaced Wavell in the Spring of 1947. Mountbatten, with the help of his brilliant and radical wife Edwina, shifted British policy towards Congress dramatically. Outwardly they embraced the cause of Indian independence and made it their own. Mountbatten insisted that a date be fixed for independence, while Edwina relaxed protocol to win over India's leaders – and began an intense love affair with Nehru, with the blessing of her husband.[7]

Mountbatten was blamed by Churchill and the tory backwoodsmen for giving up India, but he also worked hard to sell partition to the Congress leaders as a *fait accompli*. It was Mountbatten who oversaw the division, holding back details of the final lines of the map but demanding that Congress and Muslim leaders alike agree. Fierce fighting between Hindus and Muslims broke out in Bengal and the Punjab which were all divided, as the new state of Pakistan was carved out of British India. The newly founded states fought a war over Kashmir, where Sikhs and Muslims clashed, until the United Nations divided the territory.

Jinnah believed that Mountbatten had betrayed Pakistan and favoured India, but India was always going to be more important to Britain. The value of Pakistan to the British and later the Americans was that it circumscribed India's ambitions. Pakistan was important, but it was unstable – most pointedly in the division between West Pakistan and East Pakistan (that would break away and declare itself Bangladesh, with Indian support, in 1971). The state that Jinnah made would be a trenchant Cold War ally of the West, but an illiberal and fractious state.

Mountbatten sold the truncated state in part by promising to win over the independent principalities to uniting with Nehru's India. His outward support for independence was rewarded when Nehru invited him to serve a second term as Governor General of the new state. The Congress leaders had travelled a long way since they had challenged British rule in the 1930s. Then Jinnah had been one of them. In the intercommunal fighting the British-Indian army, still commanded by British officers in its senior command, was paralysed. As Jinnah demanded Britain act against India, Nehru, too, called on Mountbatten to institute martial law. Congress failed to rein in the communal divisions that destroyed the national liberation movement, and Mountbatten persuaded Nehru to stay in the new Commonwealth. Around one million died in the intercommunal violence, more of whom were Muslim than Hindu. Around 14 million were made refugees, Muslims from Delhi and the Punjab fleeing to Pakistan, Hindus fleeing from Pakistan. The violence wounded Indian nationalism, and made British rule, which had done so much to exacerbate the tensions between the two peoples, look benign to many.

PART FOUR

Commonwealth, 1947–89

Chapter Twenty-nine

COLD WAR

After World War II Britain had lost its leading position. The underlying weakness of the British Empire was made explicit in its decline in international power politics. World leadership had passed to the United States and its most serious challenger was the Soviet Union.

Britain was the leading world power at the turn of the century, and still the largest Empire in 1939. But under the surface things were already changing. In World War I Britain had been unable to resolve the European conflict. It took America's troops under General Pershing to break Germany's 1918 Spring offensive, and it took Woodrow Wilson to broker the peace at Versailles. The instability of the interwar years was in large part due to the hiatus between the leadership of the two hegemonic powers, waning Britain and waxing America.

Many commentators thought that the question of who would lead the world would be resolved by a war between Britain and America. As it turned out the transition from British leadership to American was managed not in a war between each other, but under the umbrella of an alliance against the Axis powers.

The eclipse of British power became clear first in British dependence on US lending to pay for the war. Churchill knew full well that Britain could not afford to fight a war with Nazi Germany without US loans but fought it anyway. For the British treasury John Maynard Keynes was incensed that US Secretary of State Hans Morgenthau would not lend money until the British treasury was empty (Britain had defaulted on US loans in 1933). Americans also gifted military materiel to Britain under 'lend-lease'.

America did not only exact economic advantage over Britain. US Secretary of State Cordell Hull wanted an 'Open Door' policy towards US exports to the British Empire. Foreign Secretary Anthony Eden said he was 'unwilling to barter Empire preference in exchange for ... planes, tanks, guns, goods, et cetera' – but it was hard to resist the argument.[1]

Some in the US administration wanted to go further. The alliance between America and Britain was explained in a manifesto called the 'Atlantic Charter' of August 1941. The Charter promised the 'right of all peoples to choose the form of government under which they will live'. Undersecretary of State Sumner Welles in a speech in 1941 said that 'Our victory must bring in its train the liberation of all peoples', and 'the age of imperialism is ended'.[2]

Winston Churchill reacted angrily to this and other noises coming from the American administration. He wrote to the *Times* on 11 November 1942:

> Let me make this clear, in case there should be any mistake about it in any quarter. We mean to hold our own. I have not become the King's First Minister in order to preside over the liquidation of the British Empire.

At the February 1945 Yalta conference with President Roosevelt and Marshall Stalin, the question of Hong Kong and Singapore came up. Churchill resisted the pressure for 'trusteeship' and said:

> No one will induce as long as I am Prime Minister to let any representative of Great Britain go to a conference where we will be placed in the dock and asked to justify our right to live in a world we have tried to save.[3]

For all his bluster, Churchill was dependent on Roosevelt's support.

The British tried to argue that their Empire was not a venal or selfish enterprise. Key officials like Lord Hailey and Margery Perham worked up a propaganda campaign they called the Colonial Charter, which promised economic development in the colonies. The campaign was addressed as much at Washington as it was at the Empire. Quietly the same officials put it about that America's own race relations were an embarrassment, and Britain did not need any lessons on that score. Lord Hailey's Colonial Charter would be a blueprint for the post war Commonwealth.[4]

While many US officials leaned hard on the British to yield control the approaching victory made them more cautious. With US factories making up 36 per cent of all world output it was clear that it would be shaping the post-war world. American diplomats were by 1945 more concerned with holding together a world that was falling apart than they were in pushing for change.

According to historian William Louis, at the United Nations conference in San Francisco, 1945 the 'Americans had raised expectations that they might unfurl an anti-imperialist banner' but 'when it came to the test, the United States sided with the colonial powers'.[5] The American Secretary of State Dean Acheson said it was the point he learned from the English that Americans' idea of 'the sovereign equality of states' was a 'grand fallacy' and that diplomacy was indeed 'an instrument of power'.[6]

The United States did not formally annex large territories at the end of the Second World War, or afterwards. There were American colonies – in the Philippines (1898–1942), Guam (from 1898), Hawaii (annexed in 1898 and an American state from 1959) and Puerto Rico (from 1898). American influence overseas was manifested in the North Atlantic Treaty Organisation, the Southeast Asia Treaty Organization, and in military bases around the world, so that by 1957 43 countries had more than 100 US troops stationed;[7] in economic influence – America made up one quarter of world output throughout the Cold War (1946–89) and brokered the post-war European recovery with 'Marshall Aid'; in diplomatic influence, the US created and hosted the United Nations; it also led the World Bank, the International Monetary Fund and the General Agreement on Tariffs and Trades (later the World Trade Organisation).[8]

The American challenge to British hegemony was contained within the war against the Axis powers. Setting up Britain's junior status relative to America was managed in another conflict, the Cold War.

The second challenge to Britain's status as world hegemon came from the United Soviet Socialist Republics (USSR). In 1941 the USSR was on the verge of defeat at the hands of Nazi Germany but turned the struggle around in 1942 as the Großgermanisches

Reich collapsed. Germany's eastern Empire fell to the Red Army over 1943–45 which advanced as far as the Elbe. In December 1949, Mao's People's Army defeated the Kuomintang so that China was added to the Communist world. Following the communist victory in Vietnam, a Central Intelligence Agency estimate of 9 March 1976 put the communist share of the world population at 34 per cent.[9] In truth 'world communism' was more fragmented than western fears allowed (as became clear in the Sino-Soviet split of 1961). Still, the USSR in 1950 was a formidable rival to the USA, with a parallel set of international alliances, the Warsaw Pact countries arraigned against NATO, Comecon the soviet answer to GATT and Marshall Aid, and a seat at the United Nations Security Council table. The USSR's diplomatic offensive promised 'peaceful cooperation' with the West while at the same time offering rhetorical support to those national independence movements challenging the compromised European empires.[10]

The Americans' retreat from a wholesale embrace of national liberation arose out of the fear that they would lose the support of European allies as they remade the world order, and in particular in their conflict with the USSR. 'When perhaps the inevitable struggle came between Russia and ourselves, the question would be who are our friends', US diplomat Edward Stettinus said, 'would we have the support of Great Britain if we had undermined her position?'[11]

British power projection after the Second World War was struggling to keep up with a rapidly changing world. To meet that challenge British political leaders put themselves right at the front of the campaign to defend the West against the Soviet Union. With Washington uncertain of the solidity of the western world, Winston Churchill gave a speech in Fulton, Missouri on 5 March 1946, introduced by US President Harry Truman. Churchill began by asking what was the West's 'Overall Strategic Object', and went on to ask of the Soviet Union 'what are the limits, if any, to their expansive and proselytising tendencies?' There was, he warned, 'an Iron curtain descending across Europe' between the democratic west and the communist east. Further, 'in a great number of countries, far from the Russian frontiers and throughout the world, Communist fifth columns are established and work in complete unity and absolute obedience to the directions they receive from the Communist centre'.

Churchill argued that the British Empire combined with America would be the natural counterbalance to communist tyranny:

If the population of the English-speaking Commonwealth be added to that of the United States with all that such co-operation implies in the air, on the sea, all over the globe and in science and in industry, and in moral force, there will be no quivering, precarious balance of power to offer its temptation to ambition or adventure.

Churchill was arguing the case for the British Empire as a partner to US hegemony. In time it would be clear that Britain's position would be as the junior partner, but the alliance was the best way to preserve what influence in the world Britain had. On 24 February 1947 foreign minister Ernest Bevin told the US government that Britain could no longer afford to pay for the military presence in Greece. It was a demoralising operation, that found British troops trying to hold down a popular, left-wing resistance movement. On 12 March Harry Truman announced the doctrine that America would defend nations against outside interference. American military and financial aid to the unpopular Tsaldaris government filled the gap as the British troops left. After then the United States military, and its Central Intelligence Agency, took on the role of containing radical nationalist challenges to the western way of life. US intelligence operations to defend conservative regimes were undertaken across the world, even in British colonies and former colonies. US intelligence officers financed conservative campaigns in British Guiana (1953–64), Ghana (1966), Jamaica (1976–80), Grenada (1979–84) and as we shall see, throughout the Middle East. Occasionally, British military intelligence and even political leaders would object to these incursions into their sphere of influence, but on the whole, the British policy was to cooperate with US Cold War plans.[12]

In the Foreign Office there was some optimism about the Cold War, as can be seen in policy documents from 1950. 'The Western system is coming into being under the pressure of Soviet policy', they said, adding that, 'it is probably fair to say that the system is desirable in itself'. The Foreign Office thought the Soviet threat was good for West-West relations: 'if there was no Soviet opposition to bind all the members together, friction between the different groups would be only too likely to develop'.[13] Paul Henri Spaak, the Belgian statesman who was made head of the North Atlantic Treaty Organisation, was reported as saying that there should be a statue of Josef Stalin in every NATO capital city, as a reminder of their debt to the Soviet dictator for providing the cement to bind together the Atlantic Alliance.[14]

The bogeyman of 'communist fifth columns' throughout the world was compelling and not without some basis in fact. The anti-communist scare tactics meant that the British and American political and military leadership could characterise challenges to their authority as red subversion. When the Anglo-American alliance was under strain, British leaders ramped up the Cold War talk to underline their importance to America. After US President Eisenhower attacked Britain's foolish attack on Egypt in the Suez crisis of 1956, Churchill wrote a letter begging him not to forget the real enemy:

> There seems to be growing misunderstanding and frustration on both sides of the Atlantic. If they be allowed to develop, the skies will darken indeed and it is the Soviet Union that will ride the storm.

Churchill went on:

> If we do not take immediate action in harmony, it is no exaggeration to say that we must expect to see the Middle East and North African coastline under Soviet control and Western Europe placed at the mercy of the Russians.[15]

It was an exaggeration. The bogeyman of communism seemed to loom larger when the danger of division between Washington and London threatened. After 1946 the Cold War was the glue that held the allies together.

However, many of the militant anti-colonial movements did have left wing leaders, either avowed communists or Marxists, or radical enough that they could be characterised as Moscow's 'fifth columns'. That Britain (and other European Empires) had provoked resistance to their rule quite apart from the appeal of communist propaganda was set to one side. The exigencies of the emerging Cold War between communist East and capitalist West meant that national liberation movements were a challenge that had to be defeated, or at least de-fanged.

So it was that the 1948 Commission of Enquiry to investigate disturbances in the Gold Coast found that the rising star of the nationalist movement (and future President) Kwame Nkrumah 'proposes a programme which is all too familiar to those who have studied the technique of countries which have fallen the victims of Communist enslavement' – he was arrested and threatened with deportation.[16] Similarly, Lee Kuan Yew, future President of Singapore, was put on a list of communist subversives to be arrested or shot on sight. Chin Peng, leader of the Malayan People's Anti-Japanese Army was awarded the Order of the British Empire and honoured in the 1946 London victory parade. But when his guerrillas fought on to free their country, they were discovered to have been communist subversives after all. So taken with the anti-communist ethos were the Britain's Joint Intelligence Committee that they insisted that the danger to British rule in Cyprus came from the local communist party AKEL, though it was in fact the far-right guerrillas of EOKA who were attacking British troops.[17]

The Cold War ideology was a strong bulwark holding up Britain's post-war international position. That was important because the ideology of white supremacy that had underscored the Empire before the war had less and less purchase. On the other hand, the claim that Britain was at the forefront of the fight to defend freedom rang hollow for many in the Empire. To be convincing the Empire project would have to be seriously reformed.

Chapter Thirty

THE CHALLENGE OF COLONIAL DEVELOPMENT

With hindsight many historians see the end of World War II as the end of the British Empire. But that was not how the British Government, or its senior officials and military men saw it. Though the post war government was a Labour government it was all the same committed to the idea that Britain was still a world power, and the Empire was a part of that. Britain 'is at the centre of a Great Empire and Commonwealth of Nations' Foreign Secretary Ernest Bevin chided the Labour Party conference: 'Revolutions do not change geography.' To Michael Foot, Bevin said that he was not aware of any suggestion that 'we have overnight ceased to be a great power'.[1]

Britain won a famous victory in World War II but had exhausted its reserves and borrowed from its colonies doing it. The total national debt was £21,473 million, and Britain owed India £1250 million, Ireland £250 million, Australia and New Zealand £200 million each, and further large sums to Argentina, Norway and Brazil . Banker Arthur Villiers moaned that it was 'exasperating to think that we are supposed to owe £400,000,000 to the Egyptians, one of the feeblest races in the world'.[2] The country's balance of payments was in deficit by £875 million and only American loans were keeping it afloat. In Britain wartime austerity and rationing carried on during peacetime to 'win the export war'.

After the war Britain needed to repackage the Empire. The whole idea of Empire was repugnant to many. Lord Hailey's plan to present the Empire as a project for social development was followed through. Rather cynically, Churchill had said 'British Empire or British Commonwealth of Nations – we keep trade labels to suit all tastes'.[3]

The label Commonwealth had a meaning. It was an attempt to promote the empire as a positive, not a domineering, association. In history the Commonwealth was what Britain was called when Cromwell was protector. The meaning was that the wealth was held in common for all the peoples of the Empire. The government was only managing things on behalf of those peoples.

For the decade after the war there was an attempt to organise the Commonwealth as an economic unit, as it had been during the war. The Colonial Development and Welfare Act of 1945 was followed by a Colonial Development Corporation in 1947. Arthur Creech Jones, the new Colonial Minister said that the goal was 'creating independent and responsible life in the territories and for securing better living standards and the development of economies.' The 1945 Act created a development fund and Creech Jones invited colonies to send in plans to raise 'the standards of health, education, social welfare and general well-being of colonial peoples'.[4]

Sir Alan Burns, who had served as Governor in the Gold Coast, in his book *In Defence of Colonies* wrote that 'many years ago Britain undertook the gigantic task of helping people of various under-developed territories to overcome the handicaps imposed upon them by nature and the environment'. But 'in many parts of the world the task has not yet been completed and it is inconceivable that we should abandon it half done'.[5] Burns' defence of the colonies chimed with the US government's optimism about the prospects for growth. The economist W. W. Rostow was a speech writer for President Kennedy and then a National Security Advisor to President Johnson. He set out a theory of growth that said that all countries could expect to go through a 'take-off' as first Britain and then America had done. Rostow was saying to the poorer countries that they should be patient and their turn would come. Rostow admitted that sometimes the 'take-off' was delayed by bad investment decisions or extraneous factors, but in essence his message was optimistic. Many followed Rostow in arguing that modernisation was a general trend that would lift all countries in time. This outlook became known as 'development economics'.

The goal of economic development was a key justification for the Commonwealth and often talked about in quite radical ways. 'Socialism within the Commonwealth', hoped Canadian academic and politician Frank R. Scott, 'means the end of old-style empire and a new programme of economic and social planning for the benefit of the common people of every race and creed'. In 1946 Labour's Richard Crossman led 57 backbench MPs in an amendment to the King's Speech, saying that the government should 'recast its conduct of international affairs' to 'secure full Socialist planning and control of the world's resources'.[6] The prospects that the Colonial Development Corporation would usher in a tropical social democracy were optimistic. Its stated purpose was the 'production of food-stuffs, raw materials and manufactures where supply to the UK or sales overseas will assist our balance of payments'. British colonies were made to keep their dollar reserves in a pool in London where they could be drawn on to meet payments and buy goods that Britain needed. The historian David Fieldhouse worked out that the Colonial Development fund spend a total of £40.5 million between 1946 and 1951, or about £8 million a year. Over that time colonial sterling balances held in London along with the West African market-ing board deposits represented loans of around £250 million to the British Government.[7]

Among the important dollar earning colonial exports were Malaysian rubber and tin, and Gold Coast cocoa and palm oil. In Parliament in 1952 Lord Ogmore explained that Malaysian tin and rubber had 'very largely supported the standard of living of people of this country and the sterling area ever since the war ended'.[8] The struggle to control Malaya's rubber and tin would be bitter.

In West Africa the vehicles for collecting tropical produce were the Marketing Boards set up between 1946 and 1948, to replace the statutory marketing boards set up in the war. 'Their main functions are to fix the prices which merchants pay to farmers for the main export crops throughout West Africa', Richard Acland told the British Parliament on 11 May 1951:

> they compulsorily purchase the whole of the crops from the licensed merchants; they then sell the export crops, in the case of cocoa on the market, and in the case of other crops by long-term contracts with the British Government.[9]

The Gold Coast Cocoa Marketing Board had accumulated profits of £50 million. D. M. Williams, editor of *West Africa,* said that 'the Boards' decisions about prices to be paid to producers are eagerly awaited in Lancashire no less than in Lagos or Kenem'. Williams' estimated that the annual Gold Coast cocoa sales of £60m were two-thirds of all the colony's exports.[10]

The West African Produce Board bought palm oil from farmers at £16/15s. per ton and sold it in London at £95. Groundnuts (peanuts) were bought at £15 per ton and their oil sold at £110 per ton. The venerable socialist John Strachey as Minister of Food told Parliament on 20 January 1948 that 'by hook or by crook the development of primary production of all sorts in the colonial territories and dependent areas in the commonwealth and throughout the world is a life and death matter for the economy of this country' – the country in question being Britain.

Hugh Williams for the Empire Marketing Board 1935

In the *Financial Times* economist W. Arthur Lewis wrote that 'the British colonial system has become a major means of economic exploitation':

> Many Colonies must sell their produce to Britain at prices below the world price, and, through exchange control, must buy from Britain at prices above the world price, or pay an ever- increasing sum into the Bank of England, because Britain will not deliver goods in return for what she receives.

Lewis wrote that 'Britain talks of colonial development, but on the contrary, it is African and Malayan peasants who are putting capital into Britain'. [11]

Much of the exploitation of tropical Africa was carried on by the United Africa Company a subsidiary of Unilever. The UAC proposed an enlarged groundnut scheme in East Africa, which the Government enthusiastically backed as an exemplar of what economic planning could achieve. The Government advanced the UAC £25 million and Colonial Minister Arthur Creech Jones granted some 3,250,000 acres of native land. John Strachey had 'perfect confidence that in a very few years the groundnut scheme will be one of the acknowledged glories of the British Commonwealth'. It turned out to be a disaster. Only 26,000 acres were planted at a cost of £23 million. The crop was smaller than the seed used. The eventual losses were £32 million.

In the 1940s the British took control of Italian colonies in Africa, Abyssinia (Ethiopia), Eritrea and Libya, through war and under the United Nations mandate after the war. These were plundered mercilessly. Officially, Ethiopia's King Haile Selassie was an ally. British and Indian troops fought alongside Ethiopian warriors to rid the country of the Italian occupiers. Afterwards Britain's General Wetherall commandeered the country's industrial infrastructure. Crankshaft grinders were sent to Libya to repair tanks, road-making equipment was sent to India, a brick factory was dismantled and sent to Nairobi and an Oxygen plant to Uganda (leaving the country's hospitals without). British memoranda listed goods to be taken including soap-making equipment, diesel tractors, bridges and fleets of trucks, water-boring works and oil-pressing equipment, saw-mills and mining machinery.[12]

From Eritrea the British stripped the Naval base of Massawa of a floating dock, a large dredger and equipment from a bombed aerodrome. The oil installation at Ras Dogan was dismantled as were 5.7 km of railway track 850 railway points, 3 tons of bolts, 71 trucks and 20 turntables from Zula. More railway equipment was taken from Otumlo and Agordat. The Eritrean Chamber of Commerce made a full inventory of British seizures valued at 1,700 million East African Shillings (£1.85 billion today).[13]

Limits of Colonial Exploitation

Already in 1929 more of the world's money reserves were held as dollars than sterling. In the course of the war Britain burned up its reserves relying on the US to underwrite them. But at the post war reconstruction conference at Bretton Woods in 1944 American negotiator Harry Dexter White dismissed the proposal from John Maynard Keynes to create a new international currency (the 'bancor'), by saying that they did not need one: the dollar would do the job.

Paymaster General Lord Cherwell wrote to Churchill that,

> our fundamental problem is that the Sterling Area is spending more than it is earning. We have to put that right by exporting more and importing less.[14]

The Empire was still living as if it was the economic power-house that it had been at the end of the nineteenth century, though the dynamic centre of the world economy at the end of the war was the United States.

It is pointed that when he was offered the post of Colonial Secretary in the Attlee Government, Hugh Dalton drew back. He 'had a horrid vision of pullulating, poverty stricken, diseased n****r communities, for whom one can do nothing in the short run, and now, the more one tries to help them, are querulous and ungrateful'. Another candidate who did want the post was left-winger Nye Bevan. But the official view, according to Dalton was that 'he couldn't be trusted there (a) not to waste lots of money (b) not to be carried away by his colour prejudice, pro-black and anti-white'.[15] Colonial Secretary was an appointment that was more likely to ruin your career than save it and only a dangerous dreamer would want it was Dalton's judgement.

The major problem was that most colonial production was undercapitalised. The mines, plantations and oilfields were major currency earners, and jute and cotton mills had grown up in India and Africa, but these were still a small part of the economy. South Africa's gold mines helped keep sterling afloat, but that was not enough. The price-rigging of the Marketing Boards was onerous for the cocoa farmers – but that did not make it a very efficient means of exploiting African labour as far as British capitalists were concerned.

An outward flow of capital from Britain into the colonies had taken place in 1878–90 and again between 1905 and 1913. One-sidedly, and exploitatively, that capital export drove industrial development in the Empire. But after the Second World War the centre of industrial growth shifted back to the reconstruction of Western Europe, so capital flowed out of the colonies. In parliament, Labour MP Roy Jenkins said that 'it is extraordinary that in recent months the three biggest exporters of capital in the world have been, first, the United States; second, Malaya, and, third, West Africa'.[16] 'Capital export' in the second two cases was a measure of how much those colonies were being exploited.

The settled colonies, Canada, New Zealand and Australia wanted dollars more than pounds to buy US imports, while the non-white colonies were impoverished. In 1949 the pound was devalued by 30 per cent to accommodate the fact that the economic activity denominated in sterling had declined.

It should be said that the British did not just tighten African and Asian belts in the post war years. The wartime policy of domestic rationing and austerity was not lifted until 1951. Occupied West Germany was on even harsher rations – dropping to 1100 calories a day. All effort went to increasing overseas earnings and to try to reduce the national debt.

After Nasser nationalised the Suez Canal the Americans made it clear they would not support sterling so that investors sold theirs creating a 'run on the pound'. Prime Minister Macmillan reflected,

> We have inherited an old family business which used to be very profitable and sound. The trouble is that the liabilities are four times the assets. ...we must either carry on the business with all its risks, or wind it up and pay 5s in the £.[17]

In his popular outline *British Economic Policy since the War* (1957), the City correspondent Andrew Shonfield argued that the cost of keeping a reserve currency for the sterling area was too great a burden on British industry. Defending the value of the pound kept interest rates high and hurt the balance of payments.[18]

Plans for investment in the former European colonies were frustrated by the 'shortage of capital' according to France's historian of Africa Catherine Coquery-Vidrovitch. The consequences were dire: 'Capitalism could revolutionise agriculture in Europe, but it could not do the same for Africa', wrote Guyana's Walter Rodney.[19] Between 1960 and 1980 Ghana, Nigeria, Congo, Chad and Tanzania all experienced a stagnation, if not deterioration in agricultural output. Drought and famine were the consequences, particularly in the Sahel between 1968 and 1974.

The Commonwealth, as the institution that was to carry on the traditions of Empire was a shadow of the thing it replaced. As the economies of the former colonies declined, trade relations and diplomatic relations were less important to Britain. In 1949 the British Commonwealth became the Commonwealth of Nations, and, in the words of the one-time Commonwealth Secretariat official Krishnan Srinavasan, once it became 'everybody's Commonwealth', it became 'nobody's Commonwealth'.[20]

Chapter Thirty-one

STATES OF EMERGENCY

After World War II the British Empire was challenged by social movements that quickly turned into national movements for independence. The traditional leaders of the native administrations tended to fall away. The new challenges to the Empire drew on the urban working class, as in Singapore, West Africa, and the Caribbean, but also on the rural peasantry and plantation workers in Kenya, Malaya and Guiana. Ex-servicemen, men who had volunteered (or been pressed) to work for the British victory played a part. So, too, did the growing number of younger people who were less beholden to the old order.

The intellectual leadership of the opposition drew on different sources. Some, like African leaders Jomo Kenyatta (Kenya), Kwame Nkrumah (Ghana) and Julius Nyerere (Tanzania) had been students in Britain and also moved in radical circles. Some, like Chin Peng in Malaya, were Communists allied to the USSR – though not as many as was claimed. Others, like Maasina Rule in the Solomon Islands or the Mau-Mau uprising drew on religious movements and local organisation.

Malaya and Singapore

Under the Japanese occupation Malaya's migrant Chinese population in particular were persecuted by the political police, the Kempetai. They left the towns to find safety living off the land in the countryside. Chinese were the backbone of the Malayan People's Anti-Japanese Army, under its remarkable leader Chin Peng.

In 1947 the British negotiated a new constitution for the colony with the Sultans and the United Malay National Organisation. Under the constitution, non-Malays – Chinese and Indian migrant labourers – had their citizenship rights severely restricted.[1]

As British authority was restored the MPA-JA veterans supported militant strikes by plantation workers. The British imposed a state of emergency. In April 1948 British intelligence officers worried that the United Malays National Organisation was 'steadily losing ground to left-wing organisations'.[2] Quite quickly conflict turned into all-out warfare.

High Commissioner Gerard Templer's regime waged war on mostly ethnic Chinese rebels creating 'killing zones' and relocating as many as half a million (under the 'Briggs Plan' – for its architect Lt. General Sir Harold Briggs). In 1948 soldiers of the Scots Guards shot dead 24 unarmed villagers then covered up the massacre, at the rubber plantation by Batang Kali village. Villages were bombarded from the air, though Chin

Peng's renamed Malayan People's Army fought on until peace talks with the British and
the Malay leader Tunku Abdul Rahman in 1960.[3]

*Chinese schoolgirl holds the attention of striking
workers at the Firestone factory in Kallang Road (1955).*

Singapore – lying between Malaya to the North and Indonesia to the South – was
rocked by student protests in 1954 against national service, led mostly by Chinese
Singaporeans. A young lawyer, Lee Kuan Yew, who defended the students launched a
mass movement, the People's Action Party in alliance with the trade unions that year.[4]

Solomon Islands and Fiji

Soon after the Second World War a movement called Maasina Rule took off in the
Solomon Islands. A British army campaign to 'de-louse' the islands led to the arrest of
nine chiefs or Alaha in 1947 under the Sedition Act for holding secret meetings. That
only led to further disorder and mass withholding of tax payments. Under Operation
Jericho thousands were imprisoned. Losing control of the situation the Government
had to release the chiefs so that they could negotiate with someone. In 1951, the British
had to concede a peace deal that included local self-government under the Malaitan
Congress.[5]

In December of 1959 the Shell Oil refinery workers in the Fijian capital Suva went
on strike in an action that very quickly led to rioting and a state of emergency. The strike
was led by the oil workers union secretary, James Anthony, an Indian, and Apisai Tora,
a Fijian and president of the North West Branch. The Union stoked fears among the
British settlers of a joint collaboration between Indo-Fijians and native Fijians, upsetting
the otiose racial organisation of the colony.[6]

After Fijian villagers started to collect food to help the mixed Indian and Fijian
strikers, the Fijian chiefs, were called on to talk the native population around. Official
dismay was sharpened by the dread that the more traditional natives were becoming as
militant as the rebellious Indian cane-growers unions were in the 1930s and 1940s. The
leading chiefs the Vunivalu Ratu George Cakobau and Ratu K.T.T. Mara barged their
way into the mass meetings that the union had organised and warned the Fijians against
the influence of Indian agitators. The racial divide that had been built into the colony's
constitution was activated and the Chiefs proved their worth to the British.

Governor Maddocks tended to downplay the British role in engineering the break, shifting the responsibility instead onto the Fijian chiefs. He wrote in his memoirs that

> The Fijian leaders, who greatly valued their traditional alliance with the Europeans, blamed the Indians for starting the trouble and as a result, race relations, which hitherto had been remarkably good, suffered a setback.[7]

Mau Mau

In the 'White Highlands' of Kenya the European settlers were challenged by Kikuyu militants of the Kikuyu Central Association. After the war the Europeans had already won a built-in majority on the legislative council, out of all proportion to their share of the population. The settlers faced constitutional opposition from Jomo Kenyatta's Kenyan African Union, but the more serious challenge to the colonial set-up came from a clandestine movement that came to be called 'Mau Mau' – though its members called it the Kenya Land and Freedom Army.

Mau Mau prisoners.

The Mau Mau war rallied mostly Kikuyu squatters farming on land nominally owned by settlers in the White Highlands. At Olenguruone, in Nakuro, county in June 1943 some Kikuyu argued with the District Officer about their tenure, which they understood to be secure, but were told that they were only squatters. The Kikuyu in the White Highlands were being challenged by the settlers who tried to limit their farms and reduce livestock to keep them dependent on the meagre wages the white farmers paid. At Olenguruone the Kikuyu refused to work for the settlers and protested at a visit by colonial secretary Arthur Creech Jones in 1945.[8]

At clandestine meetings Kikuyu took oaths to fight against the colony and to keep their organisation secret from government spies. They challenged settlers in a growing conflict. Between October 1952, when the State of Emergency was declared, and

1955 the Mau Mau uprising became an out-and-out war. As many as ten thousand Kikuyu were killed by the British army in a campaign to stamp out the insurgency. The Army cleared 80,000 Kikuyu from the White Highlands and put them behind barbed wire in 'Native Land Units'. This ethnic cleansing led to thousands more deaths. In the camps the Kikuyu were subject to arbitrary punishments, forced labour, torture and mutilation and many were killed.[9] Even the moderate leader Jomo Kenyatta – who had made a point of condemning the Mau Mau – was jailed by governor Evelyn Baring.

West Africa

In 1947 Kwame Nkrumah a radical Ghanaian student living in London was invited back home to help organise the United Gold Coast Convention. Nkrumah had been working with the West African National Secretariat which itself had been put together after the Pan African Congress in Manchester in 1946.

The U.G.C.C. was led mostly by Chiefs and political power brokers on the Gold Coast and among the Ashante. They were chafing at the collar of the colonial admin-istration, though not ready for the kind of change that was taking place in the new Ghana. The lion's share of the five million population were subsistence farmers, though the growth of cash crops employed many, like the 210,000 cocoa farmers (mainly Ashante). The population of the major towns – Accra, Kumasi, Sekondi-Takoradi and Cape Coast – had grown from 150,000 to 300,000 between 1931 and 1947 and there were around 100,000 wage labourers. This younger urban population played a key role in what followed.[10]

Kwame Nkrumah's tour of the country for the United Gold Coast Convention in 1947 gathered large crowds of younger Ghanaians ready for change. On 28 February 1948 a group of ex-servicemen were demonstrating against the Governor but were blocked from marching on his official residence at Christianborg Castle. Police opened fire on the men killing two and injuring five. As the news spread around Accra crowds attacked businesses – in particular the stores of the United African Company and the United Trading Company. Twenty-nine more people were killed when the police and army tried to contain the rioting and a further 237 injured.[11]

Nkrumah was arrested along with other officers of the United Gold Coast Convention and prosecuted for conspiracy. While he was in prison the authorities put pressure on the Convention to distance themselves from the man they claimed was a communist agitator. Nkrumah saw that the U.G.C.C. would abandon him and quickly set up his own new party with the core of the activists that he had recruited building the move-ment. To the dismay of the colonial authorities Nkrumah's Convention People's Party was launched at a mass rally of 60,000 and the moderates were eclipsed.[12]

Cyprus

In 1955 a guerrilla group called EOKA (National Organisation of Cypriot Fighters) took up arms against the British colonial authorities on the island. Their goal was free-dom from British rule, and 'Enosis', union with Greece and they were led by Georgios

Grivas. 'I can imagine no more disastrous policy for Cyprus than to hand it over to a friendly but unstable power. It would have the effect of undermining the eastern bastion of NATO', said the Colonial Secretary Oliver Lyttleton: 'Eastern Mediterranean security demands that we maintain sovereign power in Cyprus.'[13]

There were around 1250 EOKA fighters arraigned against 30,000 British troops. There were 1,144 exchanges recorded between EOKA and the British forces, and EOKA killed 105 soldiers and another 50 policemen. In 1959 EOKA was persuaded to lay down its arms in exchange for an independent government for Cyprus.[14]

The victor in Cyprus' first election – with 70 per cent of the vote – was Archbishop Makarios who had been exiled from the country by the British authorities. He proved a popular leader in Cyprus but was despised in London and Washington where he was called the 'Castro of the Mediterranean'.

Guiana

In Guiana British hopes of building up moderate allies were dashed when the radical Progressive People's Party led by Cheddi Jagan and Forbes Burnham won elections under a new constitution. The British Government goaded the Governor Sir Alfred Savage to support a suspension of the constitution. A strike by sugar workers added to the pretext that Jagan aimed at a communist overthrow of the colony. The State of Emergency was declared on October 1953 – though the planned clampdown had been widely discussed and Jagan and his supporters tried to make sure that they kept up their legal existence.[15]

Chapter Thirty-two

BRITAIN IN THE MIDDLE EAST

Mossadegh's Iran 1951–52

Supposedly independent Iran had been practically divided between the British and the Russians throughout the first half of the twentieth century. In World War II the British put Mohammad Reza Pahlavi on the throne. As the Shah was dependent on British control the main export earner was the British owned Anglo-Iranian Oil Company.

In 1948 Anglo-Iranian made an after-tax profit of £61 million. Of that just nine million went to the Peacock Throne as royalties. Ten million pounds of Anglo-Iranian's royalties went straight to the British government which owned 51 per cent of the company, and a further 24 million went in taxes. It also supplied all the Royal Navy's oil needs at well below market price. To officials in Washington British diplomats estimated the total cost of losing Anglo-Iranian oil would be in the region of £100 million – around one per cent of Britain's total GDP, or 35 per cent of its spending on the National Health Service. 'Without the Middle East and its oil', British Foreign Secretary Ernest Bevin said in 1946 there would be 'no hope of our being able to achieve the standard of living at which we are aiming in Great Britain'.[1]

An agreement made with Reza Shah, Mohammad's father, to increase pay and promotion for native Iranians, and to invest in local services was ignored. Once drilled, the oil was refined on the silt-made island of Abadan. Manucher Farmanfarmaian told what he found there when he became director of Iran's petroleum institute in 1949:

> The workers lived in a shantytown called Khagazabad, or Paper City, without running water or electricity, let alone such luxuries as iceboxes or fans … In every crevice hung the foul, sulphurous stench of burning oil – a pungent reminder that every day twenty thousand barrels, or one million tons a year, were being consumed indiscriminately for the functioning of the refinery, and AIOC never paid the government a cent for it. To the management of AIOC in their pressed ecru shirts and air-conditioned offices, the workers were faceless drones … In the British section of Abadan there were lawns, rose beds, tennis courts, swimming pools and clubs; in Kaghazabad there was nothing – not a tea shop, not a bath, not a single tree.[2]

Anger at AIOC's exploitation of Iran was the issue that propelled the radical nationalist Mohammed Mossadegh and his National Front to a majority in the Iranian parliament, the Majlis. Mossadegh took apart AIOC's accounts in an oil sub-committee of the Majlis. Soon after, the National Front won a majority and the Shah reluctantly appointed him Prime Minister. America's President Truman pressed Britain to renegotiate a fairer share of the profits, and the American company drilling Saudi Arabia's oil agreed a new 50-50 division of the profits with the Saudis, putting pressure on Britain to negotiate. With great rallies of support the National Front argued for nationalisation of all Iranian oil.

In response Britain tried to prosecute Iran for seizing its oil but failed. Mossadegh told the United Nations in New York in October 1951 that,

> if we are to tolerate a situation in which the Iranian plays the part of a mere manual worker in the oil fields of Masjid-i-Suleiman, Agha Jari and Kermanshah and in the Abadan refinery, and if foreign exploiters continue to appropriate practically all of the income them our people will remain forever in a state of poverty and misery.[3]

The Iranian Prime Minister was winning the argument. He impressed Americans breaking his trip to Washington to visit the Liberty Bell in Philadelphia, and then on the way back home stopped to greet cheering crowds in Egypt.

The British Navy blockaded Iran's waterways and in 1952 towed the Rose Mary carrying oil to Italy ashore at Aden. Iran's oil exports were stopped and the loss of revenue added to heightened tensions in the country.

Britain failed to convince President Truman that they had a right to Iran's oil. Christopher Woodhouse, head of the British intelligence station in Iran went to Washington in November of 1952 to argue that the real threat was as much the communist-leaning Tudeh Party that was waiting in the wings to take over. The new President Eisenhower was much more willing to support the European colonialist powers as Cold War allies.

Mossadegh at the United Nations in New York.

At a meeting of the National Security Council on 4 March US Secretary of State John Foster Dulles argued that if Iran 'succumbed to the Communists there was little doubt that in short order the other areas of the Middle East, with some sixty per cent of the world's oil reserves would fall into Communist control'.[4] Eisenhower gave the go-ahead for the Central Intelligence Agency to organise a coup to get Mossadegh out of power.

CIA Director Allen Dulles sent Kermit Roosevelt to Iran to plan the overthrow. Donald Wilber, who wrote the CIA's own internal history of the coup records that Allen W. Dulles, 'approved $1 million on April 4 to be used in any way that would bring about the fall of Mossadegh':

> The aim was to bring to power a government which would reach an equitable oil set-tlement, enabling Iran to become economically sound and financially solvent, and which would vigorously prosecute the dangerously strong Communist Party.[5]

Much of the groundwork had already been done by British MI6 and Woodhouse. They had gathered contacts in the armed forces, among southern rural town leaderships, in the Mosques and in the Majlis. The British called it 'Operation Boot' – when it was handed over to Kermit Roosevelt it was renamed 'Operation Ajax'.

After demanding that Mohammad Reza Shah surrender control of the military Mossadegh was alarming the traditionalists in the country as much as he was winning popular support in the streets. The Shah left the country, fearful of arrest. Roosevelt's agents took advantage of the polarisation to rally support. With protests and counter-protests getting more strident, America persuaded Mossadegh that he would have to use the police to rein in his more militant supporters and in particular the radicals of the Tudeh Party.

The police clampdown became a pretext for the reaction that would push Mossadegh out of power. Roosevelt organised gangs of right-wing thugs to mass outside the Prime Minister's house. He was helped by MI6 agent Norman Darbyshire and the CIA's Stephen Meade.

'My brief was very simple', Darbyshire told filmmaker Mark Anderson. 'Go out there, don't inform the ambassador, and use the intelligence service for any money you might need to secure the overthrow of Mossadegh by legal or quasi-legal means.' Darbyshire said he spent 'vast sums of money, well over a million-and-a-half pounds', adding, 'I was personally giving orders and directing the street uprising.'[6]

Fazlolla Zahedi, was declared Prime Minister over the radio as the armed forces seized control. The Shah returned to oversee Zahedi's elevation and Mossadegh's trial and imprisonment.

Iran's oil industry kept the name that Mossadegh had given it, the National Iranian Oil Company – but that was a front for the western consortium that took over. The Anglo-Iranian Oil Company (that would later change its name to British Petroleum) had a 40 per cent share, while five American companies had the other 40 per cent and the rest was handed over to Royal Dutch/Shell and Compagnie Française de Pétroles.

Post war, Britain's imperial claims in the Middle East were being overturned. British economic and military power was not ended. It was being downgraded to the role of junior to a dominant United States. The Cold War, not the imperial mandate, was the new policy framework. Those changes were not painless but led to more conflict as Britain was challenged and America stepped in.

Palestine

Out of the Arab revolution and the collapse of the Ottoman Empire Britain claimed the Protectorate of Palestine under the 1920 Treaty of Sèvres, that granted Syria to France. Palestine was home to Muslim and Christian Arabs, and a growing Jewish population. Jews had lived in that part of the world since the eighth century B.C.E. but many more came at the end of the nineteenth and in the twentieth centuries invited by the Zionist movement to build a Jewish homeland.

Zionism was in some ways a reaction to the growth of European anti-Semitism. Its nineteenth century founder Theodor Herzl had lost faith in assimilation while reporting on the Dreyfus case in France, where a Jewish officer was falsely accused of treason. From 1880 the Zionists bought plots in the Ottoman province of Palestine and moved families from Europe in. The Jewish population grew from 20,000 in 1880 to 80,000 in 1914.

Seeking to govern the former Ottoman territory the British hoped that the Jews would be a counterbalance to Arab demands. In 1917 Foreign Secretary wrote in reply to an appeal from Lord Walter Rothschild to say that a 'declaration of sympathy with Jewish Zionist ambitions has been submitted to, and approved by, the Cabinet'. Known after as the Balfour declaration, it read:

> His Majesty's Government view with favour the establishment in Palestine of a national home for the Jewish people and will use their best endeavours to facilitate the achievement of this object, it being clearly understood that nothing shall be done which may prejudice the civil and religious rights of existing non-Jewish communities in Palestine, or the rights and political status enjoyed by Jews in any other country.

Palestinians objected that their land was overwhelmingly Arab and suspected they were being undermined. To Woodrow Wilson a Muslim-Christian Committee wrote on 14 July 1918 that 'the country as well as the inhabitants are Arab', that 'Arabs are 30 times more numerous than the Jews' and that Jews own just '1/500 of the land owned by Arabs'. In March and April 1918 Arabs attacked Jewish settlements in Syria and rioted against the threatened British mandate. Palestinians protested again in 1921 but were disappointed when the League of Nations confirmed the British mandate on 24 July 1922, with the Balfour Declaration endorsed by the League.[7]

Under British rule, between 1922 and 1927 immigration pushed the Jewish population up from 84,000 to 415,000 while land bought or confiscated from Arabs for Jews grew from 79,000 to 200,000 hectares. In 1929 Palestinian Arabs clashed with a growing Jewish settlement in Jaffa, Nablus, Tiberias, Safed, Haifa, Hebron and Jerusalem.[8]

Palestinian unrest turned into a near insurrection against Britain. Muslim leader Izzedin al-Qassam was killed in fighting he led against the British in 1935 and a general strike called in 24 April 1936 dragged on till October of that year. With the Arabs in revolt, Britain relied more on the Jews as allies.

A British White Paper of 17 May 1939 proposed an independent Palestinian state with Jewish immigration limited to 75,000 a year. Zionists carried on organising illegal immigration, turning on their British allies with increasing militancy.

The holocaust in the German Reich added to the urgency of getting Jews out of Europe but set the Zionist movement at odds with Britain. Jewish militias, notably Irgun, led by Menachem Begin, and Lehi, sometimes called the 'Stern Gang' after its leader Abraham Stern, launched an armed insurrection against the British. Now it was the Jews who were put under emergency laws.

On 6 November 1944 Stern had the British Minister in the Middle East Lord Moyne assassinated in Cairo. In 1946 Irgun bombed the King David Hotel in Jerusalem – site of the central offices of the British Mandatory authorities in Palestine – killing 92 military personnel and civilians.[9]

British troops confronted by Palestinians at the Jerusalem gates in the 1929 'Buraq Uprising'.

Britain closed off Jewish migration into Palestine. In 1940, 252 Jewish refugees from Nazi Germany on board the Patria were killed when the ship was scuttled off Palestine. Another ship, the Exodus, which set off from southern France carrying 4,515 Jewish survivors of the holocaust towards Palestine was intercepted by the British and taken back to Europe. The forced disembarkation, and the implicit threat of a return to the camps turned opinion against Britain.

On 2 April 1947 the British government asked the UN Secretary General to convene a special session of the General Assembly to look at Palestine. The Special Conference on Palestine reported on 31 August 1947 proposing the division of Palestine into a Jewish and an Arab state, under the Partition Plan. In November, the General Assembly ratified the report. In it the Jewish state got 56.47 per cent of the land and the Arab state 42.88 per cent – with Jerusalem made an international zone. On the eve of the partition Jews had owned 5.6 per cent of the land and made up 36 per cent of the population. The Zionists accepted the plan, the Palestinians and the Arab states rejected it. The voting was 33 for and 13 against with 10 abstentions, including Britain.[10]

On 31 March 1948 Zionists launched attacks on Arab communities outside and in their allocated zone. The Zionist forces occupied Tiberias on 17 April, Haifa on 22 April, Safed on 7 May and Jaffa on 13 May 1948, as well as many other small towns and villages. One of the more shocking attacks was upon the village of Deir Yassin near Jerusalem where 245 were killed. Around that time 340,000 Palestinians fled to neighbouring Arab states. Arabs call this time the 'Nakba', or catastrophe. On 14 May 1948 the State of Israel was declared.[11]

The intensity of the Zionist campaign was a response to the trauma of the holocaust in Europe. Zionist leaders like David Ben-Gurion, Chaim Weizmann and Menachem Begin were determined to fight without pity because they drew the conclusion from the German 'final solution' that not to meant extermination.

By contrast the Palestinians were in disarray. The struggles of the 1930s saw many of their leaders escape the British mandate. In 1948 the Palestinians were dependent upon the support and leadership of other Arab states. King Abdallah of Jordan was committed to defend Jerusalem from the Israelis but just as sure that the Arabs of Palestine should be under Jordanian rule.

The attacks on Arab towns and the Israel's Declaration of Independence drew an answer from the Arab states but it was a feeble one. In the first Arab-Israeli war 10,000 Egyptians, 4,500 Jordanians, 3000 Syrians, 3000 Iraqis and 15,000 local Palestinian fighters took on an Israeli force of 30,000 between 15 May and 11 June. A truce was brokered by Sweden's Count Bernadotte on behalf of the United Nations. In the armistice the Israelis increased their force to 70,000 and fighting started again on 8 July, with Israel taking the towns of Ramleh and Lydda from the Jordanians easily. When the United Nations tried to sanction the belligerents Abraham Stern's Lehi organisation killed their representative Count Bernadotte. A third stage in this Arab-Israeli war began when Israel pushed south against the Egyptian Army positions. Colonel Gamal Abdel Nasser led a successful Egyptian defence against this attack, one of few Arab successes in the fighting. The Israelis moved into Galilee and Sinai. Fighting ended on 7 January 1949.

For Britain, the collapse of the Palestine Mandate was difficult. They had been seen to fail in the face of a determined national liberation movement. The creation of the State of Israel had been fostered by British divide-and-rule tactics, though it plainly had its own internal dynamic. British and American attitudes to the new Israeli state were conflicted. On the one hand Arabs were understandably angered by the loss of so much territory to the upstart Israel – and that jeopardised friendly relations between Britain and the Arabs. On the other hand it still suited Britain (and later America) to see Arab nationalists sent into disarray by this militant regional power.

Later on, in the Cold War, Israel was more clearly on the side of the West in its ideological battle with the Communist East. But that was not immediately the case. Soviet Russia was the first state to recognise Israel on 17 May 1948, and it had supported the United Nations partition plan. Only later did the USSR support radical Arab states in their regional conflict. Britain still had a crown colony in Aden and enjoyed exclusive relations with other states in the Persian Gulf. Troops were based in Aden, Cyprus, Egypt, Iraq and Libya. 'We felt that the British should continue to carry a major responsibility for its stability and security', American President Eisenhower said: 'The British were intimately familiar with the history, traditions and peoples of the Middle East.'[12]

Suez 1956

Egypt's constitutional status was ambiguous from the days of the 'veiled protectorate' right through to after the end of the Second World War. In that conflict, Fuad's successor King Farouk (r. 1936–52) was again faced with *de facto* British rule and occupation as both the North Africa campaign and the invasion of Italy were mounted from Britain's military bases in Egypt, which housed fifteen divisions, sixty-five air squadrons and the Royal Navy fleet in the Mediterranean. In the course of the war King Farouk was threatened with being deposed if he did not dismiss the elected Wafd Party government.

British demobilisation took troops out of the bases in Egypt but left *eighty thousand* in charge of the 'canal zone' base which went on ninety miles along the canal and went as far as sixty miles to the west. In 1952 nationalist feelings were running high against the British-policed canal zone. After some attacks on British troops they imposed a cordon around it searching Egyptians as they left and entered.[13]

On 25 January of that year at Ismailia about halfway along the canal a detail of auxiliary Egyptian policemen challenged the British troops' authority on Egyptian soil. The British opened fire with light arms and tanks, killing 41 and wounding another 72. Egypt erupted in rioting. British watering holes like the Shepheards Hotel, Groppi's tea rooms, Badia's Club, and the St James restaurant were attacked. At the British Turf Club nine British civilians were killed. When the Egyptian police tried to take control the fighting got worse – seventeen Europeans and fifty Egyptians were killed.[14]

That July, a radical nationalist group led by Gamal Abdel Nasser, the Free Officers took control of Army Headquarters. Two days later on 26 July 1952, King Farouk abdicated, and General Mohammed Naguib was made Prime Minister, though the head of the Revolutionary Command Council was Nasser, who became Prime Minister in 1954.

As a leader Nasser was bold, taking advantage of the divided loyalties of the Cold War by seeking arms and aid from the Soviet bloc, visiting the Soviet Union and India. He was looking for western aid for the Aswan High Dam project and when that was not forthcoming nationalised the Suez Canal to finance the dam and other modernisation projects. British Parliamentarians were scandalised.

The canal was seen as being vital to British interest. Two-thirds of the canal traffic in 1955 was made up of oil tankers going to Europe. One third of the 14,666 ships that passed through the canal were British. Sixty thousand British troops passed through the canal every year, on their way to military bases east of Aden. Britain owned 44 per cent of the Suez Canal Company and nine of its 32 directors were British. The annual dividend to Britain was about £8 million.[15]

The House of Lords was in broad agreement that Nasser was 'a kind of Arab Hitler' – or 'Hitler on the Nile' as the *Daily Mail* headlined. Even the radical left winger Nye Bevan said caustically that 'if the sending of police and soldiers in the darkness of the night to seize somebody else's property is nationalisation, Ali Baba used the wrong terminology'.[16]

In a series of editorials, probably written by David Mitrany, the *Manchester Guardian* argued that 'it was a heavy day for the world when the canal that has for so long been an international interest passed under a violently nationalist government'. Later, the *Guardian* suggested that there might 'be a way of reconciling Egypt's interests with the rest of the World by creating a new international authority for supervising the canal without ownership'. Such an authority 'could collect revenues on behalf of the Egyptian government'.[17]

With the French Prime Minister Guy Mollet and the Israelis, Eden agreed a plan that Israel would spark a conflict with Egypt, and then the British and French would invade to keep the peace. When they were planning the attack Israeli Prime Minister David Ben Gurion felt that British Foreign Secretary John Selwyn Lloyd treated him 'like a subordinate'. Ben Gurion protested at the subterfuge of 'making Israel look like an aggressor while Britain and France look like peace lovers' – but went along with it anyway.[18]

On 29 October 1956 the Israelis attacked Egypt across the Sinai desert, and the British and French (as agreed) demanded both sides withdraw ten miles. When Egypt refused to comply, British and French paratroopers invaded – landing 13,500 British and 8,500 French troops. US President Eisenhower was alarmed, not having been told of the plan, which unfolded on the eve of the US Presidential elections. Eisenhower's decision not to back the British action was costly for America, he said – 'a sad blow because, quite naturally, Britain not only has been, but must be our best friend in the world'.[19] The *New York Times* later explained that the invasion had led to 'an irrevocable loss of prestige and friendship by the British and French' – which made them less useful allies to the United States.[20] Eisenhower would not back Britain because he felt that he had been double-crossed by Eden who had 'not consulted us on anything'. The French and British even vetoed a US ceasefire resolution at the United Nations Security Council. Looking at the impact of the conflict on world oil supply Eisenhower knew that America's was hardly affected but Europe's was seriously threatened. He said, 'I'm inclined to think that those who began this operation should be left to sort out their own problems – to boil in their own oil, so to speak'.[21]

Britain was condemned in the UN General Assembly alongside its allies France and Israel (of Commonwealth countries only Australia and Canada backed Britain). Sterling was losing value hourly as US investors sold off their reserves and the US refused to bail them out until they agreed to pull out. More decisive than all of the international fall-out was the underlying weakness of Eden's domestic position. The military planning for the invasion was bungled and slow. The Cabinet was split. For the opposition Labour Party Hugh Gaitskell attacked the 'unlawful' invasion. Protestors filled Trafalgar Square demanding withdrawal.

Eden agreed to withdraw. By Christmas of 1956 all the British troops had left. Churchill said that it was stupid to invade, but that having started it was a bigger mistake to withdraw – and even Eisenhower said he was surprised that they did. British authority in the Middle East was greatly diminished.[22]

Britain's position in the Mediterranean was greatly shaken by the impact of the Nasser rebellion. EOKA's guerrilla war against the British in Cyprus had already exacted a high price, and in 1960 Britain negotiated independence with the proviso that it kept the military bases at Akrotiri and Dhekelia. In 1963 Cyprus's Turkish minority protested against President Archbishop Makarios's proposed changes to the constitution, and the British army intervened to separate Greek and Turkish Cypriots. Major-General Peter Young divided the island along a 'green line'. In 1974 Turkey invaded to take control of Northern Cyprus, while the rebuilt EOKA organisation overthrew Makarios. The division of the country led to 3000 killed and a further 2,100 missing, while 200,000 Greek Cypriots and 40,000 Turkish Cypriots were displaced in the population transfers across the 'green line'.[23]

In 1964 Britain agreed a qualified independence to Malta while retaining control of some military bases. Then in 1972 Prime Minister Dom Mintoff negotiated a leaving date of 1979, adopting a more stridently anti-British stance.

Rallying the Conservative states in the Middle East

On February 1955 British Prime Minister Eden signed an agreement with the Moslem states, Turkey, Iraq, Iran and Pakistan, the Baghdad Pact or Middle East Treaty Organisation, for a mutual defence alliance against Soviet influence in the region. The Pact was not immediately successful. In Baghdad itself, on 14 July 1958 Abd al-Karim Qasim led a coup against Prince Faisal and nationalised British Petroleum's assets in Iraq. Washington stood back from the Pact, fearing that it would be boxed in, leaving Britain to rally the conservative Middle East states.

Britain's rearguard defence against radical Arab nationalism did chime with Eisenhower's new view that order must be maintained. He announced the 'Eisenhower doctrine' on 5 January 1957 that if nations of the Middle East were threatened 'by alien forces hostile to freedom' then the US and its allies would come to their defence. Everyone understood that Eisenhower's doctrine was to fight communism. That America itself, or the former colonial powers Britain and France might be 'alien forces hostile to freedom' was of course inconceivable to Washington as it was to London or Paris.

In practice it was not the Soviet Union that pulled the conservative Middle Eastern states together, so much as the threat from Nasserite Egypt. Sudan's nationalists had been open to the strategy of union with Egypt in the 1920s and the British administration pushed 'Sudanisation' of the civil service and even a tentative offer of self-government to head off that prospect. With the overthrow of King Fuad, the appeal of collaborating with the revolutionary regime in Egypt revived, especially as the first President, Mohamed Neguib was himself half-Sudanese. Now it was the Egyptians who were demanding Sudan's independence and the British who were stalling. Unable to head off the demand for elections they were dismayed to see the most militant party, Ismail al-Azhari's National Unionist Party win the elections. Azhari was weakened by rebellions of non-Muslims in the South, and his coalition split. Soon after, military leader General Ibrahim Abboud led a coup against the civilian government with the support of the British.[24]

In July of 1957 British paratroopers were sent to Amman to help Jordan face down a Nasser-inspired revolt there. In 1962 the Royalists of North Yemen were overthrown by the Nasser-inspired national movement, immediately putting pressure on the British Aden Protectorate. British forces launched raids against Yemeni positions beyond the protectorate. Billy McLean, of the Conservative Party's 'Aden Group', helped recruit British mercenaries to fight alongside Yemeni Royalists and destabilise the Republic.

Britain's secret service chiefs organised a clandestine force of mercenaries – mostly Special Air Service (SAS) men operating off-the-books – and Saudi troops to undermine the Yemeni nationalists. More than £30million of colonial development 'aid' was wasted on bribes to venal tribal chiefs to buy their loyalty to the Saudis.

In Aden, in 1966, the British officer commanding Lieutenant Colonel Colin 'Mad Mitch' Campbell's brutal war against the guerrillas and Caesarist rule span so far out of control that he was made to resign. The officers had initiated inter-platoon rivalry by awarding Robertson's Jam golliwog stickers to units for each killing of an Arab. In time, though, it was the British position in Aden that was undermined.[25]

As well as operations in Yemen the British Army were active in Oman between 1968 and 1975. Oman, though, had never been a British colony, nor even a protectorate, but in truth it was a client state. British officers trained and led the Sultan's Armed Forces, and officials seconded from the Foreign Office advised on economic and national policy. Dhofar, in the west of Oman, had long nursed ambitions to independence and a lively secessionist movement, the People's Front for the Liberation of the Arab Gulf drew on as many as 5000 fighters. According to a British Joint Intelligence Committee report the 'majority of Dhofaris appear at least passively to support the rebels in in preference to any attractive alternative'.[26]

The Special Air Service sent 60 men under Brigadier Roderick Semple to train and lead units of the Sultan's Armed Forces in the fight against the Dhofari People's Front. In London the Joint Intelligence Committee thought that the Sultan Sa'id was the biggest barrier to success in the anti-insurgency fight because he would not fund development in the region. They speculated that a likely and favourable outcome would be the overthrow of the Sultan in favour of his son Qaboos. Qaboos was educated at a private school in England and then at the military college at Sandhurst before serving in the British Army.

Local British intelligence officer Stewart Crawford wrote that 'we would of course maintain the public position that we had no foreknowledge' and that the coup should be 'presented as an internal matter with the British hand concealed or at least deniable'.[27] Shortly after the SAS arrived in Oman Sa'id was overthrown and Qaboos took over Oman as the SAS took the war to the Dhofaris. The rebels were isolated by 1970 after Nasser's death and succession by the more pro-western Anwar Sadat. Their last big push came in 1973 and in 1975 Qaboos declared the conflict over.

The Trucial States, those Gulf Sheikhdoms that had worked with British India, valued Britain's backing against the tide of Nasserite rebels. When they heard of Britain's desire to withdraw, they proposed that they would pay the British to police the Gulf. As the historian William R. Louis explains: 'The Sheikhs under the initial shock had proclaimed themselves willing to do virtually anything to extend the British presence, including themselves paying for the upkeep of British troops.'[28]

Boys and girls of the People's Front for the Liberation of the Arab Gulf.

Though that proposal was not formally taken up, afterwards Britain related to the Arab states first and foremost as customers for weapons and military support. In 1966 Britain's Ministry of Defence set up the Defence Sales Organisation. Ten years later defence sales had risen from £150 million to £560 million, with the Gulf states chief buyers. Sales in 1976–77 included 1,200 Chieftain tanks to Shah Pahlavi's Iran and another 165 to Kuwait; Rapier anti-aircraft missiles to Iran, Abu Dhabi, Oman and Saudi Arabia; Jaguar jets to Oman and the British Aircraft Corporation's £190 million a year contract to service and maintain the Saudi air force.[29]

In September 1985 the British Government signed the Al Yamanah deal to supply Saudi Arabia 72 Tornado military jets and 30 Hawk trainer jets made by British Aerospace – a contract worth £20 billion, with payments offset against a British Petroleum/Shell agreement to receive 500 barrels a day of Saudi crude oil. The deal, that was expanded in a further agreement in 1988, also committed Britain to extensive military training and administration of the Saudi air force and air bases. A naval officer who had worked on the Royal Yacht explained that its main role was as a floating arms bazaar sailing around the Gulf, hawking hardware to Arab rulers.

British military personnel worked in the Gulf as advisors to the former Trucial States, which became the United Arab Emirates, including Dubai and Abu Dhabi. Many of those soldiers worked clandestinely as mercenaries in private security companies that worked for Arab states. Others were seconded by the Ministry of Defence or recruited directly.

In 1958 John Christie of MI6 set up a station in Kuwait and offered to update the Emir Abdullah al-Salim al-Sabah's military. To make the case that Kuwait should join the Commonwealth the British talked up the threat of an Iraqi invasion in 1960 though that never materialised. With British backing the al-Sabahs declared Kuwait an independent country on 19 June 1960. Behind the scenes the Foreign Office had drawn up plans for an invasion of Kuwait, with or without the Emir's blessing, but shelved them.[30] In 1977 there were 140 British forces personnel seconded by the Ministry of Defence to advise and train troops as part of the Kuwait Liaison Team.

Britain's relation to the Conservative Arab states in the end served it well. A triangular trade had developed where America's deficit with Europe led to dollar surpluses, that Europeans used to buy Arab oil ('petrodollars'). Those petrodollars in turn were used to buy British and American arms by conservative Arab states who were hoping to fend off popular movements, like those inspired by Nasser in Yemen and Jordan.

Chapter Thirty-three

DECOLONISATION

The loss of India in 1947, like the loss of southern Ireland in 1921, was a blow to the prestige of the British Empire, however brave a face was put on it. The nationalist challenges to British rule after World War II felt like an unavoidable tide. While the Attlee government struggled to rebuild the Empire, the retreat of the British from Suez in 1956 made it clear that Britain would have to yield more.

In 1960, British Prime Minister Harold Macmillan toured Ghana and Nigeria in West Africa before arriving in Cape Town where he gave a speech to the South African Parliament on 3 February. In the speech Macmillan said:

> the most striking of all the impressions I have formed since I left London is of this African national consciousness. In different place it takes different forms, but it is happening everywhere. The wind of change is blowing through this continent, and whether we like it or not, this growth of national consciousness is a political fact. We must all accept it as a fact, and our national policies must take account of it.

Macmillan was talking about the move towards independence, and his speech meant that Britain was embracing decolonisation. South African Prime Minister Henrik Verwoerd, objected that there would have to be justice for the white man as well as the black man, and it was the white who had brought civilisation to the continent. In the Parliament at Westminster the Monday Club was formed as a right-wing pressure group to resist the 'Winds of Change'. But Macmillan had caught the mood. Britain would embrace decolonisation, the better to manage it. That December the United Nations General Assembly, affirming that 'the process of liberation is irresistible and irreversible', passed Resolution 1514, 'on the granting of independence to colonial countries and peoples' which said 'all peoples have the right to self-determination'. Britain wanted to make sure that decolonisation was something that they stayed ahead of rather than something that was done to them.

Colonies achieving independence after World War II.

India	15 August 1947
Pakistan	15 August 1947
Myanmar	4 January 1948
Ceylon	4 February 1948
Ghana	6 March 1957
Federation of Malaya	31 August 1957
British Somaliland	1 July 1960

Cyprus	16 August 1960
Nigeria	1 October 1960
Sierra Leone	27 April 1961
South Africa	31 May 1961
South Cameroons (became part of Cameroun)	1 October 1961
Tanganyika	9 December 1961
Jamaica	5 August 1962
Trinidad and Tobago	31 August 1962
Uganda	9 October 1962
Federation of Malaysia	16 September 1963
Zanzibar	10 December 1963
Kenya	1 December 1963
Nyasaland	6 July 1964
Malta	21 September 1964
Gambia	18 February 1965
Rhodesia	11 November 1965
Guiana	26 May 1966
Botswana	30 September 1966
Lesotho	4 October 1966
Barbados	30 November 1966
Yemen	30 November 1967
Mauritius	12 March 1968
Swaziland	6 September 1968
Tonga	4 June 1970
Fiji	10 October 1970
Qatar	3 September 1971
United Arab Emirates	2 December 1971
Grenada	7 February 1974
Seychelles	29 June 1976
Tuvalu (Gilbert and Ellice Islands)	1 October 1978
St Lucia	22 February 1979
Saint Vincent, Windward Islands	27 October 1979
Kiribati (Gilbert and Ellice Islands)	12 July 1979
Vanuatu	30 July 1980
Saint Kitts-Nevis and Anguilla	19 September 1983
Hong Kong	30 June 1997

At first the Colonial Office tried to manage decolonisation by bundling the colonies into larger federations. That way Britain could retreat from domestic administration while retaining influence over the federations in their relations with one another. This was a formula that had been worked out by government advisor David Mitrany who wrote that production 'in Africa, is likely to be put on an international basis both for greater economic effectiveness and to neutralise it politically'.[1] But as it turned out these federations proved unstable: the West Indies Federation was superseded by Jamaican independence in 1962; the Central African Federation (Northern Rhodesia, Southern Rhodesia and Nyasaland) broke up in 1963 – as its African subjects feared it would be an instrument of white rule; the union of Singapore and Malaya broke up in 1965, and the Protectorate of South Arabia became independent Yemen in 1968. 'A federation was attempted in the British islands' of the Caribbean, remembered the Trinidadian historian C. L. R. James, 'the British being anxious to rid themselves of the responsibility of these islands'.[2]

The FO realised that it would have to deal directly with the leaders of independence movements – once it had managed to beat back direct challenges to its power. Julius Nyerere, Hastings Banda and Kenneth Kaunda had all been imprisoned by the British and had to be released to negotiate independence for Tanzania, Malawi and Zambia respectively.

Britain abandoned its mandate to Palestine in 1948. The British occupation of Iraq ended in 1947 and British bases there were given up in 1954. In 1951 Egypt withdrew from the Anglo-Egyptian Treaty of 1936. The same year Libya, which had been surrendered by Italy to a British and French administration in 1947, declared independence. Sudan won its independence from Britain in 1956. Singapore left the Federation of Malaya in 1965. Military bases were abandoned in Cyprus (1960), Malta (1964) and Aden (1967).

(Source: Bridgewater Associates)

Accommodating the Commonwealth

For the Commonwealth to work, Britain would have to deal with the post-colonial leaders. After centuries of dictating the terms, British Prime Ministers would have to take into account native opinion. British Prime Ministers were heavily criticised at Commonwealth summits over the colour bar in the settler colonies of South Africa and Rhodesia, as it was then known. Even Britain's domestic race relations were a source of anxiety. Attacks on Afro-Caribbean migrants to London and Nottingham in rioting in 1958 were widely condemned in the West Indies, to the embarrassment of the Foreign Office.[3]

As Britain gave up direct control of colonies it had to work out how to keep up its influence overseas. The most important direct influence was through the treaties that colonies signed up to when they got independence. It was Britain's first goal to get former colonies to join the British-led Commonwealth. After that British treaties of independence often included clauses for states that were nominally independent to accept British diplomatic, military and economic advisors. Such offers were often tied to trade deals and aid in the form of credit. Poorer countries without the resources could sign up to accept military advisors or development programmes. Under the terms of the Overseas Service Act (1961) 41 former colonies got grants to pay for 11,000 colonial service officials to stay on as civil servants.

In his 1965 book *Neo-Colonialism* Ghana's Prime Minister Kwame Nkrumah said that the other way that former colonisers kept up their influence was in the private sector. He argued that though Ghanaians had control over the political government of Ghana, this could mean very little when the same European companies that owned the industries and plantations in the country before decolonisation carried on playing a key role afterwards.

The influence of European investors over nominally independent states in Africa, Asia and the Caribbean carried on through their ownership of key industries. The monopoly over technical expertise and over access to investment funds gave Europeans – Britons in the case of Ghana – continuing control. The historian of decolonization A. J. Stockwell echoed Nkrumah's outlook when he said that 'decolonization was the pursuit of imperialism by other means'.[4]

Where indirect influence was not enough Britain would need to be able to intervene, whether through diplomatic pressure, sanctions or militarily. 'Ministers should consider the means by which we prepare to withdraw' Cabinet Secretary Burke Trend wrote about the British presence in the Gulf, 'but also to retain the capability of intervening, if necessary in the future'.[5]

Government advisors and private investors between them carried on a considerable influence over newly independent states. But as the colonial apparatus shrunk, British officials needed other ways to shape the political outcomes in former colonies.

The Information Research Department

In 1948, the Government set up the Information Research Department (I. R. D.) within Military Intelligence Department 6 (MI6). The aim of the department was to research and prepare intelligence and propaganda to promote British interests overseas. As they interpreted it, that meant fighting the influence of communism, and, in the name of anti-communism, any radical or nationalist challenge to Britain. The I. R. D. took the view that 'the British Broadcasting Corporation Overseas Service is obviously a most important vehicle for anti-Communist publicity'. The I. R. D. set about making sure its broadcasters were properly briefed.[6]

In 1956 Hugh Greene, controller of the Overseas Service of the BBC joined an I. R. D. committee on Egypt where anti-Nasser propaganda was cooked up, mostly accusing him of being a dupe of the communists.[7] MI6 and the I. R. D. set up operations in other countries, like the Arab News Agency in Egypt and the Globe News Agency in Calcutta. The Arab News Agency was resented by Reuters as a rival, so MI6 paid Reuters £28,000 a year to let the Arab News Agency be its sole distributor in the Middle East.[8] The Information Research Department also translated and published cheap editions of George Orwell's books *Nineteen Eighty-Four* and *Animal Farm* for Indian, Iranian and East European markets, hoping that their anti-Stalinist message would undermine communist influence.[9] Another press venture Background Books published booklets like *Why Communism Must Fail* by Bertrand Russell, *Trade Unions: True or False?* by Vic Feather, the assistant General Secretary to the Trades Union Congress. Brian Crozier, who would go on to work for the *Economist* wrote *The Struggle for the Third World* (1966) and *Neo-Colonialism* (which tried to rebut the argument that decolonisation was an opening to 'neo-colonialism' by the back door,

1964). The books 'were aimed mostly at readers in the Third World who were getting a higher education in English even if that wasn't their first language, e.g. university students in India and Africa', explained editor Stephen Watts. The imprint was taken over by the publishers Bodley Head.[10]

As well as the Information Research Department MI6 had many other important contacts among businessmen and government advisors working in the former colonies. Roland 'Tiny' Rowland became head of the London and Rhodesian Mining and Land Company, later 'Lonrho' and in the 1980s made connections South African and Zimbabwean national liberation movements. David Mitrany worked for British intelligence in the First World War and then writing the history of the that conflict for the Carnegie Institute. He went on to work as an advisor to the British government and Unilever from 1943, as well as a leader writer for the *Guardian* newspaper. Kenyan palaeontologist Richard Leakey worked in the 1960s to 'Kenyanise' the National Museum and then from 1989 as head of the Wildlife Conservation and Management Department, where he campaigned against poachers. Later Leakey was active in opposition politics before brokering a deal between President Daniel arap Moi and the World Bank where he led a team of 'anti-corruption' experts who helped stabilise the country in line with international donors' demands. The writer and explorer Laurens van der Post befriended Zulu chief Gatsha Buthelezi and worked as a go-between for him and the British government. All of these connections helped Britain to maintain its influence upon the developing world after independence.

Academics and the Developing World

The School of Oriental and African Studies' (SOAS) main work between the wars had been to train colonial officials. With decolonisation these were fewer over time. In their submission to the Scarborough Commission into funding higher education SOAS set out the problem that 'there has been a widespread feeling in Oriental countries that the attitude of Britain to their civilisations was highly contemptuous'. The understanding was growing that 'in the interests of good international relationships we cannot go on ignoring the manners and customs of the greater part of the world's population'.[11]

In 1949 the Foreign Office asked SOAS to teach short courses in Arabic and 260 students were sent from the armed and colonial services, with another 36 from banks and businesses attending – by 1956 about half that number went. The businesses that sent employees on short courses included the United African Company, British American Tobacco, Anglo-Iranian Oil, Burmah-Shell, Imperial Chemicals Industries and Metal Box.[12]

Research at SOAS included a big project, the 'Restatement of African Customary Law', in 1959, under Professor A. N. Allott. The study was in the Lugard 'dual mandate' mould, arguing that with rapid 'and in some places a catastrophic change', 'African governments need',

a close and accurate restatement of the present condition of the customary law, especially the customary law of land and tenure, succession, the family and marriage, all of which form part of the social bedrock.

So it was that the work on the restatement of Africa's customary law began in Bloomsbury in London.[13] The project was funded by the Nuffield Foundation.

Elsewhere in the school C. D. Cowan was drafting a modern economic history of South East Asia and the Far East with the help of the Ford Foundation. In 1966 the *New York Times* exposed the extensive but hidden Central Intelligence Agency funding and operation behind a lot of the Ford Foundation's work (as well as the Carnegie and Rockefeller Foundations). Another SOAS project that had been launched with help from the United States' Central Intelligence Agency (CIA) was the *China Quarterly*, which the school took over after the International Association for Cultural Freedom that set it up was exposed as a CIA front organisation.

A number of spies had senior positions in SOAS from the first Director of the School Denison Ross who had been head of a Military Intelligence 5 section. SOAS graduate Ann Lambton worked in the Teheran legation in the 1930s before returning to as a Professor of Persian at SOAS, in a post funded by Anglo-Iranian Oil. Lambton was said to have been one of the architects of the plan to overthrow Iranian Prime Minister Mohammed Mossadegh. Other SOAS academics were given temporary postings to the Foreign and Diplomatic Services covering their area in times of crisis, like C. D. Cowan, during the 1965 Malay-Indonesia crisis, and Paddy Honey during the Laos crisis of 1961.

The Imperialist Rearguard

From the first moves towards decolonisation right-wingers in the Conservative Party and in Military Intelligence organised to frustrate it, often working with the white settlers in the colonies.

In the House of Commons on the 21 July 1947 Labour MP Tom Driberg spoke out about the way that the intransigent rearguard of the Empire was trying to sabotage Burmese independence after the popular leader Aung San was murdered: 'the moral guilt of the assassinations attaches less to the brutal gunmen in Rangoon than to the Conservative gentlemen here who incited U Saw to treachery and sabotage'. Driberg meant the 'Friends of the Burmese Hill People', a group set up by the former colonial governor Reginald Dorman-Smith and Lieutenant Colonel John Cromarty Tulloch to undermine Burma's independence, by promoting separatism and disorder. Tulloch was helped by Frank Owen of the *Daily Mail*. Later he was exposed for sending guns to the opposition to fight against Aung San's government. Though the cause went under many names and had many different members, there was a right-wing opposition to decolonisation policy throughout the post-war era.

In 1954, leading Tory back-benchers organised as the Suez group to vote against the government's decision to withdraw from the canal zone. The leaders of the Suez Group were Captain Charles Waterhouse, MP for Leicester South-East, and Julian Amery MP for Preston and son of the wartime Tory minister Leo Amery, Victor Montagu – Lord Hinchingbrooke, Major Harry Legge-Bourke, MP for Ely who had been aide to the British Ambassador in Cairo during the war, and new MP John Biggs-Davison.

David Stirling in 1942

Afterwards, many of the Suez group became the Aden group lobbying for a more militant policy against the Nasser-inspired revolt there. They included Amery, Cabinet Ministers Enoch Powell, Peter Thorneycroft and Duncan Sandys, and the wartime Special Operations Executive officer and Inverness MP Neil 'Billy' McLean (who spent time with the Yemeni Royalist opposition leaders).[14]

The Suez-Aden group had its own publicity campaigns and the sympathetic firm Johnson Publications put out their books bemoaning the end of Empire, like Biggs-Davison's *Africa – Hope Deferred* (1972, 'his view of Africa is sombre', reported the *Times Literary Supplement*), former District Commissioner Robin Short's *African Sunset* (1973, 'how English aspirations for a better life for Africans foundered under the "Winds of Change" policy') and Michael Wright's *Zambia – I Changed My Mind* (1972, 'a Liberal criticises one-party rule in Zambia').

Colonel David Stirling, who founded the Special Air Service, organised a mercenary group Watchguard International to recruit men to fight in Aden and Oman, and also KAS Enterprises, which was active in Namibia. Stirling also began to organise a secret army in preparation for a breakdown in civil order in Britain called GB 75 but backed off when his plans were exposed in *Peace News* (the plot was parodied in Channel 4's sitcom, 'Fairly Secret Army', broadcast in 1984). Stirling was associated with the millionaires James Goldsmith and John Aspinall.

Alongside and sometimes overlapping the Suez Group were other far-right pressure groups who wanted to stop decolonisation. The League of Empire Loyalists was led by Arthur Chesterton, who had been in the British Union of Fascists, but succeeded in rallying a number of Conservative Party supporters despite the disapproval of the Party leadership. Some Empire Loyalists, like John Tyndall, Colin Jordan and Martin Webster went on to be leaders of Britain's far right parties in the 1970s. The outlook of the Suez/Aden group helped shape Margaret Thatcher's Conservative administrations of 1979–90. Peter Thorneycroft was Conservative Party chairman and John Biggs-Davison was Chair of the right-wing Monday Club.

Chapter Thirty-four

WHITE SETTLER REVOLT

White settlers in Africa commanded a remarkable degree of control over the lands they settled though they were a minority, right up to independence and, informally, beyond. European communities in Kenya, Tanzania and Uganda were privileged in political influence and social power. Independence threatened handing over political control at least to a black national leadership. In Southern Africa and Rhodesia the white settlers were deeply entrenched. They were still a minority of the population (unlike white settlers in Australia, New Zealand or Canada). But they were a large minority with a lot of control over central government and the economy. They enjoyed broad privileges over the majority black population. Decolonisation, as it had played out in West and East Africa was a real threat to those privileges. In South Africa and Rhodesia in particular 'independence' would look very different from decolonisation elsewhere.

Apartheid South Africa

South Africa's elder statesman Jan Smuts had risen from a Boer commando in the war of 1899–1902 to lead the South African Army alongside the British in the First World War, and then again in the Second, where he was made a Field Marshal and a member of the British War Cabinet. He was Prime Minister of the Union South Africa – its first – from 1919 to 1924, and then again from 1939 to 1948.

A valued champion of the British Empire, Smuts represented the common struggle of Briton and the Afrikaner to rule in South Africa and as a global power. But in 1948, along with his United Party, Smuts lost the election to Daniel François Malan's Nationalists. Smuts and Malan were both believers in white rule in South Africa, but Malan's campaign spoke to a fear that white people would have to share the government of the country with the black South Africans.

The share of the population between the races was stable at around one fifth white to two thirds black between the censuses of 1904 and 1960; the white population rose to four million by 1960, from a little over a million in 1904, while the black population grew from 3.5 million to 10.9 million in 1960. The mixed-race population – called 'coloured' in South Africa – made up a little less than a tenth of the population and around 3 per cent were Indian.

Among whites the two main groups were the English-speaking and Afrikaans-speaking (descendants of the Dutch Voortrekkers). The English speakers tended to live in the Cape and along the coast, in East London, Durban and Port Elizabeth; while Afrikaners lived inland, around Johannesburg, and north in the Transvaal (that province north of the Vaal River). Malan's Nationalist Party was more rooted among Afrikaners and played on their resentment at being the poorer whites (which they were), while Smuts' United Party had more support among white English speakers. The Nationalists warned that Smuts' 'Fagan Commission' aimed to relax restrictions on natives staying in white areas. A rival commission set up by the Nationalists argued for stricter controls.

Malan's Nationalist Party manifesto in 1948 drew on the ideas of the Pretoria University sociologist Geoff Cronjé who wrote a number of books in the forties about 'apartheid' – the separation of the races, and about the white man's responsibility of 'guardianship' towards the less developed 'Bantu'. The Election slogan ran: *Die Kaffir op sy plek en die koelie uit die land!*, or, 'the native in his place and the coolie out of the country!'

Another ideological source for the 'apartheid' idea came from the South African Bureau of Racial Affairs, which had many supporters at Stellenbosch University like the anthropologist W. Eiselen who was an advisor to the Native Affairs Secretary Hendrik Verwoerd (later Prime Minister).

The ideas of apartheid were not that different from the colour bars in operation in the White Highlands in Kenya, or the Lugard principle of 'native administration'. What set South Africa apart was that the Nationalist Party governments that ruled there from 1948 to 1994 realised their 'apartheid' policy much more rigidly and systematically.

From the moment Malan was elected separate counters at the Post Office appeared, as did separate carriages on trains in Cape Town. Soon after the Nationalist government started to put in place the legal scaffolding that would shore up the apartheid society:

- The 1950 Group Areas Act under which the Government proclaimed residential and business areas designated for different races.
- The 1950 Population Registration Act – under which all new births were recorded by race.
- The 1950 Immorality Act that outlawed interracial marriage.
- The 1950 Suppression of Communism Act.
- The 1951 Separate Representation of Voters Act.
- The 1952 Natives (Abolition of Passes and Coordination of Documents) Act – which despite the name brought in a rigorous system of passes (the 'reference book' or 'dompas' as it was called) and a vast register of natives.
- A 1952 amendment to the Native Areas Act made African women carry passes, which meant that a great many were effectively restricted to the Reserved Areas.
- The 1954 Natives Resettlement Act allowed for the clearing of unofficial townships and the relocation of their residents elsewhere.
- In 1956 the Separate Representation of Voters Act disenfranchised coloured voters.
- The 1956 Industrial Conciliation Act had a clause saying that Africans were not 'employees' so not covered by trade union legislation that protected whites.

Alongside the markedly oppressive rules demarcating black South Africans and restricting their movement, their subordination to the Native Administration was redoubled.

Verwoerd as Native Secretary commanded authority not just over blacks in the native reserves but over all blacks, on the theory that the native areas were where they belonged. The 1951 Bantu Authorities Act gave the Native Administration new powers to create 'tribal authorities' in rural African reserves. At the same time the old Natives Representative Council was abolished because, said Verwoerd, Bantu people were not meant to get involved in 'general principles of higher politics'.

In 1953, the Bantu Education Act took away secondary schooling for black South Africans but also extended it up to age eleven for all in schools in the African reserves. Africans were to be schooled to obedience, but not in mathematics or other abstract disciplines.

Protesting against the pass laws.

The apartheid system was immediately challenged by African leaders, whose African National Congress (ANC) had first been set up to fight the 1913 Land Act and was already a lively and combative organisation. A 1943 ANC manifesto, Africans' Claims, was written in response to the Allies' Atlantic Charter, and made it clear that in South Africa 'the demands of the Africans for full citizenship rights and direct participation in all the councils of the state should be recognised'. This was a long way from the old formula of asking for votes for 'civilised Africans'.

In 1946 a strike involving African miners at Witwatersrand started on 12 August 1946 and lasted a week. The strike was attacked by police. At least 1,248 workers were wounded and nine killed. In 1949, the ANC youth wing launched a programme of action against the proposed Group Areas Act and the other Apartheid legislation. They organised boycotts, strikes and civil disobedience protests. On 1 May 1950, 18 Africans were shot dead by police after a work stoppage.

Later, 26 June 1952 was named as National Day of Protest when people stayed at home rather than going to work. The tempo of the protests did not stop. In 1955 a Congress of the People was called with the participation of the ANC, the Indian Congress, the Coloured People's Organisation and the Congress of Democrats (largely made up of those who had been supporters of the outlawed Communist Party). Around 3000 delegates met in Klipstown outside Johannesburg to agree a Freedom Charter. It said that the 'rights of the people shall be the same, regardless of race, colour or sex' – a sentiment that was too revolutionary for apartheid South Africa. The Charter also said that 'South Africa belongs to all who live in it, black and white', and also that the country's mineral wealth, banks and monopoly industries should be publicly owned.

The following year 156 of those who had been involved were rounded up to face trial for high treason on the grounds that they were setting out to overthrow the government and create a communist state. The ANC leaders Albert Luluthi, Nelson Mandela and Walter Sisulu were in the dock along with Indian Congress leaders Yusuf Dadoo and Ahmed Kathrada, and communists Joe Slovo and Ruth First.

The trial dragged on as the state struggled to prove that the defendants were communists or committed to anything but peaceful means. International observers like Britain's Louis Blom Cooper watched in astonishment as the process ground on. All the time the African National Congress was growing, using the trial as a platform to establish its authority as the opposition to apartheid. ANC membership grew from 5,000 in 1948 to 100,000 by the end of the 1950s. Finally, the defendants were acquitted in 1961.

In the Reserved Areas rural peoples often rose up against the imposed chiefs of the Bantu Authorities Act. In 1950 the paramount chief in the overcrowded Witzieshoek reserve in the Orange Free State ordered cattle-culling measures only to be faced with a mass revolt. Women rose up against Chief Albert Gopane in the Western Transvaal town of Zeerust for supporting the government pass laws in 1957. When the Native Administration removed a popular chief from Sekhukhuneland in 1958 there were mass protests and the police opened fire on them. In Pondoland in the Eastern Cape in the early 1960s there were many protests against the government collaborating chief Botha Sigcau, when he was appointed to head the Transkei Territorial Authority. In nearby Tembuland there were big protests against Kaizer Mantanzima when he was made paramount chief.[1]

In October 1960 the Nationalist Party consolidated the apartheid regime with a referendum (of white voters) deciding to become a republic. Verwoerd wanted to stay in the Commonwealth but faced with sharp criticism over its racial policies at the following March summit, South Africa withdrew.

Rhodesia

Britain's initial plan for (what was then called) Southern Rhodesia was that it would be bundled together with Northern Rhodesia (today called Zambia) and Nyasaland (Malawi today) into a larger federation. The idea was that the larger unit would be easier to control by Britain, and by the white settlers. Getting a hold of Zambia's copper and other mineral wealth would depend on investment. William Batt, head of American's Economic Cooperation Administration (the 'Marshall Plan') in London had already promised £5 million for Rhodesia, and was confident Americans would 'be repaid in the fullest extent possible in raw materials in which the United States is deficient, such as cobalt, copper, tungsten and chrome'. Lord Home, then Secretary of State for the Commonwealth argued that 'the Federation was the unit most likely to attract such investment'. To Africans in Northern Rhodesia and Nyasaland the Federation looked like a bogus independence that would leave them under the rule of the white settlers of Southern Rhodesia. At a mass meeting in Ndola in the Northern Rhodesian copper belt in 1953 the speaker said that,

> in rejecting Federation with Southern Rhodesia we are not choosing between heaven and hell. Northern Rhodesia is also hell, but the door out of the Federation hell will be more tightly bolted than the door out of the present hell.[2]

The opposition to the Federation was argued by the Southern Rhodesian African National Congress (SRANC) that was founded in 1957. There had been widespread rioting in Northern Rhodesia and the Southern Rhodesian Prime Minister Whitehead suppressed the SRANC with an array of laws from the Unlawful Organisations Act to the Preventative Detentions Acts of 1959, following those up with an Emergency Powers and a Law and Order Act in 1960. There were riots in Bulawayo in June 1960, followed by more in Salisbury (the capital, now Harare), Gwelo, Umtali and Bulawayo again over the Autumn.

The depth of feeling against the Southern Rhodesian settler elite had grown up over decades. The ignominies of the 1930 Land Apportionment Act, which had restricted natives to special areas, were added to by the Land Husbandry Act of 1951. This seemed to pull in the opposite direction, promoting land development in the reserved areas and effectively locking out black Rhodesians who had left the reserves. The point was to make their labour cheaply available to white employers, and it led to a lot of hardship.

African opposition to the Federation meant that Britain granted Nyasaland (Malawi) and Northern Rhodesia (Zambia) independence, under the leaderships of Hastings Banda and Kenneth Kaunda respectively. The future of Southern Rhodesia (henceforth, plain Rhodesia) was unclear. The settlers claimed that since they had been self-governing following the all-white referendum of 1923 their road to independence ought to be straight forward. For the newly independent African states, though, South Africa and Rhodesia's independence were an affront. South Africa's withdrawal from the Commonwealth under the apartheid system institutionalised white supremacy in the independent republic. In December 1962 the Rhodesian Front, a new party led by young MP Ian Smith won the elections on a programme of keeping the white rule in Southern Rhodesia. In talks with Britain's Harold Wilson, Smith reacted against the demand for black majority rule and instead made a Unilateral Declaration of Independence in 1965.

OUTPOSTS OF EMPIRE   SOUTHERN RHODESIA

An idealised view of Rhodesia.

The British position on the white settler states of South Africa and Rhodesia was ambiguous. Publicly, and formally, Britain denounced apartheid, as it did the white supremacy laws in Rhodesia. At the same time Britain cooperated with South Africa's armed forces in the defence of the Cape, and the Royal Air Force had a Rhodesian squadron that served regularly in Aden. So, too, were there considerable British investments in South Africa especially and, to a lesser but still important extent, in Rhodesia. Culturally, there were very strong ties between Britain and South Africa. Between 1964 and 1974, 170,000 Britons settled in South Africa. Rhodesia, too, doubled its white population between 1941 and 1951 through immigration – mostly from Britain. Collaboration between the South African and Rhodesian governments on the one hand, and the British and American governments, on the other hand, in military activities against radical nationalist movements in Africa was extensive, but largely clandestine. (America and Britain both relied on the South African and Rhodesia security forces to fight wars against the MPLA forces in Angola, against the Namibian independence fighters and against Frelimo in Mozambique.)

British policy towards South Africa and Rhodesia showed up the ambiguity of its position. On each occasion that the United Nations General Assembly voted to condemn South Africa's apartheid policy, Britain voted against, until it was in a minority of two (with France) in 1960, when it changed its public position. On Rhodesia, the British Governments of Harold Wilson, Alec Douglas-Home and Edward Heath all argued with the delegations from Salisbury, pressing them to share power with black African leaders, and resisting Rhodesia's right to declare independence unilaterally.

In London the service chiefs made it plain to Prime Minister Harold Wilson that they would on no account wage war against white Rhodesia and Wilson relayed that message to the House of Commons on 1 November 1965. 'If there are those who are thinking in terms of a thunderbolt hurtling from the skies and destroying their enemies, a thunderbolt in the shape of the RAF' Wilson said, 'let me say the thunderbolt will not be coming'.[3] Ian Smith was confident of that, too, since the officers of the Royal Air Force squadron Wilson had sent to Zambia would cross the Zambezi to mess with the Rhodesian Air Force. 'To Smith and Rhodesia', was their Christmas Party toast, honouring the Prime Minister who had himself served in the RAF. Squadron Commander Arthur Bottomley let Salisbury know that they would not attack Rhodesia.[4]

Harold Wilson was persuaded by his senior civil servants that economic sanctions against Rhodesia would soon bring the country to its knees and force them to negotiate. But when those same civil servants drafted the Order in Council it was restricted to British companies, but not their overseas subsidiaries. That was a great advantage for the regime in Rhodesia since it meant that British Petroleum and Shell could trade oil to Salisbury, indirectly, so avoiding sanctions as many other companies did, and as Foreign Secretary George Brown had warned they would.[5]

In any event the differences between Wilson and Heath's governments, and Ian Smith's in Salisbury were not so great. Before it became an issue, Britain had introduced the separate voting roll for black Rhodesians (roll B). Labour and Conservative Prime Ministers agreed with the Rhodesian government that majority rule was something for the future, setting target dates of 1999 or 2035. Many British political and business leaders sympathised with the white colonialists in Rhodesia and South Africa, especially in the Conservative Party.

Bantustans

Faced with demands for black majority votes both South Africa and Rhodesia said that their black populations were represented through the native chiefs. In his memoirs, Rhodesian Prime Minister Ian Smith claimed that the 1964 decision to declare independence from Britain had the backing of native Africans: 'Six hundred and twenty-two Chiefs and Headmen gathered in Salisbury on 22 October for the biggest Indaba ever held in the country', he said. That was after a consultation with 'some 30,000 kraal-heads who, at the level of the family, represented an estimated 3 million tribesmen'.[6]

In South Africa another key Bill passed by the Parliament was the 1959 Promotion of Bantu Self-Government Act. Under that act provision was made to set up 'self-governing' and even 'independent' 'Bantustans'. That way African reserved areas were given formal self-government, with their own flags, football teams, and even security forces. Among the Bantustans were the independent states Transkei (1976), Bophuthatswana (1977) and Ciskei (1981); self-governing states included Kwazulu (1977) and KwaNdebele (1981).

When Transkei was made 'independent' in October 1976 all those with 'Xhosa' stamped in their passbooks lost their South African citizenship. The same thing happened to Tswana when Bophuthatswana was declared in December 1977, and so on. Mangosuthu Gatsha Buthelezi was one of the more successful Bantustan leaders, becoming First Minister of KwaZulu with his own Inkatha Freedom Party. Buthulezi had been a member of the African National Congress, but when he took on his new role he was denounced as a stooge of apartheid – and his chiefly authority did help deflect attacks on South Africa's government.

Minister of Plural Relations and Development Connie Mulder explained in a speech in 1978: 'If our policy is taken to its logical conclusion as far as the black people are concerned, there will not be one black man with South African citizenship.'[7]

Outside of South Africa none of these states' independence was recognised. The Group Areas Act was estimated by the South African Institute of Race Relations to have led already to the removal of 1,820,000 Africans and a further 600,000 of those they called 'coloureds'. With the Promotion of Bantu Self-governing Act, Act No. 46 of 1959 around 3 to 5 million were relocated.

The Second Carnegie Inquiry into poverty and Development in Southern Africa in 1989 summed up the impact of the Bantustan experiment. The average income of a black family in a rural area was about half that of a black family in the city. Almost nine million people were living below the breadline in the 'homelands'. By the early 1980s school spending was R1,385 for each white student and R192 for each black student.[8]

The Profits of Racial Discrimination

Unlike a lot of the British Empire, Rhodesia boomed after the war. Manufacturing output stood at £14.1 million in 1945 but reached £105.1 million by 1957; mining output jumped from £7.7 million in 1938 to £25.8 million in 1957. Tobacco exports grew from £23.2 million in 1945 to £63.8 million in 1953.

With the Unilateral Declaration of Independence Rhodesia was faced with economic sanctions from Britain and the Commonwealth and was prepared for an economic set-back. Instead, the economy boomed some more. Between 1967 and 1974 Rhodesia grew at an average of eight per cent per year. Businesses diversified and the manufacturing sector grew relative to agriculture.[9] Despite the half-hearted sanctions on Rhodesia, the struggle to substitute imported technologies with locally developed ones turned out to be a spur to growth.

South Africa, too, boomed. Over the 1960s output grew by 5.8 per cent a year. White families lived in ranch-style homes with tennis courts and swimming pools, owned Mercedes Benz cars or Toyota trucks, in the kind of suburbs they saw on American television, except that they could afford black maids and gardeners. Enjoying their state protected status, formerly 'poor white' Afrikaners could now afford a middle-class lifestyle.

One way that South Africans were paying for this lifestyle was with foreign export earnings. South Africa's trade with America grew by 79 per cent in the 1960s, and with Britain by 88 per cent. The other way that they could afford such luxury was by the exploitation of black labour. Where black South Africans had made up some of the difference in pay with whites during the Second World War, in the apartheid era their share of income was sharply cut back. Already in 1947 white employees could expect to make ten times as much as black workers made, and by 1970 that had increased to fifteen times as much. Though the black population grew, its share of income shrank to one fifth of all income.[10]

In Rhodesia, too, unrestrained white rule cut black incomes. In rural areas the average income fell from £15 a year in 1956 to £11 in 1968. Black farmers' share of agricultural sales fell from 30 per cent in 1957 to 19 per cent in 1971.[11]

The boom in these two white settler Republics encouraged overseas investors to get a share. British companies were responsible for 60 per cent of all foreign investment in South Africa – around £5 billion. Between 1972 and 1976 profits rose by 202 per cent. In 1978 British banks loaned £1.2 billion to businesses in South Africa.[12] By 1985 Britain's investments had swollen to more than £11 billion – 40 per cent of all overseas investments.

In March 1985 the *Economist* reported that the rate of return on South African mining investments averaged 25 per cent, compared with 14 per cent in the rest of the world, and in manufacturing, returns were 18 per cent, compared with 14 per cent elsewhere. The *Economist*'s cold explanation for the advantage South African investments enjoyed was that 'there is a plentiful supply of cheap labour and usually effective law and order enforcement'. Between 1977 and 1982 the British Overseas Trade Board helped 84 separate trade missions to South Africa, and in 1984 Britain's trade balance there was £497 million in the black.

British firms made good money selling to South Africa's military. Plessey made integrated circuits for weapons systems. Racal Electronics made radios and radio backpacks for the South African Defence Force and for the police. Marconi developed 'tropospheric scatter' communications systems. ICI had a 40 per cent share in African Explosives and Chemical Industries that made fertilisers for local agriculture but also teargas, nerve gas and defoliants for the South African Defence Force's war against the African National Congress's military wing, uMkhonto we Sizwe.

Throughout the sixties and seventies Britain had around £200 million invested in Rhodesia. Another important investor was South Africa. South Africa helped Rhodesia when it was under the British sanctions regime by importing and exporting across its border. Increasingly unpopular, at least in polite society, the two regimes found it useful to collaborate. That gave rise to a growing South African investment in Rhodesia, which grew to something approaching the British share.

National Liberation Struggle

The black subject peoples of South Africa and Rhodesia were understandably outraged at the perverse independence that those two former colonies claimed. Where most people understood that national independence held out the hope that black Africans would govern themselves South African and Rhodesian independence meant the opposite – that the system of white domination that held sway under the British Empire would carry on, now broken free from its original setting.

The theoreticians of the South African Communist Party (who would play a key role in developing the African National Congress's policies) called the apartheid system 'colonialism of a special type' – meaning that they saw the fight for black majority rule as an extension of the struggle against imperialism.

In other ways the perverse independence that the white settler societies fought for tempted many black southern Africans to hope that Britain (and later America) could be persuaded to make the former colonists see sense, or maybe even invade them. It was an understandable wish that the Empire would sort out the mess that it had left behind it. There were enough noises of regret coming from the more liberal end of the British Establishment – the Church of England, some radical intellectuals and MPs, authors and others – to make it seem as if Britain might do the right thing.

In Zimbabwe nationalist leaders like Joshua Nkomo and James Chikerema called outright for Britain to invade to overthrow Ian Smith's white settler regime. 'I expected the British to take some action', recalled Dzingai Mutumbuka: 'I was filled with a sense of hopelessness when they failed to do so.'[13] The African National Congress in South Africa also put great store by its links with British and other international leaders, though these rarely offered anything more than token opposition to apartheid. Military and economic links with the South African regime carried on.

The Commonwealth looked like another avenue for putting pressure on South Africa and Rhodesia to reform. More often, though, Commonwealth leaders used the ANC and the Zimbabwean opposition to embarrass Britain, but little more. The 'front-line' states, Zambia, Malawi, Botswana, and the Portuguese colonies Angola and Mozambique, and Namibia (which had been ceded to South Africa in 1948), were in no position to help. Zambia's Kenneth Kaunda gave the Zimbabwean opposition bases over the Zambesi River from which to attack the Rhodesians. But later Kaunda was under pressure himself and deported a number of fighters back to Rhodesia where they were imprisoned and some executed. At Commonwealth summits the issue was used by the leaders of now-independent former colonies to signal their continuing association with the freedom struggle, before they got down to more mundane matters of governing over their own peoples.

The substantial motor for change was not in the international community but among the African masses. Faced with seemingly insurmountable odds the leadership of the African National Congress, and the two independence groups in Zimbabwe, Robert Mugabe's Zimbabwe African National Union (ZANU) and Joshua Nkomo's Zimbabwe African People's Union (ZAPU), tried every avenue to end white minority rule. The African people in those states saw so many challenges that they had little choice but to resist. The struggle ebbed and flowed, facing crushing defeats and astonishing successes. But with remarkable fortitude the African peoples made apartheid, and the racist rule in Rhodesia close to unworkable, and then unworkable.

The key points in the contest in South Africa were many.

- The 1956 trial, where 156 leaders of the African National Congress and its allies defended themselves against the charge of treason.
- The 21 March 1960 Sharpeville Massacre, where police opened fire on a seven thousand-strong anti-passbook protest, killing 69 and injuring 180 more. Twenty-nine of those killed were children.
- The founding of the ANC's military wing, uMkhonto we Sizwe in December 1960.
- The Rivonia trial where Nelson Mandela and eight other ANC leaders were sentenced to life imprisonment in 1964.
- The Durban strikes and the resurgence of the trade union movement in 1973.
- The 12 June 1976 Soweto uprising, when tens of thousands of black students left school to protest against being taught in Afrikaans and not English. One hundred and seventy-six of the protestors were killed by police.
- The rise of the black consciousness movement in the 1970s and the death of its leader Steve Biko, killed in a police interrogation in 1977.
- The legalisation of trade unions in 1979.
- The founding of the United Democratic Front in 1983, and the subsequent wave of protests.
- The founding of the Cosatu labour federation in December 1985.

Zimbabwe's national liberation struggle was similarly marked by intense conflict, though on a narrower social base. Ian Smith's Rhodesian Front government was in many ways even more rigid than apartheid South Africa.

The determination of Zimbabweans to resist Smith made Rhodesia near ungovernable, though Britain and later the United States, too, did their utmost to impose a settlement. In 1972, British Prime Minister Edward Heath had agreed to Smith's avoidance of majority rule, but before the treaty could be signed, Heath wanted to make sure that Smith could deliver a stable black population. A Commission under the High Court Judge Edward Pearce was sent to investigate.

At each site that Baron Pearce visited – Gwelo, Umtali, Fort Victoria, Shabani and Salisbury – he was met by thousands of African protestors against the proposed settlement. On each occasion police attacked the crowds, opening fire in most cases. Prime Minister Smith's claim that the Indaba was the real representative of the African people was empty. Even in the official record 14 were shot dead in front of Baron Pearce's Commissioners and 1,500 arrested – and the true total was certainly much higher. Pearce was enough of an old-school imperialist himself to say that the repression was 'not unreasonable' but could not support Smith's claim that the settlement had native support. Mass action derailed the British-Rhodesian plan to normalise relations.

The Zimbabwean African National Liberation Army launched its military campaign in December 1972, and the next year stepped up attacks on Rhodesia, leading Smith's government to close the border with Zambia. ZANLA attacks led to the abandonment of around 2,000 of the 6,682 white-owned farms by 1979, covering several million acres.

Rhodesia's Selous scouts terrorised Shona and Matabele communities alike.

As part of its struggle to defeat the guerrillas the Smith government set out to attack their popular base. Africans were herded into 'protected villages' where they were stopped from helping the ZANLA fighters. By July 1974 the 44,000 residents of Chiweshe Tribal Trust Land north-east of Salisbury had been moved into 21 'protected villages'. By August 1977 there were 203 of these villages with 580,000 unhappy inhabitants. The Rhodesian Defence Force backed up curfews with deadly force, killing hundreds. Early in 1977 the Salisbury Regime brought in Operation Turkey which withheld food stores so that villagers could not feed ZANLA fighters. Shops and grinding mills were shut down causing great hardship and hunger.

The white settler regimes of South Africa and Rhodesia worked up the pre-war colonial colour bar into powerful engines of exploitation, making a great many inside and outside southern Africa very rich. They were states that were at war with their own African populations. The independent white republics would not survive beyond the 1980s.

Chapter Thirty-five

POST-WAR BRITAIN

Britain's Empire was renamed a Commonwealth after the war. Almost all of the colonies became independent. Britain still kept up an imperialistic attitude in its foreign policy, keeping military bases overseas, interfering in its former colonies through diplomatic and military means.

Overall, the emergence of the Commonwealth of politically independent states was a sign that the old Empire was less important to post-war Britain. Decolonisation was in the first instance a difficult encounter with the reality of independence movements. Later the Foreign Office worked hard to stay ahead of the decolonisation process, and even drove events. Britain itself was changing, and as in the past, the real driver of relations between the 'mother country' and the (now ex-) colonies was what happened in Britain.

The wartime experience wrought social changes in Britain that were even more profound than those of 1914–18. A society-wide mobilisation, not just to the services but also to industry, worked because of the wartime promise of a welfare commitment to security and prosperity afterwards. Workers' support for 'joint production committees' was rewarded with the official recognition of trade unions in industry and by government. The political mobilisation of the country around the reforms in William Beveridge's 1942 'Social Insurance and Allied Services' report laid the ground for a landslide victory for Clement Attlee's Labour Party at the end of the war.[1]

Labour was in office from 1945 to 1951 under Clement Attlee. The Conservatives were back in power from 1951 to 1964. Labour ruled from 1964 to 1970 under Harold Wilson, and then again from 1974 to 1979, interrupted by Edward Heath's Conservative administration. In 1979 Margaret Thatcher's Conservatives won the first of three elections, and Labour was not again in office until 1997.

Britain's social policy under those post-war governments changed greatly. Both parties were (until 1979) committed to a far greater welfare state, a programme of modernisation and a dirigiste industrial policy. The focus of growth had turned again, away from the global reach of Empire, inwards towards domestic investment – rather as they did in the era of the first industrial revolution.

Clement Attlee, losing the 1951 election.

Growth rates climbed in the post-war reconstruction. The most important dynamic was that between the British working class and the employers. The old colonies mattered less than the class struggle at home. That is not to say that the colonies were not at all important. They were. So, too, were relations with the wider world. But they were all secondary to the cooperation and conflict between labour and capital within the borders of the United Kingdom.

During the war capital and labour were drawn into a kind of social contract with government, sometimes called the 'tripartite system' (because it united the three powers labour, capital and government). Unions were recognised as representative of workers and drawn into a collaborative struggle to increase output. It was an arrangement that encouraged a pointedly patriotic outlook among the Labour leadership and the trade union officials. While commonwealth development was more propaganda than real, in Britain the first Labour government did work with organised labour to meet the balance of payments gap. Even when the Conservatives came to power in 1951 they kept much of the apparatus of class collaboration Attlee's Labour government made.

Attlee's determination to keep hold of the colonies was because of the need for rubber, oil, tin, cocoa and other colonial goods that could be exchanged for dollars. Later, Britain was lost interest in colonies that were often seen as holding her back. The labour economist Paul Mattick thought that 'the end of colonialism was brought about not only by the revolutionary nationalist movements growing out of impoverishment but also by the dwindling profitability of the colonies, which made it easier for their possessors to give them up'. According to the Institute for Commonwealth Studies Director,

Philip Murphy, 'from the mid-1950s to around the late 1980s, there was a fairly steady reduction in the proportion of total British exports and imports flowing to and from the Commonwealth'.[2]

Decolonisation was increasingly embraced as part of a programme for modernising Britain. After the debacle of Suez for Conservative Prime Minister Anthony Eden, his successor Harold Macmillan – also a Conservative – made himself a champion of decolonisation saying that the 'winds of change' were blowing through Africa. Decolonisation was all part of the modernisation drive.

Macmillan's government was alarmed by the rising cost of Britain's military commitments overseas – which ran to eight per cent of output and 700,000 servicemen and women in 1957. The development of Britain's 'independent nuclear deterrent' meant the country could still claim great power status and defend its seat on the United Nations 5-member security council (alongside America, the USSR, France and China). A smaller military force played a role in US-sanctioned policing operations around the world – down from 871,000 in 1952 to 434,000 in 1962.[3]

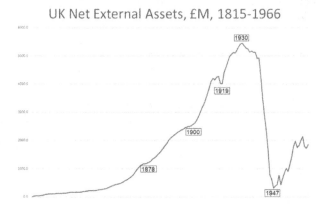

UK Net External Assets, £M, 1815-1966

The UK's overseas investments were repatriated at the end of World War II.

The colonial old guard were made to feel like dinosaurs of another age. At the Theatre shows like 'O what a lovely war!' (1963) mocked the unthinking patriotism sent millions to their deaths in 1914–18. Among the great crowds that protested against the Suez invasion were young middle-class anti-war activists who went to the Partisan Coffee House in Soho where a 'new left' was born. From 1960 many of them would join the marches organised by the Committee of 100 against Britain's 'nuclear deterrent'. British men were bound to give eighteen months' National Service in the armed forces when they got their call-up from 1948. In 1957 the decision was made to wind down National Service and the last finished theirs at the end of 1963.

International affairs were less important for most Britons than the modernisation of the country. In a post-war boom people enjoyed something like full employment and access to new consumer goods on hire purchase. Prime Minister Macmillan dared to say that the British people had 'never had it so good'.

The top British companies in 1965 included those that had been founded in the Edwardian era, like Shell Oil (1907), the British-American Tobacco Company (1902), the Imperial Tobacco Company (1901) and Ford UK (1909); there were also those that were born out of the interwar munitions boom, like Vickers-Armstrong (1928), Imperial Chemical Industries (1926), Hawker-Siddeley (1934), Associated Electrical Industries (1928) and Unilever (1929); there were also some more long-standing companies, like the P&O Steam Navigation Company (founded 1837), Bowater (1881) Courtaulds (1794), Guest, Keen and Nettlefolds (1902, but from John Guest's iron business founded 1759) Midland Bank (1836), Barclays (1690) and Lloyds Bank (1765).[4]

Growth in Britain carried on alongside a declining sterling bloc. Demands to devalue the currency, so that it was not a barrier to exports, grew. The Governor of the Bank of England countered that devaluation would damage Britain's reputation with holders of sterling overseas. Their sterling balances would be worth less than before.

In 1967, Harold Wilson had to concede that the pound would be deflated. In 1950 half of all international trade was paid for with pounds, but by 1970 only a fifth was. Devaluation cost Hong Kong £56 million of the £400 million the banks there held. Singapore lost 157 million Singapore dollars. All across the Commonwealth states that held their reserves in sterling lost out.

Shortly after deflation Wilson announced the withdrawal of British troops from bases 'East of Suez' – mainly in Malaya, Singapore and the Persian Gulf. The Overseas Empire was downsizing. In the House of Commons, on 16 January 1968, some MPs joked about the end of the Roman Empire, to which Wilson replied that maybe Kipling's 1897 poem 'Recessional' would be a better fit. The last stanza of Recessional runs:

> Far-called our navies melt away
> On Dune and headland sinks the fire
> Lo, all our pomp of yesterday
> Is one with Nineveh and Tyre.

Nine years later, a government Green Paper admitted that 'Britain is no longer an imperial power'.[5]

Growth and modernisation created new problems for Britain. Social expectations kept on rising. National pay-bargaining by sector politicised the contest over wages. Full employment gave workers the confidence to go on strike for more. Trade union officials were called in as a moderating influence on an often-militant rank and file. Unofficial strikes began to break out as younger workers' respect for seniority waned.[6]

Apart from the wage conflicts capitalist growth was by the 1970s beginning to slow down. Profit rates were falling. The industrial policy of spotting winners and giving them government backing seemed to have created some large and unwieldy monopolies that were resistant to change. Inertia and bloated inventories created a malaise. Government policy throughout the 1970s turned to restricting wages and demanding greater output from the workforce. The experiments were many, from wage freezes, a 'Social Contract', to a reform of labour agreements. These were contested by organised labour. The governments of Edward Heath, and Harold Wilson were overwhelmed by questions of labour negotiations and large set-piece strikes, alongside many unofficial disputes.

There was better news for the financial markets. Though leading bankers had warned of disaster if Britain devalued things in fact improved. The sterling zone turned out to be less important and the City did better business outside of it. A parallel market was growing up alongside the stock exchange connected to the greater flux in the world economy.

The excess dollars European companies earned but did not spend on US goods – Eurodollars – sloshed around in funds traded in London. There was a growing Eurobond market, too. As in the mid-nineteenth century, European businesses were looking to raise finance for large-scale investments, floating bonds in London. American banks put offices in London which served as a halfway house between Europe and America. A lot of the increased trade in international finance came about because European businesses had caught up with America and were overtaking it. That put big strains on an international finance system that was built around America. The agreement at Bretton Woods that the dollar would serve as an international currency, and be 'as good as gold', was wrecked in 1971 because America's deficit with Europe was too great. Fixed exchange rates were abandoned as currencies' real values diverged.[7]

Later, knock-on effects of these changes would come when the oil producing countries' cartel OPEC pushed up prices in 1973, causing shortages and triggering a recession. Western commentators blamed the Gulf States for bidding up prices. But President Nixon's response to the rising price of oil – putting a ceiling on the price of US crude oil – had the unintended consequence of winding down US production, so that American industries went abroad to buy up the world's surpluses, bidding up prices further. Some Europeans suspected that Washington had let OPEC go ahead because it would damage oil-starved Europe and Japan more.[8]

Instability caused lots of problems for British manufacturers, but for the City of London, with its specialisation in international financial trade, it was good. Large scale loans and transactions were its business. Britain's manufacturing deficit was offset by its so-called 'invisible earnings' – the profits made on financial intermediation, raising loans and banking. Asset management companies like Slater-Walker and John Bentley used cheap credit to buy up moribund firms and break them up, earning the reputation as 'asset strippers'. Big name companies like Rolls Royce, Aston Martin and Bowater were in trouble with their creditors and Prime Minister Edward Heath bearded bankers to demand why they did not invest in British industry. In February 1974, *The Banker* protested that 'the City is probably Britain's biggest exporter' and that anti-banking prejudices were misplaced. Industries, like Rolls Royce (1971), British Leyland (1975) and British Aerospace (1977), were all brought into national ownership, to prevent the wholesale de-industrialisation that threatened.

The slump of the 1970s echoed some of the features of the slump of the 1880s. The interruption in domestic growth was matched by more overseas trade and investments. Most of the international financial trade was between the developed nations. But the large funds that were accumulating were going to have an impact in the developing world, too. Foreign direct investment by UK businesses that had stood at around five per cent of all investment climbed to 15 per cent in 1973.

'The Empire Strikes Back' – migration to Britain

One important way that Britain's colonial ties impacted on domestic life was the growth in migration from the former colonies, or as it was called at the time 'coloured immigration'. Britain's economy grew post war and labour shortages were holding it back. Though it was not official government policy, some institutions like the National Health Service and London Transport set about recruiting labourers from abroad, while many individually set out to find a better life in Britain. More than a quarter of a million black West Indians arrived in Britain between 1953 and 1962, along with 143,000 from India and Pakistan.

The legal and moral basis for the right of migration to Britain was set out in the 1948 Nationality Act. The Act has often been understood as an 'open door' immigration policy that granted British citizenship to all former colonial subjects as their countries gained independence. On paper that was true. But the government had no expectation that it would literally be an open door. In the debates on the Nationality Act in Parliament it was looked on as measure that consolidated relations between countries in the Commonwealth, and also made sure that those in the colonial and military services would be free to move, get employment and marry without losing their rights.[9]

In private the British Cabinet reacted badly when the first West Indian migrants arrived at Tilbury Docks on the Empire Windrush, making around 830 Caribbean arrivals that year. Publicly Ministers said that since the immigrants had come at their own expense as private individuals there was nothing that they could do about it.[10] Migrants found that they were made subject to informal colour bars in employment and accommodation, and often persecution by the police.

In the years that followed, migration into Britain would become the focus of marked anxiety about the state of the country. Racist campaigns against migrants were stirred up and in 1962 the first restrictions on colonial migration were imposed. A cartoon by Cummings in the *Express* newspaper put a picture of colonists arriving in India next to one of Indians arriving in London, as if to say that it was Britain's turn to be colonised.

Black communities brought aspects of colonial life to Britain and reworked them. In 1959 Claudia Jones organised the first Caribbean Carnival in St Pancras Town Hall (the event was moved to Notting Hill in 1966). Jones set out to show Londoners that the West Indian community who had been targeted in rioting the year before were open and friendly people. Intellectuals like Ambalavaner Sivanandan from Sri Lanka, C. L. R. James and Darcus Howe from Trinidad raised issues both of colonial struggles and of black people's struggles in Britain, in public meetings and writing. 'We are over here because you were over there', Sivanandan explained to critics of immigration. Britain's black communities put a human face to the colonial heritage in culture and activism, and later many raised hard questions about the historical record of the Empire.

The European Economic Community

One consequence of decolonisation was that it took away one of the main limits to European cooperation. As colonial powers expanding into new territories Europeans had clashed with each other. As European powers withdrew from their colonies, they laid the basis for more regional cooperation. Though British leaders discounted Europe as a ruin immediately after the war, they came to believe that they had been too hasty as they looked on at the continent's the economic resurgence in the 1960s. In 1973 Edward Heath took Britain into the European Economic Community when turmoil in the world economy made it look like a safe refuge. The decision was confirmed in a referendum in 1975. Opposition to joining was restricted to the left wing of the Labour Party (who saw the British state as the vehicle for social reform) and the right of the Conservative Party who saw it as another backward step for the country, like decolonisation. The majority position then was for a modern country oriented towards Europe.

Conventions signed with African countries at Yaoundé in 1963 and 1969, superseded by the 1975 Lomé Convention, allocated aid to former European colonies in the ACP – African, Caribbean and Pacific – countries to moderate the impact of decolonisation.

At the time Lynn Mytelka (who would go on to hold a senior position at the United Nations Conference on Trade and Development) judged that 'the Lomé Convention will perpetuate this pattern of dependent capitalist development'. As she saw it the European states were 'anxious to guarantee preferential rights of establishment for EEC multinationals in ACP countries vis-à-vis their Japanese and American competitors'.[11] As a trading bloc the EEC and those ACP states covered by the Convention were protected against rivals, and in 1993 a trade war with America broke out over access to European markets for US companies like Chiquita bananas.

The Lomé Convention's STABEX fund was set up to shield high earning exports from former colonies, like cocoa and sugar, from price fluctuations, so securing those imports to Europe. Over time the STABEX fund came under more pressure as the terms of trade for primary goods worsened. The Convention also secured markets for subsidised European agricultural exports to those same countries, raising allegations of dumping.

For Britain, the advantage of the Lomé Convention was that it spread some of the responsibility for its former colonies which the other European powers now shared. In

1988 aid to the ACP countries under the Lomé Convention stood at £1.74 billion, of which Britain's share was £288 million.[12] When the Convention was discussed at the Commonwealth conference in 1975 Prime Minister Harold Wilson was heartened that it was a lot more popular among the Heads of Government there than the more established international arrangements. 'It was at first thought that that initiative might face heavy weather because of the very strong views of some of the Third World countries, which rather suggested that they wanted to pull down the whole of the world's economic machinery, including the IMF and the Bank', he told Parliament, but instead there was 'very warm support' for the Convention.[13]

Chapter Thirty-six

THE RISE AND FALL OF THIRD WORLD

The major upset to the post-war order was the challenge of national liberation move-ments in the 'Third World' to imperialism. From India's independence in 1947 to the mid-1980s Britain and the other European colonial powers, and also the United States, struggled to keep control. The new nations that broke free from the European empires tried to make a world that worked for them, not just for the developed world. The key questions they grappled with were the political rights to self-determination and a more equitable world economy.

In 1945 some of the future leaders of Africa and the Caribbean met in Manchester at the fifth Pan-African Conference (previous conferences had been held in 1919, 1921, 1923 and 1927, organised in the main by Afro-American W. E. B. Dubois). Dubois was at the Manchester conference, but it was organised mostly by Trinidadian radical George Padmore and Ghanaian student Kwame Nkrumah, who would go on to be president of that country. Also there were the future presidents of Malawi (Hastings Banda) and Kenya (Jomo Kenyatta), Amy Ashwood Garvey, the wife of black leader Marcus Garvey, and other delegates from the Caribbean, Nigeria and South Africa. Delegates debated imperialism in Africa and the 'colour problem in Britain'. At the same time the West Indies National Emergency Committee sent its declaration for a right to self-government to the United Nations.

An intellectual milieu that had begun with Padmore and that other Trinidadian writer and activist C. L. R. James who had worked on *International African Opinion* drew in the African delegates to the Manchester Conference. They were joined by a third Trinidadian Eric Williams, who had been James' student at school and wrote a compel-ling book *Capitalism and Slavery* (1946). They corresponded with Leopold Senghor who would become President of Senegal in 1960. James, for his part, wrote the history of the Haiti Revolution, *The Black Jacobins* as a guide and encouragement to the new anti-colonial revolt. Michael Manley, who was enrolled at the LSE in 1945 and would become a radical Prime Minister of Jamaica was also a part of that milieu.

Nehru, Nkrumah, Nasser, Sukarno and Tito.

In 1955 the leaders of the newly independent states of Indonesia, India, Pakistan, Burma (Myanmar) and Ceylon (Sri Lanka) hosted the Asia-Africa conference in Bandung in Indonesia. Though the plan was that it would be for independent states only, many national liberation movements were there. Ho Chi Minh commiserated with the Algerian National Liberation Front, and Ghana's Kwame Nkrumah rubbed shoulders with Egypt's Gamal Abdel Nasser. The conference closed with a resolution 'against colonialism and all its manifestations'. Three years later in Accra an all-African conference brought Frantz Fanon to the attention of the world. He was a psychiatrist from Martinique who had thrown in his lot with the Algerian Revolution, writing for its paper *Al Moudjahid*. Fanon's writings on Third World Revolution were as uncompromising as they were brilliant.

It was around this time that the developing world became known as the Third World, in distinction to the First World of the 'free market' West and the Second World of the Communist Bloc. In 1961 the Bandung Conference was followed up by another in Belgrade where the 'Non-Aligned Movement' was set up.

Independent African and Asian countries pushed for the United Nations General Assembly resolution 1514 that Colonial peoples should have 'an inalienable right to complete freedom, the exercise of their sovereignty and the integrity of their national territory'. 'The U. N. resolution on decolonization has created a new situation for our struggle' said Amilcar Cabral, the leader of the movement to free Guinea-Bissau from Portuguese rule, in which 'colonialism is a crime'.[1]

International Relations theorist Hedley Bull worried that,

> The revolt of non-European peoples and states against Western dominance and the expansion of the states system beyond its originally European or Western confines, have produced an international system in which the area of consensus has shrunk by comparison to what it was in 1914.[2]

Bull's colleague Professor Martin Wight was more sanguine. Asking the question whether the United Nations did achieve the generalisation of the States System was a way of asking whether those states that for doctrinal reasons challenged the 'foundations of international society' could be incorporated. Wight saw the System of States as a moderating influence: 'international revolution has never long maintained itself against the national interest'.[3] National independence pulled African and Asian countries out of

European empires but it tied them into a 'System of States' that had already been set up by – and arguably for – the dominant European and North American powers.

From the 1960s the problems that the anti-colonial movements faced were different. No longer were they rallying opposition movements against colonial authorities but were governing their own societies. As leaders of their own states the nationalists inherited all the challenges of the old authorities of how to run those countries. Kwame Nkrumah had argued at Manchester that the key issue was to take control – 'seek ye first the political kingdom', he said. The goal was 'complete and absolute independence from the control of any foreign government'.[4]

As Nkrumah and many others knew political power was not enough. They would face the problem that the private ownership of industry left much of it in the hands of European owners. Further, the newly independent states would have to manage their economies as part of a world economy. Trade with the rest of the world would be a vital source of investment capital, depending on the prices that newly independent countries could expect for their goods, which were mostly 'primary goods'. The 'terms of trade' were not generally favourable to exporters of primary goods, and in the 1960s they deteriorated. Tanzanian President Julius Nyerere explained that a tractor imported to Tanzania in 1965 cost as much as 6.3 tons of sisal, but by 1972 that had risen to 17.3 tons.[5]

As well as a disadvantageous position in the world economy the leaders of newly independent, former colonies were faced with social problems. A lot of the challenges stemmed from the low levels of development under colonialism. The division between rural villagers under traditional leadership and a somewhat smaller town-based industrial sector that was typical of colonial Africa carried on after independence. Leaders like Nkrumah, Banda, Kenyatta, Nasser and Nehru all had their main support in the towns, but they still had to deal with rural communities that were less invested in the national liberation struggles. Those divisions were often mirrored in ethnic and language differences that made it difficult for leaders to secure consent across the nation.

The days when Tin Tin would teach the Congolese about their homeland Belgium were over (1931).

In 1960 Patrice Lumumba was elected Prime Minister of the newly independent Congo Republic. The Belgian and US governments were united in opposition to this radical leader and set about destabilising his government. Belgium supported separatist movements in Katanga and Kasai to undermine Lumumba's position, and he was eventually arrested and executed in Katanga. In 1967 the secessionist Republic of Biafra, based on the Igbo people of the south, fragmented Nigeria leading to three years of warfare and the first of a succession of military governments.

To meet the challenges of securing freedom from the dominant American and European powers nationalist leaders tried to broaden their social base by making their own regional alliances. Nkrumah and Lumumba both argued for an African federation of states, on the lines of the USA. Those were ambitious proposals that aimed to break out of the relative isolation of working with the moderate resources of an African state. Nkrumah's proposals were too much for Nigeria's Nmadi Ezikiwe and Ethiopia's Haile Selassie and a more modest regional association, the Organisation of African Unity, was set up instead. The more conservative outcome was favoured by those leaders who were already struggling with the business of consolidating state power in socially and ethnically divided countries. Pragmatism won out over idealism.

In the Middle East, pan-Arabism was an important current in the attempts to break out of European domination. The national boundaries of the newly independent states of the Middle East mirrored the European powers' division of their region after the collapse of Ottoman power as much as they did the national aspirations of local elites. There were two important movements towards pan-Arabism in the post-war period. The most successful was the United Arab Republic between Syria and Egypt between 1958 and 1961. The U. A. R. was driven forward by Nasser's radical nationalist agenda and many Syrians came to view the Republic as Egyptian domination. A coup led by Syrian officers broke the union.

In Syria the main champions of the Union were the Arab Socialist Baath Party, founded by Michel Aflaq and Salah al-Din al-Bitar (Baath means 'resurrection' in Arabic). Aflaq's book *The Battle for One Destiny* (1958) made the case for pan-Arabism against the West and against Israel. Though Nasser as President of the U. A. R. commanded the dissolution of the Baath Party it was rebuilt after the end of the Union. The Baath Party was not only successful in Syria, but also in Iraq. Over time, though, the Baath Party divided as the ruling elites in each country, led by Saddam Hussein in Iraq and Hafez Assad in Syria used the organisation as a vehicle for consolidating a new ruling elite. In Iraq the Baath Party turned on the radical rivals, particularly those of the Iraqi Communist Party:

> The months between February and November 1963 saw some of the most terrible scenes of violence hitherto experienced in the post-war Middle East. Acts of wanton savagery and brutality were perpetrated by the Baath and their associates.[6]

The national aspirations of those two autocrats made a Baath Republic as difficult to sustain as the Union with Egypt.[7]

Pan-Arabism continued to be a driving force in the Middle East and was a serious challenge to US influence, as it was to that of Britain and France. Western support for Israel was in large part a strategy to keep the Arab world divided, and to frustrate radical challenges to the West. In the wars of 1967 and 1973 the Arab states found a brief and strident unity. Israeli victory in both conflicts, on the other hand left Arab unity in tatters. Those nations that took part in the wars against Israel were Egypt, Jordan, Syria, Iraq and Lebanon in 1967, when Egypt lost 15,000 troops, the Gaza Strip and the Sinai Peninsula, Syria lost 2,500 and the Golan Heights, and Jordan lost the West Bank, while Israel's losses were less than 1000 troops. In the Yom Kippur War of 1973, more Arab states joined the Egyptian-Syrian coalition, including Jordan, Algeria, Morocco, Tunisia and Saudi Arabia, but once again Israel prevailed. The impact was markedly demoralising for Arab unity, and Egypt, led by Anwar Sadat since Nasser's death in 1970 was eventually persuaded by the United States to make peace with Israel in 1979. Egypt, from being the leading challenger to western influence in the region became America's second strongest ally after Saudi Arabia. It was a change that left Syria and Libya posturing unhelpfully as main defender of the Arab world against Israel and the West – until Iran's Islamic revolution mapped out a new kind of conflict between the West and the Middle East.

As more Arab leaders entered into resentful acceptance of US hegemony in the Middle East, they assuaged their subjects' anti-imperialist sentiments by supporting the exiled leadership of the Palestine Liberation Organisation, first in Jordan and then in Tunisia. At the General Assembly Arab states vented their frustration at the settlement by sponsoring diplomatic attacks on Israel as the 'US proxy' in the region, even as they were seeking US aid to develop their industries and militaries. Syria and Libya also sponsored rival and radical Palestinian groups to attack Israel, as an extension of their foreign policy.[8]

In the Middle East, as in the rest of the Third World, attempts to build regional power blocs failed because of the lack of unity among the different national units. One of the chief barriers to unity were differences over relations to the Great Powers. Egypt's shift from a critical to a supportive policy towards the United States churned up all of its established relationships with the other Arab states. Iraq's rivalry with Iran made it an ally to America in the 1980s and a major buyer of weapons from America and Britain (only to clash spectacularly with the United States in the next two decades).[9]

Aid as Imperialism

Aware that the terms of trade were stacked against them radical nationalists tried to develop their domestic economies. Nkrumah, Nasser and Nehru all tried to redirect earnings from primary goods (cocoa, cotton and tea) into industrial investments. Large scale investment programmes – like the Volta and Aswan Dams – were taken on to boost employment and modernise their different countries. The hope was that these would shift the countries' from predominantly rural to more urban economies. They hoped to replace the expensively imported manufactured goods with locally produced equivalents, a policy called import substitution. At the same time the newly independent countries had some success in getting the radical Argentine economist Raúl Prebisch appointed as Secretary General of the United Nations Conference on Trade and Development (UNCTAD) when it was set up in 1964.

It was important to the nationalist leaders that their project was for independence from the developed west. They did not want to be dependent upon aid or too dependent on borrowing. In 1960 the Swedish development economist Karl Gunnar Myrdal had argued that the developed world would have to aid the less developed in a kind of international welfare programme (in the book *Beyond the Welfare State*). Nkrumah replied that,

> It has been argued that the developed nations should effectively assist the poorer parts of the world, and that the whole world should be turned into a Welfare State. However, there seems little prospect that anything of this sort could be achieved.

Nkrumah added that 'the less developed world will not become developed through the goodwill or generosity of the developed powers', and 'It can only become developed through a struggle against the external forces which have a vested interest in keeping it underdeveloped.'[10]

It was out of an unwillingness to be dependent upon the former colonialists that Frantz Fanon argued *against* reparations for slavery, in his 1952 book *Black Skins, White Masks*. First Fanon made the argument that the colonial revolt was not just a reaction but the beginning of something new.

> I am not a prisoner of history. I should not seek there for the meaning of my destiny.

Then Fanon goes on to ask the question:

> Am I going to ask the contemporary white man to answer for the slave-ships of the seventeenth century?

He answers:

> I do not have the right to allow myself to be mired in what the past has determined.

And insists that

> I am not the slave of the Slavery that dehumanized my ancestors.[11]

In 1962, in an afterword to the second edition of *The Black Jacobins*, C. L. R. James made a similar argument against bitterness over the past:

> The West Indian writers have discovered the West Indies and West Indians, a people of the middle of our disturbed century, concerned with the discovery of themselves, determined to discover themselves, but without hatred or malice against the foreigner, even the bitter imperialist past. To be welcomed into the comity of nations, a new nation must bring something new. …The West Indians have brought something new.[12]

It was not out of a misplaced generosity to the old imperialist masters that James and Fanon counselled against looking for redress. They were arguing for independence and a break from the past as the stronger policy for the liberation movement.

The determination to be self-supporting and independent was a part of the ideology of national liberation. Such hopes, though, collided with the reality of governing poor countries.

A slump in commodity prices in the mid-seventies undermined export earnings. Countries that had borrowed found that they could not meet their repayments, and in desperation borrowed more to cover the loans. Against their hopes many third world leaders were forced to go to the IMF to ask for assistance to cover their debt repayments. From the point of view of the IMF it seemed that the debts were incurred because of over-profligate social programmes at home.

The IMF aid packages came with strings attached – called conditionalities – meaning that the recipient countries would have to change their domestic policies to meet the conditions of the aid. The conditions that the IMF and donor countries set were for austerity. They demanded that currencies should be devalued to reduce incomes, and that state assets that development-minded countries had built up should be sold off to private industry. These were called 'structural adjustments' and were presented as technical changes though they had the effect of putting Third World wealth in the hands of first world investors. The imperialistic character of aid was exposed at the time by Teresa Hayter, who had worked in the Overseas Development Institute, and by Albert O. Hirschman, an economist who had worked at the American Office of Strategic Services and the Federal Reserve Board. In the 1990s World Bank's senior economists Joseph Stiglitz and Ravi Kanbur confirmed that the structural adjustment programmes were often destructive of development.[13]

As well as losing control over their economic policy the recipient countries had to push through unpopular economic and social policies that undermined them further in the eyes of their publics. At the extreme Bangladesh, suffering from the impact of war and famine after its break with what was then West Pakistan, became the world's greatest recipient of aid. Economist Rehman Sobhan explained that the country had become dependent on overseas aid:

> Bangladesh came to be dependent on foreign aid to fund 60 per cent of its investments, 85 per cent of its development budget and 63 per cent of its commodity imports, the level of external resource inflows was critically dependent on the volume of aid available to the economy.

Aid was choking off any domestic growth that might reverse the situation as the governing elite 'has thus come to acquire a material stake in an aid-dependent regime'. On a practical level all of the country's graduates were working for overseas aid organisations instead of working for local indutries.[14]

Aid played a significant role in the Biafran War of 1967, with aid agencies taking a stance at odds with official western policy. British policy was to support the Nigerian government in its conflict with the Igbo separatists. But it was widely criticised by aid agencies, in particular Oxfam, which ran advertisements claiming that 'the price for a united Nigeria is likely to be millions of lives'. A BBC journalist (and later novelist) covering the conflict, Frederick Forsyth published *The Biafra Story* in 1969 highlighting the hunger among the Igbo and Britain's 'treacherous' role supporting the Nigerian government. The World Council of Churches set up a relief organisation, Joint Church Aid to fly food to the fledgling Republic of Biafra. Aid activists were particularly critical of the politically neutral stance that the International Committee of the Red Cross held to, that it would not take sides in international conflicts and work with recognised governments. A French doctor with the Red Cross attacked the organisation for becoming 'accomplices to the systematic massacre of a population' arguing that aid workers had to 'bear witness' to the violations of human rights that they encountered. Bernard Kouchner helped set up the new organisation Médicins Sans Frontières (Doctors without Borders) in 1971 which married relief activities with political advocacy.

According to the veteran aid worker Conor Foley the Biafra intervention is 'now widely recognized, in humanitarian circles, as a huge error'. The impact of the aid, Foley argues, was to sustain the separatist government and to dissuade them from finding a negotiated peace, but instead led them to dig in for an unwinnable war. Though the war cost more than a million lives, the eventual peace did not lead to a Nigerian massacre of Igbo as aid organisations had warned, but rather both sides backed off from recrimination. Former Biafran fighters and officials were reabsorbed into the Nigerian Army and Civil Service. Confiscated property was returned. The aid organisations greatly overstated the extent of the threat and were lifted by the public response in Britain and elsewhere.[15]

Aid played a dramatic role in the politics of Somalia, too. In 1969 military commander Siad Barre overthrew an elected government there. Somalia was in conflict with the U.S.-backed Ethiopian government over the Ogaden at the time, and Barre turned to the Soviet Union for help. But in 1974 the Horn of Africa was turned inside out by a Soviet-inspired coup against the Ethiopian Emperor Haile Selassie led by Haile Mengistu Mariam's Derg organisation. Barre invaded the Ogaden in 1977 and the USSR having changed sides, so did the USA backing Barre's Somali regime. Ethnic Somali refugees from the Ogaden needed help and America gave generously. The aid that America and other donors gave, though, was having a bad effect on the country.

A World Bank discussion paper explained that food aid funnelled through USAID, CARE International and Catholic Relief Services was wrecking Somalia's economy. 'The share of food import in total volume of food consumption rose from less than 33 per cent on average for the 1970–79 period to over 63 per cent during the 1980–84 period.'[16]

Abdirahman Osman Raghe, who worked in Somalia's Department of Food Aid at the Ministry of the Interior explained to the journalist Michael Maren that the Barre government systematically redirected food aid through different government departments, which was then sold on for profit by Barre's flunkies. The intended target of the aid, Ogadeen refugees were held in camps but saw little of the aid. Their numbers were deliberately inflated to more than a million though there were more like 400,000. Aid workers knew that the programmes were systematically plundered but CARE International did not give up its $7million contract. Farm friendly policies in America created large surpluses that were bought up by the U.S. government under Public Law 480 – the Agricultural Trade Development and Assistance Act of 1954 – for the programme. Meanwhile farmers in Somalia abandoned their farms unable to compete with the price of USAID flour once it was sold on to middlemen in Mogadishu.

By 1988 many of the remaining refugees were drifting out of the camps, back to the Ogaden or to Mogadishu looking for work. The World Food Programme and the UNHCR decided in 1988 that they would have to withdraw their programmes but were anxious about the response of the Somali government. By then Barre was already facing a significant challenge from the Somali National Movement, and in January 1991 he fled the country.[17]

Like the World Bank and the IMF, Aid agencies had their own ideas of what was the best way that the developing world should develop – ideas that mirrored their own preoccupations and prejudices. Those ideas were summed up in reports sponsored by the aid agencies. These reports were influential upon donors of aids and loans who were setting the conditions on which funds would be extended to the developing world.

In 1980, North-South – A Programme for Survival, the report of the Independent Commission on International Development Issues dealt directly with the problem of the developed world's monopoly on technology. Under German Social Democrat and former premier Willy Brandt, the report first popularised the case for 'appropriate technology' for the less developed world. Appropriate technology is a hybrid concept. It appeals both to the demand for better technology on the part of the people of the less developed world, and at the same time calls into question the generalisation of 'Western' technology.

The Brandt report regretted that 'industrialised countries stick to a guiding philosophy which is predominantly materialistic and based on a belief in the automatic growth of gross national product'. The point of the intervention though was not in substance addressed to the developed world but the less so: 'We must not surrender to the idea that the whole world should copy the model of the highly industrialised countries'.[18]

Overall, the Brandt Report made a case for modest technologies in contrast to the grand projects and dams that had been taken on by Nkrumah in West Africa and Nasser in Egypt. Brandt wrote that appropriate technology 'can include cheaper sources of energy; simpler farm equipment; techniques in building, services and manufacturing processes which save capital; smaller plants and scales of operation which can permit dispersal of activity'.[19]

Arghiri Emmanuel, the University of Paris development economist took issue with the appropriate technology thesis. Emmanuel struck at the conservative notion of preserving cultures, writing, 'cultural authenticity is also the tourist picturesqueness of underdevelopment', and adding, 'humanity is neither a zoo nor a museum of the anthropologically exotic'. Striking at the faux-radical appeal of 'appropriate technology' Emmanuel charged that 'a certain addiction to the past' wrongly identifies 'less developed capitalist relations … as paradise lost, and slides from the criticism of capitalism in general to the denial of development within capitalism'. Emmanuel appealed to the radicals not to forget 'that if capitalism is hell there exists a more frightful hell: that of less developed capitalism'.[20]

Under Norwegian Labour Party president Gro Harlem Brundtland, the World Commission on Environment and Development declared in 1987 that 'if needs are to be met on a sustainable basis the Earth's natural resource base must be conserved and enhanced'. The Brundtland Report presents sustainable development as the more palatable alternative to absolutely limited growth. 'The concept of sustainable development does imply limits – not absolute limits but limitations imposed by the present state of technology and social organizations on environmental resources and by the ability of the biosphere to absorb the effects of human activities'.[21]

In the context of aid projects in the less developed world, sustainable development meant a lowering of expectations. Aid worker turned journalist Michael Maren recalled how 'sustainable development emerged as a reaction to criticism that most development projects for the last fifty years fell apart the moment the foreign money was pulled out'. The prefix 'sustainable' meant in effect, modest in aspiration 'so projects started referring to sustainable development'.[22]

Declining Fortunes

To force through the development programmes – often in the face of domestic opposition – many nationalist leaders, Nkrumah and Nasser included, silenced political opponents and critics. The dangers of getting things wrong were brought home to African leaders when Nkrumah was deposed in 1966 by a 'National Liberation Council'. Julius Nyerere in Tanzania and Kenneth Kaunda in Zambia shifted to more rural, village-based strategies to widen their support. Nyerere's policy was called Ujamaa, or villagization.[23]

Eric Williams had in the 1940s and 50s given intellectual and political leadership to the anti-colonial movement in the West Indies so that he was elected Prime Minister of Trinidad. By 1970, though, his government had narrowed its focus to manage the economy. A younger generation of activists inspired by the Black Power movement in America challenged Williams' authority. Large demonstrations in February led by the college group NJAC of Geddes Grainger and Dave Darbeau, bus workers' leader George Weeks, and C. L. R. James' nephew Radford 'Darcus' Howe attacked Williams as a sell-out. 'Black Massa Doing White Massa Wuk', Grainger's creole slogan ran, parodying the title of Williams' own lecture of 1961 'Massa Day Done'. Williams' swung between mollifying the protestors and repression. Williams went so far as to ban his own books for their subversive potential, saying 'they may give these half-educated negroes the wrong ideas'. In the end the movement ran out of steam, though not before Williams called on the support of the Royal Marines on board HMS Jupiter and HMS Sirius. Some of the rebels were jailed. After that Williams became more cautious of popular protest and closer to the outlook of the U. S. State Department.[24]

To defend their regimes, Third World governments sometimes also resorted to repression. Once-popular liberation leaders were reduced to the status of overseers of unpopular economic policies effectively imposed upon them by their former colonial masters. In Jamaica Michael Manley's radical government was undercut by the fall in the price of Bauxite (the country's highest earning export) and was forced to negotiate a stabilisation programme with the IMF, with privatisation of state assets and a 30 per cent devaluation of the currency. In 1980, he lost the election against the right-wing challenger Edward Seaga.

Muammar Ghadafi and Josip Broz Tito.

In Zimbabwe, the Patriotic Front's agreement with Britain and the other powers was lauded as a success. When Robert Mugabe's ZANU (PF) won the first general election he was praised. 'Some of us on this side of the House would like to congratulate Mr Mugabe both on his victory and the statesmanlike nature of his victory speech', said Tory backbencher Christopher Brocklebank-Fowler. *The Times* joined in saying that 'the British Government has rather unexpectedly got what it always wanted – the basis for a stable Zimbabwe in which the white population could stay and help'. Business partners – notably Lonrho which as London-Rhodesia was founded under the old regime – welcomed the stability that Mugabe offered.

'Yes, we've cultivated a close relationship with Britain', said Prime Minister Mugabe, 'there is no quarrel with Britain'. He made a point of saying that Zimbabwe would happily continue to enjoy the assistance of British military instructors' – as it had during the handover of power, and another 130 troops were sent to work under Major General Joss Acland. An aid package of £890 million was promised by different donors, led by Britain and America.[25]

Mugabe's electoral victory was overwhelming in most of Zimbabwe among the Shona majority but Matabeleland in the west voted largely for his rival Joshua Nkomo. In January 1983, the elite Fifth Brigade of the army that the British had trained was sent into Matabeleland to suppress those guerrilla fighters who were resistant to the new regime. Twenty thousand were killed in the fighting. The regime dealt with labour activists harshly, too, denouncing those who went on strike in 1980 hoping to win better pay in the new Zimbabwe. The once-radical Mugabe promised business leaders that 'we recognise that the economic structure of this country is based on capitalism, and that whatever ideas we have, we must build on that'.[26] Mugabe and the other Zimbabwean leaders undertook to guarantee foreign investments in industry, white seats in parliament and white owned farms, by stalling land reform for a decade. In the years that followed Mugabe's regime dealt harshly with opposition, and later took to scapegoating the remaining white farmers for the limited opportunities available to black Zimbabweans.

Those nationalist leaders who did not learn to work in the new conditions paid a heavy price. Patrice Lumumba was murdered in 1960 and his junior ally Mobutu Sese Seko built a spectacular and authoritarian regime to govern the Congo up until 1997. Milton Obote was overthrown by Idi Amin in 1971 and lived in exile in Tanzania. (Amin had taken part in the suppression of the Mau Mau revolt as a sergeant in the Kenyan African Rifles, learning many of the violent methods that characterised his eight-year rule.) Ahmed Ben Bella, Algeria's first President was deposed in 1965 and spent 14 years under house arrest, making way for Houari Boumédiène's authoritarian regime.

Nehru's hopes that India might lead an anti-imperialist alliance were dashed when Mao's China incurred on the border in 1960 and 1967. In 1970, the radical leaders of West and East Pakistan, Zulfikar Ali Bhutto and Sheikh Mujib respectively, failed to unite, so that Mujib had little option but separation – and the military drowned the fledgling Bangladeshi independence in blood. In 1977 military leader Mohammed Zia-ul-Haq overthrew Bhutto's government in (West) Pakistan and had him executed. In 1975, Nehru's daughter Indira Gandhi, having succeeded him as Congress leader and Prime Minister, brought in a state of emergency to suppress radical challenges from student protestors and trade union oppositionists.

In the 1980s under the premierships of Margaret Thatcher in Britain and Ronald Reagan in America the challenge of the Third World to the West had been largely contained. At the Cancun summit on North-South Dialogue Margaret Thatcher took heart from the way that the Soviet invasion of Afghanistan had undermined radicalism in the developing world. Now it was the communists who were cast as imperialists. The invasion, wrote Thatcher, 'divided the Third World and so weakened the pressure it could bring against the West on international economic issues':

> In these circumstances, countries which had long advocated their own local form of social-ism, to be paid for by western aid, suddenly had to consider a more realistic approach of attracting western investment by pursuing free market policies.[27]

Western attitudes towards the developing world were changing in the 1980s. Where there had been a degree of guilty self-reflection about the history of Empire, atten-tion now turned to the way that the post-colonial states were governed. Repression in Uganda, Zaire and Zimbabwe was highlighted in the press as evidence that Third World leaders were as likely to make things worse as make them better. In 1986 the American sociologist Lewis Feuer presented the end of Empire as a step backwards:

> The abrogation of imperialism brought a resurgence of tribal massacres in independent African states. Untrammelled aggression exceeded the bounds imaginable by the most sceptical Western imperialists.[28]

On the other hand, Chicago Political Science Professor Adom Getachew summarises that 'the thirty years after the end of the Second World War were characterised by a quest for a domination-free international order'. But in the 1980s the 'revival and reconstitution of an imperial world occurred as anti-colonial nationalism, faced with its own internal crises and limits, could no longer mount an effective challenge'.[29]

Rise of Islamic Fundamentalism

The decline of Third World Nationalism has been mirrored by the rise in Islamic fundamentalism. The Muslim Brotherhood which had been formed in Egypt in 1928 under Hassan al-Banna was suppressed in 1952 after being implicated in an assassination attempt on President Nasser. Its leader then, Sayid Qutb, wrote a manifesto that argued the Muslim world was no longer Islamic and would have to be overthrown to create a new Islamic law. Qutb was executed in 1966 but his ideas continued to have an underground appeal. With the decline of Arab nationalism in particular and Third Worldism in general Islamic fundamentalism would re-emerge as an expression of Arab demoralisation.

In the 1970s Britain and America gave support to Islamists in the southern republics of the USSR and in its 'sphere of influence'. Israel also supported Mujama al-Islamiya, an educational and welfare organisation founded in 1973 hoping that it would be a counterweight to the nationalist Palestine Liberation Organisation. Most dramatically Britain and America, with the assistance of the Pakistani secret services, supported the Mujahideen fighters in Afghanistan who took on the Soviet-backed government of Babrak Karmal from 1980. In time the Mujahideen would celebrate victory as the Soviet forces withdrew in 1988 having lost 15,000 troops in the conflict.

A surprising source of the influence of political Islam came with the sudden rise of a mass opposition to the Shah of Iran. Street protests made Reza Pahlavi's government untenable and he abdicated. At first the opposition was led by the constitutional nationalist Mehdi Bazargan (who had been a minister under Mossadegh in the 1950s). The nationalists by this time lacked the organisation or the will to rule and quite quickly the interim government was replaced by one supported by Iran's leading Islamist cleric, Ayatollah Khomeini, who had been living in exile in Paris. The Islamic Party of Iran outlawed all rivals and brought in a regime of religious repression. The seizure of the US embassy in the revolution, and the taking of 52 US citizens as hostages, initiated many decades of hostility between the United States and Iran. A botched attempt to free the hostages with an invasion ended in humiliation when the helicopters malfunctioned in the desert.

Iran's ability to export its Islamic revolution was limited by the religious differences between its Shi'a supporters and the Sunni allegiance of most Arabs. When Israel invaded South Lebanon in 1982 Iran sent 1,500 Revolutionary Guards to support the resistance to the invasion and train local Shi'a fighters. They helped to set up the Hezbollah organisation of Lebanese Shi'a. In 1980 Saddam Hussein invaded Iran (with the support and encouragement of the United States) in a conflict that caused more than a million dead and saw Iraq's initial advances reversed in 1984–85.

In the aftermath of the Soviet withdrawal from Afghanistan the country was riven by different factions of the opposition Mujahideen groups. An Islamist inspired movement that called itself the Taliban ('teachers') rose to power on the promise of uniting the factions and ending the fighting. Its ideology was decidedly reactionary, forcing women to cover up and excluding girls from school.[30] The Taliban enjoyed some support from the Pakistani secret services. At the same time the Saudi regime was financing overseas schools, mosques and welfare organisations under the leadership of followers of the eighteenth century Arab religious leader Ibn Abd-Al-Wahhab.[31]

What united the different Islamist groups was a disdain for secular political authority. In principle at least most were committed to the idea that true authority belonged to God and political representation suborned it. Where constitutional politics failed Islamists of different stripes took advantage to push their anti-secular ideology.

Both Hezbollah and Saudi Arabia supported volunteer Muslim fighters who went to support Izetbegovic's forces against the Serbs in Bosnia. Islamists supported the Chechen separatists in their attempt to break away from the Russian-led Confederation of Independent States in 1994. The Islamic Salvation Front took advantage of the first elections in Algeria in 1990 and 1992 to put up a slate first for the local elections which they won, and then for the General Election, only to see voting suspended and the election cancelled by the ruling Nationalist regime. An Islamist insurgency was mounted in 1994 by the Armed Islamic Group (which declared a ceasefire in 1997). From 1987 in Palestine the organisation Hamas, that drew on some of the activists behind Mujama al-Islamiya, challenged the Palestine Liberation Organisation for leadership of the struggle against Israel in the West Bank and Gaza.

Veterans of the fighting in Bosnia, Chechnya and elsewhere took refuge in Afghanistan with the tacit support of the Taliban. Among them, Osama bin Laden, from a wealthy Saudi family had been organising a group called Al-Qaeda ('the base'). Bin Laden had become disillusioned with the Saudi government over its alliance with the United States in the 1990 war with Iraq. Bin Laden had wanted to organise a Saudi force to fight against Saddam but was dismayed by the siting of US bases on Saudi soil as a part of the mobilisation. It was in his base in Afghanistan that bin Laden planned direct attacks on the United States as the main barrier to a true Islam in Arab lands. After bombing the US embassy in Kenya in 1998 Al-Qaeda mounted the attack on the Twin Towers in New York and the Pentagon, using hijacked US airline planes in 11 September 2001.

When Osama bin Laden was the West's ally against the Soviet Union.

The trajectory of Islamic fundamentalism was that it rose where the national liberation movements had reached a dead end. At its heart the Islamist movement is not a national liberation movement at all, but a religious one that seeks to end all secular political government. Practically, of course, Islamists have created social orders, in particular in Afghanistan and in Somalia, where the Islamic Courts provided some stability to a deeply divided country. Some Islamist movements have developed in the direction of stable polities, in particular in Iran, where the regime has stabilised over time, and in Sudan, where President Omar al-Bashir invited Islamist support to shore up his regime (al-Bashir was overthrown in 2019). In the main, though, Islamist regimes have proved markedly unstable, and vicious towards people without and within their rule. The record of Islamic State in Mosul and Raqqa shows some alternatives to western imperialism could be as destructive. Above all the rise of Islamic fundamentalism was a movement whose dynamism owed more to the collapse of the alternatives than it did to the intrinsic virtues of its own ideology.

Chapter Thirty-seven

COLD WAR CLIMAX

The slowdown in Britain's economy in the 1970s was not exceptional. All the developed economies, in Europe, America and even Japan were suffering a similar malaise. Between 1969 and 1975 rates of investment in the developed world fell. In Germany and Western Europe, they fell by 20 per cent; In America, by 25 per cent, and in Japan 30 per cent.[1] As investors were pulling out of domestic markets, they looked for other opportunities. In 1960 private direct investment flows to developing countries were $103 million from Germany, $226 million from the UK, $667 million from the USA. But by 1976 these had climbed to $765 million from Germany, $723 million from the UK and $3119 million from the USA.[2] By 1980 British overseas investments were earning £2.6 billion a year.

Overseas trade became more important as a share of trade overall.

Trade as a proportion of GDP (per cent)[3].

	1968	1978
UK	21	29
West Germany	21	26
France	14	20
Italy	16	24
USA	5	10

Some of the companies earning large profits in Africa in 1978 were Lonrho (which earned £66m), Unilever (£59m), Associated British Foods (£28m), British American Tobacco (£21m), Rio Tinto Zinc (£18.8m), the British Oxygen Company (£16.7m) and British Electronic Traction (£15m). Others that earned most of their profits in Africa (as Lonrho and Unilever did) included Mitchell Cotts (£21.1m) Paterson Zochonis (£10.5) James Finlay (£8.82) Eastern Produce (£3.47m).

A lot of what was classed as investment in the developing world was really just extending loans. This 'hot money' ran out of the country quicker than it came in. Growth rates in Africa and Western Asia fell from 3.9 and 6.8 per cent in 1971 to just 1.7 per cent in both regions by 1990 (though they climbed in South East Asia).[4] Lending to third world countries locked many into a spiral of debt where repayments on loans were eating up surpluses so that they had to borrow more to pay interest on their loans. In the 1980s interest rates across the world were hiked up by the developed countries – to prevent inflation they said – so that the debts were harder to service. A report commissioned by the Commonwealth

Secretariat painted a gloomy picture: 'debtor nations are being required by their debt-servicing obligations to engineer a net flow of resources to industrial countries for the foreseeable future'.[5] The Commonwealth Secretariat report listed nine countries that were in the most difficulty because they were 'countries with under $400 per capita income' with large government debts. All were former British colonies: Bangladesh, India, Uganda, Tanzania, Malawi, Ghana, Sri Lanka, Sierra Leone and Kenya. Among the next worst cases were also the former colonies of Guyana, Jamaica, Mauritius and Zambia.[6]

Foreign Direct Investment in East Africa (Kenya, Tanzania and Uganda), 1970–78 ($ millions of 1972 constant prices).

1970	1971	1972	1973	1974	1975	1976	1977	1978
23.0	11.5	20.0	26.5	20.2	14.3	40.8	43.6	27.9

Source: UNCTAD.

Radical economists like Andre Gunder Frank, Celso Furtado, Walter Rodney and Samir Amin argued that capitalism tended to develop the West but keep the rest of the world locked in a state of 'underdevelopment'. (The 'underdevelopment thesis' rang true of the state of much of the post-colonial world of the 1980s, but it did not anticipate the strong advance of many of the East Asian countries, like Korea, Indonesia, Malaya, and then later China and Vietnam.)[7]

The greater internationalisation of the world economy in the 1970s was matched with a rising tempo of international conflict. The Cold War between America and Russia imposed remarkable costs in security and cash as the two superpowers tried to manage their nuclear missile rivalry.

The Cold War also drove the main powers to seek out allies in the rest of the world to match each other's diplomatic and military reach. To many it seemed that the Eastern Bloc was winning. In 1970 the Socialist Salvador Allende was elected to govern Chile; in 1973 America withdrew its troops from Vietnam, in 1974 a Socialist revolution in Portugal not only shook Europe but handed over much of its African empire to anti-colonial forces in Mozambique, Angola and Guinea. That same year a Revolutionary government overthrew Haile Selassie's Ethiopian Empire.

In Southern Africa the victory of the liberation movements in Angola and Mozambique alarmed US Secretary of State Henry Kissinger. 'We have a stake', he said, 'in not having the continent become radical and move in a direction that is incompatible with western interests'. America and Britain supported Jonas Savimbi's UNITA guerrilla war to overthrow the radical MPLA government in Angola, and the RENAMO guerrillas fighting against Samora Machel's government in Mozambique.

The Western Allies could also take succour from the outcome of the Yom Kippur war in the Middle East, where American- and British-backed Israel inflicted a heavy defeat on the Egyptian and Syrian forces that invaded in 1973. But instability in the Middle East led to more dramatic actions by Palestinian guerrilla groups, sponsored by different Middle Eastern governments.

Britain's ruling class was in dudgeon in the 1970s. Strikes – often 'unofficial' seemed to threaten ungovernability. Conservative Minister Quintin Hogg worried that legislation regulating industry was like a ratchet-effect, only moving in the direction of socialism. Iain Duncan Smith recalled that Conservatives supported Britain's entry into the European Economic Community in 1973 because they thought the socialists would keep on winning elections to Parliament and hoped the EEC would be a limit on socialist policies.

In the still-British six counties of Northern Ireland students protested at discrimination against Catholics, and for civil rights. They drew a violent response from the Protestant-dominated regime at Stormont. As fighting broke out between militant civil rights protestors and the authorities' paramilitary 'B-Special' police force, Britain sent the army in, ostensibly to keep the peace between the 'two sides'. In August 1971 the British army raided the homes of suspected dissidents to be interned without trial, which only confirmed the civil rights protestors' view that they were in truth an army of occupation. Prime Minister Edward Heath ordered the British army to put down the protests. On 30 January 1972 Lieutenant Colonel Wilford ordered British paratroopers to open fire on a large Civil Rights demonstration, killing thirteen people. The Irish Republican Army, which had been largely dormant in the post-war era recruited hundreds to begin a long and secret war of attrition against the British Army in Northern Ireland. To retain control, the British built up a formidable machinery of repression, with special 'no-jury' courts, armed patrols and low-intensity warfare against the nationalist minority in Northern Ireland.[8]

Women volunteers of the Provisional IRA.

Margaret Thatcher's election in 1979 (like Ronald Reagan's in America) signalled a renewed determination on the part of her supporters to reverse Britain's declining fortunes. On the other side, unwilling to take power for themselves and disappointed by the Labour government's flip-flopping, working-class trade unionists had lost heart and left the field to Mrs Thatcher.

Margaret Thatcher set out to rewrite the post-war compromise between capital and labour, and rip-up the 'tripartite' agreements. Nationalised industries like British Steel, British Leyland and, eventually, British Coal were sold off to private investors (and greatly downsized). The free market, not government planners, would decide. For all the talk of freedom, Thatcher's government put legal restraints on trade union's ability to organise, blaming them for wrecking industry, and a great many other restraints on civil liberties besides.

Thatcher shared a lot of the outlook of the 'Suez Group' that Britain had given up too much in the post-war decolonization. The Suez debacle, she thought, 'entered the British soul' and the country developed 'what might be called the "Suez syndrome"', meaning that 'we exaggerated our impotence'. She thought that the retreat from the Gulf in 1970 had been a mistake, but that it and other retreats were 'held to be the inevitable consequences of British decline' – a conclusion she rejected.[9]

Thatcher met the international challenges to Britain's position in the spirit of reversing that decline. When the Soviet Union sent forces into Afghanistan to support the deposed presidency of their client leader Babrak Karmal, Britain supported America's deployment of special forces to support Mujahideen fighters against the Russians. On 30 April 1980 a group of Iraqi-backed militants occupied the Iranian Embassy in London demanding the release of political prisoners in Iran. Where other governments might have tried to negotiate, Thatcher signalled a firm stand sending Special Air Service commandos in to overpower and kill the siege-makers.

The opportunity to give substance to the new policy of 'walking tall' came in 1982 when the military Argentine government invaded the British occupied Falkland Islands 150 miles off their coast, against the wishes of the Falkland Islanders. Thatcher ordered the task force to sail across the Atlantic to engage the Argentine Fleet and take back the islands. In the fighting the Royal Navy destroyed the Argentine cruiser, the Belgrano (even though it was outside the British-declared 'exclusion zone' when it was sunk).

'Gotcha!' headlined the Sun newspaper. British paratroopers took back the Falkland Islands. In her memoirs Thatcher reflected on the meaning of the conflict:

> The significance of the Falklands war was enormous, both for Britain's self-confidence and for our standing in the world. Since the Suez fiasco in 1956, British foreign policy had been one long retreat. The tacit assumption made by British and foreign governments alike was that our world role was doomed steadily to diminish. We had come to be seen by both friends and enemies as a nation which lacked the will and the capability to defend its interests in peace, let alone in a war. Victory in the Falklands changed that. Everywhere I went after the war, Britain's name meant something more than it had.[10]

Britain's forward position in the Middle East led to the creation of a Rapid Deployment Force to help police the Gulf. The conservative rulers there were unnerved by the novel threat of Iran's Islamic Republic. In 1986 British airbases were used for an American attack on Libya in retaliation for the bombing of off-duty US airmen in a disco in Germany. The strategy of confrontation was welcomed by Mrs Thatcher as an example of what the West ought to be doing. The limits to Thatcher's international power projection were not in Moscow or the Third World but Washington. Despite the Prime Minister's fulsome support for US leadership, her objection to the 1983 US invasion of the Commonwealth nation of Grenada, in the overthrow of its far-left leadership, was heard but ignored. Britain's nuclear deterrent proved to be less than independent when American cruise missiles were sited in bases and under US control two years earlier.

Closer to home Margaret Thatcher's militantly confrontational policy left the Labour opposition first paralysed, and then demoralised. As the party lost working class voters, its trade union base was shrinking under the pressure of unemployment and the restructuring of industry. Trade union leaders, having felt that they were ill-served by the Callaghan government, withdrew, and left the Constituency Labour Parties to their hobbyhorses of town hall socialism and the 'Tony Benn for Deputy' campaign. Labour's middle-class supporters swung from one extreme to another, as many left for the Social Democratic Party from 1982. Industrial opposition to job cuts in steel, cars and the mines was faced down and isolated. The leadership of the Labour Party conceded more and more ground to the Conservatives, apparently lost for an answer to Britain's problems. Mrs Thatcher's government looked dynamic in relation to the opposition.

The Conservative government's ideological appeal was aggressively patriotic carrying the resentment of those who thought that Britain had been sold down the river. In the 1979 election campaign party leader Margaret Thatcher had worried out loud that 'people are really rather afraid that this country might be rather swamped by people of a different culture'. A British Nationality Bill of 1981 restricted rights of immigration for those of the former colonies, and black Britons were harassed by police and immigration police.

In Northern Ireland the Conservative administrations of the eighties doubled down on the suppression of the Republican movement. The security forces organised an assassination squad, the Headquarters Mobile Support Unit that took out Republicans, like Gervais McKerr, Eugene Toman and Sean Burns (11 November 1982), Seamus Grew, Roddy Carroll (12 December 1982) and Michael Tighe (24 November 1982). The security forces also collaborated with Protestant paramilitary militias who assassinated the Belfast solicitor Pat Finucane. IRA attacks and bombings of British army and government targets carried on.[11]

The British also withdrew the special status granted those political prisoners who had been imprisoned by special ('Diplock') courts. The loss of political status led to a confrontation in the prisons that escalated into the Hunger Strike of 1981 and ended with ten Republican prisoners dying after refusing food. While the strike was on, the Parliamentary seat of Fermanagh and South Tyrone fell vacant, and the hunger striker's leader Bobby Sands won a by-election with 30,493 votes. The Republicans were emboldened as they were embittered. The conflict carried on, with each side more determined to win.[12]

With both Washington and London taking on a more strident policy Third World Nationalism was being confronted. But confrontation did not make problems disappear. Many conflicts became yet more heated. In South Africa supporters of the outlawed African National Congress set up the United Democratic Front in 1983 to challenge apartheid. The governing National Party imposed a state of emergency on 20 July 1985, which was extended to cover the whole country the following year. Two-thousand three hundred and forty-six people were detained under the Internal Security Act. Still protests and strikes against the regime carried on. For Britain and America the apartheid regime was a grave embarrassment and a threat to stability across Southern Africa.

The collapse of the Soviet Union

The impact of the Cold War on the Western powers had been fractious and difficult. What few understood at the time was that the Soviet Union itself was in deep trouble. The 1970s had been years of 'zastoy' – stagnation. The Soviet economy managed great mobilisations in the eras of industrialisation and wartime defence, at terrible human cost. It proved much less effective at developing light industry and a consumer goods market. Soviet efforts involved a grinding wastage of time and resources. The Cold War in some ways leant purpose to the ill-run state, but what analyst Fred Halliday called 'the Second Cold War'[13] turned out to be too costly, and too sapping of Soviet resources to be borne. At the Novosibirsk Institute of Economics Tatyana Zaslavskaya wrote a report in 1983 that the 'productive relations' in Russia were lagging behind the development of the 'productive forces'.[14] In Marxist theory the clash of productive relations with productive forces would be the formula for a social revolution and the meaning of the report was that they would have to change course. Attempts were made by Communist Party General Secretary Andropov (1982–84) and then his successor Gorbachev (1985–91) to reform the economy, under a policy called 'perestroika', or openness.

The Soviet model of internationalism at the children's camp, Werbell East Germany.

The economic reforms were too weak to overcome the Soviet economy's fundamental problems. Worse for them, the collapse of ideological confidence meant that long-bottled up frustrations escaped rocking the whole soviet bloc in East Europe and beyond. The hard-line leaders of the USSR's allies found it difficult to cope with the new appeals to 'openness'. East German President Erich Honecker was challenged when Hungary's leaders opened the borders to let massing numbers leave the East and make their way to West Germany. In 1989 the East German government fell, and crowds gathered to smash up the Berlin Wall that divided the two Germanies. In 1991 the Soviet Union itself was beset by so many challenges that Gorbachev suspended the Union encouraging the constituent states to leave and reform themselves. The Soviet Union had collapsed, and the Cold War that had gripped the world was at an end.

The impact of the End of the Cold War was felt throughout the developing world. As an ally the Soviet Union had often turned out to be a fair-weather friend. Rhetorical support for third world liberation was often set aside as Moscow's leaders hoped to make détente with the West. The USSR backed many vicious dictatorships in its quest for allies in the world: from Kim il-Sung in Korea to Haile Mengistu Mariam in Ethiopia. On the other hand, just the fact of another pole of influence in the world did open up more options for Third World liberation movements. With the collapse of the Soviet Union the world seemed set to become unipolar, with the United States the sole superpower. The anti-western rhetoric of Third World liberation was stilled – though in other

ways the end of the Cold War led the way for the resolution of some seemingly intractable conflicts.

Throughout the post-war period, Britain's relations with the rest of the world had
been seen through the lens of the Cold War with the USSR. All the more localised
conflicts with colonised and formerly colonised peoples had been understood in those
terms. The democratic challenge posed by national independence movements for their
freedom, and for freedom from interference by the former coloniser, was reinterpreted
as communist subversion. The intense politicisation of that Cold War framework in the
1970s and 1980s effectively broke it apart. In the 1990s Britain would have to learn
to motivate its overseas policy, and in particular its policy towards the less developed
world, differently.

PART FIVE
Empire of Human Rights?
1990–2020

Chapter Thirty-eight

THE NEW WORLD ORDER

For 45 years the world had been in the grip of a Cold War, from 1945 to 1990. The international contest set the 'Free West' against the 'People's Democracies'. Fighting the Cold War gave Britain a special sense of purpose as it moved from Empire to Commonwealth. Rather than be cast as the enemy of freedom, Britain claimed to be fighting for freedom against the threat of dictatorship. In the name of meeting the Soviet challenge, Britain managed the handover to the United States as the leading western power and kept a special status as a NATO ally. Britain used Cold War propaganda to cast challengers to its authority in the colonies and former colonies as communists, or the dupes of communists. Domestic politics in Britain were also framed in Cold War terms. Radical opponents were decried as 'Marxists' and Labour politicians demonstrated their respectability by committing to the Western Alliance. Britain's national identity rested in no small part on its mission to defend the free world.

The end of the Cold War was understandably welcomed as a triumph for the free world. Margaret Thatcher told Parliament on 21 November 1990 that they had reached 'the end of the cold war in Europe and the triumph of democracy, freedom and the rule of law'. What Ronald Reagan had called 'the Evil Empire' was no more. Rand fellow Francis Fukuyama wrote in an essay that it was the 'end of history', by which he meant that the old contest between rival ideologies was over, and that liberal capitalism had triumphed.[1]

Quite soon after the end of the Cold War it became clear that it was not just the Soviet empire that had collapsed. US Ambassador to the United Nations, Jeane Kirkpatrick worried that the end of the Cold War meant that the 'structures through which international affairs have been conducted for the past 40 years have been shaken to their foundations'.[2] The mood of triumphalism shifted to one of anxiety. World leaders and security chiefs fixed on what they feared would be the new dangers, like 'rogue states', the 'Islamic bomb', international terrorism, the resurgence of Fascism in East Europe. There were elements of truth that these fears attached to, but there was also a great deal of exaggeration.

Margaret Thatcher, having stepped down from the British premiership, was invited to Fulton, Missouri on the fiftieth anniversary of Churchill's 'Iron Curtain' speech, 9 March 1996. She spoke on the theme of 'new threats for old', summarising the mood of anxiety about the post-Cold War order. The end of the Cold War had brought good, she thought, but,

> Like a giant refrigerator that had finally broken down after years of poor maintenance, the Soviet empire in its collapse released all the ills of ethnic, social and political backwardness which it had frozen in suspended animation for so long.

Thatcher highlighted in particular the menace of so-called 'rogue states' in the Third World:

> When Soviet power broke down, so did the control it exercised, however fitfully and irresponsibly, over rogue states like Syria, Iraq and Gadaffi's Libya. They have in effect been released to commit whatever mischief they wish without bothering to check with their arms supplier and bank manager.

For decades, the Soviet Union had been blamed for agitating third world nationalism, but Mrs Thatcher now complained that the Soviets were no longer around to rein in third world nationalism. She also highlighted the presumed threat of Islamic militancy:

> Within the Islamic world the Soviet collapse undermined the legitimacy of radical secular regimes and gave an impetus to the rise of radical Islam. Radical Islamist movements now constitute a major revolutionary threat not only to the Saddams and Assads but also to conservative Arab regimes, who are allies of the West. Indeed, they challenge the very idea of a Western economic presence. Hence, the random acts of violence designed to drive American companies and tourists out of the Islamic world.

Without doubt the challenge of Al Qaeda and ISIS in the twenty-first century would be a destabilising factor, though how the ground had been laid for their influence was a question that deserves investigating. What was clear in Mrs Thatcher's speech was that she was trying to imagine what kind of threat would justify Britain's continued military role in an Atlantic alliance first, and who the enemy might be second. The underlying anxiety confronting Britain's leaders was clear in Mrs Thatcher's insistence that:

> The West is not just some Cold War construct, devoid of significance in today's freer, more fluid world. It rests upon distinctive values and virtues, ideas and ideals, and above all upon a common experience of liberty.

Those words suggest that Britain's most strident peacetime premiere was unsure whether the West would endure the end of the Cold War, and whether its ideals would endure.

Peace Dividend

At the End of the Cold War there were hopes for a 'Peace Dividend'. The great mobilisation of arms and armies to guard against the Soviet threat was surely at an end. The money spent on arms could be spent instead on welfare; the armaments industries turned to civilian goods: 'They shall beat their swords into ploughshares.'

In 1990 defence procurement minister Alan Clark proposed a significant reduction in Britain's military budget and the cancellation of some missile programmes. Coming at the end of the Cold War these proposals were called a 'peace dividend' by some. Labour's Mark Fisher congratulated Clark, saying 'there are real benefits in the peace dividend', in Parliament on 4 December 1990 and Clark agreed that Britain's armaments industries 'will benefit from conversion to peaceful activity'.

In its 1991 Human Development Report, the United Nations Development Programme estimated that cuts of 2–4 per cent a year in global defence spending could free up $200 billion to $300 billion a year – leaving more for world aid. In a private conversation with French President Francois Mitterrand on 16 December 1989, US President George H. W. Bush was more circumspect, complaining that: 'there is a crazy mood in the US. Some people say we should cut $50 to 100 billion dollars in defence and give out a peace dividend in our social programs'.

UK Defence spending did fall between 1985 and 1990, and then again from 1992 to 1998, but in 2000 it began to rise again and in 2020 stands at £52 billion. The fall in spending was largely due to rationalisation and more hardware relative to troops. In terms of military engagements there has been no peace dividend, on the contrary, there were more 'hot wars', with new conflicts breaking out in the Middle East, the Horn of Africa and even in Europe. However, there would be important 'peace processes' in South Africa, Palestine and Northern Ireland as the end of the Cold War opened up the room for a readjustment or even a resolution of old conflicts (see Chapter Thirty-nine).

The crisis of legitimacy at home

Willingness to meet the communist challenge turned out to be so fundamental to Britain's international position, its military organisation and even its domestic politics, that the end of the Cold War led to disarray. It was like watching a tug-of-war competition where the winning side all fell over backwards as the losers on the other end of the rope lost their footing.

The domestic impact of the end of the Cold War, in Britain and America, was as important as the international ramifications. Domestic political life had been shaped by the contest of left and right in Britain, exemplified by the contest between the Conservative and Labour parties in parliament. The end of the Cold War did not just make Stalinism in the East look like a terrible route. It seemed to confirm the case that statist economies were destructive. That robbed the Labour Party of its social programme.

The Conservative Party ought to have been triumphant at the end of the Cold War, and its leaders claimed a victory. But in 1990 their longest serving leader Margaret Thatcher was deposed by her own MPs and John Major's government was by comparison ideologically adrift. The *raison d'être* that had sustained the Conservatives, of 'rolling back socialism' no longer had any point. The end of the Cold War seemed to be the end of ideologies, too. Tory grandee Lord Hailsham, who had been High Chancellor, fell into a deep depression in 1992, 'profoundly disappointed at the absence of improvement which had followed the collapse of Stalin's former Empire in the late 1980s'. 'Instead of the "peace dividend which we had hoped for in our optimistic mood after the breach in the Berlin Wall, the civilised world seemed to be in a state of collapse"'.[3] Without an overarching ideological appeal, both of Britain's major parties haemorrhaged members – as did mainstream parties all over Europe, and in the United States.

Without a coherent rationale British governing and cultural institutions lost legitimacy. Deference to authority fell away. Political party affiliation declined. Membership of civil associations, from trade unions to the Women's Institute fell. Even the Monarchy suffered in 1992 what Queen Elizabeth called her 'annus horribilis', with the divorce of Prince Andrew and Lady Diana's tell-all memoirs. Social scientists talked about a rising trend of individualisation as more people withdrew from public engagement.[4]

In the decades following, the main problem that governing elites had to cope with was a crisis of legitimacy as their relationship to the mass of people disintegrated. Popular enthusiasm for political parties gave way to a generalised cynicism towards government far greater than the usual background suspicion.

The themes of the World Economic Forum, the annual meeting of world business and political leaders held at Davos, gives a flavour of the growing disquiet among elites over their ability to govern. At the end of the Cold War, the Forum was discussing the 'new direction for global leadership' (1991), but as the decade wore on they worried about 'rallying all the forces for global recovery' (1993) 'sustaining globalisation' (1996) and 'managing volatility' (1998). In the following decade the themes got darker, with 'leadership in fragile times' (2002), 'Building trust' (2003), 'Taking responsibility for tough choices' (2005) and 'shaping the post crisis world' (2009).

Governing in a post-ideological age was mired in difficulty. New initiatives – like Hillary Clinton's 1993 health care plan, or Tony Blair's unfinished reform of the House of Lords – simply fell away, swamped in inertia, drawing more criticism than enthusiasm. The domestic political space was one where leaders were mocked and ignored. By contrast international politics, and in particular the apparent disorder in the developing world were an arena in which world leaders thought they could make a dramatic difference. The decades following the end of the Cold War saw a rise in diplomatic, military and aid intervention in the world.

The Gulf War 1990–91

On 2 August 1990 Iraq invaded neighbouring Kuwait - the first test of the post-Cold War world order. The United States' military was prepared. In 1989 General Norman Schwarzkopf served on the US Army's Central Command. 'I was confident of the Middle East's strategic importance and, therefore, of Central Command's reason for existence', recalled Schwarzkopf in his memoirs, but 'nobody except a few stubborn hardliners believed that we'd go to war against the Soviets in the Middle East. So I asked myself, what was most likely?'[5] As they looked around for an enemy that would justify them carrying on, Schwarzkopf and Central Command scrapped the old 'Zagros Mountain' plan, which prepared for a Soviet invasion, and drafted 'Internal Look', which changed the script, anticipating instead an attack by Iraq on Saudi oil fields.

That July Ambassador April Glaspie was asked by Iraqi dictator Saddam Hussein what the US view would be of a conflict with neighbouring Kuwait. Glaspie replied:

> We have no opinion on your Arab-Arab conflicts, such as your dispute with Kuwait. Secretary Baker has directed me to emphasize the instruction, first given to Iraq in the 1960s, that the Kuwait issue is not associated with America.[6]

Whatever Baker had the ambassador tell Saddam, the U.S. military was preparing for a war with Iraq.

In late July 1990, Schwarzkopf staged a mock-up of 'Internal Look' just two weeks before Iraq invaded Kuwait. As he says himself 'the movements of Iraq's real-world ground and air forces eerily paralleled the imaginary scenario in our game'.[7]

In the Cold War years Saddam Hussein had been an American ally and was valued by them as a counterweight to the influence of the radical Islamic regime led by Ayatollah Khomeini in Iran. Between 1982 and 1988 both America and Britain sold arms to Iraq that were used to fight a grinding war against Iran. Backing local strongmen like Saddam to defeat the communists made sense in the old Cold War framework. After 1989 Washington pundits and policy-makers recoiled from the association with Saddam. Instead, the Iraqi dictator became the first target of the post-Cold War western military.[8]

Visiting Washington Margaret Thatcher was disappointed to hear that US President George H. W. Bush was waiting to see whether an Arab League intervention would solve the border issue. 'This is no time to go wobbly, George', Mrs Thatcher said, meaning that the western alliance would need to use force against Iraq. President Bush was not going to 'go wobbly'. He discussed with his chiefs of staff the possibility that the Iraqis might back off, secretary of state Brent Scowcroft protested, 'don't you realise if he pulls out, it will be impossible for us to stay?' 'We have to have a war', said Bush, who was privately jubilant when negotiations between the Iraqi foreign minister and James Baker broke down.[9]

The conflict would become an early model for what post-Cold War engagements would be like. The first thing that made this war different was that there was no Soviet position to worry about. Soviet President Mikhail Gorbachev was preoccupied with the changes that would soon lead to the dissolution of the USSR. American and British diplomats worked hard to secure a UN Security Council resolution supporting an invasion. Not only did the Soviet Union support the action, but the Arab states Syria and Egypt, as well as Morocco and many of the Gulf States contributed forces to take part in the invasion.

The diplomatic campaign to build a coalition against Iraq was very suggestive to policy experts, and it would become a model for the conduct of international relations afterwards.

The *Guardian's* senior diplomatic editor, Hella Pick, highlighted the way that 'the United Nations emerging as a vital tool for shaping a new world order':

> For the first time since its foundation it has become possible to envisage ... the creation of a collective security system, combining mediation, peace-keeping and, if necessary, enforcement backed by UN peace-keeping forces.

The big change, thought Pick was that the Soviet Union was no longer tripping up the Security Council: 'The liberal use of the veto, especially by the Soviet Union, has made a mockery of the council's main task of maintaining peace and security until very recently', she wrote.

Pick understood that the new dispensation at the United Nations was not just about the absence of the Soviet Union as a factor. It was also about the declining authority of the non-aligned movement. Where third world radicalism had tended to enlarge its influence in the United Nations General Assembly in the 1970s, so many Arab states lining up behind a US–British coalition in the Gulf was a sign that their room for independent action had been limited. One of the major tensions in the General Assembly had been between the United States and its allies and the Palestine Liberation Organisation, which rallied third world support behind resolutions condemning US-ally Israel. In the votes over Iraq, the PLO was out in the cold, opposing western intervention by supporting Iraq. Afterwards the Palestinians' status took a dive. As Pick saw it,

> This new determination to give the United Nations a central role in the world order coincides with a virtual collapse of Third World solidarity in the UN. The stranglehold which this majority had sometimes been able to inflict on the UN's agenda has evaporated. The non-aligned group has become a shadow of its former self.[10]

Margaret Thatcher promised 'to send the 7th Armoured Brigade to the Gulf, comprising two armoured regiments with 120 tanks, a regiment of Field Artillery, a battalion of armoured infantry, anti-tank helicopters and all the necessary support'. 'It would be a completely self-supporting force, numbering up to 7,500', she said. Later Thatcher also sent,

> the 4th Brigade from Germany, comprising a regiment of Challenger tanks, two armoured infantry battalions and a regiment of Royal Artillery, with reconnaissance and supporting services. Together the two brigades would form the 1st Armoured Division. The total number of UK forces committed would amount to more than 30,000.[11]

The British forces were under General Peter de la Billière, a veteran of wars in Malaya and Dhofar. Coalition forces dropped 88,500 tons of bombs in 109,000 sorties. In all 250,000 bombs were dropped. The bulk of the bombing was carried out by B52s flying at 40,000 feet. The Iraqi death toll was around 180,000. As much as 80 per cent of the country's infrastructure was destroyed at an estimated cost of $150 billion.

The 'Highway of Death'.

Under Major General Rupert Smith Britain's 1ˢᵗ Armoured division took part in the attack on Iraqi forces retreating from Kuwait, the Battle of Norfolk, the biggest tank battle in the war, on 27 February 1991. British forces also took part in the attack on the retreating Iraqi forces on the Basra Road on the same day. The Iraqis were bottled in when Allied air forces attacked the roads out of Kuwait and destroyed them. Kill zones were assigned along the road. More than two thousand vehicles were destroyed and 25,000 killed.[12]

The Moral Rehabilitation of Imperialism

One consequence of the Gulf War was that elite attitudes towards military action overseas changed. American conservatives thought their country was suffering from 'Vietnam Syndrome' a popular disaffection with warfare after the fall of Saigon to the Viet Kong in 1975. The Gulf War was celebrated by them as a reversal of Vietnam Syndrome. In the minds of some Conservatives Britain was suffering from a similar 'Suez syndrome'. But with British troops and pilots fighting in Iraq it seemed that Britain was walking tall again. Though there was disquiet about the death toll, that was largely overshadowed by outrage at the Iraqi army's attacks on a disaffected Kurdish minority in the North, and by a general sense of triumphalism in the immediate aftermath of the war.

Editor of the *Sunday Telegraph* Peregrine Worsthorne saw vindication for his own conservative views in the turn to military action:

Refusing to adapt, as Britain is accused of doing, can sometimes pay off, since the wheel of fortune comes full circle. Possibly Britain was in danger of clinging too long to outmoded imperial values. Thank God she did. For the civilised world will soon need them again as never before.[13]

Foreign Secretary Douglas Hurd was also pleased with the idea that Britain might take more pride in its past record. 'We are putting behind us', he said, 'a period of history when the West was unable to express a legitimate interest in the developing world without being accused of neo-colonialism'.[14]

At least as interesting as the response of conservative thinkers to the 1990 Iraq War was the generally positive reaction from radicals. In the *New Statesman* the veteran Marxists Fred Halliday and Norman Geras reprimanded those who criticised the war on Iraq: 'the alternative to imperialist intervention is not non-intervention, but, rather, action in support of democratic change'. In another article, Halliday wrote that 'if I have to make a choice between Fascism and Imperialism, I choose imperialism'.[15] Geras and Halliday were not alone in crossing over to the side of enlightened imperialism. Academics and commentators from Michael Ignatieff to Robert Harris and Mary Kaldor were all gung-ho for military action overseas – on the understanding that this was a new kind of military intervention, one that was motivated by humanitarian rather than chauvinistic drives.

The writer and QC John Mortimer drew attention to this 'remarkable change in the opinions of those who either opposed the war or felt extremely doubtful about it': 'We have been hit by an unlooked for wave of liberal imperialism.'

Mortimer was surprised that the US announcement that it would leave was being criticised because it would leave the Kurds at the mercy of Saddam's army, since the critics were not the usual champions of American military action: 'Those who denounced the American invasion of Vietnam and Nicaragua are calling on yesterday's bullies not to leave the foreign soil of Iraq.'[16]

The 'wave of liberal imperialism' that Mortimer noticed was important because it would go on to help shape the character of military intervention in the next twenty years (though as it turned out the 'liberal imperialists' of 1997–2016 were not interested in restoring the reputation of Victoria's Empire, but preferred to distance themselves from it).

In the US Congress on 7 March 1991 President George H. W. Bush gave a speech marking the end of the conflict. It was an interesting speech most notably for the way that he sought to differentiate the coalition fought war from previous military adventures. 'Until now,' said President Bush, 'the world we've known has been a world divided, a world of barbed wire and concrete block, conflict and cold war.' He went on to say that:

And now, we can see a new world coming into view. A world in which there is the very real prospect of a new world order. In the words of Winston Churchill, a 'world order' in which 'the principles of justice and fair play . . . protect the weak against the strong.' A world where the United Nations, freed from cold war stalemate, is poised to fulfil the historic vision of its founders. A world in which freedom and respect for human rights find a home among all nations.

It was the phrase 'new world order' that caught the imagination. The President did set out to indicate what that might mean, suggesting a renewed push for peace between Israel and Palestine, collective action to secure the peace and an attempt to stop the proliferation of weapons of mass destruction. As important as the President's ideas about a New World Order would be the way that it was developed by those who came after him.

After inflicting a traumatic defeat on the Iraqi army and the country, British Prime Minister John Major proposed to create 'safe havens' from the air to stop attacks on the Kurdish minority. That laid the basis for RAF and USAF imposed 'no fly zones' over Iraq. As BBC correspondent Mohammed Darwish explained there were 'continued air strikes in the south and north of the country where British and American planes are attacking under the disguise of patrolling the no-fly zones'. So, on 16 February 2001 British Tornado jets joined US F-15 aircraft bombing Baghdad on the claim that Iraqi forces were set to attack the RAF imposed 'no-fly zone' over northern Iraq.[17]

Iraq was subject to an embargo of food from September 1990 under the unfortunately numbered UN resolution 666. After the war sanctions remained in place with the modification that Iraq could – on condition it surrendered its oil exports to the UN – get food aid in return (while the UN deducted a percentage for costs). Denis Halliday who managed the 'food for oil' programme resigned in 1998, saying that he was 'overseeing the de-development and deindustrialisation of a modern country', and that 'sanctions are starving to death 6,000 Iraqi infants every month, ignoring the human rights of ordinary Iraqis'.[18]

The conclusion to the 1991 war also put Iraq under a 'weapons inspection' programme, where UN officials would examine military sites in Iraq to make sure that they had no 'weapons of mass destruction' (WMDs). The weapons inspection regime failed to discover WMDs, but it did keep the issue in the public eye. Britain's MI6 had two clandestine programmes, 'Rockingham' and 'Mass Appeal' which were tasked with finding evidence from the UN weapons inspection programme to prove the existence of WMDs even though the inspectorate's actual findings were that there were none – they were destroyed in 1991. An official in Bill Clinton's administration explained that they counted on British military intelligence to help come up with the pretext for war: 'we were getting ready for action and we want the Brits to prepare'.[19]

Somalia 1991; Bosnia 1993–96

The first test of George Bush's New World Order was in Somalia. A famine in inter-riverine Somalia caught the world's attention in 1990. UN Secretary-General Boutros Boutros-Ghali argued that this was the place where a humanitarian mission was needed, and America's Congressional black caucus echoed his plea for intervention.

Siad Barre's 30-year rule had collapsed after unsuccessful campaigns to take territory from Ethiopia and Djibouti. He was ousted from Mogadishu and his retreating army helped wreck agriculture in already drought-ridden South-Central Somalia. The UN Secretary-General argued that rival clans were threatening food aid distribution.

The press in Europe and America leapt on the story of famine encouraged by the United Nations. Ever more dramatic headlines were written, and on 28 July 1992 Associated Press's story that 'The United Nations estimates 1.5 million people are in imminent danger of starving to death in Somalia while another 4.5 million are nearing a food crisis' was copied round the world. These were wild exaggerations. Somalia's entire population was only 7.2 million in 1993. The press campaign over Somalia's famine played on stereotypes of starving Africa being saved by white charity. In 1992, with the ambitions for humanitarianism writ large across the West, those images made a case for intervention.

President Bush agreed to send 25,000 US troops as part of a 37,000 strong Unified Task Force (UNITAF) under Operation Restore Hope to make the country safe for aid workers. Admiral Jonathan Howe was put in charge of the overall mission, known as UNOSOM. US news anchors Dan Rather of CBS and Ted Koppel of ABC were sent to Somalia. A study by the Refugee Policy Group found that the famine did kill between 202,000 and 238,000. That was a terrible loss of life but the study also found that it was mostly over by the time that the US troops arrived.[20]

There were many problems with the intervention. The aid organisations themselves created problems. Grain was bought from US farm surpluses under US Public Law 480. As USAID it dropped in Mogadishu depressing prices, so that Somalis abandoned their ruined farms moving to the coastal capital. Aid workers employed armed militias to secure the grain, creating rivalry.

The United Nations Security Council passed Resolution 814 on 26 March 1993 which committed UNITAF not just to peacekeeping (under Chapter VI of the UN Charter) but also to rebuilding Somalia's government as a 'peace-making' project (under Chapter VII). The idea that Somalia's government would be remade by 40,000 UN troops and personnel turned out to be wildly ambitious.

Somali leaders Mohamed Farrah Aidid of the Somali National Alliance, and interim President Ali Mahdi Mohamed were vying for power. US envoy April Glaspie and Admiral Howe favoured the weaker Mahdi, and they were jealous of Aidid's growing power base. UNITAF eventually raided Aidid's Mogadishu Radio and were confronted with thousands of protestors. In the fighting 37 Pakistani troops serving in UNITAF – and twice as many Somalis – were killed.

Admiral Howe issued an arrest warrant for Aidid, leading to an all-out war between Aidid's forces and UNITAF. On 12 July 1993, UNITAF fired missiles on a building housing a Somali peace conference in Mogadishu, killing 73. Aidid's forces stepped up attacks on UNITAF. In September they shot down a US 'Black Hawk' helicopter. On the night of 3–4 October 1993, a 160 strong UNITAF force attacked an Aidid stronghold near Bakara Market in Mogadishu, but quickly lost control when two Black Hawks were shot down with RPG missiles, and the ground force was penned in by hundreds of Somalis. A rescue force of 3,000 were sent to save them. Twenty-seven UNITAF troops – 19 of them American – were killed, and in the region of 500 Somalis. Around the world the UN peace mission in Somalia looked more and more like a US war mission. US embassies faced protests and even the Embassy in London was attacked, and for the first time in its history, breached and occupied.

In accounts of the war Admiral Howe is often blamed for taking the challenge from Aidid too personally. But the same could be said of Boutros Boutros-Ghali and of President Clinton, who fulminated:

> We're not inflicting pain on these fuckers. When people kill us they should be killed in greater numbers. I can't believe we are being pushed around by these two-bit pricks.[21]

Journalist Michael Maren says that the decision for the 12 July attack came direct from the White House.[22]

Eventually UNITAF had little choice but to sue for peace and begin a dialogue with Aidid. The mission failed because it was extravagantly overreaching, imagining that the United Nations could decide what Somalis needed better than they could themselves. Supporters of the intervention nursed intense and one-sided prejudices against those Somalis who challenged them, seeing them as tribal and backward peoples who were without morality. With hindsight it is easy to see that those beliefs solidified to justify the intervention.

Britain's contribution to the UNOSOM missions was minimal. The British role in the UNPROFOR mission in Bosnia, from October 1992 to December 1995 was larger. Britain made up the second largest contribution, after France, of 2,400 troops in a total force of 38,599.

The conflict in the former Republic of Yugoslavia began as the central government weakened at the end of the Cold War. Yugoslavia's international position as a non-aligned power not quite in the Eastern bloc gave it special status – and access to loans – with the US. Outside of the Cold War stand-off between NATO and the USSR, Yugoslavia lost a lot of overseas aid. After World War II, Yugoslavia's preponderant Serb population was contained by granting greater territory to the Slovene, Croat and Bosnian constituent Republics, meaning that the last two had a large Serb population within their borders.

Croatia declared independence on 1 June 1991, leading to fighting in the majority Serb parts of Croatia. In October the forces of the Yugoslav National Army bombarded Dubrovnik to wide condemnation. At the urging of Germany's Hans-Dietrich Genscher the 11 European Community ministers agreed to back Croatia's independence on 16 December 1991. UN Secretary-General Perez de Cuellar had urged Germany not to give diplomatic recognition to Croatia. Boutros Boutros-Ghali explained that 'if Croatia's independence were accepted internationally, other parts of Yugoslavia would declare independence as well, and a drastic struggle for territory would break out'.[23] It was a fateful decision that whipped up regional conflict even further.

For Bosnia a future tied to Slobodan Milosevic's Socialist Party regime was not the most promising prospect. The mathematics of Bosnia-Herzegovina were not very attractive either. In 1991 the population was 42.5 per cent Bosnian Muslim ('Bosniak'), 31 per cent Serb and 17 per cent Croat. An independence referendum on 3 March 1992 was boycotted by Serbs but enthusiastically supported by Bosniaks and Croats – securing a majority, but not a consensus.

Bosnian independence was initially viewed with some suspicion by Europeans but enthusiastically taken up by US Democrats in the 1992 Presidential election. When Bosniak leader Izetbegovic agreed a partition plan for Bosnia at Lisbon in February 1992, US Ambassador Warren Christopher talked him out of it. American 'policy was to break the partition plan', said one senior official.[24] Quite soon all of the powers were competing to propose the most radical break-up of the former Yugoslavia. They slipped easily into a moral rationale that the Serbs were the 'bad guys' and the Bosnians the 'good guys'. It was an approach that cast the conflict in black and white terms, leading to policies that increased tension rather than decreasing it.

At the London Bosnia Conference on 2 July 1992, Boutros Boutros-Ghali worried that the UN Security Council, 'is becoming like the General Assembly: it is using phrases and making demands that it knows cannot be implemented in order to please public opinion'.[25] On the ground the Bosnian Serb forces under Ratko Mladic, with the assistance of the government in Yugoslavia, plainly had the advantage over the amateurish Bosniak forces, and made heavy inroads. British Prime Minister John Major judged that the presence of the UN troops 'almost alone gave the "Bosnian state" meaningful territorial definition on the ground'.[26]

In Resolution 824 of 6 May 1993 the United Nations Security Council named Sarajevo, Goražde, Srebrenica, Tuzla, Žepa and Bihać 'safe havens'. The ability of the United Nations troops to keep the peace was compromised by the lack of agreement and the widespread belief that they were 'keeping the peace' by backing the Bosniaks against the Serbs. NATO action also encouraged Izetbegovic to struggle on, and 'the Bosnian Muslim government was adamant that an early end to the fighting had to be avoided at all costs'.[27]

By February of 1994 NATO forces were effectively at war with the Bosnian Serb army. Increasingly the Serb forces attacked soldiers in UNPROFOR and also Muslim civilians. In July 1995 Mladic's army took Srebrenica, which had been declared a 'safe haven' to 20,000 Muslims who had fled fighting in central Bosnia. In the massacre that followed 8,000 Muslims were killed by the Bosnian Serb Army. These were the worst of the atrocities against Muslims, but by no means the only ones – 25,609 Muslims civilians were killed in the fighting, as well as 7,480 Serbs, 2,610 Croats and others. Bosniak forces lost 42,492, Serbs, 15,298 and Croats 7,182.[28] The Srebrenica massacre was called a genocide so making the case for military action against Serbian forces.

In 1995 the RAF took part in NATO attacks on the forces of the Bosnian Serb forces in the civil war. NATO flew 3,515 sorties and a total of 1,026 bombs were dropped on 338 Bosnian Serb targets. British forces also took part in the UNPROFOR forces' artillery attacks. In the wake of the peace talks later in 1995 British forces took part in the 'Stabilisation Force' that occupied strategic points in Bosnia. Not independence but administration by the international community followed. The whole of the Former Yugoslav Republic of Bosnia-Herzegovina became a United Nations/EU protectorate placed under a United Nations 'High Representative' with dictatorial powers to direct and suspend political government. The first High Representative was Britain's Paddy Ashdown, outgoing leader of the Liberal Democratic Party. Despite hopes for a multi-cultural society in Bosnia, the country remains divided between Republika Srpska and the Federation of Bosnia and Herzegovina.

The conflict in the former Yugoslavia, like the fighting in Somalia did not lead to a reconsideration of the efficacy of humanitarian intervention. On the contrary, it was widely believed in diplomatic circles that the massacres of Bosnian civilians showed that humanitarian intervention had to be *more* decisive to succeed.

The ethos under which international relations were understood was changing. British Foreign Secretary Douglas Hurd argued that, 'it is empty to pretend we can impose peace with justice on every disorder or dispute outside our national borders'.[29] Hurd's views were widely pilloried by the new school of 'liberal internationalists', like the academics Martin Shaw and Mary Kaldor. The old idea that intervention in the world must necessarily be limited was denounced as cynical and a green light to dicta-tors to act with impunity. Radicals were as excited by the prospects for humanitarian intervention overseas as the liberal imperialists had been in the 1880s. As far as the proponents of this kind of liberal internationalism were concerned this marked the end of any kind of imperialist motivation. Liberal intervention was, according to its cham-pions, the opposite of imperialism.

Hong Kong: the Last Colony

With so much attention on the rebalancing of the world with the end of the Cold War, one question bearing on Britain seemed to be a hangover from another age. In 1898 as the British colony of Hong Kong grew, Britain leased the New Territories from the Qing China for 99 years, meaning that the lease would be up on 1 June 1997. The New Territories over time absorbed the overspill of Hong Kong's growth, so that by 1997 they were not quite two thirds of developed Hong Kong. In 1984 Britain and China agreed a broad Joint Declaration for a handover of power, with some general promises of a broad degree of autonomy.

Though the grounds for the transfer were legal the substantial basis for the change was the shift in power between Britain and China over the second half of the twentieth century. The handover was both an echo of the decolonisation era of the 1960s and a modern expression of the rise of China in the 1990s.

In the Maoist era political turmoil made small businesses leave China taking their capital with them so that the western concessions on the coastal towns of Macao and Hong Kong, and expatriate colonies in Singapore and across the Far East, once again became a refuge for Chinese traders. Hong Kong did seem like a miracle – in 1984 China's GDP was only four times greater, though its population was 200 times greater. That was because a lot of the trade that Hong Kong profited from was between China and the rest of the world. Hong Kong served as an entrepôt so that the goods that were made on mainland China were rung up on a cash register in the offshore island and counted there. Hong Kong's capitalist ascent was bound up with China's Maoist leviathan.

Deng Xiaoping kicked off the great change in China's economic system when he set up Special Economic Zones where free trade would flourish outside state control. The first zone was in Shenzhen opposite Hong Kong with the aim of attracting capital investment from there. Deng appealed to all the expatriate Chinese businessmen across East Asia to help the new China, and as much as eighty per cent of FDI came from Hong Kong. With China setting out on a new path of capitalist expansion the special role of Hong Kong as a trading point of the coast of Communist China was less distinct – Shanghai, Shenzhen and Guangzhou were fast catching up.[30]

The Conservative ex-minister Chris Patten was appointed Governor of Hong Kong – the last British Governor – in 1992. Patten sensed from the outset that the role of retreating Colonial Governor was as humiliating personally as it was for Britain. Uncomfortable with the prospect of surrendering the territory to Beijing Patten set out to emphasize the advantages of British liberty over communist tyranny and build in safeguards for those advantages.[31]

Governor Patten was hampered in this goal by Britain's actual record in Hong Kong. Though he tried to underline Britain's commitment to democratic reform by building up an elected legislature, he had to cope with the record that Britain had stood in the way of democracy throughout the 156 years it had governed. Plans to elect legislators were talked of in 1988 and in 1991, but not until 1995, with just two years left on the lease, did the Governor manage to have one third of the legislative council elected. Patten's claims to stand for liberty were undermined, too, by the British Government's 1981 decision not to honour the rights of Hong Kong people to UK citizenship.

In 2019, when the Beijing government did threaten democracy in Hong Kong there were mass demonstrations against the imposition. But in 1997, despite Patten's attempts to galvanise a democratic opposition to Beijing, most of the legislators, civil servants and businessmen he worked with were more interested in building relationships with the mainland. One by one his collaborators drifted over. Britain's departure from Hong Kong was marred by Patten's prickly fixation on prestige, and a habit of lecturing China from a position of weakness. Dictating human rights to Somalia or the Republika Srpska was ambitious, but in 1997 it was simply water off China's back.

Chapter Thirty-nine

PEACE PROCESSES

With the end of the Cold War the international realm was changed forever. Instead of two superpowers there was one. The Soviet Union under Mikhail Gorbachev changed from a challenger to a helpmate to America's leadership.

It was, said the intellectuals, the end of ideology. The differences of left and right that shaped the nineteenth and twentieth centuries were all played out, with liberal democracy winning out. The radical anti-imperialist ideology that motivated independence movements was one of those that fell by the wayside. Most of the European colonies were by this time nominally independent (even if they did bear the yoke of economic domination).

The end of the Cold War gave the United States, and its allies, including Britain, the chance to break down some of the more intractable conflicts. Where the struggle between 'western imperialism' and 'third world revolution' seemed to be set in stone, the new conditions seemed to offer a way out. As the big conflict that gripped the world was wound down, so, too, did it seem that these local and regional conflicts could be overcome.

In South Africa, and then the Middle East, and even in Northern Ireland new 'peace processes' were opened up. The peace processes were brokered by the U.S. with the help of the European Union and the United Nations, and often with Gorbachev's Soviet Union advising the anti-imperialists that they had to negotiate. The processes were infectious, each being a model for the next.

In each case the yearning for peace in communities long scarred by civil war and conflict was a compelling justification for negotiation. The pressure on the third world revolutionaries to hang up their guns was intense. Years of struggle had hardened the leaderships of these movements, but without tangible successes they were in danger of losing touch with the wider peoples on whose behalf they fought. The prospect of an honourable peace was a tempting prize.

With the possibility of dealing directly with the rebels, the Great Powers found that they had less need of the local strongmen that they had relied on to put them down. The apartheid state and the Ulster Unionists found that they were a lot less secure than they thought. Over their shoulders they could see how other strongmen, like President Marcos in the Philippines, General Noriega in Panama, the South Lebanese Army and in his own way, Saddam Hussein in Iraq could be dropped like a stone when they stopped being useful.

On the other hand, the balance of forces was not favourable for third world revolutionaries. At the very least they would have to smarten themselves up and rewrite their Lenin-inspired manifestos if they were to be taken seriously. Worse, the danger that a solution was to be imposed upon them persuaded many to try to make sure they were part of the peace process, not its targets. Often there were hard-liners who were ready to accuse the nervous penitents of selling out, whether it was the Pan Africanist Congress in South Africa, Hamas in Palestine or the breakaway 'Republican Sinn Fein' in Northern Ireland. Those critics would say that the revolutionaries of yesterday had become the deputy police chiefs of today, working on behalf of imperialism, that the end point was not so much an honest peace as the pacification of an insurgent people.

South Africa

South Africa in the 1980s had come close to revolution. The trigger was a half-baked reform, the 1983 Constitution Act, the apartheid government had brought in with the hope that it could drive a wedge between black subjects on the one hand and 'coloured' and Indian South Africans on the other. A 'tricameral' system was set up where there were different electoral rolls for Indians and coloured South Africans who sat in separate parliamentary chambers. Black subjects were to be represented in their bantu homelands through local councils.[1]

Though some coloured and Indian voters did take part in the elections, Allan Boesak led a strong boycott which undermined the legitimacy of the reforms. Only two thirds of coloured voters eligible registered to vote, and when the election took place only 30 per cent of them voted. The reforms hit black South Africans in much the same way that Britain's 1832 Reform Act, by leaving working class voters off the electoral roll, became a focal point for Chartist protests for the next 16 years.

Opposition to the Constitution Act made a bridge between the opponents of apartheid, the African National Congress, Boesak, Archbishop Desmond Tutu and the white Progressive Party. Rallying as the United Democratic Front they inspired a wave of protest across the black townships. On 3 September 1984 at Sharpeville nine anti-apartheid protestors were shot dead by police as they commemorated the massacre in 1960 and in Port Elizabeth a further 20 were killed. In the autumn 800,000 members of the only recently legalised trade union COSATU stayed away from work to protest against the new constitution. From Addis Ababa the ANC Radio called on the people to 'render South Africa ungovernable'. Their radicalism was in many ways an attempt to keep up with the grassroots campaigns in the townships that were running ahead of them. At that point the government in Pretoria had nothing to offer but a state of emergency, and as came out later, the use of clandestine 'death squads' to target activists.[2]

Late in 1984 the liberal South African MP and opponent of apartheid Helen Suzman brokered a meeting between Lord Bethell of the European Parliament and Mandela in prison. Though Mandela told Bethell he would call a halt to violence if the ANC were legalised, he refused a government offer of freedom if he foreswore violence.

The Nationalist Party Prime Minister P. W. Botha's apartheid regime was protected by Margaret Thatcher's administration, and that of Ronald Reagan in the United States who called his policy 'constructive engagement'. At the same time a growing campaign to boycott South African goods engaged popular opposition across the world.

Forty-eight US companies closed shop in South Africa in 1986 and Chase Manhattan Bank stopped all lending. By 1988 R2.7 billion had left the country. For many world leaders it seemed that they would have to strong-arm Botha into reforms or the whole system might be overthrown – and their investments lost along with it.[3]

On 18 January 1989 President Botha had a stroke. Through his illness he struggled to keep control of the Government, but that summer was forced to resign. His replacement F. W. De Klerk, though no radical, said, 'most South Africans are tired of confrontation and wish to speak to one another about the road of prosperity and justice for all'. On 2 February 1990 he announced that the bans on the African National Congress, the South African Communist Party and the Pan African Congress would be lifted, and that Nelson Mandela and other political prisoners would be released without conditions. On 11 February Mandela walked free to a hero's welcome.

De Klerk tried to moderate some of the anger that the years of repression had brought by appointing the liberal judge Richard Goldstone to head a Standing Commission of Inquiry Regarding the Prevention of Public Violence. Goldstone, who was backed by the ANC, used his powers freely, demanding access to prisoners in detention and exposing the South African security forces' role in attacking black militants. What became known as the 'Goldstone Commission' would play an important role in the transition to black majority rule and was the inspiration behind the Truth and Reconciliation Commission that investigated the crimes of the apartheid era under Archbishop Desmond Tutu.[4]

Talks about a new constitution began in March 1990. South Africa's ruling elite were not yet convinced that they could do business with the African National Congress and used Police, Defence Force, and clandestine death squads – the so-called 'Third Force' – to attack ANC supporters. The Bantustans and their governments were severely rocked by the changes, standing as they did on the grounds of cooperating with the apartheid regime. Transkei's Head of Government Bantu Holomisa told De Klerk that the homeland was 'a failed political experiment' and began talks with the ANC. Gatsha Buthulezi sent his supporters to attack ANC supporters (with financial help from the security forces).[5] At the same time the ANC was challenged by the grassroots of the township campaign at a Consultative Conference in December 1990, for giving too much ground to De Klerk to maintain white domination in a new form.

The township critics of the ANC had a point. The big change in the ANC's fortunes came not just from movement on De Klerk's side. In 1989 the ANC had adopted a policy, the Harare Declaration, that pledged the movement to equal rights and a democratic non-racial state. The Declaration also included a commitment to 'an economic order promoting the well-being of all South Africans'. At a meeting with 300 business leaders in May 1990 Mandela alarmed them explaining that the clause meant widespread nationalisation of private industry.[6] As it happened the ANC was already moving on that promise.

That February F. W. De Klerk had argued that the ANC would have to rewrite the socialist clauses in its manifesto: 'The collapse, particularly of the economic system in Eastern Europe, also serves as a warning to those who insist on persisting with it in Africa.' The President went on to say that 'those who seek to force this failure of a system on South Africa should engage in a total revision of their point of view'.[7] De Klerk was not just trying to push a change. He knew that it was already happening.

Joe Slovo was a member of the team the ANC put forward to negotiate with Pretoria. Slovo was a leading figure in the South African Communist Party. South Africa's business leaders were alarmed. But Slovo was leading the SACP as well as the ANC in a 'total revision of their point of view'. His booklet 'Has Socialism Failed?' – a response to the changes that Gorbachev was making in Soviet Russia landed on De Klerk's desk. Slovo faced the inevitable: 'For the moment the socialist critique of capitalism and the drive to win the hearts and minds of humanity for socialism have been virtually abandoned'[8] Slovo made some grand claims for the role that the communists had played, with some justification given that the SACP had been a core element of the ANC throughout the apartheid years. It was a back-handed claim though to say that: 'No one can doubt that if humanity is today poised to enter an unprecedented era of peace and civilised international relations, it is in the first place due to the efforts of the socialist world.'[9] Slovo was right in a sense. By withdrawing its support for the revolution in Southern Africa and advising Mandela to negotiate Gorbachev had made a reconciliation between South Africa's white business elite and the African National Congress possible.

In the British Parliament the Conservatives were gloating at the climb-down. 'The South African Government could not have run the risk of releasing Mr. Mandela', said Julian Amery, 'if President Gorbachev had not withdrawn his support for militant revolutionary forces in central and southern Africa'. Minister of State William Waldegrave agreed: 'The completely transformed relationship between East and West and this country, the United States and the Soviet Union has contributed to the change in atmosphere.' Waldegrave underlined 'the advice of the Soviet Union to the ANC, the South-West Africa People's Organisation and other organisations in southern Africa has been to seek dialogue and peace'.[10]

The peace process in South Africa was a remarkable success after years of violence and misery. The negotiations led to the first black majority-elected government in 1994, when 62 per cent of the nearly 20 million votes cast went to the ANC. Mandela led a government that granted voting rights to black South Africans and dismantled the formal restrictions of apartheid. It stopped short at the social transformation that many looked forward to, as industry and land remained in the hands of a mostly white elite.

Palestine

The Palestine Liberation Organisation, after years of contesting Israel for authority over Palestine, accepted Israel's right to exist on 8 December 1988. 'We accept two states, the Palestine state and the Jewish state of Israel', said chairman Yasser Arafat. That April Soviet president Gorbachev had advised the PLO that 'recognition of the state of Israel, consideration of its security interests, the solution of this question is a necessary element for the establishment of peace and good-neighbourliness in the region based on principles of international law'.[11] (The Soviet Union had long supported the diplomatic campaign that the PLO undertook to try to pressure Israel – and America

– in the United Nations General Assembly.) The 1988 overture was met coldly. Israel and America were not interested.[12]

While the PLO leadership, exiled in Tunis, were seeking peace, the Palestinians in the occupied territories were at boiling point. The previous year protests against the Israeli Defence Forces in the occupied West Bank gathered into a general wave that people called the 'Intifada', or uprising. PLO supporters were active in these protests,[13] but so, too, were the Islamic group Hamas, and other locally based organisations.

Things got worse for the Palestinians with the Gulf War of 1990–91. It was part of Saddam Hussein's strategy to try to widen the conflict by launching scud missiles at Israel. At the same time the Israeli authorities used the conflict to crack down on the protests that had been going on since 1987, the intifada. The Israeli authorities imposed a 24-hour curfew on the occupied territories from 17 January 1991. They also blocked Palestinian agricultural exports (worth around $60 million a week), laying off many of the 120,000 Palestinians who worked in Israel and closing the border crossings to them.[14] There were a number of protests in Palestine over US Operation Desert Storm against Iraq, and Arafat was isolated as a champion of an Arab solution when both Syria and Saudi Arabia backed Desert Storm. Both Saudi Arabia and Syria could have been counted on to support the PLO before, but now those regional powers had no use of the Palestinians. US President George Bush made a point of saying that Arafat had 'backed the wrong horse'.[15] Bush acceded to Israel's insistence that any future peace would be negotiated with the Arab states and exclude the PLO.

At a US- and Soviet-sponsored conference in Madrid in 1991 pressure was put on the Arab world to relax the economic sanctions it had put against Israel and reverse the UN General Assembly declaration that 'Zionism is a form of racism'. For the Palestinians, obliged to attend only as a part of the Jordanian delegation, and with PLO officials barred, the Madrid Conference offered little hope.

Secretly, though, Yitzhak Rabin's government sent Foreign Minister Shimon Peres to negotiate with the PLO's Mahmoud Abbas in Oslo. The Oslo accord gave up a great deal on the Palestinian side, but relatively little on Israel's part. A 'Palestinian Authority' was granted police powers over the Arab population in the occupied territories, but it fell far short of statehood. The Israeli Defence Forces would not withdraw, but be 'redeployed' outside of Arab towns, and Israel kept control of the border crossings into Egypt and Jordan. Israeli settlements stayed, with the IDF taking responsibility for their security. The West Bank was divided into three administrative areas each with a different status – not much more than a patchwork of Arab towns surrounded by Israeli-controlled areas.

Shimon Peres explained why the Israelis reversed their principle that they would not talk to the PLO in his 1993 book *The New Middle East,* where he looks at the way that the organisation was 'losing ground' and asks himself, 'would a collapse of the PLO benefit Israel?' Peres feared that if the PLO were to go under that the Islamic fundamentalist group Hamas – which was definitely not offering to recognise Israel – would take its place.[16] The Oslo accord gave the Palestine Authority-to-be the responsibility for suppressing Hamas and its attacks on Israel.

The Oslo Accord was topped off with a photo-shoot at the White House where an ebullient Bill Clinton cajoled a grumpy Yitzhak Rabin into shaking hand with Yasser Arafat. (Rabin's caution was understandable – hardline opposition to the deal was intense in Israel, and just two years later Rabin was assassinated because of it.) Though there was little of substance for the Palestinians they clung onto the hope that even the caricature of national independence offered. The protests of Intifada were mostly silenced, and for a while it seemed as if there might be a 'two-state solution' for Palestine and Israel.

Northern Ireland

By 1994 the British army had been stationed in Northern Ireland for a quarter of a century – in a conflict with the nationalist population that had left 3000 dead. The big change in the nature of the conflict was that in 1981 Sinn Fein, the political wing of the Republican movement, had fought – and won – the parliamentary constituency of Fermanagh and South Tyrone, standing the hunger striker Bobby Sands, so that shortly after he was elected, he died in the prison camp, Long Kesh. Sinn Fein went on to win again in the following by-election. In 1983 Sinn Fein President Gerry Adams won the Belfast West seat.

For Republicans the electoral strategy was a big departure. In 1981 Danny Morrison asked the Sinn Fein conference, the Ard Fheis, 'Who here really believes we can win the war through the ballot box?' – to which the answer was no-one. Morrison went on: 'But will anyone here object if, with a ballot paper in this hand and an Armalite in the other, we take power in Ireland?'

The movement had for decades kept up the principle that they would not sit in the colonial parliament in Westminster, nor in the partition parliaments of Stormont and the Dail in the South. Adams did not take up his seat, but the movement saw the chance of breaking out of the narrowly military conflict. In 1986 Gerry Adams told the Ard Fheis that the movement would contest seats in the Dail as part of a '32-county wide political struggle'.

Part of the pressure on the Republicans to change their methods came from the agreement made between the government of the 26-county Irish state and the British in 1985. Mrs Thatcher told the Eire government that they could have a say on policy in the North if, in turn, they cooperated with Britain on security measures against the IRA. Outside of the Republican stronghold of West Belfast Sinn Fein's strategy produced few results but it did suggest to the British security services that it might be possible to pull the Republican movement in the direction of more constitutional politics. At the same time the veteran moderate nationalist leader John Hume set out to save Sinn Fein from isolation by opening talks about a possible deal.

In 1992 Jim Gibney raised the prospect that 'republicans have been deafened by the deadly sound of our own gunfire', and asked Ard Fheis delegates to consider that 'there is a different world to the one that existed in the mid-sixties'. Gibney emphasized his theme in the pages of *An Phoblacht/Republican News:* 'the conflict has gone on long enough. It is now time to engage in talks to find a peaceful way to a new Ireland'.[17]

The thinking in the leadership of the Republican movement was not just about the pressures of war weariness at home. Gerry Adams had his eye on what was going on around the rest of the world: 'From South Africa to Palestine, we are witnessing what could be the beginning of what could become processes for the democratic resolution of these conflicts'. Martin McGuinness, the Republicans' second-in-command suggested that the British government should 'learn from South Africa and Israel', and that John Major should be 'radical' in the manner of De Klerk and Rabin. In *Republican News* the rank and file were told that 'Attempts are being made to take the gun out of South African, Palestinian and Salvadorean conflicts'.[18]

In response to these overtures the British government said through their own 'back channel' to the Republicans that 'Sinn Fein should comment in a major way as possible on the PLO/Rabin deal; that Sinn Fein should be saying "If they can come to an agreement in Israel, why not here? We are standing at the altar, why won't you come and join us?"' Ten days after this message *Republican News* did exactly that, writing that 'whatever the outcome of the PLO/Israel deal, the message which emerges, as it has elsewhere, is that inclusiveness is the way forward for all conflicts'.[19]

The change in outlook among Sinn Fein's leaders was remarkable. The leadership of the 1970s owed its place to a harsh, and deadly, contest over the way forward for the movement. The old guard (called the 'Officials') were excoriated as back-sliders, ready to sell out Ireland for a seat on the town council; the new Sinn Fein leadership (called the 'Provisionals') fought for the principle of a 32-county, all-Ireland Republic without compromise. Their attitude to the Protestants of Northern Ireland was that they would be represented by the people they elected to the Dail, but not be allowed to dilute the principle of national self-determination. By 1993 things looked very different.

'We would like to see a 32-county republic in Ireland', said Martin McGuinness, 'but what we are trying to bring about is a situation where all the people of Ireland get a right to national self-determination'.[20] Gerry Adams muddied the waters yet more:

> Whatever agreement we come up with has to be an agreement that the Unionists, like the rest of us, can give their allegiance to. They have to be part of it and have to feel that it accommodates them. [21]

Veteran socialist republican Bernadette McAliskey remembered asking Gerry Adams about the peace process strategy at the time: 'What is your Plan B if this doesn't work?' The impression she got from him was that 'he didn't have one'.[22] The peace process was the only option.

At the end of the year, the British Prime Minister and his counterpart, the Irish Taoiseach Albert Reynolds made a joint statement in Downing Street. The statement said that the most important issue was 'to remove the causes of conflict, to overcome the legacy of history and to heal the division which have resulted'. Between them they acknowledged that 'the absence of a satisfactory and lasting settlement of relationships between the peoples of both islands has contributed to continuing tragedy and suffering'. It was quite an admission for Britain that it had helped to make things worse, even if it was balanced up by including the government in Southern Ireland in the blame.

Major went further, by agreeing that the British government had 'no selfish strategic or economic interest in Northern Ireland',[23] and more, that it was 'for the two people of the island of Ireland alone, by agreement between the two parts respectively, to exercise their right of self-determination on the basis of consent, freely and concurrently given, North and South, to bring about a united Ireland, if that is their wish'.[24] In some ways this was just a repeat of the old dodge that it was the Unionists whose consent stood in the way of a United Ireland, and Britain was just making sure everything was done above board. But the statement went further. First in decrying the idea of a 'selfish interest' Britain was effectively saying that its sovereignty did not need to extend to Northern Ireland. Secondly, the agreement acknowledged a Southern interest in the settlement in Northern Ireland that went much further than the 1985 agreement, acknowledging the legitimacy of Irish national aspirations. In response Irish Taoiseach Albert Reynolds indicated that the Dublin government was ready to renounce its constitutional claim – adopted in 1939 – to jurisdiction over the six counties of Northern Ireland.

'The idea of a Joint Declaration had come from John Hume's talks with Gerry Adams which had begun in 1988', John Major recalled.[25] It seems likely that the wording was at least in part Adams's.

The Irish Republican Army declared 'a complete cessation of military operations' on 31 August 1994. 'We believe that an opportunity to secure a just and lasting settlement has been created'. To the irritation of London and of the Unionists in Ireland, IRA supporters in West Belfast and Derry came out on the streets to celebrate.

In the months that followed, British Prime Minister John Major could not bring himself to make the concessions that would have secured the peace. Pressured by his party and the Ulster Unionists to recant the apparent concessions to a Southern Irish role in the government of the North, Major insisted that he had offered no such thing. When he glossed the Downing Street declaration in his autobiography John Major wrote that 'the democratic right of self-determination had to remain within Northern Ireland', – which was rather less than was declared at Downing Street.[26]

The peace process stalled because Major's government would not go ahead with talks on the future settlement with the Republicans present. They were told that they would have to surrender their arms to an international decommissioning body, led by US Senator George Mitchell. The Republican leadership saw this as one more manufactured hurdle, with no clear promise of talks if they did surrender their arms. On 9 February 1996 the IRA announced the end of their ceasefire. An hour later a lorry loaded with explosive blew up at Canary Wharf in East London, killing two people. Later, on 15 June a massive explosion wrecked the shopping centre in Manchester.

Despite the resumption of the IRA's bombing campaign it was clear that the 'long war' was going nowhere. There was no plan B, as Bernadette McAliskey guessed. John Major's government was itself in a lot of difficulty, not because of the peace process, but because it had run out of ideas and was widely seen as corrupt. With all Britain waiting for an election and most likely a new government, the Republican leadership would do nothing to restart the peace process while Major was in power.

The Good Friday Agreement

Shortly after Labour leader Tony Blair became Prime Minister in 1997, the talks started again. Talks between the political parties in Northern Ireland, including Sinn Fein, and the leaders of the British and Irish Governments under the auspices of US representative George Mitchell ended with the Good Friday Agreement, on 10 April 1998. The guiding principle of the agreement was that the two traditions in the Six Counties, Nationalist and Unionist, would have 'parity of esteem' in the eyes of the authorities.

For ten years after the signing of the Good Friday Agreement the British Government's shuttle diplomacy between the Republican and the Unionist leaders went on. Tony Blair told (then) Northern Ireland Secretary Peter Mandelson that 'the process is the policy' meaning that if the negotiations stopped then everything would slide back into conflict.

Under the Good Friday Agreement loyalist and nationalist parties agreed to share power in a new Northern Ireland assembly, in tandem with measures to release paramilitary prisoners, decommission arms and other 'confidence building' measures. The Northern Ireland Assembly was innovative in its power-sharing mechanisms which aimed to stop the representatives of one community from capturing all the political offices.

As the process wore on the world changed so that a return to an IRA campaign seemed harder to imagine. After the September 11, 2001 Al Qaeda attack on the Twin Towers America's Irish community were less sympathetic to the 'armed struggle', and New York Congressman Pete King, a long-time friend of Gerry Adams, said that 'the time has come for the IRA to disband'.[27] On 25 July 2005 the IRA (using their Gaelic-language name) declared that 'the leadership of Óglaigh na hÉireann has formally ordered an end to the armed campaign'.

Even with the winding down of the shooting war between the IRA insurgents and the security forces, in Northern Ireland, says political analyst Liam Ó Ruairc, 'segregation and divisions have significantly increased since 1998'. There are 88 'peace walls' dividing Catholic and Protestant communities in Northern Ireland today, compared to 22 before.[28] The political settlement did not end the divisions, but rather entrenched them as the Northern Ireland Assembly works under a 'power sharing' agreement, that has institutionalised the 'nationalist' and 'unionist' political identities: all members of the legislative assembly must adopt 'a designation of identity, being "Nationalist", "Unionist" or "Other"'. Institutionalised sectarian divisions lead the politicians to compete for resources, widening the gaps even further. Ó Ruairc explains that in the new framework both Sinn Féin and the Democratic Unionist Party have become 'ethnic tribune' parties. Ó Ruairc points to the problem that these parties 'seek to maximise the group's share of resources extractable from participation in the power-sharing institution'.[29]

Northern Ireland's peace process was consolidated. In South Africa, an historic overthrow of apartheid was only tempered by the understanding that now the African National Congress would be responsible for managing capitalism. In the Middle East, the doleful position of the Palestine Authority, little more than a municipal extension of the Israeli occupation was the least successful.

Chapter Forty

HUMANITARIAN INTERVENTION

The 1990–91 Gulf War, and the war in Bosnia after it had a dramatic impact on how international relations were organised. Lessons that were laid down in the Gulf War were that military action could be taken when it was in the name of the international community. The rationale for military action (beyond the rights of self-defence) that were deemed acceptable and proper were those undertaken for humanitarian reasons, in particular to stop genocide, aggression and to prevent harm.

The working out of the new ethos of humanitarian intervention took place in a nexus of debate between Ministers and Civil Servants, the military and with a big contribution by aid and human rights organisations. Their role was considered so novel that they were gathered under the category of 'Non-Governmental Organisations' – NGOs (though sceptics pointed out that they were often largely government-funded bodies).[1] The debate over the new humanitarianism reached a curious intensity, with international trouble spots dominating the news agenda throughout the 1990s and 2000s. Arguments were overwrought with moral intensity, as it seemed that not to act would be to be complicit in atrocities or genocide. It was a debate that broke down the usual demarcation lines of 'left' and 'right', too. Many people on the left were ardently committed to military intervention, whereas many on the right were sceptical about the extension of British power beyond her national interests. It would be wrong to say that this was a debate that engaged the general public. Rather it was carried on among the liberal intelligentsia and the somewhat less liberal military and civil service.

The new humanitarian foreign policy was so different that it led to a big shift in international relations theory. Where it had been assumed that the essential building block out of which all international relations were made was the sovereign nation state, a new liberal internationalist theory downgraded the nation state as actor, elevating (in theory at least) the non-governmental actor, the 'international community' and international organisations.

The United Nations Charter of 1945, Article 2.7 reads 'Nothing contained in the present Charter shall authorize the United Nations to intervene in matters which are essentially within the domestic jurisdiction of any state'. That clause defended the ideal of national sovereignty. In the new liberal internationalism the national sovereignty clause seemed to be out of date and a barrier to humanitarian action. States could resist intervention on the grounds that the international community had no business interfering with their domestic jurisdiction. Geoffrey Robertson QC served as a Judge in a United Nations War Crimes Tribunal in Sierra Leone. His book *Crimes Against Humanity* makes the case against Sovereignty: 'The great play of sovereignty, with all its pomp and panoply, can now be seen for what it hides: a posturing troupe of human actors, who when off-stage are sometimes prone to rape the chorus'. Similarly, Kenneth Roth, executive director of the organisation Human Rights Watch argued: 'sovereignty cannot be used as an excuse to avoid human rights commitments'. Columbia University Professor Samuel Moyn, in a careful history of the emergence of Human Rights as a focus for international law explains that it was the *decline* of radical alternatives to the status quo, in particular the anti-colonial movements, that left human rights as the main arena of ameliorative action.[2]

The argument over humanitarian intervention was not academic. All of the post-cold war military interventions that Britain was involved in were undertaken in the name of humanitarianism, and self-interested motivation was denied.

These were the major military engagements British forces fought:

Gulf War (1990–91)
Bosnian War (1992–95)
Operation Desert Fox (against Iraq, 1998)
Kosovo War (1999)
Sierra Leone Civil War (2000–02)
War in Afghanistan (2001–14)
Iraq War (2003–09)
Libyan Civil War (2011)
Operation Shader, in Iraq and Syria (2014–present)
Persian Gulf Crisis (2019)

In every case apart from the Sierra Leone incursion British forces were part of a coalition with the United States, or part of a United Nations or NATO force.

Humanitarian intervention was by no means military intervention alone. United Nations' missions did much more than use military force. Missions undertook conflict resolution, capacity building with new regimes, trained police forces and undertook extensive educational and welfare roles. Most strikingly, the United Nations created ad hoc investigations into war crimes. The most important of these were the United Nations Criminal Tribunals that investigated and tried leaders in the conflicts in the former Yugoslavia (1993), Rwanda (1994) and in Cambodia (2003).

Britain's 1997 Regime Change

Tony Blair's Labour Party won a handsome victory in the general election on 2 May 1997 (and again in 2001 and 2005). The Conservative Party was exhausted, morally and programmatically after four terms of office. Blair very successfully cleansed his party's brand of its old association with top-down state socialism and the trade union leadership. Campaigning against both Conservatism and Labour's own traditional working-class base, Blair positioned it as 'New Labour' – a post-ideological party that would rule technocratically, committed to free markets and detraditionalizing society.[3] He was very successful at showing what was wrong with the old ways, but less so at setting out what was new. Though the party won the popular vote it failed to build a strongly committed following and, its critics complained, suffered from an ideological and moral vacuum at its centre.

Tony Blair advanced a political appeal that he called the 'third way' – that was neither socialist nor conservative, for markets and the state. The post-ideological approach appealed to people who could see that the older solutions were not working and chimed with a generation of world leaders from Lionel Jospin in France to Bill Clinton in America. It was less successful in presenting a positive appeal in its own right and its reforms were piecemeal and uninspiring. Many, like the 'Anti-Social Behaviour Order' (ASBO) and the Private Finance Initiative, created more problems than they solved.

Throughout his term of office Tony Blair was a militant supporter of humanitarian intervention. Where the domestic political agenda often seemed like a quagmire, dramatic action overseas was especially appealing to a leader with a keen sense of his place in history.

Through the course of the Bosnia conflict the Conservative government was put on the back foot over its cautious approach. That was a novelty in British politics. In the 1980s, especially over the Falkland conflict, it was the left that was cast as cowardly and attacked for not backing 'our boys'. Labour's policy of unilateral nuclear disarmament was scoffed at from the Tory benches. With the Bosnia conflict the cliché of right-wing belligerents versus left-wing milquetoasts was disrupted.

The Bosnia War did not influence the outcome of the 1997 election. Popular support for the war in 1993 had in fact waned by 1995. The importance of the new thinking on overseas policy was not in the polling booths, but in the confidence of the Labour Party leadership and activists that they were in the right on this issue (as on many others). Having cringed at the prospect of arguing Labour's non-nuclear alternative defence strategy on the doorsteps in the 1980s, the party was feeling ebullient. Radical intellectuals, after the Cold War, were more excited by the possibilities of military intervention overseas. Labour's policy makers were of a similar frame of mind. A youthful and energetic Labour Party won in May 1997. The liberal internationalism of the foreign policy debate shaped Labour's thinking. Foreign Secretary Robin Cook set out the approach:

> The Labour Government does not accept that political values can be left behind when we check in our passports to travel on diplomatic business. Our foreign policy must have an ethical dimension and must support the demands of other peoples for the democratic rights on which we insist for ourselves. The Labour Government will put human rights at the heart of our foreign policy.[4]

The recasting of Britain's foreign policy in 1997, marked by the change in administration from Conservative John Major to Tony Blair had wider implications – most pointedly in the Good Friday Agreement of 1998.

The Blair government also shifted Britain's policy on Europe. The previous Conservative administrations of Margaret Thatcher and John Major had been sceptical members of the European Economic Community. Tony Blair, by contrast, was an enthusiastic supporter of the European Union (as it had become under the Maastricht

Treaty of 1993). In the first instance Blair's pro-Europeanism was a challenge to the domestic audience, a way of painting both the Labour left-wing and the Conservatives, as backward-looking little-Englanders. For Blair, Britain's 'history of grudging engagement with the continent was a tragedy of missed opportunities'.[5] Blair did not see participation in the Union as the loss of British power. He told Labour's conference in 2002 that it was 'our destiny to lead in Europe'.

Britain's pro-European turn in 1997 coincided with greater prospects for the Union's Common Foreign Policy. Cambridge University's Christopher Bickerton explains that in the Cold War era European foreign policy cooperation was stymied by the way that those global tensions aggravated differences among European nations. The post-Cold War era it seemed held out new prospects for European cooperation, though, as Tony Blair highlighted the Union was a superstate but not a superpower – something that he hoped he could fix.[6] More cooperation at the European level suited his ambitions for a liberal internationalism and for international cooperation in policing the world.

Practically, though, Britain under Blair adopted international alliances in an *ad hoc* way. The European Union was a useful platform from which Britain attempted to isolate Zimbabwe President Robert Mugabe, and it shouldered some of the burden of overseeing the administration of Bosnia-Herzegovina. The Union proved to be an unwieldy vehicle for international cooperation on the whole, however, because of its incoherent policy-making process (which would become clear when it was confronted with a crisis in the Ukraine).

Kosovo 1999

The Kosovo Liberation Army was founded in 1996 to press for the separation of the Yugoslav province. The KLA took up arms against the Federal Republic of Yugoslavia in 1998 and was rewarded with a place at UN sponsored peace talks. When Yugoslav forces took action against Kosovans, NATO launched a prolonged series of air attacks in Kosovo, and against the Yugoslav capital, Belgrade. Rather than calm the conflict the intervention led to more attacks on Kosovans by Yugoslav forces.

British Prime Minister Tony Blair gave a speech in Chicago on 24 April 1999 where he argued that 'this is a just war, based not on any territorial ambitions but on values'. Blair went on to set out what he claimed was a new and different vision of the world:

> We are all internationalists now, whether we like it or not. We cannot refuse to participate in global markets if we want to prosper. We cannot ignore new political ideas in other counties if we want to innovate. We cannot turn our backs on conflicts and the violation of human rights within other countries if we want still to be secure.

The Prime Minister tried to persuade US public opinion to support a ground force in Kosovo – earning the jibe that he was willing to fight to the last drop of American blood. Relying on air power, however, the Allied forces were only committed to destruction.

On 14 April 1999 the allies bombed a convoy of Kosovo Albanian refugees at Korisa – the very people they claimed to be helping – killing 87. The Royal Air

Force played a significant role in the bombardment of Kosovo and of Belgrade. Around 600 people were killed in Kosovo and 5000 in Yugoslavia overall. The citizens of Belgrade protected their bridges from 72 days of aerial bombardment by making themselves 'human shields' – standing on the bridges at night with ironic target signs. Bomb damage to Yugoslavia was estimated at $26 billion. The USAF bombed the Chinese Embassy killing three Chinese reporters. At the time this was claimed to be a result of poor intelligence though it was later shown to be deliberate targeting.[7] In the aftermath of the conflict, 7000 British troops took part in KFOR – a 'stabilisation force'. Under its jurisdiction 20,000 ethnic Serbs were forced out of Kosovo.

When NATO targeted Belgrade bridges Serbs made themselves into human shields to protect their city.

Outside of Serbia the Kosovo war was seen as a great success. 'Nato is prosecuting a war which many liberals can hardly believe', *Guardian* journalist Jonathan Freedland told an audience at the Methodist Central Hall on 11 May 1999: 'a war fought in pursuit of a humanitarian aim', where 'the prize is not turf or treasure', but 'a noble goal'. For Tony Blair it was an opportunity to paint a very different picture of the role of Britain's military overseas. At Chicago on 24 April 1999, Blair said,

> Our armed forces have been busier than ever – delivering humanitarian aid, deterring attacks on defenceless people, backing up UN resolutions and occasionally engaging in major wars as we did in the Gulf in 1991 and are currently doing in the Balkans.

The Prime Minister's vision of the new internationalism was one that had the USA at its heart, and he used the platform to plead with Americans not to abandon her international commitments:

> I say to you: never fall again for the doctrine of isolationism. The world cannot afford it. Stay a country, outward-looking, with the vision and imagination that is in your nature.

To this extent Blair was like so many Prime Ministers before him, appealing to Atlanticism, the unity of the NATO Alliance and Britain's own perceived 'special relationship' with America:

> And realise that in Britain you have a friend and an ally that will stand with you, work with you, fashion with you the design of a future built on peace and prosperity for all, which is the only dream that makes humanity worth preserving.

One sign of the new Labour government's enhanced status in the Atlantic alliance was the choice of Defence Secretary George Robertson as head of NATO in 1999. The humanitarian values seemed to work well with those more traditional aspects of militarism.

Afghanistan 2001, Iraq 2003

The American election of November 2000 saw George W. Bush (son of President George H. W. Bush) become President. The election was closely fought (and his opponent did win the popular vote but lost the electoral college). George W. Bush's campaign took on the record of the popular but flawed Bill Clinton. George W. Bush was elected on a policy of refocussing on domestic issues away from the apparent preoccupation with international affairs. Bush's choice for Secretary of State Condoleezza Rice had argued for a shift in foreign policy in an article in *Foreign Affairs* published before the election. Rice's article was a stark attack on the liberal internationalism followed by the Democrats in the White House from 1993 to 1999. 'Foreign policy in a Republican administration will ... proceed from the firm ground of the national interest, not from the interests of an illusory international community', she promised.[8] The administration withdrew from the Kyoto agreement on climate change, the 1972 anti-ballistic treaty and stalled debt relief. It was a vision very much at odds with Tony Blair's of an Atlantic axis of cooperation. In Europe, Bush's election provoked a wave of anti-American protests from environmentalists and 'anti-capitalists'. Many Europeans saw the election as America withdrawing from its international obligations.

On 11 September 2001 the United States was attacked by a group of Islamist terrorists called Al Qaeda ('the base') organised by the Saudi Osama bin Laden, from his exile in Afghanistan. The attack was as simple as it was deadly. Four small groups hijacked separate aeroplanes leaving Logan International Airport in Boston. Two of the planes were flown into the Twin Towers of the World Trade Center, one after the other. Another crashed into the Pentagon. Passengers in the fourth plane tried to overpower the hijackers and it crashed into a field in Pennsylvania. Two thousand nine hundred and seventy-seven people were killed, as well as the 19 hijackers. Most died in the Twin Towers and in the planes. A further 25,000 were injured by the blast and collapse of the towers. Understandably, the United States was traumatised and outraged by the attack. The public mood for retribution was great.

In Britain Prime Minister Tony Blair was at the Trade Union Congress prepared to give a speech, but cut it short with the news that America had been attacked, and a denunciation of mass terrorism: 'we, the democracies of this world, are going to have to come together to fight it together and eradicate this evil completely from our world'. From that point on Blair made it his goal to stay as close to the American president and offer whatever he could in support. The United Nations Security Council quickly agreed the US proposition to attack Al Qaeda's base.

In October 2001 American and British forces attacked the Taliban government in Afghanistan. The war was initially very effective. The Taliban were unworldly in their attempts to negotiate, and the United Nations Security Council agreed to set up a NATO-led International Security Assistance Force, which invaded the country. In 2003 they helped to install Hamid Karzai as President.

In Washington, President Bush signalled that America's need for a reordering of the world was not satisfied. His State of the Union address in January 2002 set out the case that the 9/11 attacks and the rogue regime in Iraq, Iran and Kim Jong-il's North Korean dictatorship should be understood collectively as an 'Axis of Evil'. On 6 April 2002 Tony Blair met Bush and committed Britain to support a renewed all-out attack on Iraq. In 2003, though, the US was not able to get a consensus on the Security Council for an invasion, when France, Russia and Germany called for more time for diplomatic efforts to work. Instead, America organised an ad hoc 'Coalition of the Willing' (the United States, Britain, Spain, Poland and Australia initially), claiming authority under the previous UN resolutions calling on Saddam to open all sites to the weapons inspectorate.

On 19 February 2003 coalition air forces flew 1700 sorties, 504 with cruise missiles in an attempt to 'shock and awe' Iraq. Thirteen thousand cluster bombs were dropped by the Allies, 2170 by the UK. According to Human Rights Watch:

UK forces caused dozens of casualties when they used ground-launched cluster munitions in and around Basra. A trio of neighbourhoods in the southern part of the city was particularly hard hit. At noon on 23 March, a cluster strike hit Hay al-Munandissin al-Kubra (the engineers district) while Abbas Kadhim was throwing out the garbage. He had severe injuries to his bowel and liver, and a fragment that could not be removed from his heart

Human Rights Watch went on to say that:

Three hours later, submunitions blanketed the neighbourhood of Mishraq al-Jadid about two and a half kilometres north east. Iyad Jassim Ibrahim, a 26-year old carpenter, was sleeping in the front room of his house when shrapnel injuries caused him to lose consciousness. He later died in surgery. Ten relatives who were sleeping elsewhere in the house suffered shrapnel injuries. Across the street, the cluster strikes injured three children.[9]

Between 25,000 and 50,000 Iraqis were killed in the initial invasion of Iraq. But that was by no means the end of the conflict in the country. Nine thousand British troops took part in the occupation of Iraq which brutalised and killed many Iraqis. Though the Iraqi army was effectively defeated in 2003, under allied rule the country was plunged into a destructive internecine conflict, as well as several rebellions against the allied occupation that cost hundreds of thousands of lives.

In late March 2003 Britain's 7th Armoured Brigade fought the Iraqi Army's 51st Division for control of Basra. Around 500 Iraqis were killed in a tank battle fought by the Royal Scots Dragoon Guards. British losses were eleven.

Britain supplied a force of 7,200 to police Basra from 2003 to 2009. Hundreds of allegations of torture, assassination and ill-treatment have been laid against the British forces, leading to the setting up of a government Iraq Historic Allegations Team.

In Afghanistan the initial successes were undermined as the government of Hamid Karzai failed to secure support against a resurgent Taliban. The conflict has cost more than 100,000 Afghan lives, of whom two thirds were Taliban fighters, and the rest government forces or civilians. Two thousand two hundred and seventy-one Americans have been killed in the fighting, and 456 British troops. In the occupation and the prolonged (and ineffective) hand over that followed, British forces were stationed in Helmand Province in the South West of the country between 2006 and 2009.

The British presence in Helmand lacked legitimacy. When British forces handed over authority to local chiefs in Musa Qala, those same chiefs later asked the Taliban to enter the town peacefully, without a shot being fired. When the outside world got to hear about Britain's humiliation, the British army had to stage an invasion of the town they had only recently abandoned, with a force of 4,500 troops after the US Air Force bombed the town. British commander, Major-General Graham Binns asked: 'If 90 per cent of the violence was directed against us, what would happen if we actually stepped back?'

Later Afghan President Karzai protested that the British administration of Helmand Province had undermined the government's authority, ousting the local Governor, and worse bribed Taliban militias to garner support. As International Relations specialist David Chandler explains, 'The British policy of appeasing local opposition leaders, through buying their support and allowing the harvesting of opium poppies, has directly undermined the Afghan government'.[10] The last British forces were withdrawn from Afghanistan on 27 October 2014. In 2021 US forces withdrew, and the Taliban took back many towns and cities.

Looking back, Jonathan Freedland, one of many journalists who had made the case for liberal interventionism in the post-Cold War Era had to admit that 'the notion that the west has a duty to act in extreme situations has been buried in the rubble of Afghanistan and Iraq'. The Afghan withdrawal, he concluded, 'seals the fate of liberal interventionism'.[11]

Humanitarian Intervention after Iraq

Before and after the 9/11 attack on America international relations were turned upside down and then upside down again. George Bush's (and Condolezza Rice's) threatened withdrawal from the international community was halted and reversed. Under George W. Bush America was once again fiercely engaged in the world. Britain, as Tony Blair foresaw, would make a role for itself as the bridge across the Atlantic, making the case for America in Europe, and for Europe in America, so enhancing its own authority. As champion of international cooperation – albeit of a yet more militantly forward kind – Britain would secure its own status in the world.

That vision was developed by Tony Blair's growing club of admirers. In 2006 John Bew and Gabriel Glickman wrote a manifesto *The British Moment* for their think-tank, the Henry Jackson Society (named for an Atlanticist American Senator). There they tried to distil the lessons of the preceding decade:

> From the British perspective, those who support the principles of humanitarian intervention, or the spread of liberal democracy, converge on the ground of what we could call a "progressive" foreign policy.[12]

In the same collection James Rogers and Matthew Jamison set out a six-point plan to realise what they called the British Moment:

- Commitment to Britain's economic dynamism;
- Maintenance of a strong military;
- Standing against mass murder in Greater Europe and beyond;
- Support the spread of democracy;
- Commitment to universal human rights; and
- Commitment to the European Union and enhancing relations with America.[13]

Around the same time a similar group were meeting in Euston, where they set out another manifesto (the 'Euston Manifesto'). It was similar to the 'British Moment' statement, though more argumentative, making the case against anti-Americanism, for 'Historical Truth', and with a more explicit commitment to fighting racism and women's rights. The founders of the group were Alan Johnson, Eve Garrard, Nick Cohen, Shalom Lappin and Norman Geras.

What both groups had in common was the belief that British overseas intervention was a likely vehicle to achieve these goals. That way they were both defenders of the Blair government's commitment to humanitarian intervention.

The difficulty for the proponents of humanitarian intervention was that the actual interventions were looking more and more inhumane. With the death-toll in the 'coalition' wars ratcheting up from hundreds to thousands to hundreds of thousands the claim that Britain was a force for good was looking more threadbare.

In the nineties the wars against Aidid in Somalia, Milosevic in Bosnia and Kosovo, and against Saddam in Iraq were not met with mass opposition. The Iraq War of 2003 set a completely different precedent. Millions of protestors opposed the 2003 Iraq war, marching in Washington, London, Paris, Berlin, Madrid and Athens; and millions more across the Middle East. The champions of intervention had enjoyed the moral high ground in the nineties. But from 2003 they were cast as the defenders of a brutal and barbaric policy. The rationale for the Iraq War, the alleged presence of 'Weapons of Mass Destruction', failed to materialise, as also the alleged link between Saddam and Al Qaeda was never demonstrated. The moral high ground was turning into a bog. Steadfast champions of humanitarian intervention in the 1990s became opponents of war, like the campaigning journalists Ed Vulliamy and Martin Bell, while Robin Cook, the original champion of an ethical foreign policy opposed war in Parliament. In the

1990s the anti-war left, Tony Benn, Jeremy Corbyn and Diane Abbott, was isolated and mocked for being old-fashioned, while these same figures found themselves addressing crowds of hundreds of thousands of people in 2003.

In America, too, George W. Bush's very successful and popular war was slowly turned into a sour anti-insurgency that cost American lives and drained American self-confidence. In 2008 Bush was defeated by a remarkable young senator from Illinois Barack Obama, who rode into the White House on a wave of youth rebellion whipped up by a promise to get out of Iraq. Obama's political orientation was very close to Tony Blair's and his election was in no sense a repudiation of the broader project of humanitarian intervention, but his popular support was premised on a desire to end the Iraq war (among other issues that were pressing at the time, notably the financial crash of 2008).

After 2005 the case for humanitarian intervention would never again be popular with the public, though it was still fundamental to many politicians' ideas about Britain's place in the world. In 2007 Tony Blair succumbed to a sustained campaign by his second-in-command Gordon Brown to vacate 10 Downing Street. At the end of his premiership, Timothy Garton Ash asked Tony Blair what the essence of Blairism was. 'It is liberal interventionism', Blair answered, 'I am a proud interventionist'.[14]

The Meaning of Humanitarian Intervention

For the proponents of humanitarian intervention the reasons for action were easily understood. The compelling motive was the threat to human security and rights from dictatorial regimes and ethno-nationalist movements. Humanitarian intervention was an internationalist response to the problem of human security. The conceptual meaning was that the old system of sovereign nation states was solipsistic and a warrant for dictatorship and oppression. Military action in pursuit of mere national interest or worse, predatory and oppressive motives were to be abjured. The responsibility to act was an idealistic expression of human community that transcended national boundaries. The agents of intervention were armies and governments, but their selfish motives were tempered by action in concert, through international cooperation and institutions, like the United Nations, the Organization for Security and Co-operation in Europe, the Nuclear Non-Proliferation Treaty and so on; those traditional actors were added to by a new set of agents, the non-governmental organisations – aid organisations, human rights advocates, environmental pressure groups and so on. These added up, it was claimed to an international 'civil society', that would make up the legitimacy that the imperfect national polities no longer provided.

The growing ranks of the critics of humanitarian intervention saw things differently. They simply did not believe the claims to disinterested motivations on the part of the proponents of humanitarian intervention. These ideals were in the eyes of the critics just a mask for venal and vested interests. (In this way champions and critics alike tended to see themselves as the representatives of idealism, with the critics casting the champions as hypocrites.) On their marches the anti-war protestors excoriated the Prime Minister as 'Tony B. Liar'. It was, they said, a 'war for oil', not a war for democracy. Unmasking the pecuniary interests behind the high ideals was the argument they felt most comfortable making. Both champions and critics of humanitarian intervention contrasted their chosen course with the old politics of Empire. The champions had claimed that their interventions were a break with the old policies of Empire because they were not selfish or predatory. The critics struck a harsh blow when they replied that the interventions in Iraq, Yugoslavia and Somalia were examples of 'humanitarian imperialism'. Since the ideals claimed were just a disguise for selfish interests then it stood to reason that the new liberal internationalism was in truth just the old imperialism dressed up in fancy clothes.

After the Iraq debacle it was harder to argue that the investigation of war crimes by international tribunals was disinterested idealism. Rather it seemed that the selection of which belligerents might be investigated was governed by brute reality. The evidence that US service personnel had tortured and killed innocent Iraqis and ridden rough shod over their human rights was not going to be investigated at the Hague. The United States resolutely opposed submitting its nationals to the jurisdiction of the International Criminal Court. The ad hoc justice of the international war crimes tribunals punished those who were outside of western favour while protecting those who were favoured allies. The Serb leaders, Mladic, Karadzic and Milosevic, were prosecuted (the last died of a heart attack while conducting his own defence), but the authoritarian leaders of Croatia and Bosnia, Franjo Tudjman and Alija Izetbegovic were never called to account for the actions their armed forces took against civilians. Even the terms of the Rwandan tribunal excluded atrocities that the forces of the Rwandan Patriotic Front undertook before 1992 and against refugees after 1994, that fell outside of its remit. Later on, western diplomats began to suspect that their champion of human rights in Rwanda, President Paul Kagame was sanctioning the assassination of dissidents overseas.[15]

Not just the war crimes tribunals were tarnished by the selective justice of humanitarian intervention. Media outlets like CNN and the *New York Times,* and in Britain, the *Times* and the *Guardian* were seen to have carried fake stories about Saddam's 'weapons of mass destruction'. The one-sided accounts of the just allies and the evil Iraqi regime were hard to square with the dawning realisation that the coalition forces were deeply unpopular, and casually oppressive. Many journalists who had uncritically repeated British government war propaganda were invited to eat their hats when those stories turned out to be less than the unvarnished truth. Press coverage of conflicts overseas were viewed with a greater scepticism after Iraq.

Conor Foley, who had worked for Liberty, Amnesty International and the UNHCR is a defender of humanitarian intervention. Foley worried about the way that the Iraq war of 2003 had undermined the argument for intervention, trying to imagine how things looked to those people on the other side of the argument:

> For 'anti-imperialists' the invasion was the culmination of a period of misguided western intervention that has seen the weakening of both national sovereignty and international law.

Foley went on, in the voice of the 'anti-imperialists' he had argued with:

Iraq exposed the folly of the belief that human rights and democracy can ever be imposed on other countries by force of arms.

And further,

Such rhetoric, they argue, masks a more traditional concern with securing western strategic, economic and political interests. The doctrine of 'humanitarian intervention', they maintain, is just a new name for old-fashioned imperialism.[16]

The people that Foley was talking about were the anti-war left and other critics of 'humanitarian imperialism'. They included writers like the late Peter Gowan and Tariq Ali at the *New Left Review,* the veteran anti-war scholar and activist Noam Chomsky and his collaborator Ed Herman, the scholar David Wearing and Stop the War activist Lindsey German. They echoed the point of view of the activists, writing articles and books about the War for Oil, and what they called the 'humanitarian imperialism' (the title of a 2006 book by Jean Bricmont).

Though occasionally the anti-imperialist left would use the term 'New Imperialism' (the title of a 2005 book for the Oxford University Press by David Harvey), the main rhetorical strategy they adopted was to emphasize the continuity between the new humanitarian imperialism of the 1990s and the old-school imperialism of the 1890s. The human rights claims were just a façade, they said – after all the old school imperialists were missionaries who talked about anti-slavery (before clapping you in irons), too. Oil interests were the real motive for war, that and the quest for new bases overseas to intimidate the natives.

The anti-imperialists' critique of humanitarian imperialism had a point, but it also had a weakness. The emphasis on continuity between the past imperialism and the modern humanitarian intervention risked losing sight of what was new. The liberal interventionists' claim that international relations are about more than self-interested states had a point. What they were describing was a new factor in foreign policy that did not follow the self-limiting rules of sovereignty as argued by Douglas Hurd and the students of the 'Realist' school of international relations.

The argument that it was West's demand for oil that was driving the humanitarian interventions was the was hard to stand up. After all it would have been a lot cheaper to buy the oil from Saddam than spend what was estimated to be more than $1 trillion to fight the war. If the goal was only to make money the Iraq War was already a disastrous failure.

'The majority of Iraq's 200-odd state-owned factories are white elephants full of outdated equipment', reported the *Kansas City Star:* 'Still, in the fall, the coalition had to abandon its notion of rapidly privatising those enterprises after heated opposition from Iraq's Governing Council.' When the Pentagon finally did start to award contracts in March 2004, it was part of an $18.6 billion construction programme funded by the USA. In October 2003, a donor conference failed to raise the targeted $34 billion from America's allies, leaving the US to foot the bill. British oil interests were not in favour of the war. Both the Chief Executives of Shell and BP counselled against the war. After the war oil prices rose precipitately.[17]

Subtler views of the capitalistic motives of the warmongers saw the military campaigns as part of a general strategy of imposing order and warning off any opposition before it hardened up. In this view 'shock and awe' – the name of the initial bombardment of Iraq – is the central point.

The view that interventions were designed to impose order on the world were open to an obvious objection – that they did not create order, but disorder. The restless overturning of former allies, from General Noriega to Saddam Hussein all tended to make the world a *less* orderly place. Here both liberal internationalist and anti-imperialist analyses seem to be lacking. The obsessive focus on new problems was disruptive. Interventions did not bring stability but disorder that was disruptive for the people whose lives were being turned over as it was for the prospects of future trade and investment. Looking back the era of 'humanitarian intervention' is more notable for its lack of purpose than either its liberal or capitalistic order. The decades 1990–2020 are dominated instead by statesmen grandstanding for attention in a world whose essential outlines are unclear.

Michael Ignatieff, who himself played a key role in making the case for a muscular interventionism made this self-critical point:

> When policy was driven by moral motives it was often driven by narcissism. We intervened not only to save others, but to save ourselves, or rather an image of ourselves as defenders of universal decencies.

Ignatieff's reflections on the humanitarian impulse saw it as much more driven by the needs of western liberals than by events in the Balkans:

> We wanted to know that the West 'meant' something. This imaginary West, this narcissistic image of ourselves, we believed was incarnated in the myth of a multiconfessional Bosnia. The desire to intervene may have caused us to rewrite the history of Bosnia, to make it conform to our ideal of a redeemable place.

The intervention was, in Ignatieff's argument, the outward manifestation of a spiritual crisis in the west:

> Bosnia became the latest *bel espoir* of a generation that had tried ecology, socialism, and civil rights only to watch all of these lose their romantic momentum.[18]

Ignatieff had a point. One of the chief drivers of humanitarian intervention, as it had been since the End of the Cold War was an attempt to invest the Western mission with a moral purpose. The insistent note of Tony Blair's argument was the appeal to values. 'This is not a battle for NATO, this is not a battle for territory', the Prime Minister insisted at the Stenkovec refugee camp near Skopje, the Macedonian capital, in May 1999. 'This is a battle for humanity', Blair went on to say – revealingly – that 'Milosevic shall be defeated so these people can again become symbols of hope, humanity and peace.' The refugees were important to him not as people, but as symbols, symbols of suffering humanity and western largesse.

At Stenkovec the Prime Minister found a sense of purpose that eluded him in the more mundane debates over Britain's domestic political scene. The world outside Britain's borders, most of all where order had broken down, was a place where Blair, like those other activist political leaders Bill Clinton and later Barack Obama, could act decisively.

The government commissioned research from the British Council and the Demos think tank about Britain's standing abroad and were disappointed to find a reputation for colonial arrogance. They talked to advertisers like Wally Olins and BMP about rebranding Britain and tried to promote an idea of 'creative Britain' overseas. The 'ethical foreign policy' was such a rebrand.

The anti-war protestors were right in one sense about the Iraq War. It did echo many aspects of the old imperialism. At its heart it was a pointedly unequal contest, where the western powers imposed their writ on a less powerful enemy. The new United Nations and NATO administrations in Iraq, Somalia, Afghanistan and Bosnia were not Empire as it was, but they were imperialistic in their attitude to the peoples they commanded. In other respects, the war was very different from the old colonial wars. One major difference was that if you were to think of the new humanitarianism was an imperial ethos, it was markedly different from the old, in the most obvious sense that the 'Empire of Human Rights' belonged to no one particular power. Though the anti-war activists called it an American Empire, it was not that in name, but instead acted in the name of a community of nations. Michael Hardt and Antonio Negri argued in their book of the same name, that 'Empire' in 2000 was a system of global ordering that had broken free of any particular nation state. The 'humanitarian interventionists' were right to argue that the conditions were new, but ought to have understood that it was the west that had changed, more than the world beyond had. The perception that the world was dominated by rogue states and cartoon-villain dictators said more about the west's yearning to cast itself as the hero of the story than it did about real-world developments. What had changed was the West, America and Europe, in their need, post-Cold War, to define for themselves a *raison d'être*. International Relations analyst Philip Cunliffe shows how this moral imperialism made a 'de facto new standard of civilisation that inscribed a new hierarchy into international politics, by which certain states were deemed superior and others inferior.'[19] Though Cunliffe goes on to explain that this is a hierarchy that brings little order.

Woke Imperialism

Over the centuries Britain has in different eras imposed its will on peoples and nations beyond its borders. Those interventions and impositions have been different in different times, taking on the beliefs and preoccupations of the governing elite here, and imposing it on people over there. Elizabethan colonists took the rights of seizure for granted, but after the 1837 Select Committee on Aboriginal Peoples colonists started to motivate their claims as part of a civilising mission abroad, as their church missionaries argued. In the twentieth century the colonists often said that they were only looking after colonies on behalf of their native occupants and aiming to educate them to govern themselves at some point in the future. Today, too, when Britain's armed forces and government impose their will on others, they do so in keeping with the aims and sentiments of their own times.

Our own times are a lot more liberal in outlook than they were. Ideas that owe their original formulation to the struggle for racial justice and even against imperialism are today mainstream. Ideas about women's liberation and even gay liberation that were alien to our Victorian forbears have today become embedded in the outlook of mainstream society. The new laws on equality of opportunity that were passed in the later twentieth century and in the 21st have consolidated that broadly liberal trend in British society (Race Relations Acts of 1965 and 1976, Equal Pay and Sex Discrimination Acts of 1971 and 1975, decriminalisation of homosexuality in 1967, equalisation of the age of consent for homosexuals in 2000, and gay marriage in 2006, Equality Acts of 2006 and 2010).[20]

Liberal social views, however, have not done away with the encounter between a more powerful Britain and less powerful nations in the world. They can lead to some strange paradoxes, as British leaders motivate their actions overseas in ways that seem at odds with the unequal power relationship. With the 'humanitarian intervention' ethical foreign policy that Britain developed in the 1990s intervention was, as we have seen, motivated as the defence of the rights of the peoples of the countries that were being attacked, on the premise that their governments were oppressive and illiberal (which was generally true). The end point, as the critics argued, was quite often not an improvement, however.

Labour MP Ann Clwyd played a big part rallying liberal opinion in favour of the 1991 Iraq war, which she did by highlighting the plight of Iraqi Kurds who were subject to violent suppression under Saddam's regime. On 1 October 2001 Development Minister Clare Short deflected criticisms of the bombing of Afghanistan in the House of Commons by painting the British mission there as one to bring aid to the hungry, and to educate children: 'On behalf of our Government I undertook to work with the Government in the North-West Frontier province to ensure that, as rapidly as possible, boys and girls are educated.' In the *Guardian* newspaper, Katharine Viner cautioned that the US military interventions overseas that Britain was supporting were a case of 'Feminism as Imperialism', a 'theft of feminist rhetoric' in pursuit of 'national expansion'.[21]

A report by the Special Inspector General for Afghan Reconstruction into 'U.S. efforts since 2002 to support Afghan women and girls and advance gender equality' points out that the $787 million budgeted for such programmes underestimates the real figure, 'because hundreds of other U.S. programs and projects included an unquantified gender component': 'gender mainstreaming advocated bringing women's issues and perspectives into all programs or policies'. Quotas for women representatives in the Jirga, or Parliament, were so successful that 27 per cent were women – a greater share than there were in Congress. The Special Inspector General did worry that 'women parliamentarians have limited connection with their constituencies, and some have never even been to the provinces they represent'. Those fears proved prescient. The withdrawal of US military support for the Afghan government in August 2021, saw it collapse in 48 hours, as the Taliban took over.[22]

At the National Army Museum, the armed forces are presented as a changing institution that is working to overcome its history of discrimination:

> Today, the Army is lauded as an employer that celebrates diversity. Women make up about nine per cent of the current force. And, in 2016, it reached number 32 in Stonewall's top 100 inclusive employers for lesbian, gay and bisexual staff.[23]

To many critics of Britain's military role overseas the claims that the army is an equal opportunities employer ring hollow as they see the army's role overall as one of reinforcing oppression.

In her compelling analysis of western aid policy and how it works in Mozambique, LSE academic Meera Sabaratnam argues for a 'decolonisation of intervention'. Looking at the ways that aid intervention has worked to undermine native agency, Sabaratnam calls for:

> a reversed understanding of who deserves what out of intervention – in this story, it is the target of aid who is entitled to it materially by virtue of historical patterns of imperial dispossession.[24]

Sabaratnam's call for a policy of intervention to fix the impact of previous intervention is not as remarkable as it might appear to a casual reader. Under James Wolfensohn the World Bank looked again at its own record of setting conditions on loans to developing countries and found that these were often damaging to the economies that they were supposed to be helping. Instead of imposing conditions on loans, the World Bank and other international institutions insisted that they would become partners in poverty reduction. British Chancellor Gordon Brown characterised the shift in attitude:

> A century ago people talked of 'What we could do for Africa?' Last century it was 'What can we do for Africa?'. Now in 2006 we must ask what the developing world, empowered, can do for itself.

Those were big promises, but how did they work out in practice? Looking at the example of Tanzania, researcher John Pender outlines the ways that the World Bank's Poverty Reduction Schemes turned out to be just as patrician and coercive as the previous Structural Adjustment Programmes. The Bank went through the process of agreeing Poverty Reduction Schemes with the Tanzanian government. At the same time these agreements were used to sideline the Tanzanian parliament and political process.[25]

Though the new approach emphasized 'country ownership', as the humanitarian interventions in Afghanistan and Iraq claimed to be liberating the people of those countries, the conundrum remained that the developed countries were telling the less developed countries what they had to do to be free. In international diplomacy British promotion began to take on the character of a 'woke imperialism', where it seemed the Britain's mission overseas was nothing to do with advancing British interests, but instead a campaign to educate Muslim girls, stamp out racism and mend the damage caused by imperialism.

In the older imperial project those people who resisted the British presence were often traduced and dehumanised in ways that made sense to Britons in those days. Muslims were often portrayed as effete and predatory homosexuals. In 1849 Brigadier-General Williams claimed that 'had the Turks penetrated into Georgia last campaign, very few youths of either sex would have escaped pollution'. The year before the Anti-Slavery Society claimed that 'the brutish idolators and low-caste Mohamedans', who had migrated to the West Indies as indentured labourers, 'are guilty of the vile practises alleged', meaning homosexual acts.[26] Today the British Foreign Office helpfully advises lesbian and gay visitors to Saudi Arabia, Kuwait and other countries in the Middle East that homosexuality is illegal in those countries. The Foreign and Commonwealth Development Office campaigns for lesbian and gay rights to be recognised across the world.[27] Over the last 170 years it is not the Middle East that has changed to become more anti-gay, but rather Britain that has changed, liberalising its laws on gay rights as the attitudes of its citizens have become more liberal. The idea that Muslims were effeminate back then was really just an upside-down reflection of how fundamental masculine values were to Victorian society. That Britain's laws have subsequently changed makes Saudi Arabia's or Zimbabwe's intolerance on the matter stand out to a British traveller. Those are real problems that minorities in other countries face. They are also part of the account of the superiority of British society that makes it possible for Britons to believe that they have a right to reform other countries for the good of their different peoples.

When British leaders try to distance themselves from the record of the British Empire, they make intervention more palatable, but they also risk opening themselves to criticism. Prime Minister Tony Blair's address to the September 2002 Earth Summit in South Africa was upstaged by Namibia's president Sam Nujoma, who roundly attacked Blair for rallying sanctions against Zimbabwe's president Robert Mugabe. It was Britain that had created the land problem in Zimbabwe in the first place, argued Nujoma, while the British Prime Minister had to suffer the public attack. 'Woke imperialism', has its risks for political leaders, but in relations between Britain and the developing world those are bound to reflect the attitudes that Britons hold, and particularly those that are distinct from those held by other peoples.

Chapter Forty-one

IMPERIALISM TODAY

British military intervention in the Middle East continues to this day. The main areas of conflict that Britain has been involved in since the 2003 Iraq War are in Syria, Iraq, Libya and Yemen.

Protests against Syria's President Assad began in 2011 as they did against many Arab leaders as a part of a wider 'Arab Spring'. Though Syria was an important ally in the 1990–91 Gulf War, President Assad's opposition to the 2003 invasion put the country at odds with western policy. In 2005 Syria was accused of being behind the assassination of Lebanon's President Hariri and relations cooled. From 2011 both Washington and Westminster put their support behind 'opposition groups' protesting against Assad's regime.

The dilemma that has dogged western policy in the Middle East is that the two main rivals for power in many of the countries that the west has intervened in are authoritarian nationalist leaders and the Islamic fundamentalist movements known as Al Qaeda or Daesh. In the Arab Spring early protests were led by more middle class and secular democrats, but these quickly lost ground to the more dynamic Islamist movements. In Syria, the Foreign Office and the US State Department sponsored groups that they hoped were committed to democratic and liberal reform, the Syrian National Council and the Free Syrian Army. These have largely melted away as Islamic State fighters have proved a more durable challenge to the Assad regime, and in some cases were found to be masquerading as the Free Syrian Army. Western allies like Turkey and Saudi Arabia had no compunctions about funding the Islamists directly in the campaign to oust Assad.

The problem for Britain was that the IS fighters were at least as hostile to Britain (and all of the West) as they were to Assad – though they were willing to take as much military and financial assistance from the West as they could get away with. The opposition protests soon took on the character of an all-out revolt as the Assad regime fell back on violent repression.

An unintended consequence of western military support for the opposition was that the Islamic State of Iraq and Syria that Daesh built grew rapidly, taking advantage of the weakening of the Assad regime. The problem was underscored by the emigration of some 400 British citizens to the Islamic State to support its campaign against Assad and Iraq. As Philip Cunliffe argues, the Jihadis believe that they justified by a cause that rises above national borders, as in their own way, many western leaders do.[1]

British women who joined ISIL.

In 2014 as Islamic State bore down on Yazidi and others in Northern Iraq, British troops were sent to support local forces against them. Troops were sent to train Iraqi military and Military Engineers to help build the Al-Asad air base. Between December 2015 and 2017 the Royal Air Force made 85 strikes in Syria. These were undertaken after opposition defence spokesman Hilary Benn called on Parliament to put away its reluctance post-Gulf War to intervene in the Middle East, and attack Daesh.

On the ground, Islamic State was defeated by a mix of Syrian and Iraqi forces with some assistance from the West. In 2014 Assad called on Russia's President Putin for assistance and the Russian military has tipped the balance back in Assad's favour. In 2018 British media reported an alleged chemical attack by Syrian government forces on the city of Douma. The British switched sides a second time in the war between Assad and Islamic State, pleading with their US and French Allies to help attack Syria. Russia vetoed the attack on the United Nations Security Council, but the allies went ahead and bombed a chemical factory in northern Damascus.

In 2011 British, French and American leaders waged an air war on the government of Muammar Gadaffi in Tripoli, in apparent support of rebel forces attacking the capital. British ships and aircraft fired Tomahawk missiles at Al Khums naval base and other targets. The intervention was largely the initiative of British Prime Minister David Cameron and French President Nicholas Sarkozy. US President Barack Obama was persuaded by Secretary of State Hillary Clinton that the intervention was worthwhile but has since said it was a mistake. These tensions could be seen in the organisation of the offensive force, where it was announced more than a few times that NATO would be taking over leadership. British Prime Minister David Cameron was reported as saying that it was important to get Arab nations on side so that 'this did not look like a Western initiative'.

Britain, America and France could take succour from the capture and execution of Colonel Gadaffi who as an opponent – and as an ally – had been a thorn in their sides. But the opposition government that replaced him had scant authority. Active in the opposition to Gadaffi were the Islamist group Ansar al-Sharia. In 2012 that group took advantage of the defeat of the old regime and the greater US presence in Libya to attack American diplomats in Benghazi, killing the ambassador Chris Stevens and three others. Following that attack Ansar al-Sharia were listed by the United States as a terrorist group in 2014. In 2012 mass protests forced them out of Benghazi. Britain, Turkey and Italy in particular continue to support the ill-founded Government of National Accord under Fayez al-Sarraj where the Tobruk-based Libyan National Army of Khalifa Haftar is challenging it.

A substantial motive in the Syrian and Libyan policies was Prime Minister David Cameron's determination to overcome the reluctance of the Armed Forces to commit to intervention after the difficulties in Iraq and Afghanistan. Cameron wrote in his memoirs that 'our military and security services were on this issue a huge source of frustration'.[2] Cameron was frustrated, too, that in 2013 the British Parliament voted down military intervention in Syria, a position that it did not reverse until Hilary Benn's speech in 2015. These interventions were at least in part undertaken to reverse the post-Iraq malaise that Cameron and Minister Michael Gove felt had taken a hold of the British political and military establishment. Many commented at the time that Prime Minister Cameron was 'channelling his inner Tony Blair'.

The House of Commons Foreign Affairs Committee took a dim view of the Libya intervention, concluding in 2016 that,

> The government failed to identify that the threat to civilians was overstated, and that the rebels included a significant Islamist element. By the summer of 2011, the limited intervention to protect civilians had drifted into an opportunist policy of regime change.

The Committee went on to outline the damage that had been caused:

> political and economic collapse, inter-militia and inter-tribal warfare, humanitarian and migrant crises, widespread human rights violations, the spread of Gaddafi regime weapons across the region and the growth of Isil [Islamic State] in north Africa.[3]

It was a harsh judgement but justified.

Britain in the War in Yemen

In the Arab Spring of 2011, the Saudi-led Gulf Cooperation Council brokered a deal to install Vice President Abdrabbuh Mansur Hadi in the place of President Saleh, to forestall mass protests against the Yemeni government (as the only candidate in the election, Hadi won 100 per cent of the vote). Conflict broke out between the supporters of Hadi and the Houthi movement that overthrew him in the capital Sana'a in 2015. Saudi Arabia to the north used military force to support Hadi, with the support of the British and US military.

Yemen protests, 2011.

Saudi air power could not cover up the fragmentation of Hadi's forces in face of the Houthi advance, but the impact on the country has been disastrous. More than 100,000 have been killed in fighting while starvation has led to tens of thousands of deaths and an outbreak of cholera. The United Nations warns that since Saudi Arabia started its military campaign in 2015, two million people have been displaced; 2.9 million children and women are acutely malnourished; over half the population has no regular access to safe water; and less than half of health facilities are still functioning. In August 2016 hundreds of thousands of Yemenis protested against the Saudi air strikes shouting 'we won't bow down'.

The British government admits that scores of military personnel are working as part of the British Military Mission to the 130,000 strong Saudi Arabian National Guard as they wage war against the Houthi movement. The British Ministry of Defence also supply the Saudi Arabia National Guard Communications Project delivering 'a £2bn programme to modernise the Saudi Arabian National Guard's communications network'.[4]

According to Andrew Smith of the Campaign Against the Arms Trade, 'UK-made fighter jets and bombs are doing terrible damage in Yemen. The war has killed tens of thousands of people and depleted the healthcare system in a time of crisis.' In August 2020 Ahmed al-Babati, a lance corporal from the 14 Signals Regiment (Electronic Warfare), was arrested by military police while protesting outside the Ministry of Defence against Britain's support for the Saudis. Before he was taken away al-Babati said 'this government has blood on their hands, so with that being said I refuse to continue my military service until the arms trade with Saudi Arabia has been put to an end'.

Banking on the Rest of the World

British economic policy since 1998 has in many ways been a reaction against the era of deindustrialisation and restructuring of the Thatcher years. Years of high unemployment between 1980 and 1994 were reversed so that the UK workforce grew from 20 million in 1980 to 32 million in 2019. The very high interest rates of the 1980s were brought down markedly in 2001 and then again in 2008 in response to the banking crisis. The low interest rate policy was adopted to encourage investment, though rates of investment have generally been lower than in the 1970-1995 era. While the UK economy grew modestly from 1995 to 2008 labour productivity has barely grown at all. What low interest rates did achieve was a boom in lending and house prices.

Britain's specialisation in finance is remarkable. British-based (but not necessarily owned) banks held 20.1 per cent of outstanding global assets and liabilities, compared to 10 per cent in the US.[5]

That should not be taken to mean that industry is of secondary importance to the British economy. British manufacturers still export more than half as much again as the financial and knowledge economy does.[6] Britain is the ninth biggest manufacturer in the world, and exports £275 billion of manufactured goods – with Europe as its largest trading partner.

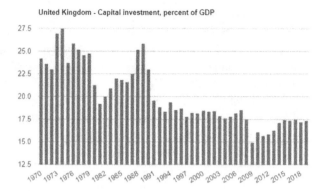

United Kingdom - Capital investment, percent of GDP

The end of the Cold War had an obvious impact on business worldwide, as the communist world was opened to trade and investment. Like the rest of the developed world Britain's larger industries have been lifted by the remarkable resurgence of capitalism in the Far East and China in particular. Britain's exports to China rose from £1.8 billion in 1999 to £16.8 billion in 2016. Much more important were the imports of intermediate goods from East Asia that massively cheapened costs for British construction and manufacturing.

In 2014 Britain's overall outward Foreign Direct Investment was more than £1 trillion – which is about one twelfth of the value of all British assets. Of that £1 trillion FDI, more than two thirds were invested in the already developed world (28.6 per cent in the USA and 40.2 per cent in the EU). In Brazil, Britons invested £14.7 billion, in Russia, £13.7 billion, South Africa £12.7 billion, in China £7.4 billion and in the Gulf Arabian countries £6.8 billion.[7]

The Bank of England's John Gieve explained that in the years since 2005 more money has been invested in Britain from abroad than the other way around:

100 years ago, the developed countries were investing in emerging markets (at the time in the Americas and Australia) which had abundant land and natural resources but scarce capital and so the returns were high. Currently, capital is flowing "uphill" from emerging to mature economies.

A major source for these investments were the 'Sovereign Wealth Funds', set up by governments to invest surpluses like those generated by Gulf Oil or Russian natural gas, as those primary producers get rich on western demand. Sheikh Khalifa bin Zayed Al Nahyan the President of the United Arab Emirates used London's overheated property market to quietly move some £5.5 billion of investments making him a bigger landlord in the capital than the Duke of Westminster.[8]

Britain is still a country that depends greatly on wealth generated elsewhere, with the City of London skimming profits off international financial transactions. In more recent times it has been the lucky recipient of investment from the wealthy overseas who want a part of Britain's heritage. These financial earnings, and inward capital flows help to offset the great imbalance on Britain's current account as the country buys more goods abroad than it sells. Britain is in the red by about 4 per cent of Gross Domestic Product on its current account – and that was before the impact of 'Brexit' and the 2020 coronavirus epidemic.

The Arms Trade

Britain's overall defence exports were worth £14 billion in 2018, grabbing one fifth of the world market, and making it the second biggest exporter after the United States (which took 40 per cent of the market). That represents 3.8 per cent of all British exports. Fully sixty per cent of all British arms exports went to the Middle East, eighteen per cent to the US and eleven per cent to Europe.[9] BAE Systems which is both a defence and aerospace company has a turnover of £18.31 billion (2019).

In the sales of just arms alone the British government issued licences for the export of £5.7 billion, of which £656 million were to Saudi Arabia, £371 million to Qatar and £116 million to the United Arab Emirates, £688 million to the USA, £632 million to India, £531 million to Italy, £522 million to Norway, £262 million to Indonesia and £45 million to China. Of those arms sales £1.3 billion were to countries that were judged 'not free' by the US government's Freedom House.[10]

As well as arms sales the Ministry of Defence trains military personnel from other countries. In 2019 spies from Saudi Arabia, the United Arab Emirates, Egypt Jordan, Oman, Cameroon, Algeria, Pakistan, Sri Lanka, India, Bangladesh Afghanistan and Nigeria attended an 11-day International Intelligence Directors Course, run by the Joint Intelligence Training Group. In 2019 the Royal Air Force trained 210 Saudis including 90 who were trained in aspects of the Typhoon fighter jet while the war against Yemen was in its fourth year. Just months before the military crackdown in Belarus, Royal Marines from 42 Commando's Lima Company were sent to train the Belarus 103rd Guards Airborne Division. The previous year, while Hong Kong's police were cracking down on democracy protestors, they were also getting training from the British Army in bomb disposal. The British Army also recruits and trains Gurkhas from Nepal to serve in the Singapore police force. Other states that received military training from Britain included Bahrain, Egypt, Israel and Uzbekistan.

The RAF Croughton camp in Northamptonshire is home to more than 1000 American intelligence officers. It was briefly in the public eye in 2019 when one

CIA agent, Anne Sacoolas hit a motorcyclist, Harry Dunn in her car, killing him, but claimed (falsely) diplomatic immunity before leaving the country. RAF Croughton is, according to the former US intelligence contractor Edward Snowdon, a communications hub for routing information intercepted by America's 'Stateroom' network of listening stations around the world. Britain's own listening station GCHQ has a £100 million account with US intelligence to gather information.

British arms sales and military training are an important export earner for the economy. They are also an important part of Britain's diplomatic and military power projection. Deep contacts with governments around the world give Britain the influence that allows it to 'punch above its weight'.

Troop Deployments

There were 145,320 personnel in the UK armed forces in 2020, 79,620 in the army, 32,940 in the air force, 26,170 in the navy and 6,590 in the Royal Marines.

The British Army keeps up bases in Afghanistan (where Afghan troops are trained) Belize, Bermuda (under the auspices of the Royal Bermuda Regiment), Brunei (home to the Royal Gurkha Rifles) Canada, Cyprus (where there are four separate sites as well as the Sovereign Base Areas of Akrotiri and Dhekelia), Diego Garcia, the Falkland Islands, Gibraltar, Germany (though these are almost all to be phased out in 2020), Nepal (under the Brigade of Gurkhas), Iraq (the Al Asad Airbase), Kenya and Sierra Leone.

In the Middle East there were in April 2019, 1,200 military personnel committed to Operation Shader (of whom 400 are in Iraq), 2,150 permanently stationed in Cyprus (as well as 1220 other Ministry of Defence personnel), 120 in Saudi Arabia, 90 in Oman, 40 in Kuwait and 20 in Bahrain. It also has 'our largest military capacity building programme in the region' in Jordan. The Royal Airforce has bases in Kuwait, Qatar, Oman, the United Arab Emirates and Akrotiri. The Navy has facilities at Bahrain and Oman.[11]

In Africa there are 100 permanent staff at the British Army Training Unit in Nanyuki Kenya, servicing 280 short tour troops. Eighty troops are training Nigeria's armed forces. Three hundred military personnel are in the UN mission in South Sudan and there are five missions in Somalia, training Somali troops and working with peacekeeping operations of the UN, European Union and the African Union. Other missions work training troops in Zambia and Uganda and 250 UK service personnel clearing mines and 'supporting the human rights of women and children' in Mali (according to the Ministry of Defence's website). A further 1000 troops are based in Kabul in Afghanistan as part of the Kabul Security Force and training and advising the Afghan army.

Around 900 troops are based in Estonia as part of NATO's Enhanced Forward Presence to warn Russia off Eastern Europe and the Baltics. In 2014, after the Russian invasion of the Crimea, and then the invasion of Eastern Ukraine in 2022, the British presence in East Europe was increased by 8000 troops, and around 22,000 Ukrainian soldiers have been trained by the British Army, many in Poland, and sent 120 armoured vehicles with short range missile launchers. The British Army calls its Global Response Force the 'tip of the spear', a 'force multiplier' and a model for the 'future soldier'.

Britain and Its Empire in 2020 – between
Brexit and 'Rhodes Must Fall!'

Throughout much of the post Second World War era Britons thought very little about the British Empire or about Britain's role in the world. The focus of public life was mostly upon domestic questions. A minority of disgruntled Empire loyalists on the one hand and ardent anti-war campaigners on the other argued about international issues. It was rare, though, that these arguments and the protests that came with them would directly impact upon the wider public.

The era from 1991 to 2010 was exceptional in that there was a large interest in international affairs in Britain, though even then this was mostly contained among the intelligentsia. Over the last five years, though, two parallel arguments about Britain's place in the world broke out into the mainstream. The most important was the argument over Britain's membership of the European Union. The other was a more academic argument about how the history of the British Empire was taught – though even that was very hotly contested for a discussion of the curriculum. The background to both is a pointed alienation that many feel with Britain's recent and more distant past.

On 23 June 2016, 33.5 million people voted in a referendum on the United Kingdom's membership of the European Union. The final result was that 17.4 million votes were cast to leave the EU and 16.1 million to stay a member. The issue was fought out again in the General Elections of 2017 and 2019, and each time the result favoured leaving, or 'Brexit' as it was called, and in January 2020 Parliament voted to leave the European Union.

Clearly, the Brexit vote showed that a great many people in Britain were unhappy with the country and its relation to the rest of the world. To many who were upset by the vote it seemed to arise out of a desire to return to the days of Empire, or out of some atavistic sense of loss. Journalist and historian Fintan O'Toole spoke for outraged Remainers when he argued that 'Brexit is fuelled by fantasies of "Empire 2.0"'. O'Toole's was just the first of a rash of books divining the Brexit vote in Empire nostalgia, from Priya Satia, Stuart Ward and Astrid Rasch, Robert Gildea, Peter Mitchell, Danny Dorling and Sally Tomlinson.[12]

Certainly, some of the rhetoric of the Leave campaign rehearsed nostalgia for Britain's glory days. Still, the evidence that Britain is in the throes of a nostalgia for Empire is hard to sustain. A poll by YouGov asked the question whether respondents thought that the Empire was more something to be proud of than ashamed of, and 32 per cent replied, yes. On the other hand, a plurality, 68 per cent did not think Empire was something to be proud of with 37 per cent thinking that it was neither that nor something to be ashamed of, and 20 per cent thought it was something of which to be ashamed. More interestingly, attitudes on Empire have shown a big shift over recent years, so while YouGov found that only 32 per cent of Britons had a positive view of Empire in 2020, that compared with 44 per cent in 2016 and 59 per cent in 2014. If

Brexit campaigners played on some nostalgic and patriotic themes, they also gave voice to a deep-seated disaffection with the drift of British society. Many in Britain's less successful towns it was reported felt 'left behind' in an era of globalisation. Some communities in the North of England, Wales and the Midlands were less impressed by the argument that membership of the European Union had improved their lives.

Though it invited less sociological analysis, the Remain camp was remarkable in its own way. After the referendum, the Remain campaign was renamed the 'People's Vote' campaign. More than 250,000 marched in London on 20 October 2018 to demand a re-run referendum vote. As Leave campaigners waved Union Jacks the People's Vote campaign adopted the European flag in a way that it never had been taken up in Britain before.[13] And though the other side of the debate have been labelled as Empire nostalgics, leading Remainers like Alasdair Campbell, Tony Blair, Rory Stewart and Dominic Grieve were all arguing for their own version of British power projection, not against military intervention overseas.[14] Pointedly it was those who were criticising the Leave campaigners who had most to say about the history of the Empire, while the Leave campaigners themselves tended to dismiss it as an issue.

The Brexit Referendum was an insight into the alienation that many voters felt towards the political establishment. The reaction to the Brexit Referendum result by the more strident Remainers was an insight into another kind of alienation, that of the middle-class intelligentsia from their fellow Britons. It was, thought Laurie Penny, 'the frightened, parochial lizard-brain of Britain' that voted Leave.[15] According to social scientist David Goodhart many metropolitan liberals felt no strong affinity to their country – they were not citizens of somewhere, but of anywhere.[16] It was an interesting idea. The imperial ideal in Britain has for a century and a half been carried by the middle classes. If they did not believe in it any more the decline in identification with Empire in the opinion polls is easier to understand.

Perhaps as important has been the declining influence of the old trade union and 'traditional Labour' leadership. The strand of 'social patriotism' that was so fundamental not only both to the Labour Party, but also to the popular support for the British Empire, was carried by a trade union leadership that identified with Britain's success. The social status of those trade union leaders, and their semi-official standing in the old 'tripartite' system of industrial organisation was dismantled by the Conservative governments of 1979-1997. The return of the Labour Party to power under Tony Blair did not reverse that change, but instead further distanced the Party from its trade union roots. 'Old Labour' was no longer there to popularise patriotism among working people.[17]

Just how the British establishment will cope with leaving the European Union is unclear at the time of writing. Before the vote, and after, many senior government ministers and civil servants were adamant that the proposal was quite simply unworkable. Many set out to show that was so and to limit its scope to a largely symbolic display of sovereignty while keeping Britain within the European Union's main institutions. Theresa May, who took over as Prime Minister after the Referendum, when David Cameron stepped down, was reported to have taken on the brief without enthusiasm, but to 'limit the damage' caused by Brexit.[18] When May's half-hearted Brexit plan provoked a rebellion in the Conservative Party, the incoming Prime Minister Boris Johnson was chosen to 'get Brexit done'. Since he was elected on that mandate in December 2019, he has clashed with many senior civil servants over the policy. As we saw, Fintan O'Toole highlighted the Foreign Office characterisation of Brexit as 'Empire 2.0'. But O'Toole played down the fact that this was the sarcastic nickname that sceptical civil servants had given the policy, because they did not believe in it.

Imperial Doubts

In 2020 a great hue and cry was raised when the British Broadcasting Corporation said that they would not have the patriotic songs 'Land of hope and glory' or 'Rule Britannia' sung at the Last Night of the Proms (Henry Wood Promenade Concerts) as was traditional. To some the lines 'Britons Never Shall be Slaves' and 'Britannia Rules the Waves' were embarrassingly out of date while others protested against the decision as another betrayal of British tradition by the BBC (the decision was reversed).

Already in 2020, a number of clashes over Britain's imperial heritage blew up in the wake of America's Black Lives Matter protests and the marches in solidarity with those in Britain. In Bristol, Black Lives Matter protestors pulled down the (already contentious) statue of Edward Colston, who was both a benefactor of that city and a slave trader. In London the statue of Winston Churchill was boarded up after it was graffitied with the slogan 'Racist' by protestors. Statues of Robert Milligan and Sir Hans Soane have been taken down from their pedestals outside the Docklands Museum and the British Museum because of their links to slavery, by authorities anticipating the criticisms of the Black Lives Matter protestors.

The challenging of slavery-linked monuments echoes similar protests in the United States, but it is also the outcome of a growing campaign to reform the teaching of history in Britain under the slogan 'decolonise the curriculum'. A number of academics have been challenging the teaching of history, English and geography for its colonial biases, including Gurminder Bhambra, Priyamvada Gopal, Robbie Shilliam and many more.[19] Conferences, papers and books aimed at 'decolonizing the curriculum' have been given and published.

Attempts to reform the curriculum to make it more inclusive for black students have been going on in British schools for many years. In the seventies John la Rose and the black schools' movement did a lot to question the pro-imperial biases in teaching, and in 1981 educationalists Nigel File and Chris Power wrote *Black Settlers in Britain* for schools. In 1982 Dawn Gill's report 'Geography in a Multi-racial Society' was refused by the School Council for its critical attitude to geography teaching, kicking off a big debate. The following year the Institute of Education organised a conference on geography teaching under the title 'Racist Society'. In 1987 'black history month', was launched, on the model of an American programme, and has been taken up by many schools and local authorities since. The complaint that the history of Empire was left out of school curricula has over the years been heard. Teacher Tarjinder Gill points out that since 2013 a critical view of Empire has been a part of the History Curriculum for both Primary and Secondary (Key Stage 1–3).[20]

In June 2021 Counter Terrorism Intelligence Officers of the government's strategy to fight extremism were invited by Derby council to audit the teaching of British history, worried that it might carry 'biases and misconceptions that may underpin far-Right extremism'. The Prevent officers' internal report praised schools for 'developing the history curriculum' so that it could 'provide a more rounded view of history', one that gave an 'alternative view of history compared to the dominant white, male, heterosexual one', and that foregrounded slavery and colonialism. It seems that even the counter-terrorism officers are doing their bit to decolonise the curriculum![21]

Edward Colston's statue pulled down in Bristol by Black Lives Matter protestors.

The argument over teaching colonial history became more heated in the years after Britain's participation in the Iraq and Afghan wars and the protests against them. In 2015 students at Oriel College, Oxford took up a campaign to take down a statue of Cecil Rhodes, and after that the National Union of Students endorsed the campaign to decolonise the curriculum. The project entails a lot more than just the reform of history teaching. Literary theorist Gayatri Chakravorty Spivak bound a new awareness of the position of people in the less developed world – under the title of 'Subaltern Studies' – to the project of the 'deconstruction' of western philosophy inspired by Jacques Derrida. Others in the post-colonial school of criticism, like Robert Young and Homi Bhabha have much grander ambitions than just the reform of history but aim at a fundamental revolution in our understanding of the world.

In 2017 Bruce Gilley, a professor of political science at Portland University had an article 'In defence of colonialism' by the journal *Third World Quarterly,* but after many on the editorial board protested, and circulated a petition against its publication. Arguing against Gilley, Kim Wagner made the good argument that historians ought not to approach the history of Empire by drawing up columns of pluses and minuses. You could go further and say that sifting through time awarding favourable judgements and condemnations is of limited value. An interest in history often begins with a degree of identification with historical figures but it ought to move beyond that to a more dispassionate understanding of what happened. The one moral obligation any historian has is to tell the truth as best she or he can (with the proviso that it is never complete). Beyond that anyone interested in the truth would surely hope for as broad and liberal an openness to competing ideas as is possible.

If one were to look at the pluses and minuses of the British Empire an answer to the critics might be that if it was as wholly destructive as they said it was, then it would never have succeeded as long as it did; and to the defenders, the answer would be if it was as positive as they said it was, it would still be with us. A great many things that British colonialists did were oppressive and destructive, as we have seen here, but it would be a travesty to imagine that there were no happy moments, great achievements or fulfilled lives under British rule.

Those students rallying and protesting in Oxford, Cape Town and Washington are right to want to see the history of colonialism's subject peoples told. The struggle to overthrow the British and other European Empires is central to the history of the twentieth century. A moderating argument is that a great many people around the world look back on colonisation as a positive part of their history to this day. In some cases such nostalgic thoughts are coupled with a disappointment with present-day leaders. Those attitudes cannot be dismissed as mere 'false consciousness' but are themselves a component part of the national sentiment in many former colonies. It would not be possible to tell the stories of India, Ireland, Nigeria or New Zealand without including some account of the years that those places were under the British Empire.

The emerging debate in Britain over the country's Empire is in part a sign of the way that Britons put less store by the colonial past than they did. It is also part of a wider questioning of traditional teaching and the ideology of 'Britishness'. The historical reflection on Britain's past is a welcome development that has deepened our understanding of world history, too.

In itself, however, a critical stance towards the British Empire in the past is something that can easily sit alongside the case for a belligerent stance in defence of the Global North today. British Prime Minister Tony Blair apologised for what Britain did during the Irish famine, but he still led the campaign to invade Iraq and it turned out that Blair had not written the apology himself, which was drafted by senior civil servant John Holmes in his absence. Prime Minister Theresa May told the House of Commons in May of 2019 that the British massacre at Amritsar was 'a shameful scar on British Indian history' and that 'we deeply regret what happened and the suffering caused' – but she also set in train a harsh regime of deportations as Home Secretary which she called a 'hostile environment' for immigrants. The new interventionism is often motivated as a movement away from the old imperialism. Indeed, each generation of British soldiers and missionaries active overseas has tended to portray its own interventions as wholly different from the patrician imperialism that went before: Britons trading opium to China were critical of the old monopolists (by which they meant not only the East India Company but also the Chinese Emperor); the 'New Imperialists' were very critical of the laissez faire indifference to native welfare; the champions of 'commonwealth development' insisted they were different from the Empire that went before; and the liberal interventionists insisted that they were nothing like the Cold Warriors of old. There is nothing new about Britain's champions of overseas action motivating their case by criticising their predecessors.

As welcome as the expanded interest in teaching the history of the Empire and as welcome as greater research into colonial history are, any historian ought to be circumspect about a movement that tears down monuments. The study of the past should aim to widen knowledge not to shut it down. The unreflective study of imperial history raised up heroes like 'Clive of India' and 'Gordon of Khartoum' into mere ciphers of Britain's supposedly civilising mission. Such hero-worship not only distorted historical understanding, it fed unhealthy ideas of British superiority over those they deigned to call 'lesser breeds'. To make our history better it is not enough simply to swap over the 'villains' and 'heroes' of the old story. We ought to hope to do more than replace one moral fable, where the white colonists are just and heroic, with a counter that makes Britons into bad guys and their opponents into saints. The study of history should not be arrested at the allocation of moral judgements but deepens and broadens all the time.

Graça Machel, who fought for many years for Mozambique's liberation, took a different view of the statues of imperial figures like Edward Colston and Cecil Rhodes. 'It is not the issue of bringing down a statue which is going to resolve the ills of the past', Machel told Radio 4 in June 2020: 'What is important is to look at the history of what is it which brought us to the situation where we are.'

Machel did not mean that history should avoid the questions of where justice lay. She went on to say:

> And of course you have to see who are the architects of the past. But I believe even it might be much more positive to keep them because you are going to tell generations to come 'this is how it started and this is how it should never be'.[22]

Britain since the Iraq War of 2003 has been grappling with its place in history and the world. Both the 'Brexit' referendum and the movement to 'decolonize the curriculum' speak to a profound sense of doubt about the way forward. Doubts and re-evaluations have many different outcomes. In 1960 doubts about the Empire began the process of decolonisation. On the other hand, anxieties about Britain's status around the end of the nineteenth century led to the 'New Imperialism'. Where the reflections on Britain's status in 2020 will lead is yet to be seen.

NOTES

Chapter One

1. 'The social order', in The World of Domesday, The National Archives, https://www.nationalarchives.gov.uk/domesday/world-of-domesday/order.htm.
2. Norman Davies, *The Isles*, Macmillan, 2000, p. 308; Conall Mageoghagan quoted in Jane Ohlmeyer, *The Cambridge History of Ireland:* Volume 2, 1550–1730, Cambridge University Press, 2018, p. 274.
3. Angus Calder, *Revolutionary Empire: The Rise of the English-Speaking Empires from the Fifteenth Century to the 1780s*, London: Pimlico, 1998, p. 27.
4. John H. Munro, 'Medieval Woollens: The Western European Woollen Industries and their Struggles for International Markets, c. 1000–1500', in *The Cambridge History of Western Textiles*, Volume 1, ed. D. T. Jenkins, Cambridge: Cambridge University Press, 2003, pp. 228–324, 304–5.
5. Alexander Anievas and Kerem Nişancıoğlu, *How the West Came to Rule*, London: Pluto, 2015, p. 194.
6. Alan Macfarlane, *The Origins of English Individualism*, Oxford: Blackwell, 1978, p. 68; Xavier LeFrance, *The Making of Capitalism in France*, Chicago: Haymarket, 2020, p. 15.
7. Christopher Hill, *Reformation to Industrial Revolution*, London: Verso, 2018, p. 35.
8. Christopher Hill, *Reformation to Industrial Revolution*, p. 92, 95.
9. Christopher Hill, *The Century of Revolution: 1603–1714*, Routledge, 2014, p. 145.
10. John Houghton, *A Collection of Letters for the Improvement of Husbandry and Trade*, London, 1681, p. 56.
11. Arnold Toynbee, *Industrial Revolution*, David and Charles Reprints, 1967, pp. 58–9, 62.
12. Sir James Steuart quoted in Michael Perelman, *The Invention of Capitalism*, London: Duke University Press, 2000, pp. 147–51.
13. Maurice Coakley, *Ireland in the New World Order*, London: Pluto Press, 2012, p. 66; Jim Smyth, *The Making of the United Kingdom*, 1600-1800, Pearson, 2001, p. 189; T. M. Devine, *The Scottish Clearances*, London: Penguin, 2019, p. 42.
14. Jim Smyth, *The Making of the United Kingdom*, p. 78.
15. Jim Smyth, *The Making of the United Kingdom*, pp. 148–9, 196, 162–3; T. M. Devine, *Scotland's Empire*, London: Penguin, 2004; John Mackenzie and T. M. Devine (eds), *Scotland and the British Empire*, Oxford University Press, 2016; Arthur Herman, *The Scottish Enlightenment*, London: Fourth Estate, 2003.
16. Maurice Coakley, *Ireland in the World Order*, p. 11.
17. Jim Smyth, *The Making of the United Kingdom*, p. 77.
18. in Liz Curtis, *Nothing but the Same Old Story*, London: Information on Ireland, 1984, p. 16.
19. Maurice Coakley, *Ireland in the World Order*, p. 21.
20. Jim Smyth, *The Making of the United Kingdom*, p. 77.
21. Sean O' Faolain, *The Great O'Neill*, Dublin: Mercier Press, 1997, p. 136.
22. O'Faolain, pp. 222–3.
23. Eli F. Heckscher, *Mercantilism*, Volume II, London: Allen and Unwin, 1955, p. 41.
24. Micheal O' Siochru, *God's Executioner*, p. 95.
25. Liz Curtis, *Nothing but the Same Old Story*, p. 23.
26. in John Rees, *The Leveller Revolution*, London: Verso, 2017, p. 293.
27. Gerard Boate, *Ireland's Natural History*, 1652, p. 95.
28. Ted McCormick, *William Petty*, and the Ambitions of Political Arithmetic, Oxford: University Press, 2009, p. 101.

29. John Prendergast, *The Cromwellian Settlement of Ireland,* LLC. 2014 (orig. 1870), p. 54–5 – the question of the 'Irish slaves' transported to Barbados has been controversial and its discussion in Sean O'Callaghan's *To Hell or Barbadoes,* Brandon, 2000, makes some overblown claims, but the point that many Irish women and men were transported to the West Indies, and made to serve indentures is true.
30. 26–7, 15–6, quoted in McCormick, *William Petty,* p. 107.
31. Karl Bottigheimer, *English Money and Irish Land,* Oxford, 1971, Appendix C. and pp. 153–5.
32. Bottigheimer, *English Money and Irish Land,* Oxford, 1971, p. 75.
33. Ted McCormick, *William Petty,* p. 117.
34. Denis O'Hearn, *The Atlantic Economy,* Manchester: University Press, 2001, p. 41.
35. quoted in Sean Callaghan, *To Hell or Barbados,* Brandon, 2000, p. 52.
36. 'Labour and Irish History', Chapter II, *Collected Works,* Volume I, Dublin, 1987, p. 33.
37. Sean Cronin, *Irish Nationalism,* Academy Press, 1980, p. 12, 16, 17.

Chapter Two

1. William Hirt Howe, 'Jus Gentium and the Law Merchant', *The American Law Register,* July 1902, no 7, 378–80; and see also Jairus Banaji, *A Brief History of Commercial Capitalism,* Chicago: Haymarket, 2020.
2. Olivia Constable, *Housing the Stranger in the Mediterranean World,* Cambridge U.P., 2003.
3. Abraham Udovitch, *Partnership and Profit in Medieval Islam,* Princeton, 1970, p. 218.
4. Janet Abu-Lughod, *Before European Hegemony,* Oxford: University Press, 1989, pp. 156–57, 213.
5. Stanley Alpern, *Abson and Company,* Hurst, 2018.
6. J. R. Green, *Town Life in the Fifteenth Century,* New York, 1898, volume 1, pp. 1–2.
7. Abram Leon, *The Jewish Question,* New York: Pathfinder Press, 1970, pp. 145–46.
8. William Stafford, *A Discourse of the Common Weal of England,* 1581, quoted in I. I. Rubin, *History of Economic Thought,* Pluto Press, 1989, p. 44.
9. F. J. Fisher, *London and the English Economy,* London: Hambledon Press, 1980, p. 95.
10. David Harris Sacks, *The Widening Gate,* Berkeley: University of California Press, 1993, p. 26.
11. Robert Brenner, *Merchants and Revolution,* London: Verso, 2003, p. 56.
12. Robert Brenner, *Merchants and Revolution,* London: Verso, 2003, pp. 66–67.
13. Ian Barrow, *The East India Company,* Indianapolis: Hackett, 2017, pp. 3–5.
14. Brenner, *Merchants and Revolution,* London: Verso, 2003, p. 49; Barrow, *The East India Company,* Indianapolis: Hackett, 2017 p. 10.
15. Barrow, *The East India Company,* Indianapolis: Hackett, 2017, p. 20.
16. Barrow, *The East India Company,* 2017, p. 26.
17. Sven Beckert, *Empire of Cotton,* 2014, p. 34.
18. Christopher Hill, *From Reformation to Industrial Revolution,* p. 162, 160; Bowen, *The Business of Empire,* Cambridge UP, 2006, p. 32.
19. House of Lords, 9 June 1698.
20. Robert Brenner, *Merchants and Revolution,* London: Verso, 2003, p. 83, 88.
21. Pettigrew, *Freedom's Debt,* 2013, p. 67.

Chapter Three

1. Janet Abu Lughod, *Before European Hegemony,* 1989, Oxford UP, p. 168.
2. Janet Abu Lughod, *Before European Hegemony,* 1989, Oxford UP, p. 255.
3. Eric Wolf, *Europe and the People Without History,* University of California Press, 1997, p. 24, 55.
4. quoted in Kirkpatrick Sale, *The Conquest of Paradise,* 1992, p. 353.
5. 'Columbus and the Making of a Historical Myth', *Race & Class,* Vol. 33, No. 3, January 1992.
6. Duncan Green, *Faces of Latin America,* Monthly Review Press, 2013, p. 102.
7. Kirkpatrick Sale, *Conquest of Paradise,* 1992, p. 74.
8. Crowley, *Conquerors,* p. 55.

9. Roger Crowley, *Conquerors*, London, Faber, 2016, p. 31.
10. Crowley, *Conquerors*, pp. 80–86.
11. Henry Kamen, *Empire: How Spain Became a World Power, 1492-1763*, Harper Collins 2003, p. 41.
12. Henry Kamen, *Empire: How Spain Became a World Power, 1492-1763*, Harper Collins 2003, p. 82–83.
13. Angus Calder, *Revolutionary Empire*, London: Pimlico, 1998, p 12.
14. Karl Marx and Frederick Engels, *Communist Manifesto*, London: Verso, pp. 35–36.

Chapter Four

1. Henry Kamen, *Empire: How Spain Became a World Power, 1492-1763*, Harper Collins, 2003, pp. 95–96, and see 98–104 for the campaign against the Nahua (Aztecs).
2. Nathan Wachtel, *The Vision of the Vanquished*, pp. 26–7.
3. John Silver, 'The Myth of Eldorado', *History Workshop Journal*, no. 34 (1992), p. 2.
4. Pierre Vilar, *A History of Gold and Money*, p. 126; David E. Stannard, *American Holocaust: The Conquest of the New World*, Oxford University Press, 1992, 215.
5. Pierre Vilar, *Spain a Brief History*, 1967, p. 40, 46.
6. John Keay, *The Honourable Company*, London: Harper Collins, 1993, p. 141.
7. K. C. Sharma, *East India Company*, New Delhi, 2007, p. 8.
8. John Keay, *The Honourable Company*, p. 146.
9. J. H. Parry, *Trade and Dominion*, p. 216.
10. 'Speech on East India Settlement, 27 February 1769', in *Writings and Speeches of Burke, II*, ed. Langford and Todd, p. 220.
11. In Niall Ferguson, *Empire*, p. 38.
12. R Palme Dutt, *India Today*, 1940, p. 112.
13. Mukherjee, *The Rise of the East India Company*, New Delhi: Aakar Books, 2011, p. 345, 347; John Keay, *India*, London: Harper Press, 2010, p. 390.
14. Lionel Trotter, *Warren Hastings: A Biography*, London: W. H. Allen, 1878, p. 66.
15. James Mill, *History of India, Vol II*, Chapter 5, Cambridge University Press, 2010 (orig. 1817–18), p. 201.
16. Jadunath Sarkar, *History of Aurangzeb*, Vol V., M. C. Sarkar and Sons, Culcutta, 1924, pp. 452–53.
17. William Bolts, *Considerations on India Affairs*, London, 1772, pp. 193–94.
18. May 1762, Mukherjee, *East India Company*, p. 304.
19. Romesh Chunder Dutt, *The Economic History of India Under Early British Rule*, p. 250.
20. Monideepa Chatterjee puts the number as high as 10 million, while Rajat Datta says it is between one and two million 'A Forgotten Holocaust: The Bengal Famine of 1770', Monideepa Chatterjee, Department of History, Presidency University, https://www.academia.edu/6977392/A_Forgotten_Holocaust_The_Bengal_Famine_of_177017, 26 November 1772, Rajat Datta, Society, Economy and the Market, New Delhi: Manohar Publishers, 2000, pp 242–8.

Chapter Five

1. David Scott, *Leviathan: The Rise of Britain as a World Power*, 2013, pp. 88–89; Neil Hanson, *The Confident Hope of a Miracle*, Transworld, 2011, p. 557, for quote from the pope.
2. Christopher Hill, *Reformation to Industrial Revolution*, pp. 78–79.
3. William Camden, *The Historie of the Most Renowned and Victorious Princess Elizabeth, Late Queen of England*, 1635, p. 492.
4. Angus Calder, *Revolutionary Empire*, London: Pimlico, 1998, p. 82.
5. Calder, *Revolutionary Empire*, p. 56, 66, 71.
6. Wim Klooster, *The Dutch Moment*, Cornell University Press, 2016, p. 43.
7. 'A Discourse of the Invention of Ships, Anchors, Compass, &c', in *The Works of Walter Raleigh*, 1829, p. 325; Eli F. Heckscher, *Mercantilism*, Vol. II, London: Allen and Unwin, 1955, p. 35.
8. Francis Bacon on Henry VII, quoted in Heckscher, *Mercantilism*, p. 16; Peter Linebaugh and Marcus Rediker, *The Many-Headed Hydra*, Boston: Beacon Press, 2000, p. 146.

9. *Reformation to Industrial Revolution,* p. 157.
10. Matthew Parker, *The Sugar Barons,* London: Hutchinson, 2011, p. 89.
11. Matthew Parker, *The Sugar Barons,* p. 117.
12. Pettigrew, *Freedom's Debt,* p. 24.
13. Michel Beaud, *A History of Capitalism,* 1983, p. 45.

Chapter Six

1. Hugh Thomas, *The Slave Trade,* London: Picador, 1997, pp. 58–59.
2. Robert Brenner, *Merchants and Revolution,* London: Verso, 2003, p. 165.
3. Samuel Pepys, *The Diary of Samuel Pepys: A Selection,* London: Penguin, 2003, p. 83, entry for 3 October 1660.
4. William Pettigrew, *Freedom's Debt,* p. 25.
5. *The Case of the Late African Company,* 1694, p. 1. Pettigrew, p. 91.
6. Minutes of the Board of Trade, 17 April 1708, CO 391/20 108. In Wm. Pettigrew, *Freedom's Debt,* 2013, p. 41.
7. 'Review of the State of the Nation', 6 March 1711, p. 591, in *Defoe's Review* 1704–13, Volume 8, Routledge, 2010 ed. John Mcveagh.
8. Transatlantic Slavery Database, https://www.slavevoyages.org/assessment/estimates; T. O. Lloyd, *The British Empire 1558-1983,* Oxford University Press, 1989, pp. 71–72.
9. *Anti-Slavery Reporter* Vol. LV; *Anti-Slavery Reporter* Vol. IV, no. XXXVII, 1 January 1849, p. 11.
10. 'Dicky Sam', *Liverpool and Slavery,* Liverpool, 1985 (1884 orig.), pp. 9–10.
11. Stanley Alpern, *Abson and Company,* Hurst, 2018, p. 24.
12. Ibid.

Chapter Seven

1. Victoria Bateman, *Markets and Growth in Early Modern Europe,* Pickering and Chatto, 2012, p. 44.
2. Robert Brenner, *Merchants and Revolution,* London: Verso, 2003, p. 106, p. 171.
3. Brenner, *Merchants and Revolution,* pp. 125–9.
4. Trevor Burnard, *Planters, Merchants, and Slaves: Plantation Societies in British America, 1650-1820,* U Chicago Press, 2015, p. 57.
5. Matthew Parker, *Sugar Barons,* London: Hutchinson, 2011, p. 145.
6. Parker, *Sugar Barons,* pp. 142–3.
7. Parker, *Sugar Barons,* p. 172; David Eltis, Frank D. Lewis and David Richardson, 'Slave Prices, the African Slave Trade, and Productivity in the Caribbean, 1674-1807', *The Economic History Review,* Vol. 58, No. 4 (November 2005), pp. 673–700.
8. Parker, *Sugar Barons,* p. 126; Lloyd, *The British Empire 1558-1983,* Oxford University Press, 1989, p. 71.
9. Lowell J. Ragatz, *The Fall of the Planter Class in the British Caribbean, 1763-1833: A Study in Social and Economic History,* New York: The Century Co., 1928, p. 205.
10. Ragatz, *The Fall of the Planter Class in the British Caribbean,* pp. 378, 93–4.
11. Ragatz, *The Fall of the Planter Class in the British Caribbean,* pp. 52–3.
12. Sally-Anne Huxtable et al. (eds), *Interim Report on the Connections between Colonialism and Properties now in the Care of the National Trust, Including Links with Historic Slavery,* National Trust, September 2020, p. 12, 34, 84.
13. Eric Williams, *Capitalism and Slavery,* New York: Capricorn, 1966.
14. Brenner, *Merchants and Revolution,* pp. 93–102.
15. Steven Katz, *The Holocaust and New World Slavery,* Cambridge University Press, 2019, section 1.2, 'The Coming into Being of New World Slavery'; and see also James Walvin, *Questioning Slavery,* London: Routledge, 1996 and Peter Kolchin, *American Slavery,* London: Penguin, 1995.
16. George Lankevich, *New York City,* NYU Press, 2002, pp. 36–7.

Chapter Eight

1. Henry Kamen, *Empire: How Spain Became a World Power, 1492-1763,* Harper Collins 2003, p. 90.
2. Kamen, *Empire,* p. 159, 161.
3. Kamen, *Empire,* pp. 184–85.
4. Kamen, *Empire,* pp. 186–87.
5. Kamen, *Empire,* p. 189.
6. Pepijn Brandon, *War, Capital and the Dutch State,* Brill, Leiden, 2015, p. 49.
7. Els M. Jacobs, *In Pursuit of Pepper and Tea: The Story of the Dutch East India Company,* Zutphen: Netherlands Maritime Museum, 1991, p. 9, 15.
8. Wim Klooster, *The Dutch Moment,* Cornell University Press, 2016, pp. 31–32.
9. Els M. Jacobs, *In Pursuit of Pepper and Tea,* pp. 73–74.
10. Jacobs, *In Pursuit of Pepper and Tea,* p. 76.
11. Jacobs, *In Pursuit of Pepper and Tea,* p. 76.
12. Bhawan Ruangsilp, *Dutch East India Company Merchants at the Court of Ayutthaya,* Brill, Leiden, 2007, pp. 19–22.
13. K. M. de Silva, *A History of Sri Lanka,* Colombo: Vijitha Yapa Publications, 2008, Chapter 13; Ruangsilp, *Dutch East India Company Merchants…,* p. 7.
14. Klooster, *The Dutch Moment,* Cornell University Press, 2016, p. 37, 40, 45, 49.
15. Jardine Lisa, *Worldly Goods,* London: Papermac, 1997, pp. 289–91.
16. Malyn Newitt, *Emigration and the Sea: An Alternative History of Portugal and the Portuguese,* London: Hurst, 2015, p. 84.
17. Newitt, *Emigration and the Sea,* p. 82.
18. Malyn Newitt, *Emigration and the Sea: An Alternative History of Portugal and the Portuguese,* 2015, p. 90.
19. K. M. de Silva, *A History of Sri Lanka,* Colombo, Vijitha Yapa Publications, p. 163.
20. Kamen, *Empire,* p. 404.
21. Kamen, *Empire,* pp. 400–02.
22. *IPENEYM ΦΙΛΑΛΕΘΙΥΜ,* 1650, pp. 4–5, quoted in Pepijn Brandon, 'Masters of war: state, capital, and military enterprise in the Dutch cycle of accumulation (1600-1795)', in the University of Amsterdam's Digital Academic Repository, 2013, p. 8. The passage incorporates many of Heraclitus' fragments on war. .
23. J. Holland Rose, 'Three Conditions of Expansion', in Harrison M. Wright (ed), *The New Imperialism,* Lexington: D. C. Heath and Company, 1961, p. 3.
24. Quoted in Pepijn *Brandon, War, Capital and the Dutch State,* p. 51.

Chapter Nine

1. Langford, *A Polite and Commercial People,* Oxford: Clarendon Press, 1998, p. 169.
2. Robert Kayll, *The Trades Increase,* 1615, in Ian Barrow, *The East India Company,* 2017, p. 32.
3. Thomas Mun, *A Discourse of Trade,* 1621, reproduced here https://oll.libertyfund.org/titles/mcculloch-a-select-collection-of-early-english-tracts-on-commerce-1856/simple#lf1372_head_023.
4. Thomas Mun, *England's Treasure by Forraign Trade,* published in 1664 – but written in 1630, quoted in Rubin, *History of Economic Thought,* p. 49.
5. D'Avenant, *An Essay upon the Probable Methods of Making a People Gainers in the Balance of Trade,* London, 1699, pp. 45–6.
6. D'Avenant, *Discourse on the Publick Revenues …,* Part II, London, 1698, p. 31, Petty in Heckscher, *Mercantilism,* Vol. II, 1955, p. 117, and Thomas Mun, ibid., p. 166.
7. *Principles of Political Economy, The Works of Sir James Steuart,* Vol. 1, London, 1805, pp. 275–6.
8. Josiah Child, *New Discourse of Trade,* 1690, p. 125.
9. Adam Smith, *Wealth of Nations,* Books I-III, Penguin, 1987, p. 472.
10. Adam Smith, *Wealth of Nations,* Edinburgh, 1827, book IV, Chapter 7, p. 247.
11. Adam Smith, *The Wealth of Nations,* Book III, Chapter 1, Penguin, 1987, pp. 483–4.
12. Henry Brougham, *An Enquiry into the Colonial Policy of the European Powers,* 1803, pp. 36–7.

13. Brougham, *An Enquiry into the Colonial Policy of the European Powers*, 1803, p. 93.
14. Andrew Ure, *The Philosophy of Manufactures*, 1835, pp. 136–7.
15. Bowen, *The Business of Empire*, Cambridge: University Press, 2006, p. 36.
16. 26 November 1772.
17. *Wealth of Nations*, Bk 4, Chapter 7, part III.
18. Nick Robins, *The Corporation that Changed the World*, p. 135.
19. quoted in John Kenneth Galbraith, *A Short History of Financial Euphoria*, 1994, p. 49.
20. David Kynaston, *The City of London, Vol. 1*, London: Chatto and Windus, p. 16.
21. Adam Hochschild, *Bury the Chains*, Boston: Mariner Books, 2006, especially chapter 9.
22. *The Anti-Slavery Reporter* Vol. 4, No. 8, 1 August 1856, p. 189.
23. Thirty-First Report of the Birmingham Ladies' Negroes'-Friend Society, in *The Anti-Slavery Reporter* Vol. 4, No. 8, 1 August 1856, p. 189.
24. Brougham, *An Enquiry into the Colonial Policy of the European Powers*, 1803, p. 47.
25. Brougham, *An Enquiry ...*, p. 70.
26. Brougham, *An Enquiry ...*, p. 72.
27. Brougham, *An Enquiry ...*, p. 76.
28. Brougham, *An Enquiry ...*, p. 77.
29. Pitt, in Eric Williams, *Capitalism and Slavery*, New York: Capricorn Books, 1966, p 146.
30. *The Anti-Slavery Reporter*, 1 December 1846, p. 189.
31. John Silver, 'The Myth of Eldorado', *History Workshop Journal*, No. 34 (1992), p. 2.
32. D. C. M. Platt. *Finance, Trade, and Politics in British Foreign Policy. 1815-1914*, Oxford: Clarendon Press, 1968, p. 312.
33. John Silver, 'The Myth of Eldorado', *History Workshop Journal*, No. 34 (1992), p. 4.
34. T. O. Lloyd, *The British Empire 1558-1983*, Oxford University Press, 1989, p 55.

Chapter Ten

1. Marx, *Capital*, Vol. I, London: Lawrence and Wishart, 1954, p. 712.
2. Bairoch, *Economics and World History*, 1993, Chapter 7.
3. Seymour Drescher, 'Eric Williams: British Capitalism and British Slavery', *History and Theory*, Vol. 26, No. 2 (May 1987), pp. 180–196.
4. Blackburn, *The Making of New World Slavery*, Verso, 2010, p. 542; Patnaik, 'New Estimates of British Eighteenth Century Trade', in *The Making of History: Essays Presented to Irfan Habib*, ed. Pannikar, Byres and Patnaik, 2010, p. 389.
5. Shashi Tharoor, *Inglorious Empire*, 2017, p. 11.
6. Brougham, *An Enquiry into the Colonial Policy of the European Powers*, 1803, p. 80.
7. *Accumulation on a World Scale*, New York: Monthly Review Press, 1974, p. 3.
8. *Capital* Vol. I in Marx and Engels *Collected Works*, Vol. 35, p. 739.
9. *Capital* Vol. III, Chapter 20, in Volume 37 of the Marx and Engels *Collected Works*, p. 325; for a different interpretation, see Glen Coulthard, *Indigenous Americas: Red Skin, White Masks: Rejecting the Colonial Politics of Recognition*, University of Minnesota Press, 2014, p 9.
10. Eric Williams, *Capitalism and Slavery*, pp. 106–7.
11. Karl Marx, *Grundrisse*, Penguin, 1973, p. 278.
12. *Capital*, Volume I, In Marx and Engels *Collected Works*, Vol. 35, p. 726.
13. *Grundrisse*, Harmondsworth, Penguin 1973, p. 651.
14. See Pernille Ipsen, *Daughters of the Trade: Atlantic Slavers and Interracial Marriage on the Gold Coast*, U Pennsylvania Press, 2015, and Finn Fuglestad, *Slave Traders by Invitation: West Africa's Slave Coast in the Pre-Colonial Era*, London: Hurst, 2018.
15. William Dalrymple, *White Mughals*, London: Penguin, 2002.
16. Holden Furber, 'Asia and the West as Partners Before "Empire" and After', *The Journal of Asian Studies*, Vol. 28, No. 4 (August 1969), pp. 711–21.

Chapter Eleven

1. In Michele Louro, *Comrades against Imperialism*, Cambridge University Press, 2018, p. 273.

2. See Lothrop Stoddard, *Racial Realities in Europe*, New York Scribner, 1924, especially chapter one, for an example of racial explanations of Europe's advantages, or Niall Ferguson, *Civilisation: The Six Killer Apps of Western Power*, London: Penguin, 2012, for a cultural explanation.
3. See John Hobson, *The Eastern Origins of Western Civilisation*, Cambridge University Press, 2004; Alexander Anievas and Kerem Nişancıoğlu, *How the West Came to Rule*, London: Pluto, 2015.
4. Kenneth Pomeranz, *The Great Divergence*, University of Princeton, 2000; and see David Landes, *The Wealth and Poverty of Nations*, Little, Brown, 1998; Hernando de Soto, *The Mystery of Capital*, 2001.
5. Paul Langford, *A Polite and Commercial People*, Oxford U. P. 1998, Chapter II, 'Robin's Reign'.
6. Linda Colley, *Britons*, London: Pimlico, 2003, p. 69.
7. Paul Langford, *A Polite and Commercial People*, p. 64.
8. Quoted in Roy Porter, *Enlightenment*, Allen Lane, 2000, p. 3 – sic on 'its self'.
9. *Wealth of Nations*, Book IV, Chapter II, New York: Bantam, 2003, p 572.
10. *Essay Concerning Human Understanding*, section 12.
11. quoted in C. B. MacPherson, *The Political Theory of Possessive Individualism*, Oxford University Press, 1964, p. 198.
12. MacPherson, *Possessive Individualism*, p. 202.
13. *Two Treatises of Government*, II, para. 184.
14. Emer Vattel, *The Law of Nations*, New York: Oceana, 1964, p. 85.
15. C. B. MacPherson, *Possessive Individualism*, p. 240.
16. Andrew Ure, *Philosophy of Manufactures*, p. 136.
17. Maxine Berg, *Age of Manufactures 1700-1820*, London: Fontana, 1985, p. 94.
18. Berg, *Age of Manufactures*, p. 39.
19. Berg, *Age of Manufactures*, p. 36.
20. Berg, *Age of Manufactures*, p. 35; Philip Sauvain, *British Economic and Social History*, Leckhampton: Stanley Thornes, 1989, p. 56.
21. David Edgerton, *The Shock of the Old*, London: Profile, 2006; Maxine Berg, *Age of Manufactures*.
22. Roy Porter, *Enlightenment*, Allen Lane, 2000, p. 431.
23. Samuel Kydd, *The History of the Factory Movement*, New York: Augustus Kelly, 1966 (orig. 1857), pp. 16–26; See also the Channel4/National Trust Quarry Bank Mill project, https://www.channel4.com/press/news/background-quarry-bank-mill-national-trust.
24. Philip Sauvain, *British Economic and Social History*, pp. 104–110.
25. Samuel Smiles, *Lives of the Engineers*, London: Folio Society, 2006, pp. 8–32.
26. Langford, *Polite and Commercial People*, p. 214.
27. O'Brien and Engerman, 'Exports and the Growth of the British Economy from the Glorious Revolution to the Peace of Amiens', in Barbara Solow (ed), *Slavery and the Rise of the Atlantic System*, Harvard U. P., 1991, p. 188.
28. Centre for Scottish and Celtic Studies, 'Slaves and Slaveowners in Eighteenth-Century Scotland', University of Glasgow, 20 November 2012, http://cscs.academicblogs.co.uk/slaves-and-slaveowners-in-eighteenth-century-scotland/.
29. Porter, *Enlightenment*, London, 2000, p. 424.
30. Adam Smith, *Wealth of Nations*, Book I, Chapter 1, Penguin, 1987, p. 117.
31. quoted by Anton Howes, in 'Age of Invention: Improveable Beings', 19 December 2019, https://antonhowes.substack.com/p/age-of-invention-higher-perfection, viewed on 10 Oct. 2020.
32. Adam Smith, *Wealth of Nations*, Book IV, Chapter 2, New York: Bantam, 2003, p 591.
33. John Vincent Nye 'The Myth of Free-Trade Britain…' *The Journal of Economic History*, Vol. 51, No. 1 (March 1991), pp. 23–46.
34. Belich, *Replenishing the Earth*, pp. 106–7.
35. Robert Blake, *Jardine Matheson: Traders of the Far East*, London: Weidenfeld and Nicolson, 1999, p. 54, 56.
36. Belich, *Replenishing the Earth*, pp. 109–11.
37. Ben Wilson, *Heyday*, London, Weidenfeld and Nicholson, 2017, p. 8.
38. Ben Wilson, *Heyday*, p. 10.
39. Quoted in Beaud, *A History of Capitalism*, p. 96.

Chapter Twelve

1. Henry Jenkyns, *British Rule and Jurisdiction Beyond the Seas*, Oxford: Clarendon Press, 1902, p. 123.
2. Paul Langford, *The Eighteenth Century*, London: Adam and Charles Black, 1976, p. 26, p. 107, p. 204.
3. Linda Colley, *Britons*, London: Pimlico, 2003, pp. 88–98.
4. See Jonathan Israel, *The Expanding Blaze*, Princeton University Press, 2017; R. R. Palmer, *The Age of the Democratic Revolution*, Vol. I *The Challenge*, Vol. II, *The Struggle*, Princeton University Press, 1959 and 1964; Jacques Godechot, *The Taking of the Bastille*, London, Faber, 1970, especially Chapter 1, 'Social Peace and Unrest in the Western World in the Eighteenth Century'.
5. Bernard Semmel, *The Rise of Free Trade Imperialism: Classical Political Economy: The Empire of Free Trade and Imperialism, 1750-1850*, Cambridge University Press, 1970.
6. Israel, *The Expanding Blaze*, pp. 118–19.
7. Israel, *The Expanding Blaze*, pp. 66–68.
8. Paul Langford, *A Polite and Commercial People*, Oxford U. P. 1998, p. 539.
9. R. R. Palmer, *The Age of Democratic Revolution*, Vol. I, p. 6.
10. Gerald Horne, *The Counter-Revolution of 1776*, 2016.
11. Israel, *The Expanding Blaze*, p. 149.
12. *New York Times Magazine*, 14 August 2019, https://www.nytimes.com/interactive/2019/08/14/magazine/black-history-american-democracy.html.
13. WSWS.org, 28 November 2019 https://www.wsws.org/en/articles/2019/11/28/wood-n28.html.
14. Carol L. Bagley and Jo Ann Ruckman, 'Iroquois Contributions to Modern Democracy and Communism', *American Indian Culture and Research Journal*, Vol. 7, No. 2 (1983), pp. 53–72.
15. Quoted in Michel Beaud, *A History of Capitalism - 1500-1980*, New York: Monthly Review Press, 1983, p. 37.
16. Beaud, *A History of Capitalism*, New York: Monthly Review Press, 1983, p. 38.
17. Beaud, *A History of Capitalism*, p. 38.
18. C. B. A Behrens, *The Ancien Régime*, London: Thames and Hudson, 1967, pp. 66–67.
19. Israel, *The Expanding Blaze*, p. 124.
20. Quoted in Israel, *The Expanding Blaze*, p. 252.
21. Quoted in John Bew, *Castlereagh*, London: Quercus, 2011, pp. 150–51.
22. Marianne Elliott, *Theobald Wolfe Tone*, p. 126, p. 215.
23. John Bew, *Castlereagh*, p. 107.
24. Marianne Elliott, *Theobald Wolfe Tone*, 279.
25. See Julius Scott, *The Common Wind*, London: Verso, 2018.
26. C. L. R. James, *Black Jacobins*, London: Allison and Busby, 1980, p. 54, 111.
27. James, *Black Jacobins*, p. 60.
28. Sometimes called Boukman Dutty, Madison Smartt Bell, *Toussaint Louverture*, New York: Pantheon, 2007, pp. 22, 25–8.
29. James, *Black Jacobins*, p. 25.
30. Bell, *Toussaint Louverture*, pp. 40–41.
31. James, *Black Jacobins*, p. 113.
32. James *Black Jacobins*, p. 140.
33. James, *Black Jacobins*, p. 200.
34. In Peter Marshall and Glyn Williams, *The British Atlantic Empire Before the American Revolution*, 1980, p. 128.
35. E. P. Thompson, *The Making of the English Working Class*, London: Penguin, 1991, p. 29.
36. Jacques Godechot, *The Counter-Revolution: Doctrine and Action, 1789-1804*, Princeton University Press, 1981, pp. 173–80.
37. G. E. Mainwaring and Bonamy Dobrée, *The Floating Republic: An Account of the Mutinies at Spithead and the Nore in 1797*, Barnsley: Pen & Sword, 2004; Lawrence James, *Warrior Race: A History of the British at War*, London: Abacus, 2002, p. 314.
38. David Andress, *Beating Napoleon*, London: Abacus, 2012, p. 42, p. 513.
39. Israel, *The Expanding Blaze*, pp. 86, 104–7, 335–37.

40. Julius Scott, *The Common Wind*, p. 150.
41. Israel, *The Expanding Blaze*, pp. 375–76; Godechot, *The Counter Revolution*, Chapters 13 and 18.
42. James, *Black Jacobins*, pp. 369–70; Napoleon quoted in Sudhir Hazareesingh, *Black Spartacus: The Epic Life of Toussaint Louverture*, London: Penguin, 2021, p. 302.
43. Israel, *The Expanding Blaze*, chapter fifteen; Andrew Robert, *Napoleon the Great*, London: Penguin, 2015, p. 303.
44. John Bew, *Castlereagh*, London: Quercus, 2014, p. 127, 173.
45. Andress, *Beating Napoleon*, p. 76.
46. John Hand, *The Life of Robert Emmett*, Liverpool: John Denvir, 1873, p. 20.
47. Lawrence James, *Warrior Race: A History of the British at War*, London: Abacus, 2002, p. 374, 391, 333.
48. Ibid., p. 271.

Chapter Thirteen

1. John Bew, *Castlereagh*, London: Quercus, 2011, p. 302.
2. David Landes, *Unbound Prometheus*, Cambridge U. P. 2003, p. 148.
3. Landes, *Unbound Prometheus*, p. 144; Napoleon quoted in Eli F. Heckscher, *Mercantilism*, Volume II, London: George Allen and Unwin, 1955, p. 20.
4. See Sidney Pollard, *Peaceful Conquest: The Industrialization of Europe, 1760-1970*, Oxford: Oxford University Press, 1981, for the account of European importing of British inventions, and also Landes, *Unbound Prometheus*.
5. Ricardo, *Principles of Political Economy and Taxation*, London: Everyman, 1984, p. 81.
6. Ben Wilson, *Heyday*, London: Weidenfeld & Nicolson, 2017, p. 9.
7. Friedrich List, *The National System of Political Economy*, 1841, excerpted in Margaret Hirst, *Life of Friedrich List and Selections from His Writings*, Scribner, 1909, p. 291.
8. List, *Outlines of American Political Economy*, Philadelphia, 1827, Appendix, p. 4.
9. Sidney Pollard, *Peaceful Conquest: The Industrialization of Europe, 1760-1970*, p. 198.
10. Franz Mehring, *Absolutism and, Revolution in Germany, 1525–1848*, Part Four, London: New Park, 1975.
11. Sven Beckert, *Empire of Cotton*, London: Penguin, 2015, p. 244.
12. Beckert, *Empire of Cotton*, p. 100.
13. Beckert, p. 107.
14. Maxine Berg, *The Age of Manufactures 1700-1820*, London: Fontana, 1985, p. 34, 39; Ure, *The Philosophy of Manufactures*, London: Charles Knight, 1935, pp. 106–7; *Anti-Slavery Reporter*, Vol. 8, No. 4 (April 2, 1860), p. 88.
15. Dodson (ed.), *Jubilee: The Emergence of African-American Culture*, Washington, DC: National Geographic Books, 2003 – for the number 1,800,000.
16. Beckert, *Empire of Cotton*, p. 110; and see Elizabeth Fox-Genovese and Eugene Genovese, *Fruits of Merchant Capital*, Oxford University Press, 1983; Jairus Banaji, *Theory as History*, Chicago: Haymarket, 2011, p. 68, 353.
17. 'Important Statistics Of The Slave Trade' Article reproduced from the *Pennsylvania Freeman* and based on 'a report leaked from the Commissioner of Patents', *Anti Slavery Reporter*, Vol. II, No. XIII (1 January 1847), p. 4.
18. *A Journey in the Sea-Board Slave States*, Sampson Low, Son, & Co., 47, Ludgate Hill, 1856, p. 166.
19. *Anti-Slavery Reporter*, Vol. Iv, No. XXXVII (1 January 1849), p. 4; Leonard L. Richards, *The Slave Power: The Free North and Southern Domination, 1780-1860*, Baton Rouge, 2000.
20. John Mitchel, *Jail Journal*, London: Sphere Books, 1983, p. xxvii.
21. in Liz Curtis, *Nothing But the Same Old Story*, London: Information on Ireland, 1984, p. 53.
22. in Liz Curtis, *Nothing But the Same Old Story*, London, 1984, p. 50.
23. *Jail Journal*, xxxii – assuming a family to be five or more which was right at the time, E. R. R. Green reckons that fully 45 per cent of holdings were under five acres, in Moody and Martin, *The Course of Irish History*, 1987, p. 267.
24. quoted in T. P. O'Connor, *The Parnell Movement*, London: Ward and Downey, 1886, p. 186.

25. Ibid.
26. Tom Crehan, *Marcella Gerrard's Galway Estate, 1820-70*, Dublin: Four Courts Press, 2013.
27. Tim Pat Coogan, *The Famine Plot*, Chapter 6.
28. John Mitchell, *Jail Journal*, p. xxxiv.
29. Cecil Woodham Smith, *The Great Hunger*, London: New English Library, 1981, p. 72, 117.
30. in Liz Curtis, *Nothing But the Same Old Story*, p. 51.
31. quoted in T. P. O'Connor, *The Parnell Movement*, London: Ward and Downey, 1886, p. 186.
32. 'Thoughts and Details on Scarcity', in *Miscellaneous Writings*, ed. Edmund Burke, Indianapolis: Liberty Fund, 1999, p. 81.
33. Tim Pat Coogan, *The Famine Plot*, Basingstoke: Palgrave Macmillan, 2012, p. 31.
34. J. S. Mill, *England and Ireland*, London, 1868, and see Murphy (ed), *Economists and the Irish Economy*, Blackrock: Irish Academic Press, 1983.
35. *Capital I*, Lawrence and Wishart, 1954, p. 657.
36. Gerald Hertz, 'The English Silk Industry in the Eighteenth Century', *The English Historical Review*, Vol. 24, No. 96 (1909), pp. 710–727; George Riello, 'When Cotton Was Banned', *Cambridge University Press Blog*, 15 May 2013, http://www.cambridgeblog.org/2013/05/when-cotton-was-banned-indian-cotton-textiles-in-early-modern-england/.
37. Michael J. Twomey, 'Employment in Indian Textiles', *Explorations in Economic History*, Vol. 20 (1983), p. 41; James Walvin, *Slavery in Small Things: Slavery and Modern Cultural Habits*, 2017, pp. 242–3 for relative productivity.
38. quoted in Sailendra Nath Sen, *History of The Freedom Movement In India (1857-1947)*, 2009, p. 4.
39. quoted in M. J. Akbar, *Nehru*, London: Penguin, 1989, p. 158.
40. Hobsbawm, *Industry and Empire*, London: Weidenfeld and Nicolson, 1969, p. 121.
41. P. J. Cain and A. G. Hopkins, *British Imperialism*, Longman, 2002, p. 246.
42. James Belich, *Replenishing the Earth*, p. 524.
43. Woodbine Parish, *Buenos Ayres and the Provinces of the Rio de la Plata*, London, 1839, p. 338.
44. House of Commons, 24 April 1849.
45. *Anti-Slavery Reporter*, Vol. IV, No. XLVII (1 November 1849), pp. 168–69.
46. David Kynaston, *The City of London, Vol I: A World of Its Own 1815-1890*, London, Chatto and Windus, p. 36.
47. Kynaston, *The City of London, Vol. I*, p. 46.
48. Hobsbawm, *Industry and Empire*, London: Weidenfeld and Nicolson, 1969, p. 91.
49. *Times*, quoted in Kynaston, *The City of London, Vol. I*, p. 240.
50. quoted in Kynaston, *The City of London, Vol. I*, p. 259.
51. Kynaston, *The City of London, Vol. I*, p. 261.

Chapter Fourteen

1. The Condition of the Poorer Classes in Ireland, Appendix G., *State of the Irish Poor in Great Britain*, HMSO, vii, 61, 1, 101, vii.
2. James Belich, *Replenishing the Earth*, p. 126; T. Devine, *The Scottish Clearances*, London: Penguin, 2019, p. 268.
3. 25 July 1836, quoted in David Kynaston, *The City of London, Vol I, A World of its Own*, 1994, p. 105.
4. David Harris Sacks, *The Widening Gate*, pp. 252–53.
5. Farley Grubb, 'The Transatlantic Market for British Convict Labor', *The Journal of Economic History*, Vol. 60, No. 1 (March 2000), p. 94.
6. Robert Hughes, *The Fatal Shore*, New York: Alfred Knopf, 1987, p. 71, 83, 105.
7. George Rudé, *Protest and Punishment*, Oxford: Clarendon, 1978, p. 63.
8. Richard Clark, 'The history of judicial hanging in Britain 1735–1964', http://www.capital-punishmentuk.org/hanging1.html.
9. James Heartfield, *The Aborigines' Protection Society*, London: Hurst, 2011, pp. 66–8.
10. Belich, *Replenishing the Earth*, Oxford University Press, 2013, pp. 126, 83–4, 147; Richard Gott, *Britain's Empire*, London: Verso, 2011, p. 205.
11. T. M. Devine, *The Scottish Clearances*, London: Penguin, 2019, pp. 319–23.

12. Coogan, *The Famine Plot,* p. 190.
13. Cecil Woodham Smith, *The Great Hunger,* p. 216.
14. quoted in Coogan, *The Famine Plot,* p. 198.
15. James Belich, *Replenishing the Earth,* pp. 145–6.
16. Heartfield, *The Aborigines' Protection Society,* pp. 20, 62–63, 208–10, 279–83.
17. Belich, *Replenishing the Earth,* p. 83.
18. Belich, *Replenishing the Earth,* p. 157.
19. David Silverman, 'Guns, Empires and Indians', *Aeon,* 13 October 2016, https://aeon.co/essays/how-did-the-introduction-of-guns-change-native-america.
20. Peter Newman, *Merchant Princes,* Vol. III, Toronto: Penguin, 1991, 35–36.
21. Lewis Henry Morgan, *League of the Ho-De-No-Sau-Nee or Iroquois,* North Dighton: JG Press, 1995, pp. 10–11, 16–20.
22. Howard Zinn, *A People's History of the United States,* New York: HarperPerennial, 2005, Chapter 3.
23. George Dangerfield, *The Awakening of American Nationalism,* New York: Harper, 1965, pp. 44–45, 272–73; Frederick Jackson, Turner, *The Frontier in American History,* University of Arizona Press, 1994, p. 69, 131, 134, 143–44.
24. Belich, *Replenishing the Earth,* pp. 383–84.
25. Malcolm Prentis, *A Study in Black and White: The Aborigines in Australian History,* New South Wales: Rosenberg, 2009, Chapter 4; Heartfield, *The Aborigines' Protection Society,* pp. 89–124, 125–159.
26. Newman, *Merchant Princes, Company of Adventurers,* Vol. III, p. 73.
27. Heartfield, *The Aborigines' Protection Society,* p. 47.
28. Jan Morris, *Heaven's Command,* London, 1998, chapter seven part five covers the Durham Report.
29. Jacques Rancière, *Proletarian Nights,* London: Verso, 2012; Karl Obermann, *Joseph Weydemeyer, Pioneer of American Socialism,* New York: International Publishers, 1947.

Chapter Fifteen

1. Brian Stanley, *History of the Baptist Missionary Society,* Edinburgh: T&T Clark, 1992, p. 6.
2. Stanley, *History of the Baptist Missionary Society,* p. 5.
3. *History of the Baptist Missionary Society,* p. 51.
4. House of Commons, 'East India Companies Affairs', 22 June 1813, The Parliamentary Debates, Vol. XXVI, *Hansard,* 1813, Col. 865.
5. Stanley, *History of the Baptist Missionary Society,* p. 45.
6. Stanley, *History of the Baptist Missionary Society,* pp. 69–71.
7. Heartfield, *The British and Foreign Anti-Slavery Society,* London: Hurst, 2016, p. 17.
8. Heartfield, *The British and Foreign Anti-Slavery Society,* p. 220, p. 222.
9. Kevin, Shillington, *Luka Jantjie,* London: Aldridge Press, 2011; Jeff Guy, *The View Across the River,* Charlottesville: University Press of Virginia, 2002.
10. Max Siollun, *What Britain Did to Nigeria,* London, Hurst, 2021, pp. 253–4, 260; Richard Temple, 'The General Statistics of the British Empire', *Journal of the Statistical Society of London,* Vol. 47, No. 3 (September 1884), pp. 468–84, 482.
11. T. Robert Malthus, *Statements Respecting the East India College,* 1817.
12. *The Hertfordian,* 17 May 1822, p. 73.
13. *Essay on Population,* 1803, p. 6.
14. J Pullen, 'Malthus: The Inverarity Manuscript', *History of Political Economy,* Vol. 13, No. 4 (1981), p. 811.
15. Richard Jones, *Literary Remains,* London: John Murray, 1859, pp. 281–90.
16. Ranajit Guha, *Dominance without Hegemony,* Harvard University Press, 1997, p. 74; Manan Ahmed Asif, *The Loss of Hindustan, The Invention of India,* Harvard U. P. 2020.
17. Zareer Masani, *Macaulay: Britain's Liberal Imperialist,* London: Vintage, 2014, p. 47.
18. Masani, *Macaulay,* p. 44.
19. House of Commons, 10 July 1833.
20. Masani, *Macaulay,* p. 114.

21. Adam Hochschild, *Bury the Chains*, Boston: Mariner Books, 2006, p. 303; *Slavery in Diplomacy*, Foreign and Commonwealth Office, History note no 17, 2007, p 1; D. B. Davies, *Slavery and Human Progress*, Oxford, 1984, p. 285; James Heartfield, *The British and Foreign Anti-Slavery Society*, London: Hurst, 2016, Chapter 4.

22. Bernard Edwards, *The Royal Navy Versus the Slave Traders: Enforcing Abolition at Sea 1808-1898*, Barnsley: Pen and Sword, 2021.

23. *The Anti-Slavery Reporter*, Vol. I, No. VII (1 July 1846), p. 114.

24. Edwards, *The Royal Navy Versus the Slave Traders*, pp. 118–19, 153–54; 1865 Select Committee Report quoted in C. P. Lucas, *A Historical Geography of the British Colonies*, Vol. III, West Africa: Clarendon, Oxford, 1894, p. 116.

25. Siân Rees, *Sweet Water and Bitter: The Ships that Stopped the Slave Trade*, London: Vintage, 2010, p. 107, 150; Alastair Hazell, *The Last Slave Market*, London: Constable, 2011.

26. Michael Taylor, *The Interest: How the British Establishment Resisted the Abolition of Slavery*, London: Bodley Head, 2020.

27. James McQueen, *General Statistics of the British Empire*, London: B. Fellowes, 1836, p. 191.

28. Heartfield, *The British and Foreign Anti-Slavery Society*, pp. 13–14.

29. J. Eastoe Teall, 'A Brief Account of the Results of Granting Compensation to the West Indian Slave holders, and the continuance of Slavery under the name "Apprenticeship"', in *Slavery in British Protectorates*, London: British and Foreign Anti-Slavery Society, 1897; Woodville K Marshall, 'The Emergence and Survival of the Peasantry', in *The Long Nineteenth Century*, Vol. IV of the *General History of the Caribbean*, Unesco, 2011; Kathleen Mary Butler, *The Economics of Emancipation*, Chapel Hill: University of North Carolina Press, 1995; Palmerston quote: *The Anti-Slavery Reporter*, Vol. 6, No. 9 (1 September 1858), p. 207.

30. James Heartfield, *The Aborigines' Protection Society*, London: Hurst, 2011; Zoe Laidlaw, *Protecting the Empire's Humanity*, Cambridge University Press, 2021.

31. Aborigines Protection Society, *Report, 2nd Annual Meeting*, 21 May 1839, p. 7.

32. UK HC Report from the Select Committee on Aborigines (British Settlements), Irish University Press Series of British Parliament Papers, 'Anthropology – Aborigines', Vol. 2 at p. 6.

33. Vivienne Rae-Ellis, *Black Robinson: Protector of Aborigines*, Melbourne University Press, 1996.

34. Jennifer Reid, *Myth, Symbol and Colonial Encounter: British and Mi'kmaq in Acadia*, University of Ottawa Press, 1995, pp. 34–41; Heartfield, *The Aborigines' Protection Society*, pp. 228–231.

35. *Aborigines' Friend*, February 1883, p. 25.

Chapter Sixteen

1. William Harrison Woodward, *A Short History of the Expansion of the British Empire, 1500-1902*, Cambridge: Cambridge Series for Schools, 1902, p. 231.

2. George Newenham Wright, *A New and Comprehensive Gazetteer*, Volume III, 1836, p. 406.

3. Alexander Anievas and Kerem Nişancıoğlu, *How the West Came to Rule*, London: Pluto, 2015, p. 271.

4. *Statements Respecting the East India College*, 1817, p. 36.

5. See Kim Wagner, *The Great Fear*, Oxford: Peter Lang, 2010.

6. Spencer Leonard, '"A Theatre of Disputes": The East India Company Election of 1764 as the Founding of British India', *The Journal of Imperial and Commonwealth History*, Vol. 42, No. 4 (2014), pp. 593–624.

7. John Keay, *India*, London: Harper Press, 2010, p. 393–97; William Dalrymple, *The Anarchy: The Relentless Rise of the East India Company*, Bloomsbury, 2019, pp. 344–54; Roderick Matthews, *Peace, Poverty and Betrayal: A New History of British India*, London: Hurst and Co, 2021, p. 91,104.

8. Dalrymple, *The Anarchy*, pp. 241–42.

9. Dalrymple, *The Anarchy*, pp. 244–45.

10. Dalrymple, *The Anarchy*, pp. 363–89.

11. Keay, *India*, pp. 418–19.

12. Keay, *India*, pp. 422–24; Queen Victoria's views on the Koh-i-Noor, R. Fulford, ed., *Darling Child. Private Correspondence of Queen Victoria and the Crown Princess of Prussia, 1871-1878*, London, 1976, p. 111.

13. Thant Myint-U, *The River of Lost Footsteps*, London: Faber and Faber, 2007, Chapter 6.
14. Keay, *India*, p. 433.
15. Richard Jones, *Literary Remains*, London: John Murray, 1859, p. 284.
16. Jones, *Literary Remains*, p. 288.
17. Charles Metcalfe in The Fifth Report for the Select Committee of the House of Commons, on the Affairs of the East India Company, in 1830.
18. Jones, *Literary Remains*, pp. 289–90.
19. Ramakrishna Mukherjee, *The Rise and Fall of the East India Company*, Aakar, 2011, p. 408.
20. Jairus Banaji, *Theory as History*, Chicago: Haymarket, 2011, p. 291.
21. Rolf Bauer, *The Peasant Production of Opium in Nineteenth Century India*, Brill, 2019, p. 2.
22. Ben Wilson, *Heyday*, p. 259; Amit K. Sharma, 'Fire-carriages of the Raj', *Essays in History*, Vol. 43 (2010), http://www.essaysinhistory.com/fire-carriages-of-the-raj-the-indian-railway-and-its-rapid-development-in-british-india/.
23. Ian J. Kerr, 'Working Class Protest in 19th Century India', *Economic and Political Weekly*, Vol. 20, No. 4 (26 January 1985); Ian J. Kerr, 'Constructing Railways in India', *The Indian Economic and Social Review*, Vol. 20, No. 3 (1983).
24. Karl Marx, 'The Future Results of British Rule in India', *New York Daily Tribune*, 8 August 1853.
25. Tirthankar Roy, *A Business History of India*, Cambridge University Press, 2018, p. 102, 113.
26. Dadabhai Naoroji, *Poverty and Un-British Rule in India*, 1901, pp. 33–34.
27. James McQueen, *Statistics of the British Empire*, London, 1837, p. 215; Shashi Tharoor, *Inglorious Empire*, London: Hurst, 2017, p. 9; Angus Maddison, *The World Economy*, Paris: OECD, 2001, p. 91.
28. G. R. Greig, *Memoirs of the life of the Right Hon. Warren Hastings*, London: Richard Bentley, 1841, p. 158.
29. Dalrymple, *White Mughals*, London: Harper Collins, 2002.
30. Sanjoy Chakravorty, *The Truth About Us*, Hachette India, 2019, p. 141; and see David Cannadine, *Ornamentalism: How the British Saw Their Empire*, London: Penguin, 2002, pp. 41–2.
31. *Code of the Gentoos*, London, 1776, Nathaniel Brassey Halhed (ed.), p. 286.
32. Dipti Mayee Sahoo, 'Analysis of Hindu Widowhood In Indian Literature', *IOSR Journal of Humanities and Social Science (IOSR-JHSS)*, Vol. 21, No. 9, Ver. 7 (Sep. 2016), pp. 64–71.
33. See Kim A. Wagner, *Stranglers and Bandits: A Historical Anthology of Thuggee*, Oxford University Press, 2009.
34. Philip Woodruff, *The Men Who Ruled India: the Founders*, London: Jonathan Cape, 1953, p. 329.
35. See David Cannadine, *Ornamentalism*, London, Penguin, 2002.
36. 'Representing authority in Imperial India', in *The Invention of Tradition*, ed. Terence Ranger and Eric Hobsbawm, Cambridge University Press, 1983, p. 193.
37. Ranjit Guha, *Dominance without Hegemony*, Harvard University Press, 1997, p. 63, 77.

Chapter Seventeen

1. George Woodcock, *The British in the Far East*, London: Weidenfeld and Nicolson, 1969, xxi, p. 3.
2. Arthur Cotterell, *East Asia: From Chinese Predominance to the Rise of the Pacific Rim*, London: Pimlico, 2002, pp. 177–80.
3. Maxine Berg, 'Consumption in Eighteenth- and Early Nineteenth-Century Britain', in *The Cambridge Economic History of Modern Britain*, 2004, p. 367.
4. Robert Blake, *Jardine Matheson*, London: Weidenfeld & Nicolson, 1999, p. 14.
5. Maurice Collis, *Foreign Mud*, New York: New Directions, 2002, pp. 34, 78–79.
6. Rolf Bauer, *The Peasant Production of Opium in Nineteenth Century India*, Brill, 2019, p. 1.
7. Ian Barrow, *The East India Company*, Indianapolis, Hackett, 2017, pp. 78–79.
8. Blake, *Jardine Matheson*, pp. 18–19.
9. Collis, *Foreign Mud*, pp. 52–6; Woodcock, *The British in the Far East*, p. 31.
10. Barrow, *East India Company*, p. 76.

11. Blake, *Jardine Matheson*, p. 45, 58.
12. Report from Select Committee on the Affairs of the East India Company, IIII. Revenue, p. 70.
13. Jasper Ridley, *Lord Palmerston*, London: Constable, 1970, p. 253.
14. Quoted in Harold Ingrams, *Hong Kong*, London: Her Majesty's Stationery Office, 1952, p. 24; Julia Lovell gives a good account of the background to the crackdown in *The Opium War*, London: Picador, 2011, Chapter 3.
15. Collis, *Foreign Mud*, p. 247.
16. James Matheson, *The Present Position and Future Prospects of Trade in China*, London: Smith, Elder and Co., 1836, p. 6.
17. Blake, *Jardine Matheson*, p. 85.
18. Collis, *Foreign Mud*, pp. 262–67.
19. Karl Marx, 'Trade with China', *New York Daily Tribune*, 3 December 1859.
20. Ridley, *Lord Palmerston*, p. 254.
21. Imperial Edict to the Grand Secretariat, June 5, 1842, in *World History in Documents, A Comparative Reader*, Second Edition, Edited by Peter N. Stearns, New York University Press, 2008, Chapter 23.
22. Ridley, *Lord Palmerston*, p. 255.
23. Ridley, *Lord Palmerston*, p. 256.
24. Ridley, *Lord Palmerston*, pp. 258–59.
25. Deng Xiaoping, *On the question of Hong Kong*, Hong Kong: New Horizon Press, 1993, p. 36.
26. J.F. Davis to Lord Stanley, 21 Dec. 1843, CO 129/4, 278, quoted in Christopher Munn, *Anglo-China: Chinese People and British Rule in Hong Kong, 1841-1880*, Routledge, 2001, p. 21.
27. Ridley, *Lord Palmerston*, p. 464.
28. Ridley, *Lord Palmerston*, p. 468.
29. Haan, J. H., 'Origin and Development of the Political System in the Shanghai International Settlement', *Journal of the Hong Kong Branch of the Royal Asiatic Society*, Vol. 22 (1982), pp. 31–64; Peter C. Perdue, 'Interlopers, Rogues, or Cosmopolitans? Wu Jianzhang and Early Modern Commercial Networks on the China Coast', *Cross-Currents: East Asian History and Culture Review University of Hawai'i Press*, Vol. 7, No. 1 (May 2018), pp. 70–92.
30. Woodcock, *The British in the Far East*, p. 42; Blake, *Jardine Matheson*, pp. 136–7.

Chapter Eighteen

1. *The Victims of Whiggery*, Hobart, 1946, p. 50.
2. John Savile, *1848: The British State and the Chartist Movement*, Cambridge University Press, 1990; and see Max Morris, *From Cobbett to the Chartists, 1815-1848*, London: Lawrence and Wishart, 1948.
3. E. P. Thompson, *The Making of the English Working Class*, London: Penguin, 1991, pp. 577, 857–887; George Holyoke, Self-Help By the People - The History of the Rochdale Pioneers, Scribners, 1893; Trades Union Congress, *The History of the TUC 1868-1968: A Pictorial Survey of a Social Revolution*, London: Hamlyn, 1868.
4. T. A. Jackson, *Ireland Her Own*, London: Lawrence and Wishart, 1991, pp. 236–47; T. W. Moody, *The Course of Irish History*, Cork: Mercier, 1987, pp. 257–61.
5. Sean Cronin, *Irish Nationalism*, Dublin: The Academy Press, 1980, p. 81; Moody, *The Course of Irish History*, p. 262.
6. Cronin, *Irish Nationalism*, pp. 82–5; Jackson, *Ireland Her Own*, pp. 247–57.
7. Jackson, *Ireland Her Own*, pp. 275–283.
8. Jackson, *Ireland Her Own*, pp. 284–9.
9. Cronin, *Irish Nationalism*, pp. 86–92; Jackson, *Ireland Her Own*, pp. 292–6.
10. James Belich, 'The Governors and the Maori', p. 85, 78 *Oxford Illustrated History of New Zealand*, 1993.
11. James Heartfield, *The Aborigines' Protection Society*, London: Hurst, 2011, pp. 92–96; Vivienne Rae-Ellis, *Black Robinson*, Melbourne University Press, 1996, pp. 214–5.
12. Heartfield, *The Aborigines' Protection Society*, p. 115.

13. Ian Hugh Kawharu, *Waitangi: Maori and Pakeha Perspectives on the Treaty of Waitangi*, Oxford University Press Australia, 1989; Heartfield, *The Aborigines' Protection Society*, pp. 125–26.
14. Tawai Kawiti, 'Heke's War in the North', *Te Ao Hou The New World*, No. 16 (October 1956), pp. 38–43.
15. John Gorst, *The Maori King Movement*, Auckland, Reed, 2001, pp. 35–41; James Belich, *The New Zealand Wars and the Victorian Interpretation of Racial Conflict*, Auckland: Penguin, 1986.
16. Judith Binney, *Redemption Songs: A life of Te Kooti Arikirangi Te Turuki*, Auckland University Press, 1997.
17. John Keay *India*, London: Harper Press, 2010, pp. 397–9.
18. Keay *India*, p. 400.
19. Kim Wagner, *The Great Fear of 1857*, Oxford: Peter Lang, 2010, p. 29.
20. Wagner, *The Great Fear*, pp. 102–04.
21. Wagner, *The Great Fear*, pp. 34, 36–8.
22. Wagner, *The Great Fear*, p. 37.
23. Wagner, *The Great Fear*, pp. 42–3.
24. Kim Wagner, *The Skull of Alum Beg*, London: Hurst, 2017, pp. 62, 6.
25. Wagner, *The Great Fear*, p. 80.
26. Wagner, *The Great Fear*, pp. 82–7, 90.
27. Wagner, *The Great Fear*, pp. 136–7.
28. Wagner, *The Great Fear*, p. 208.
29. Wagner, *The Great Fear*, p. 137.
30. Wagner, *The Great Fear*, p. 212.
31. Quoted in Wagner, *The Great Fear*, p. 18.
32. Lawrence James, *Raj: The Making and Unmaking of British India*, Abacus, 2012, p. 266.
33. *Annual Register*, London, 1857, p. 304.
34. Gad Heuman, *Between Black and White*, Greenwood, 1981, p. 121.
35. *The Anti-Slavery Reporter*, Vol. 13, No. 7 (1 July 1865), p. 167; James Heartfield, *The British and Foreign Anti-Slavery Society*, London: Hurst, 2016, pp. 109–13.
36. Gad Heuman, *The Killing Time*, London: Macmillan, 1994, pp. 58–59.
37. Heartfield, *The British and Foreign Anti-Slavery Society*, p. 117.
38. Henry Bleby, *The Reign of Terror: A Narrative of Facts Concerning Governor Eyre, George William Gordon, and the Jamaica Atrocities*, London: William Nicholls, 1868.
39. Heartfield, *The British and Foreign Anti-Slavery Society*, p. 123.

Chapter Nineteen

1. John Seeley, *The Expansion of England*, London, 1888 edition, p. 8.
2. Lenin criticises Kautsky for talking about imperialism as a policy of the capitalists: 'Kautsky detaches the politics of imperialism from its economics, speaks of annexations as being a policy "preferred" by finance capital, and opposes to it another bourgeois policy which, he alleges, is possible on this very same basis of finance capital.' *Imperialism, the Highest Stage of Capitalism*, 1916, Chapter VII.
3. quoted in Gertrude Himmelfarb, *Poverty and Compassion*, New York: Alfred Knopf, 1991, p. 276.
4. T. H. Green, *Lectures on the Principal of Political Obligation*, Cambridge University Press, 1986, p. 212.
5. *Toynbee's Industrial Revolution*, Newton Abbott: David & Charles, 1969, p. 21.
6. quoted in Himmelfarb, *Poverty and Compassion*, p. 281.
7. Mearns, *The Bitter Cry of Outcast London*, 1883, p 1.
8. 1887, quoted in Gareth Stedman Jones, *Outcast London*, 1976, p. 223.
9. L. C. Knowles, *Economic Development of the Overseas Empire*, London: Routledge, 1924, p. 28.
10. John Mackenzie, *Austral Africa: Ruling it or Losing It*, London: Sampson Low & Co, 1887, p. 76.
11. Lawrence James, *Warrior Race: A History of the British at War*, London: Abacus, 2002, p. 378.
12. James, *Warrior Race*, p. 431, 433.

13. David G. Boyce, 'Harold Harmsworth, Lord Rothermere', *Oxford Dictionary of National Biography* (2004-2014).
14. Douglas Lorimer, *Science, Race Relations and Resistance,* Manchester University Press, 2013, p. 126, 133, 144.
15. John Mackenzie, *Propaganda and Empire,* Manchester University Press, 1986, p. 205.
16. Mackenzie, *Propaganda and Empire,* pp. 48–49.
17. Mackenzie, *Propaganda and the Empire,* p. 111.
18. Mackenzie, *Propaganda and the Empire,* p. 50.

Chapter Twenty

1. Stephen Bourne, 'Progress of the External Trade of the United Kingdom in Recent Years', *Journal of the Royal Statistical Society,* Vol. 56, No. 2 (June 1893), pp. 185–214; P. J. Cain and A. G. Hopkins, *British Imperialism,* London: Longman, 2002, Chapter 5.
2. David Kynaston, *The City of London: A World of Its Own, 1815-90,* London: Chatto and Windus, 1994, pp. 390–95; G. D. H. Cole and Raymond Postgate, *The Common People,* London: Methuen, 1961, p 405.
3. in an Overseas Settlement Display at the 1924 Wembley Empire Exhibition, John Mackenzie, *Propaganda and Empire,* p 111.
4. 'Home Children, Why Were They Sent Here?' Addendum, Home Committee, Minutes of Evidence, Parliament UK, 1998, https://publications.parliament.uk/pa/cm199798/cmselect/cmhealth/755/8052025.htm and see here 'Legislation Which Governed the Migration of Children from England,' British Home Children Advocacy & Research Association, https://canadianbritishhomechildren.weebly.com/british-legislation.html.
5. Edwin Cannan, 'The Origin of the Law of Diminishing Returns', 1813-15, *Economic Journal,* Vol. 2 (1892).
6. See Sidney Pollard, 'Capital Exports, 1870-1914: Harmful or Beneficial?' The *Economic History Review* Second Series, Vol. XXXVIII, No. 4 (November 1985); William Goetzman, Ukhov, British Investment Overseas 1870-1913: A Modern Portfolio Theory Approach, National Bureau Of Economic Research, Working Paper 11266, http://www.nber.org/papers/w11266.
7. P. J. Cain and A. G. Hopkins, *British Imperialism,* London: Longman, 2002, p. 179.
8. Source: Paul Kennedy, *Rise and Fall of the Great Powers,* London: Fontana, 1990, p. 259.
9. Kynaston, *The City of London,* p. 407, 342 – the Ship Canal was successfully floated two years later by a smaller firm and opened in 1894.
10. Kynaston, *The City of London,* pp. 335, 339, 396–97.
11. Kynaston, *The City of London,* p. 423, 427.
12. The *Economist,* 17 June 1882 quoted in David Kynaston, *The City of London,* p. 338. Kynaston, *The City of London,* pp. 336–40.
13. Kynaston, *The City of London,* p. 338.
14. J. A. Hobson, *Imperialism: A Study,* London: George Allen and Unwin, 1968, p. 63, 81, 85.
15. See the *Anti-Slavery Reporter,* Series 4, Vol. XI, No. 5 (September–October 1891).

Chapter Twenty-one

1. Adapted from John Hobson, *Imperialism,* London, 1968, p. 17.
2. *Anti-Slavery Reporter,* Vol. 21, No. 5 (November 1878), p. 121; Landes, *Unbound Prometheus,* Cambridge U. P., 2003, p. 240.
3. Dr Livingstone to the Earl of Clarendon, Received 18 April 1868, *Anti-Slavery Reporter,* Vol. 16, No. 10 (1 July 1869), p. 230.
4. The story is well told in John Broich's book *Squadron: Ending the African Slave Trade,* London: Duckworth, 2017.
5. Broich, *Squadron,* pp. 217–22.
6. *Anti-Slavery Reporter,* Vol. 18, No. 2 (1 July 1872), pp. 46–49.
7. Donald Neff, *Warriors at Suez,* Battleboro: Amana Books, 1988, p. 268.

8. Neff, *Warriors at Suez*, p. 17.

9. Fergus Nicoll, *The Mahdi of Sudan*, Stroud: Sutton Publishing, 2005.

10. 23 October 1884, *Anti-Slavery Reporter*, Series 4, Vol. LV, No. 9 (5 November 1884), p. 201; P. M. Holt, *A Modern History of the Sudan*, London: Weidenfeld and Nicolson, 1961, p. 123.

11. Neal Ascherson, *The King Incorporated*, London: George Allen and Unwin, 1963, pp. 93–100.

12. *Aborigines' Friend*, May 1885, p. 175.

13. Dominic Green, *Armies of the Nile*, London: Century, 2007, pp. 253–54.

14. Hansard, HL Deb 30 August 1889, §826; and see Heartfield, *British and Foreign Anti-Slavery Society*, pp. 313–18 for an account of the Brussels conference.

15. Lilian C. A. Knowles, *Economic Development of the Overseas Empire*, London: Routledge,1924, p. 169.

16. 'The Anti-Slavery Conference of the Powers at Brussels', *The Anti-Slavery Reporter*, Series 4, Vol. IX, No. 6 (November–December 1889), p. 237.

17. *The Anti-Slavery Reporter* (March/April 1890), p. 41.

18. Vladimir Borisovich Lutsky, *Modern History of the Arab Countries*, Moscow: Progress, 1969, Chapter 18; Heartfield, *British and Foreign Anti-Slavery Society*, London: Hurst, 2016, p. 293; Cromer quoted in Hannah Arendt, *The Origins of Totalitarianism*, New York: Meridian, 1971, p. 213.

19. Nöel Mostert, *Frontiers: The Epic Story of South Africa's Creation and the Tragedy of the Xhosa People*, New York: Knopf, 1992, p. 757.

20. Nöel Mostert, *Frontiers;* Martin Legassick, *The Struggle for the Eastern Cape, 1800-1854*, Johannesberg: KMM Publishing, 2010.

21. Norman Etherington, *The Great Treks: The Transformation of Southern Africa, 1815-1854*, Edinburgh: Pearson, 2001.

22. James Heartfield, *The Aborigines' Protection Society*, London: Hurst, 2011, pp. 233–72.

23. Alan Lester, Kate Boehme and Peter Mitchell, *Ruling the World*, Cambridge University Press, 2021, p. 322; Frances Colenso, *The History of the Zulu War*, London, 1880, pp. 273–302.

24. H. Rider Haggard, *Cetewayo and his White Neighbours*, London, 1882.

25. *Aborigines' Friend*, March 1884, p. 82.

26. Jeff Guy, *The View Across the River: Harriette Colenso and the Zulu Struggle Against Imperialism*, Charlottesville: University Press of Virginia, 2002, pp. 276–97.

27. Kevin Shillington, *Luka Jantjie*, London: Aldridge Press, 2011, p. 64, 78.

28. Shillington, *Luka Jantjie*, pp. 244–62.

29. F. W. Chesson, *The Basuto War: A Brief Reply to Sir Bartle Frere's Article in 'The Nineteenth Century'*, Westminster: P. S. King, 1881, p. 9.

30. *Aborigines' Friend*, April 1903, pp. 364–5.

31. Andrew Murray, *The Imperial Controversy*, London, 2009, p. 43.

32. David Kynaston, *City of London: A History* (in one volume), London: Chatto and Windus, 2011, pp. 123–5.

33. *Aborigines' Friend*, October 1901, pp. 81–5.

34. *New York Times*, 23 March 1901.

35. in a speech just before the May 1908 Convention, in J. C. Smuts, *Jan Christian Smuts*, Cape Town: Cassell, 1952, p. 111.

36. Brian Willans, *Sol Plaatje*, Sunnyside: Jacana Media, 2018, p. 243.

37. See Robert Aldrich, *Greater France, A History of French Overseas Expansion*, esp. Chapter 1, London: Macmillan, 1996; James J. Cooke, *New French Imperialism 1880-1910*, Newton Abbott, David & Charles, 1973; David Leavering Lewis, *The Race to Fashoda*, New York: Weidenfeld and Nicolson, 1987; Charles-Robert Ageron, *Modern Algeria: A History from 1830 to the Present*, London: Hurst and Company, 1990; Magali Morsy, *North Africa 1800-1900*, London: Longman, 1984.

38. *Statesman Year-Book 1917*, p. 883.

39. Aldrich, *Greater France*, p. 40, 42.

40. *Statesman Year-Book 1917*, p. 936.

41. Charles Waldstein, *The Expansion of Western Ideals and the World's Peace*, London: John Lane, 1899, pp. 185–86.

42. Lord Hailey, *African Survey*, London: Oxford University Press, 1938, pp. 720–3, 737–8, 741, Raymond Buell, *The Native Problem in Africa*, New York: Macmillan, 1928, p. 220, 231, 322;

Census of the Cape of Good Hope, Final Report, 1891, Cape Town, 1892, p. i; T. Shepstone, 'Return of the Native Population of Natal, 1891', Minute to the *Natal Census of 1891,* Martizburg; *Census of the British Empire, 1901,* London: HMSO, 1906, p. 147, 161.

43. Frank Furedi, *The Mau Mau War in Perspective,* London: Currey, 1989, Chapter 1.
44. Buell, *The Native Problem....*
45. Mahmood Mamdani, *Citizen and Subject,* Chichester: Princeton University Press, 2018.
46. Lugard, *The Dual Mandate in British Tropical Africa,* Milton Park: Frank Cass and Co, 1965, p. 300.
47. Mahmood Mamdani, *Citizen and Subject,* Chichester: Princeton University Press, 2018, p. 67.
48. Jan Smuts, *Africa and Some World Problems,* Oxford: Clarendon Press, 1929, pp. 76–8.
49. Mamdani, *Citizen and Subject,* p. 79.
50. Mamdani, *Citizen and Subject,* p. 172.
51. Heartfield, *Aborigines' Protection Society,* pp. 272–5.

Chapter Twenty-two

1. Robert Holland, *Blue-Water Empire: The British in the Mediterranean since 1800,* London: Allen Lane, 2012, p. 104, 118, 119.
2. David Wearing, *Anglo-Arabia,* Cambridge: Polity, 2018, p. 13; Vanaraj S. Sheth, 'Growth of British Influence in South Yemen, 1839-1959', *International Studies,* Vol. 19, No. 3 (1980).
3. Lawrence James, *Raj: The Making and Unmaking of British India,* London: Abacus, 2012, Chapter 1.
4. James, *Raj,* p. 309.
5. Angus Maddison, *The World Economy: A Millennial Perspective,* Paris: OECD, p 112.
6. Tirthankar Roy, 'Inequality in Colonial India', LSE Economic Working Papers, No 286, September 2018.
7. Quoted in Rajani Palme Dutt, *India Today,* London: Gollancz, 1940, p. 183.
8. Dutt, *India Today,* p. 184.
9. Angus Maddison, *Class Structure and Economic Growth: India and Pakistan Since the Moghuls,* London: Allen and Unwin, 1971, p 46.
10. Kalyan Kumar Sengupta, *Pabna Disturbances and the Politics of Rent, 1873-1885*, People's Publishing House, 1974.
11. Mike Davis, *Late Victorian Holocausts,* London: Verso, pp. 31–2.
12. Malcolm Darling, *The Punjab Peasant,* Oxford University Press, 1947, p 4.
13. Mike Davis, *Late Indian Holocausts,* London: Verso, 2002, pp. 141–75.
14. Aditya Sarkar, *Trouble at the Mill,* Oxford University Press, 2018, Chapter 1.
15. Sarkar, *Trouble at the Mill,* p. 65.
16. Sarkar, *Trouble at the Mill,* p. 67.
17. Maddison, *Class Structure and Economic Growth,* p. 57; Tirthankar Roy, *A Business History of India,* Cambridge University Press, 2018, p. 71.
18. P. J. Cain and A. G. Hopkins, *British Imperialism,* London: Longman, 2002, p. 296.
19. Maddison, *Class Structure and Economic Growth,* p. 61; William Beveridge, *India Called Them,* London: George Allen, 1947, p 195.
20. Maddison, *Class Structure and Economic Growth,* pp. 60–61.
21. Cain and Hopkins, *British Imperialism,* p. 295.
22. See Thant Myint-U, *The River of Lost Footsteps,* London: Faber and Faber, 2007, Chapter 1; Ian Beckett, 'The Campaign of the Lost Footsteps: The Pacification of Burma, 1885-95', *Small Wars and Insurgencies,* Vol. 30, No. 4–5 (2019); Jordan Carlyle Winfield, 'Buddhism and Insurrection in Burma, 1886–1890', *Journal of the Royal Asiatic Society,* Vol. 20, No. 3 (2010), pp. 345–367. Amitav Ghosh novelised Thibaw's exile in *The Glass Palace,* London: HarperCollins, 2000.
23. Arthur Cottrell, *East Asia,* London: Pimlico, 2002, p. 180.
24. J. Hagan and A. D. Wells, 'The British and Rubber in Malaya, c1890-1940', in *The Past is Before Us: Proceedings of the Ninth National Labour History Conference,* ed. G. Patmore, J. Shields and N. Balnave, ASSLH, Business & Labour History Group, University of Sydney, Australia, 2005, pp. 143–50, p. 144 for quote on Malay peasantry.

25. Anthony Burgess, *The Long Day Wanes: A Malayan Trilogy,* Harmondsworth: Penguin, 1982, p 36.
26. Robert Bickers, *Empire Made Me,* London: Allen and Unwin, 2003, p. 49, 54.
27. J. K. Chapman, *The Career of Arthur Hamilton Gordon, the First Lord Stanmore, 1829-1912,* University of Toronto Press, 1964, p. 157.
28. James Heartfield, *The Aborigines' Protection Society,* London: Hurst, 2011, p. 199.

Chapter Twenty-three

1. L. C. A. Knowles, *Economic Development of the Overseas Empire,* London: Routledge, 1924, pp. 157–8.
2. quoted in Frank Furedi, *Colonial Wars,* London: I.B. Tauris, 1994, p. 33.
3. Anthony Kirk-Greene, *On Colonial Service,* London: I B Tauris, 1999, p. 12; Merivale quoted in R. Price, *British Society,* Cambridge University Press, 1999, p. 64.
4. Kay Saunders (ed), *Indentured Labour,* London: Croom Helm, 1984, pp. 46–7.
5. Brij Lal, 'Labouring men…', in Saunders, *Indentured Labour,* p. 126.
6. *Anti-Slavery Reporter,* Vol. 19, No. 7 (1 June 1875), pp. 172–3.
7. Brij Lal, 'Labouring men…', in Kay Saunders, *Indentured Labour,* p. 126.
8. James Heartfield, *The Aborigines' Protection Society,* London: Hurst, 2011, pp. 172–4; Amit Kumar Mishra, 'Indian Indentured Labourers in Mauritius', *Studies in History,* Vol. 25 (2009), p. 233.
9. Sources *Anti-Slavery Reporter* (January-February 1907), p. 10; *The Anti-Slavery Reporter,* Series 4, Vol. XXV, No. 1 (January-February 1905), p. 14, Citing The East Africa Protectorate – Parliamentary Papers, Africa No 15 (1904).
10. Medha Chaturvedi, 'Indian Migrants in Myanmar: Emerging Trends and Challenges', Ministry of Overseas Indian Affairs, 2015. https://www.mea.gov.in/images/pdf/Indian-Migrants-Myanmar.pdf; Samart Butkaew, Burmese Indians: The Forgotten Lives, *Burma Issues,* February 2005, p. 2; K. M. de Silva, *A History of Sri Lanka,* Colombo: Vijitha Yapa Publications, 2008, p. 375.
11. *Anti-Slavery Reporter,* January-February 1907, p. 10.
12. *Anti-Slavery Reporter,* January-February 1907, p. 12.
13. *Anti-Slavery Reporter,* July 1916, p. 30.
14. Jack and Ray Simons, *Class and Colour in South Africa,* Chapter 2, London: SADF, 1983.
15. Simons, *Class and Colour in South Africa,* p. 57.
16. Simons, *Class and Colour in South Africa,* p. 62, 275, 283.
17. Andre Astrow, *Zimbabwe, A Revolution that Lost its Way,* London: Zed, 1984, p. 7, p. 9.
18. Frank Furedi, *The Mau Mau War in Perspective,* London: Currey, 1989, p. 53, 55.
19. Thomas Holt, *The Problem of Freedom: Race, Labour and Politics in Jamaica and Britain, 1832-1938,* Baltimore: John Hopkins U. P., 1992, p. 317.
20. Holt, *The Problem of Freedom,* p. 348.
21. Holt, *The Problem of Freedom,* pp. 356, 360–2 for the Jamaica Banana Producers' Association.
22. Holt, *The Problem of Freedom,* p. 365.
23. Holt, *The Problem of Freedom,* p. 375.
24. Holt, *The Problem of Freedom,* pp. 385–6.
25. 5 November 1906.
26. Theo Rothstein, 'The British in Egypt,' *The Social Democrat,* Vol. XII, No. 1 (15 January 1908), pp. 22–31; Nathan Brown, 'Who Abolished the Corvée in Egypt…?' *Past and Present,* No. 144 (August 1994), p. 136.
27. Rusiate Nayacakalou, *Tradition and Change in the Fijian Village,* Suva: Fiji Times, 1978.
28. Geoffrey Hodges, 'Military Labour in East Africa', in *Africa and the First World War,* ed. Melvin Page, London: Macmillan, 1987, 142; Opolot Okia, *Communal Labor in Colonial Kenya,* Palgrave Macmillan, 2012, pp. 64–5, 66–7, 95–100.
29. Max Siollun, *What Britain Did to Nigeria,* London: Hurst, 2021, pp. 308, 312–4.
30. Laura Tabili, *'We Ask for British Justice', Workers and Racial Difference in Late Imperial England,* 1994, Cornell U. P., pp. 42–6.
31. Quoted in Jules Marchal, *Lord Leverhulme's Ghost,* London: Verso, p. 140.

32. Lever Brothers, Annual Reports, https://www.unilever.com/Images/1930-annual
-report_tcm244-509346_1_en.pdf, https://www.unilever.com/Images/1939-annual
-report_tcm244-509344_1_en.pdf; Reuben Loffman and Benoît Henriet, 'We Are
Left with Barely Anything': Colonial Rule, Dependency, and the Lever Brothers in the
Belgian Congo, 1911–1960, *The Journal of Imperial and Commonwealth History* (2019). doi:
10.1080/03086534.2019.1638618.

33. Maria Eugenia Mata, 'Foreign Joint-Stock Companies Operating in Portuguese Colonies
on the Eve of the First World War', *South African Journal of Economic History*, Vol. 22, No. 1–2
(2007), pp. 74-107. doi: 10.1080/10113430709511202.

Chapter Twenty-four

1. Richard Shannon, *The Crisis of Imperialism*, London: Paladin, 1976, pp. 358–9.
2. *The Picture of Dorian Grey*, Penguin Classics, 2003, Chapter 16, p. 176.
3. *The Collected Papers of Bertrand Russell, Volume 11: Last Philosophical Testament 1947-68*, ed. John
Slater, London: George Allen and Unwin, 1997, p. 103.
4. Quoted in Paul Levy, *G. E. Moore and the Cambridge Apostles*, London: Macmillan, 1989, p.
240.
5. Robert Blyth et al, *The Dreadnought and the Edwardian Age*, London: National Maritime
Museum, 2011, p. 10.
6. P. J. Cain and A. G. Hopkins, *British Imperialism*, London: Longman, 2002, p. 153.
7. from 81m to 88m, *Cain and Hopkins*, p. 156.
8. quoted in L. C. A. Knowles, *Industrial and Commercial Revolutions*, London: Routledge and
Kegan Paul, 1922, p. 342.
9. David Landes, *Unbound Prometheus*, p. 331.
10. William Woodruff, 'Lessons from the Past: Capital Markets During the 19th Century and
the Interwar Period', *International Organization*, Vol. 39, No. 3 (Summer, 1985), pp. 383–439.
11. Cain and Hopkins, *British Imperialism*, p. 161.
12. Stephen Broadberry and Kevin H. O'Rourke *The Cambridge Economic History of Modern
Europe: Volume 2, 1870 to the Present*, Cambridge University Press, 2010.
13. Maddison, *The World Economy*, OECD, p. 115.
14. K L Abercrombie, 'Subsistence Production and Economic Development', *Monthly Bulletin of
Agricultural Economics and Statistics*, Vol. 14, No. 1–8 (1965), pp. 2–4.
15. *The New Machiavelli*, New York: Duffield, 1921, p. 284.
16. Lilian Knowles, *Industrial and Commercial Revolutions*, p. 329; Rajani Palme Dutt, *India Today*,
London: Gollancz, p. 185.
17. see Kevin Gillion, *Fiji's Indian Migrants*, Oxford University Press, pp. 97–8.
18. Heartfield, *The Aborigines' Protection Society*, London: Hurst, 2011, p. 190; K. M. de Silva, *A
History of Sri Lanka*, Colombo: Vijitha Yapa Publications, 2008, pp. 500–3.
19. Anthony Kirk-Greene, *On Crown Service*, p. 13.
20. K. M. de Silva, *A History of Sri Lanka*, pp. 534–5; Kirk-Greene, *On Crown Service*, p. 37.
21. Valentin Seidler, 'Institutional Copying in the 20th Century: The Role of 14,000 British
Colonial Officers', *Journal of Contextual Economics*, Vol. 137 (2017), pp. 93–120.
22. George Woodcock, *The British in the Far East*, London: Weidenfeld and Nicolson, 1969, p. 65.
23. Robert Bickers, *Empire Made Me*, London: Allen and Unwin, 2003, p. 34, 53.
24. Kirk-Green, *On Crown Service*, p. 13, 17.
25. Ian Brown, *The School of Oriental and African Studies*, Cambridge UP, 2016, pp. 19–76.
26. Quoted in L. C. A. Knowles, *Economic Development of the Overseas Empire*, p. 158.
27. Wyndham, *The Atlantic and Emancipation*, Oxford University Press, 1937, p. xiii.
28. Wyndham, *The Atlantic and Emancipation*, 1937, p. 71.
29. Quoted in John Harris, *A Century of Emancipation*, Port Washington: Kennikat Press, 1971
(orig. 1933), London, p. 208, 210.
30. Gordon quoted in James Heartfield, *The Aborigines' Protection Society,* 2011, p. 178; and see
Peter France, *The Charter of the Land*, Oxford University Press, 1969.
31. 'Sir F. Lugard on the Backward Races', *Anti-Slavery Reporter* (April 1924), p. 2.
32. Lawrence James, *Raj: The Making and Unmaking of British India*, Abacus, 2012, p. 318.

33. John Mitcham, *Race and Imperial Defence,* Cambridge University Press, 2014, p. 29, p. 11.
34. Mitcham, *Race and Imperial Defence,* p. 30.
35. Viscount Esher, *The Committee of Imperial Defence,* March 1912, p. 14.
36. In a speech to the Royal Colonial Institute 16 June 1908, quoted I Mitcham, *Race and Imperial Defence,* p. 31.
37. Spectator, 20 April 1878, p. 494.
38. Zimmern quoted in Furedi, *The Silent War,* London: Pluto, 1998, p. 56; Spengler's *Decline of the West* was written in 1914 but published after the First World War, and translated into English in 1922.
39. Quoted in Hannah Arendt, *The Origins of Totalitarianism,* New York: Meridian, 1971, p. 219.
40. Quoted in Isaac Kramnick and Barry Sheerman, *Harold Laski: A Life on the Left,* London: Hamish Hamilton, 1993, p. 39.
41. quoted in AL Morton and George Tate, *The British Labour Movement 1770-1920, A History,* London: Lawrence and Wishart, 1979, p. 141.
42. Jack London, *People of the Abyss,* London: Pluto, 1992, p. 61.
43. quoted in John Mitcham, *Race and Imperial Defence,* p. 23.
44. Quoted in Kramnick and Sheerman, *Harold Laski,* p. 39.
45. *Native Races and Their Rulers,* Cape Town: Argus, p. 21.
46. L. C. A. Knowles, *Economic Development of the Overseas Empire,* 1924, p. 158.
47. See Greta Jones, *Social Darwinism and English Thought: The Interaction Between Biological and Social Theory,* Brighton: Harvester, 1980, for an overview.

Chapter Twenty-five

1. Martin Windrow, *Our Friends Beneath the Sands,* Hachette, 2010, p. 129.
2. Robert Aldrich, *Greater France,* London: Macmillan, 1996, p. 170.
3. Lawrence James, *Raj: The Making and Unmaking of British India,* Abacus, 2012, p. 456.
4. F. S. Northedge, *The League of Nations,* New York: Holmes and Meier, 1986, p. 193.
5. Rajani Palme Dutt, *World Politics,* London: Victor Gollancs, 1936, p. 46.
6. *The Worker,* 6 September 1919.
7. Shashi Tharoor, *Inglorious Empire,* 2017, p. XX.
8. Jonathan Glancey, *Guardian,* 19 April 2003; Marek Pruszewicz, 'The 1920s British Air Bombing Campaign in Iraq', *BBC News,* 7 October 2014 http://www.bbc.co.uk/news/magazine-29441383.
9. Captain Norman Macmillan, 'The Fourth Dimension: Begin Now to Defeat the German Spring Offensive', *Flight* (9 January 1941), pp. 33–4.
10. Christopher Bayly and Tim Harper, *Forgotten Armies,* London: Penguin, 2005, p. 451.
11. Lawrence James, *Raj: The Making and Unmaking of British India,* Abacus, 2012, p. 462.
12. Palme Dutt, *India Today,* London: Voctor Gollancz, 1940, p. 186.
13. Churchill, *The Second World War, Book IV: The Hinge of Fate,* London: Reprint Society, 1953, p. 175; Cain and Hopkins, *British Imperialism 1688-2000,* London: Longman, 2002, p. 561.
14. Madhusree Mukerjee, *Churchill's Secret War: The British Empire and the Ravaging of India During World War II,* New York: Basic Books, 2010, pp. 210–3.
15. *Times,* 12 August 1916.
16. Quoted in Sylvia Pankhurst, *The Truth About the Oil War,* London: Dreadnought Publishers, 1922, p. 17.
17. Churchill, *World War II, Vol. III: The Grand Alliance,* p. 207.
18. F. Eshraghi 'The Anglo Soviet Occupation of Iran', *Middle Eastern Studies,* Vol. 20, No. 1 (January 1984), pp. 27–52.
19. Sir John Hammerton, *The Second Great War, Vol. V,* London: Waverley, 1947, p. 1859; Reza Pahlavi, *Answer to History,* New York: Stein and Day, 1980, p. 67.
20. David Johnson, *World War Two and the Scramble for Labour in Colonial Zimbabwe,* Harare: University of Zimbabwe Publications, 2000, p. 89, 100.
21. William G. Clarence-Smith, 'The Battle for Rubber in the Second World War: Cooperation and Resistance', School of Oriental and African Studies, Commodities of Empire Working Paper No. 14, November 2009, p. 10. ISSN: 1756-0098.

22. Jules Marchal, *Lord Leverhulme's Ghosts,* London: Verso, 2017, p. 212.
23. British and Foreign Anti-Slavery Society, *Annual Report,* London, 1943, p. 2; *Annual Report,* 1946, p. 1; Bayley and Harper, *Forgotten Armies,* London: Penguin, 2005, p. 384.

Chapter Twenty-six

1. David Olusoga, *The World's War,* London: Head of Zeus, 2015, p. 104.
2. quoted in Furedi, *The Silent War,* London: Pluto, 1998, p. 39.
3. SukeWolton, *Lord Hailey, the Colonial Office and the Politics of Race and Empire in the Second World War,* Basingstoke: Macmillan, 2000, p. 40, 41.
4. quoted in Furedi, *The Silent War,* p. 40.
5. 'Capital, Labour and the Colour Bar', *Times,* 14 March 1942 in Louis, *Imperialism at Bay,* New York: Oxford University Press, 1978, p. 138.
6. UNESCO, London, 16 November 1945.
7. *The Race Question,* Unesco, 1950, point 14, page 8.
8. Herskovits quoted in David Price, *Cold War Anthropology,* Durham: Duke University Press 2016, pp. 65–6.

Chapter Twenty-seven

1. Max Beloff, *Imperial Sunset,* Vol. 1, London: Methuen, 1969, p. 315.
2. Quoted in T. Jones, *Whitehall Diary,* Vol. 3, London: Oxford University Press, 1971, p. 109.
3. Ruth Dudley Edwards, *James Connolly,* Dublin: Gill and Macmillan, 1981, p. 120.
4. Liam Cahill, *Forgotten Revolution,* Dublin: O'Brien, 1990, p. 18.
5. *Ghadr,* 19 August 1917.
6. George Antonius, *The Arab Awakening,* Libraire du Liban, Beirut, 1969, pp. 414, 170–71, Sharif Hussein set out those lands bounded on the north, 'by the line Mersin-Adana, parallel to 37° N. and thence along the line Krejik-Urfa-Mardin-Midiat-Jazirat (ibn 'Umar) -Amadia to the Persian frontier; on the east, but the Persian frontier down to the Persian Gulf, on the South, by the Indian Ocean (with the exclusion of Aden whose status remains as at present); by the Red Sea and the Mediterranean Sea back to Mersin'.
7. Ibid.
8. Kevin Rooney, James Heartfield, *The Blood-Stained Poppy,* Zero Books, 2019, pp. 27–8.
9. P. M. Holt, *A Modern History of the Sudan,* London: Weidenfeld and Nicolson, 1961, pp. 127–31.
10. Harold Isaacs, *The Tragedy of the Chinese Revolution,* Chicago: Haymarket, 2010.
11. Sun Yat Sen, *The International Development of China,* London: Chinese Ministry of Information, 1928, p. 161.
12. Geoffrey Bell, *Hesitant Comrades: The Irish Revolution and the British Labour Movement,* London: Pluto, 2016.
13. Leon Trotsky, *The History of the Russian Revolution,* London: Pluto, 1985.
14. See Michele Louro, *Comrades against Imperialism,* Cambridge University Press, 2018 for an excellent account. Also useful is Ruth Price, *The Lives of Agnes Smedley,* Oxford: Oxford University Press, 2005.
15. Quoted in James Heartfield, *Unpatriotic History of the Second World War,* Winchester: Zero, 2012, p. 208.
16. See Sugata Bose, *His Majesty's Opponent,* Belknap Press, 2011 and Mihir Bose, *The Lost Hero,* London: Quartet Books, 1982.
17. See Chin Peng, *My Side of History,* Singapore: Media Master, 2003.

Chapter Twenty-eight

1. D M Leeson, *The Black and Tans,* Oxford University Press, 2011, pp. 1, 15, 24–5.
2. Owen Dudley Edwards, *Éamon de Valera,* Cardiff: GPC Books, 1987, p. 12.

3. PRO CAB 21/1842, Report by Working Party, January 1, 1949, quoted in Brendan O'Leary, *A Treatise on Northern Ireland. Volume 2 Control, the Second Protestant Ascendancy and the Irish State,* Oxford University Press, 2019, p. 142.
4. Anthony Read and David Fisher, *The Proudest Day,* London: Jonathan Cape, 1997, p. 294.
5. Devdas Gandhi, 'A Documentary History of Indian Political Events from the Crisis of August to October 1943', *Hindustan Times,* New Delhi, 1943 – quoting from the Churchill Papers.
6. Stanley Wolpert, *Nehru: A Tryst with Destiny,* Oxford University Press, 1996, p. 370.
7. The story of the Mountbattens, Nehru and partition is told in Alex von Tunzelmann's *Indian Summer: The Secret History of the End of an Empire,* London: Pocket Books, 2008.

Chapter Twenty-nine

1. Dean Acheson, *Present at the Creation: My Years at the State Department,* New York: WW Norton, 1969, pp. 31–3.
2. Louis, *Imperialism at Bay,* New York: Oxford University Press, 1978, p. 155.
3. James Byrnes, *Speaking Frankly,* New York, 1947, p. x.
4. Suke Wolton, *Lord Hailey, the Colonial Office and the Politics of Race and Empire in the Second World War,* Basingstoke: Macmillan, 2000.
5. Louis, *Imperialism at Bay,* New York: Oxford University Press, 1978, p. 532.
6. Acheson, *Present at the Creation,* New York, 1969, p. 112.
7. https://www.heritage.org/defense/report/global-us-troop-deployment-1950-2003.
8. Stephen Ambrose, *Rise to Globalism: American Foreign Policy, 1938-1980,* Harmondsworth: Penguin, 1980; David Dimbelby and David Reynolds, *An Ocean Apart,* London: Hodder and Stoughton, 1988, Chapter 9.
9. CIA, 'Amount and Percentage of the World Population Dominated by the Soviet Union or under Communist Regimes', 9 March 1976, GC M 76-10035, https://www.cia.gov/library/readingroom/docs/DOC_0000969777.pdf.
10. Fernando Claudín, *The Communist Movement: From Comintern to Cominform,* Part Two, New York: Monthly Review Press, 1975.
11. Kolko, *The Politics of War,* New York: Pantheon, 1990, pp. 477–8.
12. David Horowitz, *The Free World Colossus,* London: McGibbon and McKee, 1965, pp. 72–3; Todd Gitlin, 'Counter Insurgency: Myth and Reality in Greece', in *Containment and Revolution,* ed. Horowitz, London: Blond, 1967, pp. 140–81; William Blum, *Killing Hope: US Military and CIA Interventions since World War II,* London: Zed Books, 1972.
13. quoted in Mark Curtis, *The Ambiguities of Power,* London, 1995, p. 38.
14. Nato Review, Vol. 38, No. 1 (February 1990), p. 7; Robert O'Neill, 'Shaping NATO for the Nineties', *The Times,* 27 December 1989.
15. Donald Neff, *Warriors at Suez,* Battleboro: Amana Books, 1988, p. 429.
16. Nkrumah, *Autobiography,* Edinburgh: Thomas Nelson and Sons, 1967, p. 86; and see Susan Williams, *White Malice: The CIA and the Neocolonisation of Africa,* London: Hurst, 2021, Chapter 38.
17. See Rory Cormac, *Confronting the Colonies,* London: Hurst, 201.

Chapter Thirty

1. Partha Sarathi Gupta, *Imperialism and the British Labour Movement,* New Delhi: Sage Publications, 2002, p. 277; Rhiannon Vickers, *The Labour Party and the World,* Manchester University Press, 2003, p. 168.
2. Alex von Tunzelmann, *Indian Summer,* London: Pocket Books, 2008, p. 192; 20 August 1947, Kynaston, *The City of London, Volume IV, A Club No More, 1945-2000,* London, 2001, p. 22.
3. talking to a group of American leaders, Louis, *Imperialism at Bay,* New York: Oxford University Press, 1978, p. 16.
4. Overseas Development Institute, *Colonial Development,* 1963, p. 33.
5. James Morris, *Farewell the Trumpets,* London, 1978, p. 507.

6. 'Socialism in the Commonwealth', *International Journal*, Vol. 1, No. 1 (January 1946), pp. 22–30; Rhiannon Vickers, *The Labour Party and the World: The evolution of Labour's Foreign Policy, 1900-1951*, Manchester University Press, 2004, p. 170.
7. in Mark Curtis, *Ambiguities of Power*, London: Zed Books, 1995, p. 14, 15.
8. Curtis, *Ambiguities of Power*, p. 57.
9. HC Deb 11 May 1951, Vol. 487, cc2321-39.
10. D. M. Williams, 'West African Marketing Boards', *African Affairs*, Vol. 52, No. 206 (January 1953), pp. 45–54.
11. *Financial Times*, 16 January 1952.
12. Michela Wrong, *I Didn't Do it For You*, 2005, p. 141.
13. Wrong, *I Didn't Do it For You*, pp. 135–6.
14. 18 March 1952, Kynaston, *The City of London*, Volume IV, London, 2001, p. 49.
15. Dalton Diary entries for 28 February and 30 October 1950, in Partha Sarathi Gupta, *Imperialism and the British Labour Movement*, p. 331, 338.
16. HC Deb, 11 November 1952, Vol. 507, §816.
17. 31 December 1956, Kynaston *The City of London, Volume IV*, p. 77.
18. Kynaston, *The City of London, Volume IV*, p. 105.
19. Walter Rodney, *How Europe Underdeveloped Africa*, Nairobi: East African Educational Publishers, 1995, p. 239; Catherine Coquery-Vidrovitch, 'Economic changes in Africa in the World Context', pp. 298–9 and Maxwell Owusu, 'Agriculture and Rural Development Since 1935', p. 332, both in *General History of Africa*, vol. VIII Africa Since 1935, ed. Ali Mazrui, Oxford: James Currey/Unesco, 1999.
20. Philip Murphy, *The Empire's New Clothes*, London: Hurst, 2021, p. 19; Norman Davis, *The Isles*, London: Macmillan, 1999, p. 764.

Chapter Thirty-one

1. See Rory Cormac, *Confronting the Colonies*, London: Hurst, 2013, pp. 23–64 for an account of Britain's developing policy towards Malaya.
2. Furedi, *Colonial Wars and the Politics of Third World Nationalism*, London: I. B Tauris, 1994, p. 162.
3. Mark Curtis, *Ambiguities of Power*, London: Zed Books, 1995, pp. 56–65.
4. John Drysdale, *Singapore: Struggle for Success*, Marshall Cavendish, 2010.
5. See Frank Furedi, *Colonial Wars and the Politics of Third World Nationalism*, I. B Tauris, 1994.
6. See James Heartfield, 'The Dark Race against the Light'? Official Reaction to the 1959 Fiji Riots', *Journal of Pacific History*, Vol. 37, No. 1 (June 2002), pp. 75–86.
7. Kenneth Maddocks, *Of No Fixed Abode*, Wolsey Press, 1988, p. 130.
8. Frank Furedi, *The Mau Mau War in Perspective*, London: James Currey, 1989, pp. 80–83.
9. Mark Curtis, *Ambiguities of Power*, pp. 65–74.
10. C. L. R. James, *Nkrumah and the Ghana Revolution*, Allison Busby, 1982.
11. Kwame Nkrumah, *The Autobiography*, Edinburgh: Tomas Nelson and Sons, 1957, pp. 76–77.
12. Nkrumah, *The Autobiography*, p. 102.
13. Hansard, Vol. 550, 28 July 1954.
14. Kevin Rooney and James Heartfield, *The Blood-Stained Poppy*, Alresford, 2019, p. 128.
15. Furedi, *Colonial Wars and the Politics of Third World Nationalism*.

Chapter Thirty-two

1. Stephen Kinzler, *All the Shah's Men*, John Wiley and Sons, 2003, p. 90.
2. quoted in Malm and Esmailian, *Iran on the Brink*, London: Pluto Press, 2007, p. 162.
3. Kinzler, *All the Shah's Men*, p. 124.
4. Kinzler, *All the Shah's Men*, p, 158.
5. James Risen, 'Secrets of History: The C.I.A. in Iran', *New York Times*, 16 April 2000.
6. Vanessa Thorpe, 'MI6, the Coup in Iran that Changed the Middle East, and the cover-up', *Observer*, 2 August 2020. When the Foreign Office heard that Darbyshire had talked to the

producers of TV Series, End of Empire, Granada TV were served with a 'D Notice' telling them they could not use the footage.

7. Omar Massalha, *Towards the Long-Promised Peace,* London: Saqi, 1994, pp. 126–7.

8. Massalha, *Towards the Long-Promised Peace,* pp. 128–9.

9. Robert Holland, *Bluewater Empire,* 2012, pp. 278–9, 288.

10. Massalha, *Towards the Long-Promised Peace,* p. 135.

11. Salim Tamari (ed), *Jerusalem 1948: The Arab Neighbourhoods and their Fate in the War,* Institute of Jerusalem Studies, 1999; Omar Massalha, *Towards...,* p. 148.

12. In Donald Neff, *Warriors at Suez,* Battleboro: Amana Books, 1988, p. 36.

13. Neff, *Warriors at Suez,* p. 69.

14. Robert Holland, *Bluewater Empire,* p. 298; Neff, *Warriors at Suez,* p. 70.

15. Neff, *Warriors at Suez,* pp. 281–2.

16. HL Deb 2 August 1956, Vol. 199, cc596-627; Bevan, HC Deb 16 May 1957, Vol. 570, §680.

17. *Manchester Guardian,* Leader, 28 July 1956; *Manchester Guardian,* 31 July 1956.

18. Neff, *Warriors at Suez,* pp. 344–5. Colonel Ezer Weizman, later commander of the Air Force, gave a good flavour of Israeli thinking when he asked himself whether 'Israel's victories in the War of Independence', of 1947, were 'a true expression of her collective ability?' He went on to answer that 'only a further military conflict could prove it beyond doubt'. Ibid., p. 364.

19. Neff, *Warriors at Suez,* p. 396.

20. *New York Times,* 17 November 1956.

21. Neff, *Warriors at Suez,* p. 375.

22. Neff, *Warriors at Suez,* p. 436.

23. Robert Holland, *Blue-Water Empire,* London: Allen Lane, 2012, p. 341.

24. P. M. Holt, *A Modern History of the Sudan,* London: Weidenfeld and Nicolson, 1961, Chapters 11–13.

25. James Heartfield, 'Yemen: taking another beating from the West', Spiked-Online, 11 January 2010, https://www.spiked-online.com/2010/01/11/yemen-taking-another-beating-from -the-west/.

26. Rory Cormac, *Confronting the Colonies,* London: Hurst, 2013, p. 174.

27. Cormac, *Confronting the Colonies,* p. 186.

28. W. R Louis, 'British Withdrawal from the Gulf', *The Journal of Imperial and Commonwealth History,* Vol. 31, No. 1 (January 2003), pp.83–108, p. 97.

29. Fred Halliday, *Mercenaries,* Nottingham: Spokesman Books, 1977, p. 11.

30. PRO: FO 3711 132779: Kuwait: Legal Aspects of Intervention in Kuwait: Eastern Department Minutes: A. R. Walmsley, 22 July 1958.

Chapter Thirty-three

1. In the Unilever internal bulletin, *Progress,* No. 222 (Spring 1949), reproduced in *Millennium: Journal of International Studies,* Vol. 5, No. 2 (September 1976), pp. 190–5.

2. C. L. R. James, *A Brief History of Pan-African Revolt,* PM Press, 2012, p. 126.

3. Kenetta Hammond Perry, *London is the Place for Me,* Oxford U. P., 2015, Chapter 4.

4. 'Malaysia: The Making of a Neo-Colony?' *The Journal of Imperial and Commonwealth History,* Vol. 26, No. 2 (1998), pp. 138–56, 160–1.

5. Quoted in Cormac, *Confronting the Colonies,* p. 183.

6. Paul Lashmar and James Oliver, *Britain's Secret Propaganda War,* 1998, p. 61.

7. Lashmar and Oliver, *Britain's Secret Propaganda War,* p. 64.

8. Lashmar and Oliver, *Britain's Secret Propaganda War,* p. 79.

9. Lashmar and Oliver, *Britain's Secret Propaganda War,* p. 96.

10. Lashmar and Oliver, *Britain's Secret Propaganda War,* p. 101, 103.

11. Ian Brown, *The School of Oriental and African Studies,* p. 119, 122.

12. Brown, *The School of Oriental and African Studies,* p. 139, 145.

13. Brown, *The School of Oriental and African Studies,* p. 162.

14. Rory Cormac, *Confronting the Colonies,* pp. 136–7.

Chapter Thirty-four

1. Saul Dubow, *Apartheid 1948-1994*, Oxford University Press, 2014, p. 79.
2. quoted in Jack Woddis, 'End this Hell in Africa', *Labour Monthly*, August 1959, pp. 336–37, where the quotes from William Batt and Lord Home are to be found, originally from the *Bulawayo Chronicle*, 6 July 1951 and the *Observer*, 5 April 1959.
3. Stephen Dorrill and Robin Ramsey, *Smear*, London: Harper Collins, 1992, p. 89.
4. Ian Smith, *The Great Betrayal*, London: Blake Publishing, 1997, p. 111.
5. Dorrill and Ramsey, *Smear*, p. 91.
6. Ian Smith, *The Great Betrayal*, 1996, pp. 80–1.
7. quoted in Joan G. Fairweather, *A Common Hunger*, Calgary, 2006, p. 84.
8. Reader's Digest, *Illustrated History of South Africa*, 2nd edition, 1992, p. 477, 482.
9. Andre Astrow, *Zimbabwe*, London: Zed Press, 1983, p. 8, 14.
10. Saul Dubow, *Apartheid 1948-1994*, pp. 100–01.
11. Astrow, *Zimbabwe*, p. 15.
12. 'British businesses at stake in South Africa', *Investors Chronicle*, 3 November 1978, pp. 348–49.
13. Astrow, *Zimbabwe*, p. 36.

Chapter Thirty-five

1. See Keith Middlemas, *Politics in Industrial Society*, Part Three, London: Andre Deautsch, 1979, for a good account.
2. Paul Mattick, *Economic Crisis and Crisis Theory*, London, 1981, p. 198; Philip Murphy, *Empire's New Clothes*, London: Hurst, 2021, p. 208.
3. Chris Cook and Alan Sked, *Post-War Britain*, Penguin, 1988, p. 142; and see *Guardian* data blog, 1 September 2011, https://www.theguardian.com/news/datablog/2011/sep/01/military-service-personnel-total#data.
4. Eric Hobsbawm, *Industry and Empire*, London: Weidenfeld and Nicolson, 1969, p. 212.
5. Home Office, *British Nationality Law*, 1977, p. 4.
6. See Huw Benyon, *Working for Ford*, London: Penguin, 1984 and Alan Thornett, *Militant Years: Car Workers' Struggles in Britain in the 60s and 70s*, IMG Publications, 2010.
7. Gregory Millman, *Around the World on a Trillion Dollars a Day*, London: Bantam, 1995; Geoffrey Pilling, *The Crisis of Keynesian Economic*, Chapter 5, London: Croom Helm, 1986.
8. Cyrus Bina, *Economics of the Oil Crisis*, New York, 1985, pp. 8–9. Bina argues that the conspiracy theory is mistaken.
9. See Major Sir David Maxwell Fyfe's speech in the House of Commons, 07 July 1948, HC Deb, Vol. 453, §399.
10. Kathleen Paul, *Whitewashing Britain*, Ithaca: Cornell U. P., 1997, p. 111.
11. Lynn K. Mytelka, 'The Lomé Convention and a New International Division of Labour', *Journal of European Integration*, Vol. 1, No. 1 (1977), pp. 63–76, 74–75.
12. HC Deb 11 July 1988, Vol. 137, c12W.
13. HC Deb 13 May 1975, Vol. 892, cc241-6.

Chapter Thirty-six

1. Adom Getachew, *Worldmaking After Empire*, Princeton, 2019, p. 73.
2. Bull, *The Anarchical Society*, London: Macmillan, 1977, p. 258.
3. Martin Wight, *Power Politics*, Pelican, 1979, pp. 92–93.
4. Getachew, *Worldmaking After Empire*, p. 93.
5. Getachew, *Worldmaking After Empire*, p. 143.
6. Marion Farouk-Sluggett and Peter Sluggett, *Iraq Since 1958*, London: Bloomsbury Academic, 1990, p. 85.
7. Eberhard Kienle, *Ba'ath Versus Ba'ath: The Conflict Between Syria and Iraq*, London, I B Tauris, 1991.

8. Bruce Jentleson, *With Friends Like These: Reagan, Bush and Saddam 1982-1990*, New York: WW Norton, 1994.

9. William Quandt, *Peace Process: American Diplomacy and the Arab-Israeli Conflict since 1967*, New York: Brookings Institution, 2001.

10. Quoted in Getachew, *Worldmaking After Empire*, p. 150.

11. Frantz Fanon, *Black Skin, White Masks*, London: Pluto 1986, pp. 229–30.

12. My thanks to filmmaker Rob Harris for pointing this out.

13. Albert O. Hirschman, Richard Bird, *Foreign Aid - a Critique and a Proposal*, Princeton, 1968; Teresa Hayter, *Aid as Imperialism*, Harmondsworth: Penguin, 1971; Stiglitz, *Globalization and its Discontents*, 2002; the World Bank first acknowledged that its free market model might not be the only way to grow an economy in the 1993 research report *The East Asian Miracle*, Oxford University Press/World Bank.

14. Rehman Sobhan, 'Bangladesh and the World Economic System: The Crisis of External Dependence', *Development and Change*, SAGE, London and Beverly Hills, Vol. 12 (1981), pp. 327–34.

15. Conor Foley, *The Thin Blue Line*, London: Verso, 2008, p. 17.

16. Y. Hossein Farzin, *Food Import Dependence in Somalia*, 1988, quoted in Michael Maren, *The Road to Hell: The Ravaging Effects of Foreign Aid and International Charity*, New York: The Free Press, 1997, p. 171.

17. Maren, *The Road to Hell*, pp. 134–35, 161.

18. Independent Commission on International Development Issues, *North-South: A Programme for Survival*, 1980 (henceforth, the Brandt Report), pp. 23–24.

19. Brandt Report, p. 195.

20. Arghiri Emmanuel, *Appropriate or Underdeveloped Technology*, London: John Wiley, 1982, pp. 102–06.

21. World Commission on Environment and Development, *Report*, United Nations, 1987 (Henceforth, Brundtland Report), p. 8, 57.

22. Michael Maren, *The Road to Hell: The Ravaging Effects of Foreign Aid and International Charity*, New York, The Free Press, 1997, p. 64.

23. C. L. R. James, *A Brief History of Pan-African Revolt*, PM Press, 2012.

24. Robin Bunce and Paul Field, *Darcus Howe: A Political Biography*, London: Bloomsbury, 2015, Chapter 6; Williams on banning himself in Farrukh Dhondy, *C. L. R. James*, London: Weidenfeld and Nicolson, 2001, p. 120.

25. Andre Astrow, *Zimbabwe*, London: Zed, 1983, pp. 159, 162–63.

26. Astrow, *Zimbabwe*, p. 174.

27. Margaret Thatcher, *The Downing Street Years*, p. 171.

28. quoted in Furedi, *The New Ideology of Imperialism*, London: Pluto, 1994, p. 100.

29. Getachew, *Worldmaking After Empire*, Princeton, 2019, p. 179.

30. See Ahmed Rashid, *Jihad: The Rise of Militant Islam in Central Asia*, New Haven: Yale University Press, 2002.

31. See Fred Halliday, *Two Hours That Shook the World. 11 September 2001, Causes and Consequences*, London: Saqi, 2001; Gilbert Achcar, *The Clash of Barbarisms*, New York: Monthly Review Press, 2002, p. 36.

Chapter Thirty-seven

1. 'New World Economic Order', *Business Week*, 24 July 1978, p. 70.

2. Helen Hughes, 'Debt and Development: The Role of Foreign Capital in Economic Growth', *World Development*, Vol. 7, No. 2 (1979), pp. 95–112.

3. Bank for International Settlements, 1979.

4. *World Economic and Social Survey*, United Nations, 2017, p. 52.

5. *The Debt Crisis and the World Economy*, Commonwealth Secretariat, 1984, p. 7.

6. *The Debt Crisis and the World Economy*, 1984, p. 40.

7. See André Gunder Frank, *On Capitalist Underdevelopment*, Oxford: University Press, 1975; Samir Amin, *Accumulation on a World Scale*, New York: Monthly Review Press, 1974 and also

by Amin *Unequal Development: An Essay on the Social Forms of Peripheral Capitalism,* Hassocks: Harvester Press, 1976.

8. Tommy McKearney, *The Provisional IRA: From Insurrection to Parliament,* London: Pluto Press, 2011; Sean MacStiofain, *Memoirs of a Revolutionary,* Saxon House, 1974; Tim Pat Coogan, *The IRA,* London: Fontana, 1987, Part Two.
9. *Downing Street Years,* Harper Collins 1995, pp. 8–9.
10. *Downing Street Years,* Harper Collins 1995, p. 173.
11. Martin Dillon, *The Dirty War,* Arrow, 1991, pp. 313–4, 399–400, xxiv.
12. David Beresford, *Ten Dead Men: Story of the 1981 Irish Hunger Strike,* London: Grafton, 1987.
13. *The Making of the Second Cold War,* London: Verso, 1986.
14. Reproduced in *Survey: A Journal of Soviet and East European Studies,* Vol. 28, No. 1 (1984); See also Hillel Ticktin, *Origins of the Crisis in the USSR,* New York: M. E. Sharpe, 1992.

Chapter Thirty-eight

1. Francis Fukuyama, 'The End of History', *The National Interest,* Summer 1989; see also Fukuyama, *The End of History and the Last Man,* London: Hamish Hamilton, 1992.
2. 'Beyond the Cold War', *Foreign Affairs.* Vol. 6, No. 1 (1989–90).
3. Lord Hailsham, *Values: Collapse and Cure,* London: Harper Collins, 1994, pp. 1–3.
4. See *Social Trends,* Office of National Statistics, London: HMSO, 1994; P. Ester et al, *The Individualising Society: Value Change in Europe and North America,* European Value Studies. Tilburg: University Press, 1993.
5. Norman Schwarzkopf, *It Doesn't Take a Hero,* Bantam, 1992, p. 286.
6. 'Confrontation in the Gulf', *New York Times,* 23 September 1990.
7. *It Doesn't Take a Hero,* p. 292.
8. Bruce Jentleson, *With Friends Like These: Reagan, Bush and Saddam 1982-1990,* New York: W. W. Norton, 1994.
9. Bob Woodward, *Washington Post,* 20 June 1999.
10. Hella Pick, 'Rebirth of Nations', The Gulf Crisis: The First Sixty Days, *The Guardian Collection,* 1990, p. 56.
11. Margaret Thatcher, *The Downing Street Years,* Harper Collins, 1995, p. 826–28.
12. Mark Curtis, *Ambiguities of Power,* p. 190, 192.
13. *Telegraph,* 11 September 1990.
14. *Financial Times,* 1 November 1990.
15. *New Statesman,* 12 April 1991; 16 March 1991.
16. *Evening Standard,* 23 April 1991.
17. Rageh Omar, *Revolution Day,* Viking, 2004, p. 73; *Guardian,* 19 February 2001.
18. Rageh Omar, *Revolution Day,* p. 36.
19. Mark Curtis, *Unpeople,* London: Vintage, 2004, pp. 48–9.
20. Michael Maren, *The Road to Hell: The Ravaging Effects of Foreign Aid and International Charity,* New York: The Free Press, 1997, p. 214.
21. Quoted in George Stephanopoulos, *All Too Human,* Little Brown, 2008, p. 214.
22. Maren, *The Road to Hell,* p. 229.
23. Boutros Boutros-Ghali, *Unvanquished, a United Nations-United States Saga,* Random House, 1999, p. 37.
24. Jean Bricmont, *Humanitarian Imperialism: Using Human Rights to Sell War,* New York: Monthly Review Press, 2006, pp. 50–51.
25. *Unvanquished,* 1999, p. 42.
26. John Major, *The Autobiography,* London: Harper Collins, 1999, p. 544.
27. John Major, *The Autobiography,* p. 546.
28. Jan Zwierzchowski and Ewa Tabeau, 'The 1992-95 War in Bosnia and Herzegovina: Census-Based Multiple System Estimation of Casualties' Undercount', Conference Paper for the International Research Workshop on 'The Global Costs of Conflict' The Households in Conflict Network (HiCN) and The German Institute for Economic Research (DIW Berlin) 1 February 2010.
29. Quoted in Tara MacCormack, *Critique, Security and Power,* London: Routledge, 2009, p. 70.

30. James Heartfield, 'China's Comprador Capitalism is Coming Home', *Review of Radical Political Economics,* Vol. 37, No. 2 (June 2005), pp. 196–214.
31. Chris Patten, *East and West,* London: Macmillan, 1998.

Chapter Thirty-nine

1. Reader's Digest, *Illustrated History of South Africa, Second Edition,* Cape Town 1992, pp. 470–71.
2. Reader's Digest, *Illustrated History of South Africa,* pp. 473–74.
3. Reader's Digest, *Illustrated History of South Africa,* p. 484.
4. Richard Goldstone, *For Humanity: Reflections of a War Crimes Investigator,* Johannesburg, Witwatersrand University Press, 2000, pp. 17–18, 69–71.
5. Reader's Digest, *Illustrated History of South Africa,* p. 492; reported the *Weekly Mail* in July 1991.
6. Reader's Digest, *Illustrated History of South Africa,* p. 502.
7. Quoted in the *Independent,* 3 February 1990.
8. *Has Socialism Failed?* South African Communist Party, 1990, https://www.sacp.org.za/docs /history/failed.html, p. 2.
9. *Has Socialism Failed?* p. 2.
10. HC Deb 12 February 1990, Vol. 167, cc21-7.
11. *Washington Post,* 11 April 1988.
12. , John and Janet Wallach, *Arafat,* London: Mandarin, 1991, p. 370; Naseer Aruri, *The Obstruction of Peace,* Monroe: Common Courage Press, 1995, p. 145.
13. Wallach, *Arafat,* p. 192.
14. Aruri, The *Obstruction of Peace,* pp. 153–4.
15. Hamed Mousavi, 'The Rise and Fall of the Israeli-Palestinian Peace Process', *Journal of World Sociopolitical Studies,* Vol. 3. No. 1 (January 2019), p. 94.
16. Shimon Peres, *The New Middle East,* Shaftesbury: Element Books, 1993, p. 19.
17. *An Phoblacht/Republican News,* 25 June 1992.
18. *Republican News,* 15 October 1992 Guardian, 18 September 1993; Republican News,11 November 1993.
19. 'Setting the Record Straight' – Sinn Fein's record of the communications between Sinn Fein and the British government, October 1990-November 1993, p. 41, *Republican News,* 16 September 1993.
20. *Guardian,* 18 September 1993.
21. *Independent on Sunday,* 3 October 1993.
22. Interview with Bernadette Devlin-McAliskey, *Jacobin,* 25 April 2016, https://www.jacobin-mag.com/2016/04/bernadette-devlin-interview-derry-civil-rights-troubles-good-friday/.
23. The claim 'no selfish strategic or economic interest' was delivered by the Secretary of State for Northern Ireland, Peter Brooke, Nicholas Watt, 'Thatcher gave approval to talks with IRA', Guardian, 16 October 1999, https://www.theguardian.com/uk/1999/oct/16/north-ernireland.thatcher.
24. British-Irish Agreement, 10 April 1998, https://www.britishirishcouncil.org/about/british -irish-agreement.
25. John Major, *The Autobiography,* London: Harper Collins, 1999, p. 447; Mark Ryan's *War and Peace in Ireland* is the best account of this period, London: Pluto Press, 1994.
26. John Major, *The Autobiography,* London: Harper Collins, 1999, p. 441.
27. Andrew Rawnsley, *The End of the Party,* London: Viking, 2010, p. 424.
28. Liam Ó Ruairc, *Peace or Pacification? Northern Ireland after the Defeat of the IRA,* Winchester: Zero, 2018, p. 109.
29. Ó Ruairc, *Peace or Pacification?,* p. 107, citing P. Mitchell, G. Evans, and B. O'Leary, 'Extremist Outbidding in Ethnic Party Systems is Not Inevitable', *Political Studies,* Vol. 57, No. 2 (2009), p. 403.

Chapter Forty

1. Hubert Vedrine, *History Strikes Back: How States, Nations, and Conflicts are Shaping the 21st Century,* Brookings Institution, 2009, p. 21.

2. Geoffrey Robertson, *Crimes Against Humanity*, New York: New Press, 2000, p. xviii; Kenneth Roth, Human Rights Trump Sovereignty in 1999, *Human Rights Watch*, 9 December, http://www.hrw.org/fr/news/1999/12/09/human-rights-trump-sovereignty-1999; Samuel Moyn, *The Last Utopia: Human Rights in History*, Belknap: Harvard, 2010.
3. Norman Fairclough, *New Labour, New Language*, London: Routledge, 2000.
4. *Guardian*, 12 May 1997.
5. He told Andrew Rawnsley, *The End of the Party*, Viking, 2010, p. 191.
6. Christopher Bickerton, *European Integration*, Oxford University Press, 2012, p. 7, Chapter 5.
7. John Sweeney, 'Nato Bombed Chinese Deliberately', *Observer*, 17 October 1999.
8. *Foreign Affairs*, January/February, Vol. 79, No. 1 (2000), pp. 45–62.
9. Quoted in Mark Curtis, *Unpeople*, London, 2004, pp. 16–7.
10. Quoted in Rooney and Heartfield, *The Blood-Stained Poppy*, Zero Books, 2019.
11. *Guardian*, 3 September 2021.
12. John Bew et al., *The British Moment: The Case for Democratic Geopolitics in the Twenty-First Century*, London: The Social Affairs Unit, 2006, p. 17.
13. *The British Moment*, pp. 31–7.
14. *Guardian*, 26 April 2007.
15. Ed Herman and David Peterson, *The Politics of Genocide*, New York: Monthly Review Press, 2010; Michela Wrong, *Do Not Disturb: The Story of a Political Murder and an African Regime Gone Bad*, 2021.
16. Conor Foley, *The Thin Blue Line*, London: Verso, 2010, p. 2.
17. *Kansas City Star*, 19 March 2004; David Wearing, *Anglo-Arabia*, Cambridge: Polity, 2018, p. 72.
18. Michael Ignatieff, *The Warrior's Honour*, 1998, p. 95.
19. *Cosmopolitan Dystopia*, Manchester U. P., 2020, p. 37.
20. See James Heartfield, *Equal Opportunities Revolution*, London: Repeater.
21. Katharine Viner, 'Feminism as Imperialism', *Guardian*, 21 September 2002.
22. Special Inspector General for Afghanistan Reconstruction, *Support for Gender Equality: Lessons From the U.S. Experience In Afghanistan*, February 2021, p. 43, 47, 79, 81.
23. 'Progress', in 'Equality and the Army', National Army Museum, https://www.nam.ac.uk/explore/equality-and-army.
24. *Decolonising Intervention: International Statebuilding in Mozambique*, London: Rowman & Littlefield International Ltd, 2017, p. 143.
25. John Pender, 'Country Ownership', in *Politics without Sovereignty*, ed. C. Bickerton et al., UCL Press, 2007, p. 123, and p. 115 for the quote from Gordon Brown.
26. *Anti-Slavery Reporter*, Vol. 4, No. 9 (September 1856), p. 202; *Anti-Slavery Reporter* Vol III, No. XXVII (1 March 1848), p. 39.
27. See John Fisher, 'Putting the "Universal" Back in the Universal Declaration', FCDO, 14 December 2010, https://blogs.fcdo.gov.uk/boblast/2010/12/14/putting-the-universal-back-in-the-universal-declaration/.

Chapter Forty-one

1. *Cosmopolitan Dystopia*, Introduction, Manchester U. P., 2020.
2. Jonathan Steele, 'Cameron's Memoir', *Middle East Eye*, 25 September 2019.
3. Quoted in Jonathan Marcus, 'An Obituary for the Age of Intervention?' *BBC Online*, 17 December 2016.
4. MoD job advert quoted in Matt Kennard and Mark Curtis, Britain's secret Saudi military support programme, *Declassified UK*, 27 September 2019.
5. Wearing, *Anglo-Arabia*, p. 94.
6. Wearing, *Anglo-Arabia*, p. 94.
7. Wearing, *Anglo-Arabia*, p. 126.
8. Harry Davies, 'Revealed: Sheikh's £5bn London Property Empire, *Guardian*, 19 October 2020.
9. Department of Trade and Industry, UK Defence & Security, Export Statistics for 2018, July 2019.

10. Campaign Against the Arms Trade, 'Human Rights Abuses', updated 10 July 2020, https://caat.org.uk/challenges/the-arms-trade/human-rights-abuses/, viewed on 22 October 2020.
11. UK forces in the Middle East region, House of Commons Library, 15 January 2020.
12. Fintan O'Toole, *Heroic Failure*, London: Head of Zeus, 2018, p. 3; Priya Satia, *Time's Monster: History, Conscience and Britain's Empire*, Ward and Rasch, *Embers of Empire in Brexit Britain*, Robert Gildea, *Empires of the Mind*, Sathnam Sangera, *Empireland*, Peter Mitchell, *Imperial Nostalgia*, Danny Dorling and Sally Tomlinson, *Rule Britannia: Brexit and the End of Empire*, Biteback, 2020, and Gary Younge, 'Britain's Imperial Fantasies have Given us Brexit', *Guardian*, 3 February 2018.
13. See Daniel Cohen, 'Loud, Obsessive, Tribal: The Radicalisation of Remain', *Guardian*, 13 August 2019.
14. See Charlotte L. Riley, 'The Empire Strikes Back', *New Humanist*, 10 December 2019; and see also Robert Saunders, 'Brexit Empire: "Global Britain" and the Myth of Imperial Nostalgia', *Journal of Imperial and Commonwealth History*, 2020.
15. *New Statesman*, 24 June 2016.
16. See David Goodhart, *The Road to Somewhere: The Populist Revolt and the Future of Politics*, Hurst & Co, 2018.
17. See James Heartfield, 'Why 'Empire nostalgia' Is Declining', *Spiked-Online*, 16 March 2020, https://www.spiked-online.com/2020/03/16/why-empire-nostalgia-is-declining/; and see also Paul Embery, *Despised: Why the Modern Left Loathes the Working Class*, Polity, 2020, for a good account of the diminished status of working class patriotism.
18. May's advisor Nick Timothy told reporter Laura Kuenssberg in 'The Brexit Storm', for BBC2's Inside Story, 1 April 2019.
19. See Gurminder Bhambra, Dalia Gebrial and Kerem Nişancıoğlu, *Decolonising the University*, London: Pluto, 2018.
20. See Tarjinder Gill, 'Teaching the British Empire', *All In Britain*, March 2020, https://allin-britain.org/teaching-the-british-empire-debunking-the-myths/.
21. Craig Simpson, 'School History Lessons May Fuel Extremism, Warn Counter-terrorism Officers', *Daily Telegraph*, 13 June 2021.
22. Mailonline, 26 June 2020, https://www.dailymail.co.uk/news/article-8462735/Archbishop-Canterbury-says-Church-think-portraying-Jesus-white.html.

INDEX

Printed in the USA
CPSIA information can be obtained
at www.ICGtesting.com
JSHW020658080724
65924JS00001BA/1